Titles in *Counseling and Professional Identity*

CCREP Standards	Sangganjanavanich, Introduction to Professional Counseling	Watson, Counseling Assessment and Evaluation	Conyne, Group Work Leadership	Parsons, Becoming A Skilled Counselor	Parsons, Counseling Theory	Wong, Counseling Individuals Through the Life Span	Duan, Becoming a Multiculturally Competent Counselor	Wright, Research Methods For Counseling	Tang, Career Development and Counseling	Scott, Counselor as Consultant	...ris, ...cal Decision Making for the 21st Century Counselor
PROFESSIONAL ORIENTATION AND ETHICAL PRACTICE	1a 1b 1d 1e 1f 1g 1h 1i 1j	1j	1b 1j	1b 1d 1e 1j	1j	1j	1j	1j	1b 1j	1b 1j	1b 1d 1e 1f 1h 1i 1j
SOCIAL AND CULTURAL DIVERSITY	2c 2f 2g	2g	2d 2e 2g	2b 2c 2g	2c 2e 2g	2a 2b 2c 2d 2e 2g	2c 2e 2f 2g	2g	2g	2d 2g	2c 2e 2f 2g
HUMAN GROWTH AND DEVELOPMENT			3f		3b	3a 3b 3c 3d 3e 3f 3g	3d 3e		3e		3g
CAREER DEVELOPMENT		4f							4a 4b 4c 4d 4e 4f 4g	4c	
HELPING RELATIONSHIPS	5a 5b 5c 5f 5g 5h		5b 5c 5d 5e	5a 5b 5c 5d	5b 5c 5d 5e 5g	5b	5b 5e		5b 5c	5b 5c 5f 5g 5h	5b 5d 5h
GROUP WORK			6a 6b 6c 6d 6e								6d 6e
ASSESSMENT		7a 7b 7c 7d 7e 7f 7g	7b	7b		7f		7c 7d 7e			
RESEARCH AND PROGRAM EVALUATION								8a 8b 8c 8d 8e			8d

COUNSELING AND PROFESSIONAL IDENTITY

Series Editors: Richard D. Parsons, PhD, and Naijian Zhang, PhD

Counseling Theory

Guiding Reflective Practice

Richard D. Parsons
West Chester University of Pennsylvania

Naijian Zhang
West Chester University of Pennsylvania

Los Angeles | London | New Delhi
Singapore | Washington DC

SAGE

Los Angeles | London | New Delhi
Singapore | Washington DC

FOR INFORMATION:

SAGE Publications, Inc.

2455 Teller Road

Thousand Oaks, California 91320

E-mail: order@sagepub.com

SAGE Publications Ltd.

1 Oliver's Yard

55 City Road

London EC1Y 1SP

United Kingdom

SAGE Publications India Pvt. Ltd.

B 1/I 1 Mohan Cooperative Industrial Area

Mathura Road, New Delhi 110 044

India

SAGE Publications Asia-Pacific Pte. Ltd.

3 Church Street

#10-04 Samsung Hub

Singapore 049483

Acquisitions Editor: Kassie Graves
Editorial Assistant: Elizabeth Luizzi
Production Editor: Libby Larson
Copy Editor: Megan Granger
Typesetter: C&M Digitals (P) Ltd.
Proofreader: Dennis W. Webb
Indexer: Jean Casalegno
Cover Designer: Candice Harmon
Marketing Manager: Shari Countryman

Printed in the United States of America

Library of Congress Cataloging-in-Publication Data

Counseling theory : guiding reflective practice / [edited by] Richard D. Parsons, West Chester University of Pennsylvania, Naijian Zhang, West Chester University of Pennsylvania.

pages cm
Includes bibliographical references and index.

ISBN 978-1-4522-4465-5 (pbk.)
ISBN 978-1-4833-1205-7 (web pdf)

1. Counseling. I. Parsons, Richard D., editor of compilation.

BF636.6.C6768 2014
158.301—dc23   2013034509

This book is printed on acid-free paper.

14 15 16 17 18 10 9 8 7 6 5 4 3 2 1

Brief Contents

Detailed Contents

2 Multicultural Considerations: Within and Beyond Traditional Counseling Theories   27

Dong Xie

3 Case Conceptualization: The Case of Y-Chun   55

Naijian Zhang and Richard D. Parsons

Faith Deveaux

5　Individual Psychology: Alfred Adler　　　　　　　　　109

Robyn L. Trippany-Simmons, Matthew R. Buckley,
Kristin Meany-Walen, and Tiffany Rush-Wilson

6   Existential Counseling and Psychotherapy   141

Mark B. Scholl, Michael Walsh, and Michelle Perepiczka

7 Carl Rogers and Client-Centered Counseling   171

Marjorie C. Witty and Ray Adomaitis

8   Gestalt Therapy   201

Joseph Spillman and Christina M. Rosen

9 Cognitive-Behavioral Theories

Julia Y. Porter

10   Behavior Theory   253

Barbara C. Trolley and Christopher Siuta

11   Reality Therapy   289

David A. Scott and Hannah G. Barfield

12   Solution-Focused Therapy   311

Brandé Flamez and Joshua C. Watson

Introduction to the Series

Counseling and Professional Identity

Counseling Theory: Guiding Reflective Practice will introduce you to myriad theories and models guiding counselor practice. This text and the theories represented will play an important role in your ongoing development as a professional counselor. Growing as a competent professional counselor requires the acquisition and employment of more complex mental structures—those that help counselors organize information and make meaning of experience in a more comprehensive, integrated, and differentiated manner. Counseling theory is integral to these processes of finding meaning and directing practice. The use of theories to guide practice enables counselors to engage in problem solving from a broader range of perspectives.

This text provides a learning experience that will foster the development of these complex mental structures. However, one text—one learning experience—will not be sufficient for the successful formation of your professional identity and practice. That will be a lifelong process—one we hope to facilitate through the presentation of this text and creation of our series of counseling books, titled *Counseling and Professional Identity*.

Counseling and Professional Identity is a fresh, pedagogically sound series of texts targeting counselors in training. This series is *not* simply a compilation of isolated books matching those already available in the market. Rather, each book in the series, while targeting specific knowledge and skills and proving valuable in and of itself, gains further value and significance as an integral part of a coordinated series of texts targeting the professional development of counselors. The focus and content of each text within the series serve as a single lens through which a counselor can view clients, engage in practice, and articulate a personal professional identity. This is one lens among the many needed to serve as a competent counselor.

Counseling and Professional Identity, as noted, is not simply a "package" of traditional texts. Rather, the series provides an *integrated* curriculum targeting the formation of the reader's professional identity and efficient, ethical practice. Each book in the series is structured to facilitate the reader's ongoing professional formation. The materials found within each text are organized to move the reader to higher levels of cognitive, affective, and psychomotor functioning, resulting in their assimilation in the reader's professional identity and approach to professional practice. The texts included within the series reflect the core courses provided in most graduate counselor education programs (see Table P.1).

Table P.1 Books and Corresponding CACREP (Council for the Accreditation of Counseling and Related Educational Programs) Competencies

Counseling and Professional Identity	
Books in the Series	**Typical Courses Served by the Text**
Introduction to Professional Counseling Varunee Faii Sangganjanavanich and Cynthia A. Reynolds	Introductory
Becoming a Skilled Counselor Richard D. Parsons and Naijian Zhang	Basic skills
Becoming a Multiculturally Competent Counselor Changming Duan and Chris Brown	Multicultural and diversity
Counseling Individuals Through the Lifespan Daniel Wai Chung Wong, Kim Hall, Cheryl Justice, and Lucy Wong Hernandez	Human development
Counseling Assessment and Evaluation: Fundamentals of Applied Practice Joshua C. Watson and Brandé Flamez	Assessment
Research Methods for Counseling Robert Wright	Fundamental research
Counseling Theory: Guiding Reflective Practice Richard D. Parsons and Naijian Zhang (Eds.)	Theories
Ethical Decision Making for the 21st Century Counselor Donna S. Sheperis, Michael Koct, and Stacy Henning	Ethics—or sections within each course covering ethical issues
Career Development and Counseling: Theory and Practice in a Multicultural World Mei Tang and Jane Goodman	Career counseling
Counselor as Consultant David Scott, Chadwick Royal, and Daniel Kissinger	Consultation and coordination
Group Work: An Introduction for Helping Professionals Robert Conyne	Group dynamics, group counseling

While each text targets a specific set of core competencies (see Table P.1), they all share a common emphasis:

1. Assimilation of concepts and constructs provided across texts in the series, thus fostering the reader's ongoing development as a competent professional

2. Blending of contemporary theory with current research and empirical support

3. Development of procedural knowledge, with each text employing case illustrations and guided practice exercises to facilitate the reader's ability to translate the theory and research discussed into professional decision making and application

4. Need for and means of demonstrating accountability

5. Fostering of the reader's professional identity and, with it, assimilation of the ethics and standards of practice guiding the counseling profession

Editors' Preface

"Why?" When asked by a curious observer of human behavior, this question, more often than not, brings responses characterized as "maybes" rather than "absolutes." Human behavior is complex. Observers of human behavior have drawn inferences and interpretations, and some have developed these into hypothetical constructs and theoretical models—all in the hope they will conform to the real, empirical world of the behavior being observed.

For counselors, theories of human behavior need to be more than just points of intellectual curiosity. Counseling theory is an invaluable tool essential to effective counseling. The value of theory rests in its use as a screen or filter—an orienting framework through which client information can be processed and better understood.

Counseling theories help counselors distinguish the relevant from the tangential. They give counselors the framework for making predictions about clients' behavior. Counseling theories provide the counselor direction as to the goals and purposes of the counseling as well as the processes and techniques needed to achieve those ends.

Counseling Theory: Guiding Reflective Practice provides an understanding of the process of change and use of both classical and cutting-edge theoretical models of change as lenses through which to process client information and develop case conceptualizations and intervention plans. This text is unique among the vast array of "theories" textbooks in that it features the following:

- *Expert practitioners as authors:* Each of the theories presented within this book is written by an expert in that theory—someone who not only understands the theory presented but also employs it as a framework for client case conceptualization and treatment planning.
- *Insight into professional identity:* The authors—who are scholars, academics, and practitioners—share the special value and import of the theories they employ, not just as a guide to their practice decisions but as an essential component of their professional identities.
- *Emphasis on application:* This book goes beyond promoting understanding of theories to facilitating their application to guide practice. It demonstrates the truth behind Lewin's statement that there is "nothing so practical as a good theory."[1] The text employs a single illustrative case and the concept of "reflective practice" as the anchor for each author's presentation of a particular theory. While articulating the history, significant contributors, and essential concepts of the theory, the primary

---

[1]Lewin, K. (1951). *Field theory in social science: Selected theoretical papers.* New York: Harper, p. 169.

focus of each chapter is on the contributor's application of that theory to the illustrative case. Each author will demonstrate, use of the theory as a tool guiding the practitioner in processing client data and formulating treatment plans. This modeling, along with the chapter's guided practices, helps the reader "see" the theory in action and employ it to guide his or her own case conceptualization and practice decisions.

- *Reflection of the reality of increasing globalization:* This book presents theories that reflect the increasing globalization and diversity of clients engaged in counseling and the issues they bring. It not only highlights the various lenses through which one must view multicultural issues but also demonstrates how each of the theories discussed, while developed in Western culture, can apply to people from different cultural backgrounds.

- *Presentation of classical and cutting-edge theories:* While the classical theories of counseling are fully presented within this text, it also provides the reader with a "peek" into the future of counseling as a profession and practice, as it takes form in emerging, cutting-edge theories that will move counseling well into the 21st century.

- *Address of CACREP competencies:* As with all the books in this series, *Counseling Theory: Guiding Reflective Practices* is most noteworthy in that it has been developed to foster the reader's formative development and professional identity. This book gains value by being a significant part of the integrated series, targeting the professional formation of counselors. As part of an integrated body of work, this book presents theory as an essential component to the counselor's identity formation and eventual professional practice, and to this end is designed to address specific competencies identified by CACREP as essential to developing an understanding of the processes of counseling and development of a counselor's professional identity. Specifically, the goals of this text are as follows:

1. Demonstrate the value of theory to a counselor's reflective practice

2. Identify the historical roots of contemporary theories

3. Present models of counseling consistent with current professional research and practice

4. Compare and contrast the major tenets of affective, behavioral, and cognitive theories

5. Apply counseling theory to material guiding case conceptualization and selection of appropriate interventions

6. Describe the "what," "when," and "why" of selecting family and other systems theories and related interventions

7. Highlight the impact of increasing globalization and diversification of the practice of professional counseling and of the clients served

We are proud to have had the opportunity to assemble such a diverse group of scholar-practitioners to share their chosen theories and unique professional identities. We know you will find their presentation valuable to your own professional practice and developing professional identity.

Acknowledgments

First and foremost, our appreciation goes to the scholar-practitioners who have contributed their time and talent to the formation of this text. In addition, we would like to recognize the valuable feedback received from our insightful reviewers: Victor I. Alvarado, Mark T. Blagen, Caroline M. Brackette, Rodney A. Bragdon, Britney G. Brinkman, Laura Cramer-Berness, Kimberly Duris, Leslie Korn, Amie Manis, G. Susan Mosley-Howard, Dale V. Wayman, and Marie Wilson.

Finally, we would like to acknowledge the word-crafting skills of Megan Granger, our copy editor, and the support, encouragement, energy, and vision provided by the people at SAGE—Maggie Stanley, Elizabeth Luizzi, and, especially, our friend Kassie Graves.

About the Contributors

Editors

Richard D. Parsons, PhD—Full professor, Department of Counselor Education, West Chester University

Naijian Zhang, PhD—Full professor, Department of Counselor Educational, West Chester University

Contributors (by Chapter)

Richard D. Parsons, PhD—Full professor, Department of Counselor Education, West Chester University (Chapters 1 & 3)

Dong Xie, PhD—Associate professor, Department of Psychology and Counseling, University of Central Arkansas (Chapter 2)

Naijian Zhang, PhD—Full professor, Department of Counselor Education, West Chester University (Chapter 3)

Faith Deveaux, PhD—Associate professor of counselor education, Lehman College/City University of New York (Chapter 4)

Robyn L. Trippany-Simmons, EdD—Residency coordinator, counseling programs, core faculty, MS in mental health counseling, Walden University (Chapter 5)

Matthew R. Buckley, EdD—Core faculty, MS in mental health counseling, Walden University (Chapter 5)

Kristin Meany-Walen—Assistant professor, School of Applied Human Sciences, Counseling Program, University of Northern Iowa (Chapter 5)

Tiffany Rush-Wilson, PhD—Clinical skills coordinator, counseling programs, core faculty, MS in mental health counseling, Walden University (Chapter 5)

Mark B. Scholl, PhD—Associate professor of counselor education, East Carolina University (Chapter 6)

Michael Walsh, PhD, LPC, CRC—Assistant professor of rehabilitation counseling, University of South Carolina School of Medicine (Chapter 6)

Michelle Perepiczka, PhD—Core faculty, Walden University (Chapter 6)

Marjorie C. Witty, PhD—Professor, Illinois School of Professional Psychology, Argosy University, Chicago (Chapter 7)

Ray Adomaitis, PhD—Adjunct professor, psychology and counseling, University of Maryland, University College Europe (Chapter 7)

Joseph Spillman, PhD—Core faculty, MS in mental health counseling, School of Counseling and Social Service, Walden University (Chapter 8)

Christina M. Rosen, EdD—Associate professor, Human Development and Psychological counseling, Appalachian State University (Chapter 8)

Julia Y. Porter, PhD, LPC, NCC, NCSC—Professor of counselor education and division head, Division of Education, Mississippi State University, Meridian (Chapter 9)

Barbara C. Trolley, PhD, CRC—Professor, Counselor Education, St. Bonaventure University (Chapter 10)

Christopher Siuta, PhD, LMHC—Assistant professor, Counselor Education, St. Bonaventure University (Chapter 10)

David A. Scott, PhD—Associate professor, Counselor Education, Clemson University (Chapter 11)

Hannah G. Barfield, M.Ed.—Counselor, Greenville Mental Health Center (Chapter 11)

Brandé Flamez, PhD, LPC, NCC—Professor, core faculty for the PhD Counselor Education and Supervision Program, Walden University (Chapter 12)

Joshua C. Watson, PhD, LPC, NCC, ACS—Associate professor, Counselor Education, Mississippi State University, Meridian (Chapter 12)

Kristi B. Cannon, PhD—Field Experience Director for the School of Counseling, Walden University (Chapter 13)

Jason Patton, PhD—Core faculty for PhD in Counselor Education and Supervision Program, Walden University (Chapter 13)

Stacee L. Reicherzer, PhD—Assessment coordinator for the School of Counseling and Social Service, Walden University (Chapter 13)

Rebecca M. Goldberg, PhD—Assistant professor of Counselor Education, Mississippi State University (Chapter 14)

Adam Zagelbaum, PhD—Associate professor, Department of Counseling, Sonoma State University (Chapter 15)

Maureen Buckley, PhD—Professor, Department of Counseling, Sonoma State University (Chapter 15)

Shana Friedman, MA—Graduate and adult admissions counselor, Dominican University of California (Chapter 15)

Kalia Gurnee, MA—Graduate, Department of Counseling, Sonoma State University (Chapter 15)

Michael G. Laurent, PhD—Chair, Marital and Family Therapy Program, California State University, Dominguez Hills (Chapter 16)

Shengli Dong, PhD—Assistant professor, Educational Psychology and Learning systems, Florida State University (Chapter 16)

SECTION I

The Value of Theory to Reflective Practice

CHAPTER 1

Theory and the Reflective Practitioner

Richard D. Parsons

Counselors, like most "helpers," tend to be doers—pragmatic in their approach. But counselors, unlike lay helpers, are professionals, and as professional counselors, they "do" what they do with intentionality and rationale.

Counseling is not a haphazard, random, hit-or-miss process. Counselors approach their work with their clients with an understanding about the human condition and the factors and processes that promote growth and well-being. As trained professionals, counselors are objective observers who deliberately gather data deemed essential both to understanding the nature of the client's concern and to the formulation of a treatment plan. The interpretation of these data and the resultant understanding are guided by the "theory" of the human condition that the counselor brings to professional encounters.

This chapter introduces you to the nature and value of theory. But beyond merely presenting the rationale for the use of theory in practice, this chapter and all those that follow attempt to help you reframe "theory" so you will value counseling theory as an essential component of effective practice, not just academic curiosity. Specifically, after reading this chapter you will be able to do the following:

1. Describe the essential qualities of a "good" theory

2. Explain the value of theory as a guide to counselors' understanding

3. Describe the connection of theory to counseling approach and treatment planning

4. Explain the role "theory" plays in the ongoing development of a counselor's professional identity

COUNSELING THEORY IN CONTEXT

Early approaches—or "theories," if you will—describing the origin, course, and even treatment of those we would now identify as having psychological problems often pointed to spiritual, or supernatural, causes. The Middle Ages were ripe with illustrations of this demonological perspective. People who we now know and were most likely suffering from psychological disorders were tortured in an effort to remove the demons and cure the affliction. Thankfully, our theories and practices have progressed from those darker days—under the guidance of the research and practice of many thoughtful pioneers.

Development of the psychodynamic approach (see Chapter 4) and the work of Sigmund Freud are often identified as a significant turning point, or even first major force, in the development of psychotherapy. Significant in this "first force" was emphasis on the natural versus supernatural nature of psychological disturbance and the rooting of its understanding in "science" and practice.

This initial formation of our understanding and practice of psychotherapy was further aided by the appearance of the research and practice of early behaviorists (see Chapter 10) and those modern theorists who followed in the tradition of cognitive-behavioral theory (see Chapter 9). This second influence turned our attention away from the determinism of early childhood experiences and unconscious drives and instincts and toward a focus on understanding the impact of learning and environmental conditions as they give shape to our thinking and actions. A final wave of theories confronted the implied negative view of man proposed by many in the psychodynamic orientation and the mechanistic view offered by many behavioral theorists. Led by Carl Rogers (see Chapters 6 and 7), this third force in psychology—the existential-humanistic orientation—emphasized the positive nature of the human condition and pointed to the importance of people taking charge of their lives in the process of finding meaning.

Since these initial "schools" of psychology, theories have continued to be created, refined, combined, and altered. According to Kazdin (2008), there are more than 500 different approaches to counseling. While this growth and refinement in counseling and psychotherapy theory speaks to the value of theory in the guidance of one's practice, it is essential that counselors learn to discern what is "good" theory.

The American Counseling Association's (ACA, 2005) *Code of Ethics* directs counselors to devise counseling plans that have a reasonable promise of success (Section A.1.c). This is a mandate that can be met by the judicious use of theories as a guide to practice decisions, assuming that counselors approach their practice and the theory(ies) they employ with a critical, evaluative attitude.

THEORY

While it may be obvious, "theory" is not "fact." A theory is a system of inferences, assumptions, and interpretations drawn from one's observations and experiences. And while we all draw inferences from our experiences or jump to conclusions based on our biases and assumptions, such meaning-making, while perhaps reflective of our personal theory, typically fails to manifest the qualities characteristic of a "good" theory: precision and testability, empirical validity, parsimony, stimulation, and practicality/utility.

Precision and Testability

A good theory in counseling or physics is general and provides clear operational definitions of its constructs that will allow others to "test" the theory, which in turn predicts future observations and stimulates new discoveries. "Good" theories present well-defined, specific, and measurable constructs (Monte & Sollod, 2008). In addition to providing precise constructs, a good theory also specifies the nature of the relationship these constructs have with one another. Such precision allows for others to investigate these constructs, their relationship, and the fundamentals of any one theory to determine the degree to which it meets the next criterion of a "good" theory—that is, empirical validity.

Empirical Validity and Stimulation

Unlike theories in arts and philosophy that explain ideas and phenomena that may not be measurable, scientific theories—including those in counseling—propose explanation of phenomena that can be tested for confirmation or falsification using scientific experiments (Edies & Appelrouth, 2010). Testing counseling theories to assess their validity or truthfulness is a difficult process. The nature of our counseling does not lend itself to the purity of a scientist's laboratory and controlled experimentation.

Over the course of the past 20 years, new research methods and statistical techniques have been developed and applied to researching counseling effectiveness and the degree to which employment of different theories contributes to that effectiveness. The findings, while generally supporting the effectiveness of counseling (Wampold, 2010), continue to find it difficult to differentiate the specific value of each theory. Most of the current research presents various theoretical orientations as equally effective with a wide variety of client issues (Wampold, 2010).

While some theories lend themselves more than others to validating research methodology, as will be noted in the upcoming chapters, all theories seek to find empirical support for their validity and effectiveness. This ability to excite the research practitioner to question and challenge is what constitutes the "stimulation" aspect of a good theory.

Parsimony

To be of value, theories should be parsimonious while at the same time comprehensive enough to address the entirety of the experience being explained. The principle of parsimony directs us to value a theory that provides the simplest explanation when confronted with the option of a simple or complex interpretation. This assumes that both explanations are equally precise, testable, and valid.

Practicality/Utility

Finally, and perhaps most importantly, a theory should be of value to the practitioners who employ it. As with all scientific theories, counseling provides explanation for various elements of the human condition that can be tested for theory confirmation or falsification. But counseling theory moves beyond describing and "explaining" the reality we experience and presents ways one can affect those realities. Our counseling theories help us articulate the assumptions, interpretations, and hypotheses we employ to understand what is happening with our clients and to make predictions about what may happen in the future. An effective counselor employs a theory to describe, explain, predict, and change behavior. A "good" theory in counseling serves as an essential ingredient to effective practice and practice decisions (Hansen, 2006, 2007).

THEORY: GUIDING PRACTICE DECISIONS AND SERVING ETHICAL PRACTICE

The National Cancer Institute's (2005) monograph *Theory at a Glance* distinguishes two types of theory, both of which hold relevance for the professional counselor: *explanatory* theory and *change* theory.

Explanatory theory helps one understand complex situations (Buchanan, 1994) and, as such, is useful to counselors as they attempt to understand the stories their clients share. As explanatory theory, counseling theories help counselors take the complexity and uniqueness of a client's presenting concerns and decompose this ill-structured problem into subproblems that can then be reconfigured in ways that allow for more meaningful resolution (Voss & Post, 1988). Consider the data shared by the client in Part A of Case Illustration 1.1. Of everything the client said, what is truly important? A counselor seeking an answer to that question and questions such as, "What does the information suggest about the client or the client's problem?" and "How might these data point to effective interventions?" may find answers within the counselor's operative model or theory, as shown in Part B of Case Illustration 1.1.

CASE ILLUSTRATION 1.1

What's It All About?

Part A

The following exchange occurred during the opening minutes of the initial "intake" session with this 37-year-old woman experiencing the break-up of a 3-year relationship.

Client: (Crying) I simply don't know what to do . . . this is devastating.

Counselor: If I understood what you shared, the ending of the relationship seemed to come "out of the blue"—totally unexpected?

Client: He's such a son of bitch. He led me on for 3 years, talking about marriage and picket fences and all that bullshit. I mean, sure we had our problems, but what relationship doesn't?

What am I to do? I'm 37 years old. Who's gonna want me? I'm going to spend the rest of my life alone. I mean, really what does this say about me? What a loser I must be! Most of my friends are all moving on—married with kids, established relationships, houses . . . good jobs. The friends I have who are single won't want me hanging with them since for the past 3 years I put Tony ahead of them. And my family—Christ, mom will be crying about no grandkids!

Who's going to want to hang with me? I have absolutely nothing to offer . . . (breaks down in tears). I don't want to be alone!

Part B

The following reflects the different focuses brought to interpretation of the client's story as a result of employing two different counseling theories. Not only do the two therapists focus on different aspects of the client's disclosure, but they are directed to two different types of interventions.

Dr. L (Cognitive theory): Well, clearly she is in pain, and I truly feel for her struggle, but I am really drawn to her conclusion that *"I'm 37 years old. Who's gonna want me? I'm going to spend the rest of my life alone."* It seems, at least in this incident, that she has a tendency to overdramatize or catastrophize problems. Assuming that is true (and I would want to elicit more data to support that), then I believe helping her see this loss for what it is and nothing more, along with helping her discern the real consequences that follow from the ending of this relationship, rather than those that she is assuming, would be beneficial.

If I can assume the relationship I have with her is strong enough, I would like to question, if not outright challenge, her on what appears to be faulty thinking. She is taking the fact that this one relationship (while 3 years long) ended as evidence that she will spend the rest of her life alone. Such catastrophizing of the event is, in my view, creating the extreme sadness and hopelessness she now experiences.

Dr. G (Solution focused): She is presenting with a failed social relationship and is narrowly constructing her sense of her world and herself as a reflection of that one failed relationship. With this view of self and the world, she is understandably feeling extremely sad and hopeless. However, as she shares her story, she hints at a goal (not to be alone) and even to the fact that she has the ability and experience to make and maintain relationships.

She seems to be sharing that, while this relationship has ended, she has in fact developed relationships with many others—some married, some single. So I guess I would like to turn her attention to looking at the statement, "I don't want to be alone," and help her reframe that to a more positively stated goal, such as, "I want to have social relationships." If I could help her focus on that, then we could look at the successes she has had in the past—with her current friends and even with Tony, during the early part of their relationship—as a way of identifying things she can do to reinstate old relationships or venture into new ones.

As demonstrated in this case illustration, a counselor's theory can serve as a meaningful framework to guide his or her understanding of the client's story. One's theory facilitates the gathering and organization of client data, interpretation of those data, and, as will be demonstrated, selection and implementation of helping strategies (Magnuson, Norem, & Wilcoxon, 2000). These characteristics of one's chosen theory are not only guides to practice decisions but essential to ethical practice.

Organizing Data

The barrage of information regularly confronting practicing counselors would be a bewildering array of random, disparate happenings without the aid of organizing conceptual theory to make sense of it all (Hansen, 2006, p. 291). Most counselors can recall their initial experiences in counselor training—either working with volunteer clients or their peers in simulated counseling experiences—and the general sense of angst from not knowing what to do at any one point in the exchange.

Perhaps you can relate to the counselor-in-training who, having mastered the fundamental communication skills, finds herself immersed in the client's story, unable to discern that which is important from that which is not, or to find the thread that ties seemingly unrelated pieces of information into a meaningful life story. That type of experience led Prochaska and Norcross (2003) to state: "Without a guiding theory . . . clinicians would be vulnerable, directionless creatures bombarded with literally hundreds of impressions and pieces of information in a single session" (p. 5).

The operative premise undergirding the teaching and utilization of theory in counseling is simply that, as counselors, we are able to observe and record real-world phenomena and, in so doing, we can glean essential features and the relationships among them. Further, it is assumed that with such observation and knowledge, we (and others in the behavioral sciences) will be able to manipulate these elements for the betterment of our clients. For an example of this, consider Case Illustration 1.2.

CASE ILLUSTRATION 1.2

Anthony—Ants in His Pants?

Background

Ms. Virginia Morton, the first-grade teacher, came to Mr. Pillagalli, the school counselor, with her concerns about Anthony, a child in her class whom she described as having either "seizures" or "worms in his pants." She wanted Mr. Pillagalli to see Anthony and assist him in sitting still during class time.

Mr. Pillagalli asked if he could come to class and observe Anthony in action. As he sat in the back of the class, he noted the following:

1. Anthony sat toward the back of the class, somewhat isolated from the others, who were working in small groups (an arrangement Ms. Morton explained was the result of his being too distracting to the others).
2. Ms. Morton was an active and engaged teacher. She would move around the room, encouraging her students as they worked on their assignments.
3. In the 40 minutes Mr. Pillagalli observed, he noted that the only time Ms. Morton attended to Anthony was to ask him to "please sit still." He noted that on one occasion she simply turned and reprimanded him, and the second time, when Anthony was actually rocking his desk, she went over to him and spent close to a minute redirecting him to his work.

Connections and Hypothesis

Mr. Pillagalli met with Ms. Morton and shared his hypothesis, drawn from observation and his understanding of behavioral theory.

The question he posed was this: "Is it possible that Anthony, being somewhat isolated from peer and even your [Ms. Morton's] attention, intentionally or even accidentally discovered that his fidgeting was a way to get the attention he desired?"

While Ms. Morton questioned why Anthony would seek such negative attention—"I did correct him in front of the class," she said—Mr. Pillagalli explained that sometimes any attention is experienced as more desirable than none at all. So what she may think was negative was actually received as positive and thus reinforced his behavior.

Ms. Morton understood the theory behind this hypothesis but remained skeptical. She did, however, develop a plan with Mr. Pillagalli to test the theory.

Plan

They decided to test this plan by doing two things. First, each time Anthony started squirming or moving in his seat, Ms. Morton would simply ignore the disruptive behavior. However, as soon as Anthony stopped his wiggling and refocused on the desk work, Ms. Morton would walk over and praise him for his attentive behavior. She would keep a record of both the frequency of his movement and the duration of each incident.

Follow-Up

One week into this plan, Ms. Morton reported that Anthony was no longer any more fidgety than the other students. She had not needed to correct his behavior or ask him to stop squirming all week, and he had rejoined his small group.

A counseling theory, when used as explanatory, offers a lens or framework through which a counselor can process a client's story. The concepts, constructs, and elements of any one theory point to the factors hypothesized to cause and maintain a client's problem. Thus, the use of theories within counseling helps the counselors not only organize that which is observed but also find a tentative explanation for its occurrence. Effective counselors call on theories to assist them in organizing clinical data, making complex processes coherent, and providing conceptual guidance for interventions (Hansen, 2006, p. 291).

As you proceed in your reading of the theories to follow, you will see this process of organizing, understanding, explaining, and affecting in action. For now, it may be helpful to see theories in action within your own life. Exercise 1.1 is provided to help you in that process.

EXERCISE 1.1

WHY DID I DO THAT?

Directions: As we navigate through our lives each day, we are confronted with choices and decisions to be made. In observing our choices at any one point and contrasting those with the alternative, we might be drawn to ask why that path was chosen. The following exercise invites you to reflect on a recent decision and draw on theoretical constructs that may help explain your choice.

Part A: Identify one decision you made within the past few days. In the space below, describe the situation, your options, and your choice.

Situation: _____

_____

_____

Possible actions/decisions: _____

_____

_____

My decision/action: _____

_____

_____

Part B: In the table below, you will find questions reflecting specific theoretical concepts or constructs. In responding to the questions, do you find any offering a better explanation of the choice you described in Part A?

Testing a Theory	Answer Applied to My Choice	Feelings About Value and Validity of Explanation
How has that action/decision worked for you in the past?		
How may your physical state at the time of your choice have contributed to that choice?		
How did your thoughts about others' reactions toward your decision guide your selection?		
To what degree was your decision guided by the internal voice of what you *wanted* versus what you *should* do?		
To what degree might your decision reflect your attempt to demonstrate that you overcame or mastered some early childhood weakness or difficulty?		
To what degree might your decision reflect your family culture and values?		

While the questions used in Exercise 1.1 are neither pure nor perfect reflections of the theories to follow, it may be worthwhile to revisit the questions and how they reflected on your decision after reading each of the forthcoming theories, as a way to see theory applied to your lived experience.

Providing Direction

Theories are more than "organizing schema." They help the counselor connect disparate areas of knowledge, allowing him or her to make more discriminating judgments about the information being presented and how best to respond. To be of real value to counselors, theories need to assist not only in organizing and understanding but also in directing counselor response.

Our clients come seeking assistance with distressing circumstances or help in their growth. However, before engaging in strategies to help, counselors need to assess the nature of the problem, identify those client factors that impede the growth they desire, and know the limits of what they can do given the context in which clients work. This information and the implied direction to be taken can be found by way of a conceptual map provided by theories. Knowing the theoretical rationale, the "why" behind the client's current condition and concerns, not only directs the counselor to intervention strategies but can help counselors create new techniques or approaches (McBride & Martin, 1990).

A counselor's orienting framework or counseling theory allows him or her to approach work with a client with a greater sense of what to do if "this or that" occurs. Theories help guide a counselor's procedural thinking—that is, viewing client data from the perspective, "If this occurs (within the client's story), then I'll do this to achieve that."

Theories help counselors understand what to do if a particular condition exists or when a specific client disclosure is made. Case Illustration 1.3 provides an example of how two counselors with different theoretical orientations may respond to a client disclosure. In both cases, the counselor is employing his or her frame of reference, theory to guide procedural thinking, to respond to the client's disclosure.

CASE ILLUSTRATION 1.3

What to Do?

Introduction: A counselor's theory provides a structure for his or her employment of procedural knowledge—that is, understanding how to proceed or what to do in a given situation. The following illustrates the unique way a counselor may respond to a single client disclosure, reflecting that counselor's goals and expected impact of the response given his or her theoretical orientation.

Counselor A: Solution Focused

Client: So really, how many times do I have to come? I really don't need counseling. I mean, I had a drink or two and I just didn't see the red light, so for such a silly mistake I have to come to counseling? This is stupid.

Counselor: Well, you are here now. So I'm wondering, what would have to happen to make it so that when you leave our session, you think, "Hey, that wasn't so bad"?

Counselor reflection: Well, there is much more to this story, but what was clear from the beginning was that he was resentful of the DUI and the court-ordered counseling. It was also clear that he had constructed a view of counseling as punitive. I wanted to attempt to shift his focus from the problem of the DUI, or being mandated to receive counseling, and get him to share his goal for coming. Hopefully, he and I could develop that goal as a target and empower him to achieve it.

Counselor B: Reality Therapy

Client: So really, how many times do I have to come? I really don't need counseling. I mean, I had a drink or two and I just didn't see the red light, so for such a silly mistake I have to come to counseling? This is stupid.

Counselor: Well, to be honest, I am a firm believer in your right to make decisions. So, truly, you don't have to come here. That would be your choice.

Counselor reflection: I believe it is important for clients not to see themselves as victims and powerless. My goal is to help my clients define their wants, evaluate their behaviors, and make concrete plans for fulfilling their needs.

Case Illustration 1.3 demonstrates two unique responses to the same client disclosure. These responses, like any counselor interventions and strategies, did not occur in a vacuum. An effective counselor's response needs to be an extension of his or her operative framework or theory (Greenberg, Elliott, & Lietaer, 1994). Thus, the point of the illustration that needs to be highlighted is not that the counselors' responses differed but that each counselor engaged in a particular response as a way of facilitating the client's movement along a continuum of helping. The response, as intervention, was selected because it reflected the assumptions about the human condition and change as articulated by that counselor's theoretical model. Further, it must be remembered that while theories can provide guidance for counselor decisions, the value and efficacy of those decisions and their impact on client welfare still need to be monitored and assessed.

With this caveat in mind, theories do serve as useful guides to counselor activities with clients. Our theory provides a road map or guide in sessions with clients and a foundation for meaningful counselor decision making and action (Stiles, 2013). And just as the counselors in Case Illustration 1.3 were directed in their responses by their theoretical models and desire to impact the client in a helpful way, both will observe the impact of their responses and assess them against that which their theories would lead them to expect. Thus, our theories also provide a method of assessing the progress and effectiveness of our counseling.

Marking Progress

The previous discussion on the value of theories as a guide to a counselor's procedural knowledge highlights the "intentional" nature of the counseling process. That is, counselors engage with clients in ways intended to facilitate the helping process. Counselors' theories help them know what they are doing, why they are doing it, and the anticipated result or impact.

An effective counselor is one who systematically reflects on practice decisions. This reflection and assessment of effectiveness should not be restricted to the evaluation of terminal goal achievement. Rather, effective counselors attempt to monitor and assess their effectiveness and progress all along the way to termination. Theory can provide "markers," or criteria against which a counselor can assess the effectiveness of interventions at any one point in the helping relationship, thus enacting the ethical mandate to monitor effectiveness (ACA, 2005, Section C.2.d).

For example, consider a counselor who employs a cognitive model of counseling (see Chapter 9). This counselor believes that the way his client views or makes meaning of a particular situation is causing his distress and, therefore, that changing his view should offer relief. With this oversimplified view of cognitive theory as a backdrop, we may find this counselor engaged in the following dialogue with his client.

Counselor: So if I understand what you are saying, you feel very angry at her because she "deliberately" cut you off in the parking lot?

Client: Yeah, I can't stand it. I'm always getting disrespected. I'm not going to take it anymore.

Counselor: So we know for a fact that she did pull in front of your car and then go into the parking spot you were hoping to get.

Client: She can't get away with such b.s. . . . that is disrespectful.

Counselor: I can hear how upsetting it is to you and that you really believe two things about this event. The first is that she did it *deliberately,* and the second is that she did it *intentionally to disrespect* you.

The counselor, using cognitive theory as his guiding framework, understands that the personalization this client is experiencing is setting the cognitive stage for his anger. The counselor attempts to "shock" the client into a different perspective, and then, if that proves successful, he will use the opportunity to educate the client about the power of his thinking.

Counselor: So I guess I'm a little confused. Do you know this woman?

Client: No.

Counselor: But somehow you feel that she knows you and intentionally wants to disrespect you?

Client: (Long pause) *According to the counselor's theory, this long pause suggests that his question is causing some cognitive disruption for the client, which is a good thing.* Well, she doesn't know me . . . but it's still pretty damn rude.

Counselor: So if you believe it was personal, you see it as disrespect, and that really makes you angry. But now . . . if you think maybe it was just rude . . . how does that make you feel?

Client: Annoyed . . .

The counselor in this situation decided to ask provocative questions as a way of challenging the client's thinking. Such an intervention is in line with his operational model of cognitive theory. However, the question remains: "Was the intervention effective?" Using cognitive theory, the counselor would be led to expect that a question truly challenging to the client's thinking would first cause clear confusion and then, ideally, would resolve in the client embracing a different perspective. Confusion and initial acceptance of an alternative perspective are markers gleaned from his theory that, once noted, would indicate progress. In this scenario, therefore, the counselor was glad to observe the client's long pause before responding, seeing it as a marker signifying that the intervention was having the expected result. And reframing of the situation from personal to less personal resulted—as predicted by the theory—in movement from intense anger to annoyance. Both the reframing and the change in affect were markers of progress and evidence for the effectiveness of the intervention.

Supporting Ethical Practice

While theories serve as scaffolds for the collection and organization of data and the selection and implementation of strategies, they also serve as a foundation for ethical practice.

Welfare of Those Served by Counselors

As noted in the ACA (2005) *Code of Ethics*, professional counselors are charged with the primary responsibility of respecting the dignity of clients and promoting their welfare (Section A.1.a). One form this promotion of welfare takes is the formulation and application of a counselor's treatment plan. The ACA *Code of Ethics* directs counselors to develop "integrated counseling plans that offer reasonable promise of success and are consistent with abilities and circumstances of the client" (Section A.1.c). Such a directive can be met by the counselor's competent and proficient use of theory as a guide to practice.

Good theories not only provide a structure for planning but also, as will become clear throughout the remainder of this text, allow for empirical testing of their component parts and thus provide practitioners with the data base on which to develop plans that "*offer reasonable promise of success*" (Section A.1.c; emphasis added).

Developmental and Cultural Sensitivity

In discussing developmental and cultural sensitivity, the ACA (2005) *Code of Ethics* recommends that, "where possible, counselors adjust their practices" to meet the unique developmental and cultural characteristics of their clients. Chapters 2 and 16 of the current text highlight this need, as well as the challenge posed by using theories that largely reflect a Western and, in most cases, Anglo view of the human condition. This limitation is being addressed with the inclusion of many techniques and theories reflecting Eastern thought, including a number of therapeutic applications based on the concept of mindfulness and Buddhist meditation.

In addition to Chapters 2 and 16, you will note that each chapter in this text addresses the strengths and limitations of the theory under discussion as it relates to the *uniqueness and diversity* of the client. This aspect of theory further reflects the ethical principle of *ensuring the welfare of our clients* (ACA, 2005, Section A.1.a) by respecting the diversity they present and allowing that diversity to inform our counseling plans as shaped by our theoretical orientations.

Informed Consent

Having an operative orientation or theory to guide one's practice also allows for the explanation of that model and its implications for the relationship and dynamic of any counseling encounter. This ability to describe what can be anticipated within the counseling process is essential if a counselor is to provide for informed consent (ACA, 2005, Section A.2).

The ACA (2005) *Code of Ethics* notes that clients must be given the opportunity to choose to enter into or remain in a counseling relationship and, as such, need information on which to base that decision (Section A.2.a). While the ACA code highlights some of the information required for informed consent (see Section A.2.b), it is particularly important to note that the code directs counselors to provide clients with information regarding the process they are about to enter, including the purposes, goals, techniques, and procedures to be employed. Without understanding and utilization of a theory to guide practice, a counselor will be at a loss to articulate these elements of the process in a way that will help a client provide informed consent. Again, it is evident that a good theory is essential not only to effective but also ethical practice.

Monitor Effectiveness

The issue of informed consent does not cease to matter following a counselor's initial encounter with a client. Allowing for the client's informed consent at each point along the journey is essential. Clients have a right to know what they will encounter as well as the degree to which these processes are effective. Once again, the ethical counselor is directed to monitor his or her effectiveness (ACA, 2005, Section C.2.d) and to help the client see this progress or understand the nature of its delay. In understanding the constructs of theories and progression of the counseling dynamic implied within these theories, a counselor can meet this mandate. Counselors with a clear sense of their operative model can contrast actual progress with that anticipated by the theoretical model being employed, thus gauging the effectiveness of their counseling.

Yes, counseling theories not only are essential to effective practice but also serve to make our practice ethical.

Boundaries of Competence

As you proceed through your reading of this text, a caution is in order. As with all our initial professional experiences, this one text or course in theories is *not* sufficient to make one a competent practitioner of any theory. As noted in the ACA (2005) *Code of Ethics*, "Counselors practice only within the boundaries of their competence" (Section C.2.a). Thus, while a reader may comprehend what is presented in this text and even find its application in case illustrations and guided exercises to be accurate and efficient, that alone does not make him or her competent to engage in counseling from any one of these theoretical models. Additional training, practice, and, most certainly, supervision in the use of these theories is essential for ethical competent practice.

THEORY–RESEARCH CONNECTION

Historically, theories have been viewed as reflections of reality, or at least attempts at being accurate reflections of reality. With this as the standard, theories were typically submitted to the rigors of research to assess their validity both in terms of the constructs employed and the predictions that would flow from them. From this vantage, it could be assumed that all traditional counseling theories map actual psychological territory. While it was fashionable to argue which theory was most right or valid, more recently, counselors have approached the evaluation of theories from a different perspective.

For most counselors, the question is less "Which theory provides an accurate description of some universal truth?" and more "To what degree does the theory serve as a useful tool or narrative structure?" (see, e.g., Hansen, 2006). Counselors engage theories for the specific theoretical constructs they offer, which in turn enables them to form strong helping relationships with the clients and incorporate strategies that have a reasonable chance of promoting the change desired. As such, most counselors select theories according to the consequences of using them in specific, local situations—not on the basis of universal truth. With this shift in emphasis, counselors have started to question not only under what circumstances certain theories, systems, or strategies will be effective but also what components across theories may be integrated into effective helping.

Though such a utilitarian view of theory may be intuitively appealing, the challenge is to avoid a shotgun, hit-or-miss approach to employment of a theory or theoretical construct. Counselors need to have a rationale for their selection of a theoretical model or set of strategies. It is essential that counselors know prior to their employment the research supporting use of specific theories or strategies emerging from theories.

In recent years, attention has turned to the research in finding empirical support for theories employed and interventions selected (Deegear & Lawson, 2003). This is not unique to the counseling profession. The U.S. surgeon general, for example, called for the increased development and proliferation of evidence-based interventions across the health services (U.S. Public Health Service, 2000). The focus on employing those theories and strategies for which there is supportive research reflects the simple belief that those with the support of sound outcome studies are more likely to prove efficacious than are those without such support (Massey, Armstrong, Boroughs, Henson, & McCash, 2005).

As you proceed in your reading of this text, you will discover that some theories have extensive empirical support, whereas others may be limited in such support. It is important that we realize the limitation of support for any one theory does not mean that theory is of little value for the professional counselor. The truth of our discipline is that our research methodology is limited when it comes to the areas of intervention and treatment outcome. Thus, while some theories fail to lend themselves easily to the traditional, randomized, control-group design of research, they may have abundant support in small-sample or single-case studies, or even in anecdotal and qualitative reporting of current practice.

Perhaps our future research will clearly identify those theories and resulting strategies proven effective under specific circumstances, but until that day, practitioners need not only to exercise care in selecting theories or theoretical constructs to be employed within their practice but also to monitor the impact of their theories.

THEORY: AN ESSENTIAL COMPONENT OF A COUNSELOR'S PROFESSIONAL IDENTITY

Professional identity has been defined as "the possession of a core set of values, beliefs, and assumptions about the unique characteristics of one's selected profession that differentiates it from other professions" (Weinrach, Thomas, & Chan, 2001, p. 168). The counselor's professional identity helps distinguish him or her from others not only across the helping professions (e.g., psychiatrists, psychologists, social workers) but also within a profession. Each counselor, while embracing the values of his or her profession, will also develop a professional identity through a process of integrating a "theoretical orientation and methodology that is consistent with the counselor's personal values and beliefs" (Moore-Pruitt, 1994, p. 34). An examination of counselor development in literature suggests that the processes of developing an integrated professional identity converge with those by which counseling students align with a theoretical orientation (James, 2011). A counselor's alignment with a particular theory or set of theories provides the language necessary for articulating his or her professional identity to self and others.

The key to our identity as counselors is the fact that we are members of a profession and, thus, unique and distinct from lay helpers. Our profession is rooted in a history and a unique body of knowledge reflecting our operational theories and research. Those who enter and practice the discipline and profession of counseling are not mere functionaries simply applying this or that strategy as if following a recipe. Unlike technicians, who also may employ strategies and techniques to solve a problem, professional counselors are able to identify the rationale (i.e., theory) and research that explain what they have observed in a client and the decisions they make in response.

Professional counselors are active pursuers of understanding. They approach their work with a perspective on the human condition and factors that facilitate growth and well-being. Theories and the theoretical orientation employed by each counselor set the framework for this understanding. Counseling theories also serve as a frame of reference for thinking about ourselves—what we do and why we do it. These are important aspects of developing professional identity, and a counselor's alignment with a particular theory or set of theories provides the language necessary for articulating his or her professional identity.

Professional counselors understand theory and have reflected on the validity of each theory as evidenced by research and utility in practice. Further, professional counselors have assimilated the assumptions, values, and hypothetical constructs offered by theories as explanations for both current client behavior and factors or strategies that can be used to facilitate change. In this way, the theory becomes part of a counselor's professional identity. Exercise 1.2 invites you to observe the connection between theory and professional identity.

In many other professions, professional identity is defined by the profession—universally promulgated and relatively fixed and congruent across all members (Rosenau, 1992). Under these conditions, those entering that profession are simply

EXERCISE 1.2

THEORY–PROFESSIONAL IDENTITY CONNECTION

Directions: As noted, a counselor's operative framework or theory reflects his or her view of the human condition, the role of counselor, and the processes that facilitate or impede personal growth. As such, theory is an integral part of a counselor's identity.

This exercise invites you to interview your professors, supervisors, or mentors. Their responses to the questions listed below will help elucidate the theory–professional identity connection.

1. What would you identify as your theoretical orientation (one or multiple theories)?

2. Was the orientation you identified the one you felt was taught, promoted, or modeled in your graduate training? If not, what led you to the adoption of this model?

3. What, specifically, in your professional experience has pointed to the utility of this theoretical orientation?

4. Do you know of research that supports the tenets of this theory (or theories) and/or its effectiveness?

5. What, if any, limitations have you encountered in using this theory to guide practice (e.g., in particular settings, with particular presenting concerns, with populations served)?

taught and enculturated into that identity. Counselors, however, find themselves in a profession that is evolving and developing. As such, counselors cannot simply be enculturated into the identity of the profession but, rather, are responsible for developing their own professional identities as counselors. Many counselors align themselves with a particular theoretical orientation, to the extent that they refer to themselves as disciples of that theory. Perhaps in completing Exercise 1.2 you found that some professors referred to themselves as existentialists, Gestaltists, or behaviorists; if so, these are examples of theory serving as foundation for professional identity. It would not be unusual to find counselors who do not align with a single theoretical model and rather claim to be eclectic, transtheoretical, or integrative. But even in these situations, the counselors are giving voice to their professional identity and the role their assimilation of theory has played in its development. Whether a counselor embraces a singular theory as a purist or employs some integrated set of theoretical constructs and strategies, the counselor's operating framework, model, or theory is a substantive part of his or her professional identity.

IDEAL TO REAL: CONSTRAINTS GUIDING SELECTION AND IMPLEMENTATION OF THEORY

While we all, as ethical counselors, will employ a theory or theories to guide our practice decisions, it can be hoped that the selection of a theory will be the result of our testing of its integrity, parsimony, and the degree to which it has empirical support. These criteria are the ideal; however, in actual practice, selection and implementation of any one theory may be influenced and even constrained by real-world conditions, including realities of the workplace, fiscal considerations, and unique cultural characteristics of the populations served.

Realities of the Workplace

While we have noted the characteristics that identify a good theory, it is important to highlight that for counselors, the primary characteristics of a good theory are that it is useful, practical, and applicable to counselor functioning. Counseling theory can serve as a framework, scaffold, or guide for making practice decisions. However, in employing a theory as a guide to practice decisions, counselors need to consider not only the integrity of the theory but also the uniqueness of the client and the client's presenting concerns, and the context within which the service is provided. It is important for counselors to ensure that their practice decisions not only reflect "best practice" but also respect and reflect the culture and realities of the context within which they work.

Consider, for example, the constraints often encountered by those counselors working within a school setting. Given the school counselor's extensive case loads, along with the role and function of school counselor to facilitate students' academic progress, engaging in long-term, dynamic counseling targeting unconscious issues or early childhood experiences would seem less than feasible.

School counseling requires approaches that are appropriate for the time constraints encountered (Littrell, Malia, & Vanderwood, 1995). For many school counselors, the contextual demands and their identified roles and functions lead them to seek strength-based approaches in the classroom and guidance office. With their focus on clients' strengths and brief therapeutic encounters, theories such as the solution-focused approach (see Chapter 12) have become a practical intervention for students, teachers, and parents of school-aged children (Franklin, Biever, Moore, Clemons, & Scamardo, 2001). In those circumstances where more in-depth dynamic (e.g., psychodynamic; Chapter 4) or family systems (Chapter 14) approaches may be required, school counselors would most likely refer to an outside agency rather than employ those techniques within their work setting.

The same could be said of those counselors working within a university setting. The use of theories and models supporting brief psychotherapy with a limited number of sessions appears more suited to a university setting wherein there may be a large demand for limited services. Turner and his colleagues (Turner, Valtierra, Talken, Miller, & DeAnda, 1996) reported on a multitude of studies that have contrasted time-limited and time-unlimited treatment modalities, with the findings showing that short-term or brief psychotherapy is a successful and useful treatment modality in its own right and is particularly useful for the college-aged population. Needless to say, findings such as these, when placed within the reality of too much demand for too little resources, will serve as constraints to the employment of theories other than those fitting this time-limited criterion.

Other work settings or contexts of service delivery and populations served may place further constraints on the use of some theories while highlighting or supporting the use of others. Consider counselors who work in a drug and alcohol treatment facility. The demands and unique needs of that population and work setting may support the counselors' use of strategies such as motivational interviewing to challenge the addictive behaviors of clients, whereas counselors working in a clinic with individuals who have eating disorders may find the use of cognitive-behavioral therapy more appropriate to the population and setting. Both of these approaches have been established as effective when attempting to change behaviors. The key is ensuring that the theory utilized by the counselor is in line with the unique needs of the client and situation.

Financial Realities

The literature suggests that changes in third-party payment procedures—including an increase in the involvement of health maintenance and managed care organizations—have had a considerable, and in some ways troubling, impact on the provision of mental health services (Rupert & Baird, 2004). Reductions in covered or allowed office visits, hospital days, diagnostic tests, and procedures have been noted (Rupert & Baird, 2004). This is understandable given that insurers, with their motive of maximizing profits, are interested in providing the least costly procedures possible (Pyles, 2003; Sank, 1997).

These economic constraints imposed by third-party payers can influence a counselor's choice of operative model or theory. Rupert and Baird (2004), reporting on psychologists in practice, found that those with high-involvement in this third-party–payer system were more likely to have a cognitive-behavioral orientation and less likely to have a psychodynamic orientation when compared with their low-involvement counterparts. Clearly, insurance payment can serve as a constraint, giving shape to the specific theories employed by service providers.

Diversity

Counselors are ethically obligated to become knowledgeable about cultural differences and to design therapeutic techniques to fit each client. This ethical obligation requires each counselor to consider not only the integrity of his or her theoretical orientation, or the degree to which the theory has found empirical support, but also the degree to which the theory is in concert with the values and mores of those with whom the counselor works.

Theories with empirical support for their effectiveness, while ideal, can still prove ineffective and perhaps even harmful when running counter to a client's culture. In the chapters that follow, the authors discuss use of their theories with diverse populations. As you will note, there is supportive evidence for the use of these theories across many different populations. But as you read on, you need to consider the constraint that diverse cultural values and beliefs, as well as lived experiences, may place on the selection, use, and effectiveness of any theory. As a brief illustration, consider the following:

Existential theory (Chapter 6): Existential theory encourages the client to order the direction of therapy, with a focus on finding personal meaning in life. Such a limited-structure approach to self-determination may be challenging for those from oppressed cultures, who may prefer a more structured and directed process or for whom talking about self-determination may be difficult.

Cognitive theory (Chapter 9): A keystone of cognitive therapy is its focus on challenging a client's dysfunctional or faulty beliefs. This challenging of potentially harmful beliefs can be a challenge itself if counselors do not know and value the client's unique cultural beliefs. Further, some clients' cultures may actually prohibit them from questioning their beliefs.

Reality therapy (Chapter 11): Reality therapy emphasizing personal responsibility, decision making, and empowerment may prove ineffective with clients who have known and may continue to experience real oppression. These clients, while desiring to take responsibility and control, are neither choosing that experience of oppression nor necessarily able to control it. The call for such self-determination may be met with client frustration and despair.

Theories are valuable to the degree that they help us understand our realities and guide our practices. The selection of a theory to guide practice is a process that needs to be informed not only by the "goodness" of the theory and empirical support for its tenets but also by the reality of the working conditions, the populations served, and the unique cultural values brought to the counseling session.

A GIFT AND A CHALLENGE

What you will discover in the chapters that follow are well-developed and well-articulated orienting frameworks that we label "counseling theory." Each theory is presented by a counselor who has embraced that theory as an essential part of his or her professional identity and practice approach. While the gift is in the clear articulation of the theory and demonstration of its utility, the challenge is for you to move beyond simple comprehension to valuing and, in so doing, to allow each theory to nurture your own developing professional identity.

KEYSTONES

- A theory is a system of inferences, assumptions, and interpretations drawn from one's observations and experiences. Theories employ constructs and concepts to explain that which is observed.
- Our counseling theories help us articulate the assumptions, interpretations, and hypotheses we employ to understand what is happening with our clients and to make predictions about what may happen in the future. An effective counselor employs theory to describe, explain, predict, and change behaviors.

- As explanatory theory, counseling theories help counselors take the complexity and uniqueness of a client's presenting concerns and decompose this ill-structured problem into subproblems that can then be reconfigured in ways that allow for more meaningful resolution.
- Effective counselors call on theories to assist them in organizing clinical data, making complex processes coherent, and providing conceptual guidance for interventions.
- Theories help the counselor connect seemingly disparate areas of knowledge, allowing him or her to make more discriminating judgments about the information being presented and how best to respond.
- A counselor's orienting framework or counseling theory allows him or her to approach work with a client with a greater sense of what to do if "this or that" occurs.
- Counselors' theories help them know what they are doing, why they are doing it, and the anticipated result or impact.
- For most counselors, the question is less "Which theory provides an accurate description of some universal truth?" and more "To what degree does the theory serve as a useful tool or narrative structure?"
- Counselors need to have a rationale for their selection of a theoretical model or set of strategies. It is essential that counselors know prior to their employment the research supporting use of specific theories or strategies emerging from theories.
- An examination of the counselor development literature suggests that the processes of developing an integrated professional identity converge with the processes by which counseling students align with a theoretical orientation.
- Professional counselors have assimilated the assumptions, values, and hypothetical constructs offered by a theory as explanations for both current client behavior and factors or strategies that can be used to facilitate change. In this way, the theory becomes part of a counselor's professional identity.

REFLECTIONS FROM THE CONTRIBUTOR'S CHAIR

Dr. Parsons, there is certainly an abundance of insightful points found within this chapter. But if we asked you to identify a single point or theme in all that is presented that you would hope would stand out and stick with the reader, what would that point or theme be?

What a question. That's like asking which of my children I like the best (laughs). Well, in reviewing what I wrote, I think the message I am trying to convey to those entering our profession is just that . . . COUNSELING IS A PROFESSION. What I hope the reader takes from the chapter is an excitement and a curiosity about the theories that follow within this text, and how these theories and the research supporting their constructs and emerging strategies are the substance guiding effective . . . professional . . . practice.

In the chapter, you refer to procedural thinking. Could you share a little about why you feel that is such an important concept?

I am a firm believer in the adage that if you don't know where you are going, you will not know when you get there, and if I could add to that—and you may not get there in the most efficient and effective way. The people who come to me for assistance are generally in pain or some distress, and I feel it is incumbent on me to help them resolve the issues concerning them and assist them in continuing along the journey toward health and well-being as quickly as possible. I believe to do that I have to develop the ability to first understand what is happening and then have a knowledge base that suggests what I can do given this type of situation in order to achieve some desired outcome. This is procedural thinking. It is the process by which I take what I know is occurring, then, drawing on my knowledge of theory and research, know what to do in order to move the helping process to a desired state.

Now, my knowledge, and to be honest, the current state of our discipline does not allow me to do this with all the specificity and accuracy that I would like. But having a theory to help me anticipate what the impact of my decisions should be provides me with markers that let me know if my intervention worked as expected and if I am moving in the right direction and, when not, what to do to correct the course.

Sorry, I know I'm getting long-winded, but one of the things I emphasize with my students is the importance of knowing why *they are choosing to do something at any one moment in their interactions with their clients. Counseling is not a random activity. Counseling is or should be an intentional act, and we need to be in touch with our intention and the rationale behind our actions. This is, for me, the value of procedural thinking.*

Dr. Parsons, you are not only an author and professor but also a professional practitioner. What might this chapter reveal about your own professional identity?

I value and hopefully embody within all that I do the importance of approaching counseling both as process and profession from the perspective of a reflective practitioner. Knowing what I am doing and why I am doing it helps me assess the effectiveness of my practice, be it in my clinical office or classroom. In addition to such reflection on and in practice, I value the science—and art—of what we are called to do. I attempt to integrate my understanding of our emerging science with an artistry that allows for adaptation of this science to the uniqueness of the person and situation with whom I am engaged. Finally, I believe that mine is a profession that demands accountability—to client and to the profession itself.

In writing this chapter, I was once again reminded of the value of theory to practice, while at the same time sensitized to the responsibility of those within the profession to test theory and to communicate, by way of both formal research and anecdotal reporting, the experienced value of those theories. I believe it is by communicating this experience that the science of our profession can be advanced.

ADDITIONAL RESOURCES

Gambrill, E. D. (2005). *Critical thinking in clinical practice: Improving the accuracy of judgments and decisions about clients.* Hoboken, NJ: John Wiley.

Hansen, J. T. (2006, Summer). Counseling theories within a postmodernist epistemology: New roles for theories in counseling practice. *Journal of Counseling and Development, 84,* 291–297.

Mobley, J. A., & Gazda, G. M. (2011). Creating a personal counseling theory. *Vistas Online.* Alexandria, VA: American Counseling Association. Retrieved from http://counselingoutfitters.com/vistas/vistas06/vistas06.31.pdf

Parsons, R. D. (2009). *Translating theory to practice.* Upper Saddle River, NJ: Pearson.

Wampold, B. E., Lichtenberg, J. W., & Waehler, C. A. (2002). Interventions in counseling psychology. *Counseling Psychologists, 30*(2), 197–217.

REFERENCES

American Counseling Association. (2005). *ACA code of ethics.* Alexandria, VA: Author.

Buchanan, D. R. (1994). Reflections on the relationship between theory and practice. *Health Education Research, 9,* 273–283.

Deegear, J., & Lawson, D. M. (2003). The utility of empirically supported treatments. *Professional Psychology: Research and Practice, 34*(3), 271–277.

Edies, L. D., & Appelrouth, S. (2010). *Sociological theory in the classical era: Text and readings* (2nd ed.). Thousand Oaks, CA: Pine Forge Press.

Franklin, C., Biever, J., Moore, K., Clemons, D., & Scamardo, M. (2001). The effectiveness of solution-focused therapy with children in a school setting. *Research on Social Work Practice, 11*(4), 411–434.

Greenberg, L. S., Elliott, R. K., & Lietaer, G. (1994). Research on experiential psychotherapies. In A. E. Bergin & S. L. Garfield (Eds.), *Handbook of psychotherapy and behavior change* (4th ed., pp. 509–539). New York: John Wiley.

Hansen, J. T. (2006, Summer). Counseling theories within a postmodernist epistemology: New roles for theories in counseling practice. *Journal of Counseling and Development, 84,* 291–297.

Hansen, J. T. (2007). Epistemic contradictions in counseling theories: Implications for the structure of human experience and counseling practice. *Counseling and Values, 51*(2), 111–124.

James, J. L., Jr. (2011). Theoretical counseling orientation: An initial aspect of professional orientation and identity. *Dissertation Abstracts International Section A: Humanities and Social Sciences, 71*(11-A), 3978.

Kazdin, A. E. (2008). Evidence-based treatment and practice: New opportunities to bridge clinical research and practice, enhance the knowledge base, and improve patient care. *American Psychologist, 63,* 146–150.

Littrell, J. M., Malia, J. A., & Vanderwood, M. (1995). Single-session brief counseling in a high school. *Journal of Counseling and Development, 73*(4), 451–458.

Magnuson, S., Norem, K., & Wilcoxon, A. (2000). Clinical supervision of prelicensed counselors: Recommendations for consideration and practice. *Journal of Mental Health Counseling, 22*(2), 176–188.

Massey, O. T., Armstrong, K., Boroughs, M., Henson, K., & McCash, L. (2005). Mental health services in schools: A qualitative analysis of challenges to implementation, operation, and sustainability. *Psychology in the Schools, 42*(4), 361–372.

McBride, M. C., & Martin, G. E. (1990). A framework for eclecticism: The importance of theory to mental health counseling. *Journal of Mental Health Counseling, 12*(4), 495–503.

Monte, C. F., & Sollod, R. N. (2008). *Beneath the mask: An introduction to theories of personality* (7th ed.). New York: John Wiley.

Moore-Pruitt, S. (1994). *Seeking an identity through graduate training: Construction and validation of a counselor identity scale.* Unpublished doctoral dissertation, St. Mary's University, San Antonio, TX.

National Cancer Institute. (2005, September). *Theory at a glance: A guide for health promotion practice* (2nd ed.). Washington, DC: U.S. Department of Health and Human Services, National Institutes of Health. Retrieved from http://www.cancer.gov/cancertopics/cancerlibrary/theory.pdf

Prochaska, J. O., & Norcross, J. C. (2003). *Systems of psychotherapy: A transtheoretical analysis* (3rd ed.). Belmont, CA: Brooks/Cole.

Pyles, R. L. (2003). The good fight: Psychoanalysis in the age of managed care. *Journal of the American Psychoanalytic Association, 51,* 23.

Rosenau, P. (1992). *Post-modernism and the social sciences: Insights, inroads, and intrusions*. Princeton, NJ: Princeton University Press.

Rupert, P. A., & Baird, K. A. (2004). Managed care and the independent practice of psychology. *Professional psychology: Research and practice, 35,* 185–193.

Sank, L. I. (1997). Taking on managed care: One reviewer at a time. *Professional psychology: Research and practice, 28*(6), 548–554.

Stiles, W. B. (2013). The variables problem and progress on psychotherapy research. *Psychotherapy, 50*(1), 33–41.

Turner, P. R., Valtierra, M., Talken, T. R., Miller, V. I., & DeAnda, J. R. (1996). Effects of session length on treatment outcome for college students in brief therapy. *Journal of Counseling Psychology, 43*(2), 228–232.

U.S. Public Health Service. (2000). *Report of the Surgeon General's Conference on Children's Mental Health: A national action agenda*. Washington, DC: Department of Health and Human Services.

Voss, J. F., & Post, T. A. (1988). On solving of ill-structured problems. In M. T. H. Chi, R. Glaser, & M. J. Farr (Eds.), *The nature of expertise* (pp. 261–285). Hillsdale, NJ: Lawrence Erlbaum.

Wampold, B. E. (2010). *The basics of psychotherapy: An introduction to theory and practice*. Washington, DC: American Psychological Association.

Weinrach, S. T., Thomas, K. R., & Chan, F. (2001). The professional identity of contributors to the *Journal of Counseling and Development*: Does it matter? *Journal of Counseling and Development, 79*(2), 166–170.

Multicultural Considerations

Within and Beyond Traditional Counseling Theories

Dong Xie

> *We may have different religions, different languages, different colored skin, but we all belong to one human race.*
>
> —Kofi Annan, Ghanian Diplomat, 7th UN Secretary-General,
> 2001 Nobel Peace Prize Winner (b. 1938)

While the truth of Kofi Annan's quote is obvious, the implications for us in the helping professions are yet to be fully realized. The clients we will see are no longer representative of only one race or one culture. The increasing globalization or flattening of our world and the impact of the multicultural and diverse nature of our societies across every aspect of our lives demand that counselors and counselor educators respond to this changing face of the client.

While each of the theories to be presented within this text has a rich history and expansive research, most—if not all—reflect a Western perspective (see Chapter 16). As the reader will note, the theories presented in the upcoming chapters address this "Western bias" and even discuss the utility of the theory with diverse populations. However, beyond understanding the applicability of any one theory across cultures or with varied, diverse populations, counselors, counselors-in-training, and counselor educators must understand the breadth of multicultural considerations in training and counseling within and beyond the traditional theoretical mainstreams in counseling and psychotherapy.

The current chapter focuses on these multicultural considerations. It is hoped that the chapter will provide a context from which to view the strengths and challenges of each of the theories to be presented. Specifically, after reading this chapter, the reader will be able to do the following:

1. Discuss the historical development and evolution of multicultural counseling

2. Describe the connection of multicultural competence to the development of a counselor's professional identity

3. Explain the standards issued by the Council for Accreditation of Counseling and Related Education Programs (CACREP, 2009) as pertaining to training of multicultural-competent counselors

4. Identify the significant multicultural considerations for each of the following theoretical approaches: psychodynamic, cognitive-behavioral, and humanistic

5. Describe the limitation of traditional approaches in counseling clients with cultural backgrounds different from those of the White dominant culture

6. Identify multicultural considerations beyond the aforementioned traditional models that counselors should consider generally in counseling practice, regardless of the theoretical orientation they endorse

DEVELOPMENT AND EVOLUTION OF MULTICULTURAL COUNSELING

Historical Development of Multicultural Counseling: 1960s to 1990s

Perhaps the earliest exploration of multicultural issues in counseling can be traced back to a few articles published in the 1950s (see review by Jackson, 1995). In reviewing these articles, Jackson noted a pattern in the early multicultural literature. These studies mainly focused on the significance of culture and the cultural bias of intelligence tests in comparing African Americans to White Americans; little attention was given to other American minorities or the relationship between the majority White counselors and minority clients.

However, since the 1960s, as a result of increased attention to civil rights issues, research has consistently documented underutilization of mental health services and high dropout rates among ethnic-minority clients (see review by Atkinson & Thompson, 1992). These studies attempted to examine factors that may account for the underutilization and high dropout rates and focused on how mental health professionals can provide better services to these groups.

The construct of "culture," as addressed within counseling, was initially narrowly defined to include race or ethnicity; within that category, the focus was on two groups—African Americans and White Americans. Many of the aforementioned studies focused only on comparisons between Blacks and Whites, with Whites as the control group. It was not until the 1980s that attention was given to within-group differences. The development of African American racial identity models marked this significant advance in development of multicultural counseling. In spite of this advancement, multicultural counseling literature in the 1980s remained limited to African Americans and American immigrants. Multicultural counseling remained only as an elective special interest in the counseling profession.

This changed in the 1990s. In a historical review of multicultural counseling, Ponterotto (2008) identified the 1990s as an era of maturation and expansion of the multicultural specialty, fueled by the increasing realization that minorities combined will become the majority of U.S. society in the near future. The multicultural literature in the 1990s was no longer limited to Black and White Americans; it expanded to non-Caucasian, non-African Americans such as Native, Hispanic, and Asian Americans, in terms of their racial/ethnic identities as well as the core values they endorse. Moreover, the construct of culture expanded to include not only the racial and ethnic aspects but also a wider range of diverse issues such as gender, sexual orientation, social class, disability, religion, and the elderly. It was during this era that the term *cross-cultural counseling*, which presumed the majority (Caucasian American) counselor/minority (African American) client dyad, was gradually replaced with the term *multicultural counseling*. Since then, multicultural counseling has endorsed a broader definition to encompass multiple dimensions of identity, including race or ethnicity, gender, sexual orientation, age, disability, religion, and social class. Multicultural counseling has come to include counseling dealing with any of these dimensions.

One significant development during this period, which marked the maturation of multicultural counseling, was the presentation of multiple theories and research on multicultural counseling competence. This had the impact of enhancing the need for and value of training of multicultural-competent counselors. The emphasis on multicultural training and education was also promoted by guidelines regarding multicultural issues, published by professional organizations and accreditation councils. For example, in its 1992 ethical principles and code of conduct, the American Psychological Association (APA) started to address ethical issues concerning psychologists' work with ethnic-minority populations. During this period of time, APA also organized task forces and committees to revise the existing ethic codes and guidelines and develop more specific guidelines concerning providing psychological services to culturally diverse populations (see, e.g., APA, 1993, 2002, 2003) and gay, lesbian, and bisexual clients (APA, Division 44, 2000).

Recent Development of Multicultural Counseling in the New Century

While all the aforementioned aspects of multicultural counseling continue to thrive in the 21st century, new trends have started to emerge in multicultural counseling. Increasing emphasis on social justice has been one of the significant new developments in this specialty. Other advances include internationalization of multiculturalism, intersection of multicultural counseling with other psychological specialties, and expansion of scientific methods in multicultural counseling research (Ponterotto, 2008).

Social justice issues include those relating to social inequalities across any aspect of our society—such as education, employment, and human rights among different social classes—and the efforts employed to reduce these inequalities. Even though multicultural counseling emerged from a social justice agenda during the civil rights era in the 1960s, the social justice voice remained silent or inaudible for the next 40 years. It was not until the beginning of the new century that the social justice issue started to reemerge, and it has ascended quickly to represent one of the defining identities of the counseling profession and to distinguish it from other mental health and psychology specialties

(Ponterotto, Casas, Suzuki, & Alexander, 2010). The prominence of social justice in multicultural counseling can be seen in the increasing number of books, chapters, and articles on the social justice topic. For example, Toporek, Gerstein, Fouad, Roysircar, and Israel published a major handbook for social justice in counseling in 2006, and almost every counseling-related handbook published so far this century features a whole section that consists of several chapters discussing various aspects of social justice in counseling (e.g., Fouad, 2012; Ponterotto et al., 2010).

The 21st century, with its emphasis on globalization, has seen an increase in focus on counseling from an international perspective (Forrest, 2011; Leong & Bluestein, 2000; Leong & Ponterotto, 2003; Leung, 2003; Nutt, 2007; Varenne, 2003). The multicultural movement found in the United States has taken on international proportions. Leung (2003) noted that the current cultural encapsulation of the profession may give a "false sense of self-sufficiency" and lead to an avoidance of looking outward for ideas. Leong and Bluestein (2000), for example, argued for the importance of developing and sustaining a truly multicultural and international perspective. They asserted that practitioners and researchers in multicultural counseling must avoid seeing American scholarship as the ideal or "truth" to be imparted to the rest of the world; instead, we need to move beyond a national multicultural perspective toward a global vision for the field (Leong & Bluestein, 2000).

While contributing to the growing need for training and culturally appropriate treatment in other countries, the American scholarship in multicultural counseling can also benefit from research and scholarship beyond its borders. Because it is now generally accepted that counseling exists in a cultural context, to "understand which aspects of counseling are culture-general and which aspects are culture-specific, we need to take a global and comparative approach to counseling" (Leong & Bluestein, 2000, p. 8). Mental health professionals will perform more effectively if they can enhance both their multicultural and international competences.

MULTICULTURAL COUNSELING COMPETENCE: ENRICHING COUNSELOR PROFESSIONAL IDENTITY

A review of the literature suggests that issues of multicultural counseling competence (MCC) have received the most attention in the multicultural counseling literature (Worthington, Soth-McNett, & Moreno, 2007). The great productivity of research and theory on MCC has greatly enhanced training of multicultural-competent counselors. Toward the end of the 1990s, MCC models had been incorporated into graduate training of counselors in the vast majority of counseling psychology programs (Constantine & Ladany, 2001). While these efforts to set standards and include MCC training in graduate programs bode well for the future of the profession, research as to the effectiveness of this training is somewhat mixed. In a national survey, professional counselors reported different competence levels on specific MCC dimensions (i.e., awareness, knowledge, and skills), and they perceived their MCC training to be less than adequate (Holcomb-McCoy & Myers, 1999). The standardization of the specific dimensions to MCC training, along with additional outcome studies, is sorely needed.

What has certainly occurred, however, is the inclusion of MCC as an important element defining both the professional helper and the helping professions. The APA, for example, has established guidelines for providers of psychological services to ethnic, linguistic, and culturally diverse populations (APA, 1993, 2003). Similarly, the current standards of CACREP (2009) have explicitly incorporated MCC in the foundation of professional identity for counseling-related professions.

The Tripartite Model of MCC and Its Revisions

The tripartite model of MCC (Sue, Arredondo, & McDavis, 1992; Sue et al., 1982) is perhaps the most widely recognized framework guiding MCC research and training, and it formed the basis for the multicultural guidelines adopted by APA (2003). This model conceptualizes MCC as having three dimensions: (1) *attitudes and beliefs*—awareness of one's own assumptions, values, and biases; (2) *knowledge*—understanding the cultures and worldviews of culturally different clients; and (c) *skills*—strategies and interventions that are culturally appropriate.

However, these competencies were only broadly defined in this original model (Sue et al., 1982). The model was later revised to include the same dimensions of counselor characteristics, creating a matrix of three characteristics by three dimensions, in which nine competence areas (31 specific competencies) were identified (Sue et al., 1992). For example, under the *awareness* dimension of counselor characteristics, the *belief and attitudes* dimension describes the elements of awareness to be focused (e.g., being aware of one's own cultural heritage, cultural background and experiences, attitudes, etc., and how they influence psychological process; recognizing limits of competencies and expertise). The *knowledge* dimension specifies the knowledge needed to help counselors increase their awareness (e.g., knowledge about their own racial and cultural heritage and how it may affect the definition of normality/abnormality and counseling process), and the *skills* dimension identifies ways to increase these aforementioned aspects of awareness and obtain the knowledge to better understand them.

It should also be noted that the traditional tripartite model was developed to address the needs of African Americans, American Indians, Asian Americans, and Hispanic Americans (Sue et al., 1982). Arredondo and colleagues (1996) further extended this model by relating the racial and ethnic identity inherent in the traditional model to more broadly defined personal dimensions of identity. Therefore, the revised model of MCC includes not only racially and ethnically different populations but also those that vary on human diversity dimensions such as gender, sexual orientation, religion, physical ability or disability, and other characteristics by which someone may prefer to self-define (Arredondo et al., 1996).

The traditional tripartite model was also revised to include factors related to the counseling process. Attention was given to the development of counselor competence in terms of multicultural counseling relationship (Sodowsky, Taffe, Gutkin, & Wise, 1994) and counseling process (Constantine & Ladany, 2001). In addition to the three original multicultural competence dimensions, three new dimensions have been discussed: *multicultural counseling self-efficacy,* counselors' beliefs that they can enact skills reflecting multicultural competence; *understanding of unique client variables,* counselors' recognition of the interplay between unique personal and situational factors; and *effective counseling working alliance,* an emotional bond between the client and the counselor and their agreement about goals and tasks, allowing explorations of racial and cultural issues (Constantine & Ladany, 2001).

Requirements of Multicultural Training in CACREP Standards

Counselors have increasingly called for the inclusion of multicultural counseling training in the formation of a competent counselor. For example, CACREP (2009), one organization prescribing standards for counselor educators includes a number of competency areas to be addressed. One of the objectives all CACREP-accredited programs must have is to train counselors with current knowledge and projected needs concerning counseling practice in a multicultural and pluralistic society (Section II, B.1). The current knowledge of counseling practice is further specified in eight core curricular areas (Section II, G).

One of the competencies in the area of "Professional Orientation and Ethical Practice" is understanding of "advocacy processes needed to address institutional and social barriers that impede access, equity, and success for clients" (CACREP, 2009, Section II, G.1.i). This competency requirement in fact reflects the "new" social justice movement in multicultural counseling, discussed earlier in this chapter's review of the most recent advances in the specialty.

The second core area, "Social and Cultural Diversity," exclusively focuses on particular MCCs. Specifically, students must have an understanding of the cultural context of relationships, issues, and trends in a multicultural society, including all of the following:

a. multicultural and pluralistic trends, including characteristics and concerns within and among diverse groups nationally and internationally;
b. attitudes, beliefs, understandings, and acculturative experiences, including specific experiential learning activities designed to foster students' understanding of self and culturally diverse clients;
c. theories of multicultural counseling, identity development, and social justice;
d. individual, couple, family, group, and community strategies for working with and advocating for diverse populations, including multicultural competencies;
e. counselors' roles in developing cultural self-awareness, promoting cultural social justice, advocacy and conflict resolution, and other culturally supported behaviors that promote optimal wellness and growth of the human spirit, mind, or body; and
f. counselors' roles in eliminating biases, prejudices, and processes of intentional and unintentional oppression and discrimination. (CACREP, 2009, Section II, G.2.a–f)

Aligned with the traditional tripartite MCC model (Sue et al., 1982, 1992), these standards emphasize awareness, knowledge, and skills. Competencies G.2.b and G.2.e in Section II concern counselors' awareness of their attitudes and beliefs about their diverse clients' experiences, as well as their own cultural and acculturative experiences. Competencies G.2.a through G.2.c in that section are all about historical development and trends of multicultural counseling, multicultural counseling theories, and racial identity models. Competency G.2.d in Section II covers needed skills in working with diverse clients, in terms of effective use of different modes of therapy and community strategies. Further, this focus on MCC can be found in the sections highlighting social justice (e.g., G.2.e and G.2.f): human growth and development (Section II, G.3), career development (Section II, G.4), counseling process in helping relationships (Section II, G.5), approaches in group work (Section II, G.6), and assessment and evaluation (Section II, G.7.f). The standards also require programs to train students in culturally relevant strategies to interpret and report research and studies of program evaluation (Section II, G.8).

While this is but one example of the type of emphasis given to the training of professional counselors, it is clear that counselor educators are invested in the development of counselors with multicultural competencies.

Multiculturalism: A Core Element to Counseling Practice

Counseling is a process that ultimately takes place in a multicultural context. And while each of the theories to be presented in the remainder of this text includes multicultural elements in its theoretical prism, these elements need to be included in every domain of knowledge in counseling practice. Unlike other counseling theories and approaches to be discussed, multiculturalism has become a philosophical foundation for counseling as a profession. Multicultural competence is *not* simply a special interest, particularly intended for ethnic-minority counselors and optional for non-ethnic-minority counselors. Multiculturalism must serve as one of the core defining elements in the identities of the counseling profession.

Developing the awareness and obtaining the knowledge and skills required to be competent as a multicultural counselor is a lifelong process. But this process can be assisted by focusing on specific components, internationalizing our perspective, and seeking supervision to guide field experience.

Focusing on Specific Components

As noted above, the tripartite model of MCC conceptualizes multicultural competence as the integration of awareness, knowledge, and skills (Sue et al., 1982, 1992). This has been the dominant model guiding research and training in multicultural competence. While the three areas are general and broad, it is important to identify and operationalize the specific components of each of these areas in training. One area of multicultural competence research is to identify predictors of multicultural competence. These studies have important implications for multicultural competence training in that they provide empirically based directions for what specific components should be targeted in training.

For example, in the *awareness* domain, studies suggested that counselors' racial microaggression or color-blind racial attitudes may impede the development of multicultural competence. Racial microaggression refers to subtle, daily, and often-overlooked expressions of negative attitudes concerning people of color. Similarly, color-blind racial attitudes are those that tend to minimize the role of race and racism in an individual's experience (Neville, Worthington, & Spanierman, 2001).

CASE ILLUSTRATION 2.1

The Case of Mara

Mara is a 20-year-old Latino American student in a small college in the Southern United States, where the majority of students are White. Mara came to her college counseling center seeking help with feelings of anxiety, depression, and isolation stemming from difficulties in both academics and the interpersonal relationship with her White American roommate. Mara was born in the United States, and both her parents are first-generation Latino immigrants.

At the receptionist desk, Mara was not verbal due to her depressed mood. The White receptionist approached her politely and told her no counselor in the center spoke Spanish, asking Mara if she could find a counselor who speaks Spanish in a community counseling center. Soon, after learning language was not an issue after all, the receptionist assigned Mara to a White male counselor. They discussed her difficulties in the first session. The counselor told Mara that he was not surprised she was struggling academically, in that he saw many Latino students having the same struggles. When Mara revealed that she was troubled by her roommate's discriminative comments about her living habits, such as her choice of food and manner of dress, the counselor encouraged Mara to focus more on the similarities, not the differences, between her and her White roommate. Mara felt misunderstood and expressed her concern that the racial difference between her and her counselor might impede her progress in counseling. The counselor then said, "When I see you, I do not see color. Race does not affect the way I treat you."

Case Illustration 2.1 provides a scenario involving demonstration of microaggression in a clinical setting.

In this case, both the White receptionist and the White counselor demonstrated several of the microaggressive attitudes identified by Sue et al. (2007). The receptionist's assuming that Mara was foreign-born and did not speak English well fits in the "Alien in Own Land" theme. The White counselor's lack of surprise about Mara's academic difficulty was a reaction of "ascription of intelligence," assigning a degree of intelligence, or lack thereof, to a person of color on the basis of his or her race. The White counselor's attempt to focus exclusively on similarities while minimizing the racial differences between Mara and her White roommate (and himself) is a form of "color blindness," indicating that a White person does not want to acknowledge race (Sue et al., 2007).

Constantine and Gushue (2003) found that expression of racism or color-blind racial attitudes—even subtly, in the form of microaggressions—can impede the counseling process for culturally diverse clients. They also found that endorsement of these racial attitudes was related to decreased ability to integrate salient cultural information into case conceptualization of minority clients. Unconscious racial bias was found to be negatively related to counselors' self-reported multicultural competence awareness and knowledge, and their ability to include race as a factor in case conceptualization (Neville, Spanierman, & Doan, 2006). African American clients perceived that racial microaggression from their counselors negatively predicted their counselors' general and multicultural competence. Intuitively, these findings might be generalized to other culturally diverse clients (e.g., with variations in gender, sexual orientation, disability, social class, etc.). These studies imply that multicultural training focused on increasing counselors' awareness of their microaggressions and color-blind attitudes, not only toward racial and ethnic minorities but also toward other culturally diverse populations, is important in multicultural competence development.

In the *skill* domain, one specific component might be affective empathy. Studies have suggested that affective empathy is a unique, significant predictor of self-reported multicultural competence (Constantine, 2000, 2001). Fuertes and Brobst (2002) also found that clients' perceptions of their counselors' empathy were associated with increased ratings of counselors' multicultural competence. Training programs can facilitate the development of students' multicultural competence by identifying strategies to increase their empathy with culturally diverse clients. Another specific skill might be counselors' ability to demonstrate attention to apparent and potential cultural contents. For example, Thompson, Worthington, and Atkinson (1994) found that African American clients tend to disclose more freely to counselors who show such empathy. Therefore, training tactics focusing on demonstrating affective empathy and attention and responsiveness to cultural contents are important in multicultural competence development.

Internationalizing Multiculturalism

In his presidential address to the Society of Counseling Psychology, Heppner (2006) stressed the importance of incorporating the international perspective in training the next generation of counselors in a culturally competent manner. Leong and Ponterotto (2003) and Heppner (2006) proposed specific training techniques from multicultural and international perspectives, such as immersion experiences in other countries, working with students and colleagues from other countries, student and faculty exchanges with other countries, and incorporating international readings into the curriculum.

For example, faculty-led, short-term study-abroad programs can provide great multicultural learning experiences. In 2011, this author (Xie) led a study-abroad program consisting of two doctoral students and a few master's-level counselors-in-training to Beijing and Shanghai, China. They stayed there for about 20 days and visited a few outpatient counseling centers and inpatient psychiatric hospitals. Students were able to observe and talk with the local people, patients, counselors, psychiatrists, and students and professors in psychology departments and counselor training programs in local universities. All the students reported wonderful experiences of being truly immersed in the Chinese social and cultural environment and felt that they would not have gained the same insights into the Chinese culture if they simply attended a classroom lecture about it.

Increasing Supervision, Practicum, and Internship Experience in Multicultural Counseling

Robbinson and Morris (2000) noted that there are too few opportunities for counselors in training to work with diverse group of clients in practicum and internship, and they argued for the increased integration of practical and intracurricular opportunities for counselors to develop multicultural counseling competencies.

Clinical supervision to process multicultural counseling issues might be useful in multicultural counseling competencies. Vereen, Hill, and McNeal (2008) found that receiving clinical supervision related to multicultural issues and conducting counseling with non-White clients are salient variables facilitating development of multicultural competencies. They recommended that supervisors should be trained to effectively integrate multicultural discussions related to awareness, knowledge, and skills into the supervision process. They asserted that "a more global and holistic approach to multicultural education, training, and supervision will provide better overall training than the current model used by many training programs where one didactic class provides the basis for multicultural training" (p. 235).

MULTICULTURAL CONSIDERATIONS WITHIN TRADITIONAL COUNSELING THEORIES

The increasing emphasis on multicultural counseling has led to increased attention on application of historically dominant counseling theories with culturally different or diverse populations. These theories were developed in a Western middle-class cultural context oriented toward individualism and independence, and they may not be readily applicable to or equivalently effective for clients from different cultural backgrounds (see Chapter 16 for more detail). This section joins multicultural counseling and the three traditional schools of counseling theories—namely, psychoanalytical or psychodynamic, cognitive and behavioral, and humanistic—with a focus on the limitations of these theories in multicultural contexts and considerations in adapting them for culturally different or diverse clients.

Multicultural Considerations Within Psychoanalytic/Psychodynamic Theories

Although the emphasis on clients' insights and understanding (of their unconscious process) fits well with the awareness focus of the multicultural movement, psychoanalytic/psychodynamic approaches have been criticized for being overly Eurocentric and culturally insensitive to the role of social forces such as the family and community. Bucci (2002) noted that psychoanalytic theories appear to be a product of wealthy Europe in the early 1900s that "focuses on the well-educated, middle-class, neurotic Caucasians" (p. 218). Thus, it might be difficult to generalize to other cultural groups. The traditional Freudian emphasis on sexual drives is starkly at odds with cultures that value suppression of sexuality. The orientation to individual autonomy under the dominant Western middle-class culture may overshadow an individual's need for society. In general, compared with the intrapsychic process, cultural and social factors have been less important for psychoanalysts. Bucci (2002) further summarized cultural conflicts inherent in psychoanalytic/psychodynamic theories. For example, theories of attachment tend to focus on a single maternal figure rather than on extended family, which is often essential for traditional Asian and Hispanic cultures. The communication style in psychoanalytic treatment focuses on verbal communication, but many Asian cultures value empathetic sensing (Bucci, 2002).

However, increasing attention has been given to the above limitations. Reaching out to diverse populations has been a recent trend for psychoanalytical and psychodynamic approaches. Psychoanalytic scholars have called for the need to challenge the universality of the intrapsychic constructs and process, and focus more attention on potential influ-ences of cultural and social factors (e.g., race, skin color, social class, urban poverty, and language) on these constructs and processes (e.g., transference, countertransference, and defense mechanism; see, e.g., Pérez Foster, Moskowitz, & Javier, 1996; Tummala-Narra, 2013). Overall, in a multicultural context, psychoanalysis should be interpreted through a broader and more inclusive lens of racial and cultural diversity and adapted to culturally different populations.

Perhaps the most important consideration in applying psychoanalytic/psychodynamic approaches to culturally different populations is the need to increase both the clients' and counselors' awareness of possible impacts of culture-related factors on the conscious and unconscious meanings accompanying clients' experiences. Sue and Sue (2008) noted that cultural and diversity issues may affect the transference and countertransference experi-ences. Psychoanalysts need to attend to factors such as cultural values, norms, and beliefs, as well as societal factors such as oppression and discrimination, because they can affect the unconscious determinants of our behavior. Clients' transference may result from experiences of being oppressed. Similarly, counselors' countertransference may result from stereotypes or specific client characteristics that are all products of various cultural and social factors.

Racial and ethnic differences, as well as their inherent cultural norms, can affect trans-ference and countertransference experiences in the therapeutic relationship. Gorkin (1996) noted that when working with Arab clients, the Jewish counselor may develop counter-transference such as guilt and aggressiveness.

CASE ILLUSTRATION 2.2

The Case of John

John was a 21-year-old African American college student, seeking therapy due to feelings of depression and anxiety. He reported that these feelings were in part due to his shaky relationship with his girlfriend. He often felt belittled and emotionally abused by her, yet he found it difficult to leave this abusive rela-tionship. His therapist, a female White American psychology intern whose theoretical orientation was object relation, attempted to collect information about John's early childhood, particularly his relation-ship with his mother. In this process, she found that John referred to two different women as his "mother," not making a distinction between them. She then quickly conceptualized that John's difficulty in leaving the abusive relationship with his girlfriend might be related to his failure to form a secure attachment with one mother "object" because he had two such objects. She then spent a great deal of time focusing on probing the intrapsychic conflicts between these blurring identities of such a crucial mother figure in his childhood development. She insisted that John tell her his early childhood memories, dreams, and fantasies about these two mothers. John told her that he believed he had very good relationships with both of them and could not identify any particular issue with them. Viewing John's claim as a denial defense, she continued to pursue this topic, but John became frustrated and terminated therapy after a couple of sessions. (Note: This case scenario is based on an example described in Tang & Gardner, 1999.)

Case Illustration 2.2 shows how the cultural variations concerning child-care practice among African American families are overlooked by an object relations therapist working with a male African American client.

Apparently, the therapist was moving in the "right" direction pursuing John's early childhood experiences related to forming relationships with two mother objects, from the perspective of object relations theory. However, her approach, due to her lack of awareness of a culture that values reliance on extended family members for child care, prevalent among African American families, was unsuccessful. For many African American families, the flexibility and exchange of roles, where extended family members often act as parents, has been well established. The child care in African American families often goes beyond the nuclear family and extends to a larger family, in which extended family members and even community members are involved. Therefore, the client's "blurring" identity in addressing two different women as his "mother" is not an experience of intrapsychic conflicts but, rather, an accurate account of his experience of "mother" within his extended family (Tang & Gardner, 1999).

A multiculturally competent therapist may engage in understanding John's relationship with his mother and his White girlfriend differently and, thus, effectively. First, the therapist could attend to the fact that she is a young, White, American female like the client's girlfriend and examine whether this might affect his transference to her and her own countertransference to the client. Second, she can put the client's referring to two women as his "mother" in the context of the client's African American family background by asking a question such as, "What would people say, I mean the people in your family or community, if you called two different women your mom?"

Tang and Gardner (1999) described their experiences as minority (Chinese American and African American) psychoanalysts working with majority (Caucasian American) clients. They discussed how their skin colors pulled a rich variety of projections, fantasies, and stereotypes from their clients. One Caucasian female client who had lost her identity and did not feel she fit in her family, because she identified her Chinese American therapist as being a minority, felt that they shared the experience of being outsiders. Another young Caucasian female client who acted out her sadomasochistic dynamics in her relationships with men fantasized that her female African American therapist was a mature blues singer. This fantasy of the Black blues singer implies the experience of suffering and transcending to turn one's inferiority into success, and the client's identification of her African American therapist's racial background allowed her to incorporate the racial aspects in a useful and creative way. Tang and Gardner concluded that for African American therapists, projections are more often based on racial stereotypes, whereas for Chinese American therapists, projections are based more on cultural assumptions. When therapists pay careful attention to the manifestations of racial and cultural stereotyping and assumptions, they can learn much more about a patient's inner life, to the benefit of the analytic work (Tang & Gardner, 1999).

The issues of skin color and traditional cultural animosity are only two among a large variety of cultural issues confronting counselors. The use of language and bilingualism may also impact intrapsychic process. The age at which a language is acquired can affect the reconstruction of early memories. When therapists speak only English while clients speak another primary language, transference and resistance issues can result (Pérez Foster et al., 1996).

Multicultural Considerations Within Cognitive-Behavioral Theories

Cognitive-behavioral theory (CBT) has been criticized for its exclusive focus on setting goals and making changes without adequate consideration of environmental, social, and cultural factors (Sue & Sue, 2008). CBT is overreliant on techniques and thus may neglect the important role of counselors' attitudes and values, and the way these interact with clients' values and beliefs. However, under the influence of the multicultural movement, the impact of person–environment dynamics has been increasingly recognized in CBT treatment. For example, Ellis (2000) acknowledged the necessity of not only working to change clients' irrational beliefs but also helping them fight against an "unfair and irrational system," the social conditions that play a role in producing psychological discomfort. The values inherent in CBT are assertiveness, personal independence, verbal ability, rationality, cognition, and behavioral change, which may run counter to many cultures that value subtle communication over assertiveness, interdependence over independence, listening and observing over talking, and acceptance over change (Jackson, Schmutzer, Wenzel, & Tyler, 2006). CBT's focus on the here and now and changing the individual through cognitive reconstruction (e.g., a client's cognition in response to discrimination) may lead to neglecting the influence of the past as well as overlooking possible environmental interventions (e.g., changing the racist environment; Hays, 2009). Acknowledgement of these environmental influences and the need for advocacy for system change is closely in line with the social justice trend in multicultural counseling.

Increasing attention has been paid to the limitations of some of the classic CBT techniques when applied to culturally different clients. For example, Socratic questioning involves the CBT counselor asking a series of questions, rather than providing information directly, to impart knowledge or deepen awareness. Chen and Davenport (2005) noted that this technique can cause anxiety for clients who feel unable to come up with a right answer to the questions. Clients from certain cultures may feel awkward with this technique because repeating questioning can be seen as disrespectful. They may also worry that their therapists are withholding the advice they want to receive directly and immediately. Moreover, assertiveness training may violate values of harmony, deference to authority, and avoiding confrontation in many Asian cultures. Clients may feel uncomfortable if being asked to challenge dysfunctional or maladaptive thoughts related to cultural values or parental authority. Because of the value of controlling emotions and the tendency to express psychological distress in somatic complaints among Asian cultures (e.g., Chinese), CBT techniques that rely on asking a client to express emotion or identify inner thoughts may be difficult for a client with such a cultural background.

CBT's emphasis on development of social skills and cognitive strategies must incorporate information based on comprehensive assessment that includes contextual factors regarding familial, cultural, and social influences. It is essential to be open to the possibility that autonomous and irrational thoughts may be the results of racism, discrimination, and other social and cultural factors.

Case Illustration 2.3 highlights the importance of placing one's theoretical constructs within a cultural context.

CASE ILLUSTRATION 2.3

The Case of Liu

Consider the case of Liu, an adult Chinese male client who came to counseling reporting feelings of guilt and depression. The counselor working with Liu was quickly able to identify the source of the depression and guilt as what the counselor believed to be dysfunctional and irrational beliefs about the absolute necessity for Liu to care for his aging parents. The counselor, lacking multicultural competence, viewed this urgent demand to care for his parents as an illustration of "musterbating," an irrational and enslaving belief that one *must* do this or that even when it is not his or her personal desire. With this as the target for the guilt and depression, the counselor began to help Liu dispute and reconstruct this thought. Further, the counselor attempted to engage Liu in assertiveness training as a way of helping him become more direct with his parents about his difficulty in taking care of them. Though Liu was compliant in all aspects of the counseling, his attempt to own the reconfigured thoughts and employ the assertive behaviors was not successful.

In seeking supervision regarding this case that had no apparent progress, the counselor was introduced to the strong emphasis within Chinese culture on filial devotion toward parents. He soon learned that *yang er fang lao* (the idea of raising children to look after their parents in old age) in Chinese culture was especially prevalent in Liu's family, and, as such, the belief that adult children must commit to the responsibility of taking care of their parents was ingrained in him. The counselor also learned that direct communication of Liu's feelings and thoughts with his parents as the goal of assertiveness training violated the value of respect and deference to parents and authorities in Chinese culture.

As evident in the simple scenario in Case Illustration 2.3, the counselor operated from the perspective of Western culture and emphasized independence and self-sufficiency (see Chapter 16). From this orientation, it was a simple step to promote the notion that adult children are expected to leave their parents and live on their own. While perhaps reflective of Western thought and values, this did not align with the client's Chinese cultural values of dependency and interdependence or reliance on the family and support of others. Moreover, the Chinese culture emphasizes respect and deference toward parents and authority figures, and being direct about one's thoughts and feelings with parents and people of higher status violates that value. Considering these cultural norms and expectations, it may be inappropriate and less effective to conceptualize thought as dysfunctional and to set up treatment goals as reconstructing a "dysfunctional" thought and developing assertiveness. Instead, a culturally informed CBT therapist can show his or her awareness of how culture may have impacted the client's thoughts, and this empathetic and culturally sensitive response will likely lead to a more effective working alliance. Helping the client understand how his culture has impacted his thoughts and enabling him to explore alternative ways to fulfill his responsibility of taking care of his parents might be more effective than reconstructing his "dysfunctional" thoughts and pushing for assertiveness training.

Based on Hispanic cultural norms, Organista (2000) proposed specific considerations for using CBT with clients from Latino cultural backgrounds. Because of the value of *personalismo* (personal relationships) within Latino culture, CBT counselors are encouraged to focus on building relationship through exchange of personal information in early sessions. Assessment should include marital and family conflict, problems with children, acculturation, cultural shock, and discrimination. While taking some time off and focusing on one's needs are common CBT recommendations in treating depression, such techniques may run counter to the Latino values of connectedness and putting family needs ahead of one's own. Thus, instead of solitary activities, clients can choose social activities such as family outings and visits. In assertiveness training, it is important to recognize the Latino cultural values of being polite and nonconfrontational and to develop culturally acceptable ways of expressing assertiveness based on status determined by age or gender. Saying "helpful thoughts" or "unhelpful thoughts" instead of labeling thoughts as "rational" or "irrational" is also recommended in cognitive reconstruction.

Multicultural Considerations Within Humanistic Approaches

The inherent limitations of psychoanalytic/psychodynamic approaches and cognitive-behavioral models when used with culturally different populations also apply to humanistic approaches. Like the other two approaches, the universality and appropriateness of the assumptions underlying humanistic approaches for clients of all cultures have been questioned. Traditional humanistic approaches promote clients' independence in making choices and defining meaningfulness at the individual level. Such an approach may not be appropriate for clients who have collectivistic orientations and whose decision-making processes are shared with family and other group members (Sue & Sue, 2008). The assumption that every individual has a natural tendency toward growth, self-determination, and autonomy may be questionable in that, for many individuals, orientation toward intimacy, sense of connectedness, and what is best for the community and the common good is far more important than self-actualization (see Cain, 2008).

For example, when individuals from Asian cultures seek therapy, it may be the last resort and they may prefer immediate advice or direction from the counselor rather than nondirective techniques such as those used in Rogers's person-centered therapy (PCT). Clients coming from cultures that value respect and taking direction from authority may feel awkward and frustrated when a counselor engages only in listening and rephrasing what the clients say (Wang, 2003).

PCT emphasizes facilitative conditions (i.e., counselor's unconditional positive regard, empathetic understanding, and congruence) that are necessary and sufficient to create a safe and nurturing relationship for clients to experience their here-and-now emotions. However, PCT counselors need to be cognizant that in many cultures, emotional expression is minimal, sometimes suppressed, and even unacceptable in some situations, and they need to modify their ways of responding to the client's emotional experience (Cain, 2008). PCT counselors must examine and modify their means of communicating these facilitative qualities to fit the needs of clients from different cultures. A counselor's direct expression of empathy might be uncomfortable for clients whose cultures value indirect communication or distance in interpersonal relationships. Similarly, expression of congruence should depend on what is best for the client.

> In this sense, the counselor must practice a kind of "controlled spontaneity"—expressing what he or she feels, what is on his or her mind, after reflecting on what is best for the client and deciding that expression to this feeling would be appropriate. (Gelso & Fretz, 2001, p. 242)

For example, Chinese culture emphasizes face (*lian*), the losing of which is associated with feelings of embarrassment, humiliation, and shame. In Chinese culture, practice of face typically occurs in relationships and must be built and maintained within each relationship. In a clinical setting, a Chinese client may try to save the counselor's face and, in the meantime, expect the counselor to save his or hers. Therefore, PCT counselors need to be cautious about being congruent with clients. Direct communication of whatever they feel and think without considering clients' cultural background may inadvertently lead to clients' feeling embarrassed, humiliated, and ashamed as a result of losing face. Moreover, the social norms and expectations of a specific culture often serve as important conditions for individuals to be viewed positively. Thus, practice of unconditional positive regard should also incorporate considerations of a client's specific cultural background. Empathetic understanding of these norms and expectations and their impact on the client's perceived positive regard from family, specific cultural groups, and communities may help the counselor communicate his or her unconditional positive regard more effectively.

Cain (2008) related the tripartite model of MCC (Sue et al., 1982, 1992) to application of PCT with clients from cultural backgrounds other than Western culture. He cited Rogers's (1977) position that clients deserve a "respectful hearing" of all attitudes and feelings, no matter how "extreme" or "unrealistic" (p. 113), to highlight the importance of PCT counselors' awareness of their values and assumptions in effectively responding to the unique values and needs of culturally different clients. Empirical research also supports the importance of PCT counselors' awareness of their own attitudes and beliefs and their impact on experience and expression of empathy to clients. Burkard and Knox (2004) found that, in responding to college students who reported depression due to active, race-based exclusion by other students, counselors with a color-blind attitude (i.e., race is not important in understanding someone's life) reported significantly less empathy for the client than did those who scored lower for color blindness. Therefore, PCT counselors need to continue to develop sensitivity to possible racial and cultural issues to increase capacity for empathy.

In addition to increasing awareness of counselors' own values and assumptions, Cain (2008) also argued for the importance of knowledge and understanding of clients' worldviews. Cain cited Rogers's (1951) assertion that "the only way to understand another culture is to assume the frame of reference of that culture" (p. 494), which is viewed as a promotion of "counselor acquisition of knowledge of clients in the cultural settings, knowledge of cultural anthropology or sociology with actual experiences of living with or dealing with culturally diverse clients" (MacDougall, 2002, p. 52). Glauser and Bozarth (2001) warned against the danger of adopting a stereotypical perspective regarding specific clients' cultural backgrounds and a shift of focus from the client to the counselor. Gelso and Fretz (2001) also noted that the facilitative conditions are much more strongly related to counseling outcomes when these conditions are based on clients' perceptions rather than on ratings made by outside judges. In other words, Rogers's focus was on the client's perception of the relationship as most indicative of the effects of conditions.

Finally, on the dimension of developing culturally appropriate interventions, Cain (2008) recommended modifying the nondirective intervention inherent in PCT for culturally diverse clients. As mentioned earlier, rigid insistence on nondirectiveness may violate clients' needs for more direct advice from authorities. Cain suggested replacing "client centered" with "client informed" or even "client directed" to highlight the importance of clients' cultures, personal experiences, learning styles, and other forms of diverse experience. MacDougall (2002) also argued that "to be truly person centered, counselors need to allow themselves to be more directive if the culture(s)/circumstances of the client warrant it" (p. 54).

MULTICULTURAL CONSIDERATIONS BEYOND TRADITIONAL COUNSELING THEORIES

Just as there have been many theoretical approaches in counseling as a whole, there have been many theories and models in its multicultural counseling specialty. Fuertes (2012) reviewed papers summarizing these multicultural counseling theories and models and identified 16 such approaches, among which models on counselor multicultural competence and racial/ethnic identity have been the most robust, in that they have continually been the focus of empirical research on multicultural counseling. The tripartite model of MCC (Sue et al., 1982, 1992) has the most relevance to the training of multiculturally competent counselors. Much of this model and its implications for multicultural training were discussed earlier in this chapter and will not be repeated here. Therefore, this section mainly focuses on models of racial/ethnic identity, acculturation, and Leong's (1996) integrative model of cross-cultural counseling, along with its most recent development, the cultural accommodation model (Leong & Lee, 2006).

Racial/Cultural Identity Development Models

Perhaps the most productive models of racial and ethnic identity development were based on African Americans. But identity development models have also been developed for racial and ethnic minorities such as Asian Americans and Latino/Hispanic Americans (see Sue & Sue, 2013, for a review). However, the identity development processes involved in all these models tend to converge at similar stages. Therefore, scholars have attempted to pull out common features that cut across the race-specific identity models to encompass a broader population.

The Racial/Cultural Identity Development Model (Sue & Sue, 1990, 1999, 2013) is one such model. It involves five identity development stages, each of which is characterized by attitudes toward self, others of the same minority, others of a different minority, and the dominant group. Specifically, individuals in the *conformity stage* will have a self-depreciating or neutral attitude toward self and others of the same minority due to low race salience. They will hold a discriminatory or neutral attitude toward members of a different minority but a group-appreciating attitude toward the dominant group. The *dissonance stage* is characterized by conflict. Individuals in this stage often experience conflict between self-depreciating and self-appreciating attitudes. While still holding a group-depreciating attitude toward their own minority and negative stereotypes of other minorities, they also start to experience the strengths of their cultural heritage and find a shared experience of oppression with members of other minorities. Conflict also exists at this stage between group-appreciating and group-depreciating attitudes toward the dominant group. Attitudes of self-appreciating, group-appreciating toward their own culture, and group-depreciating toward the dominant group become more significant at the *resistance and immersion stage*. Individuals in this stage may still experience conflict between their empathy for other minority group experiences and feelings of culturocentrism. The *introspection stage* features concern. Individuals at this stage may start to reflect on the possible biases of their appreciating attitudes toward themselves, their own minority group, and the dominant group. Individuals will achieve successful identity development in the *integrative awareness stage,* when they develop appreciating attitudes toward themselves, their own minority, and other minorities and a selective appreciating attitude toward the dominant group.

These racial and cultural identity models have important implications for multicultural counseling. They help counselors increase their awareness of the role of oppression in a minority individual's development and recognize the differences among members of the same minority group with respect to individual cultural identity. These models also allow counselors to realize the changing and developmental nature of cultural identity among clients so they will be able to anticipate the attitudes, feelings, and behaviors likely to arise in a sequence (Sue & Sue, 2013). This will help the counselor develop and modify a treatment plan based on the client's level of cultural identity.

In their Racial/Cultural Identity Development Model, Sue and Sue (2013) provide more specific therapeutic implications related to clients' attitudes in each of the stages. If clients of color are in the *conformity stage*, they may prefer a White counselor over a minority counselor. Counselors need to be aware of clients' negative, resistant, and even hostile reactions to a minority counselor and positive reactions to a White counselor. A minority counselor may help the client work through these feelings of antagonism by taking a nondefensive, nonjudgmental stance and providing a positive minority role model. Similarly, a White counselor can help the client work through his or her tendency to overidentify with the dominant White culture by modeling positive attitudes toward cultural diversity. Moreover, clients of color in the *conformity stage* often consider race- and culture-related issues, and the feelings associated with them, threatening and may prefer a task-oriented, problem-solving approach. Counselors need to be cognizant of clients' conflicting feelings between the negative and emerging positive attitudes toward themselves and their racial and cultural group when they are in the *dissonance stage*. These conflicts might be heightened when a minority counselor demonstrates good knowledge of the client's cultural group, or when a White counselor is inadvertently negligent and biased toward race and cultural issues.

Clients of color in the *resistance and immersion stage* may often take an external perspective and blame society for their issues. If they seek counseling, they may often try to recruit the counselor as an ally in blaming the external causes of their psychological issues and, if unsuccessful, may quickly discount the counselor as part of the racist and oppressive society. Sue and Sue (2013) noted that clients of color in this stage are often suspicious and hostile toward the helping profession and view the counselor, particularly a White counselor, as a symbol of oppression. They warn counselors against feeling intimidated and defensive in responding to clients' strong negative attitudes. Instead, counselors should view clients' anger as legitimate and take a nonpersonal, nondefensive posture to explore clients' feelings. At this stage, clients are receptive to action-oriented interventions targeting external change (Sue & Sue, 2013). Therefore, focus on social justice issues and help clients engage in appropriate actions to challenge the racist environment, which fits not only clients' identity development but also the social justice emphasis of multicultural counseling.

Acculturation Models

Acculturation can be viewed as "a dynamic process of change that individuals undergo as they interact with and adapt to a new or different cultural environment . . . that occurs along different life domains (e.g., language, values) at different rates of change" (Rivera, 2010, p. 331). Acculturation has emerged as an important culture-related factor in multicultural counseling and a leading variable in multicultural counseling research. In our increasingly multicultural society, acculturation has played a prominent role in our understanding and counseling of ethnic-minority clients.

Perhaps the most well-known acculturation model is Berry's (1980, 1997). According to this model, individuals acculturate along two dimensions: the degree to which they wish to retain their heritage culture and the degree to which they want to endorse and engage in the new culture and society. Berry described four acculturation strategies based on the interplay of these two dimensions. The *assimilation strategy* is to adapt the values and behaviors of the new culture and reject the values and behaviors of the heritage culture. In contrast, the *separation strategy* is to maintain the values and behaviors of the heritage culture while rejecting the values and behaviors of, and avoiding contact with, the new culture and society. The *integration strategy* describes attempts to maintain the values and behaviors of the heritage culture and embrace those of the new culture, often referred to as "biculturalism." The last strategy in Berry's model is *marginalization,* neither accepting one's own cultural heritage nor adopting the values of the new culture. Among these four strategies, studies suggest that integration is the most favorable acculturation approach and the most significant predictor of high levels of adjustment and functioning in the acculturation process (e.g., Berry, 1997; LaFromboise, Coleman, & Gerton, 1993).

Atkinson, Thompson, and Grant (1993) developed another model that involves acculturation and is more closely related to the practice of multicultural counseling. According to this model, counselors must take into account three dimensions and select roles and strategies in working with racial/ethnic-minority clients: (1) acculturation level to the majority culture (low–high), (2) locus of problem (internal–external), and (3) client's goals (prevention–remediation). The intersections of these three dimensions identify eight roles for counselors to consider. Atkinson and colleagues point out that many of these roles are not traditional for counselors. They stress that all eight possible roles need to be considered to greatly increase effectiveness in working with a full range of culturally diverse clients.

Just like racial and cultural identity models, acculturation models also help counselors recognize differences in the acculturation levels of clients with the same cultural heritage.

Increased sensitivity to these within-group differences would allow counselors to avoid getting trapped in stereotypical understandings of clients' cultural backgrounds. Understanding the client's acculturation level has important implications for effective communication with culturally different clients and provision of culturally consistent interventions. Ethnic-minority clients who are less acculturated may need more culturally adapted interventions than those who are acculturated. Therefore, counselors must make sure that they communicate with their ethnic-minority clients in a manner compatible with their acculturation levels. This can include both language and communication patterns. For example, clients who grew up in traditional Asian or Hispanic cultures and are less acculturated to American society may prefer to address the counselor in a formal mode, such as "professor" or "doctor," due to cultural values of respect and deference toward authority figures. The counselor may communicate with these clients in a manner consistent with this cultural value, rather than insisting on being addressed by first name. Showing respect is desirable regardless of the client's culture, but knowledge of the culture may help the counselor effectively communicate respect (Sue, Zane, Hall, & Berger, 2009).

Attention to clients' acculturation strategies will also help counselors effectively conceptualize their presenting concerns. Clients are likely to experience conflict with other family members if they are at different acculturation levels and use different acculturation strategies. For example, a client's assimilation strategy might be in direct conflict with his or her parents' separation strategy. Clients will likely experience depression and anxiety if they are engaged in separation from the new culture but lack support from their heritage culture or cannot identify resources from their heritage culture to anchor them in the immediate surroundings of their new culture.

Integrative Model of Cross-Cultural Counseling and Cultural Accommodation

The integrative model of cross-cultural counseling (Leong, 1996) is based on Kluckhohn and Murray's (1950) framework that asserts, "Every man is in certain respects: a) like all other men, b) like some other men, and c) like no other man" (p. 35). This model focuses on three dimensions (Leong, 1996): The *universal dimension* refers to the biological and genetic makeup common to all human beings. The *group dimension* concerns social grouping based on culture, race, ethnicity, gender, sexual orientation, social class, and so on. The *individual dimension* represents the uniqueness of each person. Leong noted that a significant limitation in multicultural counseling is the tendency to focus on only one of the three levels. He asserts that all three dimensions are equally important in understanding clients' experiences and should be attended to in an integrative manner. In addition to these dimensions, this model also incorporates the theory that a positive therapeutic relationship is facilitated by the complementarity between counselor and client. Leong (1996, 2007) proposed that complementarity will be achieved when the counselor and the client are engaged on the same dimension, and lack of complementarity often occurs when the client is experiencing and relating on one level (e.g., *group*) whereas the psychotherapist is responding on another level (e.g., *universal*). The interventions of counselors working at this level are based on general laws of human behavior and the assumption that group or cultural variation is not important. However, the counselors trained in traditional, unidimensional Western models do not have the flexibility to shift between multiple dimensions of clients' problems, and their unidimensional case conceptualizations are limited and often ineffective to the extent that group dimension variables are important to the client or therapist (Leong, 2007).

The cultural accommodation model (Leong & Lee, 2006) is an extension of Leong's (1996) integrative model of cross-cultural counseling. According to this model, the cultural accommodation process involves three steps: (1) identifying the cultural gaps or blind points in an existing counseling theory that has limited cultural validity, (2) identifying culture-specific factors and models from empirically based cross-cultural psychology, and (3) testing the culturally accommodated theory and examining its incremental validity compared with the culturally unaccommodated theory. Apparently, this model is an evidence-based approach that can be used not only to evaluate existing counseling models but also to select culture-specific variables to subject to empirical research, and then incorporate in counseling.

The cultural accommodation model encourages counselors to use empirical research databases to identify culture-specific constructs relevant to multicultural counseling. An example of such empirical research is a cross-cultural study that compared relationships between certain personality constructs and social anxiety across Chinese and White American college students (Xie, Leong, & Feng, 2008). This study found that socially prescribed perfectionism and aspects of collective self-esteem are more predictive of social anxiety for Chinese than for White Americans, implying that these constructs are culture-specific variables for Chinese clients and should be considered in counseling Chinese clients experiencing social anxiety. Leong and Lee (2006) identified other culture-specific constructs such as cultural identity, acculturation, self-construal, and high-low–context communication styles from research on Asian Americans. These variables should be incorporated into the existing counseling models so they can be accommodated to work with Asian American clients more effectively.

The implications of the integrative model of cross-cultural counseling and cultural accommodation model for multicultural counseling are obvious by themselves. The integrative model helps counselors take a more comprehensive multicultural stance to look at all three levels of clients' experiences. It also sensitizes counselors to continue examining the complementarity between them and their clients and to ensure they are working on the same dimension. All these efforts will help counselors maintain a positive therapeutic relationship with their clients, one of the most significant and consistent predictors of counseling outcomes. The cultural accommodation model can aid counselors in accommodating their orientations toward traditional and classic counseling theories. The model's emphasis on reliance on scientific literature to identify culture-specific constructs helps counselors provide evidence-based multicultural counseling, an approach that has been earnestly called for by multicultural counseling scholars (e.g., Constantine, Miville, & Kindaichi, 2008; Fuertes, 2012; Sue et al., 2009; Worthington et al., 2007).

WORKING WITH Y-CHUN FROM A MULTICULTURAL PERSPECTIVE

While it may be obvious, it is important to note that a counselor must "know" the client and his or her lived experience to be effective in counseling. While the upcoming chapters provide specific frameworks from which to "understand" clients, it is also important to remember that the essence of multicultural counseling is to incorporate as many cultural variables as possible in understanding clients' feelings and experiences, development of symptoms, and their causes, regardless of the theoretical orientation in use.

In Chapter 3, you will be introduced to a young woman named Y-Chun. Y-Chun's story is one you will revisit in each of the upcoming chapters, with each specific theory applied to her case in turn. Prior to viewing the specifics of theory application to Y-Chun's case, it is important to remember that counseling occurs within a multicultural context. Y-Chun, a 35-year-old biracial female, is like all our clients and presents with many culture-related factors that may have played and may continue to play important roles in the issues she presents.

One of the most salient cultural variables in Y-Chun's case might be her biracial identity. Born to her father as White and her mother as Asian, Y-Chun appears never to have achieved a clear racial identity. Her lack of identity is demonstrated in her uncertainty about what she wants out of a relationship and what she wants to be, and feelings of being overwhelmed and empty. The experience of being teased and called "banana" by her schoolmates might have added to the challenge of identifying with either her father's or mother's race or as a biracial individual. In the face of such a challenge, her family of origin and parents might have served as an important support system and role models for her to identify with her heritage race, or at least to buffer her experience with discrimination. However, this was not the case for Y-Chun. Apparently, neither of Y-Chun's parents achieved integrative racial identity and they seem to be dealing with their own psychological issues. Due to lack of clear identity, Y-Chun relates to her own children by adopting her mother's way of relating to her—through blaming and emotional disconnection.

Y-Chun hated her skin color and herself as a result of being teased in school. She might have identified with the dominant White culture, but probably in a negative way—by becoming rebellious, promiscuous, and using alcohol and drugs, often viewed as a "hallmark" of American (problematic) adolescents. Notice that these behaviors are in direct conflict with the values of her mother's culture, which is oriented toward self-discipline, obedience, and respect for authority. According to the Racial/Cultural Identity Development Model (Sue & Sue, 1990, 1999, 2013), in school—and possibly at the time of therapy—Y-Chun may still have been in the *conformity stage* of racial identity development, where she held a depreciative attitude toward herself and her parents. These depreciative feelings reinforced each other due to conflicts between her behavior and her parents' cultures, and, consequently, she may have been trapped in this stage.

Acculturation may be another factor in Y-Chun's case. The conflicts between her and her parents might also be the result of an acculturation gap. Sue and Sue (2013) noted that parent–child conflicts are common among Asian American college students and are often related to dating and marital issues. Inability to resolve these differences in acculturation results in misunderstandings and miscommunications. Y-Chun's experience of discrimination may be a significant acculturative stress that affected her acculturation orientation. It appears she may first have been oriented toward simulation but later turned to marginalization (disengaging from both her heritage culture and the dominant culture), the least adaptive acculturation strategy.

The racial difference between her parents (her father as White and her mother as Asian) should also be taken into account. Both parents have high expectations for Y-Chun, but they may expect different results because of their own cultural backgrounds. While independence, self-reliance, and self-sufficiency might be among her father's expectations, interdependence, caring for her parents, and devotion to family might be among her mother's. These different expectations may have confused Y-Chun and trapped her in a double-bind situation in which fulfilling her father's expectations would inevitably fail to meet her mother's.

While being sexually assaulted is a traumatic experience for anyone, Y-Chun's experience of being sexually assaulted at age 16 by her cousin must be put in a cultural context. Her traumatic experience might be particularly heightened by the importance placed on a woman's virginity in Asian culture.

While a counselor can use any theoretical approach to work with Y-Chun, he or she must take the above cultural factors into account to understand the important constructs and processes underlying such an approach. A psychoanalyst may need to consider how the aforementioned cultural factors, as well as the counselor's own racial and other cultural factors, may have impacted transference and countertransference in their counseling relationship. Would Y-Chun have a positive or negative transference toward the counselor depending on the counselor's race, age, or gender? What countertransference experience might the counselor have toward Y-Chun, given the dynamic intersection of all these cultural factors? These are important questions for a counselor to ask if a psychoanalytic or psychodynamic approach is used with Y-Chun.

A CBT counselor needs to keep these factors in mind in identifying her dysfunctional thoughts and deciding which ones need to be reconstructed. For Y-Chun, it might be helpful if a CBT counselor can explain that conflicts between Asian American children and their parents because of an acculturative gap are not uncommon, and then help her explore effective ways to resolve those conflicts.

For a PCT counselor, effectively conveying unconditional positive regard and empathetic understanding is important, but expressing congruence or genuineness might be a challenge. Therefore, the counselor may need to adopt a controlled spontaneous approach, thinking of how disclosing his or her feelings and thoughts may affect Y-Chun's experience.

KEYSTONES

- Everything occurs in a cultural context, and everything must be understood in such a context.
- Cultural factors include race, ethnicity, gender, sexual orientation, social class, disability, age, and any other dimension of diversity.

- Multiculturally competent counselors must continue to challenge the universality and appropriateness of the assumptions of the theoretical approach they are using when working with culturally diverse clients.
- Multiculturally competent counselors must attempt to incorporate as many cultural factors as possible in conceptualizing culturally diverse clients' experiences, and relate them to the constructs and processes inherent in their theoretical approach.
- Multiculturally competent counselors must be sensitive to the within-group differences among clients in certain cultural groups and avoid being trapped in stereotypes about all individuals in such groups.
- Multiculturally competent counselors must view multicultural competence development is an ongoing, lifelong process.
- Multiculturally competent counselors must continue to enhance their awareness and knowledge of their own attitudes and beliefs, worldviews, and cultural heritage, and those of their clients, and understand the dynamic effects of their and their clients' cultural variables on counseling relationship, process, and outcome.
- Multiculturally competent counselors must continue to examine the effectiveness of the techniques and interventions of their theoretical approach and accommodate the application of these techniques and interventions to culturally diverse clients.

REFLECTIONS FROM THE CONTRIBUTOR'S CHAIR

"Every man is in certain respects, like all other men, like some other men, and like no other man."---- Kluckhohn & Murray (1953).

In the simplest way, they described the most complicated nature of human being. Although such a depiction of human being was made more than half century ago, even before the emergence of the multicultural movement, its embedded interlocking circles of human universality, cultural specificity, and individual difference probably encompass all aspects of the multiculturalism that has blossomed today. It was an eye-opening experience when I first read this during my doctoral study at Ohio State University more than ten years ago and since then it has been a guiding light for both my professional development as a counseling psychologist and personal growth as an individual. This light has led me and training of my student counselors to conceptualize clients' issues with a more balanced multicultural perspective without being trapped in pitfalls of being solely etic or emic. It has helped us to develop into more versatile multicultural-competent counselors.

On a personal level, it has helped me to function as a multicultural-competent individual in an increasingly diverse society. I have come to have a more insightful understanding about myself as well as my in-group and out-group fellows, known or unknown, by constantly reflecting on the commonness, differences, and uniqueness among us. However, literature has almost exclusively related the concept of multicultural competence to training of counselors rather than training of our clients. If we can train our counselors to become versatile multicultural-competent counselors, then why can't we train our clients to become versatile multicultural-competent individuals? Perhaps it is the time that we need to incorporate multicultural training into working with our clients in a way not simply conceptualizing their issues with a multicultural perspective, but rather, training and educating them to become multicultural-competent individuals. If so, then aforementioned statement by Kluckhohn and Murray (1953) can be a good and easy start.

ADDITIONAL RESOURCES

Books

Goldstein, S. (2008). Cross-cultural explorations: Activities in culture and psychology. (2nd ed.). Boston: Allyn and Bacon.

Kluckhohn, C., & Murray, H. A.(1953). Personality in nature, society, and culture (2nd ed.). New York: Alfred A. Knopf.

Pedersen, P. B. (2004). 110 Experiences for multicultural learning. Washington DC: APA.

Smith, P. B., Bond, M. H., & Kağitçibaşi, Ç. (2006). Understanding social psychology across cultures: Living and working in a changing world (3rd ed.). London, UK: Sage.

Timothy, B. S. (2004). Practicing multiculturalism: Affirming diversity in counseling and psychology. Boston, MA: Pearson Education.

Websites

Center for Multilingual and Multicultural Research at University of Southern California
http://www.usc.edu/dept/education/CMMR/home.html
Association for Multicultural Counseling and Development (AMCD)
http://www.multiculturalcounseling.org/
The Society for the Psychological Study of Ethnic Minority Issues (APA Division 45)
http://division45.org/

REFERENCES

American Psychological Association. (1992). Ethical principles of psychologists and code of conduct. *American Psychologist, 47,* 1597–1611.

American Psychological Association. (1993). Guidelines for providers of psychological services to ethnic, linguistic, and culturally diverse populations. *American Psychologist, 48,* 45–48.

American Psychological Association. (2002). Ethical principles of psychologists and code of conduct. *American Psychologist, 57,* 1060–1073.

American Psychological Association. (2003). Guidelines for multicultural education, training, research, practice, and organizational change for psychologists. *American Psychologist, 58,* 377–402.

American Psychological Association, Division 44: Committee on Lesbian, Gay, and Bisexual Concerns Joint Task Force. (2000). Guidelines for psychotherapy with lesbian, gay, and bisexual clients. *American Psychologist, 55,* 1440–1451.

Arredondo, P., Toporek, R., Brown, S. P., Jones, J., Locke, D. C., Sanchez, J., et al. (1996). Operationalization of the multicultural counseling competencies. *Journal of Multicultural Counseling and Development, 24,* 42–78.

Atkinson, D. R., & Thompson, C. E. (1992). Racial, ethnic, and cultural variables in counseling. In S. D. Brown & R. W. Lent (Eds.), *Handbook of counseling psychology* (2nd ed., pp. 349–382). New York: John Wiley.

Atkinson, D. R., Thompson, C. E., & Grant, S. K. (1993). A three-dimensional model for counseling racial/ethnic minorities. *Counseling Psychologist, 21,* 257–277.

Berry, J. W. (1980). Social and cultural change. In H. C. Triandis & R. Brislin (Eds.), *Handbook of cross-cultural psychology: Social psychology* (Vol. 5, pp. 211–279). Boston: Allyn & Bacon.

Berry, J. W. (1997). Immigration, acculturation, and adaptation. *Applied Psychology, 46,* 5–34.

Bucci, W. (2002). The challenge of diversity in modern psychoanalysis. *Psychoanalytic Psychology, 19,* 216–226.

Burkard, A. W., & Knox, S. (2004). Effects of therapist color-blindness on empathy and attributions in cross-cultural counseling. *Journal of Counseling Psychology, 51,* 387–397.

Cain, D. J. (2008). Person-centered therapy. In J. Frew & M. D. Spiegler (Eds.), *Contemporary psychotherapies for a diverse world* (pp. 177–227). Boston: Houghton Mifflin.

Chen, S., & Davenport, D. S. (2005). Cognitive-behavioral therapy with Chinese American clients: Cautions and modifications. *Psychotherapy: Theory, Research, Practice, Training, 42,* 101–110.

Constantine, M. G. (2000). Social desirability, attitudes, sex, and affective and cognitive empathy as predictors of self-reported multicultural counseling competence. *Counseling Psychologist, 28,* 857–872.

Constantine, M. G. (2001). Multicultural training, theoretical orientation, empathy, and multicultural case conceptualization ability in counselors. *Journal of Mental Health Counseling, 23,* 357–372.

Constantine, M. G., & Gushue, G. V. (2003). School counselors' ethnic tolerance attitudes and racism attitudes as predictors of their multicultural case conceptualization of an immigrant student. *Journal of Counseling and Development, 81,* 185–190.

Constantine, M. G., & Ladany, N. (2001). New visions for defining and assessing multicultural counseling competencies. In J. G. Ponterotto, J. M. Casas, L. A. Suzuki, & C. M. Alexander (Eds.), *Handbook of multicultural counseling* (2nd ed., pp. 482–498). Thousand Oaks: CA: Sage.

Constantine, M. G., Miville, M. L., & Kindaichi, M. M. (2008). Multicultural competence in counseling psychology practice and training. In S. D. Brown & R. W. Lent (Eds.), *Handbook of counseling psychology* (4th ed., pp. 141–158). Hoboken, NJ: John Wiley.

Council for Accreditation of Counseling and Related Educational Programs. (2009). *2009 standards for accreditation.* Alexandria, VA: Author.

Ellis, A. (2000). A continuation of the dialogue on issues of counseling in the postmodern era. *Journal of Mental Health Counseling, 22,* 97–106.

Forrest, L. M. (2011). Linking international psychology, professional competence, and leadership: Counseling psychologists as learning partners. *Counseling Psychologist, 38,* 96–120.

Fouad, N. A. (Ed.). (2012). *APA handbook of counseling psychology.* Washington, DC: American Psychological Association.

Fuertes, J. N. (2012). Multicultural counseling and psychotherapy. In E. M. Altmaier & J. C. Hansen (Eds.), *The Oxford handbook of counseling psychology* (pp. 570–588). New York: Oxford.

Fuertes, J. N., & Brobst, K. (2002). Client's ratings of counselor multicultural competency. *Cultural Diversity and Ethnic Minority Psychology, 8,* 214–233.

Gelso, C., & Fretz, B. (2001). *Counseling psychology* (2nd ed.). New York: Harcourt College.

Glauser, A. S., & Bozarth, J. D. (2001). Person-centered therapy: The culture within. *Journal of Counseling and Development, 79,* 142–147.

Gorkin, M. (1996). Countertransference in cross-cultural psychotherapy. In R. M. Pérez Foster, M. Moskowitz, & R. A. Javier (Eds.), *Reaching across boundaries of culture and class: Widening the scope of psychotherapy* (pp. 159–176). Northvale, NJ: Aronson.

Hays, P. M. (2009). Integrating evidence-based practice, cognitive-behavioral therapy, and multicultural therapy: Ten steps for culturally competent practice. *Professional Psychology: Research and Practice, 40,* 354–360.

Heppner, P. (2006). The benefits and challenges of becoming cross-culturally competent counseling psychologists: Presidential address. *Counseling Psychologist, 34,* 147–172.

Holcomb-McCoy, C. C., & Myers, J. E. (1999). Multicultural competence and counselor training: A national survey. *Journal of Counseling and Development, 77,* 294–302.

Jackson, L. C., Schmutzer, P. A., Wenzel, A., & Tyler, J. D. (2006). Applicability of cognitive-behavior therapy with American Indian individuals. *Psychotherapy: Theory, Research, Practice, Training, 43,* 506–517.

Jackson, M. L. (1995). Multicultural counseling: Historical perspectives. In J. G. Ponterotto, J. M. Casas, L. A. Suzuki, & C. M. Alexander (Eds.), *Handbook of multicultural counseling* (pp. 3–16). Thousand Oaks: CA: Sage.

Kluckhohn, C., & Murray, H. A. (1950). Personality formation: The determinants. In C. Kluckhohn & H. A. Murray (Eds.), *Personality in nature, society, and culture* (pp. 35–48). New York: Knopf.

LaFromboise, T., Coleman, H. L. K., & Gerton, J. (1993). Psychological impact of biculturalism: Evidence and theory. *Psychological Bulletin, 114,* 395–412.

Leong, F. T. L. (1996). Towards an integrative model for cross-cultural counseling and psychotherapy. *Applied and Preventive Psychology, 5,* 189–209.

Leong, F. T. L. (2007). Cultural accommodation as method and metaphor. *American Psychologist, 62,* 916–927.

Leong, F. T. L., & Bluestein, D. L. (2000). Towards a global vision of counseling psychology. *Counseling Psychologist, 28,* 5–9.

Leong, F. T. L., & Lee, S. H. (2006). A cultural accommodation model for cross-cultural psychotherapy: Illustrated with the case of Asian Americans. *Psychotherapy Theory, Research, Practice, Training, 43,* 410–423.

Leong, F. T. L., & Ponterotto, J. G. (2003). A proposal for internationalizing counseling psychology in the United States: Rationale, recommendations, and challenges. *Counseling Psychologist, 31,* 381–395.

Leung, S. A. (2003). A journey worth traveling: Globalization of counseling psychology. *Counseling Psychologist, 31,* 412–419.

MacDougall, C. (2002). Rogers' person-centered approach: Considerations for use in multicultural counseling. *Journal of Humanistic Psychology, 42*(2), 48–65.

Neville, H. A., Spanierman, L. B., & Doan, B. T. (2006). Exploring the association between color-blind racial ideology and multicultural counseling competencies. *Cultural Diversity and Ethnic Minority Psychology, 12,* 275–290.

Neville, H. A., Worthington, R. L., & Spanierman, L. B. (2001). Race, power, and multicultural counseling psychology: Understanding White privilege and color-blind racial attitudes. In J. G. Ponterotto, J. M. Casas, L. A. Suzuki, & C. M. Alexander (Eds.), *Handbook of multicultural counseling* (2nd ed., pp. 257–288). Thousand Oaks: CA: Sage.

Nutt, R. L. (2007). Implications of globalization for training in counseling psychology: Presidential address. *Counseling Psychologist, 35,* 157–171.

Organista, K. C. (2000). Latinos. In J. R. White & A. S. Freeman (Eds.), *Cognitive-behavioral group therapy: For specific problems and populations* (pp. 281–303). Washington, DC: American Psychological Association.

Pérez Foster, R. M., Moskowitz, M., & Javier, R. A. (Eds.). (1996). *Reaching across boundaries of culture and class: Widening the scope of psychotherapy.* Northvale, NJ: Aronson.

Ponterotto, J. G. (2008). Theoretical and empirical advances in multicultural counseling and psychology. In S. D. Brown & R. W. Lent (Eds.), *Handbook of counseling psychology* (pp. 103–120). Hoboken, NJ: John Wiley.

Ponterotto, J. G., Casas, J. M., Suzuki, L. A., & Alexander, C. M. (Eds.). (2010). *Handbook of multicultural counseling* (3rd ed.). Thousand Oaks, CA: Sage.

Rivera, L. M. (2010). Acculturation: Theories, measurement, and research. In J. G. Ponterotto, J. M. Casas, L. A. Suzuki, & C. M. Alexander (Eds.), *Handbook of multicultural counseling* (3rd ed., 331–341). Thousand Oaks: CA: Sage.

Robbinson, D. T., & Morris, J. R. (2000). Multicultural counseling: Historical context and current training considerations. *Western Journal of Black Studies, 24,* 239–259.

Rogers, C. R. (1951). *Client-centered psychotherapy.* Boston: Houghton Mifflin.

Rogers, C. R. (1977). *Carl Rogers on personal power.* New York: Delacorte.

Sodowsky, G. R., Taffe, R. C., Gutkin, T. B., & Wise, S. L. (1994). Development of the multicultural counseling inventory: A self-report measure of multicultural competencies. *Journal of Counseling Psychology, 41*(2), 137–148.

Sue, D., & Sue, D. M. (2008). Foundations of counseling and psychotherapy: Evidence-based practice for a diverse society. Hoboken, NJ: John Wiley.

Sue, D. W., Arredondo, P., & McDavis, R. J. (1992). Multicultural counseling competencies and standards: A call to the profession. *Journal of Multicultural Counseling and Development, 20,* 64–88.

Sue, D. W., Bernier, J. E., Durran, A., Feinberg, L., Pedersen, P., Smith, E. J., et al. (1982). Position paper: Cross-cultural counseling competencies. *Counseling Psychologist, 10,* 45–52.

Sue, D. W., Capodilupo, C. M., Torino, G. C., Bucceri, J. M., Holder, A. M. B., Nadal, K. L., et al. (2007). Racial microaggressions in everyday life: Implications for clinical practice. *American Psychologist, 62,* 271–286.

Sue, D. W., & Sue, D. (1990). *Counseling the culturally diverse: Theory and practice.* New York: John Wiley.

Sue, D. W., & Sue, D. (1999). *Counseling the culturally diverse: Theory and practice* (3rd ed.). New York: John Wiley.

Sue, D. W., & Sue, D. (2013). *Counseling the culturally diverse: Theory and practice* (6th ed.). Hoboken, NJ: John Wiley.

Sue, S., Zane, N., Hall, G. C. N., & Berger, L. K. (2009). The case for cultural competency in psychotherapeutic intervention. *Annual Review of Psychology, 60,* 525–548.

Tang, N. M., & Gardner, J. (1999). Race, culture, and psychotherapy: Transference to minority therapists. *Psychoanalytic Quarterly, 68,* 1–20.

Thompson, C. E., Worthington, R., & Atkinson, D. R. (1994). Counselor content orientation, counselor race, and Black women's cultural mistrust and self-disclosures. *Journal of Counseling Psychology, 41,* 155–161.

Toporek, R. L., Gerstein, L. H., Fouad, N. A., Roysircar, G., & Israel, T. (Ed.). (2006). *Handbook of social justice in counseling psychology: Leadership, vision, and action.* Thousand Oaks, CA: Sage.

Tummala-Narra, P. (2013). Psychoanalytic applications in a diverse society. *Psychoanalytic psychology, 30*(3), 471–487.

Varenne, H. (2003). On internationalizing counseling psychology: A view from cultural anthropology. *Counseling Psychologist, 31,* 404–411.

Vereen, L. G., Hill, N. R., & McNeal, D. T. (2008). Perceptions of multicultural counseling competency: Integration of the curricular and the practical. *Journal of Mental Health Counseling, 30,* 226–236.

Wang, C. C. (2003). Cultural influences vs. actualizing tendency: Is the person-centered approach a universal paradigm? *Person-Centered Journal, 10,* 57–69.

Worthington, R. L., Soth-McNett, A. M., & Moreno, M. V. (2007). Multicultural counseling competencies research: A 20-year content analysis. *Journal of Counseling Psychology, 54,* 351–361.

Xie, D., Leong, F. T. L., & Feng, S. (2008). Culture-specific personality correlates of anxiety among Chinese and Caucasian college students. *Asian Journal of Social Psychology, 11,* 163–174.

CHAPTER 3

Case Conceptualization

The Case of Y-Chun

Naijian Zhang and Richard D. Parsons

The baby, assailed by eyes, ears, nose, skin, and entrails at once, feels it all as one great blooming, buzzing confusion.

—William James (1890/1980, p. 488)

In the quote above, William James was attempting to articulate the initial experiences of a newborn as it is first introduced to the new stimuli and circumstances of life following birth. This description may very well be applied to the experience of many counselors-in-training as they attempt to make sense of the varied disclosures of their first client. When a counselor engages with a client, especially on the occasion of his or her first experience, it becomes all too clear all too quickly that the sheer volume of information disclosed can be overwhelming. The novice counselor has so much to attend to when engaging with a client in the helping process: particular things said and certain tones used to convey them; body signals, reactions to counselor queries, and things expected but not produced; patterns and styles of communication; and likely a discernible theme to the story being shared. There are valuable notes to the client's tune, but these are often lost in the noise of the moment.

In addition to attending to and recording the data presented by the client, the counselor needs to discern which of these data are relevant, important, and necessary to understanding the client, as well as the most essential response to assist him or her in dealing with the current situations. That is, in the midst of the barrage of data, counselors need to be able to process the core of the issues and that which provides insight into the keys to helping. This ability to process and attend to the essential points is a characteristic of those we deem expert counselors.

The expert counselor calls on his or her theoretical orientation, knowledge of the research, and extensive professional experience to answer questions such as, "What is essential within all that is being shared?" "What are the core elements of the story being told?" and "What, within all that is shared, provides some insight into the nature of the concern, the desired goals, and how the client can be helped to achieve those goals?" Further, expert counselors take these data and shape them into their conceptualization of the case and the treatment plan to be enacted.

The current chapter introduces you to the concept of case conceptualization. You will have the opportunity by way of case illustrations and guided exercises to begin experiencing what it means to extract essential data from a client's story and craft those data to provide a succinct view of "what is going on," "how it came about," "what is desired as an alternative experience," and "how best to achieve that alternative."

In addition to describing the process of case conceptualization, this chapter provides you with details on the case of Y-Chun, an adult client who is a biracial, nontraditional college student. Y-Chun's case will be used throughout the text. As you will see in the upcoming chapters, experts in a particular theory of counseling will not only explain that theory but also apply it to their understanding, or conceptualization, of the case of Y-Chun. It is our hope that in viewing this single case through the lens of each of the theories to be presented, the theories will take on more life and practical value. Using this one case will provide you with the opportunity to see the unique perspective a counselor takes when employing a particular theory, but it will also begin to highlight the overlapping nature of the varied case conceptualizations across theories. The unique qualities of each theory provide a richness and diversity of treatment approaches employed by counselors of varying theoretical orientations. Finally, the chapter invites you to attempt your own initial case conceptualization for Y-Chun (see Exercise 3.1). We suggest that you use this initial case conceptualization as a pretest to measure the impact of upcoming chapters on the way you view client data. This exercise could be repeated as a self-test following your reading of any one chapter—especially if done prior to your reading of that chapter author's analysis of Y-Chun's case. It may also be helpful for you to return to this chapter and the case material to reformulate your view after reading the entire text (see Exercise 3.2). Contrasting your responses to Exercise 3.1 (prior to your reading) with those in Exercise 3.2 (post reading) will highlight both your understanding and valuing of the theories presented and provide evidence of the ongoing development of your professional identity.

Specifically, after reading and rereading this chapter, you will be able to do the following:

1. Describe what is meant by case conceptualization

2. Identify four targets for inclusion in case conceptualization, regardless of theoretical orientation

3. Identify elements of a client's story that you would deem important in understanding the nature of the presenting concern(s)

4. Understand the function of counseling theories in the process of case conceptualization

CASE CONCEPTUALIZATION

Unlike lay helpers, who can provide a listening ear and advice to a friend in need, professional counselors employ their knowledge and skills *intentionally* and *systematically* to guide the helping process toward a desired goal (Parsons & Zhang, 2013). This intentional and systematic approach starts with the initial encounter, or intake. During the initial conversation—be it a scheduled, 50-minute session in an outpatient office or a 15-minute crisis contact with a walk-in sixth-grader—professional counselors engage in a deliberate and focused process of gathering data that will serve as their basis for understanding client needs, resources, challenges, and goals. Consider Case Illustration 3.1, which contrasts the responses of a lay helper (a classroom teacher) with those of a professional school counselor.

CASE ILLUSTRATION 3.1

I Lost My Library Card

Ms. Morton, eighth-grade teacher

Ms. Morton: Slow down there, speedy. Why are you running through the halls?

Anthony: (Holding back tears) I lost my library card—I don't know where it is. (Now crying openly) I am so stupid. My mom is going to kill me, and so is Mrs. Dickinson [the school librarian].

Ms. Morton: Calm down . . . take a breath . . . do you have any idea when and where you last used it?

Anthony: (Trying to hold back the sobs) No—I had it in homeroom, and Laurie was using it to underline her name on her report.

Ms. Morton: Laurie? Laurie who?

Anthony: Williams . . . I think that is her name.

Ms. Morton: The eighth-grader?

Anthony: (Looking down, somewhat sheepishly) Yes, that's her. She's on my bus and asked to borrow it.

Ms. Morton: So Laurie may still have it?

Anthony: (Returning to sobbing) I don't know . . . I can't ask . . . she'll think I'm a real . . . (Trails off and looks down.)

Ms. Morton: Let's go find her.

(Continued)

(Continued)

Ms. Clements, school counselor

Ms. Clements:	Slow down there, speedy. Why are you running through the halls?
Anthony:	(Holding back tears) I lost my library card—I don't know where it is. (Now crying openly) I am so stupid. My mom is going to kill me, and so is Mrs. Dickinson [the school librarian].
Ms. Clements:	Calm down . . . take a breath . . . good. Slow it down . . . here, let's sit over here. (Moving to an empty classroom) Good, now start from the beginning and tell me what is going on . . . can you do that? We'll figure this out.
Anthony:	(Calming a bit and trying to hold back the sobs) Well I can't find my library card.
Ms. Clements:	Okay, so you can't find your card and that is very upsetting to you.
Anthony:	(Starts to cry again)
Ms. Clements:	Okay, now try to take a breath and calm down. I bet if we put our heads together we can figure something out. So tell me about the last time you remember having it.
Anthony:	(Calming) It was this morning on the bus. I was sitting with an eighth-grader, Laurie Williams (looks down, a little sheepishly), and she asked if I had one she could use to underline her name on her report.
Ms. Clements:	Laurie Williams? Yes, I know her—she is very nice . . . so—
Anthony:	(Smiling, interrupts) Yes, she is really nice. (Pauses)
Ms. Clements:	I guess we could check with her . . . but I'm getting the feeling that may make you feel a little uncomfortable?
Anthony:	Yeah—I don't want her seeing me crying and stuff . . . that's not cool . . .
Ms. Clements:	Well that makes sense. So what would you like us to do?

In reading the case, it should be clear that both people, Ms. Morton (the teacher) and Ms. Clements (the school counselor) care for Anthony and his current state of distress. It is also clear that both understand the issue—at least on one level—is the loss of a library card. The trained professional counselor, however, highlights Anthony's nonverbal messages as they particularly reflect on his feelings about Laurie and her perception of him. She understands that while Anthony is concerned about the real consequences of losing his library card, they are secondary to his concern about being perceived as an incompetent "little sixth-grader" who cries. As such, the counselor targets interventions such as moving out of the hallway, directing breathing as self-control, and even inviting him to give direction for what to do next, which all empower Anthony and help him feel in control. While resolving the issue of a lost library card requires some problem-solving skills, the process of helping Anthony address his concerns takes the professional well beyond this concrete problem to a focus on the person of Anthony and the social–emotional issues tied to the context of losing his library card.

So, as in the case illustration, professional counselors engage in ways that help them gather data essential to more fully understand the client and the client's story. The professional counselor crafts these data into a meaningful "picture" of the client—the client's concerns and goals—through a process of case conceptualization (Seligman & Reichenberg, 2012).

Case conceptualization is a tool or process that guides a counselor's observations, data collection, understanding, and conceptual integration of client behaviors, thoughts, feelings, and physiology from a clinical perspective (Neukrug & Schwitzer, 2006). With a foundation in research and counseling theory, case conceptualization helps counselors organize the internal complexities their clients bring into the counseling sessions (Eells, 1997). Case conceptualization serves as the counselor's hypothesis regarding the causes, precipitants, and maintaining influences of a person's psychological, interpersonal, and behavioral problems. It is the framework that guides the counseling process by helping the counselor and client identify treatment goals, appropriate interventions, and potential problems that may arise (Levenson & Strupp, 1997). Case conceptualization is clearly an essential part of the counseling process. With theory and research as the framework, a counselor, through the process of case conceptualization, finds meaning within the various, oftentimes disjointed pieces of information shared by a client—meaning that not only provides clarity to the understanding of the client's story but also gives direction to the counselor's treatment decisions.

The Process

Case conceptualization can be viewed as a three-step process (Neukrug & Schwitzer, 2006). It moves from data collection, through organization of those data, and results in finding meaning within the data collected.

Data Collection

The first step in case conceptualization involves the thorough gathering of data reflecting clients' concerns, goals, strengths, and challenges. The counselor's theory may direct him or her to pursue information about early childhood development and its implications for understanding and intervening in the current situation, or perhaps to gather observable data identifying the specific conditions when the client experiences the problem or concern. Regardless of the unique emphasis the counselor's theory may present, the goal for all counselors is to gather data that reflect the depth and breadth of clients' presenting goals or concerns.

In attempting to gain a full picture of "what is," a counselor will gather data identifying the behavioral, cognitive, affective, physiological, and sociocultural components of the client's issue. In an attempt to more fully understand the issue as well as its impact on the client's life, counselors may investigate the client's developmental and family history; previous medical conditions, including psychiatric difficulties; drug and alcohol use; previous episodes of adjustment difficulties; and specifics regarding the client's current social–emotional adjustment in major life roles and role transitions. While the types of data sought may vary according to counselors' theoretical orientations and work settings, generally, the counselor is seeking to identify the central facts of the client's life, as they shed light on the current situation.

These data may be collected by way of face-to-face interviews and/or use of various assessment instruments and intake surveys. In either case, it should be obvious that the counselor who is successful in tapping and gathering this broad base of information may soon find himself or herself with a vast array of puzzle pieces that now need to be organized.

Organization of Data

The second step of case conceptualization involves the process of organizing these data in ways that make the vast quantity of information manageable and useful to the counselor's decision making. During this part of case conceptualization, the counselor attempts to cluster or group client information into related segments to unearth problematic themes and recurring patterns that not only shed light on the nature of the issue at hand but also may provide direction for facilitating client growth. Step two of the case conceptualization process directs the counselor to organize his or her observations, assessments, or measures in a way that facilitates further interpretation and explanation of the client's current concerns (Neukrug & Schwitzer, 2006). Consider the brief case of Rosie—and her failed attempts at finding a meaningful, long-term relationship (Case Illustration 3.2).

CASE ILLUSTRATION 3.2

Rosie and the Failed Relationships

Rosie: So—I just feel so hopeless—like why bother? Clearly, I'm unlovable and I should just learn to live my life alone (sobbing).

Dr. K: Rosie, this is obviously very upsetting to you and is even challenging your belief that you will ever find a relationship. Perhaps it would help us understand what is happening if you could share a little bit more about your recent history of dating and relating?

Rosie: How far do you want me to go? . . . I mean, it's been happening since I was a kid. I never had friends for more than a few months. I don't know, maybe I was born a loser. I try . . . I've always tried to win people over, to have them like me . . . love me . . . but clearly it hasn't worked, it will never work (sobbing).

> *Dr. K:* This is upsetting, but if you could continue—maybe discussing some of your recent experiences dating, perhaps that would help?
>
> *Rosie:* Well—just even since graduating from college 6 years ago—I've had at least eight failed relationships. I just know what happens. I try every website and dating service, and I can get dates pretty easily—after all, I am smart and have a great job, and I work out so I'm in great shape . . . but it doesn't matter because it all blows after a couple of dates. I don't get it. . . . I try to be what they want. I put up with a lot of crap, because I don't want to lose them. I mean—yeah, okay—so I text a lot, and I call them at work and try to find out what they are doing or when we will get together. But that's just my way of showing them that I like them . . . that I care. I mean, I get really nervous if they don't call or contact me after a date. . . . I just know they are dumping me . . . so I try my best to hold on.

While the illustration is brief, it does provide data about the client, Rosie. The counselor in this situation may be not only gathering the data but also organizing it into some meaningful groups. For example, we have data that could be clustered under the label of "ability to make social contact." Rosie clearly has the ability to engage in social outreach (use of websites and data services) and even attract attention and initial invitations for engagement. We also have data that reflect her style following initial contact, which we could group as "style of social engagement," including her willingness to "be whatever they want" or her tendency to text and call often. And finally, there are data we could group as "perception of self and others," which would include her self-reference as unlovable, as a loser and her self-described anticipation of being rejected. While it may be easy to retain the salient information from this client's story, being that it was so brief, it is easy to see how in the continued gathering of data a counselor could be overwhelmed if not organizing those data into meaningful clusters.

Often, as will become clear in the upcoming chapters, the themes sought and the problematic patterns identified are those for which a counselor's operational model or theory best explains the difficulty being encountered. So in looking back on Rosie's case (Case Illustration 3.2), a counselor with a behavioral perspective (see Chapter 10) may ponder the possible negative effects of her behavior (e.g., excessive texting, calling) on the continuation of a relationship, whereas a counselor with a cognitive orienting model (see Chapter 9) may examine the impact of her beliefs about being a loser or living alone for the rest of her life and her prediction that a date's slow response is evidence he is planning to dump her.

Finding Meaning

The final step in a counselor's case conceptualization is to draw conclusions and find meaning in the data collected. The questions asked in this phase of case conceptualization may include, "How did the clients come to have these specific problems? Where are these problems stemming from? What are the clients' strengths? What are the goals for counseling? What specific interventions will be used to address these problems identified by the counselors and the clients?" (Arbona, 2012). The types of questions pondered, as well as the meaning attributed to the data collected and organized, will be influenced by the specific theory or model employed by the counselor.

The use of counseling theory helps the counselor infer, explain, and interpret the data in meaningful ways. For example, the counselor working with Rosie in Case Illustration 3.2 might infer that given Rosie's long-standing history of difficult relationships, she has developed a belief that she is unlovable and inevitably will be alone. Her belief that this is what life holds for her makes her desperate to find a relationship, a desperation that takes form in overbearing measures of seeking affirmation (i.e., frequent texts and phone calls), which in turn leads to the relationship's termination.

The formulation of an integrated, consistent view of the client's main issues provides the foundation for developing a coherent plan for change (Eells, 1997). Thus, the effective, competent counselor employs the process of case conceptualization—moving smoothly from data collection, through organization, and finally to the extraction of meaning—as the springboard for formulation and implementation of the treatment plan (Jongsma, Peterson, & McInnis, 2006).

Not So Easy

As a process of gathering data reflecting the client's concern and organizing those data to find meaning so patterns and themes can be explained and understood, the description of case conceptualization seems rather clear-cut and simple. Yet all who have engaged in this process—from the novice to the expert—can attest that developing a case conceptualization with any one client is a daunting task (Caspar, Berger, & Hautle, 2004). Synthesizing a large amount of complex and ambiguous information is far from easy, but you will soon discover that this is much more achievable with practice (Caspar et al., 2004) when counselors employ theories to guide both understanding and decision making.

To highlight the challenge of the process of case conceptualization, consider Case Illustration 3.3. It is important to note that this case is somewhat unrealistic in its simplicity; however, even though the behavior of concern is relatively straightforward, the process of drawing definitive conclusions about what is going on with the client, why it is happening, and, more important, what to do to help, is anything *but* straightforward.

CASE ILLUSTRATION 3.3

"Because I Screamed"

The referral came from Ms. Zaborowski, the eighth-grade mathematics teacher, and was simple enough. It read: "Please talk to Alicia about proper, or should I say improper, classroom behavior. I was in the middle of teaching my unit, and I had my back turned to the class. As I was writing an equation on the board, I became startled by a scream. As I turned, I saw Alicia standing up and hollering, to no one in particular, 'Quit it.' It was so disruptive that I had to send her down to Vice Principal Hartfelt, where I heard she spent the rest of the day.

I know this may sound silly, but the volume and tone of her scream was chilling. It startled me and most of the class. Alicia has been a handful throughout the course of the term, but nothing this bad. In the past, she has called out answers prior to being recognized or without raising her hand. And on a couple of occasions she has made a negative comment to Adriana, the student who sits beside her. But again, nothing so apparently out of control. I don't know what is going on with her, but you need to help her. This type of outburst is simply unacceptable."

Additional Information

Through conversation with Alicia and her teachers, as well as reviewing the data found in Alicia's records, the counselor was able to glean the following information:

a. Alicia's mother recently and unexpectedly separated from her husband (Alicia's father) and moved out of the house. That was 3 weeks prior to this incident, and since then, Alicia has been living with her father and her younger brother (age 11). Alicia has been taking on some of the chores around the house, including cooking and overseeing her brother's homework.

b. Alicia has been diagnosed with ADHD. In the past, she worked with a counselor and has been on medication. However, since her mother left, she has not been taking her medication or seeing the counselor.

c. Alicia sits next to Adriana, a friend with whom she has gotten into minor arguments throughout the year.

d. Alicia sits in front of Raul, who has indicated on more than one occasion and to more than one person that he is "in love" with Alicia.

e. Adriana has expressed a romantic interest in Raul.

f. Alicia has a history of being talkative and verbally disruptive in her classes, calling out answers without raising her hand and audibly commenting on other students' answers.

g. On the day Alicia was referred, she was scheduled to give her presentation on the topic of "tectonic plates" in her science class, which followed this math period. Throughout the morning, she had told Adriana that she felt sick to her stomach and as though her heart was racing.

h. Alicia has a "special–supportive" relationship with Vice Principal Hartfelt, who also serves as disciplinarian for Grades 7 and 8.

For a counselor such as the one in our case illustration to completely understand and then help a client, he or she must grasp the cognitive, behavioral, emotional, cultural, contextual, and sociopolitical aspects of the client's story. The counselor in this case may search the data for answers to questions such as, What was Alicia thinking at the time of her outburst? What role might her physiological condition (i.e., ADHD) have played in creating this situation? Did her apparent anxiety about the upcoming presentation contribute to the outburst? How might the social dynamic of sitting in front of Raul, with his romantic interests, and beside Adriana, who apparently is a competitor for Raul's attention, contribute to the situation? And, of course, how is the absence of Alicia's mother impacting her?

These are just a few of the questions pondered by the counselor and targets for the counselor's data collection. By understanding and drawing conclusions about the interplay of all the salient elements of this one story—including the ADHD, the mother's departure, the apparent performance anxiety, and the adolescent love triangle—and their role in the client's overall level of functioning, the counselor will be able to develop viable treatment strategies (Sue & Sue, 2003).

THEORY GUIDING CASE CONCEPTUALIZATION

As previously noted, a counselor's theoretical model serves as a lens through which to process and find meaning in the details of a client's story. A counseling theory provides a useful scaffold or framework on which to organize client data. A theory can direct the counselor to possible explanations of how separate elements of the client's story fit together in an interrelated and comprehensible theme. But more than simply organizing the elements into an integrated whole, a counseling theory provides clarity to a counselor's understanding of the client's presenting concerns and facilitates the counselor's ability to draw inferences and conclusions and engage in an intentional and directed helping process.

Because each theory offers a unique perspective on the human condition—targeting specific factors or elements deemed important to our well-being and healthy functioning—it should be obvious that each may result in a somewhat unique take on a client's story and the role and function of the counselor working with that client. As you proceed through the upcoming chapters, you will be able to experience just how a theory may influence the case conceptualization and treatment planning processes. But prior to moving on to a full explanation of the theories and their unique perspectives, a review of Case Illustration 3.4 will highlight this influence of theory on the case conceptualization process and the unique value and view one gains by employing varied theories as the lenses through which to process client data.

CASE ILLUSTRATION 3.4

The Case of W. J.

W. J. came to counseling after losing his job. W. J. is 55 years old and had worked at the same job (as an accountant) for the same firm since finishing graduate school at the age of 31. W. J. states that he is depressed and feels hopeless and like "less than a man" because he is no longer able to support his family. W. J. has been married to Sheila for 26 years, and they have two grown children—Robert, who is also an accountant, and Denise, who is a physician with her own practice.

W. J. was told that the company he worked for was losing money and had to cut back on the number of employees. The company "valued" his years of service but was top-heavy in the accounting division. While initially irate, W. J. quickly turned to depression. He remarked, "I should have expected this, since in all my life I have been a failure." He is now convinced that Sheila will leave him and that his children are ashamed of him. He is questioning whether or not his life is worth living.

W. J.'s mother and father were both alcoholics. As a child, he witnessed his parents' violent fights, characterized by shouting and scuffling. He remembers feeling scared at those times and trying as best he could to intervene. He felt it was his duty to protect his mom and to bring peace to the family. He was quick to note that at that point, he failed.

As a child, he did not have any friends and often stayed at his aunt's house during times of particular tension and fighting at home. He worried that he would be taken away from his mom and dad, convinced that somehow their fighting was about him.

W. J. Through the Lens of Varied Theories

Psychodynamic Approaches

The psychodynamic approaches (see Chapter 4) typically do not take the presenting problem at face value. Often, they interpret that which is presented—in this case, W. J.'s depression—as a symptom of a larger and more developed root issue. To identify such an issue, counselors operating from this orientation will most likely explore the client's early childhood experiences and the way his sense of self was developed, as well as ways he navigated stressful times. Thus, the impact of his parental conflicts, the dynamic of his "rescuing" or attempting to rescue his mother during these conflicts, and his evolving relationship with his father might all serve as targets for in-depth analysis.

As you will discover in reading Chapter 4, the salient elements affecting the client's current experience are most often hidden from his or her conscious awareness, and, thus, a goal might be to make conscious that which is hidden.

Adlerian Theory

Those counselors employing an Adlerian theory (see Chapter 5) will want to investigate clients' family constellation and early recollections of the interaction experienced within the family. The counselors employing an Adlerian frame of reference might be interested in helping the clients understand their private view of themselves in relation to others and the role they feel they must play. Thus, in this case, the counselor may want to investigate W. J.'s feelings of responsibility for parental conflict and belief in his role as a peacemaker.

(Continued)

(Continued)

Humanistic Approaches

The humanistic approaches (see Chapter 7) deemphasized the importance of early life experiences and unconscious processes. These approaches brought attention to the clients' here-and-now experiences, strengths, and abilities to cope with their lives. They also highlighted the importance of the real relationship between client and counselor (as opposed to the transference relationship) in the therapy process.

The counselor employing such a humanistic, person-centered approach may identify the client's sense of limited self-worth and recognize that this may be the result of responding to messages of external valuation (e.g., parental praise or work success) rather than employing internal standards for valuing self. The counselor may also note the difficulty W. J. has in being genuine—as opposed to always playing the role of provider or peacemaker. If these observations are made, the counselor may, through the value of his or her therapeutic relationship, help W. J. move to a more self-accepting, prizing position.

Cognitive-Behavioral Approaches

Unlike counselors operating from a psychodynamic perspective, those employing a behavioral or cognitive-behavioral orientation will tend to accept the client's presenting concern (e.g., depression due to loss of job) at face value, rather than as a symptom of a deeper issue. The counselor operating from these frames of reference will be concerned about W. J.'s current behavior and its impact on his feelings and functioning. Is he staying in bed? Is he eating? Is he engaging or withdrawing from social contact? These and similar questions may be pursued with the assumption that each contributes to the experience of depression and, thus, their alternatives (e.g., engaging with others, eating well, exercising, etc.) may help reduce those depressive experiences. Also, those operating from a cognitive perspective will be attuned to W. J.'s thought processes and beliefs. The client's association between losing his job and being a total disappointment to his wife and children is a belief the counselor will attempt to help debate and reformulate.

While W. J.'s case provides a hint of the influence choice of theory may have on case conceptualization and treatment planning, the full import of theory to practice will be addressed in the upcoming chapters.

CASE CONCEPTUALIZATION ACROSS THEORIES

While counselors with different theoretical perspectives target and emphasize various components of the client story in their case conceptualization, at least four somewhat generic elements appear to be included in case conceptualization (Kendjelic & Eells, 2007). As you read through the various theories, you will see the authors attempt to find meaning in the client's story so as to understand each of the following: (1) symptoms and problems, (2) precipitating stressors, (3) predisposing events and conditions, and (4) an inferred explanatory mechanism accounting for the previous three components.

Symptoms and Problems

When attempting to draw conclusions regarding symptoms and problems, a counselor will focus on the overt issues the client presents. But, as guided by his or her theoretical orientation, the counselor may attend to covert issues not immediately disclosed by the client or the client's "behavioral leakage" (Horowitz & Eells, 1997), which is observed behavior such as fidgetiness or perspiration that suggests unexpressed affect.

Precipitating Stressors

Precipitating stressors are events that contribute to the onset of the person's current problems or symptoms, or have increased their severity. They may not be the underlying cause of the person's current problems but may provoke them. Again, those with varying theoretical orientations will assign more or less value to the importance of such stressors.

Predisposing Events and Conditions

One's theoretical framework may direct attention to factors such as events in the client's past, learning history, attachment style, interpersonal schemas, and developmental issues that may increase vulnerability to the precipitating stressor(s) and result in a greater likelihood of symptoms developing.

Inferred Mechanisms

Where theory is perhaps most evident in case conceptualization is in the constructs or mechanisms employed not only to elaborate on each of the previous components but to explain their relationship. As you read on in this text, you will discover that one's theoretical framework may result in the creation of various hypotheses about the client's current difficulties and explanations as to how and why those difficulties came to be. Elements such as biological disposition, early childhood experiences, internalized family rules and roles, developed core beliefs, interpersonal relationships, and behavioral contingencies are all used both to explain cause of the current difficulties and to give direction to the preferred methods of helping. An example of the impact of a counselor's theoretical framework on case conceptualization can be found in Case Illustration 3.5—picking back up with Alicia from Case Illustration 3.3. In this case, it is clear that the counselor, at least initially, sees the issue as part of behavior management, whereas the supervisor seems to suspect that the behavior is merely a symptom of some underlying issue or emotional upset related to the recent change in Alicia's family relationships.

CASE ILLUSTRATION 3.5

Alicia

After gathering all available data, Mrs. Kaley decided to discuss Alicia (see Case Illustration 3.3) with her supervisor, Dr. Kathryn Lenore.

Mrs. Kaley: In some ways, it seems pretty clear—I found out from the other students that Max kept looking over to Alicia, making kissing sounds and saying things like, "When are you and Raul getting married?" "What will you name your kids?" "Kiss-kiss," etc. Ms. Morton was unaware of this, but it apparently was going on for over 15 minutes. I'm thinking, given the fact that Alicia was not on her medication, she probably didn't have the ability to inhibit her impulse—and in some ways, I'm surprised she didn't hit him.

Dr. Lenore: Seems reasonable, but I'm wondering—we know her mom left her father. Do you think she is feeling abandoned? Maybe being sent to the vice principal was seen as getting the emotional support she was desiring? You know . . . a mom substitute?

Mrs. Kaley: Surely, mom's leaving is significant—but I think this is more straightforward. Alicia has a history of calling or acting out. . . . I think this is more an issue of behavioral control—and maybe if we reduce the distracting stimuli by moving her seat, she can maintain control.

Dr. Lenore: Well that would be easy enough to do—and may be effective in reducing the calling out and disruptive behavior, but I also believe that becoming the "woman" of the house—and the fact that she might feel that her mom left her . . . and not just dad . . . is worth pursuing, and this may be your invitation to talk with her about it.

Mrs. Kaley: Makes sense. I will work with Ms. Morton to reduce the immediate problem and hopefully reduce the possibility of it occurring in the near future—but at the same time, I will see if I can spend some time with Alicia to get her to talk more about the change in her family role and relationships and her experience of having her mom leave.

THE CASE OF Y-CHUN: A CASE THROUGH MANY LENSES

In the chapters that follow, you will learn the basic tenets of the primary theories currently employed by counselors. In addition to providing an introduction and explanation of a specific theory's fundamentals, each chapter includes the application of that theory to a common case—that of Y-Chun.

The use of this single case across chapters will allow you to see how the concepts, constructs, and basic tenets of any one theory serve to guide a counselor's case conceptualization and treatment planning. We hope you will find value in the case application as it helps illustrate the conversion of theoretical constructs to counselor decisions and practices. We also hope that in understanding the uniqueness of each theory and the light it sheds on the human condition, you will begin to align yourself with the theory or theories that will guide your own case conceptualization and treatment planning and give form to your professional identity.

As you begin this journey, you may find it helpful to begin identifying the perspective you already bring to the process of case conceptualization. To that end, we suggest you complete Exercise 3.1. Upon completion, you will have your own initial case conceptualization, highlighting those aspects of the case you find essential to your understanding and eventual treatment planning. This first attempt at case conceptualization can serve as a foundation from which to develop new insights, perspectives, and understandings. We invite you to return to the case and reformulate your case conceptualization after you complete this text (see Exercise 3.2). You may discover that you now emphasize elements previously missed or deemphasize those you formerly deemed essential. Changes in your formulation mark both your understanding and valuing of the theories presented, as well as your developing professional identity.

EXERCISE 3.1

INITIAL CASE CONCEPTUALIZATION

Part I

Directions: Use the following table to gather your thoughts about Y-Chun's case. In Column 1, list a clear description of each element (including client quotes) that you feel is important to your understanding of the case. In the middle column, develop a brief explanation of why you feel that element is important. Finally, in the last column, provide the category you feel best identifies the specific data you listed in the first column. Use the following categories:

a. Biological (including genetic, hormonal, nutritional, etc.)

b. Neurological (including neurochemical)

c. Overt behavior

d. Environmental/social (family) influences

e. Conscious thoughts, beliefs, values

f. Unconscious (unaware) influences

g. Distant-past childhood or developmental experiences

h. Present life conditions and experiences

i. Future goals/dreams/expectations

- Other

(Continued)

(Continued)

Specific Data From Client's Story	Why You Feel This Is Important	How You Describe/Label the Data (Use Codes)

Source: Modified from Kopta, Newman, McGovern, & Sandrock (1986).

Part II

Directions: Review the material you collected and placed in the table, and write your responses to the following questions:

   a. How would you describe Y-Chun's "problem(s)"?

   b. What would you identify as the "cause" of her current state?

   c. What specific things do you think need to change for her to resolve her issues and move to a more desired state?

   d. List three strategies you feel could help her move from what is to what is desired.

EXERCISE 3.2

POSTTEST CASE CONCEPTUALIZATION

Part I

Directions: Use the following table to gather your thoughts about Y-Chun's case. In Column 1, list a clear description of each element (including client quotes) that you feel is important to your understanding of the case. In the middle column, develop a brief explanation of why you feel that element is important. Finally, in the last column, provide the category you feel best identifies the specific data you listed in the first column. Use the following categories:

a. Biological (including genetic, hormonal, nutritional, etc.)

b. Neurological (including neurochemical)

c. Overt behavior

d. Environmental/social (family) influences

e. Conscious thoughts, beliefs, values

f. Unconscious (unaware) influences

g. Distant-past childhood or developmental experiences

h. Present life conditions and experiences

i. Future goals/dreams/expectations

j. Other

Specific Data From Client's Story	Why You Feel This Is Important	How You Describe/Label the Data (Use Codes)

Source: Modified from Kopta, Newman, McGovern, & Sandrock (1986).

Part II

Directions: Review the material you collected and placed in the table, and write your responses to the following questions:

a. How would you describe Y-Chun's "problem(s)"?

b. What would you identify as the "cause" of her current state?

c. What specific things do you think need to change for her to resolve her issues and move to a more desired state?

d. List three strategies you feel could help her move from what is to what is desired.

THE CLIENT: Y-CHUN

Y-Chun is a 35-year-old, biracial (White and Asian) female who is a nontraditional college student. She was born into a family of low social–economic class; her father is a construction worker who originally came from Poland, and her mother is a Chinese American employed as a custodian in a nursing home. This is the second marriage for Y-Chun's father and also for her mother, with both previous marriages ending with the death of the spouse. Y-Chun's father and mother both have children from their previous marriages. Her father has one son, age 38, and her mother has a son, age 41, and a daughter, age 39. Y-Chun is the only child of both parents. All children, with the exception of Y-Chun, are married and live independently from their parents. Y-Chun moved back home because she is paying for her own college and working only part-time.

Her parents are proud of her for going to college, and both Y-Chun's father and mother held high expectations for her academic achievement throughout her childhood. Her earliest childhood memories are being told "she was the smart one" and "she would make her parents so proud."

Y-Chun is in her junior year at college. She is in a liberal arts program and is attempting to manage her schoolwork, work part-time, and raise two children—David, 15, and Jennifer, 12, who is physically disabled. As noted previously, Y-Chun has moved back, along with her children, to her parents' house. This is a major source of stress in Y-Chun's life because she feels her parents treat her and her children as though they are all *their* children.

While Y-Chun's parents support her and her two children, they can't hide their disapproval of the fact that Y-Chun does not know who the father of either child is. Y-Chun rebelled as a youth, and that rebellion took the form of drug and alcohol use and promiscuous behavior. She is dating, but the relationship is not exclusive. And while this was the agreed-on arrangement, Y-Chun is now feeling used by the man she is seeing and is unsure what she wants out of this or any relationship.

Y-Chun has come to the counseling center at her physician's suggestion. She has been complaining of headaches, upset stomach, difficulty sleeping—both in getting to sleep and staying asleep—and in general finding herself short-tempered and always on edge. Her physician felt that she was handling a number of stressful issues, such as school, parenting, living with her parents, and the problems with the current relationship, and thus recommended she seek counseling.

Five Minutes Into the Intake Session

Counselor: Now, could you tell me what brought you here?

Y-Chun: I don't know where I should start, and I'm overwhelmed with so many things in my life now. I just feel like I can't handle them.

Counselor: Can't handle them?

Y-Chun: I just feel tired all the time and have no energy or desire to go out, or to do anything, especially my schoolwork. In the past 6 months I lost about 20 pounds, and you can see I can't afford to lose any weight. (She gestures to her slight figure.) I am also finding that I can't concentrate and I'm always ready to snap . . . like I'm on edge.

Counselor:	So your energy level is low and you are on edge, and it's clear your appetite is not what it used to be and you've lost weight. . . . How is your sleep?
Y-Chun:	I sleep a lot more than before, but it doesn't seem to help me at all. My sleep is often fitful, and I have nightmares and wake still very tired, not at all rested.
Counselor:	And if I understand what you wrote in your intake form, you did see your physician?
Y-Chun:	Yes, I did. But the doctor said that everything seems okay physically, and she suggested that I see a counselor because of the stress and the way I've been feeling.
Counselor:	The way you've been feeling?
Y-Chun:	Yeah. It is hard to describe. I feel empty, down, and I find myself crying a lot. And then I start to worry about my life and my kids and what's going to happen to us. These worries bother me a great deal because I can't control them.
Counselor:	You are concerned about your future and your children. Anything else?
Y-Chun:	Yeah—the thing that seems to be a constant concern is my relationships, or lack of relationships.
Counselor:	I'm not sure what you mean . . . your relationships, or lack of relationships. Perhaps you could tell me about your relationships?
Y-Chun:	You mean my parents?
Counselor:	If that's where you wish to start.
Y-Chun:	I don't think I have ever had a normal relationship with either of them. The only time we would ever talk was when I was in some type of trouble, or had disappointed them.
Counselor:	Disappointed them?
Y-Chun:	When I was little, my parents always seemed so busy and not really interested in me. I saw that other kids had so much fun with their parents, and I was so jealous of that because I did not have it. So to get my parents' attention, I would often just get into trouble, break something or get into fight with classmates. Then they would sit down to lecture me. They wanted me to behave the way they wanted and to do the things they wanted me to do, but I couldn't. And I felt so alone and helpless.
Counselor:	Alone?
Y-Chun:	Yeah, that's it . . . I just felt disconnected, alone . . . like I had no one in my life . . . no one that really cared.
Counselor:	No one in your life?
Y-Chun:	(Starting to cry) Even my brother and sister hated me and still do because I'm the "real child" of my parents.
Counselor:	"Real child"?
Y-Chun:	You know, they were both my biological parents, and my half-siblings always said they favored me over them. I don't see that I was treated or am treated special by my parents, but they do, and growing up they would tease me and

	put me down, saying that I was weak and nobody and that I would always have to be mommy and daddy's little girl.
Counselor:	You sound very sad, as you describe their teasing.
Y-Chun:	It is still sad—it hurts. It was horrible growing up. . . . To be honest with you, I attempted to run away from home a couple of times when I was in my teens and even thought about ending my life. The worst thing was that I did not have many friends at school to turn to. Kids at school did not want to be friends with me, because I looked Asian, I don't know. But I did remember some kids called me "banana" and often gave me a hard time on the school bus. They would make faces and make their eyes slant, and many would not even allow me to sit next to them, even when the seat was empty. For these reasons, I would hate to be Asian and always want to be White.
Counselor:	I'm so sorry to hear that happened to you. That must have been very difficult.
Y-Chun:	It really was—horrible. And sometimes I just couldn't take it, so I would say something or even push the kid that was calling me names or making faces. And then when I did that, my parents would always blame me, saying that if I could not play with them I should stay away from them. They didn't get it. They didn't care.
Counselor:	I do really hear that hurt—still very deep within you. That was very difficult.
Y-Chun:	It was—and even now, when I think about it—it still hurts, and I guess it makes me mad. I find I'm getting angry a lot lately. Not sure why—but it is just like back then.
Counselor:	What did you do with those feelings?
Y-Chun:	I don't know. Back then, I would just avoid the kids or try to get out of school as soon as I could—sometimes even playing hooky to avoid them. Now I withdraw to my room or try to stay away from everyone. . . . I'm afraid of going ballistic.
Counselor:	Ballistic?
Y-Chun:	Yeah. I'm just not sure I won't hurt someone if I really get angry.
Counselor:	Have you ever really hurt someone or something—when you were angry?
Y-Chun:	No, not really—and I don't even think I could. I just say that stuff . . . but I do feel like screaming sometimes.
Counselor:	You know, Y-Chun, that growing up—you experienced quite a lot, and it sounds like much of it felt quite hurtful and scary. I'm wondering if you think there is any connection between these early experiences and your current situation.
Y-Chun:	I don't know. I know I'm still struggling with my parents, my father in particular. He never treats me like an adult and has these ridiculous gender stereotypes about how a girl should act and criticizes me for behaving any other way. He

expects me to do everything my mother has been doing—cleaning, cooking, doing laundry, and listening to him. He makes all the decisions and acts like a boss for all of us—except my brother, because he's a man. I don't think that is fair. He never does anything around the house, and expects mom or me to wait on him hand and foot, having food on the table when he walks into the house. I want to talk to him on an equal basis, but I don't think I would ever get that in return.

Counselor: You sound very frustrated.

Y-Chun: Yes, I am. I did not want to grow up being like my mother, and I did not want to be like my father, either. The problem is, while I knew what I didn't want to be . . . I was lost and did not know what I wanted to be. I just feel out of step with everyone . . . (begins to cry). I just feel so alone . . . so completely alone. I really wish I could find some kind of closeness. . . .

Counselor: When you speak of being all alone and disconnected, I wonder, how do your children fit into this story?

Y-Chun: That is also very upsetting. My two kids are not close to me either, maybe because I'm cold to them. I know I have yelled a lot, and even now I yell at them and then feel guilty afterwards. It is not that I don't want to be emotionally close to them. I just don't know how. I can see that I'm acting just like my parents—I hate it—but I don't know how to stop it.

Counselor: So you think that you are following in your parents' footsteps in terms of how you relate to the children. How about other relationships, other than with your parents, siblings, or children?

Y-Chun: I really don't have any other relationships. I mean, I hang out with a couple of people at work, and I go out once in a while with a guy . . . but I don't have a real relationship with anyone, never have . . . especially with men. I just can't allow myself to trust them.

Counselor: That's a pretty strong statement. You can't trust men. . . . Do you mean all men, in general?

Y-Chun: (Long pause and hesitation, but Y-Chun sees encouragement in the counselor's eyes and begins.) When I was 16 years old, I went with my parents, my aunt, and my cousin for a family vacation. My cousin and I were the same age and had played together since we were little. The second day of the vacation, I was playing with him in the hotel room while our parents were out shopping. My cousin was using the quilt, covering my head in the bed, and we were wrestling and playing kind of rough, and almost before I knew what was happening . . . he raped me (pauses and lowers her head).

Counselor: (Remains silent, waiting)

Y-Chun: I couldn't believe what had happened. I was scared—I felt sick, and yet I was more worried that my parents would blame me . . . just like they always did. Since then, I became a different person. I have blamed myself for years and believe that it's me who let it happen. I couldn't tell my parents what had happened because I knew they would not believe me. My parents always think that I am a rough kid or a bad kid, and they would scold me even when the trouble was caused by someone else. So I pretended that nothing had happened to me, telling myself that it was just a nightmare.

Counselor: But, Y-Chun, it is clear that you know it was not a dream, and I feel honored that you would trust me enough to share it with me. I'm sure having such a thing happen to you and feeling as if you could not tell anyone—especially your parents, whom you wish could protect you—must have been really difficult. How would you describe your feelings about the event—and the fact that you had to carry this secret alone?

Y-Chun: I have a lot of anger and guilt. I try to keep it in, I guess you could say suppress it. But it comes up in my nightmares, and I find that anytime I'm getting intimate with some guy I'm dating . . . I start to get anxious and then angry, and if we do have sex . . . it gets pretty rough. And then there's other stuff . . . not sure if it's connected.

Counselor: Other stuff?

Y-Chun: Yeah, like I got into shoplifting . . . taking stuff from the supermarket, stuff I didn't need or even use. I even got arrested. And while I can't be emotionally close to men I'm dating, I find myself hooking up with strangers . . . taking them to bed—regardless if they are married or single. And for some of the married men, I've made it so that their wives find out, and some have lost their jobs and even gotten divorces. I have even take money for sex—I don't know why I do these things (begins to cry).

Counselor: You say you don't know why you do these things—have you ever thought about how this may work for you?

Y-Chun: Work for me?

Counselor: Well, if you are doing these things—and we assume that you are getting something out of it . . . what might that be?

Y-Chun: I don't know—I guess pleasure, sexually? I know I got pregnant a couple of times and had abortions. And then one time I decided to keep the pregnancy, and that is when David was born. The problem was, I found that I disliked him. I thought that it might be that I hate men and David is a boy. So I had Jennifer, who was born with cerebral palsy. But I really have no feelings for either of them. . . . I know they can sense it.

Counselor: So even though you care for your children—you say you don't have feelings for them?

Y-Chun: Don't get me wrong—I take care of them—I want to be a good parent—I just feel empty . . . distant . . . like they are plants and I just water them. I know that sounds horrible, but that's how it feels.

Counselor: It seems horrible to you?

Y-Chun: Yes, I don't know. I feel that something is not right with me, and I don't want to be this way for the rest of my life.

Counselor: So it is clear what you don't want . . . but I'm wondering how it would be if you were living the life you wanted or being the type of person you would like to be?

Y-Chun: I don't know what kind of life I want. And even if I could think about it—I know it will never happen. It's strange that I thought about ending my life many years ago but now I'm afraid of dying. It's like I need to live to figure this out.

Counselor: So if I understand correctly—it sounds like you believe that you can figure this out, even if it is going to be difficult, and that now you want to continue to focus and work on understanding what has happened and, probably more importantly, how to make your life, yourself, the way you desire?

Y-Chun: (Tearing up) Yes—I do—I really do. I don't want to continue feeling so empty and doing such destructive things, but . . . but . . . I don't know where to begin.

Counselor: I think you have already begun. Coming here—sharing as you have—was courageous, and I feel honored to be part of this process and would like to continue. How would you feel about meeting this time next week?

Y-Chun: (With a smile) Yes, I would like that. . . .

Counselor: Before we end, are there any questions you may have for me, or on what we did today?

Y-Chun: No, I just want to thank you for listening and being here for me.

KEYSTONES

- Case formulation or conceptualization is a hypothesis about the causes, precipitants, and maintaining influences of a person's psychological, interpersonal, and behavioral problems.
- Case conceptualization guides counseling by helping identify treatment goals, appropriate interventions, and potential problems that may arise.
- Case conceptualization requires the ability to synthesize a large amount of complex and ambiguous information.
- A counselor's theoretical approach may act as a lens to filter client data and give shape to the case formulation.
- At least four, somewhat generic elements are included in case conceptualization: (1) symptoms and problems, (2) precipitating stressors, (3) predisposing events and conditions, and (4) an inferred explanatory mechanism accounting for the previous three components.

REFLECTIONS FROM THE CONTRIBUTOR'S CHAIR

Although I came from an Eastern perspective originally, I have found the Western counseling theories fascinating. The first time that I was exposed to the Western counseling theories was almost two decades ago. At that time I felt excited but challenged as well. After twenty years' studying, teaching, practicing, and doing research, I have come a long way to build my professional identity with the counseling theories that I have learned and applied.

As a child I was taught some Confucius values by my grandmother and my parents. When I was studying the humanistic counseling theories, I found some similarities between the belief of the humanistic approaches and the Confucianism. The intersection of these two beliefs made me excited and motivated, which has also led me to believe that the same world can be viewed with different lenses and different paths can lead individuals at different points of the world to the same destination. Using the case of Y-Chun throughout the entire book has reflected this belief.

I teach counseling, supervise graduate students, practice, and conduct research. All these activities have become part of my life and reflect who I am as a scientist-practitioner. I strongly believe in multiculturalism and consider multicultural counseling as an essential component of counseling theories. Applying different counseling theories to a single case with a multicultural nature in this book has manifested what I believe about counseling theories and my professional identity as a multicultural counselor.

REFERENCES

Arbona, C. (2012). *Case conceptualization outline* [Ebook]. Houston, TX: Department of Educational Psychology, University of Houston. Retrieved from http://ebookbrowse.com/outline-case-conceptualization-6-2012-pdf-d361496185

Caspar, F., Berger, T., & Hautle, I. (2004). The right view of your patient: A computer assisted, individualized module for psychotherapy training. *Journal of Clinical Psychology, 41*(2), 125–135.

Eells, T. D. (Ed.). (1997). *Handbook of psychotherapy case formulation*. New York: Guildford Press.

Horowitz, M. J., & Eells, T. D. (1997). Configurational analysis: States of mind, person schemas, and the control of ideas and affect. In M. J. Horowitz & T. D. Eells (Eds.), *Handbook of psychotherapy case formulation* (pp. 166–191). New York: Guilford Press.

James, W. (1981). *The principles of psychology.* Cambridge, MA: Harvard University. (Original work published in 1890)

Jongsma, A. E., Peterson, L. M., & McInnis, W. P. (2006). *The adolescent psychotherapy treatment planner* (4th ed.). Hoboken, NJ: John Wiley.

Kendjelic, E. M., & Eells, T. D. (2007). Generic psychotherapy case formulation training improves formulation quality. *Psychotherapy: Theory, Research, Practice, Training, 44*(1), 66–77.

Levenson, H., & Strupp, H. H. (1997). Cyclical maladaptive patterns: Case formulation in time-limited dynamic psychotherapy. In T. D. Eells (Ed.), *Handbook of psychotherapy case formulation* (pp. 164–197). New York: Guilford Press.

Neukrug, E., & Schwitzer, A. (2006). Skills and tools for today's professional counselors and psychotherapists: From natural helping to professional counseling. Belmont, CA: Brooks/Cole.

Parsons, R. D., & Zhang, N. (2013). *Becoming a skilled counselor.* Thousand Oaks, CA: Sage.

Seligman, L., & Reichenberg, L. W. (2012). Selecting effective treatments: A comprehensive, systematic guide to treating mental disorders (4th ed.). Hoboken, NJ: John Wiley.

Sue, D. W., & Sue, D. (2003). *Counseling the culturally diverse: Theory and practice* (4th ed.). New York: John Wiley.

SECTION II

Theories and Their Applications

Freud and Psychoanalytic Theory

Faith Deveaux

I have spread my dreams under your feet; tread softly because you tread on my dreams.

—William Butler Yeats (1865–1939), Irish poet

If you think dreams have meaning, then you are on your way to appreciating just one of the contributions of Sigmund Freud and the theory of psychoanalysis.

What does it mean to think like a psychoanalyst? Who was Sigmund Freud? Is it important that you know who he was, and if so, why? Are Freud and psychoanalytic ideas relevant to you today? In this chapter, you will read about the person considered the primary figure in bringing about the concepts and practices on which psychoanalysis and psychoanalytic psychotherapy were built. In counseling, we are challenged to be reflective practitioners. In many ways, we can look at Freud's contributions and the significance of psychoanalytic theory as the beginning of reflective practice and can view Freud himself as a reflective practitioner. As you read about the other theories in this book, you will appreciate that Freud started a movement of people who cared deeply about how to intervene to help others resolve their problems and lead satisfying and productive lives. Many of the theories to follow will have either begun with psychoanalytic roots and branched off in new and different directions or will be positions theorists have taken in opposition to this approach. The beginnings as well as the development of psychoanalytic thinking— from Freud to today—are relevant to both theory and practice in the helping professions.

Freud was constantly creating, analyzing, developing, revising, collaborating, experimenting, and thinking about his work. He wrote a tremendous amount, and in this one chapter you will be introduced to only some of the important basics of psychoanalytic theory. Think about what you are reading. Make connections to your everyday life and the people around you. Appreciate that you can build on what you read here, for you will reflect on yourself and on those with whom you work. As you gain experience, knowledge, awareness, and skills as a counselor, at least some part of you will likely relate to the theoretical foundations of psychoanalytic thinking. Your reflective practice will be better informed because of this.

After reading this chapter, you will be able to do the following:

1. Describe the basic assumptions and characteristics of psychoanalytic theory

2. Define the ego, the id, and the superego, and explain their roles in the structure of personality from a psychoanalytic perspective

3. Identify what techniques are used to promote adaptive change from a psychoanalytic perspective

4. Describe how psychoanalytic theory guides practice

5. Identify steps in a three- to six-session consultation with the intention of making a recommendation to the client for follow-up treatment

INTRODUCTION

On many basic issues regarding the theories and interventions in counseling and psychotherapy, there is little professional agreement (Nye, 1996). Counseling is a vibrant profession because people are interested in matters that concern the personal, social, academic, and career/college issues that impact an individual's happiness and successes in life. The public wants to know that there are professionals committed and trained to assist people with their problems effectively. There is not just one approach or theory available to you, because human beings are complex, and all the research studying human emotion, growth, and development over time is also complex.

In this book, you will read about different theoretical orientations and perspectives. I advise you to appreciate all of them. You will have favorites, and you will discover that one or another theory "speaks to you." How exciting that will be. It may be a client, a course, or a particular supervisor's approach. As you develop perspectives based on where and with whom you are working, your theoretical knowledge will guide you. Parsons (2009) rightly called counselors' attention to the idea that our work with clients will proceed more successfully and efficiently if we know what to look for, are aware of what we observe, and understand what we hear and see when we encounter a client. Familiarity with the psychoanalytic perspective can help.

Historical Background: A Profile of Sigmund Freud

The name most linked with the theory of psychoanalysis is Sigmund Freud. He has been called the father of psychoanalysis and "talk" therapy. He was born to a White, Jewish family on May 6, 1856. Freud and his family lived in Vienna, Austria, from the time he was 4 years old. As he grew up, Freud developed an interest in medicine and became a medical student and researcher in neurobiology, neuroanatomy, and neurophysiology. Freud also studied philosophy, natural science, hypnosis, literature, archeology, history, psychopharmacology, genetics, and chemistry (Dufresne, 2007). Because he was born into a Jewish family and did not convert to Christianity (although he considered himself an atheist), he was not permitted to assume the research position he desired at the university. When Freud was developing his theories, there were political, social, and ideological climate changes in Vienna. Today we know changes are occurring all over the world, and followers of Freud's psychoanalytic thinking are working to promote, develop, and adapt these theories, not only in America and Europe but also in South Africa, Latin America, and China.

Freud worked with troubled patients. His training as a doctor was instrumental in helping him see that his patients' symptoms were not caused by physical ailments. He wanted to help, but there were no guidebooks. Freud thought about his patients and how he could help them, and his ideas came from rigorous training, thoughtful work with colleagues, and close observation of patients, as well as reflections on himself. Freud was beginning to formulate his ideas and approaches at the beginning of the 20th century, and even during his lifetime his theories evolved, changed, and developed significantly.

Because he was not able to work in a university setting as he wanted, Freud treated people who suffered from nervous conditions in his own practice. He thought new theories and new methods were needed to help them. Between 1887 and 1897, the prepsychoanalytic period, Freud was committed to research and wanted to bridge the fields of neurophysiology, neurology, and psychology as he worked to improve the lives and functioning of his patients. By 1897, psychoanalysis was developing into a therapeutic approach, by which the patient's relationship with the therapist, labeled the "transference relationship," was analyzed to resolve the repetition of unresolved, repressed conflicts. Freud's theories also developed from his self-analysis, which he published in *The Interpretation of Dreams* (1900/1965).

In 1933, when Freud was already in his 70s, the Nazi party took control of Germany. In 1938, the Germans annexed Austria, and the Nazis murdered all Freud's sisters. During this time, at the age of 82, Freud moved to London and escaped the Nazis. A year later, in September 1939, Freud died in London. During his life, he published many books and articles about psychoanalysis, and his approach was adopted in Europe and also America. He had high aspirations, cared about making a positive difference in people's lives, and wanted to make a name for himself. He did, indeed, leave a legacy for counselors, psychologists, and generations of helping professionals.

Freud was a prodigious writer and thinker, and he is to be admired and respected for his desire to understand what influenced humans and how to alleviate their suffering. Scientists, researchers, scholars, teachers, and philosophers are still devoted to exploring and understanding the mind and the brain. Freud began his explorations in the 19th century, and what fascinated him fascinates us today. Thus, psychoanalysis continues to be of interest to scientists, practitioners, philosophers, and scholars in the 21st century.

Many leaders in the fields of psychology, counseling, and psychiatry have contributed to Freud's work and built on the basic principles of psychoanalysis. As you read the following chapters, you will learn that many theories and theorists had their beginnings in psychoanalytic theory. The following list introduces you to the names of some of the other leaders in the field whose work has a psychoanalytic foundation and who expanded on Freud's ideas. They cared deeply about their clients' mental health and well-being and studied the psychoanalytic writings of Freud as part of their training to address the needs of those with whom they worked. In most instances, this list is a sample of those who have branched off from Freud, developing on his ideas in their work with individuals and addressing the needs of children and families from a psychoanalytic perspective. In the reference list at the end of the chapter, you can explore samples of their writings and learn more about them.

- John Bowlby
- Erik Erikson
- Anna Freud
- Carl Jung
- Otto Kernberg
- Melanie Klein
- Heinz Kohut
- Margaret Mahler

Two people who have made contributions to the field of psychoanalytic family therapy are Nathan Ackerman and Ivan Boszormenyi-Nagy.

Areas of Development

What is the place of psychoanalysis in the 21st century? A great deal of research and writing is occurring in academic settings and among practitioners of those theories that have their roots in psychoanalytic thought—including Adlerian therapy and Gestalt approaches. There are still training institutes throughout the country where practitioners are taught the psychoanalytic approach to intervention and where trainees are required to participate in their own training analyses. These institutes are not part of degree-granting institutions, hospitals, or clinics but, rather, are independent and freestanding. In the past several decades, critics of Freud's approach have cited a lack of methodology to assess the merits of his theories (Dufresne, 2007).

Today, psychoanalysts, neuropsychologists, neurobiologists, and neuroscientists are collaborating to study the interaction of the brain and the mind, to better understand how symbolic meaning is created. In psychoanalytic thinking, the brain and the mind are on a continuum. Psychoanalysis can be explored in terms of its relation to philosophy and other modern avenues of thought, such as "feminism, critical theory, aesthetics, and the theory of culture" (Sharpe & Faulkner, 2008, p. 10). Questions now being raised by researchers and thinkers have to do with how much of human suffering is caused by psychological factors (i.e., what goes on in one's mind) or by physiological factors (i.e., what goes on in one's brain). Another area of investigation is the role genetics plays in human mental and emotional illness (Hyman, 2000; Wortis, 1954/1985).

While Freud developed his thinking with drive theory and a focus on sexual and aggressive instincts, psychoanalysis has been moving in a different direction (Greenberg & Mitchel, 1983). A more current perspective in psychoanalytic thinking, and one that can be more easily integrated with other theoretical models, is the relational perspective (Altman, 2013). Here, the focus is more on the importance of early relationships than on instinctual drives. Interpersonal relations, past and present, are considered central to understanding personal and social development. This differs from Freud's view that early childhood experiences and movement through stages are the keys to personality development and functioning. From this new psychoanalytic perspective, context is no longer excluded; so, as a practitioner, the psychoanalytically oriented counselor can use this model to learn about relational patterns and experiences within their cultural and sociopolitical contexts. These theorists view one's early relationships with caregivers as shaping later expectations for relationships. When there is dysfunction, the role of the treatment is to create a healing relationship between client and counselor so that, through treatment, the repetitive, negative, maladaptive relationship patterns the client continues to enact can be repaired. Then the client can move forward to experience more satisfying relationships and not be doomed to repeat the past.

Psychoanalytic principles are also being applied to groups, couples, and family counseling. Another field of interest is using a psychoanalytic approach to study group functioning, specifically group ideology and the political process (Kernberg, 2011).

Malan (1979) conceptualized two triangles regarding therapy: the person triangle, which includes the client, counselor/therapist, and parents or people in the client's past, and the conflict triangle, which includes the client's anxiety, defenses against anxiety, and hidden feelings not consciously acknowledged that need to be made conscious.

Current practitioners of the psychoanalytic approach focus not only on coming to terms with the past and how prior relationships and experiences have had an impact on one's feelings, thinking, and behavior; they are also interested in assessing current behaviors and concerns. Counselors working with a limited time frame focus on the clients' goals and their presenting issues, not on restructuring their personality by resolving all past, unconscious issues (Kottler, 2002). With the changes that have occurred over the past century, roles and expected behaviors are far less "determined," and we think of the personality as more adaptable.

OVERVIEW OF PSYCHOANALYSIS

With Freud's ideas, scientific thinking about the mind found its accelerant. What previously had been attributed to physical disease was now seen as having psychological meaning and implications. The person with the symptoms does not know what is wrong. These psychological factors are unconscious, outside of awareness (Breger, 2009). Thinking psychoanalytically, the counselor wants to address the underlying, root causes of clients' difficulties and not just the symptoms. Through the psychoanalytic process, people gain awareness of the unconscious, the hidden forces that are outside of awareness and impact their lives. Through talk therapy, clients can identify what may have a hold on them unconsciously, and by understanding these forces, clients can solve the underlying conflicts and gain mastery over the negative effects. By achieving new solutions, the person becomes healthier emotionally and psychologically. The relationship between the psychoanalytically trained counselor and the client is a collaborative one. With the help of treatment intervention, as problems are resolved, the client is no longer in the grasp of underlying conflicts. Improvement in behavior, relationships, and sense of self is the goal of the treatment.

View of Human Nature

Freud's view of human nature was *deterministic*. What this meant to Freud was that all behavior, including actions, thoughts, and emotions, had a cause and, therefore, could be explained (Nye, 1996). Freud placed much emphasis on the impact of what happens in a child's first 5 years of life, and he believed that one's personality, one's psychological makeup, is determined in a major way by early experiences. According to this theory, the child's individual personality is shaped in large part by what happens in the first years of life. From a modern relational psychoanalytic position, how the child is treated—whether basic needs are met, there is a caring and nurturing environment, there is adequate satisfaction, or there is too much distress or even trauma—during these early years is relevant in terms of the impact of relations on the child's developing sense of self. For Freud, the ways children advance through and negotiate what he called the psychosexual stages of development are related to later functioning and adjustment. What is most important about Freud's thinking is that the early years of one's life and the mastery of developmental tasks are significant and must be understood.

Freud developed his theories from his work with patients; meanwhile, he was a serious scholarly reader who shared ideas with learned colleagues. He considered the events taking place around him and in the world, as well as his own family and how his early life experiences shaped his personality. His self-analysis gave him his most important subject, and he developed many of his ideas based on his internal thoughts and feelings and analysis of his own dreams (Nye, 1996).

The early Freudian theorists were primarily concerned with biology and psychosexual development and their consequences. Freud's psychoanalytic theory addressed the importance of biological drives and that drives influence behavior. Given his profession and training as a physician and the time and place in which he lived, the clinical arena where he developed his ideas was relatively small. Within the context of family, life, and work, we know that the opportunities we take for granted in the United States were limited in Freud's time, as were health care, educational opportunity, career choice, and a multiplicity of other advantages afforded people now. For example, in Freud's field, gender roles and expectations were seriously determined by the European societal and familial norms of the time.

Two of Freud's colleagues, Carl Jung and Alfred Adler, did not agree with all his theoretical and therapeutic ideas, so they went on to develop their own schools (Corey, 2009).

Basic Characteristics and Assumptions of Psychoanalytic Theory

A basic assumption of psychoanalytic theory is that human beings have an unconscious mind—not an unconscious *brain* but an unconscious *mind*. What does that mean? Do you ever stop to wonder why some people repeat the same mistake in a relationship over and over again? Do you wonder why you are particularly sensitive to something someone says and why sometimes you get embarrassed? Have you ever had a slip of the tongue, commonly referred to as a "Freudian slip," when a word came out of your mouth even though you meant to say a different word? Followers of Freud would want to uncover what is in your unconscious mind to reveal the whys and wherefores of such occurrences, believing that these incidences reveal motivations and desires hiding from consciousness (Freud, 1901/1961c). Psychoanalysts believe that understanding a person's unconscious is a way to understand a person's personality.

Freud focused on the biological roots of behavior, and he thought these instinctual forces contained the energy driving a person's psyche. Specifically, he considered that sexual and aggressive drives are at the roots of how we act, think, and feel (Freud, 1905/1961b, 1905/1963) and need to be managed. Sexual energy—which Freud labeled *libido* and later came to be considered life instincts—gets built up and, according to his early theory, is experienced as anxiety if not discharged. Freud also incorporated the death drive into his conceptualizations, viewing this as the drive to discharge aggression. If a person is conflicted about sexual or aggressive drives, this leads to repression. In other words, when there is anxiety or conflict, those areas are moved out of consciousness and repressed. Those unresolved areas are then stored in the unconscious. They still need to be discharged, however, and this happens when the person develops symptoms or acts them out in a way that may be unproductive or maladaptive. These symptoms and behaviors serve the unconscious. Chancer and Watkins (2006) address the discharge of aggression across societies and examine why human beings behave in exclusionary ways. Even though the Freudian psychoanalytic approach is considered "deterministic," they actually appreciate the hopefulness embedded in the theory. Freud held the belief that people can redirect their most basic drives into constructive social activities (Freud, 1930/1961a). Through the process of psychoanalytic intervention and developing awareness of unconscious conflicts and motives, people can channel their aggressions and prejudices productively and will be less likely to act them out.

The way a child is reared in an environment, usually within the family, is assumed to be where the cultural and socialization processes interact with the child's development. Freud believed that one family member at a time should be in treatment. While he acknowledged that family members have great impact on individual functioning, he advocated against any form of family treatment. Currently, most psychoanalysts do not work with members of the same family, with some exceptions. Freud's assumption was that family members would contaminate the analytic process.

A related underlying assumption is that the dysfunctional patterns being lived out in present relationships stem from conflicts experienced in the past, usually with parental figures. These conflicts can be acted out in the present with the therapist. It is important that the therapist understands this, is able to remain neutral and objective, and can help the client work through the conflicts within the therapeutic relationship (Auld & Hyman, 1991).

CASE ILLUSTRATION 4.1

Counselor:	So you say that you have been late for work a lot and now are getting warned that you may lose your job. What do you think is going on?
Client:	Well, I've been asked to do a lot of extra work, and I get no thanks or appreciation.
Counselor:	And how do you feel about that?
Client:	Mad . . . and hurt.
Counselor:	Mad and hurt. What comes to mind when you think about being "mad and hurt"?
Client:	That's how I felt growing up, lots of demands, pressure, and no thanks or recognition. I used to sulk and try to avoid doing what was being asked of me.
Counselor:	So now that you are grown-up, what could be going on? *(Note that by referring to the client as grown-up, the counselor is engaging the client's ego, the self-reflective, conscious part of the person.)*
Client:	I'm acting the way I did as a child—only it's not working. I could lose my job. I can do more now. I can go talk to the supervisor about my responsibilities. I was doing really well until I started feeling unappreciated, and I like my work. Then I started messing up, coming in late. I don't need to do that anymore.

Note: By becoming aware of how former, repressed, and unconscious hurts are impacting current functioning, the client is able to exercise conscious decision making and connect his acting out to prior feelings and experiences.

The Structure of Personality: Id, Ego, and Superego

Freud saw that mental and emotional difficulties were complex, and he devoted his working life to finding ways to understand and explain what goes on in the human psyche. The structural theory he developed is a cornerstone of psychoanalytic thinking. Basically, Freud conceived of several levels, or structures, that develop along with someone's personality. As the personality develops over time, from birth to adulthood, and in interaction with family, friends, and the real world in which one lives, so do the structures operating in the personality. Freud called these structures of our personality the ego, the id, and the superego.

According to this theory, the ego mediates between the world of internal, unconscious, instinctual drives and the realities and impositions of the external world (Freud, 1915/1961b). The ego develops over time, modified by the influences of the real world in which the individual lives. In the modern vernacular, the ego can be considered "the self" (i.e., the self we are conscious of and perceive ourselves to be). As the child grows, the demands of reality intervene, and wishes for immediate gratification can be inhibited, prohibited, or threatened by, for example, loss of love and caring. These wants and needs are kept at a distance from conscious reality through a variety of what Freud called defense mechanisms and are removed to the unconscious part of the mind. Here they find a place to reside, and Freud called this place the id. The ego is the conscious part of the personality and takes on the psychological executive function. The ego develops as the infant grows and encounters the real world. After the baby is born, it does not take long for awareness to develop that all needs are not immediately satisfied. Ideally, the external environment is nurturing and responsive, and the ego—the differentiated self— begins to develop around 6 months of age. The individual can then begin to think about the environment and negotiate what behaviors lead to getting needs met and regaining that pleasurable feeling. Healthy ego development is key to successful functioning throughout life.

The id represents the repressed, unconscious wishes and drives that seek to be fulfilled and are frustrated and stopped by the reality principle (Freud, 1920/1970a). One can think of the id as the biological and unconscious part of one's personality. At birth, the infant is functioning on the id level (i.e., wanting to be fed when hungry, warmed when cold, dried when wet). When the id is operating, tension is not tolerated and feeling pleasure is the goal. The infant is not using reason; the goal is to get needs met. The id remains at the pleasure-seeking level throughout life, a level where neither reasoning nor thinking is taking place. One's id impulses cannot and will not be satisfied. In other words, people are not always going to get what they want when they want it. The ego, the conscious part of the personality, is able to mediate successfully between those id impulses and the real world (Freud, 1920/1970b).

EXERCISE 4.1

Observe two infants. Can you tell when they want something? What are the signs? Write them down. Are they physical, such as smiling, crying, yelling, reaching, or looking intently? Can you see that the infants are driven by their biological needs—say, for food, warmth, physical contact, or sleep? How good are you at deciphering what the infants want? Can you tell when they are satisfied and getting what they want?

In this structural schema, there is a third agent: the superego. The superego develops as the child matures and learns about societal, cultural, familial, and social norms. This is the part of one's personality that has learned what is considered socially appropriate and what is judged good or not good. Superego development is learned through one's family and the cultural transmission of values across generations, in school, and through religious education (Deveaux, 1995). Frequently, the superego is considered as aligned with what one calls the conscience. It is conceived as that part of a person that develops as the rules and responsibilities are transmitted, first by parents and family, then by the greater society. As these expectations are learned and internalized, the part of the psyche called the superego develops. The superego can be relatively benign and kind or harsh and repudiating. As a respectful guide on the path of life, the superego has a valuable role—teaching lessons helpful to the individual's success, functioning, and well-being, within the family as well as outside the home. On the other hand, an overly harsh, depreciating superego does no one any favors. When caregivers or influential others in a person's world are overly critical, hostile, or frightening, an overfunctioning, maladaptive superego develops and is internalized. The ego is then in danger of being overtaken, and the battle becomes one between the id and the superego (Freud, 1930/1961a).

Mental health relies on an ego that is an excellent mediator between the superego—representing external realities and their requirements—and the id—representing unconscious wishes and instinctual drives. The ego represents a safe, secure self equipped to balance the internal demands and wants on one hand and the real world and all it presents on the other.

Navigating this balance between the impulsive desires of the id and the socialized mores of the superego is not an easy task. Quite often, the ego experiences the id's desires as strong and may anticipate their unfiltered or unmediated and inappropriate expression. The tension that results from this anticipation has been termed *neurotic anxiety*. Consider a situation in which a person has been working diligently at a difficult task. Each time his boss passes by, rather than encouraging the man, the boss becomes hypercritical and demeaning of the amount of time the task is taking. This continues throughout the day, to the point where the worker is about to explode with anger. He feels as though he is simply going to attack his boss the next time his boss says something. The man knows this would not be wise and that he could be fired. Further, he recognizes that this is not the socially appropriate thing to do; so he begins to feel increased tension or anxiety, fearing that he may lose control. The aggressive urge is generated from the id, yet it is the ego that, in processing realities, realizes the danger that could result. The fear of loss of control in response to the impulsive id's urge to be aggressive is what would be considered neurotic anxiety. The task for the ego is to somehow dissipate the aggressive energy generated by the id in a way that would be more acceptable in the work world.

A similar dilemma can be experienced by the ego when energy is discharged in the form of a socially inappropriate behavior and results in an internalized punishment by the superego—guilt. Consider the student in class experiencing hunger. Realizing that class has yet another hour to go and she did not pack a snack, this student sneaks the crackers out of another student's backpack and enjoys the repast. For the remainder of the day, she feels uncomfortable, worrying about what she did and knowing she should apologize, but concerned about the consequences if she does. The internal tension she is feeling is the result of her superego asserting social mores and enforcing them via increased tension and the experience of guilt. Again, the ego will attempt to discharge this moral anxiety.

In both situations, the ego will attempt to cope with the imbalance of energy—the neurotic or moral anxiety—by employing an "ego defense" (see Table 4.1).

Table 4.1 A Sample of Ego Defenses

Assume that the situation is as follows: A young boy (the source) feels intense hatred (emotion) toward his father (the object) and is struggling with his desire to aggress against his father. The boy can use the following ego defenses as a way of discharging some energy in a less dangerous or socially inappropriate way.

Defense	Description	Illustration
Denial	An outright refusal to admit or recognize that something has occurred or is currently occurring	When confronted that he is being nasty (verbally) to his father, he simply denies that this is true. The source, object, and feeling all stay the same, but the person denies that reality.
Displacement	Redirecting emotions to a substitute target	In this case, the object (dad) is replaced with a substitute; thus, the boy comes home and is verbally and physically aggressive toward his younger brother.
Intellectualization	Taking an objective viewpoint	
Projection	Involves taking our own unacceptable qualities or feelings and ascribing them to other people	The boy is quite verbal about how dad hates him and wants to hurt him (object and source switch).
Rationalization	Creating false but credible justifications	In this case, the source, object, and feeling stay the same, but the child now attempts to offer a justifiable explanation—"He (dad) is always being mean to me."
Reaction formation	Overacting in the opposite way to the fear	Now the source and the object stay the same, but the intense emotion is replaced by its opposite. In this case, the boy exaggerates verbally and behaviorally how much love he has for his dad, to the point of "loving him to death!"
Regression	When confronted by stressful events, people sometimes abandon coping strategies and revert to patterns of behavior used earlier in development	The boy may return to a less mature way of responding and thus begin to aggress by having difficulty controlling his bowels. This could be a sign of regressing to an early (anal) stage of psychosexual development.
Repression	Pushing uncomfortable thoughts into the subconscious	In an attempt to rid himself of these negative feelings and aggressive desires, he may attempt to push all negative, hostile thoughts of his dad into his unconscious. While finding some relief, tension and energy remain and will need to be discharged. They may surface in other forms, such as difficulty saying "no" or asserting himself.
Sublimation	Redirecting "wrong" urges into socially acceptable actions	Sublimation would have the boy discharge his hostility in ways that would be socially valued and approved, such as being an aggressive football player or a boxer, or joining the special forces or police force.

These defenses are employed in an attempt to protect the ego from the threatening impulses of the id or the sanctions of the superego, and they share two things in common. They often appear unconsciously, and they tend to distort, transform, or otherwise falsify reality. For example, in the case of our angry worker, he may resolve the issue and discharge the energy by way of displacement. In this case, we can see that while the original target for his anger is his boss, he may redirect or displace his anger on a less threatening object, such as the noisy pencil sharpener. In this case, he is able to discharge the energy—the tension—erupting from the aggressive impulse generated by the id and do it in a way that avoids "real" danger, such as being fired.

Similarly, in the case of moral anxiety, the tension from the guilt the superego generates following the "theft" of the crackers could be discharged by way of a defense such as rationalization. In this case, our hungry student will simply develop a logical, acceptable explanation for her actions. She may convince herself that Marcia (the "victim") would have freely given her crackers and that it was better not to bother her in class by asking and instead simply take them—"After all, we always share stuff and take stuff from each other's backpacks. I'll replace them tomorrow!"

Ego defenses are useful and effective ways of dealing with the internal strife experienced while attempting to meet instinctual needs in ways that are efficient and socially acceptable. Similarly, a person who is immersed in continual rationalizations—unable to accept his or her mistakes, violations of norms, or even engagement in criminal activity—will have little chance of developing appropriate and adaptable prosocial behaviors. Defense mechanisms have useful features, however, and the psychoanalytic counselor is cautioned not to work to remove a defense without replacing it with a more realistic, ego-compatible resolution.

Everyone is thrown off balance at times. How a person handles an upset determines adaptability and the strength of his or her ego. When people seek help—for example, for a relationship disruption, change in employment status, or a loss—the psychoanalytically trained counselor's work involves strengthening the ego so these setbacks and whatever they may trigger in the unconscious are understood and worked through, ultimately strengthening the ego further.

Use With Diverse Populations and Children

An important aspect of competent multicultural counseling is being a learner. Worth noting is that while psychoanalysis for more than a century has been considered a treatment intervention for those with money enough to pay for sessions, Freud himself encouraged that psychoanalytic therapy be made available to people through free clinics all over Europe, wherever there were psychoanalytic societies (Altman, 2010; Danto, 2005). Altman suggests that those who are psychoanalytically trained today are capable of adapting a classically oriented stance with creative approaches that would accommodate settings not considered traditionally psychoanalytic. He makes the point that "community-based work requires an integration of psychoanalytic and systemic perspectives—an integration of the intra-psychic, the interpersonal, and larger systems, from families to communities and societies" (p. xxiv). Everyone needs to be aware that to be a competent counselor, one must always consider the larger cultural context—not only that of the client but also the counselor and setting.

The Western cultural roots of individualism have certainly had an impact on psychological and psychoanalytic theory. Roland (1996b), who studies Asian and North American cultures in this context, makes the point that our cultural heritage is a part of us, like an inherited mantel we wear (Deveaux, 2002). He suggests that one can understand one's own psychology with its cultural history and framework only when done so comparatively. He says, based on his own experiences with Americans and Japanese, that values and patterns—both cultural and social—frequently seem to diverge completely. Values and cultural norms speak to who a person is. For someone entering into a treatment situation, these become important components for the professional counselor to be aware of and address. "Culture and socio-historical change [have been] with rare exceptions the missing dimensions in psychoanalysis" (Roland, 1996b, p. xii). When you appreciate that the family is a central, basic unit of society, it follows that psychoanalysis must be involved with culture, because, from a theoretical perspective, the impact of family can be a key to understanding personality development. More attention, however, has been paid to how psychoanalysis can lead to understanding various areas of culture, rather than to how the theory and practice in various cultures are influenced by psychoanalysis (Roland, 1996b).

Now that psychoanalytic training institutes, actual and virtual, are emerging globally (Fonda, 2011; Yang, 2011), and since the United States and other countries are home to peoples from all over the world, culture assumes a central perspective in psychoanalytic thinking. As a discipline, psychoanalysis belongs to no one state, country, or institution (Yang, 2011). Training institutions have been established in major cities in Europe, Asia, North America, and South America. New ways of training have been developed in the recent past and are still emerging today. The Institute of Latin American Psychoanalysis was created in 2006. Garcia (2011) recognized that while there is an identifiable Latin America, it includes different social, cultural, and geographical realities, and is by no means homogeneous. Therefore, there were challenges to be faced to provide appropriate training so clinicians could receive what they needed, meet the standards of the profession, and be qualified to deliver services to people across many different regions. Also in Eastern Europe, obstacles to providing training to psychoanalysts had to be overcome (Fonda, 2011). The programs in these countries developed after the fall of the Iron Curtain in post-communist Europe.

The virtual campus has become a recent solution in Latin America, Eastern Europe, and also China, where the first Sino-German Continuous Training Program for Psychotherapists began in 1997 (Yang, 2011). For a psychoanalyst practicing in China and trained in psychoanalysis by Westerners, accommodation based on an understanding of the significance of culture, cultural practices, and values is being addressed. For example, psychoanalysis has traditionally been an individualized approach. In China, the family is central, considered the basic unit of society; the child has an obligation to the family. This differs from Western society, where the individual and the concepts of independence and autonomy are highly valued (Yang, 2011). Roland (1996a), in his psychoanalytic work, scholarly analyses, and observations, notes that there are hierarchical, reciprocal relationships in Chinese society, where the young respect and obey their elders and those who are senior are responsible for caring, advising, and guiding the young. Also, there exists a tension between being independent and dependent, and the personal and professional identity are evaluated and recognized in the family. "The construction and maintenance of one's self-esteem and self-confidence are greatly influenced by expectations and evaluations of parents, family members and other authority figures" (p. 738).

In South Africa, psychoanalytic practitioners recognize the complex relationships between events in the external, societal world and their impact on the development of the individual psyche. There is appreciation and acknowledgement that societal trauma shapes the development of individuals across generations (Walker, 2006), and the scope of treatment extends beyond the individual and the family.

There is specialized training for people who want to work with children from a psychoanalytic perspective. Anna Freud, Sigmund Freud's daughter, was interested in working with children and adolescents. She built on her father's work and began looking at the psychosexual stages of children from a developmental viewpoint. Those interested in working with children from a psychoanalytic orientation could refer to the work of Anna Freud (1936) and Margaret Mahler (1968), provided in the Additional Resources section at the end of this chapter.

EXERCISE 4.2

Ask someone you know if he or she would be willing to talk with you about his or her family of origin. What does this person know about how his or her parents and grandparents were raised? Where were they living geographically? What languages did they speak? What was the political and social climate where they grew up? How did their cultures influence their values and attitudes? Have there been any changes in values and attitudes across generations or between families?

Now think about your own family. How many different cultural aspects can you identify in your family of origin? Can you think of any expectations your family had for you that have cultural origins? What about expectations regarding gender roles, education, marriage and family, work, social class? Does anyone in your family have conflicted feelings about these expectations? How are the conflicts understood and resolved?

Note: Every family has diversity and cultural factors, both within and across generations. This exercise can help you appreciate the importance of exploring these factors with your clients.

Research, Intervention, and Supportive Evidence

Advocates of the psychoanalytic approach do disclose the limitations of the research done to demonstrate effectiveness. Like other therapeutic interventions, many of the findings reported are based on clinical case examples. While psychoanalysis has no doubt contributed to 20th century thought, practice, and culture, its scientific status is being challenged (Kernberg, 2011). Psychopharmacology has become a dominating force in the modern mental health field and is considered potentially less costly. Short-term, neurobiological and cognitive-behavioral perspectives have absorbed some of the psychoanalytic contributions to understanding psychopathology. Within this context, some advocate for the need for more research in the field of psychoanalysis, either through the development of research arms of training institutes or in university settings. Currently, a promising field of exploration and research is looking at the connections in the brain that result from psychological—specifically, psychoanalytic—treatment intervention (Kandel, 1999; Lehtonen, 2010). The boundaries between the biological sciences and psychoanalysis can be explored; so even within a biological or genetic frame of reference, interpersonal and affective factors that impact personality can be acknowledged and considered (Lehtonen, 2010).

Limitations

The contributions of psychoanalysis, psychoanalytic counseling, and psychotherapy are evident today. In a 21st century economic environment, however, there are many competing orientations and questions about the relevance of the 19th century assumptions on which psychoanalysis was built (Sulloway, 1979). In Freud's time, the climate in Vienna was less than progressive, and psychoanalysis was about being resigned to the impact of early life experiences and resolving unconscious conflicts. Today, there is a more optimistic approach about wellness, the value of psychopharmacological intervention, and a multitude of treatments that can include individual, group, couples, and family therapy, as well as yoga, mindfulness, hypnosis, and other interventions.

What insurance will cover is another consideration. In the past, psychoanalysis was reserved for those with the financial resources to engage in a long-term treatment relationship, often involving several sessions a week. Such an approach today would still be reserved for those with financial resources, since insurance companies favor shorter-term interventions, such as solution-focused, cognitive-behavioral, or psychopharmacological approaches.

A limitation in psychoanalysis has been its testability and the methodology to validate the practice. More specifically, if the theories are testable, practitioners have not been taught to test them (Sulloway, 2007). This criticism is being heard, and current research is focusing on creating clinical profiles based on observations (Sheftel, 2011). Another limitation is that short-term interventions are prized in some settings. For example, school counselors are critical players in working with students to address the emotional obstacles that interfere with their attaining mastery in school (Parsons, 2007). Given the high caseloads and limited time for individual counseling, a psychoanalytic relationship would not be recommended in the school setting. That said, however, a psychoanalytic perspective can certainly be useful in approaching an understanding of the roots of the problem, assessing whether a short-term intervention will actually be successful, and determining if a referral to a practitioner outside of the school for longer-term follow-up and treatment is warranted.

Professional Identity

Professional identity is a concept receiving much attention in both practice and accrediting organizations. Often, we define our professional selves by the work we do; however, aligning our work with a theoretical orientation broadens our identity. What does it mean to identify with a psychoanalytic orientation? To be able to call yourself a psychoanalyst, you would need to continue your training at an institute, complete a rigorous training program of usually 3 to 4 years, participate in your own training analysis, see clients and be supervised by a practicing certified psychoanalyst, and ultimately receive certification yourself. If you wish to pursue this path, there are training institutes across the United States and Europe.

If you are planning to be certified as a mental health or school counselor, social worker, or psychologist, you do not need additional certification as a psychoanalyst; however, you should continue your studies as part of your professional development and can incorporate psychoanalytic thinking into your work.

In your work as a counselor, you have a responsibility to reflect on and address your own issues. You need to understand that you may have unconscious motivations or countertransference areas needing attention. Counselors in training frequently inquire about whether participating in a counseling relationship is a good idea, and it is commonly recommended if not required (Corey, 2009). If you have an interest in psychoanalytic theory, then participating in a therapeutic relationship with a psychoanalytically oriented practitioner is an excellent idea, and training institutes frequently offer low-cost treatment. Many training institutes are located in major cities, including New York, Boston, Chicago, and Los Angeles.

CASE ILLUSTRATION 4.2

Client (age 22): I am very upset. I just learned my parents are getting a divorce. I don't even want to go to school anymore. I don't know whether to scream or cry. I think it may be my fault. I just don't know what to do. Tell me what to do. You have to tell me what to do. What's going on with me? What if it's my fault? Do you think it's my fault?

Counselor: I can hear that you are upset. We are going to set up some times to meet so you can sort out your feelings and get a better handle on what's going on. Is that okay with you?

Client: Yes, I'll meet with you. Can you tell me what to do? I have so many thoughts and feelings right now. I know we'll all be okay, but I'm just so confused.

Counselor: I'm glad we can meet together. This will give you a chance and a good place to express yourself and understand your own thoughts and feelings.

Note: This counselor's parents also divorced when she was 22. She had decided to participate in her own psychoanalytically oriented treatment to work through her feelings at the time. She is aware that this client is the same age as she was when her own parents divorced. This could potentially lead to unconscious countertransference feelings because she could project her own experiences and feelings onto the client and overly identify with her. She recognizes consciously, however, that this client is having her own unique experiences and that her role is to be an empathic listener and let the client's story unfold. Rather than give advice, the counselor can allow the client to do the work with her in the context of the treatment to resolve issues as they arise.

THERAPEUTIC PROCESS AND APPLICATION

Psychoanalytic Techniques

Freud's interest was in the human personality. He also developed an avid interest in anthropology—the study of human beings, past and present. According to the American Anthropological Association (2012), to understand complex cultures, anthropologists rely on social and biological sciences as well as the humanities and physical sciences. Their goal is to solve human problems by applying knowledge. Anthropology is a good metaphor for what Freud believed about exploring the depths of the human mind and, in particular, what is buried in the unconscious. Freud saw society as inhibiting a person's impulses and drives and believed that a process of discovery was needed. Freud's psychoanalytic treatment approach was a way of exploring with an individual his or her unconscious processes to reduce what Freud referred to as "neurotic" anxiety and suffering. His perspective was that the real work for client and analyst is in patiently uncovering hidden truths and meanings that are out of consciousness, in the same way an archeologist uncovers hidden civilizations and artifacts that need to be pieced together to make sense and advance understanding and knowledge (Altman, 2013). Since the layer of the mind that is in awareness is the conscious mind, Freud believed that once what is unconscious is made conscious, people will be free—no longer ruled by the unconscious over which they have no mindful control or understanding.

All people have to understand and cope with their emotions. According to psychoanalytic theory, dreams reside in the unconscious, and dream interpretation and free association are techniques used to understand what is going on in a person's psyche. To remain asleep, what is expressed in dreams needs to remain disguised or hidden. We can consider that parts of the dream are representations of unresolved conflicts or desires the client is dealing with. In the dream, the person is able to grapple with hidden impulses or feelings. Through analyzing the dream in a trusting treatment relationship, the person is able to untangle the meaning of the dream and give expression to what had, up to that point, been repressed.

Dreams are the way the unconscious mind deals with things the conscious mind cannot. In a dream, the content is disguised. By analyzing the dream, one's thoughts and motivations can be examined. By listening to one's associations to a dream, connections can be made to understand the motivation behind it. Past and current emotional conflicts represented in the dream can be explored. Since this is done with the client in a conscious state, these conflicts can be understood through analysis.

Dreams can be wish fulfilling and, because they are disguised, allow us to continue sleeping. There are several elements to dream interpretation. One image in a dream may represent several ideas, and meanings are symbolically represented through dream images. Dreams do not have to make sense. That is part of the disguise.

There are two ways to think about the content of dreams: The first is called the manifest content. This is the dream the way the dreamer recalls it. The other is called the latent content. This is what is revealed through free association to the dream or any part of it and, ultimately, through dream analysis.

EXERCISE 4.3

Try your own dream analysis. When you wake up from a dream, take a few minutes to remember it. Keep in mind that dreams do not have to make sense. Write down what you remember, and also identify any feelings you experienced in the dream. You now have the manifest content of the dream. Relax and let your mind wander—what is called free association—to any part of the dream, any particular image, or any feeling. Does anything come to mind? Sometimes, one part of a dream can symbolize several different things and will lead you to identify what is referred to as the dream's latent content.

Another aspect of psychoanalytic treatment is based on the notion of the client having what is referred to as a transference relationship with the trained counselor. This means that the client reenacts within the therapy his or her feelings about other people in his or her life. As the client works through these relationship conflicts and issues from the past with the psychoanalytically trained professional, they are resolved. The counselor remains neutral and maintains limited self-disclosure so clients are free to develop an understanding of the causes of their reactions and behaviors and to resolve distressing issues.

Countertransference is when the counselor projects feelings from his or her own experiences onto the client. The counselor transfers thoughts, feelings, sensations, and reactions toward the client. It is the counselors' responsibility to be aware of countertransference feelings so they do not act on them inappropriately and can remain nonjudgmental. Counselors' awareness of their personal feelings and thoughts can contribute to their empathy; however, such thoughts and feelings should not intrude on the focus on the client.

Ethical Considerations

In contemplating ethics, one usually takes into account what is right or wrong. In counseling, we reflect on the treatment goals guided by theory. In the psychoanalytic approach, the counselor is trained to attend to and help the client feel and function better. Following this model traditionally means that what matters most to the client is what matters to the counselor. In other words, secondary to the client's perceptions are those of others in the client's life. The focus is on the client's thoughts, actions, feelings, and motivations. The counselor is to remain neutral, helping the client develop awareness of his or her unconscious conflicts. The counselor's role is guided by the ability to maintain focus on improving the client's life, even though a benefit of the intervention may, of course, be improvement in the client's relationships as the treatment progresses (La Roche, 2013).

Given the importance of neutrality on the counselor's part, attention to countertransference feelings is the professional and ethical responsibility of the counselor. While the counselor allows the client to transfer subjective feelings and thoughts by remaining neutral, this is done to serve the goal of self-discovery and self-awareness on the client's part (Freud, 1933). Countertransference feelings—those feelings the counselor may feel in response to the client—cannot be acted on and must be resolved in the counselor's own supervision so they do not influence or leak into the treatment relationship.

COUNSELOR–CLIENT RELATIONSHIP

The client must be willing and able to engage in a relationship with the psychoanalytically trained counselor. Since working to achieve insight and understanding is considered important, sessions occur regularly; sessions can continue for a lengthy period of time; and, while the focus is always on the client, the direction of the sessions can shift depending on what the client brings to the meeting. Clients are free to talk about whatever they want as they participate in their treatment, and they do not have to focus on only one goal. In working within a psychoanalytic framework, the client is expected to talk freely and be interested in cognitively reflecting on the past as well as the current situation. As appropriate, clients can report their dreams and free associate to uncover unconscious conflicts that may be revealed in dreams. Since the psychoanalytic approach aims to work through long-standing personality issues and help the client gain insight, a quick solution is not to be expected.

THEORY-GUIDED CASE CONCEPTUALIZATION

Therapeutic Goals

The therapeutic goals of psychoanalysis include relief from painful anxiety and other symptomatic behavior. From a theoretical point of view, the goal is for the client to achieve a cognitive awareness of why he or she continues to repeat maladaptive behavior patterns, essentially uncovering whatever unconsciously needs to be brought into consciousness so the client will be free to make healthier and more satisfying choices. A major goal in analysis is to resolve the transference relationship with the analyst and develop a competent sense of self, able to deal with the realities of life.

Intervention and the Change Process

The change process from a psychoanalytic perspective involves making what is unconscious conscious and strengthening the individual's ego functioning. The underlying assumption is that people have developed, over time, defense mechanisms and patterns of behavior to ward off unconscious conflicts. While these have become coping strategies, they are maladaptive, which means they do not promote the client's health and well-being. Clients need help to understand what causes them to repeat behaviors and thoughts that do not work, those that do not get them what they want or need to continue to grow and develop and to experience successful social and emotional relationships.

Psychoanalytic interventions involve ongoing, consistent therapy sessions with an individual client and trained counselor. This is frequently called "talk" therapy because the client talks freely to the counselor, at times freely associating what comes to mind and saying it aloud. Together, the client and counselor explore the unconscious aspects and underlying causes of the client's difficulties. Dream interpretation is another intervention used by psychoanalysts. If a client remembers a dream, he or she retells it and then, through associating with any part of the dream, begins to explore what the unconscious mind may be revealing through it. Freud considered dreams the royal road to the unconscious (Freud, 1900/1965). He analyzed his own dreams, and this self-analysis provided much of what fed his ideas about the relationship between the unconscious mind and the structure of the id, ego, and superego.

Assessment

What influences personality? Is it static or fluid? Can we change, or are we doomed to repeat patterns of behavior? What is the counselor's stance? Do you look for causes of behavior and, if so, what causes? Your theoretical orientation and professional training will influence various aspects of assessment. In today's world, brain chemistry is a major factor in assessment, and the value of a psychotropic medication may well be part of assessment. From a biochemical perspective, a doctor—preferably a psychiatrist or psychiatric nurse practitioner trained in psychopharmacology—may prescribe medication along with counseling. A psychotherapeutic exploration and assessment of underlying causes is considered a lengthy and costly approach, and insurance companies frequently choose to support the prescription of drugs over a longer-term, ongoing psychoanalytic relationship. The psychoanalytically oriented counselor can, however, conduct a multi-session consultation to determine the best recommendation for follow-up treatment. Part of a consultative assessment for psychoanalytically oriented treatment would include seeing if the client is willing to participate in treatment and is motivated and has the ability to engage in a therapeutic relationship. The client would need to appreciate the expertise of the counselor and want to change, accepting that it could be a lengthy process of talking and examining the past as well as the present. Is the client able and willing to talk about his or her thoughts, beliefs, motivations, emotional states, and behaviors? In addition to talking, you will want to assess if the client is able to be self-reflective and has adequate resources to support and benefit from ongoing counseling.

The psychoanalytically oriented assessment process is based on the counselor's interviewing the client. For a consultation, you want to meet with the prospective client for two to six sessions before committing to or referring the client for long-term therapy. This gives the counselor the opportunity to assess the client's current level of functioning, living situation and resources, health, employment, and physical as well as substance-abuse issues that may need to be addressed prior to undertaking long-term therapy. The point of a multi-session consultative interview process is to be able to work with the client in determining what methods of intervention will be most beneficial.

Y-CHUN: THROUGH THE LENS OF A PSYCHOANALYTIC COUNSELOR

Focus and Intentionality: A Consultation Model

You are now going to put yourself in the role of a professional counselor. Your client is Y-Chun. Now consider how to think psychoanalytically as you meet her. You need to think about what you are going to observe, what to listen for, what questions to ask, and how to ask them. How much is it appropriate for you to self-disclose? Your theory accompanies you, guides you, in your meetings with the client. As a psychoanalytically oriented counselor, you will observe the client's appearance; demeanor; comfort level in talking; motivation to change repetitive, maladaptive behavior; and ability to self-reflect, form a therapeutic and productive consultation relationship, and benefit from counseling.

Several key factors are involved in conducting a counseling consultation. First, you need to engage and inform the client of your ethical and professional responsibilities. You also must have the client sign any necessary release forms so you can speak with any other professionals involved and with whom you should be consulting about the welfare of the client and services to be provided. Next, you need to undertake an assessment. This involves gathering history and hearing what the client identifies as her current issues and goals. Are the problems current, or is there a history of repeated, maladaptive patterns? You will also be assessing whether the client is interested in and would benefit from long-term, psychoanalytically oriented treatment. Finally, you discuss your recommendation with the client and make an appropriate recommendation for follow-up treatment.

Y-Chun has come to you on referral from her physician. She is a 35-year-old female who complained of physical symptoms, including fitful sleep and headaches. The physician considered the presence of several stressors in her life and thought she could benefit from counseling. Psychological factors may be involved and her feelings and stresses somatized (i.e., expressed and experienced physically). Her current stressors are lack of income, living with her parents, having two children without the support of a partner, and career uncertainty. You have made an agreement with Y-Chun to meet for three to six consultation sessions to determine the next steps and make a follow-up recommendation that will benefit her.

The Initial Steps in the Consultation

According to the profession's ethical principles and standards of practice, the counselor can work within the scope of his or her training. Contracting for a consultation allows both the client and the counselor to undertake a process of determining the most appropriate intervention based on the client's needs, goals, and resources. In the first session of the consultation, the counselor explains the limits of confidentiality—that if the client presents a danger to herself or others, confidentiality will not apply and an intervention will be initiated. The counselor will ask the client to sign a release form so the counselor and referring physician can share information. At the conclusion of the first session, the counselor and Y-Chun will review their agreement to meet for three to six consultation sessions to determine the best course to address Y-Chun's goals and needs.

In the first two sessions, Y-Chun begins to review her history. She has shared that she considers herself biracial, White and Asian, and grew up lower working class. Her father immigrated to the United States from Poland and is a construction worker. He remarried her mother, who is Chinese American, after his wife died, and he has one son from his first marriage. Her mother is a custodian in a nursing home. Her husband also died prior to her marrying Y-Chun's father, and she has a son and daughter from her first marriage. Y-Chun is not close to her half siblings, and all three of them are married and live independently. Y-Chun is living at home with her parents, supposedly for financial reasons, while she works part-time and attends college as a nontraditional student. Y-Chun herself is a mother of two: a son, age 15, and a daughter, age 12, who has a physical disability.

As Y-Chun talks to the counselor, she discloses more of the emotional issues that are troubling her and have troubled her in the past. She has not been able to maintain a healthy relationship and has struggled with drugs, alcohol, and promiscuity.

In the next session, the counselor and client begin to explore Y-Chun's family of origin, her connections to her mother's and father's culture, the environment in which she was raised, and what she recalls. It is clear that Y-Chun is able to reflect on her own issues, is thoughtful, and appears motivated to change.

Y-Chun:	As we are talking, I think I can say that I used drugs and alcohol to cope when I was younger. I would get upset at not being sure who I wanted to be and who my parents expected me to be, and then I just tried to find solace in substances.
Counselor:	It sounds like you experienced conflicts growing up that related to your very self.
Y-Chun:	I did. With my mother being Chinese—and in the Chinese culture, what elders think is very important and is to be honored—and with my father coming to this country as an immigrant, he also has strong opinions about getting ahead and what that means. I felt that they relied on me to make their dreams come true, but I didn't know how to do that, and I didn't know if I even wanted to do that.
Counselor:	So you think your parents had ideas about who you should be?
Y-Chun:	I think so. Maybe I imagined some of it because I know that both their first spouses died, and that had to be hard on them. I don't know. Maybe I feel somehow responsible for them. I know that it is time for me to lead my own life though, and take care of my children myself and be independent.
Counselor:	What comes to mind when you think about "leading your own life"?
Y-Chun:	I want to be able to be in a good relationship. I haven't been able to do that. That is one of my goals.

Y-Chun has demonstrated that she is introspective and insightful. She suggests that from the time she was very young, she felt compelled to meet her parents' high expectations, and she is aware that she has had a history of unsuccessful relationships and wants to change that pattern. According to psychoanalytic theory, the two areas that indicate successful adult functioning are the ability to love and the ability to work, and these areas both present difficulties for Y-Chun. At this point in the consultation, the counselor may begin to form a working hypothesis. The client's goals include being able to enter into and sustain a loving relationship, develop psychological and financial independence from her parents, and stop repeating self-destructive patterns of behavior. The counselor and client can begin working to determine an appropriate follow-up for the client to meet her goals.

The Middle Steps in the Consultation

After the initial meetings with the client, the consulting counselor wants to assess if the client's interest in identifying her goals and working to resolve areas of conflict continues. The counselor will also assess if there are any reasons or circumstances in the client's life that would rule against a referral at this time. The counselor wants to inform the client of what to expect out of treatment and to make a recommendation.

Counselor: Y-Chun, you seem like a very thoughtful person, and you are motivated to change some of your patterns of behavior and thinking to have a more satisfying life. Is that right?

Y-Chun: Yes, definitely. I think this is a good time for me to examine what I have been doing up until now, and maybe look at why. I'm in a good place to do this because I am living with my parents, so I have some stability for my children and me. I am also going to school, so I am sort of in a thoughtful place anyway (laughs at this).

Counselor: Okay. What do you think about starting psychoanalytic psychotherapy? Psychoanalysis is a treatment where you can talk about your past and explore further what may be the reasons for some of your behaviors that aren't working for you.

Y-Chun: That sounds good. I am also sleeping a little better now. I think I may have dreams to talk about. That's part of psychoanalysis isn't it?

Counselor: Yes, it can be. I think you have had an introductory psychology course.

Y-Chun: I did have a course in psychology, and I liked it. I may want to do some type of counseling myself in the future, maybe help people who have suffered different kinds of abuse. So I think I need to find out what's going on with me first.

Counselor: Alright. Working with someone trained psychoanalytically will help you better understand yourself and have a stronger sense of who you are, who you want to be, and how you can get what you want in the real world. I'm going to identify a possible referral for you so that you can begin. We will meet next week for our final consultation visit.

The Last Step in the Consultation

The last of the consultation sessions is as important as the first. Since you will be referring the client for treatment elsewhere, it is important that the termination session be respectful and supportive. The client has worked hard and shared her history with you, along with her goals for the future. You have successfully assessed that she is a good candidate for psychoanalytically oriented treatment, and you have identified a qualified referral resource that will be affordable.

Y-Chun:	I am looking forward to beginning therapy. How often will I go, and how much will it cost?
Counselor:	These are excellent questions. How often you schedule sessions will be determined when you meet with your psychoanalytically trained counselor. I have a referral for you to a local training institute that will work with you on what you can afford. You will be able to meet with a professional counselor who is doing advanced training at the institute and who works under supervision. You can find a counselor with whom you feel comfortable and able to talk freely, since that will be an important part of your treatment. Would you like the referral now?
Y-Chun:	Yes. I feel I am ready to confront my past to move forward.

The counselor as consultant has provided a service to Y-Chun by meeting with her, being an attentive and careful listener, and assessing the value of a referral for a psychoanalytic intervention to help her develop ego functioning and participate in a therapeutic, maturational experience.

KEYSTONES

- Psychoanalysis is a method of treatment for mental and emotional disorders.
- Sigmund Freud developed this theory as a way of conceptualizing why people behave the way they do, and he conceived of psychoanalysis as a treatment modality as well as a theory to understand personality.
- The psychoanalytic approach involves using a client's conscious mind to explore unconscious parts of him or herself so conflicts, repressions, anxieties, and fears can be brought into conscious control and understanding.
- Psychoanalytic thinking is a theoretical orientation still used today.
- Psychoanalytic theory is appreciated as well as criticized.
- Psychoanalytic thought and theory still provide the basis for helping professionals to approach how they understand and change human behavior and functioning.
- People's words and actions have meaning beyond their conscious self-awareness.
- Talking and using words is a way of resolving psychological problems.

REFLECTIONS FROM THE CONTRIBUTOR'S CHAIR

Between the time I received my master's degree in counselor education and applied for my PhD in counseling psychology, I enrolled in a 3-year psychoanalytic training program in New York City. When I began, I was volunteering at a free clinic in New York's East Village, working with walk-in clients who were facing varying degrees of physical, mental, and emotional difficulties. My supervisor was a psychiatrist, and everyone who worked there was committed to providing counseling and/or medical services and valued making these services available for all people, regardless of income. I then became the director of a federally funded, multilingual (English, Spanish, and several dialects of Chinese), community-based educational counseling program for young people who were to become the first generation in their families to attend college.

All the work I was doing was community based with multiethnic, multilingual, low-income clients dealing with a multiplicity of problems related not just to their early years but also to their social, political, economic, family, community, and health situations. When I was in the training program and working with my own training analyst, supervisors, and teachers, I knew I was not going to be a practicing psychoanalyst. In my work as a counselor, and subsequently as a professor, my clients and students did not necessarily fit the profile of those traditionally drawn to psychoanalysis. I undertook this extensive training, however, because I thought this was where I would experience the integration of theory and practice, where I would get the rigorous training to be a counseling practitioner and to integrate what I was learning at the institute with all my other academic training. After completing my PhD, I established a community counseling program in the Bronx, New York, where family members were experiencing extreme stress. I hired specialists in counseling, social work, and career counseling; in child and play therapy; and in family therapy. We created family therapy training spaces and provided professional development for staff. I continued my training in ecological and systems theories. When I became a faculty member and coordinator of the Counselor Education Program at Lehman College, City University of New York and a member of the American Counseling Association and several divisions, I found wonderful colleagues around the country who were working to promote multicultural competencies and social justice in counseling. I experienced being a faculty member as an extension of the community work I had done prior to entering an academic environment. I was now teaching and training would-be counselors, many of whom were successful first-generation college graduates themselves. Through the program, the counselor trainees are preparing to enter the schools and community as professionals. The program graduates need to use their own multicultural, multilingual, counseling competencies to intervene to help improve the lives and circumstances of their own clients. So where in all my work are my psychoanalytic roots and identifications?

My psychoanalytic training provided me with a serious and thoughtful approach to understanding others, as well as myself. I became an even more careful reader and a self-reflective practitioner. My psychoanalytic institute teachers were all practitioners themselves. Their varied experiences with helping people contributed to the learning environment. I value the part of my professional identity that has been trained in psychoanalytic theory and practice. In this psychopharmacological era and in a time when applied behavioral analysis is often prescribed, I bring the perspective that problems have underlying causes and that just treating the symptoms is not always the best intervention. I think, as counselors, we need to engage with our clients over time and be trustworthy, be ethical, and meet high professional standards. I also think counselors need to work through their own issues so the interface between counselor and clients is a collaborative, respectful partnership. I believe the psychoanalytic perspective is a valuable guide in this profession.

ADDITIONAL RESOURCES

Ackerman, N. (1958). *The psychodynamics of family life.* Oxford, UK: Basic Books.

American Psychoanalytic Association. (2013). Retrieved from www.apsa.org

Boszormenyi-Nagy, I. (1967). *Foundations of contextual therapy: Collected papers of Ivan Boszormenyi-Nagy, M.D.* Philadelphia: Brunner/Mazel.

Bowlby, J. (1990). *A secure base: Parent-child attachment and healthy human development.* New York: Basic Books.

Erikson, E. (1959). Identity and the life cycle: Selected papers. *Psychological Issues, 1,* 1–171.

Freud, A. (1936). *The ego and the mechanisms of defense.* New York: International Universities Press.

Gay, P. (1988). *Freud: A life for our time.* London: Dent.

Hale, N. G., Jr. (1971). *Freud and the Americans: The beginnings of psychoanalysis in the United States, 1876–1917.* New York: Oxford University Press.

Hale, N. G., Jr. (1995). *The rise and crises of psychoanalysis in the United States: Freud and the Americans, 1917–1985.* New York: Oxford University Press.

International Association for Relational Psychoanalysis and Psychotherapy. (2013). Retrieved from http://www.iarpp.net/

Journal of the American Psychoanalytic Association. (2013). Retrieved from http://apa.sagepub.com/

Jung, C. G. (1990). *Two essays on analytical psychology* (2nd ed.). London: Routledge.

Kernberg, O. (2004). *Object-relations theory and clinical psychoanalysis.* Lanham, MD: Rowman & Littlefield.

Klein, M. (1932). *The psycho-analysis of children* (A. Strachey, L. London, & V. Woolf, Trans.). London: Hogarth Press.

Kohut, H. (1971). *The analysis of the self: A systematic approach to the psychoanalytic treatment of narcissistic personality disorders.* New York: International Universities Press.

Mahler, M. (1968). *On human symbiosis and the vicissitudes of individuation.* New York: International Universities Press.

Makari, G. (2009). *Revolution in mind: The creation of psychoanalysis.* New York: HarperCollins.

Milton, J., Polmear, C., & Fabricius, J. (2011). *A short introduction to psychoanalysis* (2nd ed.). Thousand Oaks, CA: Sage.

Rudnytsky, P. T. (2011). *Rescuing psychoanalysis from Freud and other essays in revision.* London: Karnac Books.

REFERENCES

Altman, N. (2010). *The analyst and the inner city* (2nd ed.). New York: Routledge.

Altman, N. (2013). Psychoanalytic therapy. In J. Frew & M. D. Spiegler (Eds.), *Contemporary psychotherapies for a diverse world* (pp. 39–86). New York: Routledge.

American Anthropological Association. (2012). What is anthropology? Retrieved from http://www.aaanet.org/about/WhatisAnthropology.cfm

Auld, F., & Hyman, M. (1991). *Resolution of inner conflict: An introduction to psychoanalytic therapy.* Washington, DC: American Psychological Association.

Breger, L (2009). *A dream of undying fame: How Freud betrayed his mentor and invented psychoanalysis.* New York: Basic Books.

Chancer, L. S., & Watkins, B. X. (2006). *Gender, race, and class.* Malden, MA: Blackwell.

Corey, G. (2009). *Theory and practice of counseling and psychotherapy* (8th ed.). Belmont, CA: Brooks/Cole, Cengage Learning.

Danto, E. (2005). *Freud's free clinics*. New York: Columbia University Press.

Deveaux, F. (1995). Intergenerational transmission of cultural family patterns. *Family Therapy, 22,* 17–23.

Deveaux, F. (2002). Complexities uncovered: Intergenerational considerations of sociocultural contexts. In R. Roth & F. Farley (Eds.), *The spiritual side of psychology at century's end: Proceedings of the 57th Annual Convention of International Council of Psychologists, August 15–19, 1999, Salem, Massachusetts, USA* (pp. 57–64). Lengerich, Germany: Pabst.

Dufresne, J. (2007). *Against Freud: Critics talk back*. Stanford, CA: Stanford University Press.

Fonda, P. (2011). A virtual training institute in Eastern Europe. *International Journal of Psychoanalysis, 92,* 695–713. doi:10.111/j.1745-8315.2011.00461.x

Freud, S. (1933). *New introductory lectures on psychoanalysis*. New York: W. W. Norton.

Freud, S. (1961a). *Civilization and its discontents* (James Strachey, Ed. & Trans.). New York: W. W. Norton. (Original work published in 1930)

Freud, S. (1961b). *Instincts and their vicissitudes: Standard edition of the complete works of Sigmund Freud* (Vol. 14; James Strachey, Ed. & Trans.). London: Hogarth Press. (Original work published in 1915)

Freud, S. (1961c). *The psychopathology of everyday life: Standard edition of the complete works of Sigmund Freud* (Vol. 6; James Strachey, Ed. & Trans.). London: Hogarth Press. (Original work published in 1901)

Freud, S. (1961d). *Three essays on the theory of sexuality: Standard Edition of the complete works of Sigmund Freud* (Vol. 7; James Strachey, Ed. & Trans.). London: Hogarth Press. (Original work published in 1905)

Freud, S. (1963). *Sexuality and the psychology of love* (J. Bernays, Trans.). New York: Collier Books. (Original work published in 1905)

Freud, S. (1965). The interpretation of dreams (James Strachey, Ed. & Trans.). New York: Avon Books. (Original work published in 1900)

Freud, S. (1970a). *Beyond the pleasure principle* (James Strachey, Trans.). New York: Liveright. (Original work published in 1920)

Freud, S. (1970b). *A general introduction to psychoanalysis* (Joan Riviere, Trans.). New York: Pocket Books. (Original work published in 1920)

Garcia, J. (2011). The training of psychoanalysts in Latin American countries without IPA institutions: Antecedents, experiences and problems encountered. *International Journal of Psychoanalysis, 92,* 715–731. doi:10.1111/j.1745-8315.2011.00464.x

Greenberg, J. R., & Mitchell, S. A. (1983). *Object relations in psychoanalytic theory*. Cambridge, MA: Harvard University Press.

Hyman, S. E. (2000). The genetics of mental illness: Implications for practice. *Bulletin of the World Health Organization, 78*(4), 455–463.

Kandel, E. R. (1999). Biology and the future of psychoanalysis: A new intellectual framework for psychiatry revisited. *American Journal of Psychiatry, 156,* 505–524.

Kernberg, O. (2011). Psychoanalysis and the university: A difficulty relationship. *International Journal of Psychoanalysis, 92,* 609–622. doi:10.111/j.1745-8315.2011.00454.x

Kottler, J. (2002). *Theories in counseling and therapy: An experiential approach*. Boston: Allyn & Bacon.

La Roche, M. J. (2013). *Cultural psychotherapy: Theory, methods, and practice*. Thousand Oaks, CA: Sage.

Lehtonen, J. (2010). Dimensions in the dialogue between psychoanalysis and neuroscience. *International Forum of Psychoanalysis, 19,* 218–223. doi:10.1080/0803706X.2010.499136

Malan, D. H. (1979). *Individual psychotherapy and the science of psychodynamics*. London: Butterworth.

Nye, R. D. (1996). *Three psychologies: Perspectives from Freud, Skinner, and Rogers* (5th ed.). Pacific Grove, CA: Brooks/Cole.

Parsons, R. D. (2007). *Counseling strategies that work!* New York: Pearson Education.

Parsons, R. D. (2009). *Translating theory into practice: Thinking and acting like an expert counselor.* Upper Saddle River, NJ: Pearson Education.

Roland, A. (1996a). *Cultural pluralism and psychoanalysis: The Asian and North American experience.* New York: Routledge.

Roland, A. (1996b). The influence of culture on the self and self-object relationships: An Asian-North American comparison. *Psychoanalytic Dialogues, 6,* 461–475.

Sharpe, M., & Faulkner, J. (2008). *Understanding psychoanalysis.* Stocksfield, UK: Acumen.

Sheftel, S. (2011). Turning points in modern psychoanalysis. *Modern Psychoanalysis, 36,* 29–41.

Sulloway, F. J. (1979). *Freud, biologist of the mind: Beyond the psychoanalytic legend.* New York: Basic Books.

Sulloway, F. J. (2007). Psychoanalysis and pseudoscience: Frank J. Sullivan revisits Freud and his legacy. In T. Dufresne (Ed.), *Against Freud: Critics talk back* (pp. 48–69). Stanford, CA: Stanford University Press.

Walker, S. C. (2006). Trauma in South Africa: Psycho-analytic psychotherapy in South Africa. *Psychoanalytic Quarterly, 75,* 657–684.

Wortis, J. (1985). *Fragments of an analysis with Freud.* New York: J. Aronson. (Original work published in 1954)

Yang, Y. (2011). The challenge of professional identity for Chinese clinicians in the process of learning and practicing psychoanalytic psychotherapy: The discussion on the frame of Chinese culture. *International Journal of Psychoanalysis, 92,* 733–743. doi:10.1111/j.1745-8315.2011.00452.x

CHAPTER 5

Individual Psychology

Alfred Adler

Robyn L. Trippany-Simmons, Matthew R. Buckley,
Kristin Meany-Walen, and Tiffany Rush-Wilson

It has always been this way! I should not be surprised that my boss thinks I didn't deserve that promotion. My parents always thought my older sister was so much better than me. Clearly, my ex-husband thought his colleague was better than me, which is why he left me for her! I just never measure up.

Michelle, the client quoted above, is demonstrating a style of life that is steeped in feelings of insecurity, possibly a result of early childhood experiences in which she was compared with her older sister. It is not likely, however, that the client's experiences are factually accurate. The client experiences her subjective understanding as truth. Until she begins to challenge her understanding of those experiences, her interactions with others will likely follow this same theme.

After reading this chapter about Alfred Adler's theory of individual psychology, you will be able to do the following:

- Describe the core concepts of Adler's theory of individual psychology
- Apply Adlerian theory to case conceptualization
- Describe the role of a counselor when using an Adlerian approach
- Describe techniques this theory ascribes for intervening with clients

INTRODUCTION

Historical Background

Alfred Adler was a pioneer of counseling theory who focused on social interest, family constellation, and the development of parenting style. He initially worked closely with

Sigmund Freud and was a regular participant in Freud's discussion groups, known as the Wednesday Psychological Society (Rattner, 1983), which ended after professional and personality differences developed. The primary disagreement between Drs. Freud and Adler rested on the concept of determinism. Psychoanalysts used the term *impulse* for the fundamental process behind behavior, while Adlerians preferred the word *will* (Adler, 1931). Adler "conceived man not only as an organism, but also and even principally as a social being. . . . The only function of existence that psychoanalysis ascribes to the other ego as being an occasion for satisfaction" (Allers, 1933, p. 31). Freud, however, believed that people had no capacity to make change in their lives. Conversely, Adler noted that while challenging, perceptions of problem-genic life circumstances can change and thus allow for mentally healthier individuals (Adler, 1931). In 1912, a year after Adler and Freud parted ways professionally, Adler began theory development for individual psychology, which adduced "the artificiality of Freud's psychoanalytic theory" (Rattner, 1983, p. xii).

Adler attended Universität Wien (the University of Vienna), studying medicine, and began his career as an ophthalmologist in 1895. After meeting Freud in 1902, he became interested in psychiatry and established Adler's School of Individual Psychology in 1912. He also desired for as many people as possible to be involved in the counseling process, including teachers, parents, bus drivers, principals, and coaches. During WWI, Adler was a physician for the Austrian Army, ultimately working in the children's hospital. This experience influenced his social activist efforts training teachers and working with clinics at a state school. Adler also published texts related to his psychological interests, lectured, and advocated for all people to learn the basic principles of psychology.

Areas of Development

Adlerian followers have expanded on the philosophical underpinnings of original Adlerian concepts while maintaining the integrity of Adler's original theory. Just as persons do not remain stagnant, Adlerian theory adapts to accept societal change and deeper understanding of the human condition. Whereas all areas of development cannot be given credit in this chapter, we will provide details about a few particular areas of change.

One example of these areas of change is life tasks. Adler was a pioneer in feminist-type theory and referred to the sex task as people's challenge in defining how to relate to the *other* sex, rather than the *opposite* sex (Adler, 1927/1998). His initial view of homosexuality reflected that of the times. He described gay and lesbian people as discouraged, using socially useless behaviors to meet their needs, and failing at the life task of sex. This view has since changed, and homosexuality is understood as a normal and natural biological phenomenon. Furthermore, Adler initially identified three life tasks: society/friendship, work, and sex/love. Some current Adlerian theorists ascribe to five life tasks; spirituality and self were later added and defined by Harold Mosak (Mosak & Maniacci, 1999).

Adler desired a simple and commonsense theory. He wanted all people to be able to understand and apply his concepts. Although Adler was opposed to labels, he recognized the importance of creating a common language for the sake of simplicity. One of his applicable concepts was personality types, of which he had 14 (Mosak & Maniacci, 1999). In an effort to condense the types into a more useful system, four personality priorities were identified: pleasing, controlling, superiority, and comfort.

Another such example is child development. Adler originally identified the importance of childhood to one's development and lifestyle; he also described all behavior to be goal directed. Dreikurs (1964) developed his four goals of misbehavior as a way to delineate the goals of children's actions. By deciphering a child's goal of misbehavior, a counselor, teacher, or parent could hypothesize the child's fictional goal and develop strategies to help the child meet goals in a socially useful manner.

Adler was one of the first psychiatrists to identify the importance of working with school systems. In the late 1960s, Dinkmeyer noticed there was relatively no guidance curriculum for elementary-age children (Muro & Dinkmeyer, 1977). Dinkmeyer was instrumental in developing and implementing guidance counseling in school systems. An example of a popular school-based program is Positive Discipline in the Classroom® (Nelsen, Lott, & Glenn, 2000). Nelsen et al. emphasize the importance of cooperation among all members of the school environment, attesting that schools have the resources to teach academics as well as provide an atmosphere for nurturance and positive social behavior. Many school-based curricula have been based on the foundation of Adlerian theory. Terry Kottman (2003) later expanded on Adlerian philosophy by creating Adlerian play therapy. Adlerian play therapists use play as a way to meet the developmental needs of children. It is used by school counselors as well as counselors in private and community settings.

In addition to furthering the application of Adlerian theory to the above, other developments have centered on applying it to crisis intervention (Tedrick & Wachter-Morris, 2011), leadership development (Ferguson, 2011), work hygiene (Shifron & Reysen, 2011), eating disorders (Belangee, 2007), and couples therapy (Peluso & MacIntosh, 2007), among other areas. Additionally, the fall and winter 2012 editions of the *Journal of Individual Psychology* were dedicated to research on the efficacy of Adlerian theory with a variety of nationalities.

OVERVIEW OF INDIVIDUAL PSYCHOLOGY

Individual Psychology

Adlerian theory is often referred to as individual psychology because of the holistic and subjective nature of individuals in relation to others and their environment. Individuals act within a social context (Mosak, 2005) and according to their subjective experience of themselves within the world. Individuals view their experience through the use of imagined (fictional) goals that act as a template for an adopted style of life. Mosak noted that

> the conceptualization of humans as creative, choosing, self-determined decision makers permits them to choose the goals they want to pursue. Individuals may select socially useful goals or they may devote themselves to the useless side of life. They may choose to be task-oriented or they may, as does the neurotic, concern themselves with their own superiority. (p. 54)

Individuals are holistic in that they behave, perceive, feel, become, and strive for meaning in their interpersonal relationships and must be understood as an indivisible whole. Aslinia, Rasheed, and Simpson (2011) pointed out that Adler's German translation of the term *individual* means "indivisible." To reduce individuals to separate parts for the purpose of analysis or understanding misses their essence (Aslinia et al., 2011). Individuals engage in "cognitive organization," which helps them manage their experiences, thoughts, beliefs, and aspirations and ultimately control their lives (Mosak, 2005). Life has no significance in and of itself, so individuals' intrinsic subjective experience is reciprocally shaped and influenced by their encounters with the world. Each encounter has an additive effect. Mosak (2005) quoted Lawrence Frank, who succinctly captured this reciprocal evolution:

> The personality process might be regarded as a sort of rubber stamp which the individual imposes upon every situation by which he [or she] gives it the configuration that he [or she], as an individual, requires; in so doing he [or she] necessarily ignores or subordinates many aspects of the situation that for him [or her] are irrelevant and meaningless and selectively reacts to those aspects that are personally significant. (p. 65)

Understanding individuals as inseparable in all aspects of their lives and how they impact and are impacted by their social environment is of primary importance to Adlerian theory. The following are concepts related to individual psychology.

View of Human Nature

Basic to individual psychology is Adler's belief that the first 6 to 8 years of life influence adult life outcomes (Kottman, 2001), evident in behaviors and reactions to life situations. Thus, if a line could be drawn depicting behavior from childhood through adulthood, that line would remain relatively constant. Case Illustration 5.1 reviews the case of Michelle, the client with whom we opened this chapter, and provides her chart.

Free Will

According to Adler, people are neither exclusively preprogrammed by genetics nor solely shaped by environment; they are influenced by both. This freedom allows individuals the ability to make decisions based on an idiosyncratic personal style that results from this free will. Individuals are thus responsible for successes as well as mistakes and unhealthy decisions (Rattner, 1983).

CASE ILLUSTRATION 5.1

Michelle

The following chart highlights how Michelle perceives the various events in her life as evidence she is substandard to others. However, these events, in and of themselves, do not indicate that she is not "good enough." She uses her subjective perception of events to support her style of life, which is insecurity. Adler also felt this line could help draw conclusions regarding the future of the individual. This insight is important to understand and then change faulty beliefs and behaviors.

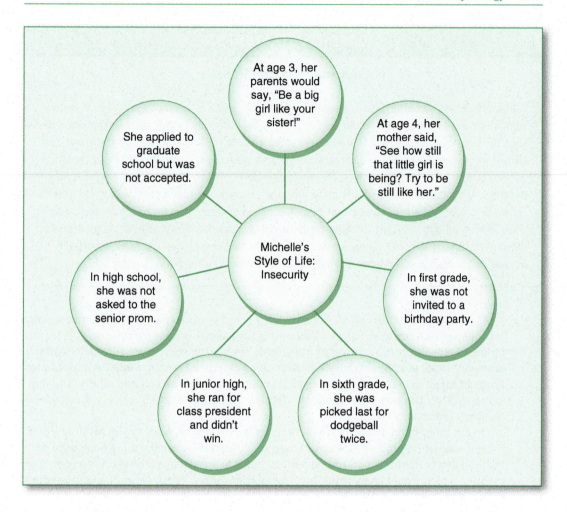

At age 3, her parents would say, "Be a big girl like your sister!"

At age 4, her mother said, "See how still that little girl is being? Try to be still like her."

She applied to graduate school but was not accepted.

Michelle's Style of Life: Insecurity

In first grade, she was not invited to a birthday party.

In high school, she was not asked to the senior prom.

In junior high, she ran for class president and didn't win.

In sixth grade, she was picked last for dodgeball twice.

Social Interest

Overriding all Adlerian concepts is *Gemeinschaftsgefühl,* or social interest. According to Adler, the root of all problems is failure of social interest. Further, the solution to mental health problems is to increase social interest (Adler, 1931, 1956/1964).

Inferiority Versus Superiority

Adler theorized a struggle between feelings of inferiority and feelings of superiority (Adler, 1927/1998) based on the motivation to find one's place in a social context (Ashby & Kottman, 1996). He found that feelings of inferiority are not accidental but, rather, inherently human and anchored in *organ inferiority* (Rattner, 1983). Organ inferiority is related to a perceived deficit that develops in childhood (e.g., unattractiveness, assessment of strength and/or ability, social and economic status, or other feelings of inferiority; Adler, 1927/1998). Consider again the case of Michelle, the client with whom we opened this chapter (see Case Illustration 5.2).

> ### CASE ILLUSTRATION 5.2
>
> ### Continuing With Michelle
>
> That Michelle was picked last for dodgeball twice in sixth grade is not concrete evidence she was inferior to others. In this case, she did not consider all the other times when she *wasn't* picked last. Thus, the two negative occurrences are the memories she held on to as validation that she was deficient. A more objective perception is that while Michelle was chosen last two times, other times, she was not chosen last. Her subjective perception supported her belief that she could not measure up to others. Ultimately, feelings of inferiority are goal directed and provide motivation for growth toward belonging. Adler emphasized that these feelings were natural and become maladaptive only when fixated on and resistant to being tested and reexamined within relationships as a person develops (Rattner, 1983). In Michelle's case, she did not take being chosen last as an opportunity to improve her dodgeball skills; rather, she fixated on the event from a defeatist perspective.

As with Michelle, a struggle for compensation and personal power is evident in striving for superiority. Adler said that social interest is the balancing force for this struggle. "Social interest helps direct the striving of individuals toward the socially useful side" (Ashby & Kottman, 1996, p. 238). Adaptive manifestations of striving for superiority will yield high levels of social interest through beneficial actions that help the self and others. The individual will set flexible, high standards that lend themselves to objective self-evaluation (Ashby & Kottman, 1996).

On the other hand, maladaptive methods of striving for superiority will result in a critical self-evaluation process of actions based on disregard for others. If Michelle used maladaptation to strive for superiority, she might begin to arrogantly claim skills in a grandiose manner, which would likely result in a loss of friendships. These neurotic manifestations will demonstrate reduced feelings of social interest, increased pursuit for personal power, and a lack of consideration for the welfare of others (Ashby & Kottman, 1996). These individuals may battle with dissatisfaction and emptiness and may become overwhelmed by feelings of inferiority instead of being motivated by them. Dreikurs (1964) described individuals in this state as "discouraged."

Style of Life

Starting in childhood, people develop beliefs about themselves, others, and the world based on early perceptions of their experiences in their environment. These beliefs help them understand, predict, and control life. This is, in essence, their *truth*. That which is created based on these beliefs and the feelings and behaviors that result from them cumulate into the individual's style of life (Adler, 1956/1964). For example, a child who has been sexually abused by a perpetrator who suggested he couldn't resist how pretty she was may develop an erroneous belief that being pretty makes bad things happen, so it would be better to "hide" behind oversized clothes, unkempt hair, and poor hygiene. One's style of life is not good or bad, right or wrong; it simply describes the consistency with which one navigates through the world toward one's fictional goal, described later (Adler, 1927/1998, 1956/1964; Mosak & Maniacci, 1999). A factor of specific importance to Adlerian theory is the concept of family constellation, including birth order (Adler, 1956/1964) and family atmosphere (Mosak & Maniacci, 1999). Let's again turn to the case of Michelle (Case Illustration 5.3).

CASE ILLUSTRATION 5.3

Michelle's Feelings of Inferiority

For Michelle, while her feelings of being inferior to others caused her a great deal of distress, she felt incongruent if she did not engage in comparisons. She always asked her friends what grades they made on tests; when she walked into a room, she would look around to see who was skinnier than her. Never did she measure up, but she could always count on her ability to measure and compare herself with others. If someone paid her a compliment, she would find a way to discount it. For example, if a friend commented on her new outfit, she would respond, "Do you really like it? I wasn't sure when I tried it on."

According to Adlerian theory, there are no mistakes in style of life. One's habits and symptoms are precisely right for attaining goals determined by one's style of life. Every person experiencing alcoholism, neuroticism, and criminal behavior makes goal-directed decisions based on his or her chosen style of life and aim to attain unmet needs (Adler, 1931).

Purposeful Behavior

Adler (1931) believed that all behavior is purposeful to fulfill one's style-of-life needs. Recognizing the purpose of behavior is crucial due to possible insight into and identification of personal goals and needs. Adlerian theory assumes that individuals' decisions are based on past experiences that impact current behaviors.

Fictional Finalism

Fictional finalism, sometimes referred to as an imaginary or fictional goal, is a term used in regard to purposeful behavior and is a central focus of the style of life (Dinkmeyer, Dinkmeyer, & Sperry, 1987). It describes an imaginary aim that influences an individual's behavior and is a manifestation of that individual's beliefs about "how the world should be" (Adler, 1929). With this fictional goal, an individual has a subjective experience in which he or she chooses what is true, what is meaningful, what behavior will serve a purpose, and how to understand and perceive events. Fictional finalism also includes subjective goals that will result in feelings of self-worth (Adler, 1929). These goals are unconscious and not based in reality.

Subjective Perception of Reality

Adler (1931) emphasized the need to analyze how an individual perceives reality, rather than actual events. If these meanings are aimed toward the good of society, then the individual is grounded in social interest. However, if the focus is on self, then the individual is engaging in what Adler (1929) called *private logic*, a hidden objective for not complying with societal norms. Adler believed that individuals resorting to a life of crime, those participating in neurosis or psychosis, those who turn to alcoholism or addiction, and other "failures" do so as a result of private logic (Adler, 1931).

Early Memories

Adler (1931) stated that early memories are the most revealing clues and are significant for uncovering the individual's style of life. These memories a person carries serve as reminders of limitations and meanings of events. There are no "chance" memories, nor will they ever run counter to the style of life (p. 73). It is not the accuracy of the memories but the value the individual places on them that is important (Adler, 1931). Memories are chosen to support how the person perceives things, to serve emotions, and to represent the story of one's life. This story is repeated to warn, confront, keep focused on goals, and prepare for the future through already-tested styles of life (Adler, 1931). If the style of life is altered, memories will be altered to fit.

Dreams

Adler (1931) wrote that dreams are similar to memories in their indication of style of life. The individual will pick out the parts of the dream with which he or she agrees and that express his or her chosen style of life. Adler stated that the purpose of the dream is to support the style of life. This support is offered through emotions that manifest in dreams. Adler (1931) stated that dreams always arouse feelings the individual needs to justify his or her style of life.

Basic Characteristics and Assumptions

The Role of the Family

Consistent with all of Adlerian theory, Adler posited that people are social beings. The family is the first social relationship an infant experiences, with intraparental relationships acting as an umbrella over the family. This relationship sets the emotional stage for traditional family norms (Dreikurs, 1964; Starr, 1973). The task of a father is to be a good "fellow man to his wife, to his children and to society" (Adler, 1931, p. 134). He is to strive to meet the three problems of life discussed earlier, and if he is meeting them in a productive manner, he is a good father and husband. The mother's task is twofold: (1) to show love and (2) to guide the child to social interest (Starr, 1973). Children need to learn that the family unit is a part of society and that they can transfer trust, knowledge, and feelings to others outside of the family (Adler, 1931). It is important to note that current Adlerians acknowledge that Adler's original statements do not mirror the family relationships of today. Family constellations can include nuclear or blended families, same-sex parents, single parents, and multiple-generational households.

Birth Order

The psychological order of birth provided a general guideline for expectations of how a person will behave and be treated within the family. Adler (1956/1964) identified typical behaviors based on one's birth order: oldest, middle, youngest, or only. Psychological rather than chronological order of birth is emphasized because of the subjective nature of human beings. For example, if the chronologically firstborn child has significant health impairments, he or she may not be functioning in the role of the firstborn and, thus, the next-born child may take the place and roles of the firstborn.

Oldest Children. The oldest child enters the family as the only child. Typically, this child is given a great deal of attention prior to the arrival of additional children. Upon the arrival of younger children, the oldest becomes a helper and contributor to the entire family (Adler, 1956/1964). Oldest children are often in leadership roles as adults in their careers, social groups, and families. Oldest children may also be aggressive, organized, compliant, logical, and scholarly (Leman, 2004). Examples of famous oldest children include Oprah Winfrey, Brad Pitt, Hilary Rodham Clinton, Bill Cosby, and Catherine, Duchess of Cambridge of Wales.

Middle Children. The second child enters the family as the youngest. This child has an older sibling who has paved the way for any future children. For a period of time, this child will be the youngest and receive attention as the baby, until another child arrives. The middle child is often fighting for his or her place in the family. Due to this child's attempt to "catch up" to the oldest child, he or she often becomes more talented than the older sibling (Adler, 1956/1964). It could also be that the second child finds a unique way to make meaning and stand out in the family. For example, if the firstborn is academically talented, the second child may choose to excel athletically (Leman, 2004). Because middle children may follow the same path as the older child or take a different route than the older child, and yet strive to stand separate from younger children, middle children are described to be in a paradox. They may be social or reserved, rebellious or compromising, diplomatic or peace seeking, and independent or stubborn (Leman, 2004). Examples of famous middle children include Donald Trump; Diana, Princess of Wales; Dr. Martin Luther King Jr.; Jennifer Lopez; and Bill Gates.

Youngest Children. The youngest child is in a unique position because his or her place in the family will not be taken; he or she will always be the youngest. This child is likely to be pampered and to become the star of the family. The youngest child is competitive, often overshadowing the older children and surpassing their talents (Adler, 1956/1964). Lastborns may even receive much of their life instruction and caretaking from their older siblings, creating a multifaceted sibling relationship. Youngest children may also be outgoing, relaxed, manipulative, entertaining, impatient, rebellious, affectionate, spoiled, and absent-minded (Leman, 2004). Examples of famous youngest children include Jim Carrey, Eddie Murphy, Whoopi Goldberg, Mark Twain, and Goldie Hawn.

Only Children. The only child is different from children with siblings because he or she has no sibling interaction, thus eliminating opportunities for social emulation and competition

(Adler, 1956/1964). The only child is the center of attention and may become demanding of this position. Additionally, due to the lack of other children living in the home, the only child may spend most of his or her free time alone—or with mother or father, modeling adult-like social interactions. Only children may be characterized as self-assured, perfectionists, self-centered, organized, cheerful, efficient, nitpicky, and dependable (Leman, 2004). Examples of famous only children include Tiger Woods, Laura Bush, Alan Greenspan, Lance Armstrong, Condoleezza Rice, and Betty White.

Because of the various compositions of families (e.g., blended, adopted, same-sex parented, single parented, traditional nuclear) and the phenomenological approach to Adlerian theory, children may perceive their role in the family to be different from what is implied by birth order. Adler (1956/1964) also described some caveats to the birth order influence, such as illness, death, gender, and gaps in age.

Consider Adler's description of the family constellation. He posited that birth order is quite influential in personality development. It seems that this is generally accepted in popular culture: People commonly reference the expected behavior of firstborns, only children, oldest children, and so on. What do you think? Take a moment to review the website of the Alfred Adler Institute of San Francisco. As you reflect on your own family-of-origin experiences and your self-concept, does it seem that your position in the family constellation impacted your personal growth? What evidence do you see?

Life Tasks

Adler (1931) identified three problems or tasks of life: task of love, task of community, and task of work. The three problems are never found separately, and all three reflect on the others; solving one aids in solving another (Adler, 1931). Adler believed that the individual's response to these three tasks reflects his or her meaning of life. He said that all three problems are aspects of the same human needs: to preserve life, to further life, and to further one's environment (Adler, 1931).

Task of Love

The task of love is based on cooperation between intimate partners: "It is only between the I and Thou and the surrender inherent in it that a person discovers his [or her] own self and his [or her] real nature" (Rattner, 1983, p. 52). This task emphasizes surrendering oneself completely to one's partner, to the point where one person is formed from the two. Mistakes in solving this task may lead individuals to ask, "What can I get out of this relationship?" rather than "What can I contribute?" (Adler, 1931, p. 265). The task of love has other benefits for society. Its primary purpose is preservation and furtherance of life (Adler, 1931). This task not only encompasses intimacy and reproduction but also encourages hygiene (Adler, 1931). Through this task or problem, individuals learn manners, how to dress, how to clean, and management or repression of desires.

Task of Community

The task of community also centers on cooperation and solving social problems. Adler (1956/1964) indicated that the family serves as the training ground for development of this task, which is then externalized to the community. To solve the tasks of work and love, the individual must first examine the social task or task of community (Adler, 1931). "Social interest is required for the solution of all tasks of life because these are always social in structure and presuppose fellow feeling" (Rattner, 1983, p. 49). To solve the task of work, one must have learned cooperation (Adler, 1931). Cooperation allows for the division of labor, which then allows for organization of different training and abilities to contribute to the common welfare and increase opportunity for others (Adler, 1931). The task of love also relies on the task of community. Between partners, a sense of cooperation or division of labor needs to exist for a successful partnership (Rattner, 1983). Adler stressed that solving the task of community helps develop courage and confidence in meeting life's problems, thus promoting the welfare of others (Adler, 1931).

Task of Work

The task of work is focused on preserving an individual's environment (Rattner, 1983). In pursuing work, an individual gains a feeling of productivity and makes an attempt to con-tribute to the welfare of society. As with the social environment, the task of work has impli-cations for the success of the family. If there is fair division of labor, a sense of cooperation will exist. Adler emphasized that the mother's role, even if she works as a homemaker, is no less important than the father's. In fact, Adler (1931) emphasized the mother's decision to be a homemaker as an occupational choice.

Use With Diverse Populations and Children

Adlerian therapy has been characterized as compatible for working with diverse popula-tions (Dinkmeyer et al., 1987). The straightforward approach of the theory and focus on the subjective view of reality from the perspective of the client does not alienate individu-als or cultures. With the emphasis on encouragement and solving the three problems of life—love, community, and work—this approach is applicable to all.

Adler (1931) was an advocate for oppressed groups and developed his theory to promote social awareness. He was interested in encouraging society to appreciate people individu-ally and accept each person as an equal (Adler, 1931). Adler (1931) advocated for the rights of everyone and dedicated some of his writings to encouraging the equal treatment of women. Key to Adler's theory is the concept of social interest, which basically promotes the idea that people who value others will work toward social interest and solve problems for the benefit of others (Adler, 1931).

The focus on inferiority lends this theory to understanding the dynamics of oppressed people (Dinkmeyer et al., 1987). The therapeutic goal of increasing social interest and redi-recting selfish manifestations of striving for superiority is conducive to working with mar-ginalized and oppressed populations, and offers a productive alternative for societal participation.

People with disabilities and special needs can also benefit from an individual psychol-ogy approach. With its emphasis on the impact of organ inferiority, a greater understanding can be gained through identification of compensation methods, striving for superiority, and style of life (Dinkmeyer et al., 1987). Clients with disabilities can benefit by increasing insight into this identification and directing compensation acts to productive areas, as well as increasing social interest.

Adler was an advocate for the teaching of gender equality in schools (Ansbacher, 1990; Rattner, 1983) and warned that maladaptive behavior patterns would develop, with boys believing they are superior to girls, resulting in decreased social interest and increased feelings of inferiority (Ansbacher, 1990). Adler (1931) further advocated for women by stressing the importance of nonhierarchical gender equity within the family, explaining that "there should be no ruler in the family" (p. 135). He suggested that many unhappy marriages are a product of role expectations that result in anger and resentment (Adler, 1931).

Strengths and Limitations

As with any theory, limitations of Adlerian theory have been identified. In particular, due to the length of time needed for assessment, there may be challenges using this work with individuals who lack insight, who are concrete thinkers, and who need immediate benefits. However, neo-Adlerians have worked to shorten this process. Others cite the need for insightful clients and inadequacy for lower-functioning clients as a problem with this theory (Allers, 1933). The simplicity of this theory is a focus of criticism in that it takes highly complex human behaviors and boils them down to need for superiority and need for community (Allers, 1933). Another criticism is the therapists' responsibility to interpret. Interpretation of material in Adlerian counseling is an oft-debated topic, and no resolution has been reached.

Professional Identity

When asked the question, "Who are you?" most people will identify gender, profession, race and ethnicity, and family role, among other factors. It makes sense that for counselors, professional identification does not encompass only one's credentials or clinical focus; it also includes theoretical orientation. Further, as it is ethically responsible for theory to inform practice, theory is at the core of *who* counselors are.

Counselors-in-training are often uncertain which theory feels right as they "try on" the various theories explored in graduate training programs. Asking these three simple questions can provide direction toward the theory that resonates most with one's understanding of humans:

What do I believe about human nature?

What do I believe about how problems develop?

What do I believe about how change happens?

The unique ways those with an Adlerian perspective would address each of these questions, and thus give shape to their professional identities, serves as the focus for the next section of this chapter.

THE THERAPEUTIC PROCESS AND APPLICATIONS

The process of Adlerian therapy is a collaborative and educational one in which the primary goal is to foster and enhance social interest by helping the client become enlightened about his or her life patterns. The gained insight allows clients to intentionally make changes in their lives. The therapist begins by building a relationship with the client. As the therapist interacts with the client, he or she is collecting information from the client to understand and interpret the client's lifestyle. As the counselor begins to develop a picture of the client's way of navigating through life, he or she makes soft interpretations and relays that information back to the client so the client can become aware of some of his or her out-of-consciousness processes. Counselors educate clients about their personal freedom to make decisions about their lives, help them create alternate goals, and encourage them to become autonomous (Adler, 1956/1964).

Change Process

Individuals also develop *fictional goals* based on their style of life. A fictional goal is what each person believes must happen or he or she must accomplish to belong and have a satisfying life (Mosak & Maniacci, 1999). Examples of fictional goals are, "I must make everyone happy" or "I must be the best figure skater in the world" or "I must protect everyone." The individual believes that only by meeting these self-created objectives will he or she be loved (Mosak & Maniacci, 1999). In most instances, fictional goals are not conscious. A focus of counseling would be to uncover the client's fictional goal so he or she can either redefine it or find more healthy ways to achieve it.

Lifestyle convictions are beliefs about the self, others, and the world created by one's lifestyle (Mosak & Maniacci, 1999). Lifestyle convictions that are not helpful in meeting the innate potential for social interest are called mistaken beliefs. Examples of mistaken beliefs are, "*I* am unworthy of trusting relationships," "*Others* are unkind," or "*The world* is unsafe." Therefore, the created justified behavior might be aggression used to protect oneself from the believed threat of others.

One goal of treatment is to challenge the lifestyle convictions—fictional goals and mistaken beliefs—formed in lifestyle development. Allers (1933) identified two aims of counseling: (1) to identify that an error exists in the style of life and how the error developed, and (2) to replace the error with goals in harmony with social interest.

Individuals' emotions and thoughts are conceptualized as purposeful and consistent with their created lifestyles even if the emotional expression, or behavior, creates problems in their lives (Adler, 1931). Behaviors can be changed if the style of life is changed. Thus, symptoms must not be the only focus of treatment. The therapist and client must cooperatively discover mistakes made in the style of life, the meaning given to life's experiences, and the actions used to fulfill perceived needs. The real task of psychotherapy, according to Adler (1931), is to uncover the development of the style of life and replace mistaken beliefs and misbehaviors with those in harmony with social interest. To uncover this, the therapist—like a detective—must gather hints from a multitude of signs, big and small, that the client provides. Adler stressed that the lifestyle is not easy to change and can be changed only by the client through insight gained into the development of his or her lifestyle. In Exercise 5.1, Cynthia provides an opportunity to apply your understanding of fictional goals, lifestyle conditions, and mistaken beliefs. It may be helpful to discuss your perspective with a colleague.

EXERCISE 5.1

Cynthia is a 27-year-old, Mexican American, middle-class female. She is the oldest of three children and the only daughter. Her mother died after a short illness when Cynthia was 7 years old. Throughout the course of her life, she has been the caretaker and primary nurturer for her younger brothers and father, who never remarried. Cynthia graduated from high school at the top of her class and went on to a local community college to stay close to her family. After graduation, she worked odd jobs that paid poorly and she did not enjoy. Currently, she is considering returning to college to study nursing. Her friends and family say she would be a good nurse, although Cynthia is more attracted to engineering. Additionally, the closest university is 82 miles from her hometown and family. Cynthia comes to your counseling office reportedly seeking help in making a decision about her education and future career goals.

Given the limited information provided in this scenario, answer the following questions:

- What might be Cynthia's fictional goal(s)?
- What are some of her possible lifestyle convictions and mistaken beliefs?
- What information in the scenario led you to develop your ideas?
- What additional information would be helpful to you to determine potential lifestyle convictions and fictional goals?

Adler (1931) believed that people have the ability to make their lives better by changing their beliefs about themselves, others, and their environment. He believed that people control their destinies; they make their fate rather than becoming victims of fate. Thus, clients are primarily responsible for change. Adler wrote that a person has the ability to take both the good and bad in life and develop his or her feelings about it. Then, he or she must work to improve this world and assume responsibility for solving its problems.

A fundamental component in Adlerian counseling is encouragement (Sweeney, 2009). Encouragement, in Adlerian terms, is belief in oneself and the courage to take risks in life (Mosak & Maniacci, 1999). With the essential element of encouragement being courage, the act of therapist encouragement empowers clients. This component of Adlerian counseling is important for success. Consistent encouragement enables individuals to accept shortcomings and focus on strengths. Sweeney (2009) promoted courage as a fundamental characteristic of truth, love, and religion, which is consistent with the Adlerian concepts of social interest and the three tasks of life.

Discouragement, negative thinking, and unrealistic expectations run counter to successful counseling (Dinkmeyer et al., 1987). Discouragement decreases an individual's faith in self to accomplish goals. Thus, these clients may feel unable to set goals and work toward them in the therapeutic relationship. Clients with unrealistic expectations, such as expecting a "quick fix," may be easily discouraged and blame the therapist for the lack of progress (Dinkmeyer et al., 1987).

An example of interaction in a counseling session is presented in Case Illustration 5.4, about Cynthia again. The case helps illustrate how fictional goals and mistaken beliefs influence actions, and how encouragement can be used to help a client see his or her beliefs more clearly.

CASE ILLUSTRATION 5.4

Cynthia

Cynthia: This is really hard. My family and especially my father want me to go into nursing and have made some big sacrifices for me to do that.

Counselor: Yes, you have talked about your passion, which is to build bridges and design structures, and believe that you would be letting down a lot of people if you chose engineering instead of nursing.

Cynthia: Yes, but it is more than that. My mother was a nurse, and I remember the care she gave me and my brothers when I was little and telling me that nursing was not just a job but almost like a ministry. *(Mistaken belief)*

Counselor: So your belief is that you might be letting your mother down if you don't fulfill her destiny for you. *(Paraphrasing her a mistaken belief)*

Cynthia: Yes, I really do. It's so weird. It's like part of honoring her memory. All I really know is how to care for others, which is what my mother taught me, especially before she died. She told me that I would be the one to help the family get through and that my father needed me. I even remember having to defend myself occasionally with friends who were irritated that I couldn't hang out with them after school because I had to go home and take care of the house or work at the restaurant. *(Early recollections)*

Counselor: So even though your brothers are grown up, finishing school and getting ready for adulthood, it's hard to see beyond your mother's vision for herself and you. I am also learning that to honor your mom's memory, you feel you must choose nursing.

Cynthia: Yeah, I guess. She sacrificed so much for us. My dad and aunts and uncles have also sacrificed so much for me. I don't want to disappoint them.

Counselor: You said something really important about defending your actions to your friends about what you had to do to keep the family going. It seems like you are doing that defending here with me in trying to resolve your struggle about what direction you will choose.

(Continued)

(Continued)

Cynthia:	Yes, I guess I am. I just don't want to make a mistake.
Counselor:	You know, Cynthia, it occurs to me that you have had some significant challenges in your life that have really pressed you into becoming resourceful and figuring a way out even though the solution wasn't really clear at the time. I wonder if the same type of thing may be happening here and now.
Cynthia:	What do you mean?
Counselor:	Look at what you have accomplished so far as a mother to your brothers and a caregiver to your father. You stepped up at a very young age with no training in how to care for a family and run a household, yet you did it. You learned, asked for help from other family members and friends when necessary, connected with others when it became overwhelming, and managed to survive and provide while working outside the home. You also were able to do this while keeping good grades in school. *(Encouragement)*
Cynthia:	I never really thought about it that way before.
Counselor:	I wonder if you can be that resourceful on a different level as you consider what needs to be done to prepare for college and especially in considering your vision for yourself and what direction is best for your career.
Cynthia:	I am scared of letting my family down.
Counselor:	Yes, I really hear that, and I also hear that you are branching out into unfamiliar territory, making a decision about something you want to do rather than what has always been expected, or what you assume others want you to do. That takes a lot of courage to do something like that. Have you ever talked with your aunt and your dad about what you want to do, the way you have shared with me?
Cynthia:	I really haven't, but I have imagined it.
Counselor:	Let's practice what you might say in a conversation like that.

The counselor in this case illustration takes an encouraging stance through validating feelings, respecting Cynthia's need to honor her mother, and continually but gently confronting the struggle between considering the needs of others and listening to her own voice about what may be right for her. Though not spoken, the counselor is also aware of the cultural influences that contribute to the belief systems and inner conflict the client experiences. The counselor helps encourage Cynthia toward action by practicing a dialogue that would help her hear her own voice describe what she wants to do as a career.

Assessment Strategies

Because Adler described humans as social beings, an individual can be further understood by evaluating his or her attitude toward others (Dinkmeyer et al., 1987). This attitude will reflect the structure of the individual's personality and level of self-esteem. In assessing individuals, Adler (1929) focused on actions rather than words. Behaviors of focus should include problem-solving methods, style of life, and manifestation of the struggle of superiority versus inferiority. Adlerian counselors use family constellations, early childhood memories, current interactions, formal assessments, group interactions, and dreams to identify the client's lifestyle. This may be done through both subjective interviews and a lifestyle assessment (Sweeney, 2009). Adlerians believe that the client is the only one who truly understands his or her problems; the counselor relies on the client to be the expert (Bitter, 1997).

The Adlerian counselor is interested in the subjective and objective experiences of the client. The subjective experiences are the ways the client experiences life. Thus, the counselor is assessing how the client views his or her world from this unique perspective (Mosak & Manniacci, 1999). Cultural worldviews are included in the subjective assessment. Counselors investigate a client's objective experiences by evaluating how the client is functioning in daily life. That is, in what ways are the client's problems getting in the way of meeting life tasks? In the case of Michelle (the client with whom we opened the chapter), her perception of not being as valuable as others may interfere with her willingness to try new things or meet new people. For example, Michelle may want a romantic relationship but may believe she is not good enough and will be overlooked by a potential partner. Her perceptions, then, would get in the way of her taking the risk of meeting someone new. From an understanding of the client's subjective and objective functioning, the counselor can appropriately challenge the client regarding faulty thinking in her style of life and work to promote social interest. *In what ways are Michelle's beliefs about being second best compromising her chances of starting a relationship?*

FOCUS AND INTENTIONALITY:
APPLYING THE THEORY IN EARLY, MIDDLE, AND LATE SESSIONS

Among Adlerian theorists, there exist many terms to describe the four phases of individual psychology. Despite the differences in terms used, Adlerians agree on the importance and process of each phase. The four phases are *building a collaborative relationship, investigating the lifestyle, gaining insight,* and *reorientation* (Adler, 1956/1964; Mosak & Maniacci, 1999, 2008; Sweeney, 2009). Here, we have chosen to use the word *phases* in place of *stages* to exemplify the fluid nature of the counseling relationship and client progress. Michelle's case will be used throughout this section to illustrate each phase of the counseling process according to Adlerian theory, and Y-Chun's case later in the chapter will provide further discussion.

In the first phase, *building a collaborative relationship,* the counselor and client start the process of building an egalitarian relationship. Different from Freud, Adler (1956/1964) believed that the relationship between counselor and client should be one of mutuality and cooperation. The counselor is merely a passenger in the client's change process, rather than the ultimate, all-knowing driver. Through collaboration, cooperation, and mutuality, the client experiences a balanced relationship, witnesses social interest, and is encouraged to make her own decisions in the process. The counselor works to understand Michelle from her perspective. Time and care are taken to build a relationship in which Michelle feels safe and believes she is a contributor to the process rather than just a recipient of therapy. The Adlerian counselor infuses encouragement into each response to build trust and empower the client toward healthier functioning.

The therapeutic relationship between client and counselor is necessary but not sufficient for client change (Adler, 1927/1998). Mosak and Maniacci (2008) list the conditions of faith, hope, and love as necessary relationship attitudes. Faith is the feeling of security and trust in the relationship, as well as the client's and therapist's belief that the therapy can and will be effective. Hope is the client's belief in self and an inner feeling of encouragement that circumstances can be changed. Love is another necessary condition. The client must feel that the counselor genuinely cares about him or her. The counselor's role is to empathize with and support the client, not pity, console, or become a victim of the client. Although techniques are acceptable in Adlerian theory, they are not to replace empathy, understanding, and compassion (Mosak & Maniacci, 1999).

Once the relationship has a steady foundation and the counselor believes the client is willing to collaborate in therapy, the counselor and client move to the next phase: investigating the client's lifestyle. However, the relationship is constantly being fostered and developed throughout the therapy process. See the guided activity in Exercise 5.2, where you will explore relationships in your own life to discover what qualities contributed to the success and meaningfulness of those relationships.

Investigating the lifestyle is the second phase of Adlerian counseling, in which the counselor and client work together by means of some of the interventions described above and possibly other interventions as well. The goal of this phase is to uncover the client's lifestyle, including goals of behavior, mistaken beliefs, feelings of inferiority, fictional goals, and

EXERCISE 5.2

Directions: Think about one of your closest, most emotionally intimate relationships, and then answer the following questions.

- How was the relationship established?
- What qualities does this person possess that contribute to the creation of a safe and mutual relationship?
- How do you know you can trust him or her?
- How do you know, or what proof do you have, that he or she cares about you?
- Of those qualities that characterize this relationship, what would you suggest a counselor provide to his or her clients?

deficits in social interest. As previously stated, Adlerian therapists frequently investigate the influences of early childhood and one's family of origin. Adlerians believe perceptions of early childhood experiences are paramount in how one perceives the significance of relationships throughout life (Adler, 1927/1998; Mosak & Maniacci, 1999; Sweeney, 2009).

Michelle is a second child who has consistently felt in competition for love and attention from her parents. She has maintained this lifestyle in a variety of her relationships, in which she continues to find proof that she is not valuable or as good as others. Michelle believes that she is not good if she is not the best. A counselor may use early childhood recollections or dream analysis (explained in the next section) to explore Michelle's lifestyle.

The next phase of counseling is *gaining insight*. Gaining insight can be considered an adjoining process to investigating lifestyle. Based on information learned about the client in the previous phase, counselors facilitate client awareness about the client's created lifestyle. When clients are aware of their goals and the purposes of their behaviors, they can consciously, and thus more effectively, make decisions as to whether and what they wish to change. Therefore, much of Adlerian therapy is concentrated on helping the client gain insight into his or her current patterns of feelings, thoughts, and behaviors (Sweeney, 2009). The counselor and client then explore how the client's current functioning is assisting or getting in the way of meeting longer-term goals. The counselor may employ a variety of techniques, which we will discuss later, to help the client become aware of his or her lifestyle, mistaken beliefs, and fictional goals. Consider Case Illustration 5.5, which provides brief examples of techniques applied to Michelle's case.

CASE ILLUSTRATION 5.5

Increasing Client Awareness

The counselor uses "spitting in the client's soup" (an intervention described in the next section) and confrontation to help Michelle become aware of her lifestyle, mistaken beliefs, and fictional goals. The counselor might say to Michelle, "You've described many instances when you were not chosen or were chosen last. It seems to me that it's easy for you to recall these occurrences. Yet you've also shared how you were captain of your high school debate team and won an art competition in college. I wonder what it does for you not to remember your successes."

Michelle becomes aware of feeling, thinking, and behavioral patterns of which she was previously unaware. Michelle and the counselor continue to cycle through describing her experiences (investigating lifestyle) and uncovering her unconscious (gaining insight) to help her become more aware of how she functions in daily life. Through this process, Michelle and the counselor also consider how her life patterns influence the greater world (social interest). The counselor also challenges Michelle to consider what mistaken goals she may be meeting by attending only to her historic "failures" rather than seeing herself in a more balanced and realistic way.

Reorientation is the final phase of Adlerian counseling. Unlike some other theorists, Adler (1956/1964) believed that insight alone is not an indicator of successful counseling. Action and change, or the intentional decision not to make change, are preemptive to successful termination. In this phase, the counselor may educate the client on specific skills or concepts, or clients may demonstrate or report changes they have practiced outside of sessions. One way Michelle might demonstrate her change is by going on a date set up by a friend. She might also make a list of examples of occasions when she succeeded. The counselor may choose to educate Michelle about Adlerian concepts of goals of misbehavior and personality priorities. Teaching Michelle about particular Adlerian concepts may help her make lasting change that she can apply throughout her life.

In the spirit of Adlerian theory, let's take action! Exercise 5.3 is designed to help you practice identifying lifestyle concepts—including mistaken beliefs, feelings of inferiority, social interest, birth order, and family of origin—and applying the Adlerian phases of counseling. You may wish to collaborate with colleagues to brainstorm your responses to the different Adlerian concepts. As you complete this activity, notice in what ways you agree and disagree with your peers. What might that indicate about understanding another person's lifestyle? How can that knowledge guide your practice?

EXERCISE 5.3

Directions: Think about a character from your favorite television show/movie that you believe you know fairly well, and then answer the following questions.

Investigating the lifestyle: What data have you collected about this character? How would you describe his or her lifestyle?

Gaining insight: What might be some effective ways to help this character gain insight into his or her lifestyle? (Note: Specific Adlerian interventions are discussed in the next section.)

Reorientation: Assume the character chooses to make changes in his or her life. What would be evidence that this person has successfully completed counseling? What, if anything, might you need to provide the client to assist in the change process?

Interventions

Catching Oneself

One technique used in the reorientation phase is catching oneself. This insight into behavior patterns can help clarify goals of behaviors that the client wants to change (Mosak & Maniacci, 2008). The purpose of this technique is to gradually learn to predict one's responses by gaining insight into the intended purpose of the behavior. Consistent with Adlerian concepts, by understanding the usefulness of one's behavior, one can choose to change it (Adler, 1931). Michelle might be instructed to monitor when she considers herself not good enough. Becoming aware of the frequency and circumstances surrounding her feelings of inferiority is meant to help her be intentional about making different choices. Michelle can also be challenged to consider what mistaken goals continue to be perpetuated through viewing herself as not good enough.

Early Childhood Recollections

The events in the memories are not important; rather, the meanings associated with the memories are important. Adlerian theorists are interested in the memories people keep. Because the lifestyle is developed in childhood, Adlerians are particularly interested in those memories of events that happened prior to 8 or 9 years old (Mosak & Maniacci, 1999). The details in the memories provide a window into patterns of beliefs the person holds. For example, a person who remembers the look of fear on his father's face as his mother belittled his father in public may have created the belief, "I must never let a woman control me," in an effort to reach his fictional goal, "I must be strong and powerful to avoid humiliation and ensure love." This intervention is commonly used during the investigation or insight phase of counseling. Michelle could be instructed to describe an early childhood memory of a time when she felt in competition with her older sister. The counselor would explore Michelle's perceptions and beliefs about this event. Through discussion with the counselor, Michelle would recognize patterns of her feelings, thoughts, and behaviors. Exercise 5.4 can help you explore your own early childhood recollections.

EXERCISE 5.4

Directions: Think back to your earliest memories. Typically, these are memories of events prior to age 5. Discuss with a partner two of your earliest memories. Share them in present tense, as if they are happening now. As you discuss these memories, include the details you remember, such as what you see, who was there, how you felt, and what you were thinking. *Note: The accuracy of the memory is not as important as the perception of the experience.*

Example: I am 5 years old. My mother and father left to pick up my younger brother from a friend's house. It is winter and snowing. I am all alone. My parents left me and didn't tell me where they were going. I overheard them talking on the phone, which is how I knew they were leaving. My parents forgot about me. I'm worried I'm never going to see them again. I am hungry and unable to cook. I find the cookies and start eating. I have eaten the whole package of cookies, and my stomach hurts. I don't feel so lonely when I eat. My parents and brother return 10 minutes later, but it feels like it's been 10 hours.

Next, make a list of the themes you notice occurring in both memories. How do these themes relate to your current functioning and lifestyle? How have you seen these patterns occur in other areas of your life? What might this indicate about your fictional goal?

Example: The world is unpredictable. The world is cold. Others leave me. Others cannot be trusted. I am alone. I am not significant. To belong and be safe, I must always be prepared to take care of myself.

Spitting in the Client's Soup

The purpose of this technique is to draw attention to the motives of certain socially useless behaviors. When clients gain conscious awareness of the goals of their misbehaviors, those behaviors become less useful and less attractive. The soup (behavior) becomes less tasty, reducing the likelihood of the client continuing to eat it (to behave in that manner; Stein, 1988). An example of this is a counselor saying to her client, "I wonder if you ignore your mother to get more attention from her." This technique is often used during the final phase of counseling to aid in overcoming maladaptive solutions. An example specifically for Michelle might be, "It may be that by believing you're not going to succeed, you've given yourself permission not to take risks and try new things."

The Question

"The question" seeks an answer to what would be different in the client's life if the identified problems no longer existed (Mosak & Maniacci, 1999). Clients respond to this question with answers to their own problems. The responses given can provide insight for a client as to what needs to change and/or how to make that happen. The therapist could ask, "How would your life be different if you didn't have this problem?"

Acting as If

"Acting as if" is often used in conjunction with "the question." When a client identifies how situations or behaviors might be improved to help his or her functioning, the counselor can encourage the client to act *as if* it is currently happening. For example, a child who wants to get good grades but believes he is not smart enough might be telling himself, "If only I were smart enough, I would get good grades." The counselor would encourage this child to act *as if* he is smart enough for the time between sessions. This allows for the client to take a positive approach in improving his perceptions of the situation. During the next session, the counselor will explore the client's interpretation of the experience. The underlying belief here is that when the client acts *as if* goals are being met, the client will perceive the situation differently and in turn change his or her behavior (Mosak & Maniacci, 2008). Michelle might be instructed to act *as if* she is the best, competent, and successful.

Dream Analysis

Counselors who subscribe to various theoretical orientations use dream analysis to assist the client in meeting his or her goal. Adlerian theorists consider dreams to be a person's attempt to solve problems (Mosak & Maniacci, 2008). Investigating dreams can assist the client in (a) gaining information about his or her style of life and (b) creating or practicing a solution to a problem. Remembering a dream may indicate readiness to take action, forgetting a dream may forecast postponement of solving a problem, and nightmares may be an indication of the direct intention to avoid something. Consistent with all Adler's teaching, dreams must be interpreted through the unique lifestyle of the client (Adler, 1927/1998). Counselors cannot understand the meaning and usefulness of the dream without understanding the dreamer.

Paradoxical Intention

Paradoxical intention is, in essence, prescribing the symptom. This technique is effective because the client's resistance is *met* rather than *opposed;* thus, the relationship is strengthened. Meeting the resistance also renders the behavior less attractive to the client. Furthermore, it allows the client to achieve a level of insight into the problem and encourages acceptance of responsibility for identified behaviors. The counselor might ask Michelle to keep a daily log for a week. She would track every time she does not succeed, is not chosen, or is second best. She might also be asked to consider it a success when she doesn't meet her own standards, for that is an indication she has the courage to face potential failure.

Task Setting

Although not unique to individual psychology, task setting is an intervention routinely used by Adlerian counselors (Sweeney, 2009). Homework assignments such as taking small steps to a larger goal, measuring one's progress, or applying skills learned in sessions to daily life situations are all examples of homework assignments. Counselors are creative when developing assignments. Assignments should meet the unique needs and desirable outcomes of clients; including clients in this process is an important part of providing encouragement. Follow-up at subsequent sessions is another important part of task setting. An example of task setting for a client who wants to lose weight and improve health is to direct the client to go on a walk at least three times in the next week. Follow-up sessions would include discussions about successes, failures, and beliefs about the experience. A task for Michelle might be to edit her résumé to apply for a promotion or different job, or to strike up conversations with a half dozen strangers during the week, with the intent to smile, be encouraging, and be supportive.

Consequences

The concept of consequences as an educational process is a focus of Adlerian theory. Adler described two types of consequences: *natural* and *logical* (Sweeney, 1989). Natural consequences occur spontaneously in one's environment without being forced by another person. People experience the natural consequences of actions regardless of their positions in society. For example, the natural consequence of not brushing one's teeth is poor oral health, which may include mouth pain, rotten teeth and gums, or need for frequent dental care. Logical consequences require intervention from another person, and the consequence is deemed to follow the behavior logically. Thus, social standing, morals, and laws will influence the responding logical consequence. An example of a logical consequence may be that a person who does not regularly attend work is fired from his or her job.

Modeling

Adlerians represent themselves as genuine, friendly, honest, and courageous enough to make mistakes (Mosak, & Maniacci, 2008). The interaction between the client and counselor is not an applied technique; rather, it is a consistent and real demonstration of social interest. To the client, the counselor constitutes what is *healthy* and *normal*. Therefore, modeling occurs throughout the counseling process. The counselor might be intentional about making mistakes and not being perfect. Through this modeling of imperfection, Michelle might recognize that the counselor can be successful and valued even when he or she is not perfect.

Y-CHUN THROUGH THE LENS OF ADLERIAN THEORY

As discussed previously, Adlerian counselors work within four phases of the counseling process: *building a collaborative relationship, investigating the lifestyle, gaining insight,* and *reorientation*. Next, each of these phases will be applied to the counselor's work with Y-Chun.

Building a Collaborative Relationship

Y-Chun came to counseling at her doctor's suggestion and began to share some important information, including physical symptoms, current level of functioning, the quality of her relationships with family members and others, childhood memories, level of suicidal/homicidal threat, and perceptions about herself and others. This information comes at a rapid-fire rate and denotes Y-Chun's desperation and desire to understand herself better (i.e., "I don't want to be this way for the rest of my life"). The counselor is patient and supportive in facilitating the flow of information in the session and gently prompts Y-Chun in areas related to assessing early recollections, sibling constellation, and style of life, which are foundational to the Adlerian approach. The counselor does not become overwhelmed with the information but remains intentional about building an egalitarian relationship with the client through empathy and basic relationship-building skills, allowing Y-Chun to feel that she is being supported and validated in her concerns and that her experiences are important ("I just want to thank you for listening and being here for me"). In this manner, the counselor models encouragement, or the instillation of courage within Y-Chun that allows for a corrective emotional experience, such that she feels understood in a way she has never before experienced in her social interactions. The manifestation of these skills and the counselor's compassionate attitude are essential to deepening trust in the therapeutic relationship. One of the most powerful concepts in Adlerian theory is encouragement, and there is nothing more encouraging than for a client in distress to learn how to trust a gifted counselor and for a counselor to model risk taking, vulnerability, and a desire to change and grow.

Investigating the Lifestyle

As previously noted, relationship building is an ongoing process throughout counseling, and the Adlerian counselor remains vigilant to continue an encouraging attitude. An outgrowth of the therapeutic relationship is the counselor assessing the client's style of life. One important approach in this assessment is tapping into early recollections. Sweeney, Myers, and Stephan (2006) noted the importance of helping clients locate early recollections on a sensorimotor level (the physical location of the emotional response) to describe connections between events (sequence and causality) through a "concrete operational style" (p. 255); to move toward formal operation, which permits clients to analyze, synthesize, and gain awareness of important connections between life events; and, finally, to develop a dialectic style of introspection, which "permits one to *empathize, understand, and analyze differing points of view,* their origin, and relative merits" (p. 256). This intentional focus on the part of the counselor parallels a developmental process that helps clients maximize past experiences in developing insight into present functioning. An important part of this insight is the ability to reconcile differences between the subjective experiences in childhood; the beliefs about self, others, and the world; and how these beliefs impact present functioning.

Y-Chun discusses her experience of not having a "normal relationship" with her parents and often feeling lonely and unwanted by them. She notes that she would often get in trouble just to be noticed by her parents, which is consistent with the concept of "goals of misbehavior" (Dreikurs, 1953) in seeking attention. It is apparent that Y-Chun has engaged in a series of dangerous and self-destructive behaviors (i.e., fighting, promiscuity, shoplifting, etc.) that emerge from her style of life and mistaken beliefs about herself and that continue to plague her life and interrupt important social relationships. The counselor could help leverage insight by focusing on early recollections and what they mean to Y-Chun, not just on reporting memories of her past. The counselor may say, "I'm wondering if you think there is any connection between these early experiences and your current situation." Helping Y-Chun report her early recollection as if it is occurring in that moment could heighten her awareness of what mistaken beliefs she carries with her. For example, she may believe the following: "I am not really wanted by anyone, and I don't really belong"; "My worth is what I can offer men sexually"; or "I am loved by my parents only if I am smart, succeed in school, and have a successful career." The counselor can also ask Y-Chun to recount the memory as a series of sequential events having causality, and then paraphrase and summarize the memory for accuracy.

The counselor could ask what the memory or the series of events means to Y-Chun and what decisions she has made about herself, others, and the world as a result. A great example of this occurs when Y-Chun makes the following confession about her children. "I just feel empty . . . distant . . . like they are plants and I just water them. I know that sounds horrible, but that's how it feels." One interpretation of this statement could be that Y-Chun feels toward her own children much the way she believes her parents felt toward her—that she was an inconvenience and a burden. An important step is helping the client articulate what rules she has learned to live by as a result of her childhood, identify her goal, and assess how well her rules are helping her meet her goal. This process helps empower the client to make decisions about how to shape the rules she has lived by (Kern, Belangee, & Eckstein, 2004).

Finally, it is important for counselors to consider how to structure the lifestyle assessment. The assessment may range from an informal one, much like the initial interaction between Y-Chun and her counselor, or a more formal paper–pencil or computer-based assessment. Kaplan (1985) suggested a set of 10 questions that can guide such an assessment. The questions are for the counselor as well as the client to consider as the client shares early recollections:

- Who is present in the recollection?
- Who is remembered with affection?
- Who is disliked in the recollection?

- What problem(s) is (are) confronted in the recollection?
- What special talent(s) or ability is (are) revealed in the recollection?
- Is the recollection generally pleasant or unpleasant?
- What is the client's level of activity in the recollection?
- What emotion does the client feel and/or show pertaining to the recollection?
- What does the recollection suggest to you about the client's social interest?
- What fictional goal(s) is (are) implied in the recollection? (pp. 526–527)

These guiding questions help frame the sharing of the experience and assist the counselor in developing some tentative interpretations she or he can share with the client to help gain insight.

Gaining Insight

Like relationship building, the development of insight is a byproduct of all therapeutic tasks and actions taken by the counselor. Through assessment, interpretation of experience, and education, clients can gain insights into themselves that will promote stronger and more intentional decision making. Another important issue the counselor begins to touch on with Y-Chun is birth order and the quality of relationships among siblings. It is not clear at this point whether Y-Chun grew up with her siblings or whether there was shared physical custody with former spouses, but one thing is apparent: the real or perceived resentment from the older siblings toward the youngest. The paternal son is 3 years older, and the maternal children are 6 (son) and 5 (daughter) years older. That Y-Chun is the youngest and the biological daughter of both parents creates an interesting and troubling dynamic, as Y-Chun is viewed as favored (and possibly pampered) by the parents and is thus teased by her older siblings. It is also important for Y-Chun's counselor to assess Y-Chun's view of herself as a biracial woman and her subjective experience of being teased by classmates and marginalized by her siblings. What racial identity does Y-Chun accept for herself? To what degree does she still feel ambivalent about who she is, and how does that impact her? Educating Y-Chun about family constellation and birth order may prove efficacious in assessing and treating her to develop insight and make tentative assumptions about her style of life and how it has influenced her present functioning. A secondary benefit is that Y-Chun might identify with positive characteristics that would trigger possibilities she had never considered.

An important area for assessment and education is Y-Chun's rape. This event is powerful and complex and accompanied by the shame she has carried throughout her life, as well as her anger and sense of betrayal from not being protected by her parents. The connection between the rape and her current sexual relationships may be clear, but normalizing this trauma through educating Y-Chun about risk factors for abuse survivors, reactions to rape, and assessment for symptoms of posttraumatic stress disorder is an important process in gaining insight. How does Y-Chun view her own vulnerability? How might her sense of helplessness be reflected in the helplessness and vulnerability of her special needs daughter? Where might Y-Chun be stuck, and where might this impasse have occurred? What is her mistaken goal, and how has she gone about achieving it? From the information gathered so far, it appears that Y-Chun has restricted her own social influence, wherein she feels she has no one to turn to and nothing much to offer.

Reorientation

In subsequent sessions, the counselor can continue to assist and support Y-Chun in building insight and examining her assumptions about herself in the context of her personal history. *Reorientation* builds on the therapeutic gains made in previous phases and allows for the client to engage in a change process that is both risky and empowering. Often, clients who are discouraged are restrictive in their social interactions and limit their risk. They see themselves as having nothing to offer and don't feel permitted to ask much of others. An important therapeutic task would be for the counselor to help Y-Chun explore areas of her life where she has felt afraid to engage, such as being a good parent to her children, negotiating her adult relationship with her parents, and learning how to choose partners who will be positive and supportive. Reframing "failures" is an important skill to help clients continue to try on new behaviors.

Helping Y-Chun prepare to talk with her parents and choose which aspects of her life she will share with them, become an effective and loving parent to her children, and contribute meaningfully to other relationships will foster a sense of social interest that will ultimately help decrease her felt sense of isolation and contribute to the social interest of her family, friends, and society. This tentative but attainable position will help Y-Chun view her present and past more realistically and help strengthen her ability to take charge and make decisions rather than be a perpetual victim of her past. A strong therapeutic relationship allows for courage to take action; understanding the past as framed within a lifestyle helps clients anticipate how they may likely respond when discouraged; gaining insight into the past and present ways of functioning helps clients anticipate how they may get in their own way in their efforts to change. Finally, reorientation allows clients to put into practice what they learn and experience much more control and self-efficacy in their relationships.

KEYSTONES

- Adler believed that humans exercise control over their behavior, having "will" and goal orientation—in contrast to the psychoanalytic conceptualization of determinism.
- Modern-day Adlerians continue to incorporate into their work Adler's philosophy that humans continuously grow and develop while adapting to societal changes that allow clinicians an opportunity for greater understanding of the human condition.
- Early Adlerian theory expressed some postmodern views. The conceptualization of the sex task is one such example, engaging an almost feminist conceptualization of homosexuality since modernized by contemporary Adlerians to reflect current understanding.
- Adlerian theory was one of the first counseling orientations to consider, and support, the importance of school systems, professional identity, and workforce treatment. School-based programs and employee assistance programs are just two examples of continuing efforts with Adlerian roots.
- Inferiority versus superiority is a core concept that encourages the Adlerian clinician to consider an individual's motivation to understand how he or she fits in the larger societal context and move toward personal growth and social affiliation.

- Style of life is a salient tenet of Adlerian theory that describes a valence-free self-perception that influences emotional reactions, thoughts, and behaviors.
- Adlerian theorists believe all behavior to be *purposeful* and useful for providing insight into a person's goals and needs.
- Among the concepts embraced by contemporary Adlerians is *fictional finalism*. This concept, along with the *subjective perception of reality*, describes an imaginary goal held by all people that is based on their understanding of "how the world *should* be" and thus influences their beliefs, behaviors, and feelings.
- *Birth order* is a prominent principle in Adlerian theory that is not based on the sequential birth chronology of a child as much as on role perceptions, treatment, and a sense of importance within the family.
- Adlerian theory identifies three important life tasks that symbolize the human needs to preserve life, further life, and further one's environment: the task of love, the task of community, and the task of work.
- Known for its support of equality and equity of all humans, Adlerian theory strongly advocates reducing social hierarchies and providing support for marginalized and oppressed groups and individuals.
- Specific techniques are involved in Adlerian work, including insight-oriented interventions such as those in which a counselor encourages the client to recollect childhood experiences, calls attention to socially useless behavior, models constructive behavior, sets goals, and assigns tasks.
- One of the ultimate goals of Adlerian theory is for the client to gain insight into his or her concerns and style of life. Adlerian therapists work to *build a collaborative relationship* with clients, *investigate the style of life,* and *gain insight,* while helping *reorient* the client toward therapeutic gains made in the previous work that are both risky and empowering.

REFLECTIONS FROM THE CONTRIBUTOR'S CHAIR

Robyn L. Trippany-Simmons

One of the most important beliefs I hold for clients is that, like Dorothy with her red slippers in *The Wizard of Oz*, they have everything they need to "get back home." As an Adlerian counselor, recognizing the power in Dorothy's red slippers is akin to clients discovering they have the ability within themselves (and have all the while) to reorient their style of life. This positive and encouraging method of helping others aligns with who I am as a person and a professional.

Matthew R. Buckley

Adlerian theory has informed my counseling practice in a variety of ways and is essential to my identity as a professional counselor. I am continually assessing how the past impacts the present through facilitating clients' sharing of early recollections. This practice is not an invitation for a client to remain a victim of the past or for a counselor to reinforce help-lessness but, rather, an opportunity to understand how growing up influences the choices we make. I believe that a significant step for clients is to say out loud their awareness of what life is (present), what it was (past), and what decisions they have made about them-selves, others, and the world. Clients can begin to draw their own conclusions about their decisions and be encouraged to make different ones if the results of their behaviors, beliefs, or attitudes are not satisfactory.

I work to encourage (and thus empower) my clients to take responsibility for their choices and to see themselves as agents of change for the benefit of others around them. I believe that at the heart of most problems and distress is the belief, "I have nothing to offer anyone in my life," which relates directly to the concept of social inter-est. In the relationships I establish with my clients, I actively attack and help my clients attack the belief that they have nothing to offer anyone. Helping clients take a break from themselves and actively serve others in some small way is therapeutic and can have powerful results. I have witnessed life-changing behaviors in the lives of those who resolved to step outside of their own suffering and make a difference in another's life.

Kristin Meany-Walen

As a counselor-in-training, I struggled to identify with a theory that most closely aligned with my beliefs about people—how people developed and changed. I knew from my first theories course that I valued much of what Adler said about people, communities, and the world. Throughout my early professional career and training, I intentionally sought to explore all theories. I found myself back at Adler time and time again.

For me, Adlerian theory was a natural fit. It confirmed much of what I already believed about people and stretched me to consider new ideas about human experi-ences. In all my helping relationships, I work from an Adlerian perspective. As a profes-sional counselor, supervisor, teacher, leader, and mentor, I apply the foundational tenants of Adlerian theory.

Tiffany Rush-Wilson

My clinical work is with clients who have eating disorders. As a consequence, many of them indicate having difficulty in their interpersonal relationships. These difficulties are often related to an expressed inability to interact socially with others, feelings of inade-quacy in their personal relationships, and not being able to navigate feelings of inferiority. Adlerian counseling principles allow for incorporation of several key factors into client treatment planning and delivery. The beauty of this modality is that it allows for the acknowledgment of how important social roles, as well as defining one's own place and purpose, can be for clients. That this modality encourages an understanding of the whole person—his or her concept of self, worth, goals, and what has been useful in his or her journey to alleviate pain—has proven quite useful.

ADDITIONAL RESOURCES

Print

Bettner, B. L., & Lew, A. (2005). *Raising kids who can.* Newton Centre, MA: Connexions.

Carlson, J., Watts, R. E., & Maniacci, M. (Eds.). (2006). *Adlerian therapy: Theory and practice.* Washington, DC: American Psychological Association.

Kottman, T. (1997). Adlerian play therapy. In K. J. O'Connor & L. M. Braverman (Eds.), *Play therapy theory and practice: A comparative presentation* (pp. 310–340). New York: John Wiley.

Kottman, T. (2009). *Treatment manual for Adlerian play therapy.* Unpublished manuscript.

Kottman, T. (2011). *Play therapy: Basics and beyond.* Alexandria, VA: American Counseling Association.

Kottman, T., Bryant, J., Alexander, J., & Kroger, S. (2009). Partners in the schools: Adlerian school counseling. In A. Vernon & T. Kottman (Eds.), *Counseling theories: Practical application with children and adolescents in school settings.* (pp. 47–84). Denver, CO: Love.

Muro, J. J., & Kottman, T. (1995). *Guidance and counseling in the elementary and middle schools.* Dubuque, IA: Brown & Benchmark.

Yura, M., & Galassi, M. (1974). Adlerian usage of children's play. *Journal of Individual Psychology, 30,* 194–201.

Websites

Adler Centre: http://www.adlercentre.ca/casc.html

Adler Graduate School: http://www.alfredadler.edu/about/theory/international-associations

North American Society of Adlerian Psychology: http://www.alfredadler.org/

REFERENCES

Adler, A. (1929). *Practice and theory of individual psychology* (Rev. ed.). London: Lund Humphries.

Adler, A. (1931). *What life should mean to you.* Boston: Little, Brown.

Adler, A. (1964). *The individual psychology of Alfred Adler: A systemic presentation in selections from his writings* (H. L. Ansbacher & R. R. Ansbacher, Eds.). New York: Harper Perennial. (Original work published in 1956)

Adler, A. (1998). *Understanding human nature.* Oxford, UK: Oneworld Oxford. (Original work published in 1927)

Allers, R. (1933). *New psychologies.* London: Sheed & Ward.

Ansbacher, H. L. (1990). Alfred Adler, pioneer in prevention of mental disorders. *Journal of Primary Prevention, 11*(1), 37–68.

Ashby, J. S., & Kottman, T. (1996). Inferiority as a distinction between normal and neurotic perfectionism. *Individual Psychology, 53,* 237–245.

Aslinia, S. D., Rasheed, M., & Simpson, C. (2011). Individual psychology (Adlerian) applied to international collectivist cultures: Compatibility, effectiveness, and impact. *Journal for International Counselor Education, 3,* 1–12.

Belangee, S. E. (2007). Couples and eating disorders: An individual psychology approach. *Journal of Individual Psychology, 63,* 294–305.

Bitter, J. R. (1997). *Counseling individuals: An Adlerian therapy model.* Paper presented at the meeting of the American Counseling Association Pre-Conference Workshop, Orlando, FL.

Dinkmeyer, D. C., Dinkmeyer, D. C., Jr., & Sperry, L. (1987). *Adlerian counseling and psychotherapy* (2nd ed.). Columbus, OH: Merrill.

Dreikurs, R. (1953). *Fundamentals of individual psychology.* Chicago: Alfred Adler Institute.

Dreikurs, R. (1964). *Children: The challenge.* New York: E. P. Dutton.

Ferguson, E. D. (2011). What Adlerians consider important for communication and decision making in the workplace: Mutual respect and democratic leadership style. *Journal of Individual Psychology, 67,* 432–437.

Kaplan, H. B. (1985). A method for the interpretation of early recollections and dreams. *Individual Psychology: Journal of Adlerian Theory, Research & Practice, 41*(4), 525–533.

Kern, R. M., Belangee, S. E., & Eckstein, D. (2004). Early recollections: A guide for practitioners. *Journal of Individual Psychology, 60*(2), 132–140.

Kottman, T. (2001). Adlerian play therapy. *International Journal of Play Therapy, 10*(2), 1–12.

Kottman, T. (2003). *Partners in play* (2nd ed.). Alexandria, VA: American Counseling Association.

Leman, K. (2004). *The birth order book: Why you are the way you are.* Grand Rapids, MI: Baker Books.

Mosak, H. (2005). Adlerian psychotherapy. In R. J. Corsini & D. Wedding (Eds.), *Current psychotherapies* (7th ed.). Belmont, CA: Brooks/Cole.

Mosak, H., & Maniacci, M. (1999). *Primer of Adlerian psychology: The analytic-behavioral-cognitive psychology of Alfred Adler.* New York: Brunner-Routledge.

Mosak, H. H., & Maniacci, M. (2008). Adlerian psychotherapy. In R. J. Corsini & D. Wedding (Eds.), *Current psychotherapies* (8th ed., pp. 63–106). Belmont, CA: Thomson Brooks/Cole.

Muro, J. J., & Dinkmeyer, D. C. (1977). *Counseling in the elementary and middle schools: A pragmatic approach.* Dubuque, IA: W. C. Brown.

Nelsen, J., Lott, L., & Glenn, H. S. (2000). *Positive discipline in the classroom.* Roseville, CA: Prima.

Peluso, P. R., & MacIntosh, H. (2007). Emotionally focused couples therapy and individual psychology: A dialogue across theories. *Journal of Individual Psychology, 63,* 247–269.

Rattner, J. (1983). *Alfred Adler.* New York: Frederick Ungar.

Shifron, R., & Reysen, R. R. (2011). Workaholism: Addiction to work. *Journal of Individual Psychology, 67,* 364–379.

Starr, A. (1973). Sociometry of the family. In H. H. Mosak (Ed.), *Alfred Adler: His influence on psychology today* (pp. 95–105). Park Ridge, NJ: Noyes.

Stein, H. T. (1988). Twelve stages of Adlerian psychotherapy. *Individual Psychology, 44,* 138–143.

Sweeney, T. J. (2009). *Adlerian counseling and psychotherapy: A practitioner's approach* (5th ed.). New York: Taylor & Francis.

Sweeney, T. J., Myers, J. E., & Stephan, J. B. (2006). Integrating developmental counseling and therapy assessment with Adlerian early recollections. *Journal of Individual Psychology, 62*(3), 251–269.

Tedrick, S. J., & Wachter-Morris, C. A. (2011). Integrating crisis theory and individual psychology: An application and case study. *Journal of Individual Psychology, 67*(4), 364–379.

Existential Counseling and Psychotherapy

Mark B. Scholl, Michael Walsh, and Michelle Perepiczka

Man can find meaning in any existence, however meager.

Existential psychotherapy and counseling is concerned with helping clients find meaning in their own existence, whatever that existence may be. Based fundamentally on the philosophy that man's ultimate responsibility is to make meaning of his existence, existential counseling has, at its roots, the belief that the act of finding meaning in existence is the ultimate expression of man's freedom. A practitioner working with an existential approach will help clients examine their own unique reality and experience and, from that experience, develop a meaning that is unique to the individual. In this way, existential counseling fits with many of the more humanistic counseling approaches. Its focus on individual experience and individual meaning encourages clients to empower themselves through their own interpretation of existence.

As you proceed through the chapter, you will discover that "existentialism is an attitude, an approach to human beings, rather than a special school or group" (May, 1962, p. 185). More specifically, after completing this chapter, you will be able to do the following:

1. Describe the philosophical roots of existential theory and how those roots extend through the counseling process

2. Explain the ways an existential approach to counseling and psychotherapy may be potentially helpful to a client

3. Identify clients that may benefit from an existential approach

4. Identify techniques consistent with an existential approach

5. Determine whether an existential approach is consistent with your own professional and personal worldview

PROFILE OF MAIN FIGURES

Victor Frankl (1905–1997)

Born in Austria and trained as a neurologist and physician, Victor Frankl studied with and was a contemporary of both Sigmund Freud and Alfred Adler. Frankl, his parents, and his wife were imprisoned by the Nazis in a series of concentration camps during World War II. Frankl's parents and wife were killed there. Frankl survived and wrote of his experiences in *Man's Search for Meaning* (1946). He went on to develop *logotherapy*, an approach to counseling and therapy based on freedom of will, will to meaning, and meaning in life. In essence, Frankl argued that man can find meaning in any existence, however meager, and that humans remain free to make and interpret that meaning. It is through this process that one achieves true freedom.

Rollo May (1909–1994)

Born in Ada, Ohio, Rollo May had a difficult childhood. He attended Oberlin College and later, during a time working as an artist in England, studied with Adler. He continued his learning at Union Theological Seminary, studying under the existentialist theologian Paul Tillich. After graduating from seminary, May contracted tuberculosis and spent 3 years in a sanatorium. During this time, facing the very real possibility of his own death, he began to read of philosophers such as Søren Kierkegaard, who influenced his thinking and formed the basis for his approach to therapy.

May approached existentialism in a way that incorporated many of the American concepts of humanism. He argued that a central concept of the human condition is *intentionality*. Similar, in some ways, to Frankl's freedom of will, May asserted that every reaction to an external pressure is a matter of choice. Anxiety, according to May, is not something to be overcome; rather, it can be channeled and used productively to move forward. May's approach to counseling is more than just a matter of technique. According to May, a key concept of existential counseling is being present and authentic with the individual.

INTRODUCTION

Foundation as a Philosophy

Existential counseling approaches are based on a philosophical movement called existentialism. A response to some of the more deterministic philosophies of the late 1800s and early 1900s, this philosophy focused on individual freedom—specifically, each individual's right and responsibility to make meaning of his or her life.

First described in Søren Kierkegaard's (1813–1855) label "existential thinker," an existentialist is one who seeks to understand the meaning of his or her existence through the lens of personal experience. As Kierkegaard put it, this meaning is "an objective uncertainty held fast in the most passionate personal experience . . . the highest truth attainable for an existing individual" (quoted in Kaufmann, 1956, p. 123).

Existentialism can perhaps best be understood in *contrast* to several other philosophies that dominated thinking in the 18th and 19th centuries. Kaufmann (1956) wrote: "Existentialism is not a philosophy but a label for several widely different revolts against traditional philosophy" (p. 11). Dominant philosophies such as *rationalism* (Hegel, 1730–1831) and *positivism* (Comte, 1798–1857) stressed "objective truth." One of the fundamental assumptions and tenets of these philosophies was that there are objective and "provable" truths in our existence and that such "truth" is immutable and intractable. Positivism holds that, for something to "exist," it must be measurable and observable. Rationalism holds that, for something to "exist," it must be understandable through common "ways of knowing," such as mathematics, ethics, or logic. In the historical context of the 18th and 19th centuries, if things didn't meet these two tests, they were unlikely to be accepted as "true." Such philosophical constructs formed the basis for modern scientific thinking, ushering in an age of orientation toward the notion that certain universal and provable realities exist. In this positivist- and rationalist-influenced worldview, the only things that really "exist" are things we can measure or observe directly. Further, those things are limited to that which we can presently understand. A rationalist or positivist may argue that anything beyond those limits doesn't really exist.

In response to—or some might say, in revolt against—these notions, Kierkegaard countered that not only was the idea of immutable truth somewhat suspect, but each individual who did the thinking for those philosophies (folks such as Hegel and Comte) was a living human being who must have, because of human nature, imbued those thoughts with some subjectivity. In other words, by Kierkegaard's reasoning, we all must view the world through the lens of our experience. He went on to argue that not only was this natural, but it is the responsibility of each individual to seek to understand the things in the world that are difficult to understand and/or that appear contradictory. Further, he argued, an essential part of being a human being is that we seek such understanding (Kaufmann, 1956).

Kierkegaard's writing influenced the thinking of several philosophers from a variety of backgrounds. We will note a select few of those key philosophical ideas in the chart that follows. For a more detailed exploration of Kierkegaard's influence on philosophers, see Kant's (1954) *Encyclopedia of Philosophy*.

Philosopher	Key Idea
Friedrich Nietzsche (1844–1900)	Human subjectivity and the vitality of the human experience of reality (Nietzsche, 1883–1885/2006).
Karl Jaspers (1883–1969)	Only through questioning one's own existence can one achieve limitless freedom (Jaspers, 1932/ 1969–1971).

(Continued)

(Continued)

Philosopher	Key Idea
Martin Heidegger (1889–1976)	The concept of "Dasein" or "there being." Only through "being there" in one's own context can one fully understand one's existence; that exploration should be done scientifically and systematically (Heidegger, 1927/1962).
Edmund Husserl (1859–1938)	Phenomenological approach. Life can be understood in terms of "phenomenology" (the things that happen in life—mentally, spiritually, and physically). Experience is the fundamental source of knowledge (Kochler, 1974).
Camus (1913–1960)	Human rights and individual freedom in the face of absurdity.
Jean Paul Sartre (1905–1980)	Elimination of the "illusion" of religion and God and an empirical examination of one's own existence (Sartre, 1962, p. 115).

Exercise 6.1 will help you more fully understand Heidegger's concept of Dasein, or "there being."

Existentialism as a philosophy, then, became associated with a phenomenological approach to existence—making meaning of our being by seeking to grapple with the contradictions and mysteries of what happens to us. This focus on making meaning of life becomes particularly important in the face of difficult or trying circumstances.

EXERCISE 6.1

BEING, OR DASEIN

The concept of being can seem rather abstract. It may sound like a philosophical debate about how we know a table truly exists if it is in the middle of the room. Just wrapping your mind around a notion like this can be a challenge, let alone learning how to apply it conceptually to a client.

Let's practice getting a handle on this concept first. Being, or Dasein, refers to being aware of where you are in the world, as of this moment, and where you are headed (Boss, 1963). To increase your awareness of your current state of being, ask yourself the following questions: (1) What am I thinking at this moment? (2) What am I doing? (3) What am I feeling? To become aware of your forward movement in the world, ask yourself these questions: (1) Where am I headed in life, or what are my goals for the next 5 years? (2) What must I do to get where I want to be?

Answering these questions can increase your insight into your own state of being and movement. You could ask yourself similar questions when trying to conceptualize a client's state of being. The concept is a tad easier to apply when you approach it from this angle.

This philosophical approach gained broader appeal as the early 20th century progressed. World War I and World War II hastened the development of the approach, with many people beginning to think about how to make sense of the devastation and death associated with war. Further, the Holocaust focused the world's attention on the potential for human cruelty and left many staring squarely at Jasper's despair or transcendence choice. It was in the context of this choice that a man named Victor Frankl developed a way of thinking that would eventually become most closely identified with existentialist thinking and, later, existential treatment approaches.

From a Philosophy to a Counseling Approach

Many within the counseling profession embrace existentialism as both a philosophy and an orienting frame of reference. This inclusion into our profession was spearheaded by the work of existentialists such as Frankl and May, whose approaches are described below.

Victor Frankl's Logotherapy

Logotherapy—from the Greek *logos*, for "meaning"—seeks to aid clients in building their own meaning within their own context. The development of Frankl's approach dates back to the 1930s. While working in Steinhof Hospital, Frankl built on what he had learned of Freud's psychoanalysis and Adler's individual psychology and developed what he termed *logotherapy*. Logotherapy, or existential analysis, is sometimes called the "Third Viennese School of Psychotherapy" (the first being Freud's psychoanalysis, and the second being Adler's individual psychology).

Logotherapy is characterized by one prime assumption: The search for meaning in life is identified as the primary motivational force in human beings (Frankl, 1946). Logotherapy also embraces three fundamental philosophical and psychological concepts (Frankl, 1946):

Freedom of will—Humans are not bound to circumstance; rather, they are free to make psychological (internal) and biological and social (external) meaning of events. Humans have, in effect, the spiritual freedom to make meaning and actively shape their lives independent of outside circumstances.

Will to meaning—Not only are human beings free to make meaning, but failure to do so may result in frustration, meaninglessness, and emptiness. It is each person's goal and drive, then, to make meaning. The process of logotherapy makes the development of meaning-making skills a priority.

Meaning in life—Meaning is an objective reality of the individual, not just some construct of the therapist. Individuals must develop and perceive meaning for themselves. In this way, the logotherapist is but a guide to a potentially changing landscape of meaning within the individual. The therapist seeks to assist the client with the openness and flexibility that enables him or her to develop meaning in his or her own context.

Rollo May's Existential Therapy

May (1962) defined the existential counseling process as a series of client–therapist encounters in which the therapist attempts to help the client identify personal sources of meaning, develop a series of goals based on those sources of meaning, and then lead life according to those goals. May eschewed techniques in favor of authentic relationships and essential exchanges of meaning.

Like Frankl's, May's approach involves some core concepts.

Anxiety. May worked extensively with the idea of anxiety, publishing his first book, *The Meaning of Anxiety*, in 1950. He postulated that there are two different kinds of anxiety:

> *Normal anxiety:* This is proportional to the threat involved and is realistic. It does not involve repression or the unconscious use of defense mechanisms. If successfully handled, it can lead to growth and positive change.

> *Neurotic anxiety:* This is disproportionate to the situation (Horney, 1950; May, 1950/1996; Yalom, 1980). Neurotic anxiety can be paralyzing, can bring about dependency on others, and may result in avoidance of issues at hand. It is commonly managed unconsciously by the development of symptoms and defense mechanisms. A person may experience feelings of despair resulting from inauthentic living, failure to make choices, and avoidance of responsibility.

The therapist's job, then, is to help the client identify the type of anxiety experienced and attempt to make meaning of it and the appropriate approach. This often involves identifying the subjective factors associated with the made meaning and also determining the subjective interpretation patterns associated with coping. The distinction between normal and neurotic anxiety can be seen in Case Illustration 6.1.

CASE ILLUSTRATION 6.1

Evelyn

Evelyn is a 23-year-old journalist. As a young girl, Evelyn was deep, reflective, and sensitive. At the age of 4, her parents divorced. On the day her father moved out of the house, she asked him to take her with him. Under the influence of alcohol at the time, he reacted angrily. Evelyn was devastated and developed strong dependency needs.

In high school, she became a reporter for the school paper, with a normal desire to be liked and included by her peers. On some level, she was aware of her strong dependency needs, but she sought to overcome them through her writing. Evelyn wrote editorial pieces in which she criticized school practices, such as the lack of nutritional options on the lunch menu. Her views became more political in college, where she majored in journalism. Self-conscious regarding some of her controversial views, she submitted her editorials to the local paper anonymously; if her articles included a byline, she would publish them in the newspaper of a city a considerable distance away.

In her junior year, she became an avid student of the readings of Saint Thomas Aquinas, who advocated for the importance of taking responsibility and openly acknowledging one's moral beliefs. This philosophical foundation made her more resolute regarding the need to acknowledge publicly her true political and moral views. By the time she completed her bachelor's degree in journalism, she consistently included a byline on her editorials, no matter how controversial the views she expressed.

However, throughout her college years, she became extremely anxious whenever required to speak in her classes. A pattern developed in which some problem would arise on the day of a public-speaking assignment; frequently, this would take the form of a sudden illness. On a number of occasions, she managed to persuade the course professor to modify the assignment so she could either submit a written paper or deliver the oral presentation in front of a smaller audience. Today, she is employed as a journalist for a small-town paper, but she is terrified by the idea of speaking in front of an audience or, heaven forbid, working as a television journalist.

Questions for Consideration

1. Identify a *normal anxiety* Evelyn experienced, and explain why this anxiety is normal.

2. Identify a *neurotic anxiety* she experienced, and explain why this anxiety is neurotic.

3. Think about your own life and attempt to identify one example of a *normal anxiety* and one example of a *neurotic anxiety* you have experienced.

Freedom. The individual is free but always lives within the context of his or her world. Thus, freedom always involves social responsibility. Awareness and confronting of limits enhances freedom rather than detracting from it. Freedom involves personal responsibility; each person has access to it but must work to achieve it internally. The purpose of therapy is to set the client free to choose his or her reaction to any given stimuli.

Power and Innocence. Innocence can be pure and childlike, or it can be an active denial of awareness. The latter form is termed *pseudo-innocence*. The first is productive at certain stages; the latter can be maladaptive. An example of pseudo-innocence would be a diverse individual who suppresses awareness of discrimination and asserts that perpetrators have the best of intentions. This puts the individual at a decided disadvantage with regard to self-advocacy.

Power is always interpersonal. Five different power "potentials" are located in each person:

1. *The power "to be":* This form of power is always present and represents possibilities.

2. *The power of self-affirmation:* All people have a need to affirm their own significance.

3. *The power of self-assertion:* This takes the form of overt behaviors to gain recognition from others.

4. *The power of aggression:* This form of power occurs when self-assertion is deliberately blocked by others.

5. *The power of violence:* This occurs when the actions of others make significance more difficult to achieve.

Examples of these forms of power can be seen in Case Illustration 6.2.

CASE ILLUSTRATION 6.2

Michael

Michael is a 55-year-old executive living in the Washington, D.C., area. He is vice president of sales for a large computer corporation. Coming from a poor farming background but possessed of a strong character, Michael graduated from high school with a clear sense of his potential to become someone successful, wealthy, and important. In this aspect, he experienced what May termed "the power to be." Over a period of 36 years, he worked hard and rose through the ranks to become a vice president of international sales. Throughout this time, Michael enhanced his sense of his own worth; this process of working hard and advancing illustrates the "power of self-affirmation."

Although he attained the position of vice president, he missed the excitement of making new discoveries and the risk of venturing into unknown territory he had experienced early in his career. He received an invitation to assume the position of president for a small software company in Silicon Valley. He had been in the position of vice president at his current company for nearly a decade, and the move to become president of another company was an opportunity to exercise his "power of self-assertion." Yet he was torn between staying in his current, stable executive position and taking a risk by accepting a position with a less established, smaller company.

He called his older brother, Kirk, a successful small-business owner in their small hometown in Virginia. He told Kirk of the invitation and that he was excited and tempted to accept the offer. Kirk's response was loud and derisive. He told Michael that he would be a fool to leave his current position for such a risky venture. But Michael recognized this as a longstanding pattern. Growing up, Kirk had strong negative reactions whenever Michael received opportunities such as starting for the high school baseball team or becoming a member of the honor society. Once again, Kirk was attempting to use the "power of aggression" to block Michael's self-assertion and eventual success. On one occasion, when Michael had entered a model-car contest, Kirk deliberately broke the hood support rod on Michael's model, interfering with the judges' ability to view the car's engine. Perhaps as a result of Kirk's sabotage, Michael did not receive any recognition from the judges that day. This act is an example of Kirk's use of the "power of violence" to reduce Michael's feelings of significance.

Through insight into these experiences, Michael recognized that his brother was attempting to discourage him out of a sense of jealousy or sibling rivalry. This realization made Michael angry, and the anger energized him to become self-assertive. He accepted the position as president for the new company and resigned from his current position.

May's Stages. May identified stages people may go through over the course of their lives. According to May (1969), these stages are not discrete in terms of age, as people of any age may find themselves dealing in one stage or another. However, certain stages may be more important at various times of life (e.g., rebellion may be more important to a teenager than, say, innocence is to an adult). Here are the stages as May saw them:

1. *Innocence:* Present among infants and young kids, mostly. This is a "premoral" stage; no real "drive" or will, just survival.

2. *Rebellion:* The natural process of separating oneself from family (e.g., terrible twos, teenage separation and identity exploration).

3. *Ordinary:* Normal adult development. This person may have learned to be responsible but is bored and seeks shelter in conformity, traditional values, or perhaps rebellion again.

4. *Creativity:* The existential stage; this person is engaged in the process of becoming and self-actualizing.

Love and Will: The Daimonic. May (1969) also made the connection between love and will in the form of a series of coping mechanisms he called the daimonic. This he defined as the overriding strategy by which one copes with the world. This coping strategy is made up of individual desires called daimons. These desires are neither good nor bad, but each has the potential to "hijack" the whole if an individual is not paying attention and making the right choices. May felt that the choice to allow one daimon to take control may lead to destructive behaviors and damage to one's sense of self.

May saw a separation of love, will, and sex. He called the choice to love an act of will and an act of intentionality. May saw the performance of sex for sex's sake as a mere expression of desire—and not an adaptive one. This would be an example of allowing one daimon to "run the show" and take over. On the other hand, if an individual viewed sex as an act that should be practiced only for procreative purposes in the context of a happy marriage, then the daimon of will would be too strong. In May's view, the balanced interplay among the daimonic elements of love, will, and sex represents optimal health.

May believed that it was important for individuals to integrate love, will, and sex in their daily lives. He viewed the "free sex" of the 1960s, with its emphasis on pornography and sexual gratification without responsibility, as seriously detrimental to human development. Another regrettable aspect of free sex is that will or reason becomes detached from emotions. If individuals believe that sex without love is socially acceptable, then they may neglect to develop mature, meaningful relationships. The sexual revolution of the 1960s, in May's view, could be detrimental to more holistic human development and, unchecked by will or reason, harmful to the future of the human race. As May (1969) noted in the closing of *Love and Will*: "For every act of love and will—and in the long run they are both present in each genuine act—we mold ourselves and our world simultaneously. This is what it means to embrace the future" (p. 325). Authentic love of an intimate partner, in May's view, entails love, liking, sex, and unselfish devotion to the partner's welfare. Review Exercise 6.2 for additional information on how to apply these concepts.

EXERCISE 6.2

FIVE TYPES OF LOVE

May stated that there are five types of love. The first type, *sex*, entails lust and the release of tension. *Eros*, the second type, is described as applying to pleasurable and sensual experiences, and is procreative. *Philia* is defined as platonic love or liking of another human. *Agape* is unselfish and involves devotion to benefiting and contributing to the welfare of others. Finally, *authentic love* incorporates the other four types into a single whole.

1. For each of the five types of love, answer the following questions and prompts:

   - Identify times in your past when you experienced this form of love.
   - How significant is this type of love in your current life, and how significant would you like it to be in the future?
   - Write a personal reflective statement explaining the meaning of this type of love for you as a part of your life.

2. Write a statement detailing how you view the five types of love as interacting to contribute to a meaningful and fulfilling life.

3. If applicable, identify one or more of these types of love that you would like to intentionally nurture and make a more central aspect of your life. For each type you identify, specify one or two actions you are committed to performing to realize this developmental aim.

Areas of Development: Recent Trends in Existentialism

Other contemporaries of May's have been active in more recent years. There seems to be a trend in the existential world away from some of the "empirical" and evidence-based movements that rely on technique and toward a less defined, less static approach to clients. The following chart highlights the developers and key ideas associated with this trend. For a more detailed exploration, see Sharf (2011).

Developer	Key Idea/Trend
James Bugental (1915–2008)	Counseling relies too heavily on theories and not enough on lived experience of clients (Bugental, 2008; Bugental & Bracke, 1992).
Irving D. Yalom	Relationships, not techniques, are critical. Attention to the actual experience of another is therapeutic (Yalom, 1980).
Virginia Satir	Problems in family systems are derived from members adopting scripted roles rather than authentically communicating their here-and-now needs, wants, and feelings (Satir, 1983).

Developer	Key Idea/Trend
Richard S. Sharf	Existential approaches seem to have the strongest support in Europe, which is where many of the first philosophers associated with the concept originated (Sharf, 2011).
Raymond J. Corsini and Danny Wedding	Criticisms of existential approaches have argued that the approaches, by nature, are difficult to research, leading to a lack of empirical data (Corsini & Wedding, 2005, p. 291).
Barry E. Wolfe and Kirk J. Schneider	Existential approaches have been combined with approaches such as cognitive-behavioral therapy (Wolfe, 2008) and a number of others for maximum benefit (Schneider, 2008).

Professional Identity in Existentialism

Existential counseling involves a level of genuine interaction between the counselor and the client that can be daunting for some counselors. Practicing as an existential counselor typically requires a commitment to explore the same types of issues that one's clients are exploring. It also often means actively taking part in one's own process of existential struggle. This enables the counselor to get a feel for his or her process and also to experience the level of insight and personal growth we want for our clients. Counselors make different choices regarding level of self-disclosure; however, a key part of a genuine relationship is typically relating the story of one's own experience connected to a given issue or, perhaps more broadly, to the overall experience.

Accompanying another human being through his or her journey of discovery can be an emotionally intense experience, depending on the type of counseling and the issues being explored. Counselors often describe the process as, at once, energizing and incredibly draining.

Counselors considering adopting an existential approach should take the time to ask themselves several questions:

1. How comfortable am I with my own personal existential awareness?

2. How comfortable would I be with a client who is exploring existential questions with which I may be uneasy?

3. How comfortable am I with the concepts in Kierkegaard's, Frankl's, and May's work?

4. Can I live in that world with a client and help him or her navigate those issues?

5. Is this approach faithful to who I am as a person? Can I be authentic in using this approach?

The last question becomes critical as we bring this section to a close. A crucial part of any existential counseling relationship, as in many of the humanistic approaches, is the quality of the relationship established between the counselor and the client. That relationship is built fundamentally on trust, genuineness, and empathetic understanding. If the approach does not fit the counselor, then the relationship may be strained. This jeopardizes the client's ability to engage fully, as well as the counselor's ability to do the same. If the answers to the above questions make you want to learn more, we will continue with an overview of the approach, followed by an illustration of its application to the case of Y-Chun.

How Existentialism Differs

Existentialism is different from other theories in various ways. Groth (2000) stated that one difference involves the anticipatory nature of *being* within the theoretical philosophy with clients. Counselors believe clients have a level of awareness of what they are doing, who they are, and how their choices impact the future. This overlaps with Heidegger's view of clients, as he stated that they are motivated to seek out authentic experiences in life (Groth, 1997).

Groth's (2000) second differentiation between existential and other theories is recognition of the spiritual dimension of being or existing. Spirituality is intertwined with the philosophical perspectives in that believing in a spiritual power and having a commitment to life have positive influences in life experiences (Wong, 2010).

Groth's (2000) third differentiation involves the connection between existential philosophical views and personality, anxiety, and mood disorders. For instance, common existential concepts of maladaptation include the client being anxious, eccentric, erratic, and fearful, which can align with personality or anxiety disorders. Clients also feeling immobilized (i.e., depressed) or scattered (i.e., manic) in terms of how they view themselves within the world and making meaning with their lives, which may also overlap with mood disorders (Burston, 2003).

Strengths and Limitations

Every theory has strengths and limitations from a practitioner's standpoint. Some of these may come into play based on the population you are working with, the work setting, or other clinical issues. The clinician will need to determine for each individual client whether the strengths and limitations apply.

Strengths

Existential theory has numerous strengths in counseling. Bauman and Waldo (1998) wrote, "Existential theory is consistent with the defining features of mental health counseling" (p. 22). For instance, existentialism emphasizes a high level of well-being and functioning for clients and does not exclusively focus on pathology or its absence (Hershenson & Power, 1987). Existentialism also promotes the concept of wellness and living an authentic life (Miars, 2002).

A second strength of existential theory is that it is developmentally sensitive to life transitions (Guterman, 1996). Existentialism can address life transitions and crises occurring in individuals across the life span (Bauman & Waldo, 1998). Personal growth during different stages of life is conceptualized through ultimate life concerns, potential growth that can be obtained, and self-transcendence over time (Yalom, 1980).

A third strength is that existentialism values the client–counselor relationship (Frankl, 1963; May, 1961; Yalom, 1980) that focuses holistically on the client's thoughts, feelings, and behaviors as influenced by society and culture. In existential counseling, the therapist helps the client explore meaning, develop a richer sense of freedom and responsibility, consider alternatives, predict possible consequences, and pursue growth.

Limitations

The shortcomings of existentialism, some of which are presented here, are debated by philosophers and existential authors. First, the concept of self-transcending (Yalom, 1980) can be complicated by cultural influences such as oppression, racism, and discrimination. Also, some cultures may not offer room for particular freedoms or choices. If a therapist is not sensitive to these issues, then he or she may not truly understand the client's world experience and the forces the client may not be able to overcome. This could cause complications within the therapeutic relationship if the client feels misunderstood or if the treatment plan is not appropriate.

Second, numerous philosophies make up existentialism. Thus, it lacks a traditional theoretical orientation structure, specific direction for the therapist, and outlined techniques or steps for treatment planning. Also, practitioners may be unsure of how to balance client freedom and responsibility in the session, or of how directive to be. Because of this, consistency across practitioners is low. This makes it difficult to identify the empirical efficacy of this theoretical approach, as the treatment provided may significantly differ across various studies.

A third challenge is that existential therapy seems to be a cognitive-based approach that best fits those who have higher-level functioning skills. Therapists may find that clients who are young, lower functioning, or lacking in verbal skills will find existential therapy difficult to understand. The therapist would need to make accommodations to the delivery of the theory to match the needs of any of these three types of clients.

Ethical Considerations

From an ethical standpoint, an existential orientation entails a great deal of respect for the client's autonomy. A primary characteristic of this approach is recognition that each individual is capable and has a right to construct his or her own personal meaning in life. As a result, existential therapists are likely to acknowledge that the client is competent to co-construct meaningful counseling goals and is also competent to provide input regarding how to achieve those counseling goals. Also, it is important to bear in mind that existential therapists adopt a variety of techniques in the service of assisting clients in achieving personally meaningful goals. For example, a therapist might employ systematic desensitization to assist a client who feels that his or her life is constricted, and less meaningful, as a result of experienced anxiety. A difference is that existential therapists tend to employ techniques more spontaneously as the need arises and within the context of existential aims.

Further, the therapeutic goal of supporting individual meaning can also lend itself to culturally responsive practice. The mental health ideal of authentic living can be promoted within diverse cultural contexts. An existential model of culture, with implications for counseling practice, has been developed by Vontress and Epp (2001). Although discussion of this model is beyond the scope of the current chapter, readers are encouraged to read their chapter for a detailed explanation of how existential counseling practice can also have a multicultural emphasis.

Research Supporting Theoretical Constructs and Interventions

The quantitative research on existential constructs and interventions is more limited in the literature (Yalom, 1980) as compared with the theoretical, philosophical, and qualitative research literature. These latter approaches focusing on depth may grasp a clearer picture of the theory and how its related therapeutic approach impacts clients (Walsh & McElwain, 2002). Empirical research on existentialism may also be difficult for researchers to conduct without sacrificing the client's freedom and responsibility in the session, which might result in straying away from the rigors of a quasi-experimental design (Bohart, O'Hara, & Leitner, 1998).

Rennie (1994), Watson and Rennie (1994), and Bohart and Tallman (1996) published qualitative studies indicating that existential constructs and processes such as self-reflection, making decisions, and considering various courses of action and possible consequences all play a positive role in existential therapy. These constructs and processes provide a guide for problem solving that can be used in-session and integrated into the client's daily life after sessions terminate.

Other researchers theorized about the effective use of existential therapy in terms of intervention. For instance, Quinn (2010) outlined how to integrate existential therapy into counseling with primary school children. Quinn hypothesized that existential therapy could relieve student distress while increasing their freedom and personal responsibility. Kitano and LeVine (1987) posited similar hypotheses but added the element of helping children understand how the social and physical environment impacts their choices and process of self-transcendence.

Researchers also focused on existentialism with adults across the life span. For instance, Cashin (2004) completed a qualitative study on the use of existentialism to understand the experience of parents raising a child with autism. Cashin found that the existential foundations helped clarify what these parents were going through. Suri (2010) studied how existentialism can be used with the elderly. Suri explained how addressing themes related to this developmental stage with existential concepts such as being, spirituality, meaning, and self-transcending can be healing for this population. Further, Mascaro and Rosen (2008) examined how increasing client awareness regarding existential meaning and addressing existential distress (anxiety and guilt) can improve depressive symptoms for adult clients over time.

Evidence for the effectiveness of existential therapy in treating trauma in victims of sexual abuse is modest (Pitchford, 2009), and practitioners are cautioned that documented outcomes are inconsistent (Miller, 2012). Victims may suffer from *enhanced integration,* or overemphasis of the traumatic event as a part of their overall self-concept (Berntsen & Rubin, 2007). In some cases, these individuals gain psychological or spiritual benefits from the quest for a reintegrated self-concept that is expanded and devoid of the traumatic event (Bonanno, 2005; Feinauer, 2003; Tedeschi & Calhoun, 2004; Tedeschi & Kilmer, 2005).

Unfortunately, numerous cases of adult victims who were not able to achieve this integration have also been reported in the literature (Miller, 2012).

Use With Diverse Populations and Children

Various researchers have cited existentialism as an effective theoretical approach for diverse populations as well as children. A brief overview of the available literature in these areas is presented here, but the reader should know there is extensive research available to be explored in this area.

Diversity

Existentialism is interwoven with multicultural sensitivity, as it is based in various philosophical views that are all related to shared human experiences (Vontress, 1988), such as ultimate concerns of the human condition (Yalom, 1980), alienation (Holcomb-McCoy, 2004), and being (May, 1961). The wide net the philosophers' views cast allows much room in counseling for sensitivity to various cultural and even global views (Van Deurzen, 2002). This is naturally incorporated into the theory, which provides a flexible basis for practitioners to exercise multicultural sensitivity.

For instance, Needleman and Binswanger (1963) discussed their views of existential being-in-the-world within the three realms of *umwelt*, *mitwelt*, and *eigenwelt*. They emphasized understanding the individual's perspective of these realms, how they impact the individual, and how the individual functions within them. In essence, existentialism promotes clinicians' understanding the client as well as the client's worldview, including spirituality. This understanding is integrated into a holistic conceptualization of the client, which fuels the formulation of an appropriate treatment plan based on the client–context relationship, promoting the client's freedom and responsibility to self and the world realms (Vontress, Johnson, & Epp, 1999).

Children

Existentialism is developmentally sensitive and can be applied to meet the developmental needs of children and adolescents (Guterman, 1996). When using an existentialist approach with children and adolescents, the therapeutic relationship in the here and now is emphasized. This is linked to Martin Buber's (1970) I/thou connection and the sense of betweenness. In an existential relationship with children, they are allowed to be with the therapist, are accepted for being (Sartre, 1956), and are validated (Spinelli, 2007). The therapeutic relationship can be healing for children.

Also, consider Heidegger's (1927/1962) statement that humans, including children, live in a world they cannot necessarily control. How children choose to react to and interpret the environment can be one of the foci in counseling. This is a positive approach, as children often have authority figures (i.e., parents, teachers, community leaders) who shape their environment for them. The emphasis on freedom, responsibility, and making positive meaning (whether with friendships, family relationships, schoolwork, or more) is a focused concept that can support therapeutic goals for children (Quinn, 2010). In addition, addressing existential anxiety that stems from life challenges can be healing (Berman, Weems, & Stickle, 2006).

Kitano and LeVine (1987) observed that the existential approach is highly compatible with child therapy, as the therapist has the flexibility to choose the techniques and approaches that best fit the child's needs. They identified six distinct phases that can be followed to facilitate a child or adolescent's attainment of goals: (1) identifying the existential problem of focus; (2) reflecting and communicating understanding of the problem, feelings, thoughts, and behaviors; (3) developing possible choices or plans of action to address the issue; (4) recognizing how concerns of the human condition such as loneliness or struggling with being responsible can be barriers to success; (5) helping the child accept responsibility, make choices, and be accountable for possible consequences; and (6) generalizing what was learned to other conflicts in which the child continues to make decisions within his or her limits.

EXISTENTIAL PSYCHOTHERAPY PROCESS AND APPLICATIONS

The therapeutic process in existential psychotherapy includes three primary phases. Phase 1 involves the cultivation of an authentic here-and-now client–counselor relationship, also referred to as the *cultivation of therapeutic presence* (Schneider, 2008). Phase 2 involves continued cultivation of the client's authentic self-expression and self-exploration. The counselor uses two interventions, *vivification* and *confrontation,* to promote the aims of this phase. Vivification involves promoting increased client contact with the ways he or she limits or blocks authentic here-and-now experiences. Confrontation calls attention to inconsistencies among behaviors, feelings, and goals to encourage risk taking and change on the part of the client. In Phase 2, the client engages in self-exploration to gain better awareness of his or her values, feelings, beliefs, and goals. The ultimate objective is development of consolidated life meanings. Finally, in Phase 3, the client seeks to actualize these life meanings in the world. The client's process is a quest to self-actualize his or her life meanings. Initially, the quest may involve expressing attitudes or feelings with the therapist for the first time. The client then may extend the quest by expressing him or herself in new ways in a group counseling setting and in life outside of therapy. The quest represents an unending self-actualization process.

Therapeutic Goals in Phase 1: Cultivation of the Relationship

Early in the relationship, and consistent with the philosophical beliefs espoused by Buber (1970), the counselor should provide facilitative conditions consistent with promoting an authentic client–counselor relationship. Appropriate conditions for establishing this type of relationship, originally identified and described by Rogers (1957), should be provided and communicated by the counselor—these are genuineness, respect, and empathy. The core condition known as *genuineness* refers to the degree to which the counselor is authentic. *Respect* refers to the counselor's unconditional positive regard for the client as a person. *Empathy* entails striving to understand and accurately describe the subjective aspects of the client's experience, including beliefs, views, meanings, and emotions.

A number of theorists have developed and described specific skills that support the counselor's efforts to provide and communicate the core conditions. Three skills in particular are relevant to existential counseling and the goal of facilitating an authentic client–counselor relationship: immediacy, confrontation, and concreteness. The use of immediacy involves the counselor's communication of his or her here-and-now experience. For example, the counselor may share subjective impressions of the client in the moment, such as, "I get the feeling that there is something deeply personal you would like to discuss but you're not sure that you're ready to talk about it."

In facilitating an authentic relationship, the existential counselor should use confrontation judiciously and be receptive to confrontation on the part of the client. A confrontational response is one in which the professional counselor describes client inconsistencies that usually fall into one of three primary categories: (1) inconsistencies among the client's thoughts, feelings, and actions; (2) inconsistencies between the client's behaviors and goals; or (3) inconsistencies between the client's self-perceptions and how the client is perceived by others. Effective confrontation requires considerable social skill on the part of the counselor, and care should be exercised to communicate respect for the client and ensure that the confrontation contributes to the client's growth and welfare.

A third counseling skill that is useful for facilitating an authentic client–counselor relationship is *concreteness,* or the ability to help a client turn the vaguely understood and intangible into something clear and concrete. Feelings, problem situations, obstacles, and counseling goals are examples of aspects of an individual's life that professional counselors help make more concrete. The counselor uses questions or leading statements to elicit concrete details from the client. In addition, the counselor provides details based on his or her observations of the client's behavior in the counseling sessions.

Change Process in Phase 2: Authenticity and Self-Exploration

As previously mentioned, Heidegger (1927/1962) emphasized that there are two basic patterns of being: authentic and inauthentic. The authentic pattern entails acting with courage and embracing one's freedom and process of becoming. The avenue to authentic living involves experiencing one's beliefs, values, and emotions in the here and now. Early in the relationship, the counselor can effectively encourage the client to be authentic in a counseling session through the use of active listening and encouraging the client to look inward to better understand his or her intrinsic wants, needs, and values. Another important counselor skill for promoting client authenticity is the use of immediacy. Immediacy is recommended early in the relationship because it is consistent with a gentle, respectful, and supportive counselor role conducive to strengthening the therapeutic alliance (Bugental, 2008). For a detailed example of an existential therapist's work with a client, the reader is referred to the two-part video featuring Bugental (1997a, 1997b).

To promote authenticity, the counselor extends an invitation to the client to experience his or her emotions more fully in the here and now. The counselor's invitation is reflective of three additional principles that are an important part of existential psychotherapy: (1) acknowledging the client's *freedom* with regard to choosing to accept or decline the invitation, (2) encouraging the client to be more *authentic* (as opposed to being controlled or preparing a public persona), and (3) encouraging the client to experience greater *contact with his or her here-and-now experience,* particularly emotions.

A classic example of the change process in Phase 2 can be seen in a session in which Bugental (1997a) counseled a client named Marie. To help Marie gain greater contact with her here-and-now authentic self, Bugental used here-and-now reflection and the skills of immediacy throughout the session. Bugental asked, "As you look back at yourself 7 years ago, what does that trigger inside of you?" In addition, there were moments in the session when the counselor noted that the client was more spontaneous and her voice more modulated. The counselor referred to these moments of greater authentic expression as the Marie behind the *public* Marie, and asked if it would be possible for this more private Marie to talk a little more. Here, one can clearly see that the counselor's objective is increasing the client's contact with and self-awareness of her authentic self.

Change Process Later in Phase 2: Authenticity and Self-Exploration

The latter part of Phase 2 is characterized by an increase in the use of active approaches, such as sharing insights. Another example of an active approach is the use of confrontation. For example, in his session with Marie, Bugental (1997a) told her that when she attempted to get in touch with her here-and-now experience, her speech was "larded with expressions such as 'I guess,' 'I think,' and 'sort of,'" indicating a cautiousness that prevented her from being fully present.

Another significant aspect of the existential counseling approach evident in this stage is that the counselor typically will direct the client to *look inward* for direction and guidance. This is also related to another important focus of this stage—*vivification, or making contact.* On one occasion during the latter part of Phase 2, Bugental (1997a) indicated that Marie's concern regarding anxiety was an important one and encouraged her to make contact with the anxiety by adding, "That's a terribly important question. Take time to check in on it."

Further, Bugental (1997a) increased the use of *concreteness,* turning the vaguely understood into something solid. For example, at one point, the client talked about her desire to find more balance between her polar styles of being in the world. The first one was her tendency to drink too much and lose control, and the second was her current mode of being overly self-controlled, reserved, and perfectionistic. She stated, "I'm searching for balance. I'm looking for it. That's my quest." The counselor observed, "Now, your words have so much inflection, because there's hope." A few minutes later, the client stated, "It's difficult to make a change." The counselor observed, "Your voice has gotten more level again." He used the counselor skill of concreteness to increase the client's awareness of her monotone voice as a substantial obstacle, or at least a clear signal that she was holding herself down.

In this stage of counseling, the existential counselor is more likely to play the role of *wisdom teacher.* In this role, the counselor serves as a more experienced guide and catalyst promoting the client's acquisition of insights (Walsh & McElwain, 2002). The existential counselor is careful to treat the client as an equal, and suggestions and interpretations are worded tentatively. For example, when Marie observed that she had a pattern of being either overly self-controlled or completely out of control, Bugental (1997a) stated, "I wonder if there's a third choice."

Change Process in Phase 3: Actualizing Life Meanings in the World

Finally, the counselor is focused on facilitating the client's quest, or process of *searching.* Searching is central to the counseling process (Bugental, 1997b). Bugental described searching as "seeking for greater richness of living, fulfillment, satisfaction, confirmation, and affirmation." He likened the client's process of searching to a blade of grass forcing its way through the earth or a crack in the sidewalk to find the sun. Searching is a client's ongoing effort to find greater satisfaction in his or her inner potential. Bugental asserted that "we all hunger to let out what we feel inside, and that's what searching's about." The counselor facilitates this process by introducing interpretations, encouraging the client to explore new perceptions and engage in life experiences that would be more fulfilling. For example, when Bugental commented, "I wonder if there's a third choice," he was encouraging the client to explore new territory or consider a new possibility for self-fulfillment.

While working with a client, Bugental (1997b) would ask himself, "Are we opening up more territory? Is that life force finding a way through a little more?" This process is anathema to a counselor's concern for efficiency. As such, existential counseling can be a long-term process lasting for years. Existential counselors view this process of searching, by opening up new territory, as a process without end.

Interventions

A common misperception regarding the practice of existential psychotherapy is the belief that therapists are necessarily nondirective or unstructured in their approach. In reality, a therapist operating from this orientation may use a wide variety of techniques or interventions to achieve the aims of existential psychotherapy. It has been noted that what is important is the therapist using these interventions with the appropriate "existential attitude" in the context of an authentic relationship (May & Yalom, 2005). Therapists borrow approaches from a wide variety of counseling orientations to help clients lead more authentic lives. For example, behavioral techniques may be incorporated into existential psychotherapy in the name of promoting broader existential goals. Behavioral techniques such as self-monitoring of behaviors and graduated exposure to anxiety-provoking situations might be employed to promote awareness and expansion where clients are viewed as constricted. Any approach (e.g., systematic desensitization) that aides in this respect can be employed in the name of helping the client counter constricting forces (e.g., anxiety) to become more authentic and actualize life meanings. Similarly, Mendelowitz and Schneider (2008) observe that existentialists are not averse to using a technique "where its use is warranted, but they tend to apply it spontaneously, as it arises in the context of a given relationship, rather than as determined by a formalized set of procedures" (p. 298). For example, an existentialist counselor working with a client who is divided between two alternative life decisions might spontaneously decide to employ the two-chair technique to facilitate increased integration for the client. An example of such a client is found in the case of Michael (refer back to Case Illustration 6.2).

Promoting Client Courage

As previously mentioned, the counselor's role may be compared to that of a wisdom teacher. The counselor encourages the client to venture into new territory, similar to the way Bugental (1997a) encouraged his client to consider exploring an alternative way of being—that is, an alternative to the polarities of being too controlled or feeling out of control. He asked his client to consider exploring new territory, a process he refers to as *searching*. This process of searching requires courage on the client's part. Maslow (1968), in a discussion of his hierarchy of needs, stated that the need for growth is counteracted by the need for safety. The energizing catalyst for pursuing growth, rather than safety, is courage (Goud, 2005).

Tillich (1952/2000) viewed courage as a form of willingness to confront one's fear and anxiety "for the sake of a fuller positivity" (p. 78). Tillich termed this willingness "the courage to be" and noted that it requires facing and overcoming obstacles, including meaninglessness, alienation, and despair. Goud (2005) made several suggestions regarding how a counselor might promote a client's courage. For example, promoting a client's sense of self-confidence is one method for engendering courage. Goud recommended constructing a "strengths inventory" for this purpose. Examples of categories in such an inventory include career, interpersonal, intellectual, physical, and emotional strengths. He explained that by making a client more conscious of his or her genuine strengths, a counselor could increase the client's confidence and the likelihood of performing acts of courage. Review Exercise 6.3 for a description of how to construct a strengths inventory.

EXERCISE 6.3

CONSTRUCTING A STRENGTHS INVENTORY

In her strength-based model, Smith (2006) presented 10 categories of strengths: (1) wisdom and spiritual strength, (2) emotional strengths, (3) character strengths, (4) creative strengths, (5) relationship skills and the ability to nurture, (6) educational strengths, (7) cognitive strengths, (8) work-related strengths, (9) ability to use social support and community resources, and (10) survival skills (pp. 28–31). The list of strengths below represents specific examples of strengths within each of these categories, as well as values (Super & Nevill, 1985), which can often serve as a source of strength.

To construct your own Strengths Inventory, write each of the following 47 strengths on 47 separate index cards. Divide the cards into three piles, ranging from most to least developed: (1) proficient strengths, (2) competent strengths, and (3) precompetent strengths. Print out a copy of the list below, and next to each strength place the number 1, 2, or 3 to record your self-assessment.

Think of a specific life challenge you are currently facing. Identify three or more well-developed strengths you possess that are particularly relevant to your life challenge. Next, identify three or more less-developed strengths that you believe would be useful for effectively dealing with your life challenge and you would like to intentionally work on developing. These relevant potential strengths may be termed "growth edges." Finally, write a narrative detailing actions you are committed to taking to develop these growth edges so in the future you can apply them to the life challenge you are facing.

Card Sort Items

Ability to endure	Empathy	Originality
Ability to form relationships	Forgiveness	Perseverance

Ability to provide for a family	Formal education	Physical exercise
Ability to secure employment	Having enjoyable lifestyle	Physical survival
Ability to use community resources	Honesty	Problem solving
Ability to use social support	Informal education	Religious faith
Achievement	Insight	Self-assertion
Altruism	Integrity	Sense of purpose
Art appreciation	Kindness	Social intelligence
Artistic ability	Knowledge	Sound judgment
Capacity for nurturing others	Maintaining one's health	Spiritual fulfillment
Compassion	Managing pain	Variety
Cooperation	Managing stress	Wisdom
Courage	Moral reasoning	Wisdom
Creativity	Optimism	Written expression
Discipline	Oral Communication	

Using the Expressive Arts in Counseling

The expressive arts may be employed to promote change in existential psychotherapy. Creative processes, such as those occurring in painting, drama, and dance, provide a framework for less threatening avenues to explore counseling concerns. Depicting a concern through an artistic medium (e.g., drawing) concretizes the concern and renders it more amenable to examination and change. Further, using the arts in therapy can be playful, freeing, and, consequently, may decrease the client's defensiveness. Using the expressive arts in therapy helps clients overcome blocks to experience and self-awareness, increases openness to feedback, and promotes the flexibility required for positive client change.

Y-CHUN THROUGH THE LENS OF EXISTENTIAL PSYCHOTHERAPY

Having covered the historical background, underlying philosophy, and nature of the process of existential psychotherapy, we now turn our attention to applying this approach to the case of Y-Chun. She is a 35-year-old college junior and the mother of a 15-year-old son and a 12-year-old daughter. She is frustrated because she and her children currently live at home and she feels as though her parents treat her like a child and insist on parenting her children. Further, she feels empty and sad and cries a lot. She reports that she lacks meaningful relationships in her life. The counselor in existential psychotherapy may draw on a wide variety of techniques in the service of achieving the aims of the three therapeutic phases. Each counselor is unique in terms of techniques employed and tailors his or her approach to the personality, needs, and characteristics of the individual client.

Phase 1: Cultivation of Presence and the Authentic Relationship

Based on the results of the intake interview, the counselor recognizes the seriousness of Y-Chun's rape experience at the age of 16. Mendelowitz and Schneider (2008) note that existential therapy cannot be all things to all people, and that highly specific problems such as this "may best be handled by specialists" (p. 316). For this reason, the counselor would work with Y-Chun on issues amenable to existential psychotherapy but would refer her to a specialist to address the emotional symptoms related to her rape experience.

One of Y-Chun's most serious existential concerns centers on the quality of her relationships. Her parents do not treat her as an adult even though she is 35 and the mother of two adolescent children. Further, she lacks meaningful relationships in her life. The counselor cultivates an authentic caring relationship, which may serve as a model for relationships outside of therapy. This relationship is founded on the primary counselor characteristics of genuineness, empathy, and nonjudgmental positive regard. The counselor is also invested in promoting an interaction that is based on presence, or interacting with the client in the here and now. Interacting in the present moment provides optimal conditions for promoting authentic dialogue as well as client self-exploration, growth, and development.

To facilitate trust and understanding, the counselor provides structure by describing the parameters of counseling. The counselor underscores the importance of an honest, authentic relationship for counseling to be successful, and adds that Y-Chun should feel free to express her here-and-now responses to the counselor without withholding or censuring her responses. The ultimate objective of counseling is for Y-Chun to successfully apply what she learns in her counseling sessions to her real life.

Phase 2: Authenticity and Self-Exploration

Early in Phase 2

Early in the session, the counselor asks Y-Chun once again to discuss some of her presenting concerns. The counselor listens intently, reflecting meaning and feeling throughout the discussion. As previously mentioned, victims of childhood sexual victimization may experience *enhanced integration* of the early victimization as an overemphasized aspect of their self-concept (Miller, 2012). The approach described in this section is intended to assist the client in developing an expanded and reintegrated self-concept that does not include the victimization experience.

The counselor presents Y-Chun with a set of index cards. On these cards are typed a variety of values, skills, abilities, and preferred activities. The counselor uses these cards to assist Y-Chun in developing a "strengths inventory" to promote her courage and self-confidence. The counselor instructs Y-Chun to sort the cards into three piles: "very much like me," "not sure," and "very much unlike me." Some of the values in the "very much like me" pile include *achievement, altruism,* and *creativity.* Some of the values in the "very much unlike me" pile include *taking risks, prestige,* and *competition.* In the following exchange, the counselor repeatedly uses the skills of immediacy and concretization to promote client here-and-now self-awareness, and enhances the client's freedom of choice regarding how to behave in the moment.

Counselor: Tell me more about what the value *creativity* means for you.

Y-Chun: When I was a young girl, my parents enrolled me in a program where I attended art classes. In the classes we would paint and sculpt and make pottery, and it was so much fun.

Counselor: It was really interesting just now when you talked about creativity. Your face lit up, and you expressed yourself with your hands. Your expression was very playful and childlike. You really seem to be enjoying yourself. And I'm wondering if maybe you could allow yourself to express yourself in that manner more in our work together.

Y-Chun: (Embarrassed) I would be willing to do that. Yes.

Counselor: But now you're more reserved. Do you see that? When I mentioned it, you became more formal and contained.

Y-Chun: It's just that in my home growing up, my parents taught us to be mature, and being playful was viewed as immature. If I were playful, they would express their disapproval and I would feel ashamed.

Counselor: So if you could go back to the point in our conversation just a minute ago, where I said it would be great if you could be more playful, can you get in touch with that moment when you felt something blocking you?

Y-Chun: Yes, it's a feeling here (touches her temples) and in my neck and shoulders.

Counselor: Would you be willing to think about the impulse to have fun and be playful, and pay close attention to that physical sensation?

Y-Chun: Okay . . . (Focuses on the feeling.)

Counselor: Just take a moment and look inward, and check on that feeling. What's that feeling like for you?

Y-Chun: It's awkward. It's a physical tension, and it's also a feeling of embarrassment like my parents are standing behind me watching and judging me.

Counselor: I want you to know that I like it when you're playful and having fun. I would like to see you express that side of yourself more in our work together. Would you be willing to try that?

Y-Chun: Yes. Okay.

Later in the same session, the counselor changes the topic to a discussion of the cards the client finds are not like her. Note the way the counselor uses immediacy and concretization again; in addition, the counselor communicates that, consistent with an authentic relationship, he or she is open to confrontation communicated by the client.

Counselor:	Now pick one of these cards in the "very unlike me" pile and tell me what it is you don't like about that card.
Y-Chun:	(Looking at the cards, a long pause)
Counselor:	It's important that you say whatever comes to mind and don't be shy in voicing what you find disagreeable. *(Information giving)*
Y-Chun:	(Looks displeased and remains silent)
Counselor:	I noticed just now when I mentioned saying whatever comes to mind that a look of disapproval crossed your face. Do you know what I mean?
Y-Chun:	Yes, I think so. It was when you said, "Don't be shy."
Counselor:	Would you be willing to take a moment and look inward to examine what happened for you when you made that expression and had that reaction?
Y-Chun:	Okay.
Counselor:	Take a moment now and relive that feeling that came over you when I said, "Say whatever you like and don't be shy."
Y-Chun:	(Takes a moment, and facial expression registers resentment)
Counselor:	Yes, that's the feeling. Check in with that feeling a little longer, and pay attention to what's happening inside for you. What were you experiencing?
Y-Chun:	My face felt like it was warm from embarrassment. I didn't like the way you said, "Don't be shy," because it felt like you were talking to me like I'm a child.
Counselor:	I like it when you tell me I've done something that makes you feel uncomfortable. I like it when you take care of yourself. That lets me know that I need to stop doing the thing that is making you feel uncomfortable.

The counselor also praises Y-Chun for taking a risk by voicing her resentment and suggests that while "taking a risk" is not a characteristic she strongly identifies with, she might consider the possibility that this is an emerging strength and, as such, potentially represents one of her growth edges.

At the end of the session, the counselor introduces the concept of "hoped-for selves" (Markus & Nurius, 1986) and asks Y-Chun to think of one or more "hoped-for selves" she would like to actualize in the next 5 years.

Later in Phase 2

The counselor asks Y-Chun what she has come up with in her thoughts about her "hoped-for selves." Y-Chun states that the ideal hoped-for self she was able to think of combines being a more effective parent and enjoying a closer relationship with her children. In addition, she hopes to hold an occupational position as an educator or school administrator in the next 5 years. The counselor uses the skills of immediacy and confrontation to encourage Y-Chun to communicate in new ways and actualize aspects of her personality (e.g., criticizing) that have been suppressed. These new forms of communication are also consistent with Y-Chun's self-identified hoped-for self.

Counselor: Take a moment and say something about one of these values or aptitudes that you placed in the "very unlike me" pile.

Y-Chun: *Criticizing* is not very much like me. I don't feel comfortable criticizing.

Counselor: (Long pause) I noticed that when you talk about things you don't like, you don't have a whole lot to say. Why do you think that is?

Y-Chun: My parents always told me that it was impolite to criticize or be negative.

Counselor: And if you voiced criticism in front of your parents?

Y-Chun: They would say they were very disappointed in me, and I would feel ashamed.

Counselor: So not criticizing . . .

Y-Chun: . . . gave me the approval of my parents.

Counselor: But now that you *are* a parent, isn't criticizing a fundamental part of being an effective parent?

Y-Chun: I guess so. I see what you mean.

The counselor uses vivification to heighten Y-Chun's awareness of her limitation related to expressing criticism. This represents a powerful block for her. Recalling Y-Chun's enjoyment of artistic expression, the counselor proposes that she use this avenue to overcome her block. After discussing possible forms of artistic expression, including music, drama, and drawing, Y-Chun decides she would prefer to give "voice" to her criticism through a pencil drawing. More specifically, she expresses her resentment and criticism of her parents through a satirical drawing. The drawing serves to *concretize* Y-Chun's concerns about the way she is treated by her parents. In the drawing, her parents are depicted as puppeteers. They are using a wooden apparatus to control strings that are attached to her arms and legs. Her parents' facial expressions appear sinister as they control her like a marionette. The drawing frees Y-Chun to give voice to feeling manipulated, controlled, and as though her parents are depriving her of enthusiasm for life. The counselor points out how the use of art has allowed her to bypass the block and allowed her to make contact with these feelings, and encourages her to continue to use artistic expression to get in touch with these types of feelings.

Phase 3: Actualizing Life Meanings in the World

Following the discussions of characteristics that were "very much like" her and of her "hoped-for self," Y-Chun committed to making some life changes that would provide a path for her on her quest to actualizing her preferred identity—she enrolled in art classes at the local community center.

In addition, she became a member of a Chinese American Assertiveness Training group offered through the Student Development and Counseling Center at her college and cosponsored by the Asian Student Association (Sue, 1997). This group is designed to acknowledge that traditional Chinese culture values being quiet and respectful as signs of filial piety. Group sessions include discussions of the impact of being a person of color on assertive behavior. Group facilitators acknowledge that assertive behaviors are appropriate in some situations but not all (e.g., those involving social interactions with traditional family members).

A slowly developing outcome of Y-Chun's investing time in her fulfillment and self-care (recall that the counselor also referred Y-Chun to a specialist to address her rape experience) was that her feelings of emptiness were replaced by feelings of fulfillment. She began to experience an increased desire for closeness to her children. To improve her relationship with her children, she initiated a conversation about recreational activities they could share as a family. They took art classes together. They also planned a family vacation that centered on visiting national park attractions all three found desirable.

KEYSTONES

- Existential humanism dates as far back as the beginning of recorded time. Some of the philosophers who contributed to this perspective include Friedrich Nietzsche, Søren Kierkegaard, Edmund Husserl, and Martin Heidegger. Nietzsche asserted that humans should strive to adopt a more spontaneous form of living. Kierkegaard, Husserl, and Heidegger urged humans to move from a mechanized life to a person-centered phenomenological existence.

- Victor Frankl and Rollo May were early leading figures in applying existential philosophy to the development of therapeutic approaches. Frankl's *logotherapy* emphasized that humans have the capacity to decide how to respond to their experiences in the world. May's *existential psychology* emphasized meaning and authentic relating rather than techniques.

- Fundamental to existential psychotherapy is the principle that human existence necessarily entails the tension between opposing dialectics, such as freedom and destiny, meaning and meaninglessness, and aloneness and relatedness. Health entails achieving a balanced interplay between the opposites within each of these dialectics.

- Central to the practice of existential psychotherapy is the client–counselor relationship. Having an authentic encounter with a trusted other can help a person transcend his or her conflicts. In the words of Martin Buber, "Meeting is healing."

- Key concepts in existential psychotherapy are *courage* and *anxiety*. Living a balanced life with regard to dialectical tensions (e.g., to embrace both one's aloneness and one's relatedness) requires courage. Anxiety is a normal concomitant to growth and is meaningful for this reason.

- The process of existential psychotherapy includes three primary phases: (1) cultivation of presence and the therapeutic relationship, (2) authenticity and self-exploration, and (3) actualizing life meanings in the world.
- The role of the counselor has been described as a "wounded healer" who has resolved a previous crisis and come to grips with his or her own mortality and limitations. The counselor is viewed as a more experienced equal who serves as a guide and catalyst for therapy.
- Existential therapy is a phenomenological approach emphasizing authentic living. For this reason, the therapist encourages the client to "look inward" or to "check in" on his or her internal feelings, beliefs, and experiences in the here and now.
- Existential psychotherapy is more of an attitude than a structured therapeutic system. An existential therapist may use more circumscribed approaches and techniques (e.g., systematic desensitization) to facilitate the goals of existential therapy, such as authentic living. However, while employing any technique, the therapist remains mindful of deeper existential themes (Mendelowitz & Schneider, 2008).
- The therapist encourages the client to explore new territory to discover alternative possibilities for fulfillment. This process is referred to as a quest or searching and continues throughout an individual's lifetime.

ADDITIONAL RESOURCES

May, R. (1953). *Man's search for himself*. New York: W. W. Norton.
May, R. (1986). *The discovery of being: Writings in existential psychology*. New York: W. W. Norton.
May, R. (1991). *The cry for myth*. New York: W. W. Norton.
May, R. (1999). *Freedom and destiny*. New York: W. W. Norton.
Yalom, I. D. (2002). *The gift of therapy*. New York: HarperCollins.

Philosophical Source Material

Kierkegaard, S. (1956). *Fear and trembling and the sickness unto death*. Garden City, NY: Doubleday.
Kierkegaard, S. (1992). *Concluding unscientific postscript to* Philosophical Fragments (H. V. Hong & E. H. Hong, Trans.). Princeton, NJ: Princeton University Press.
Nietzsche, F. (1997). *On the genealogy of morals* (K. Ansell-Pearson, Ed., & C. Diethe, Trans.). Cambridge, UK: Cambridge University Press.
Sartre, J.-P. (2007). *Existentialism is a humanism* (C. Macomber, Trans.). New Haven, CT: Yale University Press.
Shestov, L. (1969). *Kierkegaard and the existential philosophy*. Athens: Ohio University Press.

Video Resources

May, R. (2009, May 6). *Existential psychotherapy* [Video]. Retrieved from http://www.youtube.com/watch?v = Cay743y-Sak
Schneider, K. J. (2006). *Existential therapy* [Video]. Washington, DC: American Psychological Association.

REFERENCES

Bauman, S., & Waldo, M. (1998). Existential theory and mental health counseling: If it were a snake, it would have bitten. *Journal of Mental Health Counseling, 20*(1), 13–27.

Berman, S. L., Weems, C. F., & Stickle, T. R. (2006). Existential anxiety in adolescents: Prevalence, structure, association with psychological symptoms and identify development. *Journal of Youth and Adolescence, 35*(3), 303–310. doi:10.1007/s10964-006-9032-y

Berntsen, D., & Rubin, D. C. (2007). When a trauma becomes a key to identity: Enhanced integration of trauma memories predicts posttraumatic stress disorder symptoms. *Applied Cognitive Psychology, 21,* 417–431.

Bohart, A. C., O'Hara, M., & Leitner, L. M. (1998). Empirically violated treatments: Disenfranchisement of humanistic and other psychotherapies. *Psychotherapy Research, 8,* 141–157.

Bohart, A. C., & Tallman, K. (1996). The active client: Therapy as self-help. *Journal of Humanistic Psychology, 36,* 7–30.

Bonanno, G. A. (2005). Resilience in the face of potential trauma. *Current Directions in Psychological Science, 14*(3), 135–138.

Boss, M. (1963). *Psychoanalysis and daseinsanalysis* (L. E. Lefebre, Trans.). New York: Basic Books.

Buber, M. (1970). *I and thou* (W. Kaufmann, Trans.). New York: Scribner's.

Bugental, J. F. T. (1997a). *Existential-humanistic psychotherapy in action, Part 1* [Video recording]. Retrieved from http://www.psychotherapy.net/video/Existential_Humanistic_Psychotherapy

Bugental, J. F. T. (1997b). *Existential-humanistic psychotherapy in action, Part 2* [Video recording]. Retrieved from http://www.psychotherapy.net/video/Existential_Humanistic_Psychotherapy

Bugental, J. F. T. (2008). Preliminary sketches for a short-term existential therapy. In K. J. Schneider (Ed.), *Existential-integrative psychotherapy: Guideposts to the core of practice* (pp. 165–168). New York: Routledge.

Bugental, J. F. T., & Bracke, P. (1992). The future of existential-humanistic psychotherapy. *Psychotherapy, 29,* 28–33.

Burston, D. (2003). Existentialism, humanism, and psychotherapy. *Existential Analysis, 14*(2), 309–319.

Cashin, A. (2004). Painting the vortex: The existential structure of the experience of parenting a child with autism. *International Forum for Psychoanalysis, 12,* 164–174. doi:10.1080/08037060420000632

Corsini, R. J., & Wedding, D. (2005). *Current psychotherapies* (7th ed.). Belmont, CA: Brooks/Cole.

Feinauer, L. (2003). Existential well-being as a factor in the adjustment of adults sexually abused as children. *American Journal of Family Therapy, 31,* 201–213. doi:10.1080/01926180390167160

Frankl, V. (1946). *Man's search for meaning.* New York: Plenum Press.

Frankl, V. (1963). *Man's search for meaning: An introduction to logotherapy.* New York: Basic Books.

Goud, N. (2005). Courage: Its nature and development. *Journal of Humanistic Counseling, Education, and Development, 44,* 102–116.

Groth, M. (1997). Existential therapy on Heideggerian principles. *Journal of the Society for Existential Analysis, 8*(1), 57–75.

Groth, M. (2000). Existential psychotherapy today. *Existential Psychology and Psychiatry, 25*(1–3), 7–27.

Guterman, J. T. (1996). Doing mental health counseling: A social constructionist re-vision. *Journal of Mental Health Counseling, 18,* 228–252.

Heidegger, M. (1962). *Being and time* (J. Macquarrie & E. Robinson, Trans.). Oxford, UK: Basil Blackwell. (Original work published in 1927)

Hershenson, D. B., & Power, P. W. (1987). *Mental health counseling: Theory and practice.* New York: Pergamon Press.

Holcomb-McCoy, C. (2004). Alienation: A concept for understanding low-income, urban clients. *Journal of Humanistic Counseling, Education and Development, 43,* 188–196.

Horney, K. (1950). *Neurosis and human growth: The struggle toward self realization.* New York: W. W. Norton.

Jaspers, K. (1969–1971). *Philosophy* (E. B. Ashton, Trans.). Chicago: Chicago University Press. (Original work published in 1932)

Kant, I. (1954). *The encyclopedia of philosophy* (Vol. 4; P. Edwards, Ed.). New York: Macmillan, Free Press.

Kaufmann, W. (1956). *Existentialism from Dostoevsky to Sartre.* New York: Meridian.

Kitano, M. K., & LeVine, E. S. (1987). Existential theory: Guidelines for practice in child therapy. *Psychotherapy: Theory, Research, Practice, Training, 24*(3), 404–413. doi:10.1037/h0085732

Kochler, H. (1974). *Die subjekt-objekt-dialektik in der transzendentalen phänomenologie: Das seinsproblem zwischen idealismus und realismus* (Monographien Zur Philosophischen Forschung, Vol. 112.) Meisenheim am Glan: Anton Hain.

Markus, H., & Nurius, P. (1986). Possible selves. *American Psychologist, 41,* 954–969.

Mascaro, N., & Rosen, D. H. (2008). Assessment of existential meaning and its longitudinal relations with depressive symptoms. *Journal of Social and Clinical Psychology, 27*(6), 576–599.

Maslow, A. (1968). *Toward a psychology of being.* New York: Van Nostrand Reinhold.

May, R. (1961). *Existential psychology.* New York: Random House.

May, R. (1962). Dangers in the relation of existentialism to psychotherapy. In H. M. Ruitenbeek (Ed.), *Psychoanalysis and existential philosophy* (pp. 179–187). New York: Dutton.

May, R. (1969). *Love and will.* New York: W. W. Norton.

May, R. (1996). *The meaning of anxiety.* New York: W. W. Norton. (Original work published in 1950)

May, R., & Yalom, I. (2005). Existential psychotherapy. In R. J. Corsini & D. Wedding (Eds.), *Current psychotherapies* (7th ed., pp. 269–298). Belmont, CA: Brooks/Cole.

Mendelowitz, E., & Schneider, K. (2008). Existential psychotherapy. In R. J. Corsini & D. Wedding (Eds.), *Current psychotherapies* (8th ed., pp. 295–327). Belmont, CA: Thomson Brooks/Cole.

Miars, R. (2002). Existential authenticity: A foundational value for counseling. *Counseling and Values, 46*(3), 218–225.

Miller, L. (2012). Criminal victimization. In L. L. Levers (Ed.), *Trauma counseling: Theories and interventions* (pp. 231–248). New York: Springer.

Needleman, J., & Binswanger, L. (1963). *Being-in-the-world: Selected papers of Ludwig Binswanger.* New York: Basic Books.

Nietzsche, F. (2006). *Thus spoke Zarathustra.* New York: Viking Press. (Original work published in 1883–1885)

Pitchford, D. B. (2009). The existentialism of Rollo May: An influence on trauma treatment. *Journal of Humanistic Psychology, 49,* 441.

Quinn, F. (2010). The right to choose: Existential-phenomenological psychotherapy with primary school-aged children. *Counseling Psychology Review, 25,* 41–48.

Rennie, D. L. (1994). Storytelling in psychotherapy: The client's subjective experience. *Psychotherapy, 31,* 234–243.

Rogers, C. R. (1957). The necessary and sufficient conditions of therapeutic personality change. *Journal of Consulting Psychology, 21,* 95–103.

Sartre, J. P. (1956). *Being and nothingness.* New York: Philosophical Library.

Sartre, J. P. (1962). *Existential psychoanalysis* (H. E. Barnes, Trans.). Washington, DC: Gateway Edition.

Satir, V. (1983). *Conjoint family therapy.* Palo Alto, CA: Science and Behavior Books.

Schneider, K. J. (2008). *Existential-integrative psychotherapy: Guideposts to the core of practice.* Boston: Routledge.

Sharf, R. (2011). *Theories of psychotherapy and counseling.* Belmont, CA: Brooks/Cole.

Smith, E. J. (2006). The strength-based counseling model. *Counseling Psychologist, 34,* 13–79.

Spinelli, E. (2007). *Practicing existential psychotherapy.* London: Sage.

Sue, D. (1997). Counseling strategies for Chinese Americans. In C. C. Lee (Ed.), *Multicultural issues in counseling: New approaches to diversity* (pp. 173–187). Alexandria, VA: American Counseling Association.

Super, D. E., & Nevill, D. D. (1985). *Values scale.* Palo Alto, CA: Consulting Psychologists Press.

Suri, R. (2010). Working with the elderly: An existential-humanistic approach. *Journal of Humanistic Psychology, 50*(2), 175–186. doi:10.1177/0022167809335687

Tedeschi, R. G., & Calhoun, L. G. (2004). Posttraumatic growth: Conceptual foundations and empirical evidence. *Psychological Inquiry, 15*(1), 1–18.

Tedeschi, R. G., & Kilmer, R. P. (2005). Assessing strengths, resilience, and growth to guide clinical interventions. *Professional Psychology: Research and Practice, 36*(3), 230–237.

Tillich, P. (2000). *The courage to be.* New Haven, CT: Yale University Press. (Original work published in 1952).

Van Deurzen, E. (1990). *Existential therapy.* London: Society for Existential Analysts.

Vontress, C. (1988). An existential approach to cross-cultural counseling. *Journal of Multicultural Counseling and Development, 16*(2), 73–83.

Vontress, C., & Epp, L. (2001). Existential cross-cultural counseling: When hearts and cultures share. In K. J. Schneider, J. F. T. Bugental, & J. F. Pierson (Eds.), *The handbook of humanistic psychology: Leading edges in theory, research, and practice* (pp. 371–387). Thousand Oaks, CA: Sage.

Vontress, C., Johnson, J. A., & Epp, L. (1999). *Cross-cultural counseling: A casebook.* Alexandria, VA: American Counseling Association.

Walsh, R. A., & McElwain, B. (2002). Existential psychotherapies. In D. J. Cain & J. Seeman (Eds.), *Humanistic psychotherapies: Handbook of research and practice* (pp. 253–278). Washington, DC: American Psychological Association.

Watson, J. C., & Rennie, D. L. (1994). Qualitative analysis of clients' subjective experience of significant moments during the exploration of problematic reactions. *Journal of Counseling Psychology, 41,* 500–509.

Wolfe, B. E. (2008). Existential issues in anxiety disorders and their treatment. In K. J. Schneider (Ed.), *Existential-integrative psychotherapy: Guideposts to the core of practice* (pp. 204–216). New York: Routledge/Taylor Francis Group.

Wong, P. T. P. (2010). Meaning therapy: An integrative and positive existential psychotherapy. *Journal of Contemporary Psychotherapy, 40*(2), 85–93.

Yalom, I. D. (1980). *Existential psychotherapy.* New York: Basic Books.

CHAPTER 7

Carl Rogers and Client-Centered Counseling

Marjorie C. Witty and Ray Adomaitis

With a learned person it is impossible to discuss the problems of life; he is bound by his system.

—Chuang-Tse

While client-centered therapy still appears in collections of essays on theoretical orientations and Carl Rogers has been named one of the most influential psychologists of the 20th century, relatively few practitioners today identify themselves as client-centered therapists. Why is this so? A reasonable guess is that contemporary therapists believe they have absorbed the contributions of Rogers's work. Empathic understanding, acceptant caring, and genuineness on the therapist's part are significant factors in creating effective therapeutic relationships. In numerous meta-analytic studies, these "core conditions" appear to characterize the work of effective therapists across orientations (Elliott & Freire, 2008, 2010; Wampold, 2001). Given this state of affairs, does the client-centered approach still offer a unique and effective therapy?

We propose that client-centered therapy is not only still alive and growing but still distinctive among current psychotherapies. A major reason for our confidence in the future of the approach relates to Chuang-Tse's adage about learned men. Whether the system be moral or religious, political, or psychological, counselors who apply their system to a client may confuse or distract the client from expressing his or her own account of unique reality (Grant, 1990; Witty, 2004). But doesn't the client-centered approach inculcate its own theoretical and conceptual frame? By virtue of the counselor's disciplined effort to see the world from the client's frame of reference, the client's perceptions and ideas are valued above all theories. As Goethe reminds us, "All theory, dear friend, is gray, but the golden tree of life springs ever green."

During the actual encounter with the client, theory is irrelevant. Client-centered therapists have no goal to change or improve or teach the client. Thus, we do not impose a system of beliefs that others might think are more salutary for the client's mental health. As client-centered counselors listen to the client, we avoid the burden of assessing whether communications are irrational or intellectualized, delusional or a repetition of old patterns. Instead, each utterance of the client is original in that moment. Over time, clients experience that their point of view makes sense to a counselor who not only understands but respects them as persons. This process of expressing oneself and being understood leads to greater self-comprehensibility and self-respect.

After completing this chapter, you will be able to do the following:

1. Appreciate Rogers's discovery of the empathic understanding response process and its power in helping clients mobilize their own resources for self-healing

2. Understand the client-centered approach as a person-to-person means of empowerment

3. Distinguish the "nondirective attitude" from therapist passivity

4. Understand Rogers's views on difference: diagnostic categories; gender, class, racial, and religious categories; and personal identities

5. Assess the research evidence for the effectiveness of the client-centered approach

INTRODUCTION

Profile of Carl R. Rogers

Carl Ransom Rogers was born in Oak Park, Illinois, on January 8, 1902. His parents, Walter and Julia—both religious and socially conservative—moved to a farm in Central Illinois when Carl was in middle school. It was a working farm, and Rogers later attributed his keen interest in science to his years devoted to animal husbandry and agriculture (Rogers & Russell, 2002).

While at the University of Wisconsin, Rogers began to reflect more critically on his own beliefs and interests, moving toward the ministry and away from the fundamentalism of his childhood religion. Initially, Rogers pursued a career in the ministry at Union Theological Seminary in New York, but as his questions about any kind of orthodoxy deepened, in his second year he decided to move across the street to Teacher's College of Columbia University.

In 1927, Rogers applied for a fellowship at the Institute of Child Guidance in New York, with practitioners who were strongly psychoanalytic. In 1940, Rogers was hired with the rank of full professor at Ohio State University, where he proceeded to initiate the first recordings of actual therapy sessions, thereby establishing the field of psychotherapy research. The date associated with the birth of client-centered therapy is December 11, 1940, when Rogers presented a paper titled "Newer Concepts in Psychotherapy" at a Psi Chi meeting at the University of Minnesota. The original name for this practice was "nondirective therapy," based on the belief that the client's capacity for self-determination and actualization did not require an authority to direct the therapy but, rather, a warm, acceptant collaborator.

From Ohio State, Rogers moved to the University of Chicago with the goal of establishing the University of Chicago Counseling and Psychotherapy Research Center. Rogers left the academy for good in 1963. He went on to collaborate with other humanistic therapists, teachers, group workers, and educators at the Center for the Study of the Person in La Jolla, California. Rogers died in February 1987 at the age of 85, without knowing he had been nominated for the Nobel Peace Prize.

Historical Background

Rogers was a leading figure in the emergence of "the third force" in psychology. Rogers's vision of the human person as trustworthy, prosocial, and creative was and still is a radical stance.

From his time at Ohio State University onward, Rogers consistently attracted brilliant students, some of whom became his research colleagues and collaborators. Nathaniel Raskin studied the important construct of the internal/external locus of evaluation. Julius Seeman, a highly regarded theorist and researcher at Vanderbilt, devoted energy to a greater understanding of motivation and the experiencing process. Other notable contributors to development of the approach include Fred Zimring at Case Western Reserve, John Shlien at Harvard, and Barbara Temaner Brodley, whose writing about therapy practice greatly advanced and clarified aspects of working from the client-centered framework.

In 1986, the Association for the Development of the Person-Centered Approach held its first meeting in International House at the University of Chicago, with Rogers in attendance. A journal also emerged from this association, originally titled *Person-Centered Review* and continued later under a new title, *The Person-Centered Journal*.

In the late 1990s, the World Association for Person-Centered and Experiential Psychotherapy and Counseling was established, along with its journal, *Person-Centered & Experiential Psychotherapies*.

Areas of Development

Rogers became interested in the broad application of the core conditions for personality change in new arenas, such as conflict resolution, personal growth in encounter, race relations, and peace work. His ideas also were taken up by a number of helping professions, such as nursing, education, human development, management consulting, and medicine.

Marshall Rosenberg developed an approach to nonviolent communication as an application of nonjudgmental empathy. He has worked with gangs and other groups with apparently intractable conflicts in Israel and Palestine (Rosenberg, 2003). Garry Prouty, a student of Eugene Gendlin, developed a model for work with severely mentally ill persons, culminating in his book *Theoretical Evolutions in Person-Centered/Experiential Therapy* (Prouty, 1994). Thomas Gordon developed his method of Parent Effectiveness Training (Gordon, 2000), based on the theory of the conditions for change found in Rogers's 1957 paper, "The Necessary and Sufficient Conditions of Therapeutic Personality Change."

Person-centered feminist theorists within the person-centered approach have published in the spirit of deconstruction of therapy as a practice. More specifically, Irene Fairhurst (1999), Gillian Proctor (2002) and Mary Beth Napier (Proctor & Napier, 2004), Carol Wolter-Gustafson (2004), Peggy Natiello (2001), Maureen O'Hara (2006), and Natalie Rogers (1980) have offered analysis and critique of the nexus of client-centered therapy and feminism.

This approach has spread internationally and is now a global reality in terms of approaches to therapy, education, conflict resolution, health and medicine, and communication.

OVERVIEW

View of Human Nature

Rogers's Motivational Theory

Rogers (1959b) proposed that clients are innately motivated to actualize their potentialities, assuming that a psychological climate conducive to growth is provided. Rogers (1986) states:

> Practice, theory and research make it clear that the person-centered approach is built on a basic trust in the person . . . [It] depends on the actualizing tendency present in every living organism's tendency to grow, to develop, to realize its full potential. This way of being trusts the directional flow of the human being toward a more complex and complete development. It is this directional flow that we aim to release. (p. 198)

In addressing Rogers's view of human nature, we refer to his theory of motivation, development, and personality published in 1959. This theoretical statement is essential reading for any student of the client-centered approach. Rogers's statements about the human infant elucidate his belief in the innate actualizing tendency as the fundamental motivational process.

The Development of the Regard Complex

The theory posits that all human infants require warm, loving care to develop positive self-regard. While Rogers was writing long before the study of trauma emerged in psychology, he understood the consequences of suppressing and invalidating the infant's lived experiencing. As self-awareness emerges in the course of human development, the child's self-concept is constituted according to what is acceptable to those vital sources of survival—his or her parents or caretakers. Organismic experiences that cannot be allowed into awareness are said to be "subceived," a process in which the child has access only under conditions that are not a danger to the psychological self (Rogers, 1959b, p. 227).

The origin of a child's anxiety, shame, and self-hatred, Rogers theorized, lies in the *conditionality* of the parents' love and acceptance for the child. Conditionality, both positive and negative, tends to preempt the child's inner locus of evaluation by creating a desire for approval, constant reassurance, and praise. Criticizing and shaming a child alienates the child from his or her inner experiencing (e.g., screaming and shouting, enjoyment of eating, evacuating, seeking skin contact, touching genitalia). Praising the child for self-denial and conformity to the social code of conduct is destructive to the congruence between the child's self-concept and organismic valuing process. This point of view should not be construed as letting a child dictate his or her own desires to whomever and whenever he or she wishes. Parents and other social authorities can explain their requests and the consequences a child will experience without attacking the child's sense of self.

Consider your own viewpoint regarding human failings, mistakes, aggressiveness, and hurtful behavior. If we approach our client from the standpoint of judgment, we risk wounding the person's sense of self. Counseling requires that we cultivate an attitude of nonjudgmental acceptance. We offer an exercise to increase your ability to identify the experience of unconditional positive regard as you work with clients and suggest ways to cultivate this fundamentally important attitude.

EXERCISE 7.1

WHAT IS UNCONDITIONAL POSITIVE REGARD?

Rogers has described this attitude of the counselor in several ways in different writings—as nonpossessive caring, or *agape* (in contrast to a more self-interested love or love driven by desire). This inner experience of the therapist comes easily much of the time. The saying, "To understand all is to pardon all," has been our experience over the years. In spite of behavior or beliefs that may evoke a critical response in us, in the situation of counseling we say, "There but for the grace of God go I."

1. Think of how you feel when you see a rainbow or the tiny hands of a baby or the wagging tail of a happy dog. Do you typically say, "Gee, this rainbow isn't as good as the one I saw a month ago," or "That infant is already manipulating his mother," or "That dog is wagging to reinforce my treat-giving behavior"? Unlikely.

2. Your unconditional response to the beautiful in nature or in others is to behold something wondrous and mysterious and to realize that we cannot fully exhaust the depths of this being. We are never finished in our understanding of ourselves or of other people.

We recommend that you not try to alter your true and natural response to your client. You react and feel the way you feel. In the beginning of a relationship, you may have negative or critical responses. Your mission, if you decide to accept it, is to find a way to "see" the person in the light of love—in the light of how he or she might be if history, genetics, situations, deprivation had been fully conducive to growth. Labeling your clients with diagnostic terms can sometimes express your lack of understanding and acceptance. It is a way of distancing yourself from the other person.

(Continued)

(Continued)

For each of us, the practice of thinking, "There but for the grace of God go I," is a potent one. Over time, this exercise of dropping judgments leads to your ability to perceive the client's ideas, actions, lifestyle, and behaviors as his or her best solution, given the circumstances. One way of dropping judgments is to try to imagine how cruelty and neglect and constant criticism have distorted the person's growth, leading to any number of reactive injurious behaviors and attitudes toward self and others (sometimes including you, the counselor). Our work is one of love and understanding, not justice. Let others in our society bring "justice" to persons. In our hour with the client, we aim only to accept and cherish this person. We believe that this attitude is the deepest, most curative factor in counseling. We may not understand perfectly, but if we can find a way to the unconditional "rainbow" state of mind, we will be doing the most, not the least. As Rogers commented, "The most, not the least, but the most we can do for another person is to ask 'what are you going through'?" And to care deeply about the answer.

Researchers have investigated the idea that parental conditional positive regard and the converse, parental conditional negative regard, lead to several negative outcomes. Roth, Assor, Niemiec, Ryan, and Deci (2009) found that when parents make their positive regard (praise, affection, etc.) contingent on the child's compliance with their guidance and demands, internal compulsion to comply with external standards takes over the child's psychological well-being. This leads to suppressive regulatory strategies and grade-oriented achievement. Parental negative conditional regard was found to stimulate resentment and emotional dysregulation and academic disengagement (p. 1119).

These findings support Rogers's (1959b) postulate that conditionality, whether negative or positive, undermines the child's positive self-regard and ultimately the psychological freedom to experience and choose those experiences that are self-realizing. Roth et al. (2009) report that even though parental conditional negative (and positive) regard may seem less severe than direct power assertion by parents, both of these practices result in behavior contrary to parental expectations. Instead, practices of manipulating the child's contingencies and emotional rewards result in internal compulsion, academic disengagement, resentment toward parents, and amotivation, including dysregulation of anger and fear. The surprising finding was that parental conditional *positive* regard also contributed to dysregulation of anger and fear (p. 1133).

Rogers termed parents' conditionality of acceptance and frequent evaluation and judgment during a child's development *conditions of worth*. The child struggles to stay true to his or her bodily lived experiences (picture a 1-year-old squirming away from Grandpa's whiskery beard). The research programs of Richard Ryan and Edward Deci (2000) and colleagues have supplied empirical support for Rogers's theory of the regard complex.

We have found that unconditional love most truly fulfills the need for relatedness (Ryan, 1993), whereas conditional regard in our work and in Rogers's (1951) is an inherently compromised form of nurturance (Ryan, 1998, p. 127).

In our brief case conceptualization of Y-Chun in Case Illustration 7.1, the concepts of conditions of worth and the regard complex are clearly illustrated.

CASE ILLUSTRATION 7.1

Y-Chun Through the Lens of Client-Centered Theory

Rogers's theory of psychological maladjustment proposes that a lack of congruence between a person's organismic experiencing and concept of self stimulates feelings of vulnerability and anxiety. In this case, Y-Chun's organismic experiencing of physical and emotional deprivation was not available to awareness for most of her life, since no one paid attention to her. But the consequences of basic neglect may have given rise to sadness, anger, and withdrawal from others. Her evolving self-concept deriving from conditions of worth is that of an unworthy, bad, unlovable child. This incongruence intensifies as she matures and perceives her deficiencies as a mother and potential marriage partner. Her lack of love for her children and her anger in sex and rejection of intimacy are incongruent with her values and self-ideal.

Originating in Y-Chun's statements—her "reality as perceived"—we infer that her parents did not pay much attention to her, and even though they told her she was the "smart one" and would make them proud, she did not feel loved or cared for without *conditions of worth*. Apparently, parental conditional positive regard was expressed toward her in their saying, "You're the smart one" and "You're the one who'll make us proud." In spite of this rare instance of praise, she reports in the interview, "I don't think I have ever had a normal relationship with either of them. The only time we would ever talk is when I was in some kind of trouble, or had disappointed them." Whether positive or negative, the conditionality of parental love damages and distorts a child's concept of self.

Y-Chun's inherent *actualizing tendency* is assumed to have been the source of organismic valuing and enhancement for the developing self as the child acquires language for experience. In spite of all the negative aspects of her development, Y-Chun may have had many moments of full living, enjoyment of her own bodily aliveness, appreciation of nature, and the bubbling up of love for her family. This reaching out for attachment and connection can be inferred seemingly paradoxically from the strength of her desire to please her parents and to attract their attention. When children have completely inadequate attachment in infancy, they display indifference to situations that offer opportunities for connection.

Since there is no information about Y-Chun's mother's pregnancy or any difficulties prior to or following Y-Chun's birth, we assume that Y-Chun's early development was normal, that she met developmental milestones, and that her early years were uneventful in terms of trauma or family crisis. The exception to this conclusion is the possibility that either or both parents were experiencing unresolved mourning and loss from the deaths of each of their spouses. It is conceivable that the emotional neglect and lack of positive regard Y-Chun endured may have, at least in part, resulted from the unavailability of parents who were still dealing with major losses.

While her siblings teased her about being the "real child" of their parents and accused her of being favored, it may be closer to the truth to say that Y-Chun was conceived as a result of the marriage of two widowed people. Every person in the family except Y-Chun had to respond to and cope with death: the parents' loss of their spouses and her siblings' loss of a parent. Ironically, this shared

(Continued)

(Continued)

experience of loss excluded the youngest daughter in the family and may have led to her isolation. In the new blended family, the older siblings on each parent's side may have had exclusive bonds and alliances, shutting out the "different" child.

We surmise that as a small child, Y-Chun did not receive, or did not perceive, loving *positive regard* from either parent. Consequently, her self-experience was lonely, isolated, and unloved. She claims that she felt empty and alone. The *conditions of worth* she experienced as she matured were mostly negative. Her interpretation of her rebellious behavior is that she just wanted recognition or attention from her parents, whether negative or positive. She was jealous of her friends' enjoyment of their family lives, as it contrasted so dramatically with her own yearning and feelings of rejection. Y-Chun suffered a profound lack of unconditional love (unconditional positive regard) and *empathy*.

In addition to the emotional deprivation in her family, Y-Chun was socially isolated and stigmatized amongst her peers in elementary and middle school. Her childhood acquaintances ridiculed and ostracized her on the basis of her biracial identity, depriving her of another potential source of positive self-regard. Even if Y-Chun's parents had taken an active role in helping her understand and defend against racial prejudice, she would have been hurt and threatened by humiliating, cruel behavior. She was cruelly stigmatized, which made her hate her Asian heritage, exacerbating her helplessness and pain. Somewhat ironically, she also experienced being stereotyped at home as a member of the Asian "model minority," as the one whose intelligence would redeem the family and make them proud.

In high school, she was raped by her cousin. Not only did she have to endure the physical and emotional injury of this criminal sexual assault, but she was also forced into silence by her conviction that her parents would not believe her. With her self-concept so distorted, she turned to high-risk sex and petty crime. In view of these multiple traumas, it is not surprising that she considered suicide and sought connection and approval in sexual contacts. Risky sexual behavior may also have confirmed her lack of positive self-regard.

Y-Chun's organismic valuing process was and is intact, yet her self-concept cannot fully integrate her bodily experiencing. Feelings of yearning or desire for comfort or attention were eventually interpreted by the self as shameful because she was an unworthy, bad daughter. Unable to press openly for what she needed, Y-Chun suffered in silence in an emotionally deprived world.

Buffeted as she was between positive evaluation and negative judgment, Y-Chun displayed anger and resentment, ran away from home, and experienced suicidal thinking as a result of the pain of ridicule from other kids and the loneliness at home. Y-Chun's female gender also played a role in her lack of acceptance of self. She did not wish to follow a woman's role as modeled by her more traditional mother. Having been raped at the age of 16, her ability to trust men in relationships was minimal and her experiences highly ambivalent. She recalls that during these mostly brief, sometimes anonymous, encounters, she experienced anger that carried over into sex. Experiences many women find profoundly fulfilling—getting into a long-term intimate relationship, giving birth, and parenting children—seem to be, at this point in Y-Chun's development, sources of anxiety, conflict, guilt, shame, and self-hatred.

From the standpoint of Rogers's theory, the actualizing tendency is active and functioning in all systems of the organism and is present as long as the organism is alive. The later development of the self-actualizing tendency represents a subsystem of the overall actualizing tendency. As long as the actualizing tendency (expressed in the process of organismic valuing) is congruent with the self-actualizing tendency, the person can be said to be psychologically adjusted. This is not the case for Y-Chun, who is currently experiencing symptoms of depression and anxiety. These experiences, accompanied by their physical manifestations in sleeplessness, nightmares, loss of appetite, loss of the ability to experience feeling or pleasure (anhedonia), guilt, and loss of concentration, are presumed to stem from a fundamental incongruence.

We also note, however, that Rogers's theory dates from a time before the possible genetic and biological as well as social origins of some depressive symptoms became the focus of research. The diathesis for depression and the psychological condition of incongruence do not oppose each other. Psychogenic, biogenic, and sociogenic causes, singly and in combination, of various conditions termed *mental illnesses* are plausible and have evidentiary support. Attending to this aspect of the case material, many client-centered therapists view the use of psychotropic medication as they would any good experiment undertaken by an autonomous and informed client. It should be noted that many client-centered counselors oppose what they call the medicalization of distress.

In our view, counselors should not have an investment in any particular medical or psychological interventions but should support the clients' freedom to choose any type of avenue that might improve their lives, including other types of counseling. In this case, the possibility of client-centered family counseling might eventually be offered to Y-Chun as she progresses from her current serious distress to a more stable, self-affirming adjustment.

Y-Chun's resilience and strength in her survival through so many obstacles, traumas, and deficiencies is a strong indication that she can mobilize her own resources, particularly given a strong relationship with an empathic, acceptant counselor. We surmise that to accomplish a reversal of her self-negating behavior and begin to observe her "self-righting" capabilities will take more than a course of brief therapy. The evidence for brief client-centered work, however, is strong; so even if she comes to counseling for only a small number of sessions, we expect that she will make significant gains.

Characteristics and Assumptions

Rogers theorized that the client's perception of specific attitudinal conditions helps reorganize the person's self-concept. As the counselor experiences unconditional positive regard for the client, the client may experience feelings and thoughts and inner judgments. But now, in the presence of a nonjudgmental counselor who does not approve or disapprove of the behavior or thoughts, the client's own judgments and self-distrust can be safely reexamined. The client has a new experience of self in which he or she feels acceptance and respect. Defensiveness can be laid aside, and a greater sense of self-authority begins to take hold.

The client-centered therapist's capacity for acceptant, empathic understanding contributes to a new experience of self (Zimring, 2000). Rogers referred to such moments when the client's experience (and interpretation of that experience) is suddenly reorganized as "moments of movement" in therapy. If the congruent therapist experiences the attitudes of unconditional positive regard and empathic understanding of the client's internal frame of reference, and if the client perceives these attitudes over time, a powerful process of change predictably occurs (Rogers, 1957, 1959b; Wampold, 2007).

From our point of view on cross-gender, cross-racial, or cross-social class dyads, the best practice for the therapist is living the attitudes described by Rogers. The respect we feel for our clients, our openness to their questions, our abdication of power—all help lessen the very real differences in power in the therapy relationship. (See Proctor, 2002, for a discussion of issues of unequal power concerns in client-centered therapy.)

The counselor in this approach avoids imposing goals, unless the client invites the therapist's input. If the therapist believes it is his or her responsibility to move the client in the direction of greater self-acceptance, to get the client to think more rationally about himself or herself and relinquish shaming core beliefs, the therapist is not accepting the client where he or she is in that moment. Only when the therapist fully accepts the client's self-determining processes of defining his or her identity and choices about life will the client experience freedom within a caring relationship. For Rogers, the more the client can trust his or her own experience as a guide for living, the better an intuitive scientist he or she becomes. This is hardly an easy path. As Rogers said to his demonstration client, Gloria, "It's a risky thing to live."

Use With Diagnostic Groups, Age Groups, and Diverse Populations

Client-centered therapy is both universal—applicable to all diagnoses and diversities—and oriented to the unique experiential phenomenology of the individual. Rogers espoused the conviction that the therapeutic attitudes, experienced by the therapist in relation to any person, create a healing climate regardless of the client's gender, age, racial identity, sexual orientation, social class status, developmental disabilities, or diagnostic label. There is now literature on the application of the approach to the elderly, children, families, and couples; work with many types of traditional diagnoses, including Axis II disorders, paranoid schizophrenia, and multiple personality disorder; and work with groups who have been stigmatized and oppressed. For example, a session that Rogers recorded in 1962 features "Mr. Lin" (a pseudonym), a client who reveals that his problem involves homosexuality. Long before Stonewall, Rogers accepted Mr. Lin's account without pathologizing or judging. Case Illustration 7.2 focuses on diverse gender identities.

Basically, in regard to "difference," we believe that client-centered therapy is both an evidence-based and ethically based practice. Client-centered therapy is the approach least likely to do harm to clients, because we do not tamper with or try to alter the client's own personal frame of reference. Whether our clients speak from religious beliefs or political beliefs, such as Afrocentrism, feminism, conservatism, and so on, counselors seek empowerment of clients regardless of difference. From our point of view, the challenge is the person of the therapist. It is a question of whether the therapist's personal development, maturity, and openness to difference are sufficiently evolved to recognize and reflect on his or her biases. In spite of contentions that clients from collectivist cultures cannot work well with such an "individualistic"

CASE ILLUSTRATION 7.2

The Journey From James to Jamie

James was referred by another therapist for counseling. He is 38 years old, Caucasian with Ukrainian ancestry, and was raised Catholic. He attended Catholic schools from elementary through college. He struggles with his weight. James has been interested in computers and various types of programming since college, and he has found well-paying jobs in his field; however, he states that he is extremely uncomfortable in his mostly male workplace. For his coworkers, interests include sports, women, and various types of beer. In the office, many sexist, homophobic, and racist jokes are voiced, and James feels vulnerable, angry, and alienated. His interests are science fiction, his cats, and his Apple devices. He feels like an outsider and fears he is often on the brink of being bullied due to his inability to be "one of the guys." James has been a long-standing loner. He has a good female friend from college, but beyond her, he does not talk about a social life with his own friends or his wife.

James explains that this barrier between himself and his peers is due to more than just divergent interests. In fact, recently, James has identified the source of many years of depression and discomfort: He has suffered from gender dysphoria and says that, within the past 2 years, he has had to admit he is a woman. He has been feeling this way for a long time but has not disclosed this to his wife of 18 years. He dresses in women's clothes in private and, at one point, left a bra in their bathroom. When his wife found the bra, he feigned ignorance. His wife did not pursue the matter further. James and his wife have not had a sexual relationship in a number of years due to lack of interest on both their parts. He describes himself as never having had a very strong sex drive. The couple does enjoy cooking together, caring for their tropical fish, and seeing their parents for various events and holidays.

James comes to sessions dressed in his work clothes—khakis, a button-down shirt, and a light jacket. His face is stiff, and his presence in the sessions communicates general discomfort and uneasiness. He describes his life in terms of low-level depression. He is unhappy at his job, and, more important, he feels completely stuck in terms of pursuing a full transition to life as a woman.

How You Might Approach Working With James

First, the issue of whether James is a bona fide transsexual or a cross-dresser (bi-gendered) is not the counselor's prerogative. More clarity about this issue of identity will emerge through your acceptance and respect. If the client reports depression, we recommend suggesting the possibility of seeing a doctor for an evaluation to determine if antidepressant medication might help. One fact you may not be aware of is that a small dose of female hormones can be highly beneficial and may allow the client to achieve a greater degree of comfort. "I just feel more like myself," is a common response

(Continued)

(Continued)

when male-to-female (MTF) transgender persons start hormone therapy. Taking a small dose does not commit the person to a full transition (Ettner, 1999).

Second, good client-centered therapy, which has no goals for the client, will allow the client to move at his own pace. The goal must emerge from the client's genuine self-understanding, and this takes time to develop, as many transgender persons have kept their innermost selves secret for many years. They have also avoided intimacy—both emotional and physical—due to their fear of being discovered. Whether James ultimately will seek to transition fully to his true gender or whether for now he elects to get by with medication and counseling is at this point unknown, but both options are legitimate.

Third, we as counselors need to take a good look at our own biases toward persons, particularly MTFs, who challenge our gender stereotypes. We are deeply socialized to see the differences between men and women as real and immutable, and to see the sexes in terms of binary opposition. Men in dresses are figures of ridicule and often bullied, assaulted, and still seen as highly pathological. Cross-gender identity is not pathological. It is a condition that emerges early in the lives of children and, for a minority of those children, will be a lifelong reality. The effective treatment for MTFs is hormonal reassignment and surgery to feminize the body and face. For female-to-male (FTM) transgender persons, mastectomy, hysterectomy, and phalloplasty are robustly successful in confirming the person's true gender identity.

Conclusion: Providing the therapeutic conditions is our goal in this case as in any other. Honesty about our own limitations and ignorance is very important in nurturing a good relationship. At the same time, as in any other "difference," we want to learn as much as we can about gender variance, the process of transition, expanding our knowledge base, etc. The World Professional Association for Transgender Health is an international organization of surgeons, psychologists, counselors, social workers, attorneys, advocates, and transactivists, and would be a good source for information.

Questions for Consideration

1. How would you respond if your client asked permission to bring women's clothes, heels, makeup, and jewelry in an overnight bag so he could be himself as a woman in your sessions together?

2. How might you respond to his asking you, "How do I look?" (a) when he did not look good or (b) when he looked feminine and quite natural?

3. How might you respond to a request that you give your client advice on hair and makeup (assuming you have hair and wear makeup)?

4. Would you feel comfortable using his female name and feminine pronouns?

therapy or that African American clients need "structure," we respond that client-centered therapy may provide structure when clients communicate that need (depending on the therapist's ability to incorporate more structure creatively; Mier & Witty, 2004). Although we believe that the approach is empowering, we are not *trying* to empower or prompt liberal or progressive or conservative values of any kind. Politics has no place in therapy in the sense of the therapist's pushing an agenda for changing or attempting to influence the client. We should not be attempting to influence the client in any direction if we trust that the best direction is known only by the client. This stance, of course, is profoundly political in its antiauthoritarian, democratic practice.

Strengths and Limitations

We assert that there are no particular limitations to the client-centered approach. The limitation is a general one, which applies to the practice of counseling. The session is what it is. It is time-limited by virtue of the length of the session, clients' insurance benefits, or their personal circumstances. What counseling is *not* is many other practices devoted to alleviating human suffering, such as advocacy, social work, psychoeducation, and case management. While client-centered therapy occasionally has elements of all these other practices, its main focus is psychological: two autonomous human beings in a real relationship through which one person is seeking help, however "help" may come to be defined. Although the counseling situation is limited by definition, the possibilities for change are real. These psychological changes may have synergistic effects on other problems in living. As the client gains more confidence to assert himself or herself at work, to improve standards of behavior that enhance health, or to leave destructive situations, he or she moves in the direction of greater self-realization and higher functioning. Student counselors need to be clear about the nature of the practice in which they are engaged so they do not have expectations that should not reasonably be applied to therapy.

Research Supporting Constructs and Practices

In *The Great Psychotherapy Debate,* Bruce Wampold (2001) reviewed a series of meta-analytic studies of psychotherapy outcome and efficacy. He compared the medical model of treatment with what he has termed the *contextual* model to investigate the claims that psychological conditions *are comparable to medical conditions* and should be approached in the same way: assessment, diagnosis, treatment interventions, and cure. To obtain the most reliable inferential power, the double-blind study with random assignment is the "gold standard." This type of research design requires pure samples of the "disorder" with no comorbidity, random assignment to treatment conditions, and statistical procedures to assess effectiveness or potency of the proposed treatment modalities in which neither subject nor researcher knows which treatment is "active."

The gold-standard research studies require that disease entities are capable of being identified, diagnoses are clear-cut and reliable over site and time, the entities being investigated occur without comorbid conditions, participants are not clinic or walk-in patients, groups are randomly assigned to treatment conditions, and groups are comparable in terms of various demographic categories, such as age, race, gender, etc. Only when these conditions are met can a treatment be considered "evidence based" (see Bohart, 2002; Bozarth, 2002; Elkins, 2009, 2013). However, this most rigorous design has many problems. Do the patients in these strictly controlled studies represent "real-world" clients? To what extent is researcher bias controlled?

Since a thorough critique of this research model and the medical model undergirding the research enterprise is beyond the scope of this chapter, we encourage students to explore the arguments and evidence Wampold (2001) has set forth. To skip ahead to his basic conclusion, the notion that human suffering can be sorted into valid diagnostic categories is already problematic, as the current controversy surrounding *DSM-V* (fifth edition of the *Diagnostic and Statistical Manual of Mental Disorders*) attests. Is a father's "unresolved grief" a disorder if his child was killed in a shootout at her elementary school? What about the process of labeling behavior as "ADHD," a diagnosis that follows the child into adulthood and becomes an aspect of self? What is the consequence of an approach to treatment when the child is *aware* of being singled out for treatment?

The corollary to the necessity of accurate diagnostic assessment is the contention that only *specific* treatments are effective with particular diagnoses. This pursuit of specific treatments for specific disorders is, in Elkins's (2013) terms, the biggest boondoggle of the past 30 years in the field of psychology.

> Along with other relationship sciences, attachment theory provides a major science-based cornerstone for a new non-medical model of psychotherapy that places the human elements at the center of emotional healing. If, as attachment theory suggests, humans are evolved to develop, maintain, and restore their emotional well-being through supportive relationships with other humans, then this would explain why all psychotherapies, despite wide differences in modalities and techniques, are effective and equally so, and why the human elements are especially potent. Most simply defined, psychotherapy is a relationship between a human who is in need of emotional care and another human who is willing and able to give it. Thus, psychotherapy can best be understood not as a set of medical-like techniques but, rather, as a deeply human endeavor that is an expression of an evolutionarily derived capacity to heal one another emotionally. Thus, the best therapists are not necessarily those who memorize manuals and administer techniques but, rather, those who can create a therapeutic milieu characterized by care that activates and supports the healing potentials in the client, the therapist, and the relationship. This also explains why all psychotherapies are effective: all psychotherapies, regardless of their modalities and techniques, are ultimately dependent on the human elements of therapy for their effectiveness. As one of my doctoral students put it: "Techniques are fine. The only problem is that they leave out the client, the therapist, and the relationship." Science is now showing that the client, therapist, and relationship—in that order—are the major determinants of psychological healing. (p. 8)

In the meta-analytic work by Robert Elliott and Elizabeth Freire (2008, 2010), person-centered and experiential approaches were found to be equally effective when compared to problem-centered, cognitive approaches. Exceptions were found advantaging cognitive-behavioral therapy for treatment of simple phobias. Psychotherapies of all descriptions tend to be effective regardless of theoretical persuasion. As Elkins and Wampold, among others, have interpreted these findings, the human elements—the strength of the healing bond—are essential to the counseling enterprise.

Professional Identity

In the beginning, working as a counselor, it is natural to feel *un*natural—as if you are playing a role (and of course you are). At this point in your professional identity development, you may have little experience witnessing the potency of the counseling relationship over time. When a client asks if this process will be helpful for his or her problems, you may know—based on the research literature—but you do not yet know based on your own effectiveness as a helper. So we acknowledge that the first years of working are usually fraught with doubts, mistakes, and lots of no-shows. Eventually, though, the clarity of your theoretical orientation and the disciplined application of implementing healing attitudes that feel most natural for you as a helper will begin to yield more self-confidence and greater congruence.

Congruence for Rogers meant having access to the flow of your experiencing—a feeling of personal integration and relaxed well-being as you work with your clients. This work is a developmental process for the therapist as well as the client. In the end, the professional role disappears into the integrated whole person you are as you practice your approach to therapy. It doesn't mean you relax your professional identity or your ethical commitments. It *does* mean that performance anxiety and self-focus tend to recede, allowing a more immediate, personal presence to emerge.

The profession of counselor or therapist is one with its own code of ethics and theories of application. Perhaps uniquely, though, the more you are being yourself, the more effective you will be as a counselor. You should not hide behind a professional façade of expertise but should endeavor to meet each new person who comes for help as a unique, sovereign being who is giving you the privilege of helping.

THERAPEUTIC PROCESS AND APPLICATIONS

Therapeutic Goals

All therapeutic frameworks aim to free the client's capacities for self-realization and improved functioning. Therapy theories differ in terms of the processes hypothesized to achieve this ultimate goal. A client may come to therapy at any point in his or her development, at different ages, and under many different circumstances. For instance, a client who recently lost her 50-year-old mother to a massive heart attack came into therapy with the first author, saying, "I don't know who I am, and I can't decide what I am doing with my life. My mother and I spoke every morning on the phone. She helped me figure everything out, and now I can't ever talk to her again." A problem-centered therapist might suggest that the therapy focus on concrete steps to help the client become more conscious of what her own choices are and how she decides to take care of herself. A psychodynamic-relational therapist might focus on the relationship developing between the therapist and the client, with an aim to help the client achieve greater insight into her feelings and beliefs about intimacy and dependence, by attending to transferential content in the client's narrative.

By contrast, a client-centered therapist has no goals for the client except commitment to the meta-goal of empowering the client and freeing the client's inner resources for growth. The therapist supports the goals the client identifies, with the understanding that goals change as the therapy process unfolds. In the case of the young woman whose mother died suddenly, her most immediate goal was "to get help" in the face of this tragic loss. What "help" would come to mean evolved over the course of therapy. Over time, she recognized how dependent she was on her mother's approval. She was able to acknowledge that her feelings about her mother were not all positive and included elements of relief that she was free of her mother's evaluations and opinions. She acknowledged drinking too much and too often and began to moderate her consumption. Although her anxiety continued to plague her, she asked for ways to manage rumination and obsessive thinking. She became more assertive with her father, who tried to convince her to move home to be his caretaker and helper. All these changes were not just due to the therapy, of course; like many clients in client-centered therapy, her increasing self-confidence and awareness of her own needs led to improved self-acceptance and self-regulation.

In an interview with Michele Baldwin (1987), Rogers stated

> I think that therapy is most effective when the therapist's goals are limited to the process of therapy and not the outcome. I think that if the therapist feels "I want to be as present to this person as possible. I want to really listen to what is going on. I want to be real in this relationship," then these are suitable goals for the therapist. If the therapist is feeling, "I want this person to get over this neurotic behavior, I want this person to change in such and such a way," I think that stands in the way of good therapy. The goal has to be within myself, with the way I am. Once therapy is under way, another goal of the therapist's is to question: "Am I really with this person in this moment? Not where they were a little while ago, or where are they going to be, but am I really with this client in this moment." This is the most important thing. (pp. 47–48)

The client-centered therapist trusts the client's inner capacity for self-determination, including the direction of the therapy hour itself.

Change Process

Rogers once commented that one of the most common fears is that one is unlovable. In Rogers's theory of development, this fear arises from an inadequate psychological environment—through the failure of the infant's parents/caretakers to communicate empathic attunement to their child. This failure of responsiveness affects the child's self-perceptions and self-concept. A person's conviction of his or her lack of attractiveness, lovableness, and worthiness gradually changes in a loving, acceptant relationship with another—whether that other is a dear grandparent, beloved teacher, best friend, or therapist. Self-acceptance and self-respect gradually supplant distortions acquired through early inadequate or destructive interpersonal and social environments. The degree of success in moving toward Rogers's notion of the "fully functioning person" depends to a large extent on what psychotherapy researchers term *client factors* (Asay & Lambert, 1999; Bohart, 2007), in conjunction with therapist factors (i.e., the relationship).

Client Factors

Each client brings to therapy his or her genetic inheritance; history of pre-, peri-, and post-natal health and early attachments; quality of nutrition and physical safety and security; possible threats to well-being, depending on the economic status of the family; the situation in which the child was raised, and so on. Deeply held beliefs in the unacceptability of the self—the unlovability of one's body—derive from caregivers' attributions, whether negative—"You act like you think you're really something, you selfish brat!"—or positive (as in Y-Chun's case)—"You've always been the smartest, so you better ace that test!" The pressures for conformity at home, in school, and from other social institutions may create a poor fit between the growing, creative, experimenting child and social norms. In particular, gender-variant children and children whose social class, race, or religious affiliation differs from the majority suffer from physical and emotional violence. Those children whose difference is not immediately evident to others live in secrecy and isolation to protect themselves from ostracism.

In terms of client factors, the range of variability is sweeping, with some of the aforementioned factors abiding in your client's awareness and many variables unavailable to awareness. The counselor and even the client are always working with incomplete knowledge of this individual's early development; traumas involving physical injury, psychological abuse, and neglect; and impacts from family problems and sociocultural factors such as prejudice, discrimination, immigration, poverty, and war. The counselor need not feel responsible for ferreting out every conceivable aspect of the client's past or developmental history. As the client begins to trust the counselor, he or she will gradually bring out problems for the counselor to understand.

Relationship Factors

Client-centered therapists place their confidence in the centrality of the relationship between client and therapist as the most important healing factor in therapy. Bruce Wampold's meta-analyses, as well as those of Elliott and Freire, have demonstrated the specious claims of the "specificity" hypothesis—that what makes therapy work are specific techniques. Common factors research emphasizes the relationship as the factor that makes the greatest contribution to outcome, aside from client factors (Elliott & Freire, 2010; Wampold, 2001).

Most experienced counselors have had clients who rarely or never refer to inner experiencing, feelings, and the like. These clients could be described as fairly superficial and low on any measure of internal emotional processing. Yet over the course of therapy, remarkably, they reported feeling better, more positive, and very much helped by the therapy.

This makes the most sense if we consider that the gains from the therapy issue from the presence of the warm, acceptant therapist in a consistent relationship with the client. These clients at the end of therapy were not particularly articulate about their emotions, nor were they obviously self-aware. They were not likely to stop midsentence and say,

"You know, I just realized that I don't feel very warmly toward my son," or "I worry some-times that I bore you." Instead, they talked about work, their frustrations, about other people who annoyed them. During internship, one of the first author's clients discussed the furni-ture she wished to buy and her husband's opposition to her plans. Some practitioners might argue that allowing these clients to dwell in the mundane is a disservice and that through challenge and confrontation, the client should be faced with his or her "avoidance" or "resis-tance." But the therapist's willingness to stay in the moment with such a client conveys empathic understanding and respect and a nonevaluative grasp of what is truly important to the client. When students say that clients are "intellectualizing" or going over and over the same thing, we strongly disagree. What we see are novice counselors unable or unwilling to enter gently into the client's world of meanings and experiences just as it is.

Throughout the preceding, the idea of therapist respect and non-evaluative judgement of the client has been presented as an essential component of the counseling dynamic. Like

---

EXERCISE 7.2

IMPLEMENTING THE ATTITUDES

This exercise will help you implement the attitudes of nonevaluative acceptance and personal genu-ineness and will give you an opportunity to practice your empathic understanding. You can try it once or twice or practice in a series of sessions. Either way, we predict it will help you further the melding of your own real experiencing of understanding and of expressing that understanding from the atti-tudes of nonevaluative acceptance and personal genuineness.

1. This exercise is most useful if you can recruit a "practice" client for at least five 50-minute sessions, occurring weekly in a quiet, nondistracting, private place. Restaurants and coffee shops are not conducive to practice because of their background noise and lack of privacy.

2. This exercise is *not* a role play. When you invite a person to help you by being a volunteer client, explain that you are asking him or her to talk with you about a concern or problem he or she is *having right now*. Explain that you are not asking that he or she pick a topic so deeply distressing that he or she will leave the session in a state of disturbance or so private and personal that he or she may later regret discussing it. It should be a *real* concern or problem, however—one the volunteer feels reasonably comfortable speaking about with you.

3. The practice client should sign a release, giving you permission to record the session but forbidding your use of the tape for any purpose but your own personal education in learning to counsel people more effectively. After you have listened to your tape recording, you should erase it. Do not place any identifying information on the tape in case you misplace or lose it.

4. How to begin: Introduce yourself to your practice client (better if you do not know the person already) and invite him or her to think of an issue or concern he or she is willing to discuss.

You may encourage the volunteer to take a few moments to think of the concern. Explain that your aim will be simply to follow and understand. "I may occasionally ask a question for clarification." Explain the taping, and ask for a signature for permission to tape; the release should explain that you will erase each session after you have listened to it and that no tapes, audio or digital, will be saved.

5. In the half-hour practice session, as you listen to your client, relax and absorb what he or she is communicating. As you listen, you will notice that you either are following and getting his or her point *or* are unsure of what the client is expressing. The point of articulating an empathic understanding response is to orient yourself, although it also helps the client clarify his or her meanings.

6. When you speak to express your understanding, the client will sometimes respond by saying, "Yes, exactly!" You can assume then that you are capturing the client's meaning with empathic accuracy. If the client says, "Well, no, I meant that I *do* want the relationship even if it is making me very unhappy," then you have facilitated the client's process of expressing what he or she is trying to get across. So even though you aim for accuracy, mistakes can also forward the process. Try to respond completely from *within the client's frame of reference*, without adding your own point of view or interpretations, advice, or guiding questions. Remind yourself: How does the situation appear to my client? What are *his or her* values and theories, either explicit or implicit?

7. Although this kind of disciplined empathic understanding exercise should not be taken to represent a fully realized client-centered relationship, it can help you develop your ability to articulate meanings without the distraction of coming up with advice, guidance, problem solving, or other "interventions." As you grow in fluency, you will begin to observe the creativity that accompanies freeing the client to go where he or she needs to go and the "moments of movement" (Rogers's words) the client makes in the course of being understood. If the client asks your opinion or asks what to do, ask the client to try to hold questions until after the practice session is complete.

8. Finally, reflect on your own reactions during the session. Did the subject matter stimulate some anxiety in you, or did you get distracted by wanting to guide the client to a solution? Remember that solutions provided by the counselor deprive the client of the experience of learning the process of solving his or her own problems and, particularly if the advice is helpful, underscore the superior judgment of the counselor. Occasionally in client-centered work, clients ask direct questions of the counselor, and we believe that answering them is a respectful implementation of the nondirective attitude. (See Brodley, in Moon et al., 2011, Chapter 12: "The Empathic Understanding Response Process" and Chapter 17: "The Therapeutic Interview: Guidelines for Beginning Practice.")

(Continued)

(Continued)

9. Were you relaxed and at ease, trusting the client to find his or her own way, or were you squirming with nervousness when a silence occurred? In dealing with your own natural social anxiety (after all, you're a person, too), remember that the counseling relationship is different from a social relationship. In a friendship, each person usually takes a turn talking about problems, issues, and troubles. In counseling, you are trying to be of service to the client. The time belongs to the client.

10. In listening to the recording of your work after the session, pay attention to how you were feeling and reacting. Are there some issues that stimulate your judgment? Are there some types of people to whom you have a kind of knee-jerk reaction? This kind of self-knowledge is critical in your development as a counselor.

11. Finally, ask yourself as you are listening to your work: Did I grasp the point my client was trying to communicate with me? This is a better question, in our view, than, "Did I catch the client's feelings?" Don't listen with an agenda for any particular type of content or emotionality. "Did I feel a need to correct the client's thinking, to guide him or her toward more reasonable or socially consensual points of view?" This is a frequent temptation. Try to avoid it. Follow the client, and trust the process! And trust yourself.

unconditional positive regard, the ability to hold and convey a non-evaluative stance is not that easy given the strong cultural forces promoting evaluative judgment. Exercise 7.2 invites you to experience genuineness and non-evaluative judgment.

Interventions

The term *intervention* implies an action or course of action that originates in the counselor. Examples of interventions are reframing, normalizing, reassurance, interpretation, leading questions, confrontation, correcting distortions in thinking, and psychoeducational responses, to name a few. Depending on the situation, counselors may advise the client to see a doctor or go to substance-abuse treatment, see a psychiatrist, or submit to involuntary commitment. While any one of these situations may arise in client-centered counseling, they tend to be theoretically inconsistent (confrontation, correcting distorted thinking) or rare because they violate the principle of nondirectiveness, the attitude at the foundation of client-centered work (Brodley, 1997; Grant, 1990; Raskin, 1947/2005; Witty, 2004). Instead of "using skills" or "performing interventions," client-centered therapists practice a way of being (C. R. Rogers, 1980).

So the question is not how to *do* client-centered therapy or *use* client-centered therapy, as if it were a *tool* in your toolkit. The counselor's practice of this approach involves adopting the hypothesis that clients can be trusted and that they are doing the best they can under the circumstances they perceive and that are affecting them (Brodley, 1999a).

It requires relinquishing power over the client. Assessment procedures, diagnosis, treatment interventions, and the like may be required by the institutional settings in which you work, and you may need to become proficient in these procedures. However, it is important to realize that the counseling relationship is not the sum of procedures. Rogers said he did not want to see a patient's file. He wanted to encounter the other person as free from the preconceptions and diagnostic opinions of others as possible. He also stated quite emphatically that a system that places authority in the expert to guide the process eventually undermines the self-authority of the client (Rogers, 1957) and establishes an autocratic system that threatens democracy.

Rogers (1951) commented:

> It has been my experience that only when the counselor . . . has settled within himself the hypothesis on which he will act, can he be of maximum aid to the individual. It has also been my experience that the more deeply he relies upon the strength and potentiality of the client, the more deeply does he discover that strength. (p. 48)

Rogers's intention in his statement regarding "the necessary and sufficient conditions of personality change" was not to describe only client-centered therapy but to hypothesize the potent core of all therapies. The enormous amount of research on these so-called core conditions has repeatedly demonstrated the importance of the therapist conditions—that is, the relationship that arises as characterized by the conditions (see Cooper, Watson, & Hölldampf, 2010).

Rogers's genius was to innovate in his own work and then describe and teach an approach that helped the student acquire a disciplined "method" of being with the client and living out the attitudes (Rogers, 1959a). A number of approaches to therapy define a philosophical/political/moral ground for therapy but are weak in terms of specifying the actual practice. Feminist theorists, for example, have struggled with how to bring the practice of feminist therapy into a logically consistent relationship with their political analysis of the oppression of persons of all genders, although the main emphasis has been on women. If the feminist therapist takes on the role of mentor, psychoeducator, and support for clients, the power difference between the two persons is emphasized and the counselor may, without wishing to, become an authority figure for clients. We maintain that client-centered therapy is inherently empowering, thus implicitly supportive of and perhaps even isomorphic with some feminist therapy.

When client-centered students learn and practice the empathic understanding response, often called "reflecting" or "mirroring," it is critical to discriminate it from "active listening." Most of us do not want a counselor to repeat what we have just said. Instead, the client-centered counselor seeks to understand the relationship between the expressed content and the client's reason for expressing it. When a counselor attempts to verbalize the point of the client's communication, the purpose is not to prompt the client, support or reassure the client that he or she is being clear, or telegraph the expertise of the counselor-as-empathizer extraordinaire. The client-centered therapist makes empathic understanding responses for herself or himself. Serendipitously, this process of checking for understanding spontaneously conveys to the client that your intention is simply to understand, not to criticize, evaluate, or correct.

Empathic understanding responses are motivated by the inner experience of the counselor—a feeling of, "I'm not sure I'm getting this." At this point, *the counselor responds to check his or her understanding,* thus allowing the client to affirm the response—"Yes, exactly. Yes, you get it!"—and move to his or her next point, or correct the counselor by saying, "No, that's not quite what I mean. It's more like a feeling of relief." The empathic response almost always has a tentative quality, an implicit "Did I get this right?" This tentativeness is not strategic; it is sincere. It is true in the situation that the counselor is not completely sure that his or her grasp of the client's intended meaning is correct.

Accuracy in the process is an ideal, but often the interactive process corrects for the counselor's occasional inaccuracies. At first, practicing the empathic understanding response process may feel wooden and artificial to students. We recommend that you go ahead anyway, and with consistency and discipline, try to proceed with empathic understanding. Avoid leading questions. When you are anxious, try not to fall into "interviewing" the client or pursuing your own curiosities. Allow for silences. Questions for clarification are occasionally necessary but should not be motivated by the counselor's curiosity or desire to point out "patterns." Allow the client to fill in the blanks in his or her narrative as the relationship evolves. To acquire a deeper understanding of the practice, students are encouraged to read Brodley's articles "The Empathic Understanding Response Process," "Criteria for Making Empathic Responses," and "Client-Centered: An Expressive Therapy," all of which are published in *Practicing Client-Centered Therapy: Selected Writings of Barbara Temaner Brodley* (Moon, Witty, Grant, & Rice, 2011).

The empathic understanding response process is a perfect vehicle for the therapeutic attitudes of empathy, unconditional positive regard, and genuineness (Brodley, 2000). First, unless you are genuine as a real person and not just in a professional capacity, the client cannot completely trust you or know what actions you might take against him or her (even though *you* might feel your actions are in the client's best interest). Genuineness or congruence means the counselor is not attempting to play a professional role of any kind but is another human being offering help to someone who is asking for it (Brodley, 2001). Genuineness means not trying to deceive the client in regard to yourself, your experience, knowledge, training, or anything else. Most client-centered therapists are willing to answer personal questions clients pose (within limits of ethics and appropriateness), about the process of therapy and whether or not the therapist believes the client may be helped.

Second, the empathic understanding response process means the counselor has no intention other than to understand. As the counselor practices this process over time and with consistency, the client comes to understand and trust that the counselor holds no covert agenda or unspoken diagnoses about him or her. If our clients ask about our diagnostic opinions, we answer directly and honestly and walk them through our thinking as to how we arrived at this opinion (Brodley, 1999b).

Third, the counselor's warm esteem and real interest and concern for the client are implicit in the empathic understanding response.

Finally, the nondirective attitude is the hallmark of client-centered therapy. For most of us, it is a challenge to drop all judgmental and evaluative thoughts about the client. Most of us are so imbued with the habit of opining on everything from our friends' decisions in mates to how to train/educate dogs to how to eat right, dress right, think right, that thoughts of how the client can and should improve his or her life come to us in nanoseconds. Almost all these "inspirations" and desires to educate the client should be gently put to the side of your awareness during a session. Rogers advises that if you are afflicted with a persistent feeling, you should get supervision/consultation and decide whether to discuss it with the client. But these persistent feelings are mostly rare and require that you consider the client's psychological safety before you raise the issue. As Nat Raskin enjoins us: "Trust the client!" Give the process a chance. Give the client time to experience your warm, acceptant empathy and personal genuineness. As Rogers said, the more you can take a leap of faith in the client's inner resources, the more evidence of those resources will emerge in therapy.

CONCLUSION

The practice of client-centered therapy has sometimes been described as a "moral" education for the therapist. Practicing makes us better people. We tend to give others the benefit of the doubt; we imagine what could account for human failings. This approach gives the power and respect to the client. It means not indulging oneself in telling clients instances in your life that correspond to instances in theirs. It involves discipline and restraint, humility and abdication of power even in the most subtle forms. It means being on guard for your own desires to be a hero, a messiah, a rescuer. We do not aim to encourage the client to become dependent on our wise counsel; we aim to free the client to heed his or her own counsel. Therapy is not an ego trip for the therapist or a source of friends or admirers. The only legitimate rewards in therapy are the inherent pleasure gained from the process of understanding another person's intentional expressed meanings and whatever practical remuneration you receive for providing this service.

KEYSTONES

- In client-centered practice, case conceptualization derives from the client's "phenomenology"—that is, from the client's perceptions and experiences. Each person speaks from a point of view, a location uniquely his or her own. Rogers termed this viewpoint the *internal frame of reference*.
- While it is possible to hypothesize about causes, precipitants, and factors that create the client's problems in living, his or her perceptions and symptoms, this hypothetical formulation is not essential to the counseling process. Case formulations and reports may be requested by other professionals in psychiatry, social work, insurance, and medicine who seek your assessment of the client's status, diagnoses, course of treatment, and prognosis. This process of formulation and meeting the requirements of other professionals is a collaborative, transparent process between the client-centered counselor and the client.
- In client-centered therapy, counseling is not guided by the counselor's conceptualization, since the counselor's implementation of the attitudes of empathic understanding, unconditional positive regard, and genuineness is the same for all clients.

- Client-centered counselors, through their education and life experience, gain an understanding of biological, psychological, social, and economic factors that determine and influence clients' problems. This approach has a broad understanding of the factors influencing clients—that in each individual case, one factor or a combination of factors creates unique challenges, limitations, and opportunities in clients' lives. In this sense, client-centered therapy is a biopsychosocial model grounded in ethics and a politics of empowerment.

REFLECTIONS FROM THE CONTRIBUTOR'S CHAIR

Marjorie C. Witty

My introduction to the client-centered approach came serendipitously through taking a community practicum in client-centered therapy in 1972 at the Chicago Counseling and Psychotherapy Research Center. There, I met my lifelong mentor, therapist, and teacher, Barbara Temaner Brodley. Her inspiration came not just through the ideas about client-centered therapy—although they were and are powerful and significant to me—but through her example in how she interacted with me and other people. Her understanding, compassionate attitude has given me a therapeutic compass. I also am fortunate to have had Nat Raskin as a professor at Northwestern University. He taught me, "Trust the client!"—a revolutionary idea to this day. My colleagues and dear friends Susan Pildes, Carolyn Schneider, Sharon Mier, Ted Welsch, Barry Grant, Kathryn Moon, and Bert Rice remain faithful sources of consultation, new theory, and evolutions in practice.

Ray Adomaitis

Freedom is not having to carry around a mask.

Growing up in a large Lithuanian immigrant–refugee family with minimal formal education, in diverse, racially divided neighborhoods in Chicago, I have been educated among both the poor and affluent, and by extraordinary mentors. I came to trust the person-centered approach after years of working with children and adults—individually and in groups; in crisis or coming face-to-face with themselves; making important decisions in their lives, whether problem solving or striving to live life on their own terms; and with persons of diverse backgrounds battling prejudice, discrimination, oppression, inequality, and poverty. The person-centered approach is an accepting, optimistic, empowering, warmly human, and honest way of approaching life and being in relationship with others. The organizing principles are empathy, positive regard, and, most important for me, genuineness—a reminder and call to reflect on self and endeavor to be most fully oneself.

In the sphere of my professional activities, my teacher, mentor, and therapist of nearly 30 years, Nathaniel J. Raskin at Northwestern University, was undoubtedly most influential in helping me appreciate the nuances of being a person-centered counselor, through our discussions but mostly from his personal example. He introduced me to Carl Rogers at the Evolution of Psychotherapy Conference in 1984, which prompted me to hasten my studies and both embrace the client-centered way and ask, "What do we mean by 'being genuine'?" Another mentor at Northwestern University, Kenneth I. Howard, encouraged me similarly to find my way through the maze of theories and practices with an open mind and a love for psychotherapy research that was punctuated with Rogers's attitude that "the facts are always friendly."

ADDITIONAL RESOURCES

Graduate Education

Illinois School of Professional Psychology in Chicago and Argosy University in Schaumberg, Illinois, offer classes in the theory and practice of client-centered therapy, advanced client-centered therapy, and client-centered groups. These schools offer a vital minor in clinical psychology in client-centered therapy, and a number of students have trained in practica at the Carl Rogers Institute, the training arm of The New Center.

Two other training sites in Chicago—Chicago Counseling Associates (www.cca-cct.com) and Client-Centered Counseling Associates (ccca-online.com)—offer specific education in practicing client-centered therapy. Another group for learning and community networking is the Chicago Area Person-Centered Network, which meets once a month for discussion and encounter.

Books

The most comprehensive source for books on the client-centered, person-centered, and experiential approach can be found on the website for PCCS Books (www.pccs-books.co.uk).

Rogers, C. R. (1951). *Client-centered therapy.* Boston: Houghton Mifflin.

This is an essential text for students of the approach. In Chapter 2, "The Attitude and Orientation of the Counselor," Rogers explains the philosophical and political basis of his approach to working with persons.

Rogers, C. R. (1959). A theory of therapy, personality and interpersonal relationships as developed in the client-centered framework. In S. Koch (Ed.), *Psychology: The study of a science; Vol. III: Formulations of the person in the social context* (pp. 184–256). New York: McGraw-Hill.

Often referred to as Rogers's magnum opus (great work), this is the most formal and clear statement of his theory. To understand this approach, it is critical reading.

Rogers, C. R. (1961). *On becoming a person.* Boston: Houghton Mifflin.

With the publication of this book, Rogers became well-known to the general public. In this book, he describes what he has learned about the characteristics of the fully functioning person. This book aids the reader in understanding how Rogers views the end goals of therapy.

Moon, K. A., Witty, M. C., Grant, B., & Rice, B. (Eds.). (2011). *Practicing client-centered therapy: Selected writings of Barbara Temaner Brodley.* Ross-on-Wye, UK: PCCS Books.

An essential text for counselors interested in working from the client-centered approach. Brodley addresses specific issues related to answering questions, self-disclosure, responding to requests, and the like. She also helps students understand how the counseling relationship differs from other practices oriented toward aiding persons.

Organizations and Websites

Association for the Development of the Person-Centered Approach (www.adpca.org)

Publishes the *Person-Centered Journal,* formerly the *Person-Centered Review.* This is the official website of the U.S. and international organization of which Rogers was a member. Founded in 1986 at a conference in Chicago, the organization sponsors an annual conference and listings of other workshops, continuing education opportunities, and trainings that can provide counselors a home in the person-centered approach. For counselors and researchers, the annual conferences provide a safe, supportive, and appreciative environment for presentations, papers, and posters. This conference is distinctive by virtue of the daily small-group experience and nightly large-group community meetings.

World Association for Person-Centered and Experiential Psychotherapy and Counseling (www.pce-world.org)

This organization was founded in 1997. It is the most broadly international organization for person-centered and experiential counselors, therapists, researchers, educators, and workshop conveners. The organization sponsors conferences every other year and publishes the international journal *Person-Centered and Experiential Psychotherapy Abstracts* in English, German, French, Spanish, and Japanese.

The Person-Centered Website (www.pca-online.net)

Peter F. Schmid, PhD, a major theoretician in the approach, has maintained a vital and rich website of resources in the person-centered and experiential traditions. He is professor at the University of Vienna, Austria, with particular interests in philosophy, ethics, anthropology, and phenomenology. This remarkable, comprehensive site, with bilingual resources in English and German, contains a wealth of published papers and books. Additionally, all the international forums and conferences are listed on Peter's site.

Archives

Alberto Segrera, PhD, Professor Emeritus at Universidad Iberoamericana, has established an archive of person-centered writings at his university in Mexico City. This archive, available at www.uia.mx.aeicp/ingles.htm, is a comprehensive collection of books and articles published in multiple languages.

Transcripts

Barbara Brodley and Germain Lietaer, University of Leuven, Belgium, have compiled a large number of the extant transcripts of the interviews with Carl Rogers. Contact Kathy at kmoon1@alumni.uchicago.edu for further information. Transcripts can also be found in the Library of Congress.

REFERENCES

Asay, T. P., & Lambert, M. J. (1999). The empirical case for the common factors in therapy: Quantitative findings. In M. A. Hubble, B. L. Duncan, & S. D. Miller (Eds.), *The heart and soul of change: What works in therapy* (pp. 23–55). Washington, DC: American Psychological Association.

Baldwin, M. (1987). Interview with Carl Rogers on the use of the self in therapy. In M. Baldwin & V. Satir (Eds.), *The use of self* (pp. 45–52). New York: Haworth Press.

Bohart, A. C. (2002). A passionate critique of empirically supported treatments and the provision of an alternative paradigm. In J. C. Watson, R. N. Goldman, & M. S. Warner (Eds.), *Client-centered and experiential psychotherapy in the 21st century: Advances in theory, research, and practice* (pp. 258–277). Ross-on-Wye, UK: PCCS Books.

Bohart, A. C. (2007). The actualizing person. In M. Cooper, M. O'Hara, P. F. Schmid, & G. Wyatt (Eds.), *The handbook of person-centered psychotherapy and counselling* (pp. 47–63). Houndmills, UK: Palgrave Macmillan.

Bozarth, J. D. (2002). Empirically supported treatment: Epitome of the "specificity myth." In J. C. Watson, R. N. Goldman, & M. S. Warner (Eds.), *Client-centered and experiential psychotherapy in the 21st century: Advances in theory, research, and practice* (pp. 168–181). Ross-on-Wye, UK: PCCS Books.

Brodley, B. T. (1997). The nondirective attitude in client-centered therapy. *Person-Centered Journal, 4*(1), 18–30.

Brodley, B. T. (1999a). The actualizing concept in client-centered theory. *Person-Centered Journal, 6,* 108–120.

Brodley, B. T. (1999b). Reasons for responses expressing the therapist's frame of reference in client-centered therapy. *Person-Centered Journal, 6*(1), 4–27.

Brodley, B. T. (2000). Client-centered: An expressive therapy. In J. Marques-Teixeira & S. Antunes (Eds.), *Client centered and experiential psychotherapy* (pp. 133–147). Linda a Velha, Portugal: Vale & Vale.

Brodley, B. T. (2001). Congruence and its relation to communication in client-centered therapy. In G. Wyatt (Ed.), *Rogers' therapeutic conditions: Evolution, theory, and practice: Vol. I, Congruence* (pp. 55–78). Ross-on-Wye, UK: PCCS Books.

Cooper, M., Watson, J. C., & Hölldampf, D. (Eds.). (2010). *Person-centered and experiential therapies work: A review of the research on counseling, psychotherapy, and related practices.* Ross-on-Wye, UK: PCCS Books.

Elkins, D. N. (2009). *Humanistic psychology: A clinical manifesto.* Colorado Springs, CO: University of the Rockies Press.

Elkins, D. N. (2013, February 27). *Human elements in psychotherapy.* Paper presented at the Society of Humanistic Psychology Annual Conference (Division 32, American Psychological Association), Santa Barbara, CA.

Elliott, R., & Freire, E. (2008, November). Person-centered and experiential therapies are highly effective: Summary of the 2008 meta-analysis. *Person-Centered Quarterly,* 1–3.

Elliott, R., & Freire, E. (2010). The effectiveness of person-centered and experiential therapies: A review of the meta-analyses. In M. Cooper, J. C. Watson, & D. Hölldampf (Eds.), *Person-centered and experiential therapies work: A review of the research on counseling, psychotherapy, and related practices* (pp. 1–15). Ross-on-Wye, UK: PCCS Books.

Ettner, R. (1999). *Gender loving care: A guide to counseling gender-variant client.* New York: W. W. Norton.

Fairhurst, I. (Ed.). (1999). *Women writing in the person-centered approach.* Ross-on-Wye, UK: PCCS Books.

Gordon, T. (2000). *Parent Effectiveness Training: The proven program for raising responsible children.* New York: Three Rivers Press.

Grant, B. (1990). Principled and instrumental non-directiveness in person-centered and client-centered therapy. *Person-Centered Review, 5,* 77–88. Reprinted in D. J. Cain (Ed.). (2002). *Classics in the person-centered approach* (pp. 371–377). Ross-on-Wye, UK: PCCS Books.

Mier, S., & Witty, M. (2004). Considerations of race and culture in the practice of non-directive client-centered therapy. In R. Moodley, C. Lago, & A. Talahite (Eds.), *Carl Rogers counsels a black client* (pp. 85–104). Ross-on-Wye, UK: PCCS Books.

Moon, K. A., Witty, M. C., Grant, B., & Rice, B. (Eds.). (2011). *Practicing client-centered therapy: Selected writings of Barbara Temaner Brodley.* Ross-on-Wye, UK: PCCS Books.

Natiello, P. (2001). *The person-centered approach: A passionate presence.* Ross-on-Wye, UK: PCCS Books.

O'Hara, M. (2006). The radical humanism of Carl Rogers and Paulo Freire: Considering the person-centered approach as a form of conscientização. In G. Proctor, M. Cooper, P. Sanders, & B. Malcolm (Eds.), *Politicizing the person-centered approach: An agenda for social change* (pp. 115–126). Ross-on-Wye, UK: PCCS Books.

Proctor, G. (2002). *The dynamics of power in counselling and psychotherapy: Ethics, politics, and practice.* Ross-on-Wye, UK: PCCS Books.

Proctor, G., & Napier, M. (2004). *Encountering feminism: Intersections between feminism and the person-centered approach.* Ross-on-Wye, UK: PCCS Books.

Prouty, G. (1994). *Theoretical evolutions in person-centered/experiential therapy: Applications to schizophrenic and retarded psychoses.* Westport, CT: Praeger.

Raskin, N. J. (2005). The nondirective attitude. *Person-Centered Journal, 12*(1–2), 5–22. (Original work published in 1947)

Rogers, C. R. (1951). *Client-centered therapy.* Boston: Houghton Mifflin.

Rogers, C. R. (1957). The necessary and sufficient conditions of therapeutic personality change. *Journal of Consulting Psychology, 21,* 95–103.

Rogers, C. R. (1959a). The essence of psychotherapy: A client-centered view. *Annals of Psychotherapy, 1,* 51–57.

Rogers, C. R. (1959b). A theory of therapy, personality and interpersonal relationships as developed in the client-centered framework. In S. Koch (Ed.), *Psychology: A study of science: Vol. 3. Formulations of the person and the social context* (pp. 184–256). New York: McGraw-Hill.

Rogers, C. R. (1980). *A way of being.* Boston: Houghton Mifflin.

Rogers, C. R. (1986). Client-centered therapy. In I. L. Kutash & A. Wolf (Eds.), *Psychotherapist's casebook* (pp. 197–208). San Francisco: Jossey-Bass.

Rogers, C. R., & Russell, D. E. (2002). *Carl Rogers: The quiet revolutionary.* Roseville CA: Penmarin Books.

Rogers, N. (1980). *Emerging woman: A decade of midlife transitions.* Point Reyes Station, CA: Personal Press.

Rosenberg, M. B. (2003). *Nonviolent communication: A language of life.* Encinitas, CA: PuddleDancer Press.

Roth, G., Assor, A., Niemiec, C. P., Ryan, R. M., & Deci, E. L. (2009). The emotional and academic consequences of parental conditional regard: Comparing conditional positive regard, negative regard, and autonomy support as parenting practices. *Developmental Psychology, 45*(4), 1119–1142.

Ryan, R. M. (1993). Agency and organization: Intrinsic motivation, autonomy, and the self in psychological development. In J. Jacobs (Ed.), *Nebraska symposium on motivation* (Vol. 40, pp. 1–56). Lincoln: University of Nebraska Press.

Ryan, R. M. (1998). Commentary: Human psychological needs and issues of volition, control and outcome focus. In J. Heckhausen & C. S. Sweck (Eds.), *Motivation and self-regulation across the life span* (pp. 114–133). New York: Cambridge University Press.

Ryan, R. M., & Deci, E. L. (2000). Self-determination theory and the facilitation of intrinsic motivation, social development, and well-being. *American Psychologist, 55*(1), 68–78.

Wampold, B. E. (2001). *The great psychotherapy debate: Models, methods, and findings.* Mahwah, NJ: Lawrence Erlbaum.

Wampold, B. E. (2007, November). Psychotherapy: The humanistic (and effective) treatment. *American Psychologist, 62,* 857–873.

Witty, M. C. (2004). The difference directiveness makes: The ethics and consequences of guidance in psychotherapy. *Person-Centered Journal, 11,* 22–32.

Wolter-Gustafson, C. (2004). Towards convergence: Client-centered and feminist assumptions about epistemology and power. In G. Proctor & M. B. Napier (Eds.), *Encountering feminism: Intersections between feminism and the person-centered approach* (pp. 97–115). Ross-on-Wye, UK: PCCS Books.

Zimring, F. M. (2000). Empathic understanding grows the person. *Person-Centered Journal, 7*(2), 101–113.

CHAPTER 8

Gestalt Therapy

Joseph Spillman and Christina M. Rosen

I am a full-time student, I work full-time, and I am a single parent. Sometimes I feel that I need to clone myself; there is so much to do and so little time. I am so tired that I could fall asleep right here, but I can't give anything up (sighs). I just have to keep pushing myself and hope for the best.

Although not all clients will have this specific issue, the dynamics of this complaint are seen with many clients. The struggle between attending to external drives (work/school, kids, etc.) and internal drives (self-care) is common. This vignette is an example of what Gestalt therapy (GT) identifies as a *split*—a classic case of a client experiencing two different and competing needs and feeling powerless to change her situation. By focusing on external factors, the client will likely remain stuck. To help the client become unstuck, the Gestalt counselor would help her into full awareness by focusing on her physical, emotional, cognitive, and spiritual responses to this situation. With full awareness, the client will be able to make a decision on how to resolve the conflict.

In addition to detailing the importance of awareness, this chapter focuses on the uniqueness of GT, along with its fundamental concepts. Upon completion of this chapter, readers will be able to do the following:

1. Describe the history, development, and main figures of GT

2. Explain the basic philosophy, assumptions, and principles of GT

3. Articulate the model of mental health and emotional disturbance

4. Describe the counselor's role

5. Understand the counseling process, from initial meeting to termination

6. Apply specific Gestalt techniques

7. Analyze research on the efficacy of GT with diverse populations

8. Assess the strengths and limitations of GT

INTRODUCTION

Historical Background

Fritz Perls and Laura Posner-Perls are the most popular Gestalt figures. They introduced GT in 1947 with the publication of *Ego, Hunger and Aggression*. The oppression and intense anxiety people felt during the two World Wars solidified many of the main Gestalt principles.

Fritz was passionate about people living a "Gestalt way of life" (Bowman, 2005) and becoming more alive and aware of themselves, rather than allowing external events to dictate their lives. He highlighted the concepts of awareness of self and authenticity, which lead to recognizing one's own power to effect change (Bowman, 2005).

Fritz's confrontational style, personality, and demonstrations made GT appear easy. His personality helped promote GT and led to the creation of training institutes that flourished under Laura's guidance (Bowman, 2005). Fritz's notorious confrontational manner created a perception that his style was the only way. However, in contemporary GT, more attention is focused on the importance of having a strong theoretical and skill foundation that comes from one's own personal style (Mann, 2011).

Profile of Main Figures

Fritz Perls was born in Germany in 1893. Although he was born into a Jewish family, he did not fully identify with his Jewish heritage. He was a bright student, fluent in Latin, Greek, German, and English, and he was also a pilot. In 1914, World War I began and Fritz took a leave from college, volunteered for the Red Cross, and later joined the German army as a medic. In 1918, Fritz returned to college and completed his medical degree.

After college, Fritz worked with Kurt Goldstein at the Institute for Brain Damaged Soldiers, where he was exposed to Goldstein's approach of treating patients as a whole rather than separate parts. In the 1930s, Fritz and Laura fled ahead of the Nazi movement in Germany and eventually landed in South Africa. They stayed there until the last half of the 1940s, when they moved to New York City.

Lore (Laura) Posner was born in Germany in 1905. Laura loved the arts, playing the piano and dancing from an early age, which she incorporated into GT. She went to a humanistic gymnasium, uncommon for females at the time, and spoke German, French, Greek, Latin, and English. Laura earned her doctorate in psychology from Frankfurt-am-Main University, where she worked with Goldstein and was, likewise, influenced by his holistic approach. She was trained in psychology and later as an analyst. Laura was an existentialist and phenomenologist who worked with both Martin Buber and Paul Tillich. Laura and Fritz had two children, and Laura carried many of the parental responsibilities in addition to her professional endeavors.

After immigrating to New York, Laura began her counseling practice and cofounded the New York and Cleveland Gestalt Institutes. She contributed significantly to GT yet received little formal recognition. When asked about this, she stated that she was satisfied to leave the glory to Fritz. She independently contributed to *Ego, Hunger and Aggression,* writing the dummy complex and insomnia portions. After Laura and Fritz separated, she remained in New York and continued to run the NYC Gestalt Institute. She remained an active therapist and mentor, and promoted GT until she died in 1990.

OVERVIEW OF THE GESTALT APPROACH

I do my thing, and you do your thing.

I am not in this world to live up to your expectations

And you are not in this world to live up to mine.

You are you, and I am I,

And if by chance we find each other, it's beautiful.

If not, it can't be helped.

GT is a process- and relationship-oriented approach that focuses on client awareness (Zinker, 1978). GT integrates existentialism, phenomenology, and experiential approaches. This approach is existential in the belief that the process of living naturally involves the search for meaning and purpose in life. It is experiential in that all people have the ability to make some choices, regardless of their particular circumstances. It is phenomenological and therefore values the client's view of reality (De Reit, Korb, & Gorrell, 1980). A GT counselor does not presume to "own" the clients' reality, nor does the counselor tell clients what or how to think. So, while I am an expert at GT, the clients are the experts in their own lives. GT is a collaborative approach where the counselor and client combine their respective areas of expertise and work together to achieve success.

Human Nature

GT is rooted in holism (Smuts, 1926), organismic functioning (Goldstein, 1939), and field theory (Lewin, 1951). From a holism/holistic perspective, Perls (1973) stated,

> The basic premise of Gestalt psychology is that human nature is organized into patterns or wholes, that it is experienced by the individual in these terms, and that it can only be understood as a function of the patterns or whole of which it is made. (p. 3)

From an organismic functioning perspective, all organisms seek balance and are continually self-regulating to find that balance. According to Perls, "Clients will seek counseling when they are out of balance, as "when the homeostatic process fails to some degree, when the organism remains in a state of disequilibrium for too long a time and is unable to satisfy its needs, it is sick" (p. 4).

Lewin's (1951) work on field theory is integrated into GT. Lewin believed that each person exists in multiple fields. Some examples of fields are geographical locations, roles, religion, age, sexual orientation, race, and culture. All fields will impact your clients, so you will need to know what they are and how they affect each client.

Basic Characteristics and Assumptions

Counselors need to be well grounded in Gestalt characteristics and principles to avoid practicing gimmickry and risking harm to clients (Bowman, 2005). Perfection exists in the eye of the beholder, and humans are a work of art in progress (Zinker, 1978); therefore, no one can live a perfect Gestalt way of life. However, being as mindful, aware, and genuine as possible is critical to the ethical practice of GT.

Self-Awareness

Self-awareness is the ability to know your thoughts, feelings, and beliefs so you can make informed choices (Lobb, 2005). As the reader, you might be thinking, "Well, of course." We challenge you to stop reading for a moment and try this exercise.

EXERCISE 8.1

SELF-AWARENESS

Take a series of deep, slow breaths: Breathe in for a count of 2 and out for a count of 4. Then list what you notice now that you did not notice while you were reading—that is, what you hear, see, smell, and touch. Take a slower and longer series of breaths; what else has moved into your *awareness?* The purpose of this experiment is to demonstrate that oftentimes people think they know what they are doing, feeling, etc., but the reality is that most of us live on autopilot and are not truly connected to our experiences or aware of the effects of our actions on ourselves, our environment, and others.

Acceptance

Acceptance is the ability to see our true selves, including the shadow side. Our shadows hold qualities about ourselves we tend to reject or deny and see as negative (i.e., feeling guilty or afraid; Perls, 1969). A person talking from his or her shadow side may use words such as *never*, *always*, "not me," or "not possible." The hallmark of a mentally healthy person is someone who can make authentic contact with self, others, and the environment.

Authenticity

An authentic person is honest with self and others (Perls, 1947) and decides when to share any feelings, thoughts, and attitudes (Lobb, 2005). Such a person does not manipulate his or her feelings for others. People can be authentic and still have a private and public self. Someone watching another person cannot determine if that person is being authentic, since it is impossible to know another's true feelings, thoughts, and motives. For example, Mary expresses her anger differently in certain situations. She expresses anger calmly to her husband if the children are around. Mary chooses not to express her anger directly with her employer. At work, she delays her expression of anger to increase awareness, process, and think before taking action or being reactive, thereby allowing herself to *stay* with her anger (i.e., become aware of her feelings, thoughts, attitudes, and consequences). However, as a mom, she is already aware of her needs, thoughts, and feelings, and does not need to stay with her anger before acting. Because of this, she may seem inauthentic, as she appears less reactive in one situation and more reactive in another. In actuality, as a parent she may need to react quickly, while as an employee she may regret being reactive.

The Here and Now and Being Present

Being present is being aware of only the current moment (the here and now; Perls, 1947) and avoiding distractions, preoccupations, and multitasking. Furthermore, eliminating language referring to the past and future is necessary to be in the present. Past and future concerns are brought into the present by the counselor's encouraging the client to speak in the present tense. The present can be changed; the past and future cannot. For example, Christina says, "I wish I had attended my nephew's wedding." The counselor asks Christina to say that again using present-tense language. Christina responds, "Today is the first anniversary of my nephew's wedding. I feel sad I missed his wedding." In this way, the counselor is dealing with current feelings related to a past event (regrets). The same technique is used for future events. For example, Christina is worried about retirement. The counselor asks Christina to speak in present tense. Christina says, "I am scared that I will not have enough money to retire in 10 years."

Being present with yourself and others requires intense self-awareness and the ability to shift focus from self to others. Self-awareness is not being self-centered or navel-gazing, which blocks authentic self-awareness. Being present is suspending judgment and labeling. It is listening, watching, and receiving without analyzing, rationalizing, or intellectualizing. The Gestalt vocabulary eliminates *should, could, must, ought, good,* and *bad,* as these are labels and defensives that block exploration. Being present means paying attention to what is occurring internally and externally in the moment.

EXERCISE 8.2

BEING IN THE MOMENT

This exercise may increase the reader's awareness and ability to be more present to what is occurring now. (We will also use this for the cycle of experiences covered a bit later in the chapter.) Please get a pen and paper (no electronic devices allowed). Notice what you feel. How does the pen feel in your hand (i.e., cold, warm, hot, soft, hard, sticky)? Describe the process and sensations you experience (i.e., "My fingers have started tingling"; "I notice that my hand wants to hold the pen by bringing my forefinger and thumb together"; "I notice that the following thoughts are in my head . . ."). As you are writing, what do you notice? Pay attention to the muscles in your hands and arms, which muscles are working, and how you hold your head. As you complete this experiment, did you notice how present you were as you focused all your attention on writing and being in the *moment*?

In doing this experiment, your attention was focused on the *here and now.* We increased your cognitive awareness of the activity of writing, which brought you into the space to be present with yourself. However,

(Continued)

(Continued)

being present is more than just being in the *here and now*. Multitasking happens in the present moment (here and now) and can be done on autopilot. For example, as you are texting, you may be thinking about something else, walking, or watching TV. Being present to self and others means you are aware of your breathing, feelings, thoughts, posture, etc.—you are also aware of the other person's, without judging or labeling or looking for an outcome. There is a lack of preoccupation with anything else. You are observing without labels, without thinking, "I should say" or "What do they think of me?" Instead, you are being objective in describing your sensations. For example, "The pen I am holding is smooth, hard, and there is some weight. I notice as I grasp the pen that my breathing increases and my mind begins to race. I feel a sense of energy."

Figure and Ground

Figure and ground are forever changing. Ground includes any unfinished business (i.e., anything repressed, oppressed, ignored, or denied), our environment, experiences, interactions, behaviors, emotions, cognitions, and reactions. Figure is that which is most salient in the moment (Polster & Polster, 1974). For example, you may not be aware of your breathing rate, which makes breathing a background event. However, when you walk quickly, you become aware of your breathing, making it figure. In our subconscious, we are constantly deciding what is figure and what is ground.

Cycle of Experience

Table 8.1 Gestalt Cycle of Experience

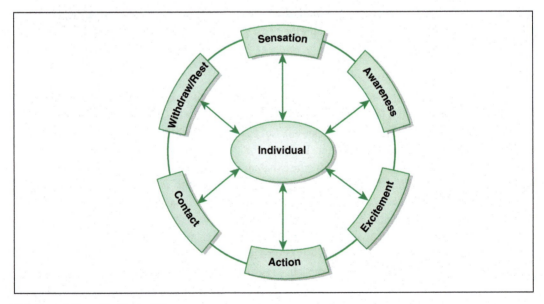

© Spillman & Rosen Graphics by KGS

The cycle of experience is a process, such as those in Exercises 8.1 and 8.2. An example of an awareness exercise in action is provided in Case Illustration 8.1.

CASE ILLUSTRATION 8.1

Tom

Counselor: Tom, I hear you talking about your struggles with Marie, your daughter. While speaking about her, I noticed that you also report having headaches. *(The counselor is attempting to stop the "talking about," which is keeping the client from noticing his physical experience while talking.)*

Client: Yes, I do have headaches—not bad, just those dull headaches. You know, right at the base of my head. The doctor says it's from stress.

Counselor: You have a dull headache. Can you describe "dull" using adverbs or sensations, or show me in a motion? *(The counselor is working with the client to use descriptive words and avoid labels, such as "dull." The counselor is moving the client from thinking about to feeling the experience (i.e., the actual physical sensations). By doing this, the client is becoming aware of what is occurring now in the present, rather than in his intellect. This increase of awareness brings different information regarding the stress and/or relationship with his daughter.)*

Client: Hum, well, I'm not sure if I can. (He raises his hand and makes a fist. He starts to pump his fist. The pumping movement is slow, and the fist remains tightly closed.) I sense a slow rhythm that is constant and steady. Is that what you mean?

Counselor: Yes, I noticed your hand is making a movement. *(The counselor is keeping the client focused on what is occurring in the present so they can explore the client's needs. Increasing what is happening around that need can lead the client to identify the unfinished need, whereas talking about the events or another person does not help the client identify his needs.)*

Client: Hum, yeah, that is how my head feels. Wow, my headache (pumping his fist faster) is really pounding now. My teeth and jaw feel tight. I never realized that before!

Counselor: Okay, pay attention to your hand, your headache, teeth, and jaw.

Client: Hum, okay. (Three seconds elapse.) Wow (moving his jaw around), my jaw really hurts and is tingling. I need it to relax.

Counselor: Before you do that, what about your headache? *(The client's processing led him to awareness of his tightened jaw; however, it is important not to lose track of the headache since that is where the process started and we need to see if there is a connection.)*

Client: Hum, it seems (slowing down arm movement and loosening fist) . . . my headache seems to be almost gone. Maybe the doctor is right, and it is stress.

This awareness exercise is typically and easily used at the beginning of the counseling relationship. This type of exercise helps assess the client's ability to develop awareness and work with Gestalt techniques.

Pick up your pen again and follow the cycle of experience. Experiences begin with sensations, so we'll start at the top of the diagram. The *sensations* of the pen are the adjectives (i.e., smooth, hard, and light). *Awareness* occurs through paying attention to the sensations—for example, noticing that the forefinger and thumb are coming together to hold the pen. The *excitement* is the energy of engaging sensations and awareness. Your fingers touch the pen, and you move into *action* by putting the pen to paper. The *contact* is your recognition of the whole process; the Gestalt is experiencing that your internal need is satisfied (e.g., you made contact after becoming aware of your excitement and energy to write).

Withdrawing is stopping the action of writing, and the consequence of not withdrawing in time is muscle fatigue. Ignoring the sensation and continuing to write creates muscle soreness (unfinished Gestalt). An unfinished Gestalt would also be avoiding writing or stopping writing prematurely; the consequence of either of these might be an unsettled feeling. The withdrawing phase is just as important as all other points in the cycle. Multiple cycles of experience occur all the time (Zinker, 1978) outside of our awareness, since only the most salient experience is the figure and the others are the ground. A mentally healthy person becomes aware of the cycle of experience. He or she allows completions (i.e., Gestalt) even with unpleasant feelings and recognizes resistance and the need to withdraw prematurely or block completion of the experience.

Resistances

Resistances are a part of human nature that protects us from perceived harm and can be healthy or unhealthy (Polster & Polster, 1974). GT works with resistance to increase self-awareness and integration. The resistance mechanisms are introjection, retroflection, projection, confluence, and deflection. Before we discuss the different types of resistance, we'll first talk about polarities.

Polarities can occur in any of the five forms of resistance, and we have never-ending sequences of polarities—evident when a person is experiencing two opposing thoughts or messages. As GT works with resistance, the polarities will arise—meaning the work on the figural resistance allows the polar opposites (i.e., shadow) to emerge from the ground. Integration occurs when enough energy emerges for both polarities to be acknowledged and worked with, which is necessary for good mental health (Polster & Polster, 1974).

When a polarities phenomenon occurs, it creates the sense of a tug of war, with opposite needs pulling for attention: "top dog" and "underdog." A useful technique to address this conflict is the "empty chair," which reveals the client's internal dialogue. This technique requires two chairs—one for the client to sit in and an empty one to face the client—and includes four steps.

The first step is for the client to imagine who (e.g., parent, partner, friend, coworker, or unaccepted part of the client's self) is sitting across from him or her in the empty chair. The client expresses his or her thoughts and emotions to that person/part of self by saying what he or she has not been able to say before. As the client is articulating these thoughts and emotions, it is important for the counselor to monitor this process to ensure that the client is expressing and not "talking about."

The second step involves asking the client to move to the empty chair. In that second chair (i.e., the formerly empty one), the client becomes the person/part of self he or she just spoke to. The client is then asked to reflect on what he or she just heard—as if the client were that other person/part of self. The third step is for the client to speak as if he or she were that other person. The client is now talking to the first chair, which is where the client started out the exercise. Therefore, the client is now speaking to himself or herself and from the perspective of the other person/part of self—meaning the client is responding to what he or she initially said to the empty chair.

Once that third step is completed, the client returns to the original chair. Once there, the counselor asks the client what he or she heard and if there is anything else to say. The swap between the two chairs occurs as often as needed. Finally, after the exchanges, the counselor helps the client process this experience to help with integration. The processing questions for the client are, (a) What are you experiencing now? (b) What did you discover? (c) Is there anything else?

This technique helps the client work through incongruent needs he or she is experiencing (self-care versus caring for the other first), allowing for both of these needs to have a "voice," and then negotiate those needs so integration can occur. Additionally, the projections or introjections are revealed because the client is putting into words what he or she thinks the other person/part of self would say or what the client would like to hear that person/part of self say. For example, consider the case of a client struggling with the desire to care for himself versus the desire to care for others (see Case Illustration 8.2).

CASE ILLUSTRATION 8.2

Empty Chair

Client: I am so exhausted. I wish I could just rest. But there is no time to rest—I have to take the kids to baseball practice, cook dinner, clean the house, and this is after working all day *(top dog; defensive stand)*.

Counselor: You feel exhausted, and you have no help. *(Providing an empathy state helps the counselor communicate what he is hearing.)*

Client: Well, my husband works really hard, and when he comes home he just sits on the couch and does nothing. I wish I could do that. I need to rest more *(underdog; projection; defensive stand)*.

Counselor: You wish you had the time just to rest and that your husband would help you more. I wonder what happens when you ask him to help. *(The summary statement gives the counselor a chance to communicate his understanding of the client's statements. The question can assess what the client has done to obtain help from her husband.)*

Client: He just sits there all day and says he is sore and tired from working *(projection; underdog)*. *(This is a projection, because most people really do not sit around all day. What we do not know is whether her husband has a medical condition creating increased soreness or how the client has asked him for help.)*

(Continued)

(Continued)

Counselor: Would you be willing to try something? I want to understand your experience better. *(From the client's responses, the counselor believes he has enough information and a pretty clear case conceptualization of the dynamic happening for the client. He conceptualizes that the client is struggling with two disparate needs—perhaps the need for rest and the need not to fail anyone.)*

Client: Hum, sure.

Counselor: Would you allow me to hear both sides of your needs—one to take care of the kids and your husband and another to take care of yourself? What I would like you to do is give each side a name. And then you will talk from each side to the other side. This empty chair will hold one of the two sides. After one side talks, I will have you switch chairs so the other side can have a voice. How does that sound? *(Here, the counselor is asking for the client's consent to initiate the experience. In doing so, the counselor is working within the American Counseling Association's code of ethics by informing the client what the experiment is and what will be required of the client.)*

Client: Hum, okay, but what are you saying—there are two of me?

Counselor: No, not two of you; however, I hear two needs that seem to be opposing each other, and I want to hear more from both.

Client: Hum, well, it sounds weird, but okay. *(The counselor is aware of the client's hesitation and natural resistance to this technique. This information is helpful, as it tells him to move slowly and push gently.)*

Counselor: Let's call the responsibility side that does not have time to rest Anna, and the other side Annie.

Client: Sure, Annie is a nickname. You know, my dad told me I always had to give 110%.

Counselor: Okay, Annie *(underdog)*, tell Anna *(empty chair, top dog)* about being exhausted and what you need. *(The counselor starts with the underdog. Typically, the underdog is not heard, so it is important to give it the voice first. If the top dog is given the voice first, then there is a chance the underdog will not talk, especially since the client is already hesitant about the exercise.)*

Client: (Her lower lip is shaking, and she bites it.) Well, I am exhausted, and I can't stand up to your demands. It seems unfair that George is resting and watching TV. It would be nice to do that, too, so I can feel rested.

Counselor: Annie, you just want to rest, and you feel unheard. You look scared. *(The counselor is using advance empathy to communicate to the underdog that she is being heard. This is important for clients who are hesitant and first learning Gestalt techniques. Later in the counseling relationship, when enough trust is established, the counselor will not want to interrupt the process of the experiment.)*

Client:	Yes, I am scared.
Counselor:	Can you tell Anna your fear? (*It is important to move the client away from talking to the counselor and toward making contact with herself. This allows the experiment to be more impactful by increasing her awareness when she connects to herself.*)
Client:	Hum, well, sure. (In a soft voice, looking away from the empty chair) Anna, I am scared to tell you that I want to rest. You never seem to want to rest—you just go and go and go. I am not sure how you do it. Can't we just rest? When is enough, enough? (Tears slowly fall.)
Counselor:	I see your tears. (*Because the underdog is talking and the client is still developing trust, the counselor highlights his awareness by using empathy and describing his observations. This means the counselor is combining two techniques to help the client feel heard and safe.*)
Client:	Yeah, I was not aware of how exhausted I feel and how demanding I am toward myself.
Counselor:	Let's hear from the other part of you, Anna. Can you switch chairs for me? (*Although the client's awareness is increased, there is no aha moment yet; so the counselor understands that more work is needed, as awareness in and of itself does not produce change.*)
Client:	Well, okay, but this is odd. (As she switches chairs, her tears continue to fall slowly and softly.) (*The counselor hears this as more resistance yet willingness to try. This tells him that the client has developed some trust and is finding this experiment beneficial.*)
Counselor:	Anna, you heard Annie—she is scared, exhausted, and feels unheard. She does not believe she can live up to your standards. What would you like to say? (*The counselor continues to be the go-between since this is the client's first experiment. Working in this abstract way takes practice, and many times clients need concrete help until they are familiar with the process. Additionally, this summary statement helps the client know that the counselor is listening.*)
Client:	(Speaking as Anna to the counselor) Well, Annie is lazy. If she had her way, she would lie around all day and do nothing. It is bad enough that she sleeps in on the weekend. (Voice sounds tense, and affect is mad.)
Counselor:	(Pointing to the empty chair) Can you tell Annie? (*Because the client is talking to the counselor instead of the empty chair and using third-person language, he redirects the client. Redirecting helps facilitate the client's contact with herself.*)
Client:	I just did. She heard me. (*Gestalt counselors perceive this as resistance. The client is struggling with making direct contact with her internal messages. She is prematurely withdrawing during the excitement stage, thereby interrupting the completion of the cycle of experience [see Figure 8.1] and not moving to the action stage.*)

(Continued)

(Continued)

Counselor:	Hum, I thought you were telling me, since you were looking at me and used the words "she is." Can you look at Annie and tell her what you told me? I understand you think she does not work hard enough. Can you tell Annie how you feel? I noticed your voice was a bit tense and your face had an angry expression. (*Because the counselor understands that natural and normal resistance is occurring, he matches the resistance with a gentle tap. It is important for him to be patient and explain without using jargon.*)
Client:	Oh, okay! Annie, I am angry about your whining. We get 8 hours of sleep on the weekend, and we watch an hour of TV daily. We have responsibilities that need to be met! I am not too demanding. You are too lazy! (Her eyes get wide, and she shakes her head.) Wow. I sound like my dad! (*This is an aha moment. The client has moved into the resistance—introjection—and taken action. She connected with herself and discovered something in her shadow. She has completed the cycle of experience for now.*)
Counselor:	Oh, how? (*The counselor recognizes this as one level of completion; however, it is important to understand the client's meaning making of this experience. He is keeping his response limited to avoid distraction.*)
Client:	(Starts crying) He used to call me lazy because I would sleep an extra hour on the weekends and watch an hour of TV or daydream. If I was not moving, I was lazy (tears increasing). (*The client has made full contact with the introjection that she swallowed as a child and never confronted. She recognizes that she is repeating her father's unrealistic demands, and so the cycle of experience is complete for now. It is important for the client to withdraw and process so integration can occur. If the counselor pushes too much, he risks overstimulating the client and losing the awareness she gained from this experience.*)

The counselor might stop here and process so the client can absorb and begin to integrate this new awareness. The relationship with the client is moving from the beginning stage to the middle stages of treatment. This experience has demonstrated the usefulness of the experiment and the power of the cycle of experience; however, these facts and jargon are not initially helpful to clients. The counselor wants the client to honor the aha moment (the Gestalt experience) and stay with her experience by staying in the present and processing the moment so her awareness is absorbed. Although this is a mini Gestalt, the aha indicates that she did have a Gestalt. The client determines when to stop (unless time is a factor), and so the counselor also asks her if there is more she feels she needs to do at this point. This process of heightening awareness often occurs over the course of the counseling relationship. This is especially true for clients new to Gestalt counseling. As she increases her awareness of the power of the projection—which stems from an introjection—through completing cycles of experience, she will gain more power to challenge her introjections and then change.

A common metaphor for growth is an onion, with the core of the onion being the most potent and sweetest part—and the most difficult to access. The cycle of experience continues to work to heighten a person's awareness, which leads to action and change. The goal is to achieve a Gestalt experience (i.e., an aha moment; Zinker, 1978). In Case Illustration 8.2, Anna worked with the outer layer of the onion and became aware of her internal message from childhood. This one session created awareness of, not permanent change in, attitudes toward self and others. She has begun the process of change by challenging her introjections, which we will discuss next in more detail.

Introjection. In the dialogue with Anna (Case Illustration 8.2), her introjection is revealed to be her father's message, "Always do 110% to be good enough"—but obeying this message makes her feel exhausted, irritable, and taken for granted. She wants to lie down on the couch and watch TV, but she will not let herself and resents her husband for taking time to relax. By not challenging her father's message, she feels unable to take care of herself and listen to her own needs. She denies her need to rest out of fear of not being good enough.

Projection. Projection is ascribing one's own feelings, thoughts, and attitudes to others (Polster & Polster, 1974). This happens when, instead of confronting someone or sharing one's thoughts/feelings/attitudes, one assigns thoughts/feelings/attitudes to that person. This is evident in the use of words such as *always* and *never*. For example, Anna's projection (in Case Illustration 8.2) is that her husband is not willing to help her around the house: "He just sits on the couch and does nothing." This is evident in her hesitation to ask him for help because she believes she already knows what he will say. Even though the counselor deals mainly with the introjection, Anna's projection is obvious. Anna wants to do what her husband is doing (lie on the couch); however, she will not give herself permission to do so because she fears being "lazy" and thus projects laziness onto her husband by exaggerating the length of time he actually spends relaxing.

Retroflection. Retroflection concerns a person's need to be self-reliant (Polster & Polster, 1974) and messages related to the values of strength and independence. Retroflection involves avoiding getting hurt or asking for help, believing that one should not ask for help because it will be seen as weak, demanding, or a nuisance. Such a person's muscles, posture, and gait are tight and breathing shallow—as if he or she is wearing body armor (Mann, 2011). For example, Anna (in Case Illustration 8.2) is not asking for more help from her husband or her kids. If the counselor sees any or all of the signs of retroflection—clinched teeth, shallow breathing, tight muscles, and a posture that is straight and almost ridged—she might decide to work with Anna's retroflection.

Deflection. The person using deflection appears to be making contact but is actually *avoiding* intimate contact. The contact is only surface level, leaving the "contactee" unsatisfied with the connection. Such a person will be verbose and vague in language use, talk about things in the past, and/or act the part of the clown (Polster & Polster, 1974). The counselor may also see the client as distracted, presenting shallow breathing and/or fleeting eye contact (Mann, 2011). The counselor working on Anna's deflection (in Case Illustration 8.2) would redirect

Anna's attention to her experience of herself, asking her to use "I" statements (avoiding "talking about" and clowning) or to pay attention to her breathing—or both.

Confluence. Confluence is loss of self to the environment, and a person experiencing confluence surrenders his or her boundary, choices, or ability to others; thereby, the external world defines this person's identity. He or she puts little energy into asserting self, preferring peace to conflict, and avoids deep intimate relationships by not challenging or confronting the other person, thereby keeping the relationship surface level. This person does not want to upset the peace and so expresses agreement when he or she really disagrees (Polster & Polster, 1974). The client's body appears soft, and he or she seems to flop into the chair. This person is unable to take an independent stand or express an opinion (Mann, 2011).

Counselors seek to find how each type of resistance blocks the client's full self-contact. The goal is for the counselor to assist the client in moving through the cycle of experience (see Figure 8.1) by recognizing what is stimulating the resistance and then guiding the client to awareness through shared observations. The counselor then uses an experiment to increase awareness and move the client to excitement. In time, the goal is to move through excitement without withdrawing before action and decision are achieved. Sometimes, change is not the goal, as resistance can provide a benefit by keeping the client safe in some way; therefore, clients are not forcefully pushed through their resistance.

Research and Supportive Evidence

There is increasing process and outcome research supporting use of GT for a variety of client issues (Strümpfel & Goldman, 2002). Strümpfel and Goldman conducted a comprehensive literature review exploring the research on GT. They found that GT was effective for clients affected by depression, anxiety, schizophrenia, compulsiveness, substance abuse, psychosomaticism, chronic pain, and other issues.

Further, specific Gestalt experiments were studied and found to be effective for particular client issues. The most famous research experiments associated with GT are the empty-chair experiments (Greenberg & Dompierre, 1981; Greenberg, Elliot, & Lietaer, 1994; Greenberg & Rice, 1997; King, 1988; Paivio & Greenberg, 1995). There are two types of empty-chair experiments: one-chair and two-chair experiments.

In the one-chair experiment, clients can address unfinished business with others who are not present by either choice or circumstance. This can be an effective way to help clients process unresolved issues with deceased loved ones, domestic violence assailants, and any others who will not or cannot attend counseling sessions. Paivio and Greenberg (1995) found that the one-chair dialogue was effective for resolving unfinished emotional business with significant others or someone from the client's past. In another study, King (1988) compared the one-chair experiment with empathetic reflection and found that the one-chair experiment resulted in greater tolerance for the client's significant other. While the one-chair experiment helps clients address unresolved business with significant others, the two-chair experiment addresses splits or polarities within the self.

In the two-chair experiment, the client plays both parts of the internal split or conflict. A split is essentially two competing parts of the self. For example, a person may be in conflict about whether to go through the divorce process or stay married and work out the issues. In this experiment, the client will physically move back and forth from chair to chair and work through both sides of the issue, with the Gestalt counselor helping facilitate the process.

For clients who experience "stuckness," or difficulty choosing a course of action, the Gestaltian two-chair experiment has been shown to be more effective than behavioral problem-solving techniques in reducing indecisiveness (Clarke & Greenberg, 1986). Additionally, the Gestalt two-chair experiment has been shown to be effective in increasing client awareness and ability to connect deeply to his or her internal emotional process (Greenberg, 1979). While awareness and connecting deeply to one's feelings is not important to all counseling theories, it is a critical aspect within the humanistic and existential schools of thought; so this research is an important component that supports this worldview on how client change takes place. While the above research gives us a glimpse of the power of GT, more research is warranted.

Use With Diverse Populations

Corey (2009) stated, "There are opportunities to sensitively and creatively use Gestalt methods with culturally diverse populations if interventions are timed appropriately and used flexibly" (p. 221). Field theory is a critical component and can contribute to effective work with diverse populations. The strength of the approach is that different cultures value different ways of working through problems, with some placing a higher value on cognitions, emotions, behaviors, or spiritual aspects of self for healing. Still, there may be some combination of those factors that individuals will need to become *unstuck*. Within the Gestalt framework, counselors are free to shift focus to any area or utilize any combination of areas mentioned above to help clients work through their presenting issue(s). Although some clients will not want to work in collaboration with their counselors, many will appreciate being involved in the process. Collaboration is an important part of Gestalt work. The counselor collaborates with the client in determining what will work best for him or her and, at the same time, challenges the client, where appropriate, to integrate disowned aspects of self so he or she may feel whole.

GT has been used with diverse populations around the world; however, a paucity of research exists on the use of GT with diverse populations. To better grasp the impact of using GT with diverse populations, more research is warranted.

Strengths and Limitations

One specific strength of this theoretical approach is the Gestalt founders' desire for GT to be a way of life, not just a theory (Woldt & Toman, 2005)—believing that anyone willing to increase his or her awareness can be taught about the cycle of experience and can discover the benefits of increased growth (Melnick & Nevis, 2005). A healthy, well-adjusted person completes each experience and then moves to the next with little disruption, occasionally choosing to postpone completion because of another priority (Mann, 2011).

Another strength of this approach is that GT is internationally recognized. It is creative and experiential, which provides the counselor flexibility but also consistency—especially for well-trained counselors working from the Gestalt philosophies and principles

(Woldt & Toman, 2005). The room for creativity is an important strength, as no two experiments look the same due to the fluid dynamic between counselor and client (Mann, 2011). Yet empirical research also perceives this as a challenge because of the difficulties in conducting research. Because Gestalt counseling is not divided into parts (variables) or molded techniques, it leaves the researcher uncertain of which variable to credit with therapeutic success. Creativity needs to be grounded in GT principles for effective and safe experiments to occur (Bowman, 2005).

The main limitation is the additional 3 years of advanced post-master's-degree training required. Without this additional training, counselors practicing GT have a high likelihood of committing ethical violations and harming the client (Bowman, 2005).

Therapeutic Goals

The overarching goal of GT is to help clients gain awareness and self-support. The goal is for clients to become aware of what and how they are doing something and the ways they can change while learning to accept and value themselves (Perls, 1973). This goal is achieved through experiential interactions (experiments), as opposed to *talking about* the client's problems. GT attempts to increase client awareness of the physical, emotional, cognitive, spiritual, and external (everything outside the client's skin). Once the client experiences these different awarenesses, he or she will be in a position to resolve the presenting issue(s).

Therapeutic Process

A full psychological Gestalt can take weeks, months, or years. In a typical counseling session, the client moves a little at a time through each part of the cycle of experience and can achieve increased awareness with each session. The counselor works with the client to discover his or her process within the cycle of experience (i.e., awareness; areas that are blocked, avoided, or where premature withdrawal occurs) and then works with the client to *make contact* (e.g., to experience the situation genuinely). The client can experience a Gestalt (i.e., make a connection to self). This experience is not dramatic because pieces of the work are happening over time. Think of the process as chipping away at a stone, with many small hits needed to reveal the form of a statue. Gestalt techniques move the client through the cycle of experience via challenging the client's defenses. For the success of the therapy and to prevent harm, it is important for the technique to match the defenses and the client. The reader will see this dynamic occurring throughout the case of Y-Chun.

Focus and Intentionality: Application to the Case of Y-Chun

Y-Chun's case provides one way to explore a potential application of GT. Each counselor will use his or her own style with the GT techniques. Yet, regardless of the uniqueness of any one interaction, those employing a Gestalt orienting framework have the same goal of increasing the client's ability to be present and genuine through increasing self-awareness.

Y-CHUN THROUGH THE LENS OF GESTALT THERAPY

A Gestalt counselor perceives Y-Chun as bicultural, in her mid-adult development, mother of two children, and living with her parents while attending school. Her responses to the intake indicate that both cultures are important to her, although she has strong Asian values. Her American values and beliefs are secondary, as evidenced by her affect and wording, which are highlighted throughout the case dialogue.

The counselor recognizes that from the *ground* (i.e., Y-Chun's experience, culture, family life, and career pursuits), several potential *figures* have arisen (i.e., the impact of the culture clashes on her relationship with her parents and boyfriend, and her physical alignments). With this *awareness,* the Gestalt counselor will be mindful of the influence of both cultures, especially as related to Y-Chun's relationship with her parents. Y-Chun's parents continue to have a major influence in her adult life, even though she desires to be independent of them.

For the Gestalt counselor, it will be important to develop experiments with consideration for the demands of both cultures to avoid any counselor biases. It is important for Y-Chun to decide, without due influence, which culture's values, norms, and beliefs she will integrate as she continues the acculturation process. For example, Y-Chun was raised in America and has started the acculturation process; however, her father and mother are first-generation Polish and Chinese, respectively. Her mother has not acculturated to America and has strong Asian roots that she desires to pass on to Y-Chun. Therefore, Y-Chun experiences culture clashes between her collectivistic (Asian culture) values and the materialistic, strong independent values of the American culture, as discussed in the case dialogue.

To be culturally sensitive, the Gestalt counselor is careful to avoid setting up an experiment that would sway Y-Chun to embrace one culture's values, norms, or beliefs over the other's. Moreover, it may be difficult to establish a counseling relationship with Y-Chun based on mutuality. In many Asian cultures, counselors (e.g., healers) give advice and tell the client what to do; however, in American culture, in general, we expect counselors to work with us to solve problems (Baruth & Manning, 2012). If Y-Chun perceives the counseling relationship more from her Asian culture, the Gestalt counselor may struggle to develop a mutual relationship and will need to work at co-creating sessions with the client. That is, the client is the expert of herself and the counselor is the expert of the theory. Therefore, except for certain times during the experiment, Gestalt counselors are client centered and not directive. A counselor who is client centered may clash with many Asian cultures, where counselors are supposed to be directive. In addition, some of the awareness techniques may need to move slower, as Y-Chun may not be comfortable showing emotions to a stranger.

Y-Chun has answered some of the intake questions. At the point when the transcript picks up, she has begun to show some emotions. The counselor uses a Gestalt awareness technique to process these emotions.

Counselor: Y-Chun, I notice tears falling down your left cheek, you are doing something with your lips, and you are no longer looking at me. I believe my question has touched on something. I invite you to share what you are experiencing right now.

Notice the lack of labeling. The counselor is using only descriptive words, reporting what she is observing. This is intentional to increase awareness of self (for Y-Chun) and to maintain focus on the experience rather than talking about the experience (see Figure 8.1, the cycle of experience). The counselor is reporting to the client the counselor's sensations (i.e., what she sees) and invites Y-Chun to attend to this experience. In general, someone holding Asian cultural values would avoid putting someone in an awkward or bad situation, which could lead to losing face. The counselor is attempting to honor Y-Chun's Asian cultural values by using the words, "I invite you to . . ." This is common language for some Asian cultures. Either someone from an Asian culture or someone with a strong American cultural orientation can reject the invitation and still show respect for the other person. If Y-Chun responds with a puzzled look, then the counselor can determine that this form of invitation is not familiar to her and therefore will not assist in developing rapport. In the counselor's response, she is assessing Y-Chun's level of self-awareness and resistance to sharing her emotional reaction.

Y-Chun: No, not really. (Slowly lifting her head, without making full eye contact, and holding her breathe) I am damaged goods and can't live up to my parents' expectations.

The counseling relationship is in the beginning stage, and this "yes, but" or "no, but" response (denying the emotional impact, then sharing that she is damaged goods) is seen as a natural and normal form of resistance; however, the counselor will not directly confront this resistance at this stage. Y-Chun is experiencing a polarity in her need to protect herself and her desire to make contact with the counselor. Y-Chun is also communicating that she is aware of her thoughts, her awareness of her own nonverbal cues is limited, and/or she does not yet trust this process.

Counselor: Living up to your parents' expectations is very important to you. You are the smart one, and you are supposed to succeed.

The counselor is increasing Y-Chun's awareness by using Y-Chun's own words and checking for the figural focal point so exploration can start, while also moving with the resistance. The counselor is using a summary statement so Y-Chun can hear the resistance in her own words.

Y-Chun: (Makes eyes contact and takes shallow breaths) Yes, you understand my situation.

Counselor: (Nods, smiling slightly) Okay. I notice your breathing is very shallow. What is happening for you right now?

The counselor is affirming Y-Chun and attempting not to take on the authority role. The counselor's desire is to keep the focus on Y-Chun's process by having her attend to her experience (i.e., the way her body is responding, communication of resistance, etc.), thus increasing Y-Chun's awareness without directly confronting the resistance or labeling her as resistant. The counselor is moving with the resistance by sharing her observations, using summarizing and paraphrasing statements. It is important for Y-Chun to insert her own interruptions and make her own meaning.

Y-Chun: Yes, I never told anyone about my rape. I never realized that I felt that way. I just knew I did not like myself and was not worthy. I think I should leave now.

Counselor: I feel honored that you trust me enough to share your feelings around your rape. I hear that you feel uncomfortable. I wonder if you are scared. I wish there was a way to help you stay.

Here, the counselor realizes that maybe the awareness is too much too fast, as Y-Chun is withdrawing before a complete contact has occurred (see Figure 8.1). The counselor believes that Y-Chun is genuinely concerned about losing face. The counselor recognizes the courage it takes for anyone to admit to being raped, especially someone from an Asian culture. According to many Asian cultures, Y-Chun is disgracing her family by making such information public. Rape is typically a shaming and disgraceful event that the family handles privately. The counselor continues to use language (e.g., "I am honored" and "I wonder") that supports a sense of understanding of Y-Chun's feelings, without being too direct, and invites Y-Chun to stay with counseling.

Y-Chun: (Makes eye contact and sighs) You are not angry with me for what I have done?

Counselor: Y-Chun, I feel connected to you. I am beginning to feel that you trust me. I see you as a courageous lady.

Notice that the counselor does not answer the question directly. Instead, she shares her genuine feelings and keeps the focus on the present.

Y-Chun: (Crying and beginning to breathe more deeply) Oh, hum, you are not mad at me?

Counselor: I see your breathing is deeper and steadier now. You have more tears. Do you notice anything else?

Notice the lack of labeling, interruption, or meaning making. The counselor keeps the focus on the here and now and avoids directly answering Y-Chun's question to keep the focus on Y-Chun's experience, eliminating "talking about" the experience. The counselor's response keeps the focus on the counselor's observations, thus increasing Y-Chun's awareness of her experiences.

Y-Chun: I feel sad. I did not realize how much I was holding onto. My stomach was hurting, and I haven't been sleeping well. My stomach feels more relaxed now.

Counselor: You are sad, and your stomach feels different.

The counselor purposefully restates the connection the client is making between her sadness and her stomach hurting, which heightens the client's awareness of the body and mind connection. Again, she avoids labeling, such as saying Y-Chun is feeling relief.

(The hour is nearly up.)

Counselor: Y-Chun, our time is coming to a close. Would you like to reschedule?

Y-Chun: Hum, perhaps.

Counselor: Perhaps.

The counselor repeats Y-Chun's word so Y-Chun can hear her own hesitation to reschedule. The counselor respects the hesitation and sees this as a normal and natural part of resistance after sharing such intimate and traumatic information so early in the counseling relationship.

Y-Chun: Well, yes, it seems to be helping already.

Counselor: Okay then, would you be willing to do something for me this week? I would like you to pay attention to your breathing. Please make a note regarding what is going on when your breathing becomes shallow versus more steady and deep. Notice your thoughts, sensations, feelings, your environment, and what you are doing. How does that sound to you? (Y-Chun nods in agreement.)

The homework is meant to increase the client's awareness without making a change yet. The theory of awareness is that the act of paying attention to a behavior, feeling, thought, or symptom without labeling allows for increased energy and the power for acceptance and, if necessary, change.

Gestalt counselors ask for permission to do an experiment or to give homework assignments. A Gestalt counselor does not push a client through resistance. The objective is to work with the resistance and avoid pushing a client longer or harder than the client can go. Working with the resistance includes honoring and recognizing its purpose.

After Y-Chun leaves the session, the counselor, during supervision, processes her own feelings and the effect of the session on her. The counselor feels sadness and hope. She is amazed with Y-Chun's strength and courage, including her ability to connect her emotional reaction to her stomach pain. But the counselor wonders if Y-Chun shared too much personal information too quickly, which could prevent her from returning to counseling. The counselor knows there was some resistance (i.e., the "yes, but" dynamic in the first response and the "I should leave" statement), as well as growth with the increased insight and awareness (i.e., Y-Chun recognizing the relationship between her stomachaches and her sadness). Y-Chun has numerous strengths and some boundaries. She is open to the Gestalt counseling process, and she has desire to change, which will assist her in reaching her goals. The counselor gives Y-Chun homework to keep the momentum of growth going between sessions. The goal of this homework is to give Y-Chun a chance to live the Gestalt principles, continue to grow, and make intentional changes between sessions.

Y-Chun attends three more sessions before asking to schedule counseling for every other week. During the three sessions, Y-Chun begins to notice several changes: reduced physical symptoms, decreased family stress, and feelings of success at school and with her boyfriend. Y-Chun has made a connection between holding her breath and increased stomachaches and headaches. However, she has not identified any common triggers or patterns for when she holds her breath. Before counseling sessions began, Y-Chun felt she was always holding her breath; however, now she holds her breath only a couple of times a day and feels less anxious. She has used therapeutic journaling as a means of increasing her awareness of her physical symptoms and emotions. She has noticed a pattern of muscle pain and biting her lip before exams, which she believes is her expression of fear because her thoughts are of failing, falling short, and losing her good standing with her parents. She has increased successful communication with her parents and her boyfriend by expressing her likes and dislikes clearly and respectfully. Y-Chun is also happier with her own parenting style. She has begun to discuss parenting issues with her mom.

Y-Chun has made great progress in her ability to recognize her feelings and needs. She has learned to communicate with others directly instead of blaming others or feeling shame/guilt. A Gestalt counselor understands that this progress is typical; that is, increased awareness initially creates energy and empowerment. The increased energy and empowerment occur because clients are living more in the present instead of avoiding or ignoring events or their feelings; however, the amount of change reported is not typical. Y-Chun requested that the counseling sessions move to every other week. The previous session with Y-Chun was 2 weeks ago, when she felt successful and generally happy.

The counselor recognizes the power of completing Gestalts. The new energy and successes Y-Chun is experiencing are most likely happening because of this new way of interacting with her environment, through being more authentic and present rather than using energy on self-protection. But the counselor is concerned that too many changes are occurring at one time and Y-Chun is not taking time to integrate all the changes; therefore, a natural regression in this new growth is likely.

Middle Stage of the Counseling Process

At the middle stage of the counseling process, the counselor would expect forward progress, with more awareness, less premature withdrawal from the cycle of experience (see Figure 8.1), and more contact with self and others. However, to sustain such movement, deeper work is required, which invites stronger resistance and regression in growth.

When Y-Chun returns to counseling, her breathing is shallow, she is biting her lips, and her affect is angry and anxious.

Counselor: Y-Chun, how are things going?

Y-Chun: The first several days after our last session, everything continued to be good. Then school demands increased, and so have the fights with my boyfriend. The kids have stopped listening to me. I am confused about what happened to all the changes. Did I do something wrong? I was working really hard.

Y-Chun is experiencing a natural regression in her growth, which is expected since so many changes happened at once. Growth is rarely a straight movement forward without some regression. Because of her strong emotions and need to fill in the details, the counselor allows Y-Chun to ramble for several minutes. This enables Y-Chun to feel heard by the counselor and herself. The counselor allows the rambling to occur when stress is being released and assesses for a shift or change in Y-Chun's anxiety before suggesting an experiment. This assessment helps the counselor know when to start the intervention (experiment). The counselor stops the rambling when the anxiety increases, as evident in a surge of pressure and increased rate of speech, shallow breathing, lip biting, and repetition. Alternatively, the counselor stops the rambling if there is a loss of energy along with repetition of information. The counselor intervenes by being "therapeutically rude" when Y-Chun's eye contact is good. Y-Chun is having difficulty sitting still, her breathing and speech rate are quick, and she does not pause to take a long breath.

Counselor:	(Interrupts—being therapeutically rude—changing her own breathing pattern by slowing down and using a soft voice) Y-Chun, let's take a pause here for a moment and catch our breath.
Y-Chun:	Oh, okay. Wow, I did not realize how quickly I was breathing.
Counselor:	Yeah, I feel as if a tidal wave just hit us both.
Y-Chun:	(Eyes wide) Yeah, me too.
Counselor:	These last 2 weeks have been difficult for you. Can we try something? I would like to focus on just one of the many things that happened.

The counselor is moving from "talking about" to working/action (see Figure 8.1). The counselor brings the session into the present (the here and now) by sharing her immediate and genuine observations and attempting to target one figural event from Y-Chun's story. The counselor is also moving into an experiment. The counselor asks permission to shift the session and to try an experiment. Informed consent is sought through the counselor's explaining what she would like to try. The client always has the option to say no.

Counselor:	I would like to pay attention to your body and notice where in your body most of your energy is located. It is important to take one symptom at a time and explore what that symptom is telling us.

The counselor is more directive as she sets up the experiment, by asking Y-Chun to pay attention to her body and to discover where most of her energy is located. The purpose of this experiment is centering (grounding) Y-Chun in her experience and sensations to get her out of her head and away from "talking about," which only increases her stress. Ideally, this occurs by moving Y-Chun's attention to her sensations (depending on what happens in the course of the experiment, since nothing is guaranteed). The idea is to have her pay attention to the location of most of her energy, then move to awareness, and then to excitement and potential actions (see Figure 8.1).

Counselor:	(Introducing the experiment and seeking informed consent) This can feel funny or odd at first. You may not like it. If that happens, then we can stop and process. This type of work initially feels hard to most clients. You may even feel unable to do what I am asking of you, and that is okay. Just let me know, and we will do something different. You are always in control, and you can stop this at any time.
Y-Chun:	(With a puzzled look) Hum, did I do something wrong? What are you asking me to do?
Counselor:	(Recognizing that Y-Chun's resistance is a normal response) Y-Chun, you have not done anything wrong. My goal is to increase your focus, reduce your anxiety, help identify your experience, and explore one thing at a time using present-tense language instead of talking about the past. Even though this past is recent, I want us to bring it into the *here and now.*
Y-Chun:	Oh, what do you mean? What would be different in the use of my language?

In the previous couple of interchanges, the counselor recognizes Y-Chun's hesitation and is gently working with it. To accomplish the goal of the experiment, the counselor needs to work with Y-Chun's resistance, which is normal and healthy. Her growth is obvious, as she is challenging the counselor (i.e., chewing on her decision to participate in the experiment through asking questions) rather than just agreeing (confluence) with the person in authority. Therefore, Y-Chun is working against both introjection and confluence.

Introjection is the question, "Did I do something wrong?" By asking this question, she is verbalizing an internal message rather than just assuming that the message is correct. Therefore, the act of saying it aloud and checking in with the counselor means she is not just "swallowing" the message; instead, she is "chewing" on it. Confluence would be just agreeing with the counselor and going along with whatever the counselor asks her to do. Y-Chun has a desire to please and begins to feel guilty when the counselor suggests changing her language, even though no judgments were being made. Because this is a growth, the counselor answers Y-Chun's question about whether she did something wrong.

Counselor: Y-Chun, in this experiment, when you speak about where most of your energy is stored in your body, I would like you to use present-tense language and give that portion of your body a voice. For example, I would say, "I am feeling short of breath as I am speaking. I notice I am talking quickly, and my shoulders are hard like rocks." I would then give my shoulders a voice: "I am hard like a rock because of the work I do and the pressure I feel." Does that example help?

Y-Chun: (With another puzzled look) Hum, well, sort of. It sounds a bit crazy.

Counselor: (Smiles slightly, recognizing that Y-Chun's reluctance is another sign of growth, as her thoughts are genuine and unfiltered. Y-Chun is showing signs of trust, finding her own voice, and allowing her reactions to be said aloud.)

The counselor is accepting the client's resistance and focusing on her growth. The counselor is gently pushing and accepting Y-Chun's need to push back. The client's leading and the counselor's dialogue are moving back and forth with just enough tension for each person to follow or lead. The counselor is gently pushing back yet staying with the resistance, since the client is not ready to move. Without a gentle push, no growth can occur; however, too much pushing from the counselor will throw the client off balance, causing her to prematurely withdraw or become overly stimulated before achieving a complete Gestalt.

Counselor: I know it sounds crazy. (Y-Chun nods her head.) When I say give your symptom a voice and listen to the voice, I am using a metaphor. (*Note: During the intake interview, it was clear that Y-Chun has never had and is not currently having a psychotic episode; therefore, this experiment should be safe for her.*) The first time clients do this experiment, they report feeling odd. However, they state that this was very helpful with increasing their awareness of the symptom. You may notice at first you cannot think of anything to say, but as you pay attention, you will become aware of sensations and words. In Gestalt counseling, we sometimes ask the person to give something a voice. By doing this, you and I can hear what is happening. How does that sound?

Y-Chun: So it is still me, but I am pretending the symptom has a voice? I am not sure I can do this, but I will try. This is crazy to me.

Counselor: Yes, I think you understand, and yes, at first it will seem crazy. If it does not work, then we will try something else.

Y-Chun: Well, okay, everything else has worked.

Counselor: Thank you for being willing to try this experiment. Can you tell me where most of your energy is in your body? Pay attention to that location. Keep your focus there, and as you become aware of the location, notice the sensations you are feeling. Try using only adjectives. Try to share your observations of the sensations and avoid labeling. When you are ready, I would like you to start talking aloud, using present-tense language.

Y-Chun: Yeah, okay. So notice where most of my energy is locate (closes her eyes), and see what happens.

Counselor: (With an inviting smile) Yes, exactly.

Y-Chun: Okay, here it goes. I am paying attention to my breathing, like we have done in past sessions—okay?

Counselor: (Nods) Keep your breath the same while you pay attention. (Y-Chun's breathing is shallow.)

Y-Chun: (Eyes open after less than 10 seconds) Huh, nothing is there.

Counselor: Okay, stay with it. (Y-Chun is holding her breath.)

Y-Chun: I can't breathe if I stay like this. I feel like I will choke.

Counselor: What is the purpose of choking?

Y-Chun: (With a puzzled look) To stop me! (She then sighs deeply.)

Counselor: You are stopping Y-Chun? (*Note: To stay in the experiment, the counselor clarifies Y-Chun's statement of holding her breath and addresses the symptom as a separate entity. Specific, present-tense language is important in keeping the client responsive to the sensations in the here and now, and in making a connection to whatever needs attention.*)

Y-Chun: No (talking as her symptom, as her breathing), she does not allow me to support her and give her energy. She holds me back.

Counselor: Who is she?

Y-Chun: (Still speaking as her breathing) Y-Chun. She takes me in and then will not let me out. She just holds on to me as if I am the one causing the trouble. I am not. If she would let me out (breathing returning to a normal rate), then I could give her more energy and support her. I could help her.

The counselor notices a change in Y-Chun's breathing pattern, which signals that something has shifted. This might be the end of the work for now. A shift indicates something has occurred, such as an increase in awareness or an aha moment; therefore, it is important to check in with the client to see if this is enough or if continuing exploration is possible.

Counselor: I notice a change. What happened?

Y-Chun: (Opening her eyes and talking as herself again) I have been holding my breath, thinking that was helping and giving me more control over my emotions. During the week, I also tried to force myself to breathe deeply, but I could not. It was as if I had no control over my breathing.

Counselor: Let's stay with this a bit longer. Could you pay attention to your breathing again?

The counselor is continuing because Y-Chun seems to have only a partial awareness, and the counselor wants to see if there is additional information available to Y-Chun about the role of holding her breath and how doing so affects her.

Y-Chun: Okay.

Counselor: Speaking as your breath again, could you fill in the blank? I am . . .

Y-Chun: (Speaking as her breath) I am important. I am energy. I am automatic if you let me be. I work with your feelings. I wish I could do my job without you forcing me to stop or to go. Just let me be who I am. (Tears begin to fall.)

Counselor: (Observing another shift in Y-Chun's affect and breathing) What just happened?

Y-Chun: I hold my breath when I think it is unsafe for me to be who I am. I just want to be me and sometimes I do not know who me is, so to fit in I control what I say and do. People get mad at me when I speak up. So I go along with the crowd or my parents, and then I feel guilty and helpless.

Y-Chun is describing the process of confluence, in that she is afraid of other people's anger and not fitting in (i.e., being rejected). Therefore, she attempts to be what other people want her to be. She believes the confluence protects her, but this protection comes at a price. In this protective mode, she is not authentic and is therefore unable to build intimacy in relationships and be herself (i.e., know and share her likes, dislikes, values, etc.).

Counselor: You do not trust yourself and are afraid of being rejected. You want to be yourself, and you are not sure what that means. I wonder if you are afraid of being yourself and of what would happen if you were yourself all the time, especially with your parents.

The counselor just took a big risk and pushed through the resistance a bit by adding the last statement. This was done with the intention of helping the client see that the counselor understands the potential value clash. The counselor trusts the rapport she has with Y-Chun and believes their counseling has moved to the work stage. If the counselor is correct, then the intervention has the potential to expand the client's awareness of her own process and struggle between the two cultures. If the counselor is wrong, the client has the chance to correct the counselor and experience one way of being in conflict. Alternatively, the client could feel insulted and not return to counseling.

Y-Chun: Hum, I am not sure. I never thought about it that way. I am not sure what would happen.

Counselor: Okay, so during this week, can you sit with what I said? That would mean paying attention to what happens and any impact my comment might have on you this week.

Sitting, in this context, means for the client to pay attention (i.e., to any sensations, thoughts, emotional reactions, and new awareness), to stay with something and try not to change anything. This is a way to increase awareness. In this case, the counselor is inviting Y-Chun to "chew" on this all week and pay attention to potential consequences.

Y-Chun: Hum, yeah, I am glad we can meet next week.

Typically, at this point, the client would move back to being seen every week to help reduce the amount of stress she was under at the beginning of this latest session. Particularly, the counselor is considering the importance of not jeopardizing Y-Chun's living arrangement and help with her children.

Y-Chun returns for several more sessions and discovers that she can blend both cultures, develop an adult relationship with her parents, finish school, and then explore her relationship with her boyfriend. She wants to hold on to some of her mother's traditions but enjoys many of the American ways of doing things. She decides that she wants her mother's help with the kids because her mom is attentive and a positive influence on them. She decides to accept her mother's parenting, which is nurturing. However, Y-Chun is doing more activities with the kids away from home to build her relationship with them. Y-Chun decides to get to know herself and stop saying yes when she really wants to say no. She decides to include the children in more activities with her boyfriend, to see what will happen. A Gestalt counselor works with these goals by helping Y-Chun become aware of when she tends to "follow the crowd" and encouraging her to think about what is best for her and the children before just doing something someone has asked her to do (i.e., "chewing" versus "swallowing").

KEYSTONES

- GT was co-created by Fritz Perls and Laura Pozner-Perls in or around 1947.
- GT is rooted in holism, organismic functioning, and field theory.
- GT is a present-focused, humanistic, holistic, integrative, creative, experiential, phenomenological, and process-oriented theory.
- Humans are self-actualizing and continually seek homeostasis.
- The counselor–client relationship is interdependent; the counselor is the expert of the theory, and the client is the expert of his or her experience.
- The main goals of GT are awareness and self-support.
- A Gestalt occurs when the client has a complete experience that connects the body/mind and spirit in meaning making (an aha moment).
- An uncompleted Gestalt leaves unfinished business and jeopardizes a person's overall wellness.

- The cycle of experience is a road map for understanding the Gestalt process.
- Counselors need to be well grounded in all aspects of GT to avoid practicing gimmickry and causing harm to clients.
- Resistances are a normal and natural part of the counseling process.
- GT is appropriate for most populations.

REFLECTIONS FROM THE CONTRIBUTOR'S CHAIR

Joseph Spillman

From its philosophical foundations to the role of the counselor, GT has always resonated with me. I have used a GT approach my whole life, yet I did not realize it until I "found" GT in my counseling studies. GT is a dynamic and creative process that allows me to use my personhood to assist clients in their change process. Focus on relationship, honesty, awareness, congruence, and working collaboratively with clients are all essential elements for long-lasting change.

Christina M. Rosen

When I saw Fritz Perls working with Gloria in the "Gloria tapes," during my master's program, I disliked GT. However, about a year later, I attended a professional workshop that used GT but was gentle, not as confrontational. From that experience, GT resonated with my values and philosophy on life. In 1992, I entered the Greater Cincinnati Gestalt Institute and completed 3 years of training, which made me a more effective counselor. I joined the Appalachian Gestalt Training Institute after moving to North Carolina.

ADDITIONAL RESOURCES

Journals

Association for the Advancement of Gestalt Therapy (www.aagt.org/)

Gestalt Australia and New Zealand (www.ganz.org.au/)

Gestalt Review (www.gestaltreview.com)

International Gestalt Journal (www.igjournal.org/)

Gestalt Institutes

Gestalt Institute of Cleveland (www.gestaltcleveland.org)

Gestalt Institute of New Zealand (www.gestalt.org.nz)

New York Institute for Gestalt Therapy (www.newyorkgestalt.org)

REFERENCES

Baruth, L. G., & Manning, M. L. (2012). *Multicultural counseling and psychotherapy: A lifespan approach* (5th ed.). Upper Saddle River, NJ: Pearson Education.

Bowman, C. E. (2005). The history and development of Gestalt therapy. In A. L. Woldt & S. M. Toman (Eds.), *Gestalt therapy: History, theory and practice* (pp. 3–20). Thousand Oaks, CA: Sage.

Clarke, K. M., & Greenberg, L. S. (1986). Differential effects of the Gestalt two-chair intervention and problem solving in resolving decisional conflict. *Journal of Counseling Psychology, 33,* 11–15.

Corey, G. (2009). *Theory and practice of psychotherapy* (8th ed.). Belmont, CA: Brooks/Cole.

De Reit, V., Korb, M. P., & Gorrell, J. J. (1980). *Gestalt therapy: An introduction.* New York: Fairview Park.

Goldstein, K. (1939). *The organism.* New York: American Book.

Greenberg, L. S. (1979). Resolving splits: The two-chair technique. *Psychotherapy: Theory, Research, and Practice, 16,* 210–218.

Greenberg, L. S., & Dompierre, L. M. (1981). Specific effects of Gestalt two-chair dialogue on intrapsychic conflict in counseling. *Journal of Counseling Psychology, 28*(4), 288–294.

Greenberg, L. S., Elliott, R. K., & Lietaer, G. (1994). Research on experiential psychotherapies. In A. E. Bergin & S. L. Garfield (Eds.), *Handbook of psychotherapy and behavioral change* (4th ed., pp. 509–539). New York: John Wiley.

Greenberg, L. S., & Rice, L. N. (1997). Humanistic approaches to psychotherapy. In P. L. Wachtel & S. B. Messer (Eds.), *Theories of psychotherapy: Origins and evolution* (pp. 97–129). Washington, DC: American Psychological Association.

King, S. (1988). *The differential effects of empty-chair dialogue and empathetic reflection for unfinished business.* Unpublished master's thesis, University of British Columbia, Vancouver, Canada.

Lewin, K. (1951). *Field theory in social science: Selected theoretical papers* (D. Cartwright, Ed.). New York: Harper & Row.

Lobb, M. S. (2005). Classical Gestalt therapy theory. In A. L. Woldt & S. M. Toman (Eds.), *Gestalt therapy: History, theory and practice.* (pp. 21–40). Thousand Oaks, CA: Sage.

Mann, D. (2011). *Gestalt therapy: 100 key points and techniques.* New York: Routledge.

Melnick, J., & Nevis, S. M. (2005). Gestalt therapy methodology. In A. L. Woldt & S. M. Toman (Eds.), *Gestalt therapy: History, theory and practice* (pp. 101–116). Thousand Oaks, CA: Sage.

Paivio, S. C., & Greenberg, L. S. (1995). Resolving "unfinished business": Efficacy of experiential therapy using empty-chair dialogue. *Journal of Consulting and Clinical Psychology, 63*(3), 419–425.

Perls, F. S. (1947). *Ego, hunger and aggression: A revision of Freud's theory and method.* London: Allen & Unwin.

Perls, F. (1969). *In and out of the garbage pail.* Lafayette, CA: Real People Press.

Perls, F. (1973). *The Gestalt approach and eye witness to therapy.* Palo Alto, CA: Science & Behavior Books.

Polster, E., & Polster, M. (1974). *Gestalt therapy integrated: Contours of theory and practice.* New York: Vintage.

Smuts, J. (1926). *Holism and evolution.* Highland, NY: Gestalt Journal Press.

Strümpfel, U., & Goldman, R. (2002). Contacting Gestalt therapy. In D. J. Cain & J. Seeman (Eds.), *Humanistic psychotherapies: Handbook of research and practice* (pp. 189–219). Washington, DC: American Psychological Association.

Woldt, A. L., & Toman, S. M. (Eds.). (2005). *Gestalt therapy: History, theory and practice.* Thousand Oaks, CA: Sage.

Zinker, J. (1978). *Creative process in Gestalt therapy.* New York: Vintage Books.

CHAPTER 9

Cognitive-Behavioral Theories

Julia Y. Porter

Men are disturbed not by things, but by the view which they take of them.

—Epictetus in *The Enchiridion*

What an interesting quote, and an even more interesting concept: We are not disturbed by things but, rather, by the view we take of them. So I guess the message we give to ourselves so often, the message that *someone else* has really made us mad, wouldn't sit right with Epictetus. Nor, as you will find out, would it sit well with those counselors who use a cognitive-behavioral frame of reference.

Cognitive-behavioral theories examine the relationship between thoughts, which are the view we take of life, and behaviors, which are our actions in response to our thoughts. Thoughts and behaviors can be healthy and beneficial or unhealthy and harmful. Cognitive-behavioral therapy (CBT) focuses on helping clients identify harmful thoughts and the resulting dysfunctional emotions and behaviors from those thoughts so they can change harmful thoughts into healthier, more adaptive ones, which in turn result in healthier emotions and behaviors.

After reading this chapter, you will be able to do the following:

1. Describe the development of CBT

2. Identify techniques and approaches that can be used in CBT to help clients change

3. Utilize the rational emotive behavior therapy A-B-C-D-E process for disputing irrational thoughts and behaviors and learn how to replace irrational thoughts and behaviors with rational ones

PROFILE OF MAIN FIGURES

CBT integrates principles and constructs taken from cognitive therapy, which focuses on thoughts, with those from behavioral therapy (see Chapter 10), which focuses on actions. What follows is a brief review of the major contributors to the development of CBT.

Behavior Theories

Much of the early foundation for behavior theory took root in research conducted in animal laboratories—including those of Ivan Pavlov and B. F. Skinner. Their research took a behavioral point of view—that is, a stance that behavior, whether functional and adaptive or dysfunctional, is learned (see Chapter 10). Those embracing this theory believe that the same mechanisms of learning can be used to help a person unlearn undesired behavior and/or learn new, more desirable behavior instead. Major figures in the development of this theory include the following:

- *Ivan Pavlov,* a Russian physiologist, conducted behavioral experiments in the early 1900s that examined responses to stimuli. Pavlov's research resulted in a type of learning called classical conditioning (Miltenberger, 2008).
- *B. F. Skinner* developed operant conditioning based on behavioral experiments that examined the use of reinforcement and punishment to shape and control behavior (Corey, 2013).
- *Joseph Wolpe* was one of the early innovators in behavior theory, taking the principles learned in the laboratories of Pavlov, Skinner, and others and applying them to humans experiencing difficulty with anxiety. Wolpe developed a technique called systematic desensitization, which employs relaxation techniques paired with controlled exposure to a feared stimulus. Since an individual cannot be in a state of relaxation and tension at the same time (Seligman & Reichenberg, 2010), the pairing of the two conditions serves to negate the person's "learned" fear response to that stimulus.

Cognitive Theories

Cognitive theories can be characterized as time-limited, structured, active, here-and-now approaches that target the way a client makes or gives "meaning" to lived experiences. Cognitive theories posit that an individual's behavior and mood are largely determined by the way he or she psychologically perceives the world. The focus of these theories is, therefore, on identifying the beliefs, underlying assumptions, and even personal philosophies that color one's interpretation of life experiences. Cognitive theorists examine the primacy of an individual's perception of the problematic situations and the cognitions (ideas and thoughts) that arise as a result. It is believed that these cognitions, beliefs, assumptions, and fundamental philosophies serve as the source of our adaptive and maladaptive feelings and behaviors. The main proponent of this model was Aaron Beck.

Beck began developing cognitive therapy in the 1960s (Beck & Weishaar, 2011). Working with depressed clients, Beck noted that his research showed a relationship between negative thoughts and depression. From his research, he postulated that thoughts—the way individuals give meaning to their lived experiences—were related to the emotional reactions. He suggested that a person's thoughts could be "adaptive" or "maladaptive," with the latter type creating problems for the individual. Beck, being a methodical researcher, was cautious in extending his cognitive model of depression to other mental disorders; however, many followers, including his daughter, Judith Beck (2011) have successfully applied cognitive therapy to a wide range of problems. Cognitive therapy and Beck's work have been expanded to address and treat issues of anxiety, eating disorders, various personality disorders, adolescent conduct disorders, and substance-abuse disorders (Murdock, 2013). Extensive research supports the efficacy of Beck's model, and he has written 17 books and more than 400 articles about his work (Corey, 2012b).

Cognitive-Behavioral Theories

It is generally agreed that the first integration of cognitive and behavioral constructs into a discrete form of CBT occurred in the 1950s with the work of Albert Ellis. However, many others, including Donald Meichenbaum and Edna Foa, have significantly furthered the development and expansion of CBT.

- *Albert Ellis* started one of the earliest forms of an integrated CBT. His theory, initially called rational emotive therapy (RET), was developed in the 1950s and expanded into what is now known as rational emotive behavior therapy (REBT; Corey, 2012b). REBT views thoughts, feelings, and actions as intertwined and addresses them as a complex unit in therapy. Ellis thought that people, rather than being mentally ill, became disturbed because of irrational thoughts based on faulty assumptions and rules about life. REBT is considered one of the major approaches to psychotherapy and is widely used today internationally (Murdock, 2013). A more detailed description of REBT is included in a later section of this chapter.
- *Donald Meichenbaum* developed cognitive behavior modification (CBM), which focuses on helping the client become aware of how he or she impacts others and how he or she thinks, feels, and behaves (Corey, 2012b). According to CBM, becoming aware of self-talk is essential for a client to be able to change his or her behavior. CBM is less direct than REBT and utilizes self-instructional training to help the client learn to become more aware of his or her self-talk.
- *Edna Foa,* another significant figure in CBT, employed the basic tenets of CBT in the treatment of those experiencing posttraumatic stress disorder (PTSD), with a method she calls prolonged exposure therapy (PET). PET is based on the idea that avoidance and negative thoughts prevent clients from working through traumatic experiences. PET employs numerous cognitive and behavioral strategies not only to educate clients about the causes, symptoms, and treatment of PTSD but also to have them experience and confront the situations that produce anxiety.

INTRODUCTION

As the field of counseling has evolved, our understanding of humans has grown. With this increased knowledge has come the understanding that, because of the complexity of human beings, a single theory of human thinking and behavior cannot address all the complexities of the human psyche. Research has shown that the cognitive and physical domains are integrated, and that addressing both in counseling practice yields more effective results than practicing either cognitive therapy or behavioral therapy in isolation.

Historical Background

As noted above, RET was the first CBT therapeutic approach developed. In the mid-1950s, Ellis developed RET because he thought psychoanalysis was inefficient and nondirective (Seligman & Reichenberg, 2010). RET is based on the work of the Stoic philosophers Epictetus and Marcus Aurelius (Parsons, 2009). Epictetus wrote in *The Enchiridion,* "Men are disturbed not by things, but by the view which they take of them."

In addition to philosophy, Ellis included elements of behavioral therapies in his theory. RET also contains elements from psychoanalysis (see Chapter 4), based on the belief that people seek pleasure and avoid pain, and from Adler's individual psychology (see Chapter 5), which posits that people have a desire to be loved and appreciated. After additional research, Ellis modified his model and renamed his theory rational emotive behavior therapy, or REBT (Murdock, 2013).

Areas of Development

CBT has been the source of interest and research since its foundation. Most recently, attention and research have focused on the areas of rational living therapy, dialectical behavior therapy, and mindfulness.

Rational Living Therapy

Rational living therapy (RLT) is an instructive therapy based on Aldo Pucci's work that emphasizes both counselor skills and client rational self-counseling skills. The counselor uses persuasive techniques to "sell" the client on the concept of rational self-counseling. These persuasive techniques help decrease client resistance and thus increase the chance of client success in therapy. Techniques used in RLT include rational motivational interviewing techniques to identify the client's desires for change. As with all cognitive therapies, RLT focuses on underlying assumptions for thinking and on irrational labeling. RLT counselors do not use the *Diagnostic and Statistical Manual of Mental Disorders* (American Psychiatric Association, 2013), since they believe this is a form of irrational labeling that may lead to hopelessness in clients.

Dialectical Behavior Therapy

In the early 1990s, Dr. Marsha Linehan developed dialectical behavior therapy (DBT), a cognitive-behavioral treatment designed for females who engage in suicidal or self-harming behavior. Linehan found that many of her patients did not respond well to the continual emphasis on change found in conventional CBT. One of the core philosophies of DBT is "radical acceptance." According to Linehan, acceptance was missing from traditional CBT. DBT advocates the bringing together of seemingly contradictory ideas into a greater whole in which the conflict is resolved (Linehan, 1993).

People who have experienced trauma often react abnormally to emotional stimulation. Symptoms of mental distress caused by both PTSD and bipolar disorder often result in the clients' living in a crisis mode and experiencing rapidly fluctuating emotions (Linehan, 1993). These clients either do not have coping skills or their coping skills are inadequate to help them deal with the intense emotions they are feeling. To address these symptoms, DBT teaches four core skills that clients learn in therapy: emotional regulation, interpersonal effectiveness, distress tolerance, and core mindfulness. The overall goal of DBT is to develop the client's skills so he or she is able to have "a life worth living" (Linehan, 1993). More detailed information about DBT is provided in Chapter 10.

Mindfulness-Based Cognitive Therapy

The foundation of mindfulness-based cognitive therapy can be traced to Eastern meditation practices that are part of religions such as Buddhism. Mindfulness practices that are more than 2,000 years old have become popular for use with any individual who is interested in developing a greater awareness of and ability to live in the here and now (Begley, 2007; Hayes, 2005; Kabat-Zinn, 2005). Mindfulness and mindfulness meditation, when employed as elements of cognitive therapy, help the client become aware of all incoming thoughts and feelings and simply accept these as they are, without attaching meaning or reacting to them. The goal of mindfulness-based cognitive therapy is to teach clients to focus less on reacting to incoming stimuli and instead simply to accept and observe them without judgment (Felder, Dimidjian, & Segal, 2012). This mindfulness practice allows the participant to notice when automatic processes are occurring and to alter his or her reactions to be more reflective.

For example, Dan, a client in his early 30s, drives to work every day on a highway that hugs one of the most beautiful coastlines in the world. Dan has made this 30-minute drive for 8 years, and he spends the drive focusing on problems in his life and trying to figure out solutions. He is experiencing high levels of stress and seeks counseling because he is afraid by the time he reaches 40, he will be "burned out" because of his stress level. In your first counseling session with Dan, as the two of you discuss the intake questions that evaluate Dan's current functioning, you discover that Dan spends all his waking time thinking about and solving problems. Dan's goal is to learn to relax. Based on your training in mindfulness techniques, you ask Dan to start consciously thinking about his thoughts while he is driving to and from work. In his busy life, Dan's drive time is the only consistent waking time he has to relax his mind. Dan is to consciously focus on the beauty of the drive he is taking and use all his senses to appreciate what is happening in the moment. If thoughts about problems come to mind, Dan is to refocus on the present. Research shows that mindfulness techniques are effective in helping clients cope with stress, pain, chronic illness, anxiety, and depression.

Acceptance and Commitment Therapy

Acceptance and commitment therapy (ACT; Hayes, 2005; Hayes, Strosahl, & Wilson, 2011) is one of the newer iterations of CBT. Like DBT and mindfulness-based cognitive therapy, ACT has a spiritual, or at least spiritually friendly, tone. ACT integrates fundamental cognitive concepts with mediation-oriented mindfulness to teach people how to "detach" from upsetting thoughts and simply step back to peacefully and acceptingly observe these thoughts as simply that—thoughts, not necessarily reality. This process has been labeled "cognitive defusion" and is based on the premise that we become tightly "fused" with our thoughts and thus fail to see alternatives.

Professional Identity

REBT is directive and confrontational, with the counselor being the authority (Ellis, 1995). As part of this directive role, the counselor teaches the client how to dispute irrational thoughts using the A-B-C-D-E model (Ellis & Ellis, 2011). While the client is a student in therapy who is learning healthier ways of thinking, feeling, and acting, he or she needs to be actively involved in the counseling process and persistent about change. As part of the process for encouraging and supporting clients to change, the REBT counselor accepts the client with unconditional other acceptance. Because clients usually take themselves, their problems, and the world too seriously, REBT counselors often use humor in sessions to help clients develop a new perspective.

While a warm counselor/client relationship is considered preferable, Ellis does not think it is necessary for successful counseling to occur. Because the REBT counselor is directive and some clients may expect the counselor to have all the answers, an ethical concern for REBT counselors is not allowing clients to become dependent on the counselor.

OVERVIEW OF REBT

As should be apparent from even the brief history provided above, CBT has evolved in many directions, with many subtle iterations. The nature of this text, along with the reality of page constraints, does not allow for a full and complete explication of CBT in all its manifestations. As such, the remainder of the chapter focuses on one model of CBT—that is, REBT, the model that most believe serves as the foundation for all that followed.

REBT is a directive therapy approach that focuses on integration of client thoughts, emotions, and behaviors. A key factor of the theory is that humans are or can be irrational and that we often set unrealistic (irrational) expectations for ourselves, which leads to self-criticism and "awfulizing." Irrational thoughts focus on absolutes that are unattainable, such as, "I must always be perfect" or "I should never be angry." When clients cannot meet their own unrealistic expectations, they participate in critical self-talk such as, "I can never do anything right" or "I am a loser."

Ellis thought that everyone needs to select goals and that it is important to evaluate the success or failure of goals. However, Ellis thought we should not rate ourselves as "good" or "bad" based on something that is a part of us but does not represent all of us (Ellis, 2005). It is important to be able to separate the evaluation of one act or characteristic of an individual from an overall rating of the individual. Each of us displays desirable and undesirable behaviors, but we should not be judged and/or judge ourselves based on one behavior. We are constantly changing, so an evaluation of our thoughts, feelings, and actions 6 months ago may not be an accurate evaluation of those same aspects of us today. For example, 6 months ago, summer school was ending. I was under a lot of pressure to grade projects and research papers quickly and did not have the time to review them as thoroughly as I would at a less busy time—for example, returning papers to students with my edits and allowing them to revise and resubmit the assignment. Because I was not able to follow a practice that I knew would enhance learning experiences for students, I could have decided that "I am a terrible teacher" (irrational) or that "I would have preferred more time to enrich the students' learning experiences, but because of the short, intensive nature of summer school, I was not able to include all the learning experiences that would have helped students" (rational). Ellis thought that unconditional self-acceptance is key to being healthy and happy.

People often think events cause consequences. Just think of the person who is angry because another person called her a name and "made her mad," or the person who no longer wants to live because his spouse is seeking a divorce. While these events certainly have consequences, the emotional reactions and behaviors that follow are controlled by the "meaning" the person gives to the event and not by the event itself. Two people can have the exact same experience but have different reactions that reflect variations in their interpretation of the experience. Consider the two individuals presented in Case Illustration 9.1.

CASE ILLUSTRATION 9.1

The Car Accident

Consider two college graduate students, each just having purchased his or her first brand-new car. As they drive off their separate lots, both get into accidents, totaling their new cars.

Assume that both students have insurance and are unharmed physically. In fact, they will both be able to continue to work, function, and live with minor disruption while their cars are replaced at no cost to them, and there will be no increase in their insurance premiums (since they were not at fault). If the incident, the actual event, is similar for both students, how do we explain the fact that one (Student A) is hysterical, uncontrollably crying and feeling as though the world is coming to an end, and the other (Student B) is merely concerned, disappointed, and frustrated? The answer may be found if we "listen" into the thoughts each student had at the time of the accident, thoughts that gave meaning to the event and generated each student's reaction.

Student A: How could this happen to me? Oh, no . . . I can't believe this—I never get a break. How am I going to pay for this? I'll never be able to drive again. How am I going to get to work? I'll probably lose my job . . . this can't be happening.

Student B: Whew—where did he come from? I had the green light! Yikes—the car is demolished. Thank God I'm okay. I hope the other driver is okay. I have to call Dad and check on who I should call. This is going to be a pain in the ass with the insurance—but, hey, at least I got it.

While it is clear that, should the accident experienced by Student A in our illustration have been accompanied by a loss of job, a failure to drive again, or a major disruption now and in the future to that student's life, perhaps emotions and reactions stronger than those exhibited by Student B would have been in order. The problem is, those consequences were not part of this reality and the student was reacting *not* to the event's actual consequences but to their misinterpretation and the irrational creation of assumed consequences. While this is a somewhat simple example, other, more poignant examples have been demonstrated by individuals who experienced childhood abuse.

For example, two children are sexually abused. One of the children grows up and becomes a pediatrician who specializes in abuse cases. His rational thoughts include, "When I am an adult I will be safe" and "I will help children be safe so they do not have to live in an abusive situation." The other child, who has similar family circumstances and trauma experiences, chooses to abuse his own child. The child who becomes an abuser as an adult has irrational thoughts such as, "This is a rotten world and everyone is abused." He extends his irrational thinking to include, "It is better for me to abuse my child than for a stranger to do it."

EXERCISE 9.1
EMOTIONAL AWARENESS EXERCISE

The following activity will help you become more aware of your own emotions and your responses to those emotions in your everyday life.

1. Identify an emotion that you had trouble with in the past week.

2. What made the emotion a problem for you?

3. Did you express the emotion?
   a. If yes, how did you express it?
   b. If no, why did you not express it?

4. Did the way you expressed the emotion improve your situation, have no effect on your situation, or make your situation worse? Why?

Since our reactions to life are rooted in our beliefs and interpretations of life events, when our beliefs result in dysfunctional feelings and behaviors, we can, according to Ellis (1995), change those beliefs to more rational, adaptive responses to the event.

REBT has been used effectively with a variety of mental health problems, including depression, anxiety disorders, and PTSD (Corey, 2012b). For the adult in the example above who abused his own child, he can learn to dispute the irrational belief that everyone is abused. He can also dispute the irrational belief that it is better for him to abuse his own child than for someone else to do it. Rational beliefs might include, "Child abuse is rotten and needs to be stopped" and "To stop child abuse, all adults need to protect children." By choosing more rational beliefs, this client can change his behavior.

View of Human Nature

Every individual has rational and irrational thoughts that affect his or her emotions and behavior. According to Ellis, irrational thoughts are not supported by facts so do not reflect reality and do not position a person to feel and act in adaptable ways. On the other hand, rational thoughts are logical and supported by facts, and they result in adaptable ways of feeling and acting that benefit self and others. For example, a client may have irrational thoughts about her body but rational thoughts about her ability to perform her job well. The client is 5'6" and weighs 128 pounds. Every time she gets dressed, she tells herself that she is fat and unattractive. Because of her constant irrational thoughts about her appearance, she does not develop habits of dressing attractively or presenting herself with confidence. Her irrational thoughts become a self-fulfilling prophecy. However, she is a certified public accountant (CPA) and is confident in her ability as an accountant because she has earned the prestigious CPA credential.

Basic Characteristics and Assumptions

Cognition is the way we think about something, and behavior is the way we act in response to our thoughts. According to Ellis (1995), events don't cause emotions; our thinking about events causes emotions. For example, anxiety is a normal, adaptive emotion and physiological response to "danger." However, irrational thoughts such as, "No one will like me" and "I will probably fail at this because I always fail at everything" can cause a client's anxiety level to rise to the fear level, and the client may then develop a phobia. It is quite common for a graduate student who is giving a presentation in class to have a high level of anxiety. The student's heart is pounding, palms are sweating, and mouth is dry. He or she would like to skip class. Why? While the presentation is important, it is not life threatening. Maybe this student is thinking, "I'm going to blow this presentation and make a fool of myself," and then, "If I blow the presentation, everyone will think I am dumb and no one will like me," and then, "I'll have to drop out of the program and I won't graduate." Wow! While this student could earn an F on the presentation if he or she messes up, the presentation is not a "test" of whether the student is a failure as a human or whether other students will like him or her. The student's thoughts have irrationally elevated this event in importance and danger.

Ellis believed that our responses to events are a combination of biological and environmental influences but that we can learn to control our thoughts, feelings, and behaviors through determination and persistence. REBT views people as being basically neutral, with the capacity for good or evil. According to Ellis (1995), people have a tendency to take their personal preferences and desires and present them as absolute musts and shoulds, which results in irrational thoughts that Ellis called "musturbation." An example is this: "Everyone must like me." While it would be great if we were liked by everyone we meet, in reality there will be some people who like us to different degrees, some people who are neutral (neither like nor dislike us), and some people who dislike us to different degrees.

REBT focuses on identifying irrational thought patterns that are causing distress and replacing those irrational thoughts with more rational ones, such as, "I would like for everyone to like me, but that is probably not going to happen" (Ellis, 1995). Ellis thought that our emotional disturbances are caused by our own unrealistic demands, absolutes, and shoulds. The following is a list of some of the most common unrealistic demands we place on ourselves, others, and the world:

1. *Demand on self:* I must do well and be approved at all times, or I'm no good. I must be loved by the significant people in my life, or I'm a failure.

2. *Demand on others:* Everyone must treat me well at all times, or they are no good.

3. *Demand on the world:* Life must be fair, easy, and hassle free at all times, or life is no good.

Ellis developed the A-B-C-D-E model to help clients learn to think more rationally and thus change their emotions and behavior to be more adaptable.

The process of identifying irrational thinking can be taught to clients, and clients can use the process in other situations. The A-B-C-D-E model includes the following aspects (Ellis, 1995):

Activating event: Through our senses, we become aware of something. We may not have any control over the activating event.

Beliefs about the event: We believe something about what our senses have told us. These thoughts can be good (rational), neutral, or bad (irrational). Based on these thoughts, there is a reaction. We can control our beliefs and thoughts, but it takes practice.

Consequence of our beliefs about the event: Our thoughts cause our feelings and behaviors. We often attribute our feelings and actions to something beyond our control, but we have the ability to control our emotions and actions as well as our thinking. People usually seek counseling because they do not like consequences from an event. For example, a client is furious that he did not receive the promotion he thinks he deserves, so he screams at his boss and is fired. The client comes to counseling to learn anger-management skills so he can get another job. The consequence of losing his job because of his angry outburst has motivated him to change.

Sometimes clients come to counseling not to change themselves but to get help from the counselor to change others. We often see clients like this in marriage counseling. For example, a wife comes to counseling because her husband is unfaithful, and she would like the counselor to help her change him because he must be faithful or she just can't stand it.

Disputing irrational thoughts: Clients are taught to analyze irrational thoughts and dispute them. This process focuses on separating the clients' preferences from the absolutes and musts that clients tell themselves are required for happiness.

Effective new emotions and behavior: These are a result of replacing irrational thoughts and behaviors with rational thoughts and behaviors—by consciously choosing better responses.

Figure 9.1 Albert Ellis's (1995) A-B-C-D-E Model for Disputing Irrational Beliefs and Replacing Them With Rational Ones

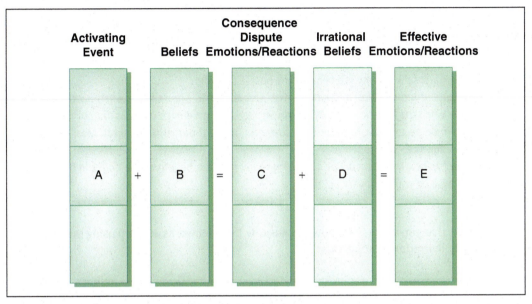

The connection of thought to feelings and behavior, as well as the value of debating irrational thoughts and employing a more adaptable way of viewing a situation using Ellis's A-B-C-D-E model, is presented in Case Illustration 9.2.

CASE ILLUSTRATION 9.2

Using the A-B-C-D-E Model to Think Rationally

Example 1

- *Activating event:* I met my in-laws for the first time and really wanted to impress them. In my eagerness to impress them, I kept interrupting them.
- *Belief (irrational):* I'm a terrible person, and I never do anything right. My in-laws will hate me and never speak to me again.
- *Consequence:* I am angry with myself, so I am avoiding contact with my in-laws.
- *Dispute irrational belief and replace with rational belief:* I don't like how I interrupted my in-laws when we were talking. I'll be more considerate the next time I talk with my in-laws.
- *Effective new emotion/behavior:* I am disappointed in how I responded to my in-laws, but I am looking forward to getting to know them better and to them getting to know me.

(Continued)

(Continued)

Example 2

- *Activating event:* My boss was having a bad day, and he snapped at me about a project we are working on.
- *Belief (irrational):* I can't stand the way my boss spoke to me. He shouldn't be that way.
- *Consequence:* I quit my job because my boss is so awful.
- *Dispute irrational belief and replace with rational belief:* I don't like it when people are rude when they speak to me. My boss was rude today. Perhaps my boss did not realize how rude he sounded because he is stressed out about our current project. Most of the time, this is a great job.
- *Effective new emotion/behavior:* I will give my boss the benefit of the doubt in this case because he usually is very polite.

Now that you understand how the A-B-C-D-E model works, let's try using this technique to dispute irrational thoughts.

EXERCISE 9.2

The worksheet below uses Ellis's A-B-C-D-E model for learning to think more rationally. Select a "disturbing" event that occurred in the past week, and complete the worksheet.

Activating event: _____

_____

_____

Belief (irrational): _____

_____

_____

Consequence: _____

_____

_____

Dispute irrational belief and replace with rational belief: _____

_____

_____

Effective new emotion/behavior: _____

_____

_____

Research Supporting Theoretical Constructs and Interventions

Emotions range on a continuum from numbness (no expression of emotions) to hypersensitivity (strong emotions expressed about most events; Porter, 2011). Research indicates that the four strongest emotions are anger, sadness, fear, and joy. Three of these—anger, sadness, and fear—are considered to be negative (Ellis, 1999) because they can create barriers that contribute to clients' not functioning in healthy, adaptable ways.

Figure 9.2   Dimensions of Negative Emotions (Ellis, 1999)

Most people do not start out at the hypersensitive emotional state but, rather, progress in stages. For example, a wife may be frustrated when her husband corrects her grammar. If the correcting behavior continues over time without the wife addressing her frustration, she may begin to make irrational statements to herself such as, "He doesn't love me or he would not correct me" or "I can never do anything right." Frustration that is not addressed will build over time to anger, and anger that is not addressed can build to rage. While clients can make irrational decisions at any emotional stage, the stronger the emotional stage, the higher the possibility that an irrational decision or reaction will result.

More than 240 research studies of REBT were conducted before 1995 (DiGiuseppe, 1996), and many research studies have been conducted since that time. REBT has been subjected to research, showing good results with many diagnostic and outcome measures (Leichsenring, Hiller, Weissberg, & Leibing, 2006).

The constructs in REBT of irrational beliefs, rational beliefs, unconditional self-acceptance, unconditional other acceptance, and unconditional world acceptance are hard to define and measure. Many of the research studies about REBT have used non-experimental methods and have focused on the effectiveness of REBT outcomes. Ellis (1996) agreed with DiGiuseppe's criticism of the research efforts to validate REBT and expressed concern that without empirical support, REBT would suffer as a recognized theory. The following is a summary of some of the research findings related to REBT:

1984   McGovern and Silverman reviewed research studies published between 1977 and 1982 using a standard summary review format. They concluded that there was significant support for the use of REBT.

1992   Silverman, McCarthy, and McGovern reviewed 89 outcome research studies conducted between 1982 and 1989. They found that 49 of the studies showed REBT to be more effective than other theoretical approaches.

2004   Gonzales and colleagues examined 19 studies of REBT with children and adolescents using meta-analyses. They found a moderate effect size (0.50).

Use With Diverse Populations and Children

REBT has been used successfully with individuals, couples, families, and groups (Ellis & Dryden, 2007). Since REBT, in its standard format, requires the application of a process requiring not only the identification of one's cognitions but the rational debating and reformulating of those cognitions, the ability to engage in higher-order thinking, conduct analyses, and think abstractly is certainly seen as valuable to the effective implementation of this theory. Having said that, however, REBT has also been shown effective in work with children and adolescents for whom these cognitive skills of higher thinking may be underdeveloped.

Child-oriented REBT practice takes into account the child's cognitive-developmental status in selecting appropriate cognitive assessment and intervention procedures (see, e.g., Vernon & Clemente, 2006). For example, REBT practitioners are aware that children, especially at the earlier developmental levels, are active learners and that knowledge acquisition is facilitated by "doing" and "seeing" as much as by "hearing." As such, those working with younger children often employ materials such as picture and storybooks, imagery strategies, and behavioral rehearsal. An excellent and comprehensive resource for those seeking more information about REBT's application to childhood disorders is Ellis and Bernard's (2006) *Rational Emotive Behavioral Approaches to Childhood Disorders*.

In terms of the utility of REBT with culturally diverse populations, Sapp (1996) noted that REBT emphasizes the value of identifying and building on a client's cultural and individual strengths, rather than letting the client accept a victim's status. It should be noted, however, that even though REBT has been rigorously studied for efficacy and effectiveness, like the other CBT approaches and techniques, it has little empirical research supporting its adaptation to characteristics of individuals coming from diverse backgrounds, including ethnicity, race, sexual orientation, and disability (Pantalone, Iwamasa, & Martell, 2010).

Strengths and Limitations

One of the greatest strengths of REBT is that it teaches clients how to change their thinking and behavior and empowers them to help themselves after the counseling process ends. REBT helps clients think about their thinking and become aware of their thought processes. REBT is adaptable to a wide variety of problems and can be used for prevention and psychoeducational programs as well as for treatment.

Limitations for some clients include the directive, confrontational nature of REBT, which does not work for clients from some cultures. Another limitation is that the analysis process necessary to implement the A-B-C-D-E model for disputing irrational thoughts may be too complicated for some clients, such as those with cognitive impairments or very young children, to implement. Ellis (1987) recommended that clients be over the age of 8 and of average or above-average intelligence.

One final "challenge" or limitation to the use of REBT comes in the form of an ethical consideration. Needless to say, as with all techniques, counselors employing REBT are ethically bound to be competent in its application. It is essential to have proper training and supervision with the use of these approaches, as well as sensitivity to the potential ethical issues involved in using "confrontational" techniques with some clients—or targeting cognitive disputing of beliefs that the client culturally, or perhaps religiously, embraces. The concern for the ethical application of REBT has been center stage among those practicing REBT, to the degree that the Association of Rational Emotive Behaviour Therapy (2011) has developed a specific code of ethics and standards to guide practice.

THE THERAPEUTIC PROCESS AND APPLICATIONS

Therapeutic Goals

The goal of REBT is to help clients be healthier and happier (Ellis, 1995). To reach these goals, REBT helps clients learn cognitive skills so they can think more rationally. While each of us has the ability to think rationally or irrationally, healthy people rely mostly on rational beliefs that can differentiate preferences from absolutes and thus allow the person to be more flexible and adaptable when solving problems in daily life (Dryden, 2011). All people have goals—for example, to be loved, to be successful, to have power, to have freedom to choose, and to have fun. When our goals are threatened or blocked, we experience frustration, anger, and anxiety (Ellis, 1999). REBT helps clients become aware of their thoughts, emotions, and behaviors so they can learn to separate the person from the behavior. Part of this separation process involves developing unconditional self-acceptance, unconditional other acceptance, and unconditional life acceptance (Ellis & Ellis, 2011). For example, a child throws a temper tantrum because he or she wants a candy bar at the checkout counter of the grocery store. The temper tantrum is bad behavior triggered by the child's belief that he or she must have a candy bar. The child's bad behavior does not make the child bad; the focus is on changing the bad behavior, not on labeling, which could further damage the process of developing rational thoughts, emotions, and behaviors.

Properly implemented, REBT results in rational thinking, which helps clients accept themselves and others. As a result of thinking rationally, clients experience greater happiness.

Interventions

Ellis (2004) said he became a psychotherapist because he wanted to help people be healthier and happier and also to help himself be healthier and happier by being less anxious. In this quest for a better life, Ellis developed techniques that he often first tested on himself.

When he was young, Ellis (1997) was afraid of many things, including public speaking and girls. He decided to face his terror of public speaking, with the idea that the worst that could happen was he would die from fear. From this self-experiment to overcome his fear of public speaking, Ellis developed a technique known as *shame attacking* (Ellis, 2002).

Encouraged by his success with the public-speaking experiment, Ellis (1997) decided to apply shame-attacking techniques to his fear of girls. Ellis lived in New York City, close to the Bronx Botanical Gardens. He decided that he would go to the gardens every day in July and approach at least one woman sitting alone on a bench, sit down beside her, and talk with her for one whole minute. At the end of July, Ellis had approached 130 women. While 30 of them had gotten up and walked away, Ellis did talk to the other 100 women, and one of them made a date to go out with him. Unfortunately, she did not show up for the date, but Ellis was pleased that none of the women screamed at him or called the police. Based on the success of this experiment, he decided to continue it. Out of the next 100 women Ellis talked to, he was able to make three dates. At the end of the experiment, Ellis had gotten over his fear and could talk to women at any time and in any situation.

In shame attacking, the client does something related to the issue that is the focus of counseling, something that has the potential to be very embarrassing. The purpose of this technique is to help clients lessen their anxiety about a particular situation by realizing they will not die of embarrassment.

The REBT counselor teaches the client the A-B-C-D-E model to help the client understand the complex way thoughts, feelings, and actions interact and to help the client learn to dispute irrational beliefs (see pp. 238–240 in this chapter for a more detailed explanation of the A-B-C-D-E model). The *D* in the A-B-C-D-E model stands for "dispute." *Disputing* irrational beliefs is the major REBT technique. As part of the disputing process, the counselor uses questioning to help clients identify irrational beliefs. Dryden (1994) emphasizes that counselors need to be careful in using disputing techniques with clients who have been abused or have suffered some other type of traumatic event. Additional REBT techniques include the following:

- *Bibliotherapy* is the use of books and assigned readings to help the client understand how to make desired life changes. Ellis wrote extensively about REBT, so there are several hundred articles that clients can be assigned as homework to better understand how to dispute irrational thoughts.

- *Homework* is an essential part of REBT because it helps clients apply skills learned in the REBT process to their lives on a daily basis. Ellis (1995) thought that transferring learning from therapy sessions to the real world was important to sustain therapy results. The counselor and the client collaborate to select homework assignments. Another benefit of homework is that clients are more likely to understand and be able to use the REBT process after therapy sessions end.

- *Humor* can help clients see how irrationally they are acting. Ellis set humorous song lyrics about irrational beliefs to familiar tunes such as "Yankee Doodle Dandy" and "Tea for Two." He used the songs with clients to bring humor into the counseling sessions and as a reminder for them to change irrational thoughts. Clients can also be asked to write their own lyrics.

- *In vivo desensitization* is a technique developed in behavior therapy to help clients overcome fear. The client is gradually and systematically exposed to the fear until he or she can more effectively deal with it. For example, a client who is afraid of mice would be asked first to picture a mouse and think about walking into a room with a mouse in it. The client would then be taught relaxation techniques to help him or her deal with anxiety from the thought of being in a room with a mouse. Gradually, the client would be moved from imagining the situation to actually being in a room with a mouse.

- *Rational coping statements* are written by the client and repeated during the change process to help the client dispute his or her irrational beliefs and change thinking to rational beliefs. For example, a man is laid off from work after 19 years because his company is downsizing. He is eligible to draw unemployment while he is searching for a new job. His coping statement might be, "I would prefer to stay at my old job; however, I do have unemployment income while I find a new job."
- *Recordings* of counseling sessions are often made and a copy given to the client for use as homework, to review what happened during sessions. Listening to the recordings helps the client learn to dispute irrational beliefs.
- *Stop and monitor* is a reminder technique that places cues in the client's environment to remind him or her to stop and monitor thinking. For example, a client had the irrational thoughts, "I am a loser" and "No one likes me." She had these irrational thoughts for many years and was having trouble disputing them. To help her replace these irrational thoughts with rational ones, her counselor helped her select a door as an environmental cue. Anytime she walked through a doorway, she was to check her thoughts and redirect them by saying, "I am a winner, and many people like me."
- *Skill training* is used to help clients develop skills that will help them achieve their therapy goals. Assertiveness training to help clients set appropriate boundaries and be able to say "no" to people they want to please is an example of skill training.

In addition to the techniques developed by Ellis and other REBT counselors, REBT counselors can use techniques from other theories or develop their own creative techniques to help clients dispute irrational beliefs.

Assessment Strategies

The first step in the REBT counseling process is an assessment of the client to determine his or her belief structure. During this assessment process, REBT counselors identify client's underlying irrational beliefs that are causing dysfunction and distress. There are many formal and informal assessment techniques that can be used in this part of the counseling process.

Formal assessments are usually research based and include standardized instructions for use. One of the most widely used formal assessments for all mental issues is the *Diagnostic and Statistical Manual of Mental Disorders* (*DSM*), a medical model for diagnosing mental illness based on client symptoms (American Psychiatric Association, 2013). REBT counselors who use the *DSM* might use the structured clinical interview to assess clients for major psychiatric disorders. These would include depression, anxiety disorders, bipolar disorder, attention-deficit hyperactivity disorder, autism spectrum disorders, anorexia nervosa, bulimia nervosa, and schizophrenia (American Psychiatric Association, 2013).

Some REBT counselors do not use the *DSM* because they disagree with the concept of labeling clients as mentally ill. They are concerned that labeling may add to a client's irrational beliefs. These REBT counselors might use a problem-focused interview assessment to look for a client's underlying irrational beliefs, as well as to assess the client's ability to adapt to change and solve problems.

Some clients are more articulate than others and are more open to discussing their emotions using traditional "talk" therapy. For resistant clients, Dryden (1995) suggests the following creative assessment strategies:

- *Guided imagery:* Using visual aids such as photographs or drawings can help some clients better describe their emotions. For example, a 40-year-old male client believes that men should never express emotions. This client is resistant to reporting or discussing any emotional problems. He is in counseling because his wife threatened to leave if he does not change. She says that he is cold and unfeeling. He says he loves her but doesn't know how to show her. For this client, a creative assessment technique might be to ask him to bring photographs of experiences he and his wife have shared over the years. When the client brings the photos, the counselor asks that he describe what is happening in each photo and then describe what he was thinking and feeling at that time. Focusing on the events rather than on the client may give the client the freedom to discuss how he was and is feeling.
- *Interpersonal nightmare*: The client writes a brief script in a play format about the event he or she fears most. The counselor assesses the script to identify the client's personal beliefs.
- *In vivo assessment.* The client and counselor visit the site of the problem during the assessment process. In the example of the client who is having marital problems, the client and counselor may conduct the assessment session at the client's house.
- *Rational emotive problem solving:* The counselor may re-create a problem situation from the client's life during the therapy session. In the counseling example above, where the man is in counseling because his wife says he does not show emotion, the counselor may scream at the client, "You don't care anything about me. You never show emotion."
- *Vivid assessment:* Vivid assessment includes overemphasizing a concept. An example of overemphasis is using words and a tone of voice that are more emotional and dramatic than those used in normal conversation. For example, Ellis had a reputation for using salty language, including curse words, not considered appropriate for polite society. Ellis's language had "shock" value and often elicited strong emotions from clients.

Dryden (1995) suggests that creative techniques should be used with caution, as they can be risky. He cautions counselors to carefully monitor client reactions and make adjustments as appropriate in the use of these assessment techniques.

FOCUS AND INTENTIONALITY: APPLYING THE THEORY IN EARLY, MIDDLE, AND LATE SESSIONS

Early REBT sessions focus on educating the client to identify and dispute irrational thoughts. Clients are taught the A-B-C-D-E model for disputing irrational thoughts and the irrational emotions and behaviors that accompany irrational thoughts, and replacing them with more rational thoughts, feelings, and behaviors. While the client is involved in the counseling process and is an active participant in change during the early stage of counseling, the counselor is directive and authoritative.

In the middle stage of therapy, the client begins to assume more responsibility for identifying and changing irrational beliefs. The counselor, while still authoritative and an expert, begins to assume more of a support and encouragement role in the counseling process.

In the later sessions of successful REBT counseling, the client has become an expert in disputing and replacing irrational beliefs. The counselor continues to collaborate with the client to plan client change and to encourage and support the client's ability to become healthier and happier.

Y-CHUN THROUGH A CBT LENS

In working with Y-Chun, as a CBT counselor, my job is to help her identify irrational thoughts that are causing her distress and to teach her the process of disputing irrational beliefs and replacing them with rational ones. If counseling is successful, Y-Chun will be able to think more rationally, will exhibit better emotional health (be less disturbed), and will select more adaptable behaviors. After Y-Chun learns to identify and dispute irrational beliefs, she will be able to apply the techniques used in counseling to other irrational beliefs in her life.

This is the second session with Y-Chun. The first was an intake session (see Chapter 3).

Counselor: Hello, Y-Chun. We will be recording today's session so you can take the tape with you at the end of the session and use it to review what we discussed. Last week, in our first session, when we completed the intake forms and assessment, you talked about your family—your parents, your children, and your siblings. You were feeling all alone and like a failure at relationships. While you expressed concern about all your family relationships, you talked most about your relationship with your parents. So let's start with your relationship with them and talk about your belief system. When I say "belief system," I am talking about the messages that you give yourself about your relationship with your parents. Messages like, "My parents should love me. My parents should take care of me." Can you pick up here and talk about your beliefs related to your parents?

Y-Chun: Okay. I'm not sure I can do what you want. I might get it wrong.

Counselor:	Do you mean not give me the right answer?
Y-Chun:	(She nods her head.)
Counselor:	Counseling is not about being right or wrong. It's about identifying thoughts that are a problem for you so you can choose more rational ways of thinking that work better for you. Now let's give it a try. Your parents should . . .
Y-Chun:	I have always thought that my parents did not want any more children. They already had children before they married, so there was no need for me.
Counselor:	What made you think that?
Y-Chun:	My parents were always busy with work and each other. And then there were my stepbrothers and stepsister. They hated me too.
Counselor:	Did your stepbrothers and stepsister live with you and your parents?
Y-Chun:	Yes, we all lived together in a very small house. I just want them to love me as much as they love my brothers and sister.
Counselor:	What makes you think that your parents love you less than they love your brothers and sister?
Y-Chun:	They always expect more of me. I have to go to college so they'll be proud of me.
Counselor:	You would like for your parents to be proud of you?
Y-Chun:	Yes, so they will love me.
Counselor:	Are you thinking, "I must be perfect and do everything my parents want or they won't love me"?
Y-Chun:	Yes, that's pretty much it.
Counselor:	What we think affects our feelings and our actions. Can you look back and see when you started thinking, "I must be perfect and do everything my parents want or they won't love me"?
Y-Chun:	Um . . . it was a long time ago. Maybe when I was 10 or 11. My oldest brother kept telling me that my parents were too old and did not want me.
Counselor:	Tell me what is different about your thoughts now when you think about your parents than when you were 10 or 11.
Y-Chun:	Um . . . I guess I haven't changed my thoughts since then. I'm still thinking maybe my parents really did not want me and that I need to please them to be loved.
Counselor:	So you have to earn their love, and it will be awful if you can't do that?
Y-Chun:	Yes! Sometimes, like when I sleep around, I just get so tired of trying to be perfect so they will love me, so I just give up trying and quit being good for a little while.

Counselor:	What if your thinking is wrong? Could your parents love you as you are? They have let you and your children move in with them, and they are taking care of the three of you while you attend college. Do you think they would do that if they didn't love you?
Y-Chun:	Well . . . I guess it could be possible. I've just thought that they didn't love me for so long . . .
Counselor:	Is it possible that you took a childhood thought process that your parents didn't love you into your adult life without examining whether the facts supported that thought? Do you think your parents might love you whether or not you are perfect?
Y-Chun:	It's hard to imagine because I've thought I had to be perfect for so long . . . but they are kind to my children and me.
Counselor:	You can dispute false thoughts and replace them with true thoughts. Are you willing to try some homework this week to help you change your thinking about trying to be perfect for your parents to love you?
Y-Chun:	Okay. I do want my life to change, so I'll try the homework.
Counselor:	Great! What names do you call your parents?
Y-Chun:	Mother and Father.
Counselor:	Your schedule is very busy, so you have a limited amount of time each day with your parents. Whenever you walk into a room where they are, think, "Mother loves me; Father loves me. If they didn't love me, I would still be okay." Will you try this for a week?
Y-Chun:	Yes.
Counselor:	Then we will discuss how this experiment went in our session next week. Is there anything else that you would like to talk about before our session ends today?
Y-Chun:	I can't think of anything.
Counselor:	Here is the tape from the session. I'll see you next week.

KEYSTONES

- While we are not able to control all the life events that come our way, what we can control is whether our responses to those events are irrational or rational.
- REBT and other forms of CBT help clients examine their thinking so they can choose healthy, rational thoughts and beliefs that will result in healthier emotions and behaviors.

- Much of our irrational thinking as adults is a result of taking our thinking from childhood, when our thinking processes were not fully developed, into adulthood without examining that thinking.
- REBT is brief therapy that focuses on the here and now.
- We create our own dysfunction and emotional disturbance because of our irrational thoughts about events. Some of the results of this dysfunction can be rage, depression, and fear.
- Thoughts, feelings, and actions are interrelated.
- We take what are actually our preferences for the way we would like things to be and elevate them into absolute demands that are impossible to achieve—for example, "Everyone must love me."
- Clients are taught the A-B-C-D-E model so they can learn to identify irrational beliefs and, through disputing, replace those irrational beliefs with rational ones. This process can be applied to other issues in the clients' lives.

REFLECTIONS FROM THE CONTRIBUTOR'S CHAIR

Working with students and adults, I have found that their irrational thoughts often cause them psychological stress. For example, prom is coming up and a high school student decides that she cannot go unless the "right" person invites her. As prom approaches, she realizes that time is running out and the "right" person has not asked her yet. She begins to place irrational absolutes on the situation, such as, "I won't be able to go to school anymore," "Everyone will laugh at me," or "I am totally undesirable and unlovable." Using REBT, the student can learn to dispute these irrational beliefs and choose more rational thoughts that acknowledge her disappointment and frustration about not being asked to the prom by someone she likes, without "awfulizing" the situation.

On a personal note, I feel strongly about issues and have struggled with letting emotions dictate my choices. Learning to control my emotions has been very freeing.

Julia Porter, PhD, LPC, NCC, NCSC, is a professor of counselor education and associate dean of the Division of Education at Mississippi State University–Meridian. Her work focuses on wellness issues.

ADDITIONAL RESOURCES

Albert Ellis and Gloria: Counselling (1965) full session [Video]. (2013, May 14). Retrieved from http://www.youtube.com/watch?v = odnoF8V3g6g

The Albert Ellis Institute. (2013). Retrieved from http://www.rebt.org/

Albert Ellis (REBT): Conquering the dire need for love (Part 1) [Audio]. (2011, April 17). Retrieved from https://www.youtube.com/watch?v = aKby0E_U_F4&feature = related

Beck Institute for Cognitive Behavior Therapy. (n.d.). Retrieved from http://www.beckinstitute.org/

A conversation with Aaron T. Beck [Video]. (2012, March 27). *Annual Reviews*. Retrieved from http://www.youtube.com/watch?v = POYXzA-gS4U

Eisendrath, S. (2012, May 31). *Applying mindfulness-based cognitive therapy to treatment* [Video]. Retrieved from http://www.youtube.com/watch?v = 5eQ3MWz4yrI

International Association for Cognitive Psychotherapy. (2010). Retrieved from http://www.the-iacp.com/

Meichenbaum, D., & Firestone, L. (2011, November 14). *Road map to resilience: Ways to bolster resilience and well-being* [Video]. Santa Barbara, CA: Glendon Association. Retrieved from http://www.youtube.com/watch?v = MvkBH9gnZW8

Mindfulnet: The Mindfulness Information Website. (n.d.). Retrieved from http://mindfulnet.org

National Association of Cognitive-Behavioral Therapists. (2013). Retrieved from http://nacbt.org/

Rational Living Therapy Institute. (2011). Retrieved from http://rational-living-therapy.org/

REFERENCES

American Psychiatric Association. (2013). *Diagnostic and statistical manual of mental disorders* (5th ed.). Washington, DC: Author.

Association of Rational Emotive Behaviour Therapy. (2011). *Code of ethics and required standards of conduct and performance in the practice of rational emotive behavioural therapy*. Retrieved from http://www.rebt.bizland.com/pdf/Code_Of_Ethics.pdf

Beck, A. T., & Weishaar, M. E. (2011). Cognitive therapy. In R. J. Corsini & D. Wedding (Eds.), *Current psychotherapies* (9th ed., pp. 276–309). Belmont, CA: Brooks/Cole.

Beck, J. S. (2011). *Cognitive therapy: Basics and beyond.* New York: Guilford Press.

Begley, S. (2007). *Train your mind, change your brain: How a new science reveals our extraordinary potential to transform ourselves.* New York: Ballantine.

Corey, G. (2012a). *Student manual for theory and practice of group counseling* (8th ed.). Pacific Grove, CA: Brooks/Cole.

Corey, G. (2012b). *Theory and practice of group counseling* (8th ed.). Belmont, CA: Brooks/Cole, Cengage Learning.

Corey, G. (2013). *Theory and practice of counseling and psychotherapy* (9th ed.). Belmont, CA: Brooks/Cole, Cengage Learning.

DiGiuseppe, R. (1996). The nature of irrational and rational beliefs: Progress in rational emotive behavior therapy. *Journal of Rational-Emotive and Cognitive-Behavior Therapy, 14,* 5–28.

Dryden, W. (1994). *Progress in rational emotive behavior therapy.* London: Whurr.

Dryden, W. (1995). Vivid methods in rational-emotive therapy. In W. Dryden (Ed.), *Rational emotive behavior therapy: A reader* (pp. 151–174). London: Sage.

Dryden, W. (2011). *Understanding psychological health: The REBT perspective.* New York: Routledge.

Ellis, A. (1987). The evolution of rational-emotive therapy (RET) and cognitive-behavior therapy (CBT). In J. K. Zeig (Ed.), *The evolution of psychotherapy* (pp. 107–133). New York: Brunner/Mazel.

Ellis, A. (1995). Rational emotive behavior therapy. In R. J. Corsini & D. Wedding (Eds.), *Current psychotherapies* (5th ed., pp. 162–196). Itasca, IL: F. E. Peacock.

Ellis, A. (1996). Responses to criticism of rational emotive behavior therapy (REBT) by Ray DiGiuseppe, Frank Bond, Windy Dryden, Steve Weinrach, and Richard Wessler. *Journal of Rational-Emotive and Cognitive-Behavior Therapy, 14,* 97–120.

Ellis, A. (1997). REBT with obsessive-compulsive disorder. In J. Yankura & W. Dryden (Eds.), *Using REBT with common psychological problems: A therapist's casebook* (pp. 197–222). New York: Springer.

Ellis, A. (1999). Treatment of borderline personality disorder with rational emotive behavior therapy. In C. R. Cloninger (Ed.), *Personality and psychopathology* (pp. 475–496). Washington, DC: American Psychiatric Press.

Ellis, A. (2002). *Overcoming resistance: A rational emotive behavior therapy integrated approach* (2nd ed.). New York: Springer.

Ellis, A. (2004). Why I (really) became a therapist. *Journal of Rational-Emotive and Cognitive-Behavior Therapy, 22,* 73–77.

Ellis, A. (2005). *The myth of self-esteem: How rational emotive behavior therapy can change your life forever*. Amherst, NY: Prometheus Books.

Ellis, A., & Bernard, M. E. (Eds.). (2006). *Rational emotive behavioral approaches to childhood disorders*. New York: Springer.

Ellis, A., & Dryden, W. (2007). *The practice of rational emotive behavior therapy* (2nd ed.). New York: Springer.

Ellis, A., & Ellis, D. (2011). *Rational emotive behavior therapy*. Washington, DC: American Psychological Association.

Felder, J. N., Dimidjian, S., & Segal, Z. (2012). Collaboration in mindfulness-based cognitive therapy. *Journal of Clinical Psychology, 68*(2), 179–186.

Gonzales, J. E., Nelson, J. R., Gurkin, T. B., Saunders, A., Galloway, A., & Shwery, C. S. (2004). Rational emotive therapy with children and adolescents: A meta-analysis. *Journal of Emotional and Behavioral Disorders, 12*, 222–235.

Hayes, S. C. (2005). *Get out of your mind and into your life: The new acceptance and commitment therapy*. Oakland, CA: New Harbinger.

Hayes, S. C., Strosahl, K. D., & Wilson, K. G. (2011). *Acceptance and commitment therapy: The process and practice of mindful change* (2nd ed.). New York: Guilford Press.

Kabat-Zinn, J. (2005). *Wherever you go, there you are: Mindfulness meditation in everyday life*. New York: Hyperion.

Leichsenring F., Hiller, W., Weissberg, M., & Leibing, E. (2006). Cognitive-behavioral therapy and psychodynamic psychotherapy: Techniques, efficacy, and indications. *American Journal of Psychotherapy, 60*(3), 233–259.

Linehan, M. (1993). *Cognitive behavioral treatment of borderline personality disorder*. New York: Guilford Press.

McGovern, T. E., & Silverman, M. S. (1984). A review of outcome studies of rational-emotive therapy from 1977 to 1982. *Journal of Rational Emotive Therapy, 2*(1), 7–18.

Miltenberger, R. G. (2008). *Behavior modification principles and procedures* (4th ed.). Belmont, CA: Thomson Learning.

Murdock, N. L. (2013). *Theories of counseling and psychotherapy: A case approach* (3rd ed.). Upper Saddle River, New Jersey: Pearson Education.

Pantalone, D. W., Iwamasa, G. Y., & Martell, C. R. (2010). Cognitive-behavioral therapy with diverse populations. In K. S. Dobson (Ed.), *Handbook of behavioral cognitive therapies* (pp. 445–464). New York: Guilford Press.

Parsons, R. D. (2009). *Thinking and acting like a cognitive school counselor*. Thousand Oaks, CA: Corwin.

Porter, J. Y. (2011, March 26). *Coping with the rollercoaster: Effectively handling emotions triggered by disasters*. Presented at the American Counseling Association Conference and Exposition.

Sapp, M. (1996). Irrational beliefs that can lead to academic failure for African American middle school students who are academically at-risk. *Journal of Rational-Emotive and Cognitive-Behavior Therapy, 14*, 123–134.

Seligman, L. W., & Reichenberg, L. W. (2010). *Theories of counseling and psychotherapy: Systems, strategies, and skills* (3rd ed.). Upper Saddle River, NJ: Pearson/Merrill/Prentice Hall.

Silverman, M. S., McCarthy, M., & McGovern, T. (1992). A review of outcome studies of rational emotive therapy from 1982–1989. *Journal of Rational-Emotive and Cognitive-Behavior Therapy, 10*, 111–186.

Vernon, A., & Clemente, R. (2006). *Assessment and intervention with children and adolescents: Developmental and cultural considerations*. Alexandria, VA: American Counseling Association.

CHAPTER 10

Behavior Theory

Barbara C. Trolley and Christopher Siuta

I know when I enter a department store I need to avoid going near the open jewelry counters. If I can't see the small, sparkling items, I am less tempted to pick them up and drop them in my purse. While I have to use all my old jewelry, I haven't shoplifted any precious gems in years!

This client's behavior has many layers that need to be peeled back and addressed, and the practicality of circumventing jewelry counters indefinitely is questionable. However, this may be but the initial step in gaining control over her behavior and is a useful strategy for avoiding environmental cues that invite such unwanted behavior.

In this chapter, you will be introduced to behavior therapy and its evolution. Specifically, after reading this chapter, you will be able to do the following:

1. Identify the major contributors to the field of behavior theory and their theoretical influences

2. Explain how behavior theory may be effectively utilized with a plethora of presenting problems and populations

3. Describe the strategies, therapeutic process, and applications of behavior theory

INTRODUCTION

Historical Background

Behaviorism has a long, rich history in the field. Different from other theories of psychotherapy, behaviorism was heavily influenced by the experimental psychology domain and information about the learning processes of humans and animals (Scharf, 2000). As far back as the start of the 20th century, the world was exposed to the notion of behavior modification when Thorndike (1911) mentioned "modifying behavior" in his now-renowned essay "Provisional Laws of Acquired Behavior or Learning." Almost a decade later, the infamous "Little Albert" experiment occurred. In further developing Pavlov's work with salivating dogs (Todes, 2002), John Watson applied these principles of classical (or response) conditioning to humans. The subject of Watson's experiment, a young baby called "Little Albert," developed an intense fear of a stuffed white rat, along with other fluffy toys, because his playing with them would trigger a loud noise (Watson & Rayner, 1920). Today, the ethical concerns of creating possible trauma for a baby would most likely have eradicated this type of experimentation.

Research continued, and near the end of World War II, Clark Hull (1943) published *Principles of Behavior*. In this same decade, B. F. Skinner (1948) published an additional cornerstone of behavior theory, *Walden II*. In this writing, Skinner discussed a utopian society based on behavioral principles. Skinner, along with colleagues such as Joseph Wolpe, was the first to coin the term *behavior therapy*, which included the findings of Hans Eysenck (Clark, Christopher, & Fairburn, 1997; Lindsley, Skinner, & Solomon, 1953; Wolpe, 1958). Eysenck's work took the concepts of behaviorism beyond their original roots of dismissing personality traits to include the environment, behavior, and personality traits (Yates, 1970).

Later in the 20th century, applied behavior analysis (ABA) was born out of Skinner's work. During this historical time frame, cognitive principles also began to be applied to those of behaviorism, thus giving birth to cognitive-behavioral theory and rational emotive behavior theory (REBT; Ellis, 2008). (Since cognitive-behavioral theory is presented in detail in Chapter 9, it will be only briefly mentioned here.) In addition, Bandura (1977) developed social learning theory, based on the premise that people learn by imitating, modeling, and observing others. Krumboltz, Mitchell, and Jones (1976) addressed this theory as it applied to career development.

While social learning theory has frequently been used in the classroom and at home to assist youth in learning new behaviors, it has been widely used elsewhere as well. Wells-Wilbon and Holland (2001) explored the use of this theory in relation to the impact on African American children of having male role models in the classroom. Furthermore, Datti (2009) used this theory in assisting lesbian, gay, bisexual, transgender, and questioning youth with their career decision making. An innovative study looked at the social learning environment in organizational settings and compliance with privacy policies (Warkentin, Johnston, & Shropshire, 2011). It is important to note that models need to be similar to clients in characteristics such as age, gender, prestige, ethnic background, and attitudes if learning is to occur (Hackney & Cormier, 2013). Clearly, behaviorism has a rich and diverse history, further explored in the next section.

Areas of Development

Dialectical behavior therapy was developed in the late 1980s and has been widely used with people who have borderline personality disorders (Linehan & Dimeff, 2001); those with substance-abuse problems and borderline personality disorders (Dimeff, Rizvi, Brown, & Linehan, 2000; Linehan et al., 1999); the elderly and adolescents who are depressed; individuals who are suicidal (Lynch, 2000; Miller, 1999; Rathus & Miller, 2002); and those with binge eating disorders (Telch, Agras, & Linehan, 2001).

More recently, behavioral principles and the Internet have been integrated. Hedman and colleagues (2011) found that cognitive-behavioral methods applied via a virtual psychiatric setting were equally as effective in treating social anxiety disorder as when delivered in a cognitive-behavioral group. Similarly, Christensen, Griffiths, and Korten (2002) discovered that web-based interventions were effective in preventing depression and anxiety in the general public. In another study, it was proved that the amount of knowledge conveyed in face-to-face versus Internet cognitive-behavioral training of substance-abuse counselors was similar, thus proposing the use of mixed education delivery systems (Weingardt, Villafranca, & Levin, 2006). Paradoxically, cognitive-behavioral therapy has shown to be an effective treatment for those with Internet addictions (Young, 2007). In the next section, a summary of the professional identity of a behaviorist and how it applies to our own identities is shared.

OVERVIEW OF BEHAVIOR THEORY

View of Human Nature

In its purest form, behaviorism posits that people are neither inherently good nor bad but, rather, are born as blank slates (i.e., tabula rasa) and develop as a result of the environmental experiences they encounter throughout their lives. Behaviorists tend to ignore the notion of "free will," a view that does not allow people much control over their fate. As Hackney and Cormier (2009) indicated, people's failures and mistakes are seen as the cause of their behavior. Some behaviorists have even taken the extreme view that people are slaves to their environment. That is, people tend to develop patterns of behavior that seem to "work" for them while rejecting those that fail to work or result in negative experiences. For example, if you are on a diet and you know that putting your picture on the refrigerator is a deterrent to binging but going out to dinner triggers a landslide backward, then eating out will be put on hold and the picture will stay hung. While the above presents the more "orthodox" behavioral approach, it has been modified by the work of those such as Bandura (1986) and Meichenbaum (1985), as well as those introducing cognitive principles to behavior theory (e.g., Weinrach, 1980).

Basic Characteristics and Assumptions

Behavior as Learned

One basic assumption held by behaviorists is that all behavior, adaptive and maladaptive, is learned. It is therefore believed that maladaptive behavior can be changed through learning. For example, if a child grows up observing a parent binging on food during times of stress, it would not be surprising if the child resorts to a junk-food marathon after every bad college test grade. The same could be true for the individual who learned that drinking alcohol removed his social anxiety and thus made it easier for him to engage with others. According to the behaviorist, these behaviors were not hard-wired but were learned by way of experience. Thus, in attempting to work with these individuals and undesirable behaviors, the behavioral counselor would try to construct conditions that increase desirable alternatives for addressing stress or reducing social anxiety while reducing the value and utility of the undesirable behavior.

Focus on Overt Behavior

For those with a strictly behavioral orientation—in contrast to cognitive behaviorists—the focus is on overt behavior, and behaviorists tend to reject the notion that human personality is based on traits. An often-heard behaviorist credo is, "If you can't see it and can't measure it, it doesn't exist." Within the therapeutic context, goals must be well defined, observable, and measurable. Consider the scenario in Case Illustration 10.1.

CASE ILLUSTRATION 10.1

Defining Goals: Scenario and Script

Consider the parents of young children who, like most children, are not that concerned with making their beds or picking up after themselves. The parents could certainly identify the problem as their children being "sloppy." But just labeling the behavior provides little direction for how one could intervene or what such an intervention would look like once accomplished. Under these conditions, the behavioral counselor may assist the parents in redefining the goal so it is more concrete, observable, and measurable. In this case, the counselor helps specify the goals in the following scenario:

Counselor: You indicate that you want your children's rooms to be less sloppy. Can you tell me exactly what you mean by "sloppy"?

Client: Their toys are all over the floor, their beds are unmade, and their laundry is not put away.

Counselor: Have you told your children that the goal before they leave for school is to have their beds made, the floor cleared, and their clothes put in their drawers the night before?

Client: I guess I haven't. I just go in at night and get upset, and tell them how sloppy they are and they better change if they want to do things on the weekend. Being specific with chores and deadlines probably would help.

Counselor: Perhaps you could set a specific time after dinner, but at least an hour before bedtime, that the clothes need to be put away and the floor picked up, thus avoiding confrontation right at bedtime. You could do similarly in the morning by stating the beds need to be made before they come down for breakfast.

Client: Yes, that sounds very good. I think being specific with my children will help them know what is expected and will decrease my need to talk several times and/or resort to yelling.

Reflection: You are the parents' counselor. Devise a behavior chart to assist them in developing the desired behaviors. You may find the following websites helpful:

"Child Behavior Charts: How to Use Behavior Charts Effectively" (http://www.empoweringparents.com/How-to-Use-Behavior-Charts-Effectively.php)

"Using Behavior Charts" (http://www.freeprintablebehaviorcharts.com/usingbehaviorcharts.htm)

You may also choose to type the keywords "behavior charts for kids" into your favorite image search engine.

A sample chart is provided below:

Single Behavior Chart

								Total
Monday								
Tuesday								
Wednesday								
Thursday								
Friday								
Saturday								
Sunday								

© Legacy Publishing Company

SOURCE: http://www.empoweringparents.com

As you can see from Case Illustration 10.1, defining the term *sloppy* in a clear, concrete, observable way not only reduces confusion that could occur because of subjective definitions of *sloppy* but also provides the children with specific actions that can be checked off, as a form of goal achievement measurement. The defining of our goals in objective terms is not always easy. Exercise 10.1 is offered as an opportunity for you to engage is such "operationalization" of your goals.

EXERCISE 10.1

TRANSLATING PERSONAL GOALS

Directions: Below, you will find a series of goals often expressed by undergraduate and graduate students. Take each goal, which in its current form is vague, open to interpretation, and difficult to measure, and reframe it so it is observable, concrete, and measurable. As a way of checking your rewrites, consult with a colleague or classmate to see if they would be able to measure that which you intended as your goal. One of the best ways to make goals measurable is practice! If you were the counselor, ask yourself, "How would I know if this goal was obtained?"

Goal (Vague)	Goal (Measurable)
Example: Get organized.	Employ a calendar listing all assignments and due dates.
Eat better.	x
Be a better student.	
Be assertive.	
Drop some weight.	
Define your personal goal.	

You may find the following website helpful in completing this exercise:

Writing Measurable Short and Long Term Goals (http://fl.eqhs.org/Portals/1/Goal%20Writing%20 for%20Therapy%20Provider%20with%20Final%20AHCA%20edits%20%201%2013%2012.pdf)

Here-and-Now Focus

In addition to targeting that which is observable and measurable, behavioral therapists focus on the "here and now," rather than spending time unearthing hypothesized historical issues. While other theorists may focus on a seminal argument that occurred in the first years of marriage, behaviorists would be more concerned about the husband's behavior of storming off after a heated dispute in the current stage of a 30-year marriage.

Value of Therapeutic Alliance

A prevailing misconception about behavior therapy is that the counseling relationship is unimportant. Wilson (2000) brought to light the fallacy of this assumption. Even when behaviors are the focal point, individuals must have some sense of communication with and trust in their counselors if principles are to be followed and change is to occur. For example, a client seeking help for weight issues who is told by the therapist to lock up the candy must have some degree of trust in the therapist to disclose these issues and follow the therapist's directives.

Use With Diverse Populations and Children

Behavior theory and associated therapy have been deemed the evidenced-based approach most effective with a wide variety of presenting problems. Behavior therapy has been the treatment of choice for individuals with depression (Kanter, Cautilli, Busch, & Baruch, 2011), anxiety disorders (Hopko, Robertson, & Lejuez, 2006), eating disorders (Lappalainen & Tuomisto, 2005; Tobin, 2000), substance-abuse issues (Smith, Milford, & Meyers, 2004), and attention-deficit disorders (Lufi & Parish-Plass, 2011; Novotni & Petersen, 2000). Programmed instruction, discussed earlier, has been useful in working with clients with aphasia (Goldfarb, 2006) and in parenting children with conduct disorders (Patterson, 1971).

Many families have also addressed their children's problem behaviors through the use of behavior charts and associated reward systems. In developing such behavior charts, it is essential that expected behaviors be broken down into measurable terms, rewards be given immediately after the behavior has occurred to develop the desired behavior, and a separate incentive be given for each behavior defined. It is not sufficient, for example, to use "Change your attitude" as a key goal in a behavior chart. Rather, it is better to state specific goals such as, "Child will not talk back to parents when given a chore to complete." Duke University has such an evidence-based program for parents, called parent–child interaction therapy (see epic.psychiatry.duke.edu/our-work/projects/parent-child-interaction-therapy).

In regard to children, positive behavioral interventions and supports (PBIS) and applied behavior analysis (ABA) have grown in their use, especially in working with youth with special needs in school settings, at home, and in the community (George & Horner, 2002; Johnston, Foxx, Jacobson, Green, & Mulick, 2006). PBIS is based on a problem-solving model that targets inappropriate behavior through instruction and reinforcement of appropriate behaviors (OSEP Technical Assistance Center, 2013b). The use of data, evidence-based practices, multitier teams, and belief in the ability of all children to behave appropriately are premises of PBIS (OSEP Technical Assistance Center, 2013a). An entire journal, *Journal of Positive Behavior Interventions,* has been devoted to this topic.

Behavior therapy, especially ABA, has also been used with families that have a child on the autism scale (Blackledge & Hayes, 2006; Sanders & Morgan, 1997). In essence, ABA is the functional evaluation of a targeted behavior in relation to the environment; experimentation is used to identify variables responsible for behavior change, and the focus is on improving socially significant behavior (Baer, Wolf, & Risley, 1968; Cooper, Heron, & Heward, 2007). ABA principles have been used extensively with myriad populations—for example, with youth, to help develop socially appropriate behaviors (Dillenburger & Keenan, 2009); for children with developmental behaviors, helping them learn to identify which behaviors under which conditions will result in the desired consequences (Sy & Vollmer, 2012); and with the elderly, to determine their preference for leisure and edible reinforcers (Ortega, Iwata, Nogales-González, & Frades, 2012). Behavior therapy has also been used to address various problems in diverse countries (Hays, 2007, 2008, 2009; Hays & Iwamasa, 2006; Papas et al., 2010). Behavioral tenets should be tailored to the theoretical constructs of each culture.

Strengths and Limitations

As with most counseling theories, there are strengths and limitations associated with behavior therapy. Starting with the benefits, this approach deals with observable symptoms that most clients express coming into counseling; therefore, immediate help to clients is foreseeable. In this day and age of managed care and economic hardships, funding for therapeutic interventions has diminished. The focus on the here and now, without devoting attention to the client's past, may shorten intervention time and save the client money. Since the focus is on behavior, most clients can understand what the counseling process is about and are not confused by psychotherapeutic jargon. Furthermore, numerous techniques exist in behavior theory, many of which have been integrated in the routine work of counselors operating from different theoretical bases. These tools include, but are not limited to, behavior modification and management, systematic desensitization, shaping, generalization, behavioral analysis, token economies, observational learning, and modeling (see Table 10.1). Many methods may be used, and therapy is tailored to the individual's needs (Hackney & Cormier, 2009).

Table 10.1   Fundamental Tools and Strategies in a Behavioral Approach

Tool	Definition	Illustration
Behavior modification via contingency management	Influencing behavior through manipulation of the consequences of that behavior	A child calls out in class rather than raising his hand to be recognized. The teacher chooses to ignore his "calling out" behavior but smiles, calls on him, and praises him for raising his hand. If the hand raising increases in frequency, we can assume the teacher's behaviors are modifying that response.
Shaping	Reinforcement strategy in which successive approximations of a desired behavior are reinforced, building to the final targeted behavior	While the client may wish to train for a mini-marathon, the fact that he has not exercised in years necessitates a program of small, successive steps. First, a walking routine, then a walking and jogging routine, etc. Further, each time the client engages successfully in one of these steps, he receives a reward (a pleasing consequence).

Tool	Definition	Illustration
Token economy	A form of contingency management in which the consequences are first delivered in the form of a symbol or token (e.g., a check mark or bingo chip) that can be exchanged for items and privileges the client finds desirable, thus acting as a reinforcement	In attempting to help the client improve his grades in math, the counselor develops a system in which, at the end of each day, the client receives 1 point for volunteering an answer in class and 2 points for completing all seat work in math. At the end of the week, these points can be exchanged for a variety of items (a sticker) or privileges (1 hour to play a video game).
Observational learning	A social learning strategy emphasizing 'watching' others.	In attempting to increase his 'dating' skills, Tom watched as his best friend invited a girl to the prom.
Modeling	Developing new behavior through observation and rehearsing a demonstrated behavior	Tom (an individual seeking to improve his dating skills), watched his friend invite a girl to the prom (observational learning) but still was having difficulty translating what he saw into his own behavior. As a result, Tom began to practice—in the mirror, then with his friend—adjusting his action with the feedback received until he felt he had developed the "winning" approach.
Systematic desensitization	Procedure of reducing anxiety symptoms by presenting the stimuli eliciting anxiety in a graded order, systematically paired with a relaxation response	A client—once bitten by a dog—demonstrates irrational behaviors when presented with any situation involving a dog. Even a picture of a dog elicits a hysterical response. The client is taught to relax and, in this relaxed state, is presented with increasingly fearsome stimuli (e.g., picture of a dog, a puppy, a growling dog on a leash, etc.). Progression continues as long as the client can remain relaxed in the presence of the stimulus.
Generalization	When one learns a new behavior under specific conditions and is able to employ those behaviors under similar conditions, thus transferring a learned response	Alex was taught to say "excuse me" when attempting to get his parents' attention. During his first-grade class, when all the children were firing questions at the teacher, Alex, to the teacher's surprise, initiated his contact by saying, "Excuse me."

Behavior theory is also grounded in extensive research supporting its efficacy. The theory and research have been supported by several national and international associations, including the Association for Behavioral and Cognitive Therapies and the International Association for Behavioral Analysis, and have been presented in numerous professional journals.

As with all theories, behavior theory has its limitations. Many argue that the theory focuses on one isolated aspect of people—that is, their behavior—and does not look at people holistically, considering their developmental stages, past histories, or unconscious drives. This theory can also be seen as a mechanical application within the counseling process and may not be as easily replicated in counseling as within controlled conditions. James and Gilland (2003) addressed further concerns about the theory in that it limits creativity while encouraging conformity, fails to focus on higher concepts such as self-worth, and encourages people to work on the most minimal, tolerable behavioral levels. In addition, this theory works best when individuals are interested in working on a few discrete behaviors, have a strong goal orientation, and are action oriented (Hackney & Cormier, 2013). These characteristics are not descriptions of a large portion of those who seek and/or are involved in the counseling process, thus eliminating a large group who may benefit from the interventions.

It would be remiss not to address ethical considerations associated with this theory that, if not followed, could not only limit the theory's effectiveness but result in ethical and/or legal breaches. Since clients are active participants in the goal-setting process, informed consent is essential (Hackney & Cormier, 2013). If clients have a major mental disorder, such as psychosis, a team of professionals should be involved in setting objectives. As always, counselors need to be aware of their own values and biases, and how these influence the counseling process. To ensure the safety of clients, caution must be exercised when using techniques such as flooding. A benefit of this theory is the clear respect for clients' dignity and the social role influence. Several areas associated with professional identities and behavior theory are discussed in the next session, with ethical considerations at the core of this development.

OVERVIEW OF PROFESSIONAL IDENTITY

As far back as the 1970s, behaviorists were seen as ignoring interpersonal relationships, using punitive techniques, and being mechanical in their approaches (Lamontagne, 1977). These perceptions have persisted for decades, with those aligned with behavior therapy being associated with laboratories and animal experiments. A veil of ethical questions also obscured the identity of behaviorists, following the experiments conducted with Little Albert. It behooves the reader to become aware of current tenets associated with each theory and how these principles are translated into practice, rather than relying on stereotypes.

Current applications of behavior therapy have been used to address issues of personality disorders and acceptance of pain and have been associated with complex case conceptualizations (Augustson, 2000; Farmer, 2005; Phelps, 2001). Clearly, behaviorists are no longer confined to the laboratory and controlling their clients but, rather, are working with a range of presenting problems, engaging in therapeutic relationships, and focusing on basic counseling skills. In fact, Norcross, Hedges, and Prochaska (2002) predicted that cognitive-behavioral therapy would be one of the psychotherapies to increase in use internationally. Solem, Vogel, and Hofmann (2010) indicated that technological advances will assist in the further use of this therapy in treatment and supervision, thereby possibly increasing the awareness of these principles and practitioners. Tryon (2010) further stated that it is important to have an open mind about professional identities, to focus on learning rather than interventions, and to emphasize the common interest in learning.

With these tenets in mind, how does behavior theory apply to our professional identities? In our direct service work with clients, behavioral principles have frequently been used in family therapy and parenting sessions to develop new, improved behaviors and eliminate unwanted ones. Similarly, in work with clients who are athletes, a schedule of reinforcement could be developed whereby a set time for studying, once successfully completed, is followed by an hour of relaxation on the court or field.

These principles are also a part of our professional identities as instructors. Classroom management is a fundamental concept that applies at all levels of schooling, even the graduate level. "Good" behavior (e.g., not talking in class, not texting) may be reinforced by a little longer break, while inappropriate behavior may be "punished" (e.g., a late assignment lowered a grade, an extra assignment given to a student who misses a class session). We shape what students learn by breaking it down into smaller units, and we continue to review their work and give feedback as a means of reinforcement.

A related concern is that of test anxiety, which frequently surfaces in the classroom, especially when taking a national comprehensive examination. Relaxation principles are often shared with students, and soothing music may be played when they enter the examination room prior to taking the test. In addition, behavioral principles are pertinent to the process of supervision. As supervisors, we frequently shape our supervisees' behaviors using verbal reinforcement, and they typically learn new behaviors through our role modeling. Behavior theory has a place in all aspects of our pedagogical tasks.

In the last section of this chapter, some "keystones" of behavior theory are presented.

THERAPEUTIC PROCESS AND APPLICATION

In this section, specific behavioral techniques used to enhance and secure behaviors (operant strategies), to reduce and eradicate behaviors (extinction strategies), and to replace behaviors (counterconditioning strategies) are discussed.

The Use of Operant Strategies: Developing and Increasing Strength of Behavior

At times, a counselor and client may identify as their therapeutic goal either the development of a new behavior or the strengthening and increased frequency of a behavior the client already employs. Perhaps the client is seeking assistance with exercising more often, studying more efficiently, or even developing the ability to be assertive in times of interpersonal conflict. When the goal of the counseling is to develop or increase the strength of a behavior, systematic use of operant strategies may be the intervention of choice.

Operant strategies are defined as those that affect the frequency of behaviors based on the manipulation of the consequences of those behaviors. This manipulation of consequences of a particular behavior is called "contingency management." The successful employment of this approach has been well documented with a variety of presenting concerns and client populations (Kazdin, 2001). However, the research demonstrating the impact of the manipulation of consequences on the modification of behavior has a long and impressive history, starting with the early experimental work of B. F. Skinner (1953, 1968, 1974).

The basic tenet underlying the use of contingency management as a way of modifying behavior is that people may develop and maintain a particular behavior because it is followed by consequences they find pleasing or, conversely, may surrender a behavior if it fails to result in satisfactory consequences.

In the therapeutic process, the goal is often to assist clients in developing new behaviors. For example, clients may come to counseling needing to learn how to speak up and assert their opinions, or perhaps they are interested in engaging in an exercise program. Under these conditions, where the clients are seeking to develop new behaviors, the following techniques may be of use:

- *Positive reinforcement:* A consequence that causes a behavior to occur with greater frequency by having a rewarding stimulus follow the specified behavior

  Example: If every time a person played the slot machine, he or she received money back, that person's likelihood of playing the slot machine would increase.

- *Negative reinforcement:* The removal of an aversive consequence when the desired behavior occurs

  Example: When someone is arrested and demonstrates respectful behavior, Taser shocks are removed.

- *Shaping:* The reinforcement of successive approximations of the desired behavior

  Example: A student in a classroom who consistently yells out the answer to a question is first reinforced (e.g., given a candy or called on first) when he or she raises a hand and yells out the answer. Eventually, the student is reinforced when he or she raises a hand and does not speak until called on by the teacher.

- *Observational learning:* The process of learning new behaviors by observing those of models

  Example: Interns sit in on their supervisors' counseling sessions to better learn communication and session-management skills.

- *Chaining:* A set of behaviors whereby each behavior is both the consequence or reinforcement of the prior behavior and the stimulus for the next behavior

  Example: A person with a developmental disability is taught to open a locked door by first inserting a key into the door, turning the key, and then opening the door. This strategy illustrates a chaining operation.

- *Stimulus control:* The process whereby a person behaves one way in the presence of a stimulus and another way in its absence

  Example: If a driver sees a stop sign approaching, the general tendency is to start braking and slowing down the car. In the absence of the stimulus (the stop sign), the person will most likely continue driving at the same speed. While this is an adaptive response helping maintain driver safety, consider the behavior of an alcoholic who in merely seeing a bottle of alcohol is drawn to engage in drinking. Clearly, the stimulus control in this situation results in dysfunctional behavior, and clients and counselors would engage in ways to either lessen the strength of that stimuli or develop an alternative, healthier response to it.

The following examples, in Case Illustrations 10.2, demonstrate the application of these behavioral strategies.

CASE ILLUSTRATION 10.2

Development of Behaviors

Example 1

An out-of-control fan rooting for the visiting team is removed by security guards. The star player of the home team is then better able to make his foul shots [negative reinforcement]. In contrast, right before he shoots, he blesses himself, a behavior that has more often than not been reinforced with his making a basket [positive reinforcement]. Leading up to the game, this athlete watched tapes of the highest-scoring foul shooter in the league [observational learning], and each time he got closer to his coach's goal of a 90% success rate—starting with 70%, then 75%, and so forth—he was allowed a 20-minute break [shaping].

Reflection: You are a sports counselor and must improve your player's success with foul shots. What would you do? The following websites may be of help to you:

Game Time Tips (http://basketball.lifetips.com/cat/65503/game-time/index.html)

Reinforcement and Punishment (http://exactsports.com/blog/reinforcement-and-punishment/2012/07/30/)

Cognitive Techniques (http://www.safetyxchange.org/training-and-leadership/cognitive-techniques-2)

(Continued)

(Continued)

Example 2

The following is a description of how both positive and negative reinforcement can be used to develop behaviors.

A baby's crying can be an aversive stimulus to parents. New parents typically run to their crying baby and pick him or her up [the baby is positively reinforced]. The parents are negatively reinforced by the cessation of the baby's crying. However, now the baby will most likely cry more frequently to receive the special reinforcement of being cradled by mom and dad.

Reflection: If you were the parents' counselor, what interventions would you develop, using behavior theory strategies, to address this cycle of reinforcement and help them get some sleep? See the following websites for ideas:

"Ferberizing, cry-it-out, and attachment parenting, what is the best baby sleep solution?" (http://communities.washingtontimes.com/neighborhood/parenting-first-time-through/2012/sep/13/ferberizing-cry-it-out-attachment-sleep-training/)

Gentle Infant Sleep Training (http://www.parentingscience.com/infant-sleep-training.html)

Strategies to Reduce or Eliminate a Behavior

In addition to the development of new, positive behaviors in counseling, there is often a need to reduce or eliminate maladaptive behaviors. This may be the case with the child in school who continues to tap on her desk, or the person with diabetes who cannot stop eating sugary foods, or perhaps even someone you know who wishes he could stop smoking. The following are strategies employed by behavioral counselors to decrease and eliminate undesired behaviors:

- *Negative punishment:* The removal of a pleasant reward when an undesired behavior occurs

  Example: A child's favorite toy is taken away when the child screams at a sibling.

- *Positive punishment:* A negative consequence following the undesired behavior

  Example: Every time a dog goes to the outer boundary of the property, it receives an electric shock from the charged invisible fence.

- *Extinction:* A behavior no longer followed by the consequence (positive or negative reinforcement), leading to a decrease in that behavior

  Example: A whistle (conditioned stimulus) in a factory is paired with the smell of food (unconditioned stimulus) for the workers at lunchtime, thus evoking hunger (conditioned response). The whistle is no longer blown when there is a smell of food, thereby decreasing the hunger response. Note: In classical conditioning, the unconditioned stimulus is one that unconditionally, naturally, and automatically triggers a response, whereas the conditioned stimulus is a previously neutral stimulus that, after becoming associated with the unconditioned stimulus, eventually comes to trigger a conditioned response.

- *Covert sensitization:* Pairs an aversive stimulus with a behavior clients wish to reduce or eliminate

    Example: A 6-year-old continues to suck his or her thumb at home. The parents place a nontoxic, edible substance such as lemon juice on the child's thumbs to decrease the likelihood of the child sucking them.

See Case Illustration 10.3 for an integrated application of these principles in the reduction and elimination of a behavior.

CASE ILLUSTRATION 10.3

Reduction and Elimination of a Behavior

A child who was once bitten by a dog (unconditioned stimulus) now becomes emotionally upset and runs (conditioned response) even from little puppies (conditioned stimulus). The parents are concerned about their child's growing fear of dogs and decide to get him a puppy. While the puppy is initially kept on the parents' laps, the child remains apprehensive and fearful, keeping his distance. However, in contrast to the initial experience the child had with a dog, which was associated with pain, seeing the puppy on his parents' laps is connected with playfulness and fun. In the absence of being bitten and thus pairing the presence of the dog with pain, the fear previously associated with being bitten slowly begins to subside. This is only the first step in a longer process of bringing the dog in closer contact with the child (systematic desensitization). But as long as the sight, then eventual touching, and then holding of the puppy all occur in the absence of pain, the learned fear response will eventually be extinguished.

Reflection: Your client comes into your office and wants to stop smoking. Using behavior theory, design a program for your client. The following websites may be of assistance to you:

"Smoking Cessation" (http://www.aafp.org/afp/2002/0315/p1107.html)

"A Meta-Analysis of Teen Cigarette Smoking Cessation" (http://psycnet.apa.org/journals/hea/25/5/549/)

Replacement of Behaviors

Oftentimes, it is not simply a matter of developing a new behavior or getting rid of a dysfunctional behavior. There are times in the counseling process when the focus is on the replacement of the old, unwanted behavior with a new, more adaptive behavior. These strategies are helpful in this process:

- *Counterconditioning:* The strategy whereby undesirable behaviors are turned into wanted behaviors by pairing a positive action with the stimulus

  Example: In the process of training a dog, the owner pets the animal to calm it when it reacts anxiously to a stimulus, such as the door bell ringing.

- *Systematic desensitization:* Discovered by Joseph Wolpe (1958), it is a type of counterconditioning often used to treat anxieties and phobias whereby the person is taught relaxation skills to extinguish anxiety and fear responses to specific phobias

  Example: A client dreads any thought of flying. The client is first taught relaxation skills. Once the relaxation skills have been mastered, they are paired with a hierarchy of the client's fear of flying, from lowest stress to highest—from looking at a picture of a plane to actually taking a trip. The next item in the hierarchy isn't addressed until the fear is extinguished with the present item. The fear responses are incompatible with the relaxation responses, thereby eliminating the phobia of flying.

- *Flooding:* A similar technique to systematic desensitization, but the client is exposed to the highest item in the hierarchy; requires the presentation of the feared stimulus (i.e., in vivo exposure) rather than asking the client to imagine that stimulus (i.e., imaginal exposure) (Virtual reality programs have been deemed effective in the use of flooding.)

  Example: A person who was involved in a fatal car accident and has repressed reactions to the trauma is brought back to the accident scene.

- *Contingency management:* The process whereby desired behaviors are reinforced while undesired behaviors are punished or reinforcement is withheld

  Example: Returning to the child raising her hand in class, the teacher will give the child a small treat when she raises her hand and does not speak until called on; spontaneous responses will be ignored and not rewarded.

While each of the above examples illustrates the individual development of replacement behaviors, Case Illustration 10.4 demonstrates a number of these principles.

A variety of behavioral techniques have been described in this section, and applications of these strategies have been shared in the presentation of diverse cases. In the following section, a guided practice of how to utilize some of these techniques is presented.

CASE ILLUSTRATION 10.4

Replacement of a Behavior

Your adult client has a fear of riding store elevators. This started in childhood when he was 4 years old and let go of his mother's hand just as she was stepping onto the elevator; he was left alone while the elevator took his mother down and away. You could start with the muscle relaxation strategy described earlier and add an image of the client's most soothing place (e.g., a deserted beach with the waves crashing, sun shining, and birds singing). Then, once a hierarchy of items associated with elevators is established—from the least feared to the most feared (e.g., from seeing the word *elevator* in print to riding an elevator)—systematic desensitization can begin. In addition, counterconditioning can take place in the store, whereby your client will receive an item he wants as he is stepping onto the elevator (obviously a small item, to prevent the client's falling and creating a whole new set of fears); your client's fear will be replaced with the joy of obtaining that desired item. Or you could use the process of flooding and bring your client immediately to a store that has multiple elevators. Counterconditioning would involve rewarding your client's positive reaction to getting on the elevator with a $25 shopping spree on the next floor; this reward would be taken away if your client backed away from the elevator or started crying.

Reflection: Choosing two to three different strategies utilized in behavior theory, how would you address your client's elevator phobia? See the following websites for assistance:

"What is the Fear of Elevators?" (http://phobias.about.com/od/phobiasatoh/f/What-Is-The-Fear-Of-Elevators.htm)

"Treatment for Phobias" (http://phobialist.com/treat.html)

GUIDED PRACTICE

In working with a case, a practitioner must begin to conceptualize the purpose of behavior rehearsal, which is used primarily for when a client does not have but needs to learn the necessary skills to handle a situation. This is called *response acquisition*. One must also teach the client to discriminate between appropriate and inappropriate times and places to use the skills, better known as *response facilitation*. Furthermore, an important step within the behavior rehearsal process is to sufficiently reduce the client's anxiety symptoms to allow the client to use skills already learned that may be inhibited by anxiety. This process is called *response disinhibition*.

Two widely used behavioral techniques to reduce physical anxiety symptoms are deep abdominal breathing and progressive muscle relaxation. These techniques are described in Case Illustration 10.5. Another technique that may be employed, once trust has been developed between therapist and client, is systematic desensitization. This is an anxiety-reduction intervention based on the learning principles of classical conditioning, which pairs a neutral event with a stimulus that already elicits or causes a reflexive response, such as fear or anger. Counterconditioning is employed with the individual, where one type of response is substituted for another, desensitizing the client to higher levels of fear or anxiety. The relaxation responses learned are used to replace anxiety on a step-by-step basis. This strategy is also shown in Case Illustration 10.5.

CASE ILLUSTRATION 10.5

Abdominal Breathing, Relaxation, and Counterconditioning Case and Script

In practicing deep abdominal breathing, a client is asked to hold her dominant hand over her belly as she breaths in through her nose and exhales out through her mouth, stretching each for 10 seconds. This process is repeated if the client does not experience relief. The goal of holding a hand over her belly is to feel the breath going in and out, imagining the belly to be a balloon that is inflated with the breath in and deflated with the breath out.

Progressive muscle relaxation is a technique employed to tense and relax each muscle group, usually beginning at the head and progressing down to the feet. After the longer form of this exercise is accomplished, the client is instructed to practice tensing and relaxing her entire body at once, within a span of 10 seconds.

In addition, a counselor may set up a counterconditioning strategy with a client in the following way: The counselor would have the client construct a hierarchy of emotion-provoking stimuli based on the presenting core issue. Then the therapist would use graduated pairing, joining imagery of the items on the hierarchy with the relaxed state of the client. There are six main steps within this desensitization process. The first step between the client and therapist is coming up with a signal whereby the client can indicate when she begins to feel anxiety (usually by raising an index finger). Second, using the client's chosen relaxation scene, the counselor invokes that scene to help her achieve a state of relaxation. Third, when the client is deeply relaxed, the counselor describes the least emotion-provoking item on the hierarchy, asking her to imagine it. The first time, the counselor introduces the item only briefly—for about 10 seconds—provided the anxiety signal does not go up. If the client remains relaxed, the counselor switches back to the pleasant or comforting scene, staying there for at least 30 seconds.

The fourth step is returning to the first step on the list, describing it one more time and remaining in it this time for 1 minute. If the client again indicates no anxiety, the counselor has the option to repeat the third and fourth steps or move to the second item in the hierarchy. Typically, the counselor should wait until 3 to 10 repetitions have occurred without any anxiety. If the client returns to therapy for her next session, the practitioner may want to repeat the last scene one more time at the beginning of the session for consistency and practice.

The fifth and last step is when the therapist is trying to move the client into the higher levels of her hierarchy. If this client experiences mild to moderate anxiety, the counselor must revert back to the lower level of the hierarchy. Gradually, the counselor works back to the hierarchy level where anxiety was experienced. If anxiety is experienced again, the counselor will repeat the process with the client. Usually, within two to three repetitions, the client is able to move through this level of the hierarchy without experiencing anxiety. If the client continues to experience anxiety for a given item, one of three things could occur: The therapist could add a less-anxiety-producing item between the two items the client is struggling with, present the same or previous item to the client again for a shorter time period, or assess whether the client is revising or drifting from the scene during the imagery process.

For example, using the case of Y-Chun, she experiences much anxiety in relation to memories of her rape. She could develop a hierarchy of anxiety-producing stimuli. Perhaps toward the bottom of the hierarchy would be a memory of an event with her cousin that was innocent and pleasurable and occurred prior to the rape. This could be followed by a picture of her cousin and then a visit to the room where the rape occurred. Y-Chun's anxiety would be evaluated at each step of the hierarchy. If she experiences anxiety while visiting the room, the counselor could revert back to the previous item on the hierarchy, insert an item between the two—such as Y-Chun's written description of the room—and/or assess whether she is still focused on the imagery and relaxation.

Reflection: If you were to go through progressive relaxation, what guided image would be helpful to you? See the following websites for samples of relaxation and imagery scenarios:

http://www.innerhealthstudio.com/guided-imagery-scripts.html

http://www.ncbi.nlm.nih.gov/pubmed/16541998

http://wholesomeresources.com/library/meditation-guided-imagery/

The following are counseling scripts that discuss the behavioral therapy technique of systematic desensitization and shaping. This client has come to therapy with the acute issue of not being able to drive anywhere in her car. She is having panic attacks as she walks to the vehicle in her driveway. There have been some preceding anxious symptoms in the past, but this response has been extreme. What follows are three scripts from the therapeutic exchange between this client and her therapist.

Session 1

Therapist: Hello. On the phone, you told me that there have been some anxious feelings as of late that are preventing you from taking care of a normal task that you normally have no issues with.

Client: Yes, although I have had nervous feelings in the past, I have always been able to get through it and "deal."

(Continued)

(Continued)

Therapist:	I see. It must be very uncomfortable for you.
Client:	I basically cannot get in my vehicle to drive to the store, to the mall, to pick up my children, nothing!
Therapist:	How long has this been happening to you?
Client:	About 3 months. It has never been this bad.
Therapist:	When you say "it," you mean the stress and anxiety, correct?
Client:	Yeah, I mean can you believe I just can't get in my car to drive somewhere? I have been doing that since I was 18. I am 42 now!
Therapist:	How difficult that must be. Can you tell me what happens in your body when you begin to experience those feelings?
Client:	I feel like my chest is tightening inside me. I also feel as though I will stop breathing. There is this pressure inside and I just know that my heart is racing in my chest.
Therapist:	When that comes on, what have you been doing?
Client:	I normally just go back in the house and wait it out. If I really have to get somewhere, I get someone else to drive me.
Therapist:	So it is not that you can't be in the car, it is that you personally have difficulty driving.
Client:	Yes, that is right.
Therapist:	Okay, so I have this correct. For 3 months, you have not been able to drive from your home to anywhere in the community. It is something that is normally very easy for you. You are okay with being in a car with someone else in the driver's seat. There are anxiety attacks that overwhelm you when you try to walk out to your vehicle.
Client:	Yes. So, I heard you could maybe do some hypnosis with me or something like that to help me.
Therapist:	Well, something like that. It is a progressive behavioral strategy that is called systematic desensitization. Would you be interested in trying this and seeing if it provides relief?
Client:	Yes, very much. I will do anything. How long will it take?
Therapist:	I will try to get you moving within the next three sessions or so. We can take as long as we need though. Every person responds differently to these strategies. Let's work on two strategies right away though. I have found that if these two behavioral tools are practiced regularly, they can help alleviate and control anxiety symptoms when the need arises.

Client:	That sounds wonderful.
Therapist:	Okay, so I found that to control the mind and think more rationally, it is necessary to understand what is happening within the body and get control of our breathing, muscles, etc. The first technique that I would like to teach you is called deep abdominal breathing. If you feel comfortable, close your eyes and just pay attention to my voice. Please take your dominant hand and place it over your belly. Hold it there. Now, for 10 seconds, breathe in through your nose. Now, for 10 seconds, exhale out through your mouth. Repeat that again, in through the nose and out through the mouth. Enjoy the fresh air that is circulating through your body and, most importantly, your lungs. When you are ready, you can open your eyes.
Client:	That felt wonderful. So relaxed. Thanks. I actually just realized like a dummy that I don't pay attention to my breathing at all. I think I am holding my breath a lot.
Therapist:	Yes, that is what we see a lot. People forget to breathe. Although it sounds strange, they tend to neglect themselves the clean, positive air that is around them. When this happens and anxiety sets in, a person is prone to hyperventilation. All of that air gets trapped up high in the lungs. This technique teaches a person to breathe deeply down below, within the abdominal cavity. It helps circulate more healthy air within the body.
Client:	That makes sense. I really should have thought of that. Listening to you talk, I know I probably have hyperventilated on a couple of occasions.
Therapist:	If you could just practice that 5 to 10 times per day in between our sessions, that would be great. We will be using this technique often as we learn how to control the stress that you are feeling.
Client:	Sounds like a plan. I am feeling hopeful that there are some things that will help me.

Session 2

Therapist:	Hello. How are you? Just curious about your thoughts from our previous session and how things have been this past week.
Client:	Actually a little better. I seem to be able to stay outside near the car a little longer than I was before. I find myself talking to the car that it is not going to beat me!
Therapist:	That is great! You are battling with the stress and taking it on. A little of that goes a long way!
Client:	That breathing helps. It seems to clear my mind.

(Continued)

(Continued)

Therapist:	Today we will be doing two things. The first is something called guided imagery. We are coming up with a relaxing scene that is comforting to you. Can you tell me of a scene that is relaxing for you?
Client:	I definitely wish I could be on a beach!
Therapist:	Okay, let's do that. Please close your eyes for me once again. Take a deep breath in through your nose and out through your mouth. Repeat that once more. As your body becomes relaxed, let your mind drift to a beach scene. See yourself on the beach, lying in the sand. No one is around for miles. As you lie there, you feel the sun beating down on your face. Your hands are touching the sand. A gust of wind from the ocean bristles through your hair. Seagulls are faintly heard in the distance. Take in this entire scene as you become peaceful and serene. You are at peace not only with yourself but the universe. There is a confidence about you that you have not felt in some time. Take this all in, as it will give you complete control over your life. Enjoy this scene for another moment. Just as you would, take a snapshot of this scene so you can always revert back to it for peace and relaxation. When you are ready, you can come back to me.
Client:	Wow, that felt great. I forgot for a moment why I was here.
Therapist:	Good. We will be building on that today. So, what I would like to do is find out what your stress hierarchy is. Rank your least anxiety-provoking situation to your highest anxiety-provoking situation on this pyramid, for the problem we are trying to overcome. Think of them as little steps as we gradually lessen the stress, overcoming the obstacle of driving your vehicle.
Client:	(Client lists her anxiety hierarchy for the therapist on given hierarchy handout.)
Therapist:	Thanks. Okay, so you have three situations listed. (1) Walking out to the car and entering car. (2) Starting the car and putting it in drive. (3) Driving to a destination.
Client:	Those are them. Does that make sense? Should I have added more steps? I guess we have already made progress, because I used to stress and panic when I thought about going out and driving. That is pretty low on the hierarchy.
Therapist:	No, perfect. So we will break this down into three steps.
Client:	You got it.
Therapist:	I will have you practice your breathing, going to your peaceful scene, and pairing the stressful scene with the relaxing scene. If you feel any anxiety that is becoming too overwhelming, raise your index finger as a signal. I will stop and back up from that point. Are you ready?

Client:	Yep
Therapist:	Please close your eyes and get control of your breathing. Do that three times. Then, think about that beach scene that was so relaxing for you. Take in all the sights, sounds, feelings, and thoughts as your mind goes there. Enjoy the relaxation for a moment. Now, switch your thoughts to yourself walking out to the car and getting in. You are in the driver's seat and are confident that you can drive. Stay there just for a few seconds, experiencing what it feels like to be in that seat. Now, go back to your beach scene. Remember to concentrate on your breathing as you control this situation. Enjoy the control that is coming over you. Take it all in and stay there for just a bit more. When you are ready, please come back to me. What did you feel? Any anxiety? Did you fully see yourself in that driver's seat?
Client:	So far, so good. Not a lot of stress. Pretty minimal. Yes, I was in my car!
Therapist:	Okay, let's move forward. Close your eyes and imagine yourself on that beach once again. Get full control of your breathing. Now, as you are relaxed, see yourself gripping the ignition key on the key chain. Insert it in the ignition and start the car. As you start the car, feel the energy as you are able to gain control of this next step in your hierarchy. You do this within a peaceful state. You now take control of the gearshift and put it in drive. Your foot comes off the brake. Stay there and see yourself doing this activity. You are achieving what you set out to do. Take it all in for just a few moments. When you are ready, open your eyes and let me know what happened for you.
Client:	Unbelievable, I did not feel much stress at all. I am surprised, but it was controlled.
Therapist:	Do you think that before our next session, you would feel up to trying this activity in real life? Only do what you can without experiencing anxiety. If the anxiety is controlled, continue. If not, cease immediately.
Client:	Yes, I am actually excited to see if it works.
Therapist:	Okay, let's see how it goes, and we will continue with your hierarchy next week.

Session 3

Client:	I tried what you had asked, and it worked! I was able to put it into drive. I actually drove down to the end of the driveway. The anxiety started up again, so I decided to stop and wait to see what magic you have for me today.
Therapist:	Yes, now we need to practice our driving skills! Let's take it one step further and get you out of that driveway! Ready?

(Continued)

(Continued)

Client:	As always!
Therapist:	Okay, close your eyes and get control of your breathing. Go to your beach scene and take it all in. Strive for that balance and relaxation that has been working for you as you progress through these steps. Enjoy the stillness and peacefulness. See yourself walking up to your car, getting in, and starting the ignition. You are confident just as you were before. You are ready to move forward. You place the car in drive and are driving to the end of your driveway. You go into the street and drive to the end of your block. You now turn to get to the main expressway as you are driving to the supermarket one town away. See yourself driving. You are comfortable and at ease. Your mind is controlling what your body is doing. You are rational and positive. The hope that you feel is overflowing. You are able to drive to the supermarket. You pull in to a space, put the gear in park, and turn off the engine. Savor the success you have just felt before you exit your vehicle. Enjoy. When you are ready, take one last deep breath in and out and open your eyes.
Client:	Awesome. I feel ready to do it. There is a little nervousness, but I think it can be controlled. Is that my next homework assignment?
Therapist:	Yes, if you feel up to the task!
Client:	I do. This has really helped me gather some perspective.
Therapist:	Thanks for the feedback. Good luck this week.

Case and Script

Several different methods could be used with clients. The first is that of identification and assessment of the client's problem. The counselor would be looking for initial occurrence, severity, and frequency. Then the counselor would conduct a functional analysis of the client's problem, attempting to identify specific personal and environmental variables that could be enabling maladaptive thoughts, feelings, and behaviors.

In regard to this assessment process, behavior therapists ask how, when, where, and what, not why, questions to assess the client's worldview. Nothing said will be taken at face value; inconsistencies, evasiveness, and distortions will be brought to the forefront (Corsini & Wedding, 2008). The therapist will rely heavily on self-reports to assess for congruent thoughts and feelings as they attribute to certain behaviors. Self-report has often proved to be a superior predictor of behavior when compared with clinicians' judgments or scores on personality tests (Mischel, 1981).

Another method for assessing clients' reactions to situations is to have clients symbolically re-create a problematic life situation, a technique called *guided imagery*. Clients are asked to conjure up an image of a situation, then to verbalize any thoughts that come to mind as a way of uncovering their specific thoughts associated with the given event. *Role playing* is another option, where clients are asked to act out a situation lending itself to the assessment of interpersonal problems. The therapist adopts the role of the person with whom the client is experiencing problems, providing the therapist with a sample of the problem behaviors that may be present within the two individuals. The client could also be asked to keep a daily journal of particular events or psychological reactions that the behavior therapist is helping the client self-monitor. For example, an individual who is trying to exercise more often for good health could monitor daily schedules, with the goal of finding themes for obstacles to exercising more consistently (de Shazer, 1991). In this case, clients may keep a daily record of how many times a reckless behavior occurs and track the triggers associated with that behavior. Each step or situation that comes up prior to that particular behavior is written down to discuss in more detail within the therapeutic process.

Now that the reader has been presented with an understanding of behavioral principles and has seen how they might be applied, the specific case of Y-Chun will be discussed in light of this theory.

Y-CHUN THROUGH THE LENS OF BEHAVIOR THEORY

In this section, the principles of behavior theory are applied to a specific case, that of Y-Chun.

Assessments

To assess Y-Chun's values and beliefs, which have a direct impact on the origin and reinforcement of her current problems, and potential avenues of change, a scale such as the Asian American Values Scale (Kim, Li, & Ng, 2005) or the adapted Acculturation Attitude Scale (Leong, Kim, & Gupta, 2011) could be used. Y-Chun's perceptions of the counseling process could be ascertained via the Attitudes Toward Seeking Professional Psychological Help Scale (Leong et al., 2011). It is important to assess Y-Chun's willingness to seek counseling as a starting point to the therapy.

In any therapeutic process, it is essential to conduct a thorough assessment of the client's problems prior to adaptation of an intervention plan. An overall assessment that might be completed is a functional behavioral assessment (FBA), a method of identifying the reasons for undesirable behaviors and needed program interventions to develop appropriate behaviors.

Specifically, the following steps would be taken: Identify (1) the behavior in concrete, measurable terms; (2) when the behavior is most/least likely to occur; (3) triggering events; and (4) the function of the behavior. A sample of an FBA in relation to Y-Chun's physical complaints is shared below. Note that a medical evaluation is essential to rule out biological etiology of these symptoms.

Counselor: You indicated that you are experiencing a variety of physical complaints. Please define what they are, when they are most likely and least likely to occur, and what immediately precedes each of these physical complaints.

Y-Chun: I am always tired, I have headaches, and I have lost weight.

Counselor: Can you tell me when you are most tired during the day, how it is expressed, and what events happen right before this feeling?

Y-Chun: It usually occurs by 4 p.m. each day. I have difficulty finishing any projects for school or work at home. It usually starts right after I have seen my parents and talked with them.

Counselor: Can you describe the headaches, when they most frequently occur, and what might be the triggers of these?

Y-Chun: They seem to occur most in the morning, when I first wake up, especially after I have had a nightmare about the rape.

Counselor: Can you tell me more about the weight loss in terms of how much, when it started, how it is being maintained?

Y-Chun: I started hooking up with strange men about 6 months ago, as I have been feeling very lonely and depressed. My father about the same time started criticizing me even more that I am not like my hardworking mother. I guess I started feeling worthless on all levels, and unattractive. I stopped eating regular meals, as I felt guilty that I didn't do anything to prepare them, and I felt like I was getting fat. I lost about 20 pounds.

From the above exchange, the counselor can deduce that the physical complaints appear to primarily occur at home (setting) and that when stress occurs in the form of parental communications or reoccurring nightmares (triggers), physical complaints surface (behavior) to avoid dealing with feelings of guilt and shame (function of the behavior). It would be important to ascertain baseline behaviors at the start of counseling. A behavior intervention plan, discussed in the "Interventions" section, may be developed in conjunction with the findings of the FBA.

In addition, more detailed information about Y-Chun's depression could be assessed by using the Beck Depression Inventory (Beck, Ward, Mendelson, Mock, & Erbaugh, 1961). Based on her reported depression, a lethality assessment should be conducted. A standard mental health status examination can be used if adapted for any cultural concerns. Throughout the course of treatment, progress toward goals should be assessed. Progress could be measured by the number of conflicts with parents she has experienced each week, the number of strange males she has had intimate relationships with over the course of a month, the length of time she has spent in positive interactions with each of her children, any decrease in her physical complaints or weight gain, and decrease in the number of nightmares about the rape. Y-Chun's increase in civil communications with her father when he starts criticizing her (i.e., stimulus cues), replacing her rebellious behavior and/or emotional outbursts, is another measure of potential progress.

Therapeutic Goals

Numerous goals could be established in the case of Y-Chun, as gleaned from the above discussion. One of the most important considerations is that of her culture and how the problems are conceptualized. Kim et al. (2005) have stressed the importance of understanding specific Asian value orientations when looking at the therapeutic process and outcomes. Wang & Kim (2010) further indicated that, for clients who are Asian, it is essential to look at the need for self-control and discomfort at times in the process of sharing personal problems. In a study of Asian American college students, it was found that "loss-of-face" concerns and level of acculturation impacted student attitudes toward seeking mental health services (Leong et al., 2011). In an earlier study, it was found that Asian Americans were more likely to phrase their problems in educational or vocational contexts rather than emotional ones (Tracey, Leong, & Glidden, 1986). It is not uncommon for these clients to phrase problems as medical complaints, as found in the case of Y-Chun. Additional cultural considerations that counselors should be aware of include the paternalistic attitudes and value for respect for elders in the Asian culture.

Based on these cultural considerations, two of the first therapeutic goals would be to alleviate the physical symptoms Y-Chun is experiencing and to increase the clarity of her educational and vocational goals. Once a therapeutic, trusting relationship develops, multiple additional goals can be developed. The prioritizing of these goals would be based on the level of distress she is experiencing from each problem, which goal may be most easily addressed, her acknowledgement of the problems and perceptions of the importance of the goals, and the therapist's assessment as to the prominence of the issues. Such goals would include enhanced communication and bonding with family members, decreased intimate encounters with strange males, elimination of shoplifting behaviors, and enhancement of social skills and relationships.

Change Process

Much of the change process for Y-Chun will take place within the context of individual counseling. A starting place might be to explore the array of irrational thoughts Y-Chun has exhibited and their impact on her behavior. For example, if she is still traumatized by the rape and blaming herself, her choice of male relationships may be negatively impacted. Unresolved and repressed issues regarding the rape could be further addressed through the use of systematic desensitization, whereby Y-Chun is taught relaxation techniques and then pairs these skills with an ascending hierarchy of items related to the rape. The last step on the hierarchy could involve going back to the room where the rape took place and/or seeing the alleged perpetrator. Likewise, if she perceives that she is not loved by her parents or siblings, sees their comments as a catastrophe, and believes she is worthless, this is a fertile area to address.

Change may also be facilitated through family counseling. However, this modality must be approached carefully in light of the shame often associated with talking and counseling, and the generational differences in traditional values between Y-Chun and her parents. Group counseling, in addition to offering her the universal aspects of groups—such as support, normalization of her issues, and validation of her feelings—may also give

Y-Chun the opportunity for observational learning, positive reinforcement, and shaping of behaviors. Specifically, Y-Chun could learn how to better communicate with her parents and siblings, and parent her children, through observation of others' behavior in the group. If Y-Chun met a stranger at a bar and reports to the group that she did not go home with him, she could be positively reinforced by the praise expressed by group members. Y-Chun's parenting skills might be shaped and reinforced if each week in group, she plans and then takes successive steps to get closer to her children. For example, the first week she may decide to spend 15 minutes every day with each of her children. The following week, she may spend more time with each and ask both her son and daughter about their favorite foods and activities. It would be important to first gain Y-Chun's trust, identify the behaviors that need to be changed and/or developed, and increase her acceptance of discussing her problems with others, such as her family or group members.

Interventions

The use of REBT has been previously described, and interventions such as systematic desensitization and stress management through relaxation were discussed earlier under "Guided Practice." Returning to the FBA as related to Y-Chun's physical complaints, a behavior intervention plan could be developed. Specifically, the target behaviors of the physical complaints would be delineated (fatigue, headaches, and weight loss) and replacement behaviors described (increased energy, decreased headaches, and weight gain). Intervention strategies would then need to be defined, such as implementation of an exercise routine, development of a journal to record nightmares, and a behavior chart for weight gain. It is crucial that the positive and negative consequences, persons responsible for implementing these strategies, nature and method of data collection, timeline, and outcomes be specified in this intervention plan.

Utilization of techniques from the prior section could also be applied to Y-Chun's case. For example:

- *Positive reinforcement:* After Y-Chun gains back each of the 5 pounds she lost, she buys herself a new item of clothing.
- *Negative reinforcement:* When her father begins to criticize her, she removes herself from his presence.
- *Shaping:* Y-Chun contracts to complete her coursework for one semester, talk to the college counselor about careers, and then take a vocational test to explore her interests and abilities. These are small steps that shape her ability to make long-term educational and vocational decisions.
- *Stimulus control:* Y-Chun, in the presence of strange males at a bar, drinks nonalcoholic beverages. When Y-Chun is out with female peers, she limits herself to two alcoholic drinks.
- *Observational modeling:* A successful woman who is Asian and in a similar position to Y-Chun's assists Y-Chun with parenting skills and communication with her parents.
- *Positive punishment:* Y-Chun is heavily fined if she shoplifts.

- *Negative punishment:* If Y-Chun loses the weight she puts on, she must return the clothing item she purchased.
- *Covert sensitization:* Every time Y-Chun has a negative self-thought, she snaps a rubber band on her wrist.
- *Counterconditioning:* When Y-Chun becomes stressed when initiating conversations with her parents, physical aspects of anxiety are replaced with a deep breathing exercise.
- *Contingency management:* If Y-Chun ignores her children, she writes an apology letter to them. If she spends time with each of them on a regular basis, she treats herself and them to a pleasurable activity, such as a movie.

The pattern of negative attention-seeking behavior with her parents, from childhood to the present, can be confronted, and positive interactions that achieve the same goal can be established. An outline of triggers of parental conflict, typical negative responses, and outcomes is developed, and the negative responses are replaced with alternative positive responses:

Triggers → → → → → → →	Negative responses → → →	Negative outcomes
Comparisons to her mother → → →	Y-Chun gets angry → → →	A fight with her father ensues
Confrontation about unknown fathers → → →	Y-Chun is ashamed → → →	She engages in self-destructive behaviors such as shoplifting, substance abuse, and/or sexual encounters with strangers
Flashbacks of the rape → → →	Onset of physical → → → complaints	Poor physical well-being

Triggers → → → → → → →	Positive responses → → →	Positive outcomes
Comparisons to her mother → → →	Y-Chun agrees with → → → her mother's positive qualities, cites her own	Father's defenses go down and insight is raised
Confrontation about unknown fathers → → →	Y-Chun accepts → → → → responsibility, highlights positives of having grandchildren	She learns from past maladaptive behaviors and begins to reframe having children in a positive light
Flashbacks of the rape → → →	Y-Chun does → → → → → relaxation exercises	Sense of calm ensues

It would be important to generalize her positive work in counseling to settings outside of the office. Generalizations are seen in the following scenario:

Counselor (male): Y-Chun, it appears that you have demonstrated very appropriate behavior in sessions. You have kept very good boundaries and acted in a respectful, responsible manner.

Y-Chun: I guess. But I know this is a professional relationship, and I would never cross a boundary and be flirtatious with you.

Counselor: You have excellent self-control in sessions. How can this be generalized to outside situations when in the presence of male strangers?

Y-Chun: Well, I could limit conversations to non-intimate topics, keep a decent amount of personal space as I do in here.

Counselor: Great ideas regarding appropriate behaviors! I also wanted to address the fact that you have never gotten angry in these sessions when I have given you feedback about your behavior. How is this different from your behaviors with your father?

Y-Chun: You never criticize me like he does or make comparisons to my mother or siblings. Your feedback is concrete and positive, while his is general and negative.

Counselor: What could you do with your father, as opposed to getting angry, that would approximate our interactions in here?

Y-Chun: I could ask him to please stop criticizing and instead give me feedback about my behaviors that are constructive. I could ignore these comments and not respond, hoping they would eventually stop.

The above scenario is a sample of how gains made in the therapeutic session could start to be generalized to the outside. Counseling-related homework assignments, such as defining the patterns of triggers and behaviors, could be assigned to facilitate the gains made in counseling and assist with this process of generalization.

In addition, a counselor may ask Y-Chun to reauthor her childhood story using principles from narrative therapy. Specifically, she could be asked to rewrite her interactions with her parents to include those that interested her and had more meaning. She could also adjust her relationships with her half-siblings as she was growing up to be ones that were more supportive, understanding, and close. Finally, Y-Chun could re-do the events of the rape, perhaps by choosing not to go there, not being alone, and/or responding differently when it happened. As can be seen, a plethora of behavioral strategies could be used to assist Y-Chun in achieving her goals.

FINAL REFLECTION

As indicated in this review, behavior therapy could be a beneficial tool in therapeutically assisting Y-Chun. It is vitally important that counselors not only be well versed in the behavior theory described but also demonstrate multicultural competencies in the attitudes, knowledge, and skills domains espoused by the American Counselor Association, American Psychological Association, and Council for Accreditation of Counseling and Educational Programs. Counselors need to

- understand their own biases and stereotypes,
- adopt culturally supported behaviors that promote optimal wellness and growth for individuals,
- be social advocates for diverse populations,
- work to diminish prejudice and discrimination,
- fight for social justice,
- possess basic counseling and communication skills (with an awareness of linguistic diversities, both spoken and unspoken), and
- be adept in the use of a variety of culturally sensitive techniques and various counseling modalities.

While many therapies based on different theoretical concepts may be utilized to assist Y-Chun, the focus on concrete behaviors, which are impacted by her thoughts, fits well with her cultural imperatives of self-control and the focus on medical/vocational responses rather than affective ones.

KEYSTONES

- Different from other theories of psychotherapy, behaviorism was heavily influenced by the experimental psychology domain and information about the learning processes of humans and animals.
- In its purest form, behaviorism posits that people are neither inherently good nor bad but, rather, are born blank slates (i.e., tabula rasa) and develop as a result of the environmental experiences they encounter throughout their lives.
- One basic assumption held by behaviorists is that all behavior, adaptive or maladaptive, is learned.
- Within the therapeutic context, goals must be well defined, observable, and measurable.
- Behavioral therapists focus on the "here and now," rather than spending time unearthing hypothesized historical issues.
- Behavior theory has extensive research support for its successful application with diverse populations, including children and families.
- Behavior theory is also grounded in extensive research supporting its efficacy.
- As with all theories, behavior theory has its limitations. Many argue that it is vulnerable to unethical use of its principles.
- Developing and increasing strength of behavior occurs by way of operant strategies (i.e., those that affect the frequency of behaviors based on manipulation of the consequences of given behaviors).
- Reducing or eliminating behaviors is often accomplished using strategies such as punishment, extinction (e.g., flooding), or developing alternative responses (e.g., counterconditioning).

REFLECTIONS FROM THE CONTRIBUTOR'S CHAIR

Barbara C. Trolley

It has been almost three decades since I walked into my doctorate internship site, convinced I was a Rogerian therapist. While I use many of the principles set forth by the humanistic tradition, I was in for a rude awakening! I was interning at a children's agency that serviced youth ages 4 to 18. My mentor, with a smile on his face, asked how I would ask a 5-year-old about becoming self-actualized. I soon became appreciative of behavioral principles such as reinforcement and behavior charts when working with parents, school issues, and play-therapy groups. I further began to utilize systematic desensitization strategies when working with youth experiencing test anxiety. As I later entered private practice, I began to have an adult caseload of clients, many of whom were struggling as adult children of alcoholics. I found that using REBT was effective in assisting these clients with their extensive irrational thoughts and feelings of low self-worth. I also used stress-management and imagery techniques, especially in my work with clients who had experienced trauma such as abuse. Now, as an educator of graduate students, not only do I teach behavior theory and techniques, but they still come in handy with academic assignment completion and refinement of professional dispositions. Last, as the parent of five children, ages 10 to 23, behavioral principles come in handy on a day-to-day basis!

Christopher Siuta

I am constantly in discussion with students about holding a strong theoretical orientation with their clients. I seem to revert to the cognitive-behavioral orientation. Although this may be my base for all the therapy I provide with individuals, couples, and families within my private practice, discussions always end with clients' decisions and choices. Those decisions and choices are behaviors. They may be based on thought patterns, but they are behaviors nonetheless. When individuals are engaging in self-destructive behaviors, substance abuse, unhealthy sexual behaviors, and so forth, they need to make better choices behaviorally first, before any true work can begin. It is difficult to change faulty thought patterns if the person is not safe or behaviors are erratic and unhealthy. Our initial job is to make sure there are safeguards for our clients. Once those safeguards are in place, an individual can take a step back and reconstruct the past to reinvent the future.

ADDITIONAL RESOURCES

Barlow, D. H. (2008). Clinical handbook of psychological disorders: A step-by-step treatment manual (4th ed.). New York: Guilford.

Martin, G., & Pear, J. (2011). Behavior modification: What it is and how to do it (9th ed.). Upper Saddle River, NJ: Pearson/Prentice Hall.

Miltenberger, R. G. (2012). Behavior modification: Principles and procedures. Belmont, CA: Wadsworth.

Antony, M. M., & Roemer, L. (2011). Behavior Therapy. Washington, DC: American Psychological Association.

Spiegler, M. D., & Guevremont, D. C. (2010). Contemporary behavior therapy. Belmont, CA: Wadsworth.

REFERENCES

Augustson, E. (2000). Issues of acceptance in chronic pain populations. *Behavior Analyst Today, 1*(1), 14–17.

Baer, D. M., Wolf, M. M., & Risley, T. R. (1968). Some current dimensions of applied behavior analysis. *Journal of Applied Behavior Analysis, 1*(1), 91–97.

Bandura, A. (1977). *Social learning theory.* New York: General Learning Press.

Bandura, A. (1986). *Social foundations of thought and action.* Englewood Cliffs, NJ: Prentice Hall.

Beck, A. T., Ward, C. H., Mendelson, M., Mock, J., & Erbaugh, J. (1961). An inventory for measuring depression. *Archives of General Psychiatry, 4,* 561–571.

Blackledge, J. T., & Hayes, S. C. (2006). Using acceptance and commitment training in the support of parents of children diagnosed with autism. *Child and Family Behavior Therapy, 28*(1), 1–18.

Christensen, H., Griffiths, K. M., & Korten, A. (2002). Web-based cognitive behavior therapy: Analysis of site usage and changes in depression and anxiety scores. *Journal of Medical Internet Research, 4*(1). Retrieved from http://www.jmir.org/2002/1/e3/

Clark, D. M., Christopher, G., & Fairburn, C. (1997). *Science and practice of cognitive behaviour therapy.* New York: Oxford University Press.

Cooper, J., Heron, T., & Heward, W. (2007). *Applied behavior analysis* (2nd ed.). Upper Saddle River, NJ: Pearson.

Corsini, R. J., & Wedding, D. (2008). *Current psychotherapies.* Belmont, CA: Brooks/Cole.

Datti, P. (2009). Applying social learning theory of career decision making to gay, lesbian, bisexual, transgender, and questioning young adults. *Career Development Quarterly, 58*(1), 54–64.

de Shazer, S. (1991). *Putting difference to work.* New York: W. W. Norton.

Dillenburger, K., & Keenan, M. (2009). None of the A's in ABA stand for autism: Dispelling the myths. *Journal of Intellect Developmental Disabilities, 34*(2), 193–195.

Dimeff, L., Rizvi, S., Brown, M., & Linehan, M. (2000). Treating women with methamphetamine and BPD. *Cognitive and Behavioral Practice, 7,* 457–468.

Ellis, A. (2008). Rational emotive behavior therapy. In R. J. Corsini & D. Wedding (Eds.), *Current psychotherapies* (8th ed., pp. 187–222). Belmont, CA: Thomson Brooks/Cole.

Farmer, R. (2005). Temperament, reward and punishment sensitivity, and clinical disorders: Implications for behavioral case formulation and therapy. *International Journal of Behavioral Consultation and Therapy, 1*(1), 56–65.

George, S., & Horner, R. (2002). The evolution of discipline practices: School-wide positive behavior supports. *Child and Family Behavior Therapy, 24*(1–2), 23–50.

Goldfarb, R. (2006). Operant conditioning and programmed instruction in aphasia rehabilitation. *SLP-ABA, 1*(1), 56–65.

Hackney, H., & Cormier, S. (2009). *The professional helper: A process guide to helping* (6th ed.). Upper Saddle River, NJ: Pearson.

Hackney, H., & Cormier, S. (2013). *The professional helper: A process guide to helping* (7th ed.). Upper Saddle River, NJ: Pearson.

Hays, P. A. (2007). A strengths-oriented approach to psychotherapy with Middle Eastern people. In C. Muran (Ed.), *Dialogues on difference: Studies of diversity in the therapeutic relationship* (pp. 243–250). Washington, DC: American Psychological Association.

Hays, P. A. (2008). *Addressing cultural complexities in practice: Assessment, diagnosis, and therapy* (2nd ed.). Washington, DC: American Psychological Association.

Hays, P. A. (2009). Integrating evidence-based practice, CBT, and multicultural therapy: 10 steps to culturally competent practice. *Professional Psychology: Research and Practice, 40,* 354–360.

Hays, P. A., & Iwamasa, G. Y. (Eds.). (2006). *Culturally responsive cognitive-behavioral therapy.* Washington, DC: American Psychological Association.

Hedman, E., Andersson, G., Ljótsson, B., Andersson, E., Rück, C., Mörtberg, E., et al. (2011). Internet-based cognitive behavior therapy vs. cognitive behavioral group therapy for social anxiety disorder: A randomized controlled non-inferiority trial. *PloS ONE, 6*(3). Retrieved from http://www.plosone.org/article/info%3Adoi%2F10.1371%2Fjournal.pone.0018001

Hopko, D. R., Robertson, S., & Lejuez, C. W. (2006). Behavioral activation for anxiety disorders. *Behavior Analyst Today, 7*(2), 212–233.

Hull, C. L. (1943). *Principles of behavior.* New York: D. Appleton Century.

James, R., & Gilland, B. (2003). *Theories and strategies in psychotherapy* (5th ed.). Upper Saddle River, NJ: Pearson.

Johnston, J. M., Foxx, R. M., Jacobson, J. W., Green, G., & Mulick, J. A. (2006). Positive behavior support and applied behavior analysis. *Behavior Analyst, 29*(1), 51–74.

Kanter, J. W., Cautilli, J. D., Busch, A. M., & Baruch, D. E. (2011). Toward a comprehensive functional analysis of depressive behavior: Five environmental factors and a possible sixth and seventh. *International Journal of Behavioral Consultation and Therapy, 7*(1), 5–14.

Kazdin, A. E. (2001). *Behavior modification in applied settings* (6th ed.). Pacific Grove, CA: Brooks/Cole.

Kim, B., Li, L., & Ng, G. (2005). The Asian American Values Scale–Multidimensional: Development, reliability, and validity. *Cultural Diversity and Ethnic Minority Psychology, 11,* 187–201.

Krumboltz, J. D., Mitchell, A. M., & Jones, G. B. (1976). A social learning theory of career selection. *Counselling Psychologist, 6*(1), 71–81.

Lamontagne Y. (1977). Implantation of behavior therapy in the psychoanalytic milieu. *Canadian Psychiatric Association Journal, 22*(1), 11–17.

Lappalainen, R., & Tuomisto, M. T. (2005). Functional analysis of anorexia nervosa: Applications to clinical practice. *Behavior Analyst Today, 6*(3), 166–175.

Leong, F., Kim, H. W., & Gupta, A. (2011). Attitudes toward professional counseling among Asian-American college students: Acculturation, conceptions of mental illness, and loss of face. *Asian American Journal of Psychology, 2*(2), 140–153.

Lindsley, O., Skinner, B. F., & Solomon, H. C. (1953). *Studies in behavior therapy* (Status Report I). Walthama, MA: Metropolitan State Hospital.

Linehan, M. M., & Dimeff, L. (2001). Dialectical behavior therapy in a nutshell. *California Psychologist, 34,* 10–13.

Linehan, M. M., Schmidt, H., III, Dimeff, L. A., Craft, J. C., Kanter, J., & Comtois, K. A. (1999). Dialectical behavior therapy for patients with borderline personality disorder and drug-dependence. *American Journal on Addictions, 8*(4), 279–292.

Lufi, D., & Parish-Plass, J. (2011). Sport-based group therapy program for boys with ADHD or with other behavioral disorders. *Child and Family Behavior Therapy, 33*(3), 217–230.

Lynch, T. (2000). Treatment of elderly depression with personality comorbidity using dialectical behavior therapy. *Cognitive and Behavioral Practice, 7,* 468–477.

Meichenbaum, D. (1985). *Stress inoculation training.* New York: Pergamon.

Miller, A. (1999). DBT: A new treatment for parasuicidal adolescents. *American Journal of Psychotherapy, 53,* 413–417.

Mischel, W. (1981). A cognitive-social learning approach to assessment. In T. V. Merluzzi, C. R. Glass, & M. Genest (Eds.), *Cognitive assessment* (pp. 479–500). New York: Guilford Press.

Norcross, J. C., Hedges, M., & Prochaska, J. O. (2002). The face of 2010: A Delphi poll on the future of psychotherapy. *Professional Psychology: Research and Practice, 33,* 316–322.

Novotni, M., & Petersen, R. (2000). *What does everybody else know that I don't?: Social skills help for adults with attention deficit/hyperactivity disorder (AD/HD).* North Branch, MN: Specialty Press.

Ortega, J. V., Iwata, B. A., Nogales-González, C., & Frades, B. (2012). Assessment of preference for edible and leisure items in individuals with dementia. *Journal of Applied Behavior Analysis, 45,* 839–844.

OSEP Technical Assistance Center on Positive Behavioral Interventions and Supports. (2013a). Primary prevention. Retrieved from http://www.pbis.org/school/primary_level/default.aspx

OSEP Technical Assistance Center on Positive Behavioral Interventions and Supports. (2013b). Response to intervention (RTI) and PBIS. Retrieved from http://www.pbis.org/school/rti.aspx

Papas, R. K., Sidle, J. E., Martino, S., Baliddawa, J. B., Songole, R., Omolo, O. E., et al. (2010). Systematic cultural adaptation of cognitive-behavioral therapy to reduce alcohol use among HIV-infected outpatients in Western Kenya. *AIDS and Behavior, 14*(3), 669–678.

Patterson, G. R. (1971). *Families: Applications of social learning to family life.* Champaign, IL: Research Press.

Phelps, B. J. (2001). Personality, personality "theory" and dissociative identity disorder: What behavior analysis can contribute and clarify. *Behavior Analyst Today, 2*(4), 325–336.

Rathus, J., & Miller, A. (2002). Dialectical behavior therapy adapted for suicidal adolescents: A pilot study. *Suicide and Life Threatening Behavior, 32*(2), 146–157.

Sanders, J. L., & Morgan, S. B. (1997). Family stress and adjustment as perceived by parents of children with autism or Down syndrome: Implications for intervention. *Child and Family Behavior Therapy, 15*(4), 19–32.

Scharf, R. (2000). *Theories of psychotherapy and counseling: Concepts and cases* (2nd ed.). Belmont, CA: Wadsworth.

Skinner, B. F. (1948). *Walden II.* Indianapolis, IN: Hackett.

Skinner, B. F. (1953). *Science and human behavior.* New York: Free Press.

Skinner, B. F. (1968). *The technology of teaching.* New York: Appleton-Century-Crofts.

Skinner, B. F. (1974). *About behaviorism.* New York: Alfred A. Knopf.

Smith, J. E., Milford, J. L., & Meyers, R. J. (2004). CRA and CRAFT: Behavioral approaches to treating substance-abusing individuals. *Behavior Analyst Today, 5*(4), 391–402.

Solem, P., Vogel, A., & Hofmann, S. (2010). An international comparison between different theoretical orientations of psychotherapy: A survey of expert opinions. *Behavior Therapist, 33*(1), 1–7.

Sy, J. R., & Vollmer, T. R. (2012). Discrimination acquisition in children with developmental disabilities under immediate and delayed reinforcement. *Journal of Applied Behavior Analysis, 45,* 667–684.

Telch, C., Agras, W., & Linehan, M. (2001). Dialectical behavior therapy for binge eating disorder. *Journal of Consulting and Clinical Psychology, 69*(6), 1061–1065.

Thorndike, E. L. (1911). Provisional laws of acquired behavior or learning. In *Animal intelligence.* New York: McMillian. Retrieved from http://archive.org/stream/animalintelligen00thor/animalintellig-en00thor_djvu.txt

Tobin, D. L. (2000). *Coping strategies for bulimia nervosa.* Washington, DC: American Psychological Association.

Todes, D. P. (2002). *Pavlov's physiology factory.* Baltimore, MD: Johns Hopkins University Press.

Tracey, T., Leong, F., & Glidden, C. (1986). Help seeking and problem perception among Asian Americans. *Journal of Counseling Psychology, 33*(3), 331–336.

Tryon, W. (2010). Professional identity based on learning. *Behavior Therapist, 33*(1), 7.

Wang, S., & Kim, B. (2010). Therapist multicultural competence, Asian American participants' cultural values, and counseling process. *Journal of Counseling Psychology, 57*(4), 394–401.

Warkentin, M., Johnston, A., & Shropshire, J. (2011). The influence of the informal social learning environment on information privacy policy compliance efficacy and intention. *European Journal of Information Systems, 20,* 267–284.

Watson, J. B., & Rayner, R. (1920). Conditioned emotional reactions. *Journal of Experimental Psychology, 39*(1), 1–14.

Weingardt, K. R., Villafranca, L. C., & Levin, C. (2006). Technology-based training in cognitive behavioral therapy for substance abuse counselors. *Substance Abuse, 27*(3), 19–25.

Weinrach, S. (1980). Unconventional therapist: Albert Ellis. *Personnel and Guidance Journal, 69,* 152–160.

Wells-Wilbon, R., & Holland, S. (2001). Social learning theory and the influence of male role models on African American children in PROJECT 2000. *Qualitative Report, 6*(4). Retrieved from http://www.nova.edu/ssss/QR/QR6-4/wellswilbon.html

Wilson, G. T. (2000). Behavior therapy. In R. J. Corsini (Ed.), *Current psychotherapies* (6th ed., pp. 205–240). Itasca, IL: F. E. Peacock.

Wolpe, J. (1958). *Psychotherapy by reciprocal inhibition.* Palo Alto, CA: Stanford University Press.

Yates, A. J. (1970). *Behavior therapy.* New York: John Wiley.

Young, K. S. (2007). Treatment outcomes with Internet addicts. *CyberPsychology and Behavior, 10*(5), 671–679.

Reality Therapy

David A. Scott and Hannah G. Barfield

CHOICES

We all have choices. Some may not be ideal, but we still have them. Many times, clients come in for counseling because they feel as though they do not have any options to improve their situation. While some external forces and environmental situations can clearly limit a person's options, the key to reality therapy is to help clients understand that they can still make choices to change their thinking and behaviors. Reality therapy is based on the client–counselor relationship, working with clients to learn that they can exercise more control in their lives and increase their sense of inner control. Reality therapy has been used with clients from diverse backgrounds and is focused on each individual client and his or her specific needs. Reality therapy is taught and used in all types of counseling settings all over the world (Wubbolding et al., 2004).

This chapter discusses the basic concepts of reality therapy developed by William Glasser and reviews aspects such as choice theory and the five basic needs in reality therapy. After reading this chapter, you will be able to do the following:

- Understand the development of reality therapy
- Define the five basic needs in reality therapy
- Identify the basic constructs of choice theory and reality therapy
- Apply the goals of reality therapy with a client
- Identify and evaluate the WDEP (wants, doing, evaluate, plan) system

INTRODUCTION

Historical Background

In Reality Therapy we are much more concerned with behavior than with attitudes.

—Glasser (1965, p. 27).

What if someone told you that the veteran who sleeps outside your favorite coffee shop is not mentally ill but, rather, making a choice to live on the streets? Or that your aunt who has been diagnosed with depression could regain control of her life by making the right decisions? You might be slightly offended at first, but that is exactly what William Glasser, the theorist behind reality therapy and choice theory, believed. Although initially trained in psychoanalysis, which states that humans are motivated by unconscious drives, Glasser believed that humans make choices to fulfill certain needs and that an internal locus of control can help free clients from past experiences that are holding them hostage (Wubbolding, 2007).

> Thus although the past has propelled us to the present, it need not determine our future.
>
> —Wubbolding (2007, p. 293)

Reality therapy is a present-centered mode of therapy whose goal is to empower clients to take responsibility for their choices as well as learn and implement healthier behaviors and decisions to fulfill universal innate needs. A useful and empathic way to conceptualize even cases of severe mental illness is to consider that people will function the best they can to meet their needs. As a therapist, your goal in reality therapy is to help clients recognize that they are capable of making better choices and, thus, receiving better results.

Glasser adamantly disagreed with the notion of "mental illness"—except in cases of severe psychosis, where biological causes constitute the only *real* mental illness. And in those instances, patients can benefit more thoroughly from a neurologist than a therapist (Howatt, 2001). An underlying assumption of reality therapy is that diagnostic labels (i.e., those found in the American Psychiatric Association's [2013] *Diagnostic and Statistical Manual of Mental Disorders*) are better understood as constellations of negative symptoms than as chronic or persistent illnesses (Wubbolding, 2007). Glasser believed that these negative symptoms of different psychological disorders (e.g., anxiety, depression, insomnia) are due primarily to choices we make in our lives and not to any sort of pathology (Howatt, 2001). In fact, Glasser (1998) took up the practice of adding *-ing* to the end of symptoms to further demonstrate the role of choice. An easy example is a client who has racing and intrusive thoughts and displays significant checking behaviors. This client is *obsess-ing*. Someone who has difficulty sleeping, a decrease in appetite, feelings of sadness, and suicidal ideations is *depress-ing*. Note that this distinctive language for describing mental issues is not an adjective to describe someone but, rather, a gerund that describes his or her choice to feel and engage in particular symptoms.

Glasser began his career as a chemical engineer but felt called to psychology. After obtaining an undergraduate and graduate degree in clinical psychology, he felt he could make a greater difference as a psychiatrist. Glasser enrolled in medical school and in 1961 became a board certified psychiatrist. During the era of Glasser's training, Freudian theory reigned supreme as the standard for psychological and psychiatric training, but Glasser was a skeptical student.

Glasser and the Development of Reality Therapy

Glasser noticed during his tenure in graduate and medical school that much of what he was being taught was incongruent with what he was witnessing his professors demonstrate and practice. Sigmund Freud's psychoanalysis, which focused on unconscious drives and early developmental experiences, was the predominant psychological theory at the time. G. L. Harrington, one of Glasser's mentors, had also become cautiously skeptical of psychoanalytic theory and encouraged Glasser to explore his ideas and put them into practice.

Glasser first implemented his unique views on helping people change at a veteran's hospital affiliated with the University of California, Los Angeles. According to Wubbolding (2000), Glasser grew frustrated with constantly hearing patients blame others and their surroundings for their current problems. Glasser wanted his patients to take responsibility for their own thoughts and behaviors and understand that they were in control of these aspects of self. Glasser began to encourage his clients to take responsibility for their actions and realize that they had to make the decision to change themselves (Wubbolding, 2000).

In addition to the anecdotal evidence supporting Glasser's beliefs, he designed and implemented several experiments. During his residency at the veteran's hospital, Glasser conducted an informal experiment to confirm his assumptions (Howatt, 2001). First, he moved all the pinball machines in the ward into one corner and set up a distinct boundary around the area, marking the entrance with a sign. Then Glasser informed all the staff and patients that no "crazy behavior" would be tolerated inside the game area and anyone who did so would be removed. He found that most of the patients were able to function very well inside the game area once they were aware of the consequence of "acting crazy." Glasser concluded that the desire to play pinball was, in that moment, superior to the need to "act crazy" (Howatt, 2001).

This simple experiment confirmed that people do have self-control and choice in their behaviors. This stood in contrast to the prevailing Freudian belief that the unconscious dictates and rules one's behaviors (Howatt, 2001). In another example of Glasser's research, he implemented a reality therapy program in a psychiatric hospital where the typical duration of treatment was 15 years in a unit of 210 men. In 2 short years, 75 men were discharged, and only 3 of those ever returned (Wubbolding, 2007). Glasser's groundbreaking theory was formally presented to the public in his book *Reality Therapy* in 1965. Glasser's theory was considered a radical shift from the mainstream theory of Freud's psychoanalysis, which was the standard theory of the time.

Basic Needs in Reality Therapy (View of Human Nature)

Although warm and cuddly, babies are perhaps the most controlling people in the world. They are genetically compelled and driven during infancy to fulfill the need for *survival.* Crying is a universal indicator that a baby needs to be fed or wants to sleep or needs a diaper change. At this point in human development, survival is the only real need infants have, and most are adept at *forcing* their mothers to take care of them. It goes without saying that survival is a need that follows people throughout their whole lives. The dietary choices we make contribute to whether we develop heart disease or diabetes. Whether we smoke a pack of cigarettes a day is significantly correlated to whether we develop lung cancer. In situations where individuals are hungry or deprived of basic health care, survival is not a choice; however, in many cases (e.g., those listed above), we have numerous choices in terms of how we survive (Glasser, 1998). (See Case Illustration 11.1 for an example.)

CASE ILLUSTRATION 11.1

Graduation

Maddie, a 22-year-old White female, is one semester away from her college graduation, but she failed a required math class and must stay an extra semester to retake the class in the summer, when it is next offered. Distraught, she seeks counseling. She is emotional and frustrated with her academic advisor for holding her back. She says she feels helpless and misunderstood. I ask Maddie if she really has no control over her situation. She explains that her academic advisor refuses to meet with her or take her dad's phone calls, so her hands are tied. I tell her I understand, but I want to know what she can do, starting today, to improve her situation so she doesn't repeat the mistakes of her previous semester. She says she needs to stop partying during the week. This confession opens the door to my helping her take ownership of an internal locus of control.

I encourage Maddie to engage in more self-evaluation, and we establish that she needs to do better this next semester. I then ask if her current behavior is going to lead to achieving her goals. She says no; so I tell her to come up with a plan that's conducive to succeeding in school and reaching graduation. Maddie decides she needs to take studying more seriously, buy a planner to write down her assignments every day, and stop partying during the week. She commits to attend tutoring two times a week, party only once over the weekend, and schedule weekly meetings with her academic advisor to show him that she is taking school seriously. This will also keep her accountable. We discuss Maddie's psychological needs, such as her need for fun and freedom, and how her partying behaviors have met these needs in the past. The question, then, is whether her plan is realistic and attainable. How is she going to meet her psychological needs in a way that will not detract from her academic goals? Maddie decides to join a dance team at school, which will be a good social activity and stress reliever. I remind Maddie that graduation is a choice and that she, not her academic advisor or the university, is responsible for earning her degree.

As babies grow into adolescents and young adults, different psychological needs begin to emerge. If survival is a physical need, the next four needs are integral to psychological health: *love and belonging, power, freedom,* and *fun.* Every person who reads this book has struggled with fulfilling the need for love and belonging—some more than others. Glasser maintained that friendships are infinitely easier to sustain than sexual love because they feature no illusions of ownership or control. This reiterates the idea that external control does not lead to fulfillment of our needs. All relationships, be they romantic, platonic, or familial, deteriorate when we begin trying to control one another (Glasser, 1998).

But how does one satisfy the next basic need, *power,* if controlling others is unhealthy? In our culture, objects such as cars, houses, and money define power. According to choice theory, power is neither good nor bad and can be used in many ways. The minimum requirement to fulfill our need for power is to have someone who listens to us. In moments when people feel as though they are not heard or respected, they feel powerless (Glasser, 1998). A victim of sexual assault feels powerless when she is attacked, and even more so if no one believes her and she is unable to obtain justice for the crime committed against her. A student who is allowed to share his own ideas and creations feels powerful when his teacher and classmates acknowledge him. Ultimately, there is far more power in getting along with people than in controlling them (Glasser, 1998).

Freedom is the quality we gain from not being controlled by others. People with freedom are able to make their own choices about their lives and well-being, and no one else dictates what they do or say (Glasser, 1998). Few people are ever totally free from others' need for external control. When we can begin to focus on our own internal control and choice, however, it becomes less important to please and satisfy anyone but ourselves.

Finally, *fun* is an essential part of a psychologically healthy mind. Because Glasser considered needs biological drives, fun is conceptualized as a genetic incentive for lifelong learning. Humans never stop playing or learning, and maintaining a consistent feeling of fun and lightheartedness is crucial for our relationships and personal mental health (Glasser, 1998).

As you might expect, certain needs aren't as salient to some people as they are to others. In a study evaluating the importance of basic needs among children ages 8 to 16, Harvey and Retter (2002) found distinct differences between girls' and boys' desire to fulfill each of Glasser's five basic needs. Using data obtained from the Basic Needs Survey (Harvey & Retter, 1995), the researchers found that younger girls indicated a higher desire to satisfy their need for love and belonging, whereas younger boys were more concerned with fun. As girls entered adolescence, the need for love and belonging decreased, although it was still higher than for adolescent boys. Both boys and girls seemed to desire power and control at younger ages and later transitioned into a greater need for freedom during adolescence. These findings are congruent with classic gender and developmental theories (e.g., Erikson, 1950; Gilligan, 1982) and should inform both clinicians and teachers as they work with children who have behavior problems and emotional issues (Harvey & Retter, 2002). Additionally, the notion that some needs are more important to clients than others should inform counselors as they work to identify barriers to and dysfunctional methods of satisfying needs.

Current Trends in Reality Therapy

Reality therapy continues to find its way into the treatment options for various issues within mental health. Addictive behavior is one of the many areas where reality therapy/choice theory is being used as a treatment option. Kim (2007) applied a group counseling model that used reality therapy in treating college students in Korea struggling with Internet addiction. Although Glasser (1984) discussed years ago the use of reality therapy in treating addictions, clinicians are now seeing its usefulness when discussing options for (or additions to) Alcoholics and Narcotics Anonymous programs. Howatt (2003) also proposed the choice theory model as a treatment option for addictions. He went on to explain that it does not matter what type of addiction someone has; the "one variable that is universal is that the person must make the choice to want to stop" (p. 12). More recently, Graham, Sauerheber, and Britzman (2013) supported the use of reality therapy by mental health professionals working with families. They pointed out that, even though choice theory and reality therapy have not been viewed as a treatment modality for families, the basic concepts in reality therapy provide many useful therapeutic tools for effective counseling. Robey and Cosentino (2012) recently published an article outlining the idea of using reality therapy/choice theory in counselor supervision. The authors suggest that counselor educators and counseling supervisors could frame supervision using choice theory as the theoretical model and reality therapy to establish and work on present and future goals.

SUPPORT FOR THE USE OF REALITY THERAPY/CHOICE THEORY

Evidence-Based Support for Reality Therapy/Choice Theory

Reality therapy and choice theory are now considered one of the mainstream counseling theories and techniques for mental health professionals around the world. In his ongoing attempt to gather data on the effectiveness of choice theory and reality therapy, Glasser (2010) called for continued independent research and published articles in journals such as the *International Journal of Choice Theory and Reality Therapy.* The William Glasser International Institute (www.wglasser.com/) reports that more than 75,000 individuals worldwide have been trained in reality therapy/choice theory since 1967. Reality therapists acknowledge the need to continue producing peer-reviewed quantitative and qualitative research examining the effectiveness of reality therapy and choice control (Wubbolding, 2012).

In 2007, Litwack commented that despite years of using reality therapy in the field, there remains a need for peer-reviewed, published data on the efficacy of reality therapy and choice theory. Litwack reported that there is a growing body of research on reality therapy and choice theory, including doctoral dissertations. This doctoral dissertation research has spanned more than 30 years. Litwack also pointed to the reviews and analyses of doctoral research that have been published in the past 20 years (e.g., Barry, 1996). Franklin (1993) published an article providing a bibliographic listing of 82 dissertations supporting the use of reality therapy and choice theory. Radtke, Sapp, and Farrell (1997) reported a medium effect size from their meta-analysis of 21 studies examining reality therapy. The authors did view this as promising and commented that the small sample size ($n = 21$) could have played a role in finding only a medium effect in the studies. Wubbolding (2007) has collected and cited numerous research articles that provide evidence-based support for reality therapy and its use as a form of treatment.

Use With Diverse Populations and Children

Applicability of a theory and its techniques to diverse populations is a critical consideration when choosing theories to include in one's counseling techniques toolbox. Wubbolding et al. (2004) reported that reality therapy and choice theory have been used and researched all over the world: "Validated by research studies, it has been used successfully from Kuwait to Korea, from Salisbury to Singapore and from Cincinnati to Colombia" (p. 227). Further, Wubbolding (2011) has taught reality therapy in various countries all over the world. Glasser pointed out that reality therapy works across cultures and that our basic needs (choices) are biological (Nystul & Shaughnessey, 1995). Radtke et al. (1997) also support the use of reality therapy with a wide range of clients and settings. Seligman and Reichenberg (2014) do caution that mental health professionals working with severe psychiatric issues (i.e., psychotic disorders, schizophrenia, etc.) will have to examine any current research as to the effectiveness of reality therapy with these types of disorders. The authors go on to state that reality therapy in these cases "will probably need to be combined with medication and other treatment approaches" (p. 380).

Wubbolding stated that everyone has choices, regardless of race, culture, or gender, going on to say that the "element of choice" is somewhat universal and can be embraced by people from all backgrounds (Robey, 2011, p. 237). At the same time, as Corey (2008) pointed out, it is important to let clients know that they are being heard when they discuss the realities of environmental/social barriers that indeed limit some of the choices they can make. Wubbolding et al. (2004) also support this key element in working with clients from diverse backgrounds, and remind counselors to adjust reality therapy to fit the client's needs, background, and environmental situation. So, in review, clients may have limited choices, but they still have choices.

Elizabeth Tham (2001), in an equally ethnographic and psychological article, described the implementation of choice theory in 1968 with a group of generationally oppressed Albanian women. She wrote, "Freedom from external coercion is only one aspect of Choice Theory" (p. 5). Tham went on to describe how women living in a practically medieval culture were unable to instigate a cultural revolution but were able to achieve balance by reflecting on questions such as, "Will feeling upset and angry get you what you want?" and "Is it important for you to be strong and logical in the way you express yourself?" (p. 5).

Glasser also mentioned that it is up to the therapist to blend reality therapy with a person's culture. Knowing how to ask culturally sensitive questions is one key to using reality therapy with diverse clients (Nystul & Shaughnessey, 1995). Graham et al. (2013) pointed out that reality therapy lends itself to use with immigrant families by incorporating both respect and understanding for the family unit (and their needs), as well as for the individual person (and his or her needs). Wubbolding et al. (2004) emphasized that the importance (and one of the basic premises) of reality therapy is the relationship between client and counselor and between client and family/friends. Even when diversity differences exist between client and counselor, creating a safe place may enable the client to share and work on issues with a counselor who is different.

Ososkie and Turpin (1985) supported the use of reality therapy in rehabilitation services for clients with various disabilities. The researchers pointed out that reality therapy could help clients understand what is in their control (what they do) and what is out of their control (their disability). Turpin and Ososkie (2004) suggested that mental health professionals using reality therapy discuss with disabled clients opportunities to become involved with community projects and grow positive relationships with their families. The researchers went on to say that reducing a client's self-critical talk and replacing negative addictions with positive ones can be beneficial to the client's success in counseling. In a similar treatment area, Sherman (2000) reported significant positive results in using reality therapy with clients suffering from chronic pain. Prenzlau (2006) reported statistically significant results from using reality therapy to reduce rumination and somatization behaviors in clients with posttraumatic stress disorder. This developing research and support for reality therapy could have implications for bolstering available resources in crisis intervention counseling.

Mickel (1991) and Okonji, Ososkie, and Pulos (1996) support the use of reality therapy among counselors working with African Americans. Holmes, White, Mills, and Mickel (2011) contended that reality therapy may be beneficial in working with and understanding the issues of Black women. Mickel (2013) supports the use of reality therapy for African American's working on developing their parenting styles. Mickel uses the term, "African-centered reality therapy" (p. 278) and discusses the common themes of belonging, personal responsibility, basic needs, and involvement in a person's life—all basic components of choice theory/reality therapy.

Seligman and Reichenberg (2014) support the use of reality therapy for adolescents (considered at-risk youth) being treated for various issues such as oppositional defiant disorder, conduct disorder, and substance abuse in residential and hospital settings. Cameron (2010) reported positive effects for both foster parents and their clients who utilized choice theory and reality therapy in therapeutic foster homes. Lawrence (2004) found positive results for using reality therapy among individuals with developmental disabilities, in comparison with using a mutual support group. Lawrence used group reality therapy to help the participants with self-regulation and making choices in their lives. Kianipour and Hoseini (2012) found support for using reality therapy in teacher training, which led to improved academic performance among students. Corey (2008) supported the use of reality therapy when working with groups. Corey went on to discuss the importance of the group leader's developing a comfort level in the use of reality therapy and how that can assist in the effectiveness of the group. More recently, Robey, Wubbolding, and Carlson (2012) coedited a book on using reality therapy and choice theory when working with couples. The text describes numerous issues couples may face and how reality therapy and choice theory can be used to address these issues in counseling.

Strengths

A large part of the appeal of reality therapy/choice theory is its applicability to many different symptoms and populations, as noted earlier. Wubbolding (2007) further explained that mental health professionals in other areas of the world who use reality therapy adapt the basic WDEP (wants, doing, evaluate, plan) system, described in detail later in this chapter, or tenets of choice theory to their cultures.

The emphasis on deliberate choice of behavior in reality therapy allows for broad application to many different issues and symptoms. The layman may assume that reality therapy requires that one make the easy and obvious choice to stop being depressed/anxious/guilty. In actuality, reality therapy achieves much of the client's emotional and thought transformation by changing behaviors first. Behaviors and actions are easier to control than thoughts, feelings, and perceptions; thus, altering the behaviors clients engage in automatically produces different thoughts and feelings (Wubbolding, 2007). For example, the emotions that follow an interaction with a client's brother or sister are directly related to the nature of that interaction. So, instead of insisting that a child love and get along with his or her sibling, it's likely more effective to teach each sibling effective communication skills that entail respect and kindness. This communication will elicit different thoughts and emotions than would an interaction characterized by screaming and name calling. Further, studies have shown that short-term reality therapy can be effective in influencing clients' locus of control, sense of personal responsibility, self-determination, self-regulation, autonomy, psychological empowerment, and self-realization (Kim, 2002; Lawrence, 2004).

Limitations

If you were somewhat unnerved by the introduction to this chapter, you will likely agree that a limitation of reality therapy/choice theory is its total lack of emphasis on the past. Many agree that to change behavior in the future, one must gain insight into past behaviors and experiences. Clients who feel compelled to resolve early conflict or emotionally process past trauma may understandably feel neglected in the application of reality therapy.

Another critique entails the explicit lack of feminist or multicultural consideration within the theory. Mary Ballou, a feminist professor, first criticized the absence of any feminist perspective in reality therapy in 1984. Ballou criticized reality therapy's "unidimensional" conceptualization of diverse clients and its rejection of experience. In denying one's experience, Ballou asserted, intersections of power and privilege related to gender, sexuality, race, ethnicity, and socioeconomic status are neglected. Linnenberg (2006) further explained Ballou's belief that this theory does not explicitly acknowledge the different experiences of gender, sexuality, race, ethnicity, and socioeconomic status and that the emphasis on internal control undermines systemic oppression that often disempowers minorities. Those who are underprivileged or oppressed are not allowed to exert control or choice over much of their lives, and insisting that they do so can be even more oppressive (Linnenberg, 2006). Additionally, Ballou (1984) pointed out that an absolute focus on internal control is detrimental to social progress, as it leads to a failure to recognize ways an individual can influence social change, ways that could result in empowerment for the client. Furthermore, if no one ever acknowledges that social injustices exist, progress can never occur to dismantle systems of oppression (Ballou, 1984). Linnenberg (2006) countered that although there has been no effort to incorporate feminist theory into either reality therapy or choice theory, many counselors do employ multicultural awareness in the counseling process due to the emergence of multiculturalism in counselor training.

Additionally, the lack of technical verbiage in this theory and the seemingly basic concepts may insinuate for some that the application of reality therapy is easy. In fact, to be a proficient reality therapist, one must undergo thorough training, practice, supervision, and lifelong learning (Corey, 2008; Wubbolding, 2007).

PROFESSIONAL IDENTITY AND OVERVIEW OF REALITY THERAPY: WHY USE REALITY THERAPY

Many graduate students struggle to decide what counseling theories they will use in their counseling sessions. What makes a theory useful to one person and his or her personality will not necessarily be the same for another person. Deciding on when and how to use a specific theory will depend on many factors. The personality and needs of the client, the counselor's personality, and knowledge pertaining to a specific theory are just a few of the variables to ponder when choosing a theory. We can't tell students which theories to use, but we can describe some of the factors associated with reality therapy and choice theory. Incorporating reality therapy into a toolbox of counseling techniques will enable the clinician to help clients understand that they are in control of their choices when it comes to behaviors and thoughts. Most clients think they do not have a choice in how they feel and behave. While clients may have limited resources and opportunities (e.g., due to socioeconomic conditions, governmental unrest, racism, oppression), these obstacles don't necessarily remove all their choices.

As you are deciding what theories you want to use in your counseling career, take a few minutes to answer the questions in Exercise 11.1. Instead of providing several paragraphs about reality therapy and professional identity, we decided to encourage students to think about their own professional identities and learn about the framework of reality therapy through this guided exercise. The questions and related information provided below will give students a general outline of the framework of reality therapy and choice theory.

EXERCISE 11.1

REALITY THERAPY AND YOU

As you read through the following questions, take some time to think about your own personality and whether the basic concepts of reality therapy match up with it. We have provided a short explanation of some basic concepts of reality therapy for you to review after you answer each question.

Question 1: When you think of your preferred counseling setting, do you feel more comfortable remaining in a traditional office or see yourself in more diverse settings? Explain your answer.

_____

_____

_____

_____

Reality therapy is often used in nontraditional counseling settings. Ivey, D'Andrea, Ivey, and Simek-Morgan (2007) pointed out that clinicians who use reality therapy may find themselves doing counseling in the field. The counseling setting could be a wilderness program, residential facility (e.g., group home, detention center, halfway house), or even the playground of a local school. Ivey et al. went on to state that reality therapy is useful when working with resistant clients and can include brief encounters instead of the more traditional 50-minute sessions. Reality therapy can also be used in more traditional settings.

Question 2: When you think about your orientation to time, are you past, present, or future oriented? Explain your answer.

_____

_____

_____

_____

Reality therapy is basically present oriented. Glasser (1965) reminded us that the past is important and cannot be completely discarded but the client must deal with the issue in the moment. Glasser wrote, "It may be interesting to talk about past errors with friends and family, but it is a waste of time to discuss them with the therapist" (p. 32). A therapist using reality therapy wants to know *what* the client is doing, not necessarily *why*. Reality therapists want to know a client's plan for action. Instead of recounting past issues, clients need to be thinking about and creating a plan for how to move forward.

Wubbolding (2007) postulated that reality therapy's goal-oriented style is in line with many of the brief therapy (solution-focused) models encouraged by today's insurance providers. While we are not supporting the views of insurance companies, understanding the basics of reality therapy may be helpful if you decide to apply to be an insurance provider.

Question 3: Medication is big business. In recent years, antidepressants have been the most widely prescribed medication in the United States. What is your view of clients using psychotropic medications? Explain your answer.

_____

_____

_____

_____

Glasser (1984) supported the use of medication only in situations where the client's life is out of control and only to help the person regain control. After the initial stabilization, the client should make life changes without the use of psychotropic medications. Glasser reminded us that even though he was a psychiatrist, he never wrote a prescription for a psychotropic medication (Glasser, Haight, & Shaughnessy, 2003). Therapists using reality therapy may struggle with this concept and may not stand as firmly against the supervised use of psychotropic medication as Glasser did.

(Continued)

(Continued)

Wubbolding (2012) provided a critical lens for this issue, suggesting that use of reality therapy is not contingent on beliefs regarding the use of psychotropic medications; rather, this decision is up to each individual clinician in conjunction with the client.

Question 4: What are your thoughts about internal or external reasons for a person's behaviors, thoughts, or mental illness? Are clients driven by external forces that make them think and behave in certain ways? Explain your answer.

_____

_____

_____

_____

Glasser believed that clients are in control of their thoughts, behaviors, and mental health (not mental illness; Glasser et al., 2003). He went on to say that clients get into trouble when they blame others or their environment for their problems. No matter how badly another person hurt the client or how bad the client's environment, the client is in control of how he or she interprets the situation and chooses to deal with the issue at hand. Glasser also warned against using the term *mental illness*, advocating instead for talking about improving the client's "mental health" (Glasser et al., 2003). When clients hear terms such as *mental illness*, they may think they need medication and can't help themselves, which is not true in the eyes of a reality therapy practitioner.

   Wubbolding's (2000) WDEP system provides counselors a structure to build on and use in the counseling sessions. It is important to remember that not all counseling sessions will go exactly as planned, but the WDEP system offers a general guideline for using reality therapy.

Question 5: Describe your thoughts and views on the importance of the counselor–client relationship. Do you see clients as people who need a diagnosis and treatment from afar? Do you think that any self-disclosure on the part of the counselor is opening up too much to the client? Explain your views.

_____

_____

_____

_____

Reality therapy views the therapist–client relationship as one of the building blocks of therapy. Similar to other counseling theories, reality therapy views this relationship as a way to generate trust in the therapist and in the process. Glasser (1965) discussed how traditional therapy was not concerned with entering into a professional relationship with clients. Therapists were taught to remain objective at all times. Empathy and seeing the world through the client's eyes will require a genuine and honest professional relationship with the client. Are you ready and willing to enter into this type of relationship with your clients?

THERAPEUTIC PROCESS AND APPLICATION

Choice Theory Constructs

The terms *choice theory* and *reality therapy* are often used interchangeably. Glasser applied the idea of control theory, which describes biological and engineering feedback, to a clinical setting and created the foundation for what is now called choice theory (Wubbolding, 2007). More simply put, reality therapy is the therapeutic practice based on choice theory. For many of us, our everyday lives revolve around a belief in *external control*. This can mean that we are attempting to control others by using force or intimidation to make them comply with our wishes. It can also mean that others are controlling us. For example, we may believe that our partner or spouse has made us angry by forgetting our anniversary or that our family is making us behave in a way we normally would not. Under this assumption, the existence of personal freedom progressively erodes (Glasser, 1998).

Choice theory revolves around the concept of *internal control* (Glasser, 1998). Other people's reactions and behaviors are simply information. They help us make informed decisions and evaluations about how we behave and what we believe. If someone consistently belittles you, that information will compel you to stop interacting or change the way you interact with that person. It does not mean that the criticism is truth or that it should affect your self-esteem. You have the control to make that decision. In essence, internal control suggests that the locus of what we do and why we do it is located within ourselves. Even more simply put, we can control only ourselves, and that control is total.

As you are probably well aware, the *Diagnostic and Statistical Manual of Mental Disorders,* published by the American Psychiatric Association (2013), is a several-hundred-page clinical digest that assists mental health professionals in diagnosing, labeling, and predicting many psychiatric disorders. According to the tenets of reality therapy, however, all mental illnesses can be easily described as one's inability to fulfill the previously discussed basic needs. Some clients may express their failure to fulfill these needs as anxiety, depression, or even psychosomatic symptoms such as migraines or stomach ulcers. Regardless of the symptomatology, the underlying cause is the same (Glasser, 1965). Choice theory proposes that we are each born with five basic needs, previously discussed in this chapter, and that we are genetically predisposed to try our best to satisfy those needs. As mentioned, dysfunction and emotional disturbance occur when the needs are inadequately fulfilled (Glasser, 1998).

Choice Theory and Schools

In addition to psychological and counseling research and publications, Glasser was quite prolific in writing about and researching education. This chapter is not the appropriate outlet to debate education reform; however, the authors would be remiss in not mentioning the important role choice theory plays in educational affairs. The primary problem with current education, according to Glasser (1999), is the focus on external control. The vast majority of schools operate on the notion that students must learn certain predetermined facts and will be punished for failing to do so. Glasser emphasized the need for useful knowledge as opposed to facts alone, along with loving and patient relationships with teachers (Glasser, 1999). Useful knowledge is understood to be skills and information that can be readily used in real-world settings. As it stands, students in most schools are merely controlled and molded by teachers and administrators, with little to no control over what they learn or how they learn it. Glasser had some interesting ideas about how to improve education, including assigning students to be teacher assistants, eliminating ranking, and establishing parental support groups to help facilitate choice theory at home. For more information about reality therapy in schools, see the "Additional Resources" section at the end of this chapter. See Case Illustration 11.2 for an example of reality therapy applied in a school setting.

CASE ILLUSTRATION 11.2

Sulli

Sulli has been having a difficult time in school since her parents decided to divorce. She is an 11-year-old biracial female who attends fifth grade at a public elementary school. Lately, her teachers have noticed that her grades are plummeting and her peer relationships have started to suffer. Additionally, she has become defiant and unwilling to follow rules in the classroom. Once a vibrant and well-behaved child, she is now disruptive and difficult to manage.

The school counselor meets with Sulli to explore this abrupt change in her behavior and discovers that she is very angry. At first, she is guarded and sits in silence until she is allowed to return to class. Over several meetings, however, she becomes more willing to share as she draws and plays with the toys in the counselor's office. She tells the counselor about her parents' divorce and how she often hears them screaming at each other after they think she's fallen asleep.

"I don't want my family to break up!" she screams during one emotional meeting. "I have to be angry! Nobody is listening!" This statement is the beginning of the counselor and Sulli's exploration into her actions and their consequences. The counselor quietly asks Sulli if being angry has led to more people listening to her. "No," she says. "My mom just gets upset and goes to her room. My sister won't play with me anymore because she says I'm mean." The counselor listens supportively and reflects that it's much easier to listen to her when she speaks like this instead of yelling.

Over the next few weeks, the counselor and Sulli start to identify behaviors and unhelpful choices that lead to unwanted consequences. They focus on specific real-life scenarios and explore how each choice affected Sulli, as well as what might have happened if she had chosen to react differently. For example, the counselor helps Sulli recognize that she often criticizes her peers when they don't want to play with her. Sulli agrees that she doesn't like to play with friends who are mean to her and can understand why her friends and sister are reluctant to play when she acts that way. The counselor also helps Sulli learn to generate other options, or *choices,* that could help her achieve a desired consequence. So instead of bullying her friends when they don't want to play the same game as she does, Sulli starts to propose other options, such as playing another game first and her chosen game next.

The counselor and Sulli are able to recognize and modify various behaviors in her life at school; however, her parents' divorce isn't something she can *choose* to make go away. After Sulli's behavioral issues have begun to improve and her grades are almost back to normal, Sulli and the counselor begin to discuss her feelings related to her father moving out of their house and her mom going back to work. Although an abstract concept, the counselor uses elementary words and explanations to help Sulli grasp the difference between internal control and external control. Based on the foundation that certain choices lead to negative consequences, the counselor helps Sulli explore the idea that there are some things we don't have a choice about at all. Sulli eventually begins to understand that reacting negatively to situations outside of her control only makes her feel bad and, in fact, has no effect on the situation at hand.

Ultimately, Sulli is able to assert control and choice over her impulses and reactions in a way that leads to more positive consequences. Her parents' divorce remains difficult to cope with, and she often feels sad; however, her sadness is no longer manifested in ways that negatively affect her, such as poor grades, lack of social support, and getting in trouble at school.

Wubbolding's Description of Choice Theory (The WDEP System)

As mentioned above, choice theory is the theoretical framework that informs the practice of reality therapy. Robert Wubbolding, cited often throughout this chapter, developed a useful acronym to encompass the interventions associated with reality therapy—the WDEP system. Unlike the A-B-C-D-E model of cognitive-behavioral therapy that describes one concept, the letters in WDEP represent broader themes and a variety of possible interventions (Wubbolding, 2000; Wubbolding et al., 2004). Table 11.1 provides a quick-reference guide to Wubbolding's WDEP system.

Table 11.1 Wubbolding's WDEP System

W What Wants Worldview	• "What do you want from this counseling?" • "What would it be like if you didn't have this problem?" • "What would a loving relationship look like to you?" • "How much energy are you willing to invest in trying to turn your relationship around?"
D Direction Describe Doing	• "Have your arguments ever gotten violent?" • "What is a typical example of what's been happening?" • "When did you stop doing enjoyable things together?" • "When was the last time you had a good time in the relationship?"

(Continued)

(Continued)

E Self-Evaluation	• "What is one thing you could do today that you think would help make the relationship better?" • "If you change nothing and do everything the same as over the past 2 years, do you think your relationship will get better?"
P Plan	• "What can you do in the future to demonstrate that you care about your partner?" • "How will you know that your relationship has improved?"

Note: Extracted from sample counseling probes quoted in Wubbolding et al. (2004, pp. 224–226) and applied to relationship counseling.

W represents the client's *what, wants,* and *worldview.* First, it is essential for the client to develop goals and establish *what* exactly he or she *wants* to accomplish throughout the counseling process. Additionally, the therapist and client explore the client's worldview, or how the client views himself or herself in relation to other people. Where does he or she exist in the world? This information helps guide the therapist and client in clarifying attainable goals, as well as in gauging the client's level of commitment to change. It may also help uncover the client's *inner and outer worlds,* which inform beliefs about the ability to exert control in life (Wubbolding, 2000; Wubbolding et al., 2004). Remember the core concepts of inner and external control?

D is used to characterize interventions related to helping clients *describe* their life *direction,* their relationships, and how they are fulfilling their most basic needs (i.e., what are they *doing*?). Most clients do not seek therapy because they are pleased and content with the direction of their lives at the moment. In asking clients to describe the world around them, the therapist can help them identify ways their choices are inhibiting their ability to achieve their goals. A transition in the actions we choose leads also to a transition in the feelings and emotions we experience (Wubbolding et al., 2004).

E indicates *self-evaluation* (Wubbolding, 2000; Wubbolding et al., 2004). Clients must have a realistic view of their own behaviors and choices, and how their actions influence the quality of their lives. As Wubbolding et al. (2004) aptly stated, "It would (amusingly) appear to be that part of being human is the undying belief that when a behavior fails, choose it more often and more intensely" (p. 225). Through the practice of self-evaluation, clients should experience (to borrow from another theory) cognitive dissonance and ultimately recognize that their current dysfunctional behaviors are preventing them from achieving their fundamental goals.

Finally, P refers to the development of a concrete *plan*. To be effective, the plan must be "simple, attainable, and measurable" (Wubbolding et al., 2004, p. 226). Plans enumerate goals as clarified by the clients, identify current behaviors that are interfering with those goals, and include specific changes in the behaviors in which clients choose to engage. See Case Illustration 11.3 for an example of the WDEP system in action.

CASE ILLUSTRATION 11.3

The WDEP System

Linda, a 35-year-old African American female, seeks counseling for her depression. She explains in the intake session that she was abused by her ex-husband for 5 years and is struggling with feelings of low self-worth and fear of never finding real love. Using Wubbolding's WDEP system, I first help Linda clarify her present wants, needs, and perceptions so we are both clear about her subjective reality. We then look at the direction in which her life is heading as a result of what she is doing, and evaluate whether she is pleased with her path. When she says she is not headed in the direction she would like to go, we make a plan to redirect her toward what she desires. I ask her to create realistic goals for herself. As a reality therapist, I am direct in my approach to help her see that she is responsible for choosing how to live and, to an extent, for how she feels. The unhappiness and depression she feels are a choice. I call these "paining" behaviors, because Linda is choosing to be unhappy. She explains how she struggles with feeling weak and incapable, which is an appropriate time to explain to her the difference between her perceived world—her subjective reality, which holds her past memories and present perceptions—and the quality world she aspires to live in. My intention is to help Linda see that she gets to decide whether or not she'll live the life of a victim or an able, determined survivor. I ask her what she needs to do to accomplish her goal of meeting a wonderful, loving man. Whenever she expresses doubt or makes excuses, I remind her that it's her responsibility to meet her own needs. Finally, I encourage Linda to be patient with herself, reminding her that it will take time to redirect her life.

Y-CHUN THROUGH THE LENS OF REALITY THERAPY

Now that we have reviewed reality therapy and choice theory, we can take a look at the case of Y-Chun through the lens of a reality therapist. Y-Chun is a 35-year-old, biracial (White and Asian), nontraditional college student. Y-Chun has three half-siblings and is mother to a 15-year-old boy and 12-year-old girl. Y-Chun's family is described as having a low socioeconomic status, with both parents currently working. Y-Chun's parents are proud of her for going to college and have high expectations for her academic achievements. Y-Chun has come to counseling at the suggestion of her doctor, after reporting a number of physical symptoms such as headaches, upset stomach, difficulty sleeping, and anger issues. During the intake session, Y-Chun discloses that she feels stressed, overwhelmed, empty, and alone, and that she cries a lot. Y-Chun also discloses a past history of substance abuse and oppositional and defiant behaviors. She talks about her struggles maintaining a "normal" relationship with her family members and others. She also shares that her cousin raped her when she was 16 years old. Y-Chun states that she is tired of feeling this way but doesn't "know where to begin." The initial session ends with the counselor providing empathy and supporting her decision to come to counseling.

The first several sessions will be geared toward providing empathy and establishing a professional relationship based on trust and hope. While reality therapy is focused on the present and future, letting the client know she is being heard and can trust the counselor will be a top priority in the beginning sessions and throughout the counseling experience. Although the primary goal of reality therapy is to select the best choices to help the client achieve her goals, Wubbolding (2007) cautioned against arguing or even providing constructive criticism to clients, as it may lead to resistance. Glasser, Wubbolding, and other reality therapists constantly discussed the importance of the relationship between therapist and client. Without this trusting relationship, counseling will be unable to proceed. It is a precarious task to neither criticize clients nor accept excuses from them (Wubbolding, 2007).

Y-Chun mentions a key term used in reality therapy numerous times in her initial session: *want*. Y-Chun *wants* many things—better relationships, less stress, more connections, and less feelings of aloneness. She wants all these things but does not know where to start to obtain them.

A key principle in reality therapy is this notion of dysfunctional relationships. The helping relationship between counselor and client is of utmost importance; however, the counselor's primary role is to facilitate the improvement of the client's relationships. Wubbolding et al. (2004) stated, "Initiating and enhancing interpersonal relationships almost always alleviates or at least lessens human suffering" (p. 222). Y-Chun is likely experiencing stress related to her own network of dysfunctional relationships. She mentioned several times that she feels alone and disconnected from the people around her (parents, children, intimate partners, etc.). This *want* falls directly in with Wubbolding's (2000) *W* in the WDEP system. By exploring with Y-Chun her wants (and needs) for improved relationships, the therapist is on the way to helping her establish goals for counseling. Some of Y-Chun's *wants/needs* are based on these poor relationships in her life.

The *direction* of Y-Chun's life and what she is *doing* appears to be somewhat varied. Like most, she is content with certain aspects of her life (e.g., going back to school) and unsatisfied with many other components. The therapist here is assessing the *D* in WDEP. Y-Chun undoubtedly has a harrowing past fraught with drug abuse, sexual assault, and other defiant behaviors. Reality therapy stresses the importance of empathy when discussing these events but also emphasizes focusing on the present (Glasser, 1965). How does she currently spend her time? What does her inner dialogue or self-talk sound like? Where will she be in 2 years if she continues to do exactly what she's doing now?

After examining what Y-Chun is currently doing, it is time to *evaluate* (the *E* in WDEP) how those actions both limit and promote her personal success and progress toward the wants she enumerated in the first sessions. Wubbolding (2007) described this part of the therapeutic process as a "pivotal moment," when cognitive restructuring can begin. Ideally, Y-Chun will realize some inconsistencies in the way she is currently living and how she wants to live. Evaluation is a delicate process that must not be critical or judgmental. It contains many elements, including the evaluation of behavioral direction, specific actions, wants, perceptions and viewpoints, new directions, and a plan (Wubbolding, 2007).

Creating a *plan* represents the last letter in WDEP; however, this step will probably require review, modification, and more self-evaluation. A plan for Y-Chun may include better communication with her children and engaging in deliberate activities with them each week. It will be part of the therapist's role to help Y-Chun explore and understand which aspects of her relationships are in her control. The therapist will help Y-Chun make a *plan* for how she will work on her relationships with her family and others. One part of the plan could be for Y-Chun to evaluate her current thoughts and behaviors to see if they are leading to what she wants and needs out of her relationships (Corey, 2013). Glasser (1965) continually emphasized the importance of the client's making a plan. Such a plan will give Y-Chun a concrete and measurable way to set realistic goals and chart her progress. It will also empower her to see that she is in control and place the responsibility for her happiness back on her. Glasser (1965) reminded us that individuals need at least one important person in their lives who cares about them and whom they care about. With Y-Chun, making a plan to work on her relationship with one or two people to begin with may make the task more attainable in the early stages of counseling.

Last, Y-Chun's seemingly external locus of control epitomizes reality therapy's key principle. Throughout her initial session, Y-Chun discussed how others have affected her thoughts and behaviors. As we know, having an external locus of control can lead to feelings of helplessness and loss of personal control in a client's life. Y-Chun clearly stated experiencing aspects of helplessness, with her fear of never having the kind of life she *wants* and even entertaining suicidal ideation at one point. There is no denying that some terrible things have happened in Y-Chun's past. Reality therapy stresses the importance of empathy when discussing these events but also emphasizes focusing on the present (Glasser, 1965). Using reality therapy, the counselor can work with Y-Chun to understand that we can't change the past but we can change the present through our decisions. After the history-gathering portion of the initial sessions is complete, the counselor using reality therapy may not encourage continued discussions about past negative experiences and failures. The goal for counseling will be to start developing *plans* to help Y-Chun attain her *wants/needs*.

KEYSTONES

- Reality therapy was developed as a counseling therapy to empower clients and let them know that they have choices concerning their thoughts and behaviors.
- Reality therapy/choice theory can be used with a diverse range of clients and mental health issues.
- Reality therapy is a present- and future-oriented style of therapy.
- The WDEP system is a useful tool when using reality therapy/choice theory.
- Reality therapy states that there are five basic needs integral to our psychological health: *survival, love and belonging, power, freedom,* and *fun.*

REFLECTIONS FROM THE CONTRIBUTOR'S CHAIR

David A. Scott

From my early years as a beginning counselor, I was curious about the incongruent nature of clients' thoughts, motivations, and behaviors, and their struggles to make lasting changes in both. So many times, I worked with clients who would recant their past issues but could not take the next steps to improve their mental health. I was excited to utilize my training in various counseling techniques but found myself always going back to reality therapy. As I learned more and more about reality therapy and choice theory I began to realize that these counseling concepts worked well with many of my clients and also were a good fit for my personality and counseling style. I was also able to work with some great colleagues who had mastered the use of reality therapy, and we spent many supervision sessions discussing the pros and cons of different counseling techniques. I found reality therapy to be useful as I transitioned my counseling career into working with at-risk youth and their families. Probably the most important aspect of reality therapy for me is the concept that we all have choices. Our life stories and environments may be filled with heartache and oppressive conditions, but we can still decide how we deal with these issues. Helping empower clients to understand they do have control over their thoughts and behaviors and not letting them fall into the trap of external control over their lives has had lasting effects for the clients I have worked with over the past 20 years.

Hannah G. Barfield

As a counselor working in a state-funded mental health agency, reality therapy has proven to be an effective mode of therapy for the wide range of mental health problems my clients experience. In addition to addressing varying symptoms, reality therapy is also an effective brief therapy that I can use when time is limited or sessions are scheduled far apart. Setting measurable goals allows clients to monitor their successes and choose which behaviors will help them achieve those goals, and which ones will not. Finally, the majority of my clients are underprivileged and disempowered. Reality therapy gives them back control over their lives and allows them to determine (sometimes for the first time) where their lives are headed.

ADDITIONAL RESOURCES

Glasser, W. (2010). *Choice theory in the classroom*. New York: HarperCollins.
Glasser, W. (2010). *The quality school: Managing students without coercion*. New York: HarperCollins.
Glasser, W. (2011). *Schools without failure*. New York: HarperCollins.

Websites

The Center for Reality Therapy. (2013). Retrieved from http://www.realitytherapywub.com/
The William Glasser Institute—US. (2010). Retrieved from http://www.wglasser.com
William Glasser International. (n.d.). Retrieved from http://www.wgai.net/index.php/home

REFERENCES

American Psychiatric Association. (2013). *Diagnostic and statistical manual of mental disorders* (5th ed.). Washington, DC: Author.
Ballou, M. B. (1984). Thoughts on reality therapy from a feminist. *Journal of Reality Therapy, 4*(1), 28–32.

Barry, J. (1996). Fifteen RT/CT doctoral dissertations 1990–1995. *Journal of Reality Therapy, 15,* 100–101.

Cameron, A. (2010). Utilizing choice theory and reality therapy in therapeutic foster care homes. *International Journal of Choice Theory and Reality Therapy, 30*(2), 9–16.

Corey, G. (2008). *Theory and practice of group counseling* (7th ed.). Belmont, CA: Brooks/Cole.

Corey, G. (2013). *Theory and practice of counseling and psychotherapy* (9th ed.). Belmont, CA: Brooks/Cole.

Erikson, E. H. (1950). *Childhood and society.* New York: W. W. Norton.

Franklin, M. (1993). Eighty-two reality therapy doctoral dissertations written between 1970–1990. *Journal of Reality Therapy, 12*(2), 76–82.

Gilligan, C. (1982). *In a different voice: Psychological theory and women's development.* Cambridge, MA: Harvard University Press.

Glasser, W. (1965). *Reality therapy.* New York: HarperCollins.

Glasser, W. (1984). *Control theory: A new explanation of how we control our lives.* New York: Harper & Row.

Glasser, W. (1998). *Choice therapy.* New York: HarperCollins.

Glasser, W. (1999). *Choice theory: A new psychology of personal freedom.* New York: HarperCollins.

Glasser, W., Haight, M., & Shaughnessy, M. F. (2003). An interview with William Glasser. *North American Journal of Psychology, 5,* 407–416.

Graham, M. A., Sauerheber, J. D., & Britzman, M. J. (2013). Choice theory and family counseling: A pragmatic, culturally sensitive approach. *Family Journal, 21,* 230–234.

Harvey, V., & Retter, K. (1995). The development of the Basic Needs Survey. *Journal of Reality Therapy, 15*(1), 76–80.

Harvey, V., & Retter, K. (2002). Variations by gender between children and adolescents on the four basic psychological needs. *International Journal of Reality Therapy, 21*(2), 33–36.

Holmes, K. Y., White, K. B., Mills, C., & Mickel, E. (2011). Defining the experiences of Black women: A choice theory/reality therapy approach to understanding the strong Black woman. *International Journal of Choice Theory and Reality Therapy, 31*(1), 73–83.

Howatt, W. A. (2001). The evolution of reality therapy to choice theory. *International Journal of Reality Therapy, 21*(1), 7–12.

Howatt, W. A. (2003). Choice theory: A core addiction recovery tool. *International Journal of Reality Therapy, 22*(2), 12–15.

Ivey, A. E., D'Andrea, M., Ivey, M. B., & Simek-Morgan, L. (2007). *Theories of counseling and psychotherapy: A multicultural perspective.* Boston: Pearson.

Kianipour, O., & Hoseini, B. (2012). An examination of the effectiveness of choice theory on teachers' teaching effectiveness and students' subsequent academic achievement. *International Journal of Choice Theory and Reality Therapy, 31*(2), 55–63.

Kim, J. (2007). A reality therapy group counseling program as an Internet addiction recovery method for college students in Korea. *International Journal of Reality Therapy, 26*(2), 3–9.

Kim, K. (2002). The effect of a reality therapy program on the responsibility for elementary school children in Korea. *International Journal of Reality Therapy, 22*(1), 30–33.

Lawrence, D. H. (2004). The effects of reality therapy group counseling on the self-determination of persons with developmental disabilities. *International Journal of Reality Therapy, 23*(2), 9–15.

Linnenberg, D. M. (2006). Thoughts on reality therapy from a pro-feminist perspective. *International Journal of Reality Therapy, 26*(1), 23–26.

Litwack, L. (2007). Research review dissertations on reality therapy and choice theory: 1970–2007. *International Journal of Reality Therapy, 27*(1), 14–16.

Mickel, E. (1991). Integrating the African centered perspective with reality therapy/control theory. *Journal of Reality Therapy, 11*(1), 66–71.

Mickel, E. (2013). African-centered reality therapy parenting: An alternative paradigm. *Journal of Human Behavior in the Social Environment, 23*(2), 278–286. doi:10.1080/10911359.2012.747347

Nystul, M. S., & Shaughnessey, M. (1995). An interview with William Glasser. *Individual Psychology: Journal of Adlerian Theory, Research and Practice, 51,* 440–444.

Okonji, J., Ososkie, J., & Pulos, S. (1996). Preferred style and ethnicity of counselors by African American males. *Journal of Black Psychology, 22*(3), 329–339.

Ososkie, J. N., & Turpin, J. O. (1985). Reality therapy in rehabilitation counseling. *Journal of Applied Rehabilitation Counseling, 16*(3), 34–38.

Prenzlau, S. (2006). Using reality therapy to reduce PTSD-related symptoms. *International Journal of Reality Therapy, 25*(2), 23–29.

Radtke, L., Sapp, M., & Farrell, W. R. (1997). Reality therapy: A meta-analysis. *Journal of Reality Therapy, 17*(1), 4–9.

Robey, P. A. (2011). Reality therapy and choice theory: An interview with Robert Wubbolding. *Family Journal, 19,* 231–237. doi:10.1177/1066480710397129

Robey, P. A., & Cosentino, A. R. (2012). Choice theory and reality therapy in counselor supervision. *International Journal of Choice Theory and Reality Therapy, 31*(2), 31–41.

Robey, P. A., Wubbolding, R. E., & Carlson, J. (2012). *Contemporary issues in couples counseling: A choice theory and reality therapy approach.* New York: Routledge.

Seligman, L., & Reichenberg, L. W. (2014). *Selecting effective treatments* (4th ed.). Hoboken, NJ: John Wiley.

Sherman, K. (2000). CT/RT in chronic pain management: Using choice theory/reality therapy as a cognitive-behavioral intervention for chronic pain management: A pilot study. *International Journal of Reality Therapy, 19*(2), 10–14.

Tham, E. (2001). The meaning of choice theory for the women of Albania. *International Journal of Reality Therapy, 21*(1), 4–6.

Turpin, J., & Ososkie, J. N. (2004). Reality therapy. In F. Chan, N. L. Berven, & K. R. Thomas (Eds.), *Counseling theories and techniques for rehabilitation health professionals* (pp. 196–210). New York: Springer.

Wubbolding, R. E. (2000). *Reality therapy for the 21st century.* Philadelphia: Brunner Routledge.

Wubbolding, R. E. (2007). Reality therapy theory. In D. Capuzzi & D. Gross (Eds.), *Counseling and psychotherapy* (pp. 289–312). Upper Saddle River, NJ: Pearson.

Wubbolding, R. E. (2011). *Reality therapy: Theories of counseling series.* Washington, DC: American Psychological Association.

Wubbolding, R. E. (2012). Reality therapy. In J. Frew & M. D. Spiegler (Eds.), *Contemporary psychotherapies for a diverse world* (Rev. ed., pp. 339–372). New York: Routledge/Taylor & Francis.

Wubbolding, R. E., Brickell, J., Imhof, L., Kim, R., Lojk, L., & Al-Rashidi, B. (2004). Reality therapy: A global perspective. *International Journal for the Advancement of Counselling, 26*(3), 219–228. doi:10.1023/B:ADC0.0000035526.02422.0d

CHAPTER 12

Solution-Focused Therapy

Brandé Flamez and Joshua C. Watson

If it works do more of it; if what you do does not work, do something different.

—Steve de Shazer

The above quote from Steve de Shazer, founder of the solution-focused brief therapy model, relates the fundamental premise of the solution-focused approach. Clients are encouraged to find what is working in their lives. Those areas featuring discord between desired goals and actual behaviors are addressed, and problematic behaviors are replaced by productive, goal-oriented ones. Since the development of the solution-focused approach in the 1980s, it has grown in popularity and become a widely used treatment for many practicing counselors and other mental health professionals. In this chapter, you will learn more about how this approach can be used with a variety of clients with different presenting issues.

This chapter reviews solution-focused therapy as a theoretical framework for understanding how clients view the world. Included is a review of research-supported techniques and interventions proven to deliver meaningful change. After reading this chapter, you will be able to do the following:

1. Describe how the causes of dysfunction that lead to problems and issues clients face are conceptualized in solution-focused therapy

2. Explain three golden rules of solution-focused therapy

3. Identify techniques and interventions associated with solution-focused therapy

4. Integrate solution-focused therapy in your work with diverse clients

PROFILE OF MAIN FIGURES

Perhaps the most recognized contributors to the development of solution-focused therapy are Steve de Shazer and Insoo Kim Berg. In 1978, they founded the Brief Family Therapy Center in Milwaukee, Wisconsin, as a nonprofit research and training center focused on providing family therapy services and training. In working with clients, de Shazer and Berg realized that the majority of their time was spent talking with clients *about* their problems, rather than focusing on ways to *solve* problems. As a result, many clients remained stuck in their current state of dysfunction and did not achieve progress. This revelation led to the development of a new approach to counseling that became known as solution-focused brief therapy. Their work served as a starting point for others to build on and advance solution-focused therapy.

INTRODUCTION TO SOLUTION-FOCUSED THERAPY

Solution-focused therapy represents a marked deviation from the traditional forms of counseling and psychotherapy. Rather than focusing on problem formation and resolution, the solution-focused approach takes an active stance toward helping the client. Solution-focused therapy represents a strengths-based approach in which counselors emphasize the resources their clients possess and how their strengths can be applied to create change. As de Shazer and his colleagues (1986) noted, using what clients possess to help them meet their own needs and build satisfactory lives for themselves is a fundamental premise of the solution-focused approach. According to Trepper, Treyger, Yalowitz, and Ford (2010), "this small but iconoclastic shift has resulted in an approach that has become increasingly popular all around the world" (p. 35). In addition to anecdotal support from clinicians, the amount of research supporting the efficacy of this approach is growing (Kim & Franklin, 2009).

The popularity of solution-focused therapy lies in its flexibility, collaborative nature, and focus on client strengths (Kim, 2008). Rather than spending valuable clinical time trying to discover why a client's problems are occurring, the solution-focused approach allows counselors to focus on resolving current problems by looking forward rather than backward. In contrast to most talk therapies, this approach is less concerned with the cause of a problem; it does not matter when or how the problem began as long as the client discovers how to change and solve it. The client and counselor work to find solutions with the greatest likelihood of producing change. In co-constructing solutions, clients can find the ones that fit their particular worldview (De Jong & Berg, 2001).

Table 12.1 highlights differences between traditional and solution-focused approaches.

Since its development nearly 30 years ago, the solution-focused approach has steadily gained in popularity. A growing body of research focuses on fine-tuning the approach and assessing its efficacy with a diverse group of clients and presenting issues. The following section provides a brief overview of the historical development of solution-focused therapy.

Table 12.1   Comparison of Traditional and Solution-Focused Approaches

	Traditional	Solution Focused
Role of counselor	Expert	Collaborator Consultant
Role of client	Learner	Expert Teacher
Focus is on . . .	Past and present Origin of the problem Deficits Limitations Stability	Future and present What is already working Attempted solutions Competencies Possibilities Change
Goals	Set by counselor Absence of the problem	Developed jointly by client and counselor Presence of solutions

Historical Background

The origins of solution-focused therapy can be traced back to the work of noted psychiatrist Milton Erickson. In the 1960s and 1970s, Erickson began experimenting with a radical new approach toward patient care. He did not believe in diagnostic labels, viewing them as anchors that keep clients attached to problems. Instead, he believed in individuals' personal power to solve their own problems; he saw his role as helping clients apply their strengths to new situations. From Erickson's perspective, his work with clients did not have to be lengthy and involved (Jones-Smith, 2012). Even small changes in a client's way of thinking and interacting with his or her environment were beneficial because these small changes served as motivation for larger ones. Accounting for his success with clients, Erickson noted three basic principles of his work: (1) meet clients where they are, (2) help clients gain control by changing their perspectives, and (3) allow for change that meets clients' needs (de Shazer, 1982). These principles formed the basis for the solution-focused therapeutic approach developed by de Shazer and Berg.

Another influential figure in the development of solution-focused therapy is Gregory Bateson. Bateson was an English anthropologist whose research foci were systems theory and cybernetics. He believed that the social system (i.e., environment) in which people function is important to the development and resolution of problems (Visser, 2008). Bateson's work led to Don Jackson's creation of the Mental Research Institute (MRI) in Palo Alto, California, in 1958. MRI was established as a nonprofit corporation to explore and encourage the use of interactional, systemic, and strategic concepts in working with the community, schools, and businesses to effectively resolve human problems with individuals, couples, families, and other levels of social organization (MRI, 2008). In addition to their work toward further understanding interactional and systemic therapy, the therapists at MRI developed an innovative model of brief therapy.

In the 1960s, a research associate at MRI, Richard Fisch, proposed the idea of studying the effects of short-term interventions for treatment. The brief therapeutic model developed at MRI was a new goal-oriented and pragmatic approach to therapy. Because Fisch and other MRI therapists saw client problems as existing in the present, they also saw the solutions to these problems as existing in the present. Therapists focused on helping clients understand what they were doing in their lives that enabled their problems to persist. Once troublesome behaviors were identified, they were replaced by effective behaviors, leading to new results for clients. By focusing on the here and now, MRI therapists were eschewing the previously held belief that therapy had to include a discussion of clients' pasts to determine how problems developed initially or how clients and their social systems nurtured the development of these problems. The brief, future-focused approach was inspiring to de Shazer and Berg and became a part of their solution-focused model.

In the late 1970s, de Shazer and Berg left MRI to begin a private practice. Berg, who had lived in the Midwest since emigrating from South Korea in 1957, convinced de Shazer to move with her to Milwaukee, where they founded the Brief Therapy Family Center, a non-profit research and training institute, in 1978. In 1982, the solution-focused approach began to take shape as a distinct model of counseling.

Throughout the 1980s, de Shazer, Berg, and the other therapists at the Brief Therapy Family Center built on early successes by applying the work of Erickson and the MRI Brief Therapy Institute in developing solution-focused therapy. They found that the practice of analyzing and diagnosing client problems could be removed from the therapeutic process without affecting the quality of services provided to clients. By focusing on what works for clients, treatment can be successful. The success of this approach is measured by the progress clients make toward their goals, rather than the number of sessions a client spends in counseling (de Shazer, 1985, 1988).

Areas of Development

The solution-focused approach remains a popular therapeutic tool among counselors and therapists, but it has also become a major influence in many other fields, including business and industry, social policy, education, criminal justice systems, and athletic coaching (Jones-Smith, 2012). Today, the approach is known by many names (e.g., solution-focused therapy, solution-oriented therapy, solution-focused brief therapy, problem-focused brief therapy); however, they all relate to the same fundamental approach begun by de Shazer and Berg.

Professional Identity

The counseling profession, as noted by Remley and Herlihy (2009), is based on a philosophy that views clinical practice as a wellness-based approach conceptualizing clients from a developmental perspective. Counselors believe that the problems clients present in counseling are developmental in nature; they are normal problems people deal with as a part of being human. In addition, counselors focus on client empowerment, which is implemented through an emphasis on personal strengths and prevention practices to curb the continuation of serious mental illness or pervasive life issues.

The solution-focused approach embodies elements of what makes counseling unique as a profession and professional service. Its perspective is developmental in nature, emphasizing finding solutions to the problem rather than trying to understand the cause of the problem. The solution-focused counselor posits that clients' presenting problems are temporary. By focusing on the future, counselors and clients can work to make changes that help clients grow and learn from their experiences. The approach also strives to empower clients, another core principle of the counseling profession, by actively working to include them in the treatment process as they co-construct their solutions. Because the solution-focused approach views client problems in a different light than do most theoretical approaches, Exercise 12.1 invites you to reflect on your current view of the nature of clients' problems.

EXERCISE 12.1

REFLECTING ON PERSONAL VIEWS

Directions: Ask yourself the following questions, and think about how you conceptualize client problems and the counseling process. Perhaps the solution-focused approach is a model that fits you.

1. When clients present with problems, do I view the problem as more internal (related to who the client is as a person) or external (something with which the client must deal) in nature?

2. Are all problems solvable? Or do some problems not have solutions, meaning the focus of counseling should be on developing coping skills?

3. Is it important to know the history of a problem to treat it? Or is it usually unnecessary to know a great deal about the complaint to resolve it?

Other Questions for Consideration

1. Do I believe complex problems do not necessarily require complex solutions?

2. Do I believe every complaint pattern involves some sort of exception?

3. Do I believe change is constant and inevitable?

Exercise 12.2 is designed to help you better understand the problem- versus solution-focused approaches.

EXERCISE 12.2

THINKING ABOUT THE SOLUTION-FOCUSED APPROACH

Directions: Answer each of the questions below. You can complete this exercise on your own or interview a classmate. After completing the exercise, ask yourself, "What are some of the differences I noticed between the two categories of questions?" "What are some of the differences I noticed in my responses to the two categories of questions?"

Problem-Focused Approach

1. What has been the most frustrating problem for you this year?

2. What did you do to solve this problem?

3. Did it work?

Solution-Focused Approach

1. How would you like things to be this year?

2. When was the last time you were even just a little successful in achieving this goal?

3. How were you able to do that?

OVERVIEW OF SOLUTION-FOCUSED THERAPY

The solution-focused approach is based on three premises: (1) If it isn't broken, don't fix it; (2) if it works, do more of it; and (3) if it doesn't work, do something else (Sklare, 2005). To assist in differentiating the solution-focused approach from other forms of psychotherapy, O'Hanlon and Weiner-Davis (2003) identified a list of 10 assumptions that counselors can use to guide their work with clients. These 10 basic assumptions are as follows:

1. *Clients have resources and strengths to resolve complaints.*

   All clients have the knowledge and potential required to solve their own problems. By focusing on their problems, clients often lose sight of the strengths and resources they possess. The counselor's role is to help clients remember their strengths and how they can put them to work in solving their current problems.

2. *Change is constant.*

   Solution-focused counselors instill in their clients the belief that change is an ever-present and inevitable part of life. Portraying change as a constant occurrence gives clients hope for the future and allows them to see that their current state of affairs does not have to persist. Solution-focused counselors lead their clients to see that the odds of change occurring in their lives are so great, it would be a rarity if they were to stay in their current situation much longer. Simply ask yourself, What was the most important activity in your life at the age of 6? How about 16? How about now? Certainly, this simple reflection highlights the degree to which your life has changed throughout the years.

3. *The solution-focused counselor's job is to identify and amplify change.*

   Although clients have the potential to solve their own problems, counselors play a pivotal role in guiding the process. They are responsible for creating an environment conducive to change by helping clients determine what issues they should focus on and how change should occur. Using a directive approach, the solution-focused counselor leads the client through a process of identifying what is working, labeling it, and ensuring that it has a high likelihood of happening more frequently by encouraging and praising their successes and accomplishments.

4. *It is usually unnecessary to know a great deal about the complaint to solve it.*

   The solution-focused approach assumes that counselors often learn too much about their clients' problems and focus more on pathology than solutions. Problems exist, and they cannot be erased from existence; they can, however, be changed to minimize future occurrence. When you visit a doctor, the physician questions you about current symptoms and begins a treatment protocol aimed at addressing those symptoms moving forward; the goal is to find new methods for solving current problems. In a counseling context, discovering what the client tried in the past and what was successful allows the counselor to pick up from that point and move forward, which prevents trying what has already proven to be ineffective in producing change.

5. *It is not necessary to know the cause or function of a complaint to solve it.*

   Clients often present an erroneous belief that they need to know the origin of their problems. According to O'Hanlon and Weiner-Davis (2003), most clients operate under the impression that the solution to a problem arises once the cause of the problem is identified. As a result, these clients spend a lot of time searching for the root cause of their problems and never dedicating time to changing what they do not like. Imagine walking into a room and attempting to turn on a lamp, only to find that it won't turn on. After a quick investigation, you realize the light bulb in the lamp has burned out. The fastest way to solve the problem is not to find out why or when the bulb burned out; it is to replace the bulb. Replacing the bulb does more to solve the problem than examining the past working history of the old bulb. The solution-focused counselor attempts to change this way of thinking by helping clients see that their end result—resolution of the original problem—can be achieved without first going back to discover why the problem began.

6. *A small change is all that is necessary; a change in one part of the system can affect change in another part of the system.*

Sometimes all a client needs is positive momentum; experiencing small successes allows clients to realize that change is possible, which empowers them to strive for greater change. Once the client takes initiative to enact meaningful change, the counselor stays out of the way. Clients can achieve small successes that build on one another in a cumulative manner, reaching a state of change that can be generalized across multiple settings and situations. Small children must learn to crawl before they can walk. As parents, it is important to encourage children's initiatives to begin crawling and provide a safe environment for them to move about in. The more success they have, the more likely they will be to try new behaviors such as walking.

7. *Clients define the goal.*

The assumption is that clients know best what they want to achieve in their lives. As O'Hanlon and Weiner-Davis (2003) note, there is no "right" way to live, so health and happiness will look different for each client. Since there is no universal end result all clients are aiming for, letting the client choose the goals to pursue makes logical sense. Not all students want to attend college. As a high school guidance counselor, it is important to make sure that attending college is something the student desires before making that a goal. By having the client establish the goal to be worked toward in the counseling relationship, the client will be invested in the process of seeking change and achieving personal happiness.

8. *Rapid change or resolution of problems is possible.*

The solution-focused counselor does not see counseling as an extended process. Within the solution-focused approach, the first session is seen as the most important, as counselors and clients work collaboratively to reframe the problem and identify the clients' natural strengths. Encouraged by positive progress, clients are more likely to work on their issues outside of the counseling relationship to maintain positive momentum. The continual work toward change in and out of session helps clients see results quickly compared with other therapeutic approaches.

9. *There is no one "right" way to view things; different views may be just as valid and fit the facts just as well.*

Although there are multiple ways to approach a problem, many clients restrict their way of thinking and focus only on select ways. In this book, you learned there are many theoretical approaches to counseling and all have their own merits. Several different approaches could be successfully used with the same client. The same principle applies to how clients view their current situations. The solution-focused counselor is tasked with helping clients see that while their approach may be one way to address the problem, there might be another, more economical and beneficial way. Many clients operate under the assumption, "If at first you don't succeed, try again." This approach typically leads to the same unsatisfactory result. Trying a new approach may be more beneficial to them and lead to the results they desire. A client may report that he always resorts to problem behaviors (e.g., drinking, drug use, disorderly conduct) when he gets together with a certain group of friends. Although he might try to be strong mentally and resist the desire to follow the crowd, he inevitably gives into peer pressure and engages in behaviors he later regrets. Rather than continuing down this road, the client may be encouraged by the counselor to consider alternative solutions, such as determining where the group goes to minimize access to alcohol or drugs, or choosing a new group of friends with whom to associate.

10. *Focus on what is possible and changeable rather than what is impossible and intractable.*

Counselors should engage their clients in activities that lead to change in situations where change is possible. Since the solution-focused approach promotes small changes that build momentum, targeting problems that cannot be changed is a counterproductive activity. "If everyone else would just live by my values and expectations, I would not get so stressed every day," a client may say to you. A more productive use of time would be to help this particular client change his or her reactions to others, rather than helping him or her change how other people think or behave.

View of Human Nature

Unlike other theories, an underlying conceptualization of human nature is not included in the solution-focused approach. As Murdock (2013) noted, solution-focused therapy is a theory of practice rather than a theory of human nature. This approach operates under the principle that treatment should be future oriented and less concerned with why problems began. It embraces the philosophical principles of social constructivism and humanism, which serve as foundational tenets. Combined, these principles work to empower clients to make necessary changes in their lives in meeting their goals.

The first principle underlying the solution-focused approach is social constructivism. Social constructivism states that a singular absolute reality does not exist; reality is viewed as a subjective experience. Each individual creates his or her own reality based on individual observations and experiences. Reality represents the combination of lived experiences, shared social interactions, and cultural influences that impact an individual. We see cultures with different views of reality, and even individuals within those separate cultures with differing ideas as to what is real and not real. For example, one need only tune in to the daily news to hear how members of the different political parties represented in our government describe what our nation needs to do to prosper. Their views of the current reality are often vastly different. As a result, any attempt by a counselor to understand an individual client's perspective must consider the various cultural and societal influences in that client's life.

The second underlying principle is humanism. The solution-focused approach presents a view of individuals as good people who have the innate ability and wherewithal to solve their own problems. Furthermore, the humanistic perspective posits that people have an inherent desire to change for the better and the capacity to make that change occur

(Gladding, 2005; Walter & Peller, 2000). Problems currently experienced are seen as the result of temporary blockages that need to be overcome. In counseling, the focus becomes helping people identify their strengths and then apply them in a problem-solving manner.

Research Supporting Theoretical Constructs and Interventions

The early history of solution-focused therapy provides little empirical research on its effectiveness (Seligman & Reichenberg, 2010). De Jong and Berg (2002) offer extensive clinical support for the effectiveness of this approach. Additionally, a study by De Jong and Hopwood (1996) conducted among clients seen at the Brief Family Therapy Center over a 1-year period indicated that 45% of the clients surveyed reported having reached their goals, and another 32% reported that they had made some progress toward meeting their goals.

Since these studies, more research has focused on a systematic attempt to document the efficacy of the solution-focused approach. Studies by Stams, Dekovic, Buist, and de Vries (2006), Kim (2008), and Kim and Franklin (2009) all provide support for this approach.

Use With Diagnostic Groups, Children, and Diverse Populations

Diagnostic Groups

Results from studies examining the efficacy of the solution-focused approach in clinical settings appear to provide evidence that clients treated with this approach experience positive therapeutic benefits significantly faster than do clients treated with alternative approaches (Gingerich & Eisengart, 2000; Knekt et al., 2008; Lambert, Okiishi, Finch, & Johnson, 1998; Ziffer, Crawford, & Penney-Wietor, 2007).

Although research is limited, some success is reported in the treatment of abuse (Froeschle, Smith, & Ricard, 2007; Li, Armstrong, Chaim, Kelly, & Shenfeld, 2007; Ray & Pierce, 2008; Smock et al., 2008) and chronic and severe mental illness (Chung & Yang, 2004; Lee, Sebold, & Uken, 2003; O'Hanlon & Rowan, 2003). Researchers such as O'Hanlon and Rowan (2003) demonstrate the successful use of solution-focused therapy with clients who have long histories of treatment and suffer from chronic and severe mental illness. However, this approach should be used with great caution and may not be sufficient for people with certain illnesses or disorders, including suicidal ideation, psychosis, dissociative identity disorder, dementia, Alzheimer's disease, or eating disorders (Talmon, 1990).

Children

Solution-focused therapy is demonstrated as both child friendly (Lethem, 2002) and effective with children experiencing clinical problems, such as mental health issues (Daki & Savage, 2010; Franklin, Moore, & Hopson, 2008; Frels, Leggett, & Larocca, 2009; Kvarme, Eboh, Teijlingen, & Love, 2008), behavior problems (Cepukiene & Pakrosnis, 2010; Emanuel, 2008; Enea & Dafinoiu, 2009; Franklin et al., 2008; Shin, 2009; Vostanis, Anderson, & Window, 2006), and less clinical school-related and academic problems (Corcoran, 2006; Franklin & Hopson, 2008; Franklin, Streeter, Kim, & Tripodi, 2007; Froeschle et al., 2007; Metcalf, 1995; Murphy & Duncan, 2007; Newsome, 2004; Osenton & Chang, 1999; Webb, 1999).

Multicultural Groups

Postmodern approaches, specifically those based on the ideas from social constructionism, such as solution-focused therapy, are currently used in a variety of multicultural settings. De Shazar (1988), Berg and Miller (1992), and O'Hanlon and Weiner-Davis (2003) all conclude that solution-focused therapy is sensitive to cultural factors because the model respects each client's uniqueness and worldview. Oliver, Flamez, and McNichols (2011) found that constructivist models such as the solution-focused approach challenge dominant stories and cultures, which leads to creating room for marginalized voices and providing alternative ways of examining difficulty in clients' lives.

Research has demonstrated the effective use of this approach when employed in various ethnic populations. Berg and Miller (1992) report on its effectiveness with culturally diverse clients treated at their Brief Family Therapy Center in Milwaukee, Wisconsin. Further studies, such as those by Seidel and Hedley (2008) and Cruz and Littrell (1998), point to the utility of solution-focused therapy among Mexican adults and Hispanic American college students, respectively.

While assumptions of solution-focused approaches appear to translate across cultures, those from the nondominant cultures can address how well they translate. While solution-focused counselors use a variety of tools and techniques, much research needs to be done to examine the place this approach may have in work with other cultures (Oliver et al., 2011).

Strengths and Limitations

While the viability of using the solution-focused approach should be evaluated on an individual basis with each client, the following represent some of the more commonly cited strengths and limitations of this approach in the professional literature.

Strengths

Clinical researchers found solution-focused therapy and long-term treatment to be equally as effective in helping clients reach their goals. This approach is appealing to health management organizations because it claims to provide the briefest therapy compared with others, incurring less cost per client. Given the short-term nature of solution-focused therapy, it appears ideal for crisis counseling in which clients have an emergency and need short-term solutions or when clients are unable to attend six to eight sessions (Zuben & Townsend, 2000). In addition to time and cost savings, this approach offers many other advantages, including higher-frequency client satisfaction and improved client outcomes (Miller, 1994).

Limitations

Despite the advantages of using a solution-focused approach, some limitations are noted in the literature. Relatively little attention is focused on the client's past history of behavior and how a problem developed. Many theorists and practitioners argue that behavior and thought patterns are cyclical; thus, if we are unable to find the sources of these dysfunctional thoughts and behaviors, we will be unable to prevent them from reoccurring in the future. A second limitation is that a cogent theoretical framework for the approach does not exist. This may be a necessary evil if the solution-focused approach continues to endorse the ability to effect quick and practical change. With the change process moving rapidly for most clients, it is impossible to formulate a theory of how change works. Finally, another limitation of this approach may be the strength it purports: its ability to effect change in clients. Some counselors argue that clients present serious issues they may need time to process and discuss (e.g., trauma and abuse). Clients might not be ready to change at the current moment because they need more time to process what happened and to make peace with the issue.

THE THERAPEUTIC PROCESS AND APPLICATIONS

Therapeutic Goals

O'Hanlon and Weiner-Davis (2003) identified three goals the solution-focused counselor should aim to reach, regardless of the problem the client presents:

1. Change the *doing* of the situation that is perceived as problematic.

2. Change the *viewing* of the situation that is problematic.

3. Evoke *resources, strengths,* and *solutions* to bring to the situation perceived as problematic.

To accomplish the first goal, the solution-focused counselor works with the client to discontinue counterproductive behaviors. In other words, *if it ain't working, do something else.* To accomplish the second goal, the solution-focused counselor helps clients identify the difference between what is a problem and what is not a problem (de Shazer, 1988). The counselor provides clients with new perspectives and ways of viewing their problems by reframing them as manageable and amenable to change. Finally, to accomplish the third goal, the counselor helps clients identify the set of internal resources they already have to achieve the goals they identify in counseling. The counselor encourages, challenges, and sets up expectations for change (Gladding, 2005). Clients are then motivated to apply what they learned and use their own internal strengths to solve their problems.

To accomplish these goals, the counselor is tasked with setting the groundwork for how change will occur both during sessions and between sessions. The change process does not occur as a singular event; rather, it occurs in a series of stages that clients navigate. The following section describes the change process.

Change Process

Change plays a central role in the solution-focused approach. Clients are encouraged to make changes in their lives that will allow them to reach their goals. The counselor serves as a catalyst to initiate the change process. However, once progress is made and momentum is built, clients are encouraged to keep the success going by using their strengths and abilities. According to de Shazer (1985), the therapeutic change process occurs in a series of seven stages.

1. *Identifying a solvable complaint*

   Before a solution can be created, the problem to be solved must be established. Once a problem is identified, the counselor and client begin developing a strategy and planning interventions to make changes that will lead to achieving goals. When identifying the complaint, it is important for the counselor to stress that the problem is solvable. For example, a teenager identifying the complaint of *making a parent understand him or her better* would present a challenge because clients cannot realistically change the behavior of others. On the other hand, a more effective complaint for the teenager to focus on would be *learning to express feelings in a more appropriate manner.*

2. *Establishing goals*

   The counselor and client engage in conversations to discover ways of solving the identified complaint, which is achieved by establishing goals. These goals allow both client and counselor to see that progress is occurring. Goals do not have to be complex or difficult to obtain. In fact, it may be more beneficial to begin with small goals the client can readily achieve. By succeeding at reaching early goals, clients gain confidence in their abilities and are encouraged that change is possible.

3. *Designing interventions*

   To meet the goals established, interventions need to be designed. In the following section, some common interventions used in the solution-focused approach are described. The choice of interventions used should be a joint decision. Ensuring client buy-in at the beginning helps keep both parties focused on the task and moves the client closer to the desired change.

4. *Assigning strategic tasks*

   To promote the change desired, counselors assign strategic tasks to their clients. These tasks are intentionally designed to engage clients and promote their working toward solving their own problems. Clients are praised when they successfully complete a task and are reminded of the personal strengths and attributes they drew on to complete the task. The scope of tasks can be broadened to more closely address the presenting problem brought forth by the client.

It is important that the assigned task match the client. To help with this selection process, de Shazer (1988) identified three types of clients who might present for counseling: *visitors, complainants,* and *customers.*

Clients who are *visitors* present relatively few complaints. They fail to see themselves as part of the problem or as part of the solution. They seem to be just "along for the ride." Assigning tasks or homework to these types of clients is often unproductive because they have not yet invested in the process. A more productive approach would be to offer compliments highlighting their strengths until they are willing to begin working on making changes.

Clients who are *complainants* often have little difficulty describing their current situation and problems; however, they fail to recognize how they can be a part of the solution. They see the problems as the result of others' actions and themselves as innocent victims. In counseling sessions, these clients will placate the counselor by suggesting that a change *may* be a good idea or a certain task *might* be helpful. Since these clients still do not see the personal power they have to make their own changes, a more meaningful task to assign these clients would be one that requires them to observe their problems. By encouraging them to focus on the issues involved before jumping into action, they may find a new perspective on the problem.

Finally, clients who are *customers* describe their problems and identify their role in perpetuating these problems; they are often eager to take an active role in solving problems. These clients have reached a breaking point and are willing to do what it takes to change their current state of affairs. They are prime candidates for behavioral tasks; tasks assigned should both empower clients and effect change in their lives (Seligman & Reichenberg, 2010).

5. *Identifying changes made and emphasizing positive new behaviors*

The counselor processes with clients their experiences with the task. Questions are used to guide the discussion and encourage clients to think about the various stages of the change process they experienced. Examples of such questions include, "How did you make it happen?" "What did it feel like for you to see it change?" "How did other people react to it happening?" and "What did you learn from that happening?" The problem the client presents is referred to as "it" or "that" to emphasize that the issue is external from who the client is as a person. To keep the momentum flowing, counselors compliment clients on their successes, no matter how small.

6. *Stabilization*

The stabilization stage is a time when the change process becomes more about maintaining current gains than making radical change. This is similar to the phases a person goes through when dieting. Initially, they are invested in the process and may notice significant weight loss. Eventually, the novelty of the process wears off, and weight loss may slow to a barely noticeable amount. During these times, people may become discouraged and revert to old habits. In the counseling process, counselors work to ensure that their clients stay focused on the future and do not revert to old behaviors. Clients are engaged in a process of reworking their goals and adjusting their views of success.

7. *Termination*

Termination occurs when clients reach the level of change they desire. They no longer feel burdened by the stress of their problems and are able to live more happy and healthy lives. Because the solution-focused approach works in the here and now and does not address past issues, it is assumed that additional problems will arise in the future. Clients are reminded that the solution to their current problem came from their strengths and abilities. In the future, they should be willing to conduct a self-inventory and see what assets they might use to help them solve new problems.

Interventions

Solution-focused therapy uses a broad range of strategies and interventions. Solution talk is an important aspect of this approach. Counselors choose their words carefully to help clients identify and use the strengths and resources they already possess. The following list represents a collection of some of the more common therapeutic interventions used by solution-focused counselors (De Jong & Berg, 2001).

First-Session Task

The first-session task was designed by therapists at the Brief Family Therapy Center to focus clients' attention on future expectations of change. In the first-session task, the counselor might say to the client, "Between now and the next time we meet, I would like you to observe so you can describe to me next time what happens in your (pick one: family, life, marriage, relationship) that you want to continue to happen" (de Shazar, 1985, p. 137). This intervention allows for clients to think about and catalog the resources they already possess to help solve a problem, as well as to identify when a problem occurs and possibly gain perspective on that problem. When clients appear for the following session they are in a better place to begin exploring new solutions to the problem.

Miracle Question

One of de Shazer's most recognized contributions is his introduction of the miracle question (Berg, 2005). Inspired by Erickson's crystal ball technique, the miracle question asks clients the following: "Suppose that one night, while you were asleep there was a miracle and this problem was solved. How would you know? What would be different?" (de Shazer, 1988, p. 5).

The question is designed to allow clients to determine what they desire from the therapeutic process without contemplating the cause or source of the original problem. The miracle question serves two basic purposes: It helps clients determine the goal or solution they are searching for and allows them to see what they are currently doing that might be helping them reach that goal or impeding their progress. When clients respond to the miracle question, counselors ensure that the responses are not too vague or general. An example of a vague response would be, "I just want to feel better." To achieve the added specificity needed to build change, counselors may ask the client to reframe this response by asking, "What does better feel like?" or "Tell me what you would need to experience to know you were feeling better?" To further expand on the solutions generated from answering the miracle question, a common follow-up approach is to use a set of scaling questions, discussed in the next section.

Exercise 12.3 will help you experience the power and value of the miracle question. Remember, the main purpose is to help clients focus on the future without emphasizing the problem. By forming a clear view of how they want their lives to function, they can construct future-oriented goals.

EXERCISE 12.3

THE MIRACLE QUESTION

Directions: With a client, classmate, or colleague as your partner, invite him or her to imagine that a miracle happened overnight and when he or she awoke the following morning, the world had changed and his or her current complaint no longer existed. How would this person know that the complaint had been resolved? What would he or she think, feel, or do differently? How would others respond to this person differently? As he or she responds to the miracle question, make note of the common themes and noticeable change indicators referenced. These will serve as the solution or outcome goal with which you will codirect the counseling process toward achieving change.

Example: Suppose tonight, while you sleep, a miracle occurs. The miracle is that this problem bothering you is solved just like that. But because you are asleep, you don't know that this miracle has happened. So when you awake tomorrow, what are some of the things you notice that tell you life has suddenly gotten better? What is the first thing you notice that *you* are doing differently? Talk to me about times when this is happening now, even a little bit.

If your partner is unable to think of what he or she would be doing differently, you might ask, "What might you be saying to yourself or to someone else that is different?"

If your partner's response focuses on what *others* might be doing, you might ask, "So, when they are acting this way, what will you be doing differently?"

Scaling Questions

Scaling questions are often used to help clients quantify present feelings, attitudes, motivations, and thoughts, as well as future possibilities. Scaling questions instill a sense of change, progress, and movement. They allow counselors and clients to assess how treatment is progressing and identify when a change in direction is needed. Furthermore, scaling questions allow the client to take control of the change process and evaluate the progress made in therapy. For example, "On a scale of 1 to 10, 1 being *completely petrified* and 10 being *as confident as you could possibly be,* where would you say you are now (or where would you like to be) in relation to trying out for the school play?" Scaling questions also ask how other people would answer the question for comparison. With less verbal clients, such as children, counselors may consider using faces instead of numeric rankings (e.g., similar to those used to assess pain levels in many hospital emergency rooms).

Scaling questions can be used to gauge where a client stands with a current complaint. By knowing how the client perceives his or her current problem, the counselor can determine how to structure treatment and implement specific interventions or techniques. Exercise 12.4 can be used to place the client's current level of function, help the client focus on concrete goals, and assess the client's perspective on the severity of the problem, as well as his or her motivation to change.

EXERCISE 12.4

SCALING QUESTION

Directions: Ask a partner to imagine that there is a line drawn from 1 to 10. "The number 1 is at this end and stands for _____, and the number 10 is at this end and stands for _____."

Example: I want you to imagine a scale ranging from 1 to 10. On one side, we have the ideal situation for you. This is how you would like your life to be. We will call this 10. On the opposite side, we have 1. This represents being as far from where you want to be as possible.

Stand up, and place yourself where you are on the scale right now. Using the scale, answer the following questions:

- What number are you on the scale right now?
- How did you get to where you are now?
- What number were you on the scale when the problem was at its worst?
- Where do you want to be on this scale? Please move to that place.
- Imagine that you have done all you need to do to achieve your goal and get to that place on the scale. What would be different for you if you moved up a point (from, say, 2 to 3) on the scale?
- What is one thing that is different now that you are where you want to be on the scale?
- What was the first small step you took to get to that place? What difference did this step make?

Coping Questions

According to Clark (1997), coping questions have the potential to help victims focus on their resourcefulness and strengths rather than on the painful event. People who have been victimized do not need to relive or recount the pain; they have been living with it and are perhaps too familiar with it already. A more therapeutic approach is to foster a sense of satisfaction and accomplishment, pointing out that they survived in the face of adversity. Coping questions that attempt to identify past successes might include, "How have you managed to prevent it from getting worse?" "This sounds hard. How are you managing to cope with this to the degree that you are?" "How do you have the strength to go on?" or "What would others say are the qualities you have that keep you going?" (Davis & Osborn, 2000, p. 71). Coping questions are often used when working with people who have physical disabilities, chronic mental illness, or HIV/AIDS, or whose significant others are drug dependent because of long-term debilitating issues.

Exceptions

In solution-focused therapy, one way to find solutions is to explore those times when the problem does not occur. Exception questions minimize the pervasive nature of the issue and emphasize clients' current capacities, rather than teaching new skills. If clients are unable to identify exceptions, the counselor can ask about when a problem was less severe, less frequent, less intense, or shorter in duration (O'Hanlon & Weiner-Davis, 2003). Once the client reveals some exceptions, the counselor can ask questions to discover resources the client drew on and details of the context. Examples of questions counselors might ask include the following:

How: "How did you get that to happen?" "What strengths, talents, or qualities are you drawing on?" "It seems that you were able to successfully _____ today. How were you able to do that?"

Who: "Who was there?" "What did you do?" "How was that helpful?"

What: "What did you do differently?" "What was different for you during those times?" "What would your (best friend, teacher, etc.) say about how he or she can tell the problem is not as severe?"

When: "When was the problem a little better?" "At what times of the day and on what days?"

Where: "Where is the exception occurring?"

Exercise 12.5 focuses on the use of exception questions. As stated above, exceptions encourage exploration of those times when the problem does not occur. But what do we do with the exceptions? Identifying exceptions can meet criteria for establishing well-defined goals, and gathering meaning from a client's point of view makes exceptions more likely to endure. As you complete this exercise, ask yourself if any of the exceptions noted by your partner can be bridged as the goal of therapy?

EXERCISE 12.5

EXCEPTION QUESTIONS

Directions: With a classmate or friend as your partner, invite him or her to talk about the times when the problem you have been discussing is just a little bit better or gone for even a short time. Ask the following questions:

- "What was different for you during those times?"
- "What would your best friend say about how he or she can tell the problem is not as severe?"
- If your partner states a goal rather than a problem, consider asking, "When are you doing some of what you want to happen already?"
- If your partner makes a problem statement, consider asking, "When doesn't the problem happen?"
- When your partner mentions that things are a little better or something is different, ask, "How is that different or better?"

Fast-Forward Questions

Fast-forward questions are useful to progress treatment when clients cannot conceive of exceptions to their current situation (O'Hanlon & Weiner-Davis, 2003). Using this technique, counselors ask clients to envision themselves in the future (e.g., 6 months from now, a year from now, in 5 years) when the issue is no longer a problem. Because this exercise is speculative, clients are required to provide specific details about what this future time will look like, how they will act, and how the world around them will seem different. In describing the future, the client proceeds as if problems have already dissolved.

Using Solution-Focused Language

Solution-focused counselors use definitive language such as *when* and *will,* instead of tentative language such as *could* or *if,* to imply that change will occur and work will be successful. Slight shifts in language help promote an internal rather than external locus of control in clients and help them become accountable to the change process. Additionally, Corcoran (2005) noted that counselors should give clients more control in the direction counseling will take. She suggested using questions such as, "What would you like to see happen as a result of our talking?" instead of "How can I help you?" In the former instance, the client replies by describing what solutions are needed or steps must be taken to achieve success; in the latter, the client allows the counselor to determine what should be done in counseling. Another language shift solution-focused counselors often use is in how they refer to the client's presenting complaint. Solution-focused counselors intentionally avoid using the word *problem,* instead using words such as *concern* and *issue* to help the client see the presenting complaint as something that can be resolved.

Using the Client's Language

O'Hanlon and Weiner-Davis (2003) stated that a true principle from the work of Erickson and others is that counselors should try to mirror the language clients use in session. Using the words clients use as a means of joining with them is an effective way to build rapport. The assumption underlying this intervention is that clients feel that the counselor better understands, appreciates, and identifies with their subjective experience. Corcoran (2005) also advised counselors to refrain from using professional jargon. In solution-focused therapy, clients are seen as the experts of their lives, and professional jargon emphasizes the counselor's expert role over the client's. For example, if a counselor has a client who describes feeling "blue" or "down in the dumps," then the counselor should use these words rather than the more clinically appropriate term *depression.*

Relationship Questions

Often, people become stuck in a problem and are unable to think of alternatives to their current functioning. Relationship questions, derived from the family systems therapy intervention of circular questioning, allow clients to view themselves from the perspective of another (De Jong & Berg, 2001). A question such as, "What would your closest friend say needs to happen in our work together to know that our time has been successful?" allows the client to consider other possibilities. By assuming an outsider role, the client is free to view the complaint for what it really is and not simply how it impacts him or her at present. For many people, it is often easier to see where others may need to change to better their situations.

Compliments

When counselors hear a client doing something positive or solution promoting, they should make every attempt to highlight the positive trend (O'Hanlon & Weiner-Davis, 2003). In their work on solution-focused therapy, De Jong and Berg (2002) discussed a form of complimenting called "indirect complimenting," in which positive behaviors are implied. Rather than directly telling clients what they did well, counselors lead clients to describe what they did well. An example of a question that could be asked to indirectly compliment a client is, "How were you able to figure that out?" Clients answer the question by sharing what they did to solve the issue. Not only do they receive positive affirmation for doing something productive, but they also benefit from knowing they recognized the productive steps they took.

Normalizing

Another technique counselors may use is normalizing, where the counselor tries to normalize the complaint for the client, framing it as a common issue (De Jong & Berg, 2002). The value of normalizing comes from the cognitive shift it produces in clients as the problem no longer appears unmanageable. Clients begin to believe that if others have dealt with the same issue and succeeded, they can succeed as well. When this technique is applied inappropriately or at a time when the client is not ready, the counselor may be perceived as trivializing the client's struggles. Sufficient rapport with the client must be developed before such an intervention can be used effectively. Counselors should gain a clear sense of what is normal for their clients and how the current issue fits in that definition.

Assessment Strategies

Assessment assumes a different role in the solution-focused approach compared with other psychotherapeutic approaches you have read about in this book. The client creates the solution or end goal. The client determines his or her success and how he or she feels about the issue presented at the beginning of counseling. Throughout the process, the counselor and client collaboratively work to assess how well they are doing in changing the current situation. Questions are the primary assessment tool used by the solution-focused counselor. Scaling questions and coping questions, for example, can assess where clients currently stand with their situation and where they hope to be in the future. Questions also allow for the assessment of progress and what approaches were beneficial and not.

Focus and Intentionality

The emphasis in the solution-focused approach is on helping clients find solutions to presenting complaints that can be maintained over time using strengths and abilities they already possess. Initial sessions help clients identify the problem they want to work on. If several complaints are noted, they can be ranked by priority and individually addressed. When several complaints are addressed simultaneously, the focus is lost and clients can become overwhelmed. To assist in determining the course of therapy, the counselor engages the client in a process of identifying the presenting problem. Additional questions may include the following:

- When does it occur?
- What is different during problem times than during other times?
- What are the exceptions to the rule (when is the problem not a problem)?

Once the primary complaint is identified, a solution can be discovered. The miracle question is a great way to establish a concrete picture of what the client would like the future to look like and, thus, the solution to the current problem. During the working stages of therapy, the focus is on helping the client make progress toward his or her self-identified solution. Scaling questions can ascertain how much progress the client is making. Counselors can keep clients motivated by discussing exceptions to the rule, normalizing the problem, and praising small gains. The key is to remain positive and solution focused.

As therapy terminates, the focus is on helping clients understand how the skills and abilities they used to solve their current problems are transferable to other problems. The counselor should remind clients of a fundamental tenet of solution-focused therapy: Change is inevitable. Communicating to clients that changes will occur again in the future is essential because it helps them normalize and prepare for the day when a new problem will occur. Despite having the innate tools needed to create their solutions, clients are encouraged to seek professional help when needed.

Y-CHUN THROUGH A SOLUTION-FOCUSED LENS

The two guiding principles of solution-focused therapy are as follows: (1) Individuals possess the innate ability and wherewithal to solve their own problems, and (2) all people construct realities from subjective life experiences. We can apply a future-oriented approach to the case of Y-Chun (see Chapter 3 for an introduction to this case). The details of the case paint a picture of a hardworking, biracial woman who has confronted many life challenges. Y-Chun sought counseling on the advice of her medical doctor, who could not find physiological explanations for her symptoms of nausea, headaches, sleeping problems, irritability, and always feeling "on edge." As you review the details of her concern, note that she reports feeling overwhelmed, constantly tired, and a lack of motivation; in addition, she states that she is feeling "empty" and crying a lot due to worries about the future. While Y-Chun provides information about her history, including being bullied as a child and raped as a teenager, the solution-focused counselor will help her focus on her strengths. This process progresses through several stages, which we will examine in some detail.

Stage 1: Joining With the Client

In order for solution-focused therapy to be successful, the counselor and client must establish a strong relationship.

Counselor: Thank you for coming in today, Y-Chun. I have been thinking about our first session and want to tell you again how courageous it was for you to make that appointment and share so much with me. Have you thought about what we talked about last week?

Y-Chun: You know, I have. When I left, I thought about what you said about my being "courageous" to come to counseling. I never thought about it that way. I was just looking for ways to fix my problems. "Courageous" kind of stuck with me. I don't think anyone has ever called me that before.

Counselor: Tell me what "courageous" means to you.

Y-Chun: Well, I am so used to making bad decisions and then feeling guilty. I never thought about making a good decision. (Smiles.)

Counselor: We will talk more about this, Y-Chun. From the little I know about you, you have made some very good decisions.

Y-Chun: And very bad ones!

Counselor: But isn't this true for most people? I don't know anyone who hasn't made some bad decisions. It is what we do next that makes all the difference.

Y-Chun: Maybe, but I've disappointed many people, including myself. How can I change how I feel about that?

Counselor: Let me ask you, what needs to happen today so that when you leave you'll think, "This was a good session"?

Y-Chun: Hmmmm . . . if I could just find something to hold on to, something that might help me feel not so guilty and worthless.

Counselor: We will work on discussing things you have done well and see if we can make a plan to continue along that path.

The counselor has set the tone with Y-Chun that all her decisions have not been bad, and has begun to instill hope in this downtrodden client.

Stage 2: Describing the Problem

The next step in solution-focused therapy is helping the client articulate what is happening in her life to help her realize that possibilities exist for future change.

The miracle question: This opens up a range of future possibilities by allowing the client to imagine a life not full of problems. We want the client to identify possibilities rather than problems.

Counselor:	Y-Chun, I want you to suppose that one night while you are asleep, a miracle happens and one of your problems is solved. Because you were asleep, you don't know the miracle happened. So when you wake up, how will you know a miracle happened? What will be different?
Y-Chun:	Gosh! I have no idea!
Counselor:	Think about your morning. What might be different if, during the night, a miracle occurred?
Y-Chun:	(Laughing) Well, my kids would be up and ready for school, my mom and dad would be eating breakfast, and I would come out to find coffee already made. That *would* be a miracle!
Counselor:	That sounds like a nice way to start the day. We'll talk more about how you can help make this happen.
Y-Chun:	I already have one idea.
Counselor:	What's that?
Y-Chun:	Instead of me yelling at the kids to get up, I could get them each an alarm clock. I'm so used to being the one to get things going in the morning that I just rush around and yell. Even I don't like myself when I'm like that.
Counselor:	So you are already seeing small ways that you can begin to make a few changes. What might happen then?
Y-Chun:	If I wasn't yelling, everybody might be a little bit nicer to each other.
Counselor:	If that were to happen, what would that look like?
Y-Chun:	Wow! Maybe we could all begin to appreciate each other. I spend so much time telling everyone what is wrong that I'm sure they dread when I walk into the room.
Counselor:	So are you willing to try a slightly different approach?
Y-Chun:	Can't hurt, right?

Exception questions: A client's problems do not occur all the time, and exception questioning helps Y-Chun focus on times when the problem did not exist, allowing her to become motivated to work toward solutions in the future.

Counselor:	Y-Chun, you mentioned that your parents are disappointed in you and never encourage you. Is that right?
Y-Chun:	Totally! Not only them, but my older sister and brothers, too. They hate me! They say I was spoiled. If they only knew!
Counselor:	Well, I know it is hard living with your parents. You mentioned they always act like they are the parents to your kids, and that makes you angry and frustrated.

Y-Chun:	Yes, they do that! Even when I try to be a good parent, they jump in with some criticism, like, "David can't watch television, because he has a test tomorrow," or they argue with me about what school is right for my daughter who is handicapped. No matter what I do, they criticize me!
Counselor:	Tell me, is there ever a time when your parents do not criticize you?
Y-Chun:	Ummmm. Yes, they love it that I am in college and I get really good grades. They even brag about that to my brothers and sister.
Counselor:	So they praise you for this?
Y-Chun:	Yes, but I feel guilty because me and my kids are basically living off them. The little money I make I have to spend on gas, school supplies for all of us, and a few things for the kids. Sometimes my mom and dad, especially my dad, says we are not grateful for what we have.
Counselor:	Does this come up every day? How often?
Y-Chun:	Well, not that much, really. I just feel guilty because I know they work hard and don't earn much for themselves, so I feel like I am taking too much from them.
Counselor:	I'm wondering if they mind so much or if it is your guilt that is bothering you. What would have to happen for you to feel less guilty? Or for them to stop saying you don't appreciate them?
Y-Chun:	They don't say it that much, but I can feel it! I suppose I could say "thanks" once in a while, or the kids and I could do something nice for them.
Counselor:	Like what?
Y-Chun:	Let's see . . . my daughter loves to draw. She could make a card. My son loves to fix pizza. We could surprise them with dinner one night as a "thanks for having us here all the time" kind of thing.
Counselor:	How do you think your parents might react?
Y-Chun:	They'd be shocked! They would wonder what I was "up to." Just kidding.
Counselor:	What would happen to your guilt feelings if you did something like this?
Y-Chun:	I suppose I would not have guilt feelings over this, but how does that help me with other things?
Counselor:	How might that help? What would you be doing differently?
Y-Chun:	I'd be showing my parents that we *do* appreciate them, and for sure that would help them and me.
Counselor:	I want to go back to something you said earlier about your parents being proud of the fact that you are going to college. Tell me about that.

Y-Chun:	They never got to go to college and always pushed me to do well in school. I tried, but I was bullied by kids for the way I looked, and made fun of. It took all the joy out of school, so I gave up.
Counselor:	But now you are back in college and doing well.
Y-Chun:	Yes, what else could I do? I have to try to make a better life for all of us. I hope to one day get a good job and help my parents, too.
Counselor:	Do you think that your parents' belief in your abilities to succeed in school had anything to do with your going to college?
Y-Chun:	Wow! It sure did, but I never thought about that. All I think about is how they tell me what to do. Maybe it is just their way. They grew up so poor that they want my life to be better.

Scaling questions: Scaling provides an opportunity for Y-Chun to self-assess the problem and identify self-induced solutions.

Counselor:	Y-Chun, let's talk a bit about your communication with your dad.
Y-Chun:	You mean, how he never treats me like an adult and expects me to conform to his old-fashioned stereotypes about women?
Counselor:	You seem upset and frustrated about this and have mentioned that this bothers you a great deal.
Y-Chun:	Yes, I feel his disapproval of everything, like even the way my daughter and I dress. He thinks all women should wear dresses all the time! He is way out of touch!
Counselor:	Let's look at it this way: Think of a scale from 1 to 10, with 1 meaning that you have no control over your anger/frustration with your dad and 10 meaning that you have complete control over your feelings of anger. Where would you place yourself right now on that scale?
Y-Chun:	One, no question!
Counselor:	Now, think about what it would take for you to move up that scale, even a little bit?
Y-Chun:	Hmmm. I'd have to think about that. I know that I react quickly and violently to things he says. Maybe I could find a way to "simmer down" a little.
Counselor:	What would that look like?
Y-Chun:	When he says any little thing, I argue with him. It doesn't even matter what he is talking about. I talk back. I could probably keep my mouth shut once in a while and just let him vent.
Counselor:	How would that help your angry feelings?

Y-Chun:	When I talk back to him, he gets louder, then I get louder, and pretty soon we are screaming at each other and saying awful things.
Counselor:	So if you just said nothing, kind of absorbed his words on some issue or another, do you think your anger would go down?
Y-Chun:	I do! I think I could move myself pretty far down that scale to a 3 or a 4 just by not talking back! I think I'll try that. I want to see how my dad reacts to that!

Stage 3: Goal Setting and Future Orientation

The client should keep goals concrete and attainable. Each of the counselor's following questions can be framed with a future focus as Y-Chun takes ownership and learns that she possesses solutions to her problems.

- How will you know if things are getting better?
- How will your mom and dad know things are getting better? Your kids?
- How will you know that you are feeling less stressed?
- How will your family members know that you are doing better?
- How will you be able to show your children, mom, and dad that you really do care for them?
- How will you feel when you complete your college degree?
- What would a healthy, stable, intimate relationship look like for you?

Stage 4: Break and Ending the Session

Solution-focused therapists often take a short break (about 5–10 minutes) to allow time to reflect on the session and provide the client with a summary, which includes feedback that compliments the client on positive behaviors, affirms the client's progress, and suggests tasks the client can complete before the next session. Self-monitoring and reporting back to the counselor will help the client pay attention to changes. By giving the client tasks, the client is required to do something to work toward positive solutions; this frames the solution as something the client can control.

KEYSTONES

- Solution-focused therapy, developed by Steve de Shazer and others, is a treatment model emphasizing client strengths, resources, and abilities.
- Noted psychiatrist and hypnotist Milton Erickson, as well as the philosophies of social constructivism and strategic family therapy, influenced solution-focused therapy.
- Rather than focusing on the past and history of the problem, this approach focuses on the present and the client's strengths.
- Progress is measured by results, not by the number of sessions a client attends.

- Collaboration between the client and counselor is essential; three types of client relationships—customer, complainant, and visitor—may develop.
- Strategies such as scaling questions, use of exceptions, the miracle question, and solution-focused language build clients' awareness of strengths and empower them to view themselves as capable.

REFLECTIONS FROM THE CONTRIBUTOR'S CHAIR

The solution-focused method represents an excellent way to approach counseling a client, because it empowers clients to be the change they seek from counseling. In this approach, counselors form collaborative relationships with their clients that allow them to identify problems and co-construct solutions that have the potential to lead to meaningful change and goal resolution. Whether you are working in schools, agencies, or private practice, the solution-focused approach is a great way to help your clients achieve success quickly and effectively. Because clients already possess the strengths necessary to succeed, they simply need someone to identify and help them redirect their strengths into goal-directed avenues. The solution-focused approach is seen as a preferred method among managed-care organizations, agency clinical directors, and school administrators. As the counseling field continually develops and new treatment modalities are implemented, the solution-focused approach will continue to be successful as a straightforward method that resonates with clients and produces results.

ADDITIONAL RESOURCES

Books

De Jong, P., & Berg, I. K. (2012). *Interviewing for solutions*. Belmont, CA: Brooks/Cole.

This book provides a solution-oriented approach to interviewing and providing feedback to clients. Evidence-based practices and working with clients in crisis are also addressed.

de Shazer, S., & Dolan, Y. (with Korman, H., Trepper, T., McCollum, E., & Berg, I. K.). (2007). *More than miracles: The state of the art of solution-focused brief therapy*. Binghamton, NY: Haworth Press.

This book is the final work of Steve de Shazer and Insoo Kim Berg, the original developers of solution-focused brief therapy. It provides new advances for this approach, as well as real-life case examples.

Metcalf, L. (2008). *Counseling toward solutions: A practical solution-focused program for working with students, teachers, and parents*. San Francisco: Jossey-Bass.

This book utilizes exercises and tasks written for teachers, administrators, and school counselors who would like to approach school populations with a more positive, solution-focused method.

Nelson, T. (2005). *Education and training in solution-focused brief therapy*. New York: Haworth Press.

A collection of articles and exercises that focus on teaching and training solution-focused brief therapy.

Handouts

Coffen, R. (n.d.). *Do one thing different*. Retrieved from http://www.andrews.edu/ ~ coffen/Do%20 one%20thing%20different.pdf

de Shazer, S. (2000). *The miracle question*. Retrieved from http://www.netzwerk-ost.at/publikationen/ pdf/miraclequestion.pdf

Pennsylvania Child Welfare Training Program. (n.d.). *Miracle questions*. Retrieved from http://www. pacwcbt.pitt.edu/curriculum/207%20SoltoEngFmlinFGDMProc/HO/HO6%20MirclQuest.pdf

Trepper, T. S., McCollum, E. E., De Jong, P., Korman, H., Gingerich, W., & Franklin, C. (n.d.). *Solution-focused therapy treatment manual for working with individuals*. Retrieved from http://www.sfbta. org/Research.pdf

Training in Solution-Focused Therapy

Bill O'Hanlon (http://www.billohanlon.com/)

The Brief Family Therapy Center (http://www.psyctc.org/mirrors/sft/bftc.htm)

Videos

Berg, I. K. (n.d.). *Solution-focused therapy* [Video]. Retrieved from http://www.psychotherapy.net/video/ insoo-kim-berg-solution-focused-therapy

This video demonstrates the solution-focused approach as applied by Insoo Kim Berg in a clinical session.

Associations

Brief Therapy Institute of Sydney (http://www.brieftherapysydney.com.au/btis/links.html)

Solution-Focused Brief Therapy Association (http://www.sfbta.org/)

REFERENCES

Berg, I. K. (2005). The state of miracles in relationships. *Journal of Family Psychotherapy, 16,* 115–118. doi:10.1300/J085v16n01_11

Berg, I. K., & Miller, S. D. (1992). Working with Asian American clients: One person at a time. *Families in Society, 73*(6), 356–363.

Cepukiene, V., & Pakrosnis, R. (2010). The outcome of solution-focused brief therapy among foster care adolescents: The changes of behavior and perceived somatic and cognitive difficulties. *Children and Youth Services Review, 33,* 791–797. doi:10.1016/j.childyouth.2010.11.027

Chung, S. A., & Yang, S. (2004). The effects of solution-focused group counseling program for the families with schizophrenic patients. *Taehan Kanho Hakhoe Chi* [*Journal of the Korean Academy of Nursing*], *34,* 1155–1163.

Clark, M. (1997). Interviewing for solutions. *Corrections Today, 59*(3), 98–102.

Corcoran, J. (2005). *Building strengths and skills.* New York: Oxford University Press.

Corcoran, J. (2006). A comparison group study of solution-focused therapy versus "treatment-as-usual" for behavior problems in children. *Journal of Social Service Research, 33,* 69–81. doi:10.1300/J079v33n01_07

Cruz, J., & Littrell, J. (1998). Brief counseling with Hispanic American college students. *Journal of Multicultural Counseling and Development, 26*(4), 227–239. doi:10.1002/j.2161-1912.1998.tb00201.x

Daki, J., & Savage, R. (2010). Solution-focused brief therapy: Impacts on academic and emotional difficulties. *Journal of Educational Research, 103,* 309–326. doi:10.1080/00220670903383127

Davis, T., & Osborn, C. (2000). *The solution-focused school counselor: Shaping professional practice.* Ann Arbor, MI: Edwards Brothers.

De Jong, P., & Berg, I. K. (2001). Co-constructing cooperation with mandated clients. *Social Work, 46*(4), 361–374.

De Jong, P., & Berg, I. K. (2002). *Interviewing for solutions* (2nd ed.). Pacific Grove, CA: Brooks/Cole.

De Jong, P., & Hopwood, L. E. (1996). Outcome research on treatment conducted at the Brief Family Therapy Center, 1992–1993. In S. D. Miller, M. A. Hubble, & B. L. Duncan (Eds.), *Handbook of solution-focused brief therapy* (pp. 272–298). San Francisco: Jossey-Bass.

de Shazer, S. (1982). *Patterns of brief therapy.* New York: Guilford Press.

de Shazer, S. (1985). *Keys to solutions in brief therapy.* New York: W. W. Norton.

de Shazer, S. (1988). *Clues: Investigating solutions in brief therapy.* New York: W. W. Norton.

de Shazer, S., Berg, I., Lipchik, E., Nunnally, E., Molnar, A., Gingerich, W., et al. (1986). Brief therapy: Focused solution development. *Family Process, 25,* 207–222.

Emanuel, C. (2008). Anger management. *Solution Research, 1*(1), 3–10.

Enea, V., & Dafinoiu, I. (2009). Motivational/solution-focused intervention for reducing school truancy among adolescents. *Journal of Cognitive and Behavioral Psychotherapies, 9*(2), 185–198.

Franklin, C., & Hopson, L. (2008). Involuntary clients in public schools: Solution-focused interventions. In R. H. Rooney (Ed.), *Strategies for work with involuntary clients* (2nd ed.). New York: Columbia University Press.

Franklin, C., Moore, K., & Hopson, L. (2008). Effectiveness of solution-focused brief therapy in a school setting. *Children and Schools, 30*(1), 15–26. doi:10.1093/cs/30.1.15

Franklin, C., Streeter, C. L., Kim, J. S., & Tripodi, S. J. (2007). The effectiveness of a solution-focused, public alternative school for dropout prevention and retrieval. *Children and Schools, 29*(3), 133–144. doi:10.1093/cs/29.3.133

Frels, R., Leggett, E. S., & Larocca, P. (2009). Creativity and solution-focused counseling for a child with chronic illness. *Journal of Creativity in Mental Health, 4*(4), 308–319. doi:10.1080/15401380903372646

Froeschle, J. G., Smith, R. L., & Ricard, R. (2007). The efficacy of a systemic substance abuse program for adolescent females. *Professional School Counseling, 10,* 498–505.

Gingerich, W. J., & Eisengart, S. (2000). Solution-focused brief therapy: A review of the outcome research. *Family Process, 39,* 477–498. doi:10.1111/j.1545-5300.2000.39408.x

Gladding, S. T. (2005). *Counseling theories: Essential concepts and applications.* Upper Saddle River, NJ: Pearson.

Jones-Smith, E. (2012). *Theories of counseling and psychotherapy: An integrative approach.* Thousand Oaks, CA: Sage.

Kim, J. S. (2008). Examining the effectiveness of solution-focused brief therapy: A meta-analysis. *Research on Social Work Practice, 18*(2), 107–116. doi:10.1177/1049731507307807

Kim, J. S., & Franklin, C. (2009). Solution-focused brief therapy in schools: A review of the outcome literature. *Children and Youth Services Review, 31,* 464–470. doi:10.1016/j.childyouth.2008.10.002

Knekt, P., Lindfors, O., Härkänen, T., Välikoski, M., Virtala, E., Laaksonen, M. A., et al. (2008). Randomized trial on the effectiveness of long- and short-term psychodynamic psychotherapy and solution-focused therapy on psychiatric symptoms during a 3-year follow-up. *Psychiatric Medicine, 38,* 689–703.

Kvarme, L., Eboh, W., Teijlingen, E. V. D., & Love, J. (2008). Use of solution-focused brief therapy in bullying. *British Journal of School Nursing, 3*(7), 346–348.

Lambert, M. J., Okiishi, J. C., Finch, A. E., & Johnson, L. D. (1998). Outcome assessment: From conceptualization to implementation. *Professional Psychology: Research and Practice, 29*(1), 63–70. doi:10.1037/0735-7028.29.1.63

Lee, M. Y., Sebold, J., & Uken, A. (2003). *Solution-focused treatment of domestic violence offenders: Accountability for change.* Oxford, UK: Oxford University Press.

Lethem, J. (2002). Brief solution focused therapy. *Child and Adolescent Mental Health, 7*(4), 189–192. doi:10.1111/1475-3588.00033

Li, S., Armstrong, M. S., Chaim, G., Kelly, C., & Shenfeld, J. (2007). Group and individual treatment for substance abuse clients: A pilot study. *American Journal of Family Therapy, 35,* 221–233.

Lindforss, L., & Magnusson, D. (1997). Solution-focused therapy in prison. *Contemporary Family Therapy, 19*(1), 89–103. doi: 10.1023/A:1026114501186

Mental Research Institute. (2008). About us. Retrieved from http://www.mri.org/about_us.html

Metcalf, L. (1995). *Counseling toward solutions: A practical solution-focused program for working with students, teachers, and parents.* San Francisco: Jossey-Bass.

Miller, S. (1994). The solution conspiracy: A mystery in three installments. *Journal of Systemic Techniques, 13,* 18–37.

Murdock, N. L. (2013). *Theories of counseling and psychotherapy: A case approach* (3rd ed.). Upper Saddle River, NJ: Pearson.

Murphy, J. J., & Duncan, B. S. (2007). *Brief interventions for school problems* (2nd ed.). New York: Guilford Press.

Newsome, S. (2004). Solution-focused brief therapy (SFBT) groupwork with at-risk junior high school students: Enhancing the bottom-line. *Research on Social Work Practice, 14,* 336 – 343.

O'Hanlon, B., & Rowan, T. (2003). *Solution-oriented therapy for chronic and severe mental illness* (2nd ed.). New York: W. W. Norton.

O'Hanlon, W. H., & Weiner-Davis, M. (2003). *In search of solutions: A new direction in psychotherapy.* New York: Guilford Press.

Oliver, M., Flamez, B., & McNichols, C. (2011). Postmodern applications within Latino/a cultures. *Journal of Professional Counseling: Practice, Theory, and Research, 38*(3), 33–48.

Osenton, T., & Chang, J. (1999). Solution-oriented classroom management: Application with young children. *Journal of Systemic Therapies, 18*(2), 65–76.

Ray, R., & Pierce, K. (2008). Solution-focused group therapy for Level 1 substance users. In E. Kaufman & P. Kaufman (Eds.), *Journal of marital and family therapy, 34,* 107–120.

Remley, T. P., & Herlihy, B. (2009). *Ethical, legal, and professional issues in counseling* (3rd ed.). Upper Saddle River, NJ: Pearson Merrill Prentice Hall.

Seidel, A., & Hedley, D. (2008). The use of solution-focused brief therapy with older adults in Mexico: A preliminary study. *American Journal of Family Therapy, 36*(3), 242–252. doi:10.1080/01926180701291279

Seligman, L., & Reichenberg, L. W. (2010). *Theories of counseling and psychotherapy: Systems, strategies, and skills* (3rd ed.). Upper Saddle River, NJ: Pearson.

Shin, S.-K. (2009). Effects of a solution-focused program on the reduction of aggressiveness and the improvement of social readjustment for Korean youth probationers. *Journal of Social Service Research, 35*(3), 274–284.

Sklare, G. B. (2005). *Brief counseling that works: A solution-focused approach for school counselors and administrators.* Thousand Oaks, CA: Corwin Press & American School Counselor Association.

Smock, S. A., Trepper, T. S., Wetchler, J. L., McCollum, E. E., Ray, R., & Pierce, K. (2008). Solution-focused group therapy for Level 1 substance abusers. *Journal of Marital and Family Therapy, 34*(1), 107–120. doi:10.1111/j.1752-0606.2008.00056.x

Stams, G. J., Dekovic, M., Buist, K., & de Vries, L. (2006). Effectiviteit van oplossingsgerichte korte therapie: Een meta-analyse [Efficacy of solution-focused brief therapy: A meta-analysis]. *Gedragstherapie [Behavior Therapy], 39*(2), 81–94.

Talmon, M. (1990). *Single session therapy: Maximizing the effect of the first (and often only) therapeutic encounter*. San Francisco: Jossey-Bass.

Trepper, T. S., Treyger, S., Yalowitz, J., & Ford, J. (2010). Solution-focused brief therapy for the treatment of sexual disorders. *Journal of Family Psychotherapy, 21,* 34–53. doi:10.1080/08975350902970360

Visser, C. (2008). *A brief history of the solution-focused approach.* Retrieved from http://articlescoert-visser.blogspot.com/2008/02/brief-history-of-solution-focused.html

Vostanis, P., Anderson, L., & Window, S. (2006). Evaluation of a family support service: Short-term outcome. *Clinical Child Psychology and Psychiatry, 11*(4), 513–528. doi:10.1177/1359104506067874

Walter, J. L., & Peller, J. E. (2000). *Recreating brief therapy.* New York: W. W. Norton.

Webb, W. H. (1999). *Solutioning: Solution-focused interventions for counselors.* Philadelphia: Accelerated Press.

Ziffer, J., Crawford, E., & Penney-Wietor, J. (2007). The boomerang bunch: A school-based multifamily group approach for students and their families recovering from parental separation and divorce. *Journal for Specialists in Group Work, 32*(2), 154–164. doi:10.1080/01933920701227141

Zuben, C., & Townsend, S. (2000). Readers react to Stalker, Levene, and Coady's solution-focused brief therapy [Letter to the editor]. *Families in Society, 81*(2), 219–220.

Relational-Cultural Theory in the Context of Feminism

Kristi B. Cannon, Jason Patton, and Stacee L. Reicherzer

I want to feel closer to my partner, but I just don't. I find myself arguing, shutting down, and even avoiding interactions with him. Then, I think to myself, it's just me—no wonder things are so bad between us. I wouldn't want to talk to me either.

The client above is responding in a way known as the *central relational paradox,* a primary theme in relational-cultural theory (RCT): The client so yearns for connection that she actively keeps parts of herself hidden away or out of connection with her partner for fear of rejection. Within this chapter, you will become further acquainted with how the central relational paradox plays out in relational interactions and how we all strive toward connection with others—this is from whence true growth and change emanate.

The current chapter outlines the origins of RCT as an outgrowth of larger feminist theory and will explore the underpinnings of our relationality. Readers should hold these goals in reading the chapter:

1. Understand the history of feminist theory and the development of RCT as derived from feminist thought

2. Explain key RCT concepts and how they differ from traditional psychological theory

3. Conceptualize connections and disconnections in your own life and how to cocreate healthier relational functioning

4. Evaluate how your own power and privilege impact your worldview and interactions

5. Understand the application of RCT in a therapeutic setting

Profiles of Main Figures

Jean Baker Miller: A psychiatrist whose relational model evolved into RCT, which conceptualized the centrality of growth-fostering connections in women's development. Her best-known works include *Toward a New Psychology of Women* (Miller, 1976) and a collection of coauthored RCT working papers, *Women's Growth in Connection: Writings From the Stone Center* (Jordan, Kaplan, Miller, Stiver, & Surrey, 1991).

Judith Jordan: A psychologist and original RCT scholar whose efforts have been to reexamine developmental psychology and clinical impacts for women. Jordan is best known for *Relational-Cultural Therapy* (Jordan, 2009) and *Women's Growth in Connection* (Jordan et al., 1991), along with her edited texts *Women's Growth in Diversity* (Jordan, 1997) and *The Complexity of Connection* (Jordan, Walker, & Hartling, 2004).

Irene Stiver: As a psychologist and cofounder of RCT, Stiver's contributions largely came from her desire to reframe models of clinical treatment of women. Her primary works include the coauthored *Women's Growth in Connection* (Jordan et al., 1991) and *The Healing Connection: How Women Form Relationships in Therapy and in Life* (Miller & Stiver, 1997).

Janet Surrey: A psychologist and cofounder of RCT, whose work emphasizes mother–daughter relationships and gender issues. Her best-known works include the coauthored *Women's Growth in Connection* (Jordan et al., 1991) and coedited *Mothering Against the Odds: Diverse Voices of Contemporary Mothers* (Garcia Coll, Surrey, & Weingarten, 1998).

Maureen Walker: A psychologist whose work has served to advance RCT in the areas of race, power, culture, and the concept of *controlling images*. Her primary works include *How Connections Heal* (Walker & Rosen, 2004) and *The Complexity of Connection* (Jordan et al., 2004).

INTRODUCTION

Feminist counseling practice is rooted in the larger sociopolitical and cultural concerns of equality and justice (Gilligan, 1982; O'Mahoney & Donnelly, 2010). To this end, feminist counselors are primarily concerned with addressing issues of social inequity, trauma, and humiliation experienced by women and men in both clinical settings and the relational and societal contexts in which these occur. Feminist theory is a broad, social justice–oriented model that guides feminist counseling practice. To understand how RCT is rooted in feminist counseling practice, it is necessary to examine the evolution of feminism from a series of women's movements that occurred primarily during the 19th and 20th centuries to the current multifaceted and culturally dynamic force it is today.

Historical Background

The feminist movement in the United States is often interpreted (Budgeon, 2011; Gillis, Howie, & Munford, 2007; Gilmore, 2007; Heywood & Drake, 1997) as the series of historical actions clustered around what are referred to as first-wave feminism, including the efforts of Susan B. Anthony and the suffragettes in both the United States and Great Britain; second-wave feminism, which arose and became most visible during the 1960s with Betty Friedan's (1963) *The Feminine Mystique* and the women's rights movement in the United States; and post-1980s third-wave feminism, which has included efforts by feminists of color and different spiritual/religious backgrounds in the United States, Africa, and Asia; transgender and gender-queer feminists; and eco-feminists. This chronological interpretation is more reflective of historical biases in recognizing the interests of middle-class White women in seeking voting rights (first wave) and, later, freedom to work outside the home and enjoy professional mobility (second wave) over the needs and struggles of women of color and working-class women—struggles largely unannounced and unchampioned, and occurring well prior to the "third wave." This biasing of a feminist agenda was profound in the United States (Collins, 2009; Davis, 1983; hooks, 2000) and in physically and psychologically colonized world regions, such as Southern Asia (Spivak, 1988) and Latin America (Anzaldúa, 2007; Moschkovich, 1983).

Whereas feminists in positions of relative power (White, heterosexual, able-bodied, economically privileged) have largely held the privilege of defining feminism and its agenda, it is more constructive to approach feminist theory and its practice in counseling from the confluence of multiple struggles of women of color (Davis, 1983, 1999; hooks, 2000); the lesbian, gay, bisexual, and transgender community (Lorde, 2007; Smith, 2000); working-class women (hooks, 2000); Third-World women (Anzaldúa, 2007); and women described by all these characteristics (Moraga & Anzaldúa, 1983). To that end, we must consider that even women who lacked the sociocultural, economic, or political mobility to be seen as part of the women's movement were, nevertheless, present in efforts to liberate others from daily lived experiences of pain and trauma.

Early feminist developments in mental health discourse began when Karen Horney (1993), one of the first female psychoanalysts, renounced Freud's theory of the Oedipal complex as particularly denigrating to women and therefore inaccurate. During the 1970s, some of the most revolutionary advancements for feminist counseling occurred. Of note were three significant developments: Carol Gilligan (1982) began her research of women's moral development, which presented the emphasis on relationships and an ethic of caring as an area in which women were different from men, not weaker, as had been identified in the dominant psychological literature at the time. During this same period, Jean Baker Miller and a team of women colleagues began asking what a psychology that highlighted women's focus on relationships would entail, and how it would be used to address issues better than the dominant mental health paradigms were (Jordan et al., 1991). Finally, Judith

Herman and Lisa Hirschman, working with women in poverty, refuted the overwhelming body of psychological literature that interpreted incest in families as very rare and also advocated alongside veterans for the acceptance of the posttraumatic stress disorder diagnosis by the American Psychiatric Association (Robb, 2007).

In the years that followed the establishment of feminist theory in counseling practice, many women's voices joined to enrich the conversation with discussions of cultural complexity in experiences of racism, homonegativity, and other forms of marginalization. One of the most noteworthy is Patricia Hill-Collins's dual concept of the matrix of domination and intersecting oppressions. As Collins (2008) explained:

> Intersectionality refers to particular forms of intersecting oppressions, for example, intersections of race and gender. . . . Intersectional paradigms remind us that oppression cannot be reduced to one fundamental type, and the oppressions work together in producing injustice. . . . The matrix of domination refers to how these intersecting oppressions are actually organized. Regardless of the particular intersections involved, structural, disciplinary, hegemonic, and interpersonal domains of power reappear across quite different forms of oppression. (p. 21)

Areas of Development

The community of practitioners engaged in different forms of feminist practice has carried out a number of significant actions that have advanced the rights and dignity of severely imperiled communities and individuals. These actions include naming the prevalence of child sexual abuse and developing a national mental health agenda for addressing it (Herman, 1981; Robb, 2007); leading efforts to address domestic violence awareness through research and social policy (Frieze, 2008); addressing ways discrimination results in mental health barriers for women of color (Copeland & Butler, 2007), including those who are immigrants (O'Mahoney & Donnelly, 2010) and transgender (Patton & Reicherzer, 2010); and supporting men harmed by dominant expectations of manhood and masculinity, particularly when conflated with violence (Kahn, 2011).

Feminist practitioners are also working to address broad, global issues that have included lesbian and transgender concerns (Matebeni, 2009), sexual assault recovery for women in Africa (Bryant-Davis, Cooper, Marks, Smith, & Tilman, 2011), sex trafficking in India (Gangoli, 2007), and civil conflict and loss of voice for women in Thailand (Norsworthy, 2011). In addition, a number of issues are being addressed within the praxis of feminist counseling, including mass media's influence on relational aggression amongst girls (Goldberg, Smith-Adcock, & Dixon, 2011), group counseling for survivors of partner violence (Singh & Hays, 2008), and postpartum depression and other issues for mothers (Davis-Gage, Kettman, & Moel, 2010; Trice-Black & Foster, 2011), as well as its use as a foundational theory in therapeutic interventions such as eye movement desensitization and reprocessing (Reicherzer, 2011).

RCT scholars understand that the social justice concerns of feminism exist in the contexts of relationships. Within this framework, feminist counselors who practice RCT posit growth-fostering connections as the foundations for wellness, and isolation and disconnection as reflective of human suffering (Jordan, 2004). As such, RCT places particular emphasis on a counselor's understanding of the need to foster a safe relational template in the counseling setting, which the client then uses in her or his life outside of the counseling experience. The emphasis of the remainder of this chapter will be on a deeper discussion of RCT, therapy, and related concepts as they stem from the larger feminist model.

OVERVIEW OF RCT

View of Human Nature

The specific origins of feminist theory, particularly RCT, can be seen primarily as a shift in the view of human nature from an individualistic perspective to one founded on interconnectedness. RCT specifically developed as an outgrowth of the need to further explore and better explain the complexities of women's psychological development. For example, rather than pathologizing a woman's need for connection as being overly enmeshed, RCT emphasizes the inherent value of connection among individuals. The underlying core beliefs of this theory are that (a) growth occurs in connection; (b) all people, not just women, yearn for connection; and (c) the healthiest relationships foster growth and develop through a process of mutuality (Jordan et al., 1991). To the extent that these elements can be fulfilled, individual growth can and does occur for all involved (Miller, 1986). Thus, someone who is seen as psychologically healthy is not someone who has developed a strong sense of self in isolation (i.e., autonomy) but, rather, someone who has engaged in strong and mutually empathic relationships and feels individually empowered as a result.

When an individual is unable to have mutually empathic, empowered relationships, this leads to feelings of isolation. Over time, if the individual is unable to or unwilling to engage in relationships with others based on prior experiences of being injured in relationships that lacked mutuality, he or she may choose to stay out of relationships altogether or alter the way he or she behaves in relationships. This is known as the *central relational paradox* (Miller & Stiver, 1997); it reflects the point at which a person may choose to keep parts of herself or himself out of the relationship, hidden, to maintain a façade. Within RCT, these feelings of isolation and disconnection ultimately lead to suffering on the part of the individual and will result in the need for therapeutic intervention. Clinically, this frequently presents as low self-esteem or a sense-of-self issue. For example, a client who is naturally outgoing and outspoken may have begun to limit her or his opinions and preferences and defer largely to a partner in an attempt to make this partner "happy." Thus, in striving to connect with another person, clients can, and often do, shift out of authentic interaction with others only to become increasingly dissatisfied themselves.

Basic Characteristics and Assumptions

RCT not only views psychological development from a relational perspective but also seeks to depathologize or reframe much of the language, characteristics, and behaviors that have previously been used to negatively define women and cultures who demonstrate increased familial or relational interconnectedness. Specifically, RCT challenges the original notion of need for individuation as the primary driving force of development and seeks to dispute and contextualize such terms as *overly enmeshed, emotional,* and *dependent,* which are associated with pathology within other theoretical perspectives. The fundamental tenet of RCT is that true growth occurs through connection. The following concepts highlight this paradigm shift.

Mutuality

In RCT, mutuality is viewed as paramount and is a prerequisite to empathy and empowerment. *Mutuality* occurs when both participants in the relationship are open to being moved, changed, or affected by the other (Jordan, 1991). In this sense, mutuality is not considered "equality" in the relationship; rather, it is the quality of both parties being open to the other's experience and willing to hear and engage at an authentic level. For example, when all individuals in a relationship are open to being impacted by the other and contributing to the growth of the overall relationship, they are engaged in a mutually empowering relationship. At times, one person might be contributing more time or investing more toward compromise, but the end result is strengthening for all.

Growth-Fostering Relationships and the Five "Good Things"

RCT-oriented scholars and practitioners espouse that relationships are paramount to psychological development, and mutuality is the first step in this process. Other required elements include relational authenticity (i.e., being "real" and allowing one's true nature and feelings to be expressed), mutual empathy (i.e., all individuals can understand the perspectives of the others), and mutual empowerment (i.e., all individuals are impacted and encouraged by the experience) (Jordan, 2003). When this mutuality is achieved, the following five "good things" (Miller, 1986) result:

1. Each person feels a greater sense of zest (vitality, energy).

2. Each person feels more able to act in and beyond the relationship.

3. Each person has a more accurate picture of herself or himself and the other person(s).

4. Each person feels a greater sense of worth.

5. Each person feels more connected to the other person(s) and feels a greater motivation for connections with other people beyond this relationship. (p. 2)

To understand the concept of the five good things, think back to a time when you felt really connected to someone. Likely, you had the feeling of being heard and valued—as though the other person really "got you." You probably felt as though you wanted to spend more time with that person because you felt safe and real in her or his presence. The expectation in this concept is that she or he felt the same way, too, leading to a higher level of connection between the two of you and a stronger willingness to further connect with each other and with others.

In contrast, those relationships that lack the five good things leave us feeling depleted, unsatisfied, and yearning for more. Just as in the previous paragraph, think back to a time when you were in a relationship that felt unsatisfactory. You probably felt inauthentic—as though you could not be yourself in the relationship. Or perhaps, in being your true self, you felt unappreciated or unaccepted for who you were. In either case, you likely felt increasingly alone and disconnected from the other person. It was hard to stay engaged. Further, if this relationship went on for an extended period of time, you quite likely began to see a negative impact on your own sense of self. Thus, those relationships that lack the five good things often lead to disconnection from others around us and a lower sense of individual worth.

Cycle of Connection and Disconnection, Relational Paradox, and Condemned Isolation

RCT relationships are seen as existing in a fairly constant state of flux, shifting between periods of connection and disconnection. *Connection* is defined as the point at which all parties are engaging with one another in such a way as to foster and deepen everyone's psychological development (Miller, 1988). As such, connections are made when individuals are willing (a) to engage authentically, (b) to be emotionally accessible (Miller & Stiver, 1991), (c) to be open to the vulnerability required to be fully present (Jordan, 2003), and (d) to be impacted (Jordan, 2003). Engaging at this level requires a great deal of trust and can be understandably scary. For that reason, mutuality is deemed important to growth-fostering relationships. However, when true connections are made, the result is growth enhancing, allowing each individual and the relationship to function at their best. This is an impetus for improved connections in other relationships—an awareness of how connections can be empowering and a movement beyond previous negative relational experiences to those that can promote growth in the future (Fedele, 2004).

The importance of connection and growth-enhancing relationships may be made clear by your own self-reflection (see Exercise 13.1).

EXERCISE 13.1

FELT CONNECTION

Consider a time when you realized that the person you were with really *got it.* How did this experience impact you? Did you change your approach in other relationships based on how well this one went?

Now that you think back on this relationship and instance, did the other individual experience the same from you? How did you offer this? Were there things that made your ability to connect easier? Another way to look at this might be in terms of barriers to connection. In what ways were you alike? What did you share? Of the differences you can name, what might have been dangerous, and why was it not?

Write a letter, which you will plan to keep to yourself, that expresses the above information. How might you relay your gratitude for the connection you experienced? If your relationship has grown, what do you want to say? If you have moved out of this relationship, what have you taken with you? What might you say to this person about how you have become more yourself as a result of this interaction?

Disconnections arise in relationships when there is movement away from mutuality, most frequently when one or more members of the relationship are not engaging authentically (Miller, 1988). Disconnections are characterized by a decreased sense of vitality and connection with the other person that ultimately leads to a questioning of self. This can lead to confusion, a decreased sense of worth, and less knowledge of ourselves and the other(s). When not repaired, this sense of disconnection can result in turning away from others, toward a place of isolation (Miller & Stiver, 1991). This action is the basis for human suffering (Jordan, 2004a; Miller, 1988).

Over time, inauthentic relationships can lead to further disconnection and questioning of all relationships. For example, attempts to maintain the relationship can begin to feel burdensome and hurtful—such as for a child who is overwhelmed with the pressures of "performing" the role of a good child or who realizes he is being accepted only because he is acting in ways that may be inauthentic to his experience. As a result, we begin to develop *strategies of disconnection,* which can be seen as ways of self-protecting and providing safety (Jordan, 2003). Common examples of strategies of disconnection include shutting down, lashing out, and isolating. Carrying forward with our example, this is the point when the child starts to "rebel" and act out at home. In essence, he wants to feel connected to his parents, but in feeling unaccepted and unloved for who he is, he acts out in ways that would keep his parents from accepting or loving him.

The more a person engages in the strategies of disconnection, the stronger she or he becomes. Thus, in our attempts to really connect with another, we often create situations in which we actively disconnect because we are wounded, feel vulnerable, or find that we are unsafe in those relationships. Over time, if an individual faces these types of nonmutual relationships and continues to need to employ strategies of disconnection, the individual will begin to suffer from diminished self-worth and may question the value of authentic engagement with others. In other words, some individuals can lose the ability to connect in a real and meaningful way, leading to a process of *condemned isolation,* or inability to connect with others.

Much like relational connection, the concept of relational disconnection can best be understood through personal application (see Exercise 13.2).

EXERCISE 13.2

CORRECTIVE EMOTIONAL EXPERIENCE/MOVING OUT OF DISCONNECTION

Remember a time in your life when you felt hurt, betrayed, or misled by someone but were able to move out of this with her or him (you were able to heal together). This circumstance need not be a huge violation such as a physical altercation; rather, it might be something as simple as being let down or hearing that she or he had spread information you wanted kept secret. This was a relational violation. In the case of an altercation, it can be advanced to the point of relational rupture—you cannot even imagine the relationship being reestablished, as the potential for mutuality has been subverted.

As you consider this instance, think about your emotions in the process. Try to picture what occurred for the other individual, too. Tell your story first with acknowledgement of how it ended ("In the end, we were closer than ever after talking about it," for instance), but then take time to detail the circumstances of the disconnection. What role did you play? What was an invitation to move out of disconnection and back into connection? What did you and the other person do, individually and together, to make it possible? How did this impact you in the future? What have you learned? How are you different than before?

Relational Images, Controlling Images, and Relational Competence

As an individual engages with others and begins to understand her or his role in relationships—connecting and disconnecting—*relational images* develop. In other words, one's prior experiences in relationships begin to shape the picture or ideology of how relationships work; these become the basis for understanding current and future relationships (Miller & Stiver, 1995). This can be particularly burdensome for individuals who have a history of poor relationships (i.e., abusive or highly restrictive relationships). Not only can an individual learn that relationships are unsafe and vulnerable, but these negative relational images may also lead to heightened self-blame, or the sense that the relationship is not unhealthy and nonmutual but, rather, the individual is to blame (Miller & Stiver, 1995). As such, creating meaning out of negative relational experiences can result in feelings of loss of worth and overall lack of trust in relationships. This is often further complicated by a tendency to lack authenticity as individuals learn unhealthy relational styles. Typically, relational images are associated with individual experiences a person has with others throughout life; however, Walker and Miller (2001) also asserted that many relational images stem from the larger society and demonstrate inequalities and roles of dominance that exist within the larger culture. These are known as *controlling images*. Thus, a person's relational images may be partially composed of larger controlling images learned from the broader culture.

Fortunately, relational images do not have to be negative. Positive interactions can also lead to expectations about oneself or others. Positive relational images can and do form when mutuality and authenticity are present in a relationship (Miller & Stiver, 1995). Further, while disconnections could lead to the utilization of strategies of disconnection, in relationships that are based on mutuality, disconnections can be transformed into stronger and healthier reconnections. Disconnections, in and of themselves, are not bad—it is how the disconnection is addressed and whether or not the element of mutuality is present that shapes the ability to reconnect or tendency to further disconnect. When an individual learns to overcome a rupture in the relationship by engaging more fully in an empathetic and authentic way (and when this is further received and shared by the efforts of the other party), she or he is fostering improved positive relational images and demonstrating relational competence.

The concept of *relational competence* is seated in one's ability to understand and gain insight into the cycle of connection and disconnection and his or her particular role in that cycle, coupled with the ability to take action as a result of that knowledge. Jordan (2004b) defined relational competence as "the capacity to move another person, to effect change in a relationship, or affect the well-being of all participants in the relationship" (p. 15). A person who is able to use this information for good is relationally competent. Honing this ability is the ideal goal for the counseling process.

To understand this from a clinical perspective, you may find it helpful to apply it to your own experiences (see Exercise 13.3).

Research and Supportive Evidence

The formation of RCT derived from biweekly meetings between Miller and early RCT scholars Jordan, Stiver, and Surrey in 1978, during which the key concepts and framework were born.

EXERCISE 13.3

CONTROLLING IMAGES

Consider the fact that the assumptions you hold about yourself and others are the result of both personal and societal experience. They may fall anywhere on the continuum from accurate to inaccurate, damaging, and hurtful. If you think of controlling images as stereotypes, with embedded messages about the capacities and implicit characteristics of a given individual or group, you can likely understand that a good many people hold a number of inaccurate assumptions about people in their lives, including themselves. These images range across time, culture, and so forth. How do these images play out in your society? One example of a typical American controlling image is related to scholastic ability: While some ethnicities are assumed to be less intelligent or lazy, others are thought to be good at science and math. The assumption might be that someone of East Asian descent will excel in these courses and have a high earning potential. However, this expresses equally as many limitations—most might not as naturally assume that a first-generation Asian American man, for instance, will excel at a sport such as football. Consider the impact of these beliefs. How are they instilled? What purposes do they serve?

By yourself, write out some of the controlling images that may lie unexamined in your own life. What did you tell yourself you could or could not do with your life? How might reexamining these areas be of value, even if you make no changes?

If you feel safe and establish an environment of radical respect, this exercise might be experienced with a partner (including a counselor). Perhaps an honest assessment of what you believe the other thinks of you could bring out some interesting information. Would it be possible to name controlling images that one holds for another? What is the danger in exploring this? If you move forward with this exercise with another person, how will you tend to the relationship should unexpected material arise?

In the early 1980s, Miller was hired as the first director of the Stone Center at Wellesley College, where she and her fellow RCT scholars continued to research and publish in the areas of psychological development and prevention of psychological issues. Built largely on the collaborative efforts of scholars and researchers, RCT has amassed more than 100 "Works in Progress" papers, which delineate the core fundamental concepts.

In 1995, the Jean Baker Miller Training Institute was developed as part of the Wellesley Centers for Women, and emphasis was placed on continuing to research RCT concepts as well as training. RCT was initially anecdotally and clinically driven but has since been heavily researched. This research has demonstrated efficacy in treating many issues often associated with relational and social contexts, such as eating disorders (Tantillo, 2006; Tantillo & Sanftner, 2010; Trepal, Boie, & Kress, 2012), adolescent relationships (Cannon, Hammer, Reicherzer, & Gilliam, 2012; Tucker, Smith-Adcock, & Trepal, 2011), and connectedness in motherhood (Paris & Dubus, 2005).

In an effort to better understand and assess the constructs within RCT, additional research has been conducted to create valid and reliable assessment measures that can be used to measure change associated with the implementation of RCT in practice. Such measures include the Relational Health Indices Survey Form (Liang et al., 2002), a scale designed to assess growth-fostering relationships (i.e., engagement, authenticity, and empowerment/zest), and the Connection-Disconnection Scale (Tantillo & Sanftner, 2010), a self-report measure designed to assess the perceived mutuality in relationships of women with eating disorders.

Use With Diverse Populations

In the years since its initial development, RCT has expanded to include evaluation and reframing of how we view and normalize developmental processes in diverse populations (Garcia Coll, 1992; Turner, 1987). Now, the emphasis on cultural diversity is seen as fundamental to the theory (Garcia Coll, 1992). As such, all issues are evaluated, assessed, and addressed from this contextual perspective. For example, a client's strong Mexican cultural identity is not viewed as simply a part of the client's background but, rather, becomes the lens through which the client's world is viewed. What is "normal" for this individual may vary drastically from what another client considers "normal." Considering each client's specific cultural identity from the core perspective of culture and context allows therapists to understand what is not fit for a particular client, rather than for people in general.

Because RCT emphasizes a bidirectional therapeutic process—meaning the client impacts the therapist, who then impacts the client—the additional element of cultural awareness that differentiates this theory dictates the therapist's need also to self-assess her or his own culture, developmental context, and biases. This includes having an awareness of the prejudices and privileges we hold that may impact our understanding or assessment of the client (Garcia Coll, 1992). So, rather than simply understanding a client's cultural history and makeup, as counselors, we must also consider how our own cultural and developmental experiences shape who we are and how we then interact and view others, especially clients. For example, how might the therapist's experience as a Caucasian female from a Westernized middle-class family impact her view, assessment, and proposed interventions for her male, working-class, Japanese client?

Marginalization, Power-Over, and Privilege

It is essential that therapists understand the larger concepts of power and privilege at play in relational interactions. In RCT, there is a strong emphasis on understanding the larger dominant society and how efforts to maintain levels of power can result in the marginalization and division of less powerful groups. Power is defined as a situation in which one group has more influence, resources, and opportunities than another group, and can thereby exert some level of control over others (Miller, 2003). Specifically, the concept of exerting will, or "power-over," on another is most fundamental to RCT (Miller, 2003). Walker (1999) noted that it is not the differences in group membership that pose the problem but, rather, the stratification—the concept that one group is superior or inferior to another—that results in oppression and marginalization. Notice the connection to the larger feminist movement and how this allows for an understanding of how dominant cultural groups exist and function.

When viewed through the larger lens of connections and disconnections, power and privilege can be understood to impact opportunities for growth and change. Ultimately, in an effort to protect opportunities and privileges that may exist in a dominant group, barriers to change are created or enforced (Miller, 2003). By using social, political, or economic fear, such as silencing, isolating, or shaming (Jordan, 2002), dominant groups can work toward maintaining a status quo that keeps less powerful groups functioning in the margins and with minimized power. Examples of marginalized groups include those in minority cultures—race, class, gender, sexual preference, religion, and so on. (Miller, 2003). Because these minority groups yearn to maintain some level of power—even if diminished—they will often conform to the needs or requirements of the larger dominant group. From an RCT perspective, instances such as these prevent true change from occurring and create culturally based shame (Walker & Miller, 2001).

Application to Diverse Clientele

RCT's emphasis on understanding and evaluating the impact of cultural identity makes it useful for working with diverse cultures and populations. By evaluating sociopolitical factors that shape an individual's experience, RCT provides a methodology from which to respond to oppression (Comstock et al., 2008). The collective research on RCT further tends to support the need for using pluralistic and more relationally driven therapeutic modalities with minority cultures, whereas oppressive factors and specific cultural context can be integrated into the assessment and treatment process.

Limitations

While the benefits of utilizing RCT are vast, some limitations are associated with this theory as well. As with other foundational theories of human development, RCT is limited in its empirical support due to the inability to observe, measure, or assess "feelings" directly. The concepts that RCT are founded on are theoretical in origin and, though strong in application, can be difficult to assess or truly measure when applied in a therapeutic setting. Though a considerable amount of writing and scholarship exists regarding the tenets of RCT, the vast majority of relevant publications are concept and case conceptualization driven. While it can be argued that case studies and applied research are useful in theory development, more stringent empirical validation is needed to assess its impact.

Another notable limitation of this theory is that while it actively seeks to depathologize behavior and experiences of marginalized cultures, this may lead to minimization of a client's true psychopathology. Miller and Stiver (1991) assert that mental health diagnoses can and should be viewed from a perspective of disconnection; they are essentially strategies of disconnection themselves. When seen from this perspective, efforts can be made to support connections and increase a client's relational competence, thereby alleviating the symptoms and diagnosis. Unfortunately, while this perspective does lend itself to a strength-based approach to counseling and situational experiences, it does not fully address all potential elements, including how to respond to individuals who may be presenting with biologically predisposed or true neurological disorders.

Finally, the concept of "boundaries" can pose challenges to a clinician who does not fully understand or appropriately implement RCT. Whereas boundaries are often considered points of separation and distance in other theories, within RCT, boundaries are places of joining and opportunities for creating a safe space for mutuality among individuals. Given the emphasis on mutuality and movement from a power-over to a power-with perspective, when not appropriately applied in the therapeutic setting, there is a risk of committing ethical violations such as dual relationships.

THE THERAPEUTIC PROCESS

Theory-Guided Case Conceptualization

The previous section noted the primary concepts associated with a relational-cultural framework. Now the goal is to help the reader better understand how these concepts are specifically utilized in a therapeutic environment. This section will explore the fundamental goals of an RCT-based therapeutic approach and provide a clinical guide to the various phases of the therapeutic process.

Therapeutic Goals and Guiding Framework

Fundamentally, an RCT approach is guided by the principle that individual growth occurs in and through relationships. This occurs as a byproduct of our ability to engage with others in a mutually empowering way. To achieve this mutual empowerment, we must engage in healthy relationships to experience the *five good things*. Thus, the overarching goal of the therapy process is to attain the mutual empowerment that results from increased connection (Miller & Stiver, 1991) and to grow further in relational competence.

The framework for therapeutic intervention comes from understanding and being able to apply to the client's life the cycle of disconnection and connection. In other words, it is the clinician's role to attend to the process of connection or disconnection that she or he and the client may experience during the counseling process (Miller & Stiver, 1991). To the extent that the client is connecting and becoming more aware, both with the therapist and with others, progress is being made. When clients engage in behavior that keeps them from connecting in session (i.e., talking the entire session so there is no space for input from the therapist), then the therapist will understand that they are using a strategy of disconnection. This may be indicative of prior negative relational images that cause the client to fear engaging authentically. If this occurs, these strategies are likely also employed outside of the office. Therefore, these types of client behaviors may signal the need to further attend to prior relational images or work to develop new positive images.

Ultimately, all problems brought forth in the therapeutic environment are seen as resulting from the central relational paradox—the strong desire to connect with others, to the extent that the client keeps parts of herself or himself out of the relationship. As such, diagnoses such as depression, dissociation, and paranoia are viewed as manifestations of strategies of disconnection, rather than as pathology (Miller & Stiver, 1991). By engaging with the client in ways that foster mutual empathy, the client can move toward increased empowerment and relational fulfillment. In this way, the therapeutic environment is seen as a model for relationships outside of the session. When the counselor can feel the experiences of the client and allow herself or himself to be moved through those experiences, the client is able to witness and experience that movement in session. In turn, the client will be moved and further empowered. Through this bidirectional process of relational engagement, change occurs in the therapy setting (Miller & Stiver, 1991) and beyond.

Focus and Intentionality

To fulfill the goal of increased mutual empowerment for the client, the counselor must first set the stage for this to happen. Unlike other therapies in which the counselor's role is to be distant, neutral, or nondirective in the session, RCT requires the counselor to be an active participant in fostering a safe environment for the client; a strong, genuine empathic response; and the appropriate relational context in which the client–counselor relationship can develop (Miller & Stiver, 1991). As a client's presenting issue is largely the result of disconnections and poor relational experiences, it is of the utmost importance that the client–counselor relationship be one of authenticity and mutuality. Therefore, before therapy even begins, a counselor wishing to use RCT must not only understand the concepts and processes of the relational-cultural model but also be willing to be affected by the client—to anticipate and experience, through empathy, what the client's prior life experiences have been and how they might impact current and future client functioning. Further, the counselor must be willing and able to demonstrate this understanding back to the client to bring the experience full circle.

Applying the Theory in Early Sessions

The initial stages of an RCT session are largely designed to provide a supportive and safe environment that can ultimately foster increased mutual empowerment. As noted, this requires a great deal of effort on the part of the therapist to demonstrate authenticity and a true desire and willingness to be affected by the client's experiences. Here, the counselor will gather information on the client's prior experiences and begin to conceptualize those experiences in the framework of connections and disconnections, relational images, and the relational paradox. At this level of the therapeutic exchange, the counselor may work with the client to educate her or him on the key concepts of RCT and how those might apply. As such, this phase of the therapeutic process is largely built on information gathering, conceptualizing, and educating. It is also the period of time during which the counselor is working with the client to foster a new and positive relational image, based on their early interactions and the safety provided in the counseling session.

Applying the Theory in Middle Sessions

The second phase of therapy from a relational-cultural framework is a much more active phase of the counseling process. Here, the client is moved beyond exploring experiences and deconstructing them, to a place of working through actual disconnections he or she may face or may have faced in the past. The ultimate goal of this phase of therapy is that disconnections be navigated in such a way that they result in improved connections or new connections with others in the client's life. While somewhat simple in theory, the ability to move into connection requires the toughest work in the therapy process—challenging and moving away from the strategies of disconnection the client has been using (Miller & Stiver, 1994). As would be expected, this can be intensely uncomfortable for the client and is one of the more difficult parts of the change process.

For the counselor, understanding the significance of moving away from these strategies for disconnection is paramount (Miller & Stiver, 1994). It is important for the counselor to remember that strategies of disconnection originate from extremely difficult relational interactions—those that may have even been dangerous or violating in some way. Thus, these strategies are put in place by the client for a reason. As such, in this phase of the counseling process, the counselor must remain empathic to the client's need for these strategies and the specific fears and barriers that may come up when the client is challenged to work through and disregard them. Rather than attempting to view the client as "resistant," "manipulative," or "difficult," the counselor should maintain empathy for this side of the relational paradox and understand the difficulty associated with letting go of these previously used strategies of disconnection (Miller & Stiver, 1994).

Applying the Theory in Late Sessions

The final phase of the therapeutic process within RCT involves bringing the client full circle. Efforts to have the client practice and use the new language and constructs identified in the first phase of therapy are continued. There is, simultaneously, an increased effort to have the client continue to confront strategies of disconnection and work toward new connections with others. Ultimately, the therapy process, and the final stages in particular, should focus on having the client put more and more of herself or himself into functional relationships with others (Miller & Stiver, 1994). As the client becomes increasingly comfortable growing in connection, she or he should experience a concomitant increase in authenticity, having learned it is safe to do so in many relationships. As such, this process is considered a continuation of the growth process; the more mutually empowered we are in building connections with others, the more we feel the desire to engage further with those individuals and others.

Further, and equally important, is the need to have the client begin to evaluate relational connections for mutuality. While many relationships have the capacity to cycle through connections, ruptures, disconnections, repairs, and reconnections, many relationships simply are not mutual and will not provide the client with the ultimate fulfillment and empowerment desired. Recognizing this can be hard; however, a large element of increasing one's relational competence is knowing when relationships have the ability to be mutual and when they do not. In the latter case, it is important to help the client determine how to avoid, move on, or end those relationships. Developing a strong sense of connection and relational competence is the primary goal of the therapeutic process within RCT and culminates in the final phase of the therapy process.

Professional Identity

What does it mean to be an RCT-oriented practitioner? We, the authors, truly believe that to embrace RCT means to *live it*. Once one has a conceptual understanding of how connections heal, and how societally based oppression and other relational forces can serve in many ways to cut us off from our experiences, it becomes intolerable to continue functioning in ways that do not foster growth and mutuality in both the counseling clinic and one's personal relationships. Many RCT clinicians find that they have been experiencing unhealthy, disconnected relationships for a long time, or perhaps for their entire lives.

One of the true gifts of RCT is that it entails a mutual exchange. In this exchange, both people are expected to bring themselves more fully into the relationship. We realize that the structures of a therapeutic relationship might make that statement hard to swallow, but as long as therapy is moved along, ethics are held high, and the client feels as though she or he is getting something valuable from the relationship, good things are indeed happening. This also means that the therapist should feel empowered by the work, too; in effect, she or he is also expected to change and grow continually. In this sense, one who has practiced RCT for any amount of time has undoubtedly grown in relational competence and reverence for the power of *we*. How could one be comfortable living without authenticity in this way?

The questions asked by those who practice RCT generally merit responses that sound increasingly complex, compared with those from a number of other orientations. As an astute and non-risk-averse student once noted to one of the authors, some believe that RCT is "just like every other theory, with the word *relational* thrown in before every bit of the normal jargon." This perspective is understandable, but it misses the most basic underlying principle: the primacy of relationships. Our understandings of ourselves, our joys and pains, and the manifestations of what we believe to be psychopathological all occur in the context of relationships. (One can even begin to think of a relationship with oneself or one's relational images, for example. Many a client has said, "I just don't like myself," to his or her RCT clinician.)

Establishing an identity that includes RCT indicates a counselor's sincere interest in letting others know that they matter; this is almost definitely an extension of the counselor's own need to feel as though she or he matters, too. This implies a willingness to be vulnerable—to have difficult conversations in which an individual might learn she or he is decidedly in the wrong or things are worse than once thought. The distinction is that through the power of a growth-fostering relationship, these moments of vulnerability deserve a response that *holds* the other individual. In other words, what we do with our clients and when they do it, by degree, in return, provides clear indication of relational movement.

This level of relational awareness and responsibility extends beyond just the interpersonal counseling environment. How could one come to understand the need for, and power of, healthy connection but not need to spread this message? Perhaps this is why so many RCT clinicians are involved in any number of social change and social justice efforts. True to their feminist roots, RCT practitioners remain firmly committed not only to naming injustice and oppression but also to working to change things that keep others from fully being.

Our shared understanding of what it means to be RCT practitioners emerged as a series of conversations about how we feel supported, bigger (expansive in acceptance and awareness), and compelled to do the same with others, as all deserve this in full measure. As this progressed, we realized that talking about connection is truly supportive of connection. In some ways, this experience can feel deeply powerful, spiritual, uplifting, and, in cases where difficult truths are painfully clear, bittersweet. In all, though, there is hope for positive change as long as there is a relationship out there.

Y-CHUN THROUGH THE LENS OF A RELATIONAL-CULTURAL COUNSELOR

The case of Y-Chun demonstrates a number of the concepts salient to the RCT practitioner. A brief overview of Y-Chun's life presents the following key aspects: (1) She is biracial, of Polish and Chinese descent, for which she has experienced marginalization and discrimination; (2) she has two children—a 15-year-old boy and a 12-year-old girl—from different, nonparenting fathers; (3) she is experiencing physical and emotional symptoms unrelated to illness, including headaches, nightmares, and agitation; (4) she was raped by her cousin when she was 16 and suffered the effects in silence; and (5) she has some drive for healthy relationships but cannot name successful ones now or in her past.

A relational understanding of Y-Chun's current symptoms and perpetuated sense of pain and loneliness emerges through examination of her past and present cultural and contextually relevant information. Y-Chun's statements suggest that she has a history of feeling as though no one cares about her, that she cannot trust men, and that her general sense of worth and relational ability are low—statements indicative of someone who exists in a state of *condemned isolation.* Central to her dissatisfaction and feelings that she will always be alone and nothing can really change is a mistaken, learned understanding of her relational worth—that she is not only unworthy of meaningful, uplifting relationships but also incapable of creating and sustaining such relationships in the first place.

Y-Chun has attributed her relational worth and relative lack of competence and relational acumen to a series of what an RCT practitioner might call *relational violations,* such as those from her siblings, peers in early school life, and the serious marker event of an incestuous rape during her formative years. It seems possible that Y-Chun's general assessment of her current relational style is in some ways accurate, as she implies that these events have had lasting, negative impacts on how she views herself, relationships in general, and, more specifically, men. The relationally rupturing event of her rape is likely inextricably tied, as she has intuited, to how she interacts with men. One wonders if her eventually aggressive reactions after a sexual encounter are symbolic re-creations of the sexual assault, in which she now takes the reins to experience a seemingly more positive and powerful result. Presently, she tends to have brief, sexual encounters, after which she sometimes effectively punishes partners by exposing their infidelity to wives and girl-friends. She seems to suggest that she is not happy with how she treats others in these instances; furthermore, alludes to a belief that she should act in a kinder, healthier way.

Y-Chun's RCT-oriented counselor would experience and express compassion for her feelings of being lost and alone during those moments of relational violation. There is no prescribed method for addressing the condemned isolation that emerged as a result of these painful experiences, coupled with a context of ethnically based oppression and unsatisfactory gender-based expectations from family and society. It stands to reason, though, that Y-Chun is in need of assurance that she is deserving of powerful connections and relationships and can develop the capacity to create and sustain them. An RCT practi-tioner might self-disclose the impact of receiving these painful memories and words as an invitation to create a different kind of (therapeutic) relationship. This new kind of relation-ship could help transform the impact of these experiences and, ideally, support movement into other relationships that are mutually growth fostering. A foundational component of RCT work is the understanding that the therapeutic relationship represents a microcosm in which to practice new ways of receiving and responding. These new efforts endeavor to transform relational templates; in other words, Y-Chun's relationship with her counselor can change her understanding of her own relational worth, work to increase her ability to create and participate in successful growth-fostering relationships, and help her define and create a new sense of happiness and fulfillment that has been lacking for her.

There are assumptions, partial truths, and untruths that an RCT-oriented counselor will want to invite Y-Chun to examine thoroughly. Though she expresses that she wants her parents to be proud, and notes that they are proud of her for attending college, she also discusses never having a "normal relationship" with them. The expectations placed on her to form a traditional family and such are outside of what she sees as possible. Additionally, she expresses ambivalence and some guilt about the way she treats and cares for her chil-dren, especially her son. How did she establish expectations for herself related to caring for her children? Though it is understandable that she might feel displeased with her par-ents' still trying to act in parental roles with her, how is it troubling to her that they do the same with her children, since she alludes to her apparent discomfort with the parent role? An RCT practitioner might ask Y-Chun to question the development of her expectations for herself. Of particular importance might be consideration of the *controlling images* she maintains. What limitations on her experience lie within her conscious or unexamined beliefs about what she could or should be in her life. Is she supposed to want to be a mother, and is it right to endeavor to fill the role even if she does not want to or finds she is not suited for it? Should she want to be in a committed, long-term relationship with a man, and if so, why? What would that relationship need to look like, and how did she come to develop these beliefs about what a relationship should be? What is the relevance of her biracial identity and other cultural elements? What expectations or messages are hidden in this? What does it even mean to be a woman? A mother? A daughter?

In many cases, controlling images serve the purpose of locking us into seemingly inescapable circumstances. Examining the underpinnings of these beliefs and perhaps letting go of inauthentic or extremely limiting ones can often be a tremendous relief. An RCT therapist would want to begin this process with Y-Chun after establishing an environment of trust. One can imagine the liberating effect of receiving *radical respect* in this exploratory phase. To know that one truly matters, without reproach or qualification, while reconsidering even some of the most basic life assumptions—perhaps traditional gender roles and the expectations tied to women, mothers, lovers, and the like—could be life affirming and changing in and of itself. Though RCT presupposes the importance of healthy, growth-fostering relationships, there is also room for interpretation of what that means for all participants. Y-Chun could decide that she has been fighting against an internalized belief that she should be someone different from her true self. A part of this journey also often uncovers manifestations of the *central relational paradox,* which for Y-Chun might be her keeping her true desires and wants out of relationships because she sees them as unacceptable.

The process of counseling with Y-Chun would be dependent on needs, emerging trends, and any changes in circumstance, through a natural progression of connection and disconnection with the counselor. However, one might expect Y-Chun's work to progress along somewhat predictable lines. First, again, the RCT practitioner would work to cocreate an environment of warmth, filled with the expectation that Y-Chun will be held in full, radical respect, no matter what. This establishes the foundation to allow Y-Chun to share any elements of her past and present she feels are relevant. A primary focus on how things progress within the therapeutic relationship is equally important, though. The counselor would begin helping Y-Chun identify the things that bring the two of them closer into connection, starting to name when there are shifts and movements closer. Similarly, an explanation of barriers to mutuality, such as the effects of institutionalized racism, histories of trauma, differences of power, and so forth, would be discussed. These would need to be bravely examined by client and counselor, as they are best directly addressed; as RCT is rooted in feminism, the examination of power is particularly important, and the therapist would work to ensure that Y-Chun is understood to be an expert of her own life. Furthermore, her agency in establishing change should be constantly affirmed.

Particulars of cultural and contextual relevance should never be avoided, though they should be intentionally considered, as reactivity would constitute a potential disconnection, which might be especially challenging early on. For example, this might occur if the ostensible gender of the therapist is male (we specify "ostensible," as gender is, in our postmodern, transgender, subjectivity-informed understanding, a nonbinary, potentially fluid concept). Consider the major hurdle of this reality, given Y-Chun's self-protectiveness against men, one of whom has hurt her greatly. The counselor must be brave and willing to be vulnerable in this process, too, as Y-Chun is necessarily vulnerable in this potentially unbalanced power exchange. Additionally, consider the impact of having an outwardly appearing White counselor, perhaps with a wedding ring on. How might all this serve to keep client and counselor out of connection? What can a practitioner do or say to make it known that she or he is most interested in creating an environment of safety that supports mutuality? These discussions can be intense and frank. The counselor should know to tread with caution but, nevertheless, to be assured that the best relationships are authentic ones.

After the initial phase of the therapeutic process, Y-Chun should have a well-developing understanding of how connections can serve as healing mechanisms; she and her counselor will have discussed the changes she has already experienced and those to which she looks forward. During both the beginning and middle phase, disconnections could easily occur. As Y-Chun's history indicates, attention has most often come to her in times when she acts out, sometimes directly attacking a loved one. It is possible that elements such as this could manifest in session. If so, a skilled RCT clinician would want to convey understanding, even then. Inauthenticity in acting completely unaffected would be unproductive. Perhaps a gentle observance of the hurtful incident would be of value. Consider the following advanced self-disclosing statement:

> Y-Chun, when you called me that name and told me that I was, to you, like all men—only a means to achieve what you want—I have to tell you that statement both surprised and saddened me. I am only beginning to know the hurt you have experienced in those past relationships with men, but I yearn for this one to be different. I think it can be. What I want you to know is that I am here, regardless. I don't believe that I am worthless, but I respect your expression of what feels most real to you right now. For now, let's call this what it is: a shift. I don't even want to say "setback" because this is just an occurrence—information. What I want to offer you is the awareness that I would like things to be different with us, and I will continue to invite that, because we both deserve it, and we can both benefit from this relationship.

In the above statement, which is both more detailed and disclosing than what might typically be offered in any counseling session, the counselor has named the disconnection. He confessed that it was impactful but there is hope. Simultaneously, he did not back down from his expectation that they treat each other with due respect, but he did so in a way that did not invalidate Y-Chun's immediate needs or experience. Though this approach is potentially dangerous (especially to classically trained clinicians), RCT practitioners consider the possible positive outcome well worth the risk. In any case, the counselor has abided by his own rule of maintaining the authenticity he would like to inspire in his client. Many RCT practitioners can recount isolated instances when self-disclosures during the course of a potential disconnection, violation, or possible rupture did not serve to create the intended outcome. However, it is important to consider the possible impact such an event might have on the client. The underlying intent is relational movement. The vehicle of this movement is respect and held mutuality despite a violating incident. This is fully supportive of the kind of trust that mutually empowering relationships must feature. The counselor's training assists him in understanding that self-disclosures are perfectly appropriate, so long as they move therapy along. This disclosure, though deep and potentially hard to receive, represents a new way of interacting—with *realness,* a word that many of us use to demystify the word *authenticity*.

During the intermediate stages of counseling, Y-Chun would also begin to act on the identifications she has made in the current relationships in her life. She might make strides to create mutuality when possible. This process will likely be difficult, so she should be encouraged to bring in the developments that result from her efforts. Many clients move quickly through these stages, as once the ball gets rolling, they realize the benefits of authenticity, mutuality, and the resultant liberation of these intimately intertwined concepts. But this can be tumultuous, just as it may be rapturous. The important step for the counselor in all this is to keep the client accountable in her efforts but to remain the embodiment of acceptance. There may be times when violations and ruptures occur in her personal relationships (as a result of, or despite, her attempts to change in relationships); an RCT practitioner feels comfort *joining* the client. If the client feels betrayed, the counselor is free to "be with" this emotion. We believe it is okay to be impacted by clients. If a client is hurt to tears, how could it hurt to cry with her or him? In other words, could it not be beneficial to the client to have tears shed on his or her behalf in response to real pain and degradation? This is not to suggest a therapist should blubber at every emotional whim; rather, it is acknowledgement of the power of realness in relationships.

As the intermediate period ends and the counselor and client move toward termination of their relationship (some RCT practitioners, being strengths based, prefer the term *graduation*), preparations for how to operate best in the future are made. Most likely, the counselor would share with Y-Chun that, though their time is coming nearer to a close (with emphasis on Y-Chun's considerable efforts and laudable growth), she is welcome to come back in the future. As relationships serve as legacies, it would not be uncommon for the counselor to say to the client (and for the client to say in return):

> This is tough. It is bittersweet knowing that we won't be seeing each other as often, but what I want you to know is that I am filled with such joy and confidence for where you are headed. You know that I will be welcoming you back with open arms should you ever request to come back—you're always welcome to reestablish therapy should you wish. Part of what I want you to take with you, though, is my confidence in you, and I wanted to tell you that I am going to be taking something from our work together, as well. I think of each of my clients as having an impact on my future clients, because not only have I learned from you, but I learned more about myself, too. As I mentioned to you as you joined me, this is a "practice," and only my clients can make it perfect. Thank you, Y-Chun.

Y-Chun would, of course, do almost all the talking, but it is important to remember that an RCT-oriented counselor knows her or his assertion of relational worth and space is, in many ways, as important as offering it. Y-Chun should know that she has exactly the same worth and potential as her counselor; we are all equal in our entitlement to mutual, growth-fostering relationships. Work will be needed to prepare for future connections and disconnections, but by this time, Y-Chun will have made strides toward developing relational competence; so she will be able to adapt accordingly.

One last thought about RCT in work with Y-Chun is that vulnerability invites vulnerability. Y-Chun disclosed a lot in her first session (see Chapter 3). She may need to be prepared for the emotion of feeling "exposed." However, a counselor's willingness to hold these disclosures and not fear disclosing in return is important. If the counselor's disclosures are helpful and not solely self-serving, then Y-Chun will, most likely, feel safe to bring more of herself into the relationship, in turn. Mutual exchanges can result in less triggering and less engagement in the central relational paradox. Simultaneously, Y-Chun may be able to define for herself new images and possibilities. Finally, movement out of a state of condemned isolation might result in an alleviation of the symptoms she has been experiencing. It is important to note that many RCT therapists would conceptualize something like what the *Diagnostic and Statistical Manual of Mental Disorders* (American Psychological Association, 2013) refers to as a personality disorder (histrionic personality disorder, for instance) or major depressive disorder, as a manifestation of relational trauma. These things are healable, in the *we*.

KEYSTONES

This chapter was designed to introduce you to and allow you to further explore the concepts of RCT. Below are some of the primary takeaways from this theory:

- RCT is a feminist theoretical model.
- This theory is context driven and further encourages us to evaluate client issues from a perspective of power, privilege, and marginalization from the dominant culture.
- This theory espouses that we grow by participating in empowering and mutual connections.
- RCT involves identifying and deconstructing obstacles to mutuality within relationships.
- RCT emphasizes the belief that movement toward mutuality, rather than separation, results in improved functioning.
- This theory purports that the goal of the therapeutic process is increased connection with others, resulting in increased relational competence that allows for the future development of growth-fostering relationships.

REFLECTIONS FROM THE CONTRIBUTOR'S CHAIR

Kristi B. Cannon

While in my master's program, I was challenged to identify a theoretical orientation that would initially ground my work with clients. I found this process to be particularly difficult, as I was both torn by my appreciation of elements of many of the major theorists and discouraged that none of the therapeutic approaches appeared to be comprehensive of all my beliefs. Fortunately, in my doctoral program, I was exposed to RCT and finally found the sense of completion I had been looking for in a theory. This particular theory seemed a natural fit for the way I viewed the world and my individual experiences; it seemed the perfect intersection of relational emphasis, context-driven awareness, and emerging thought that I had been searching for.

As a woman of a great many privileges, my work as a counselor has really helped shape my understanding of power, oppression, and marginalization. Being able to work with clients who are underserved and in need helped me expand and understand the fundamental need of exploring context in the lives of my clients, and people in general. I came to fully conceptualize what it means that we do not all have the same opportunities in life and that being aware of the experiences of others only serves to better understand them. Ultimately, my identity as a counselor is one of wanting to engage authentically with people. RCT allows me this opportunity, both in professional practice and in my everyday existence.

Jason Patton

My introduction to feminism and RCT occurred during a time of great flux and the emergence of a new, more inclusive, strengths-oriented perspective in my life. My traditional education included a primary identification with the medical model and a psychopathology-minded perspective of psychology and counseling. I was fortunate to find a well-rounded, strong Council for the Accreditation of Counseling and Related Education Programs master's program. The program addressed a great variety of theoretical orientations, and it was a revelation to me that there were professionals who touted the complicity of the mental health industry in "blaming the victim" and how at least some diagnoses were so stigmatizing that professionals wrote off their clients as being beyond help or "lost causes." I was touched by this profound, invigorating assessment. I realized that part of what drew me to the mental health field was the evidence I had in my life that perseverance and constructive, healing relationships really may be all it takes to survive oppression. I know that I had believed, intuitively, that counselors would support these efforts. Coming out as gay in a small, conservative town to parents and other influences who were convinced that I had sealed my eternal damnation by being honest about the kind of person I want to love resulted in distrust and relational trauma that I felt was un-healable. Fortunately, a family of choice and the support of people who were genuinely interested in seeing me succeed moved me through this period.

When I heard an instructor talk about the healing power of growth-fostering relationships and the *five good things* we can expect to gain by engaging in these relationships, I realized my need to have compassion for my own experience, appreciation of those who helped me succeed, and drive to constantly question my environment and embrace positive social change. In particular, the *zest*ful component felt most real to me. I know that those relationships I experienced as growth fostering had supported a sense of passion, general positivity, and movement. I learned that there was a time in my life during which I existed in *condemned isolation;* rather than being overwhelmed by this, I felt affirmed and proud to have experienced movement out of this state. I learned, too, that the proof in the relational pudding made me realize that the sickness in my life came from without, not within. I felt compelled to spread the message of the power of *we* to those who had been told they were unworthy of love and admiration. The process of becoming an RCT practitioner was not all sunshine and lollipops, though. Sure, learning how to further my own relational competence and move through barriers to connection was revelatory, but the price was also the identification of a number of relationships that were most certainly not creating any of the five good things. I quickly became far less tolerant of engagements with those who did not wish to be strengthened through their efforts to strengthen me. This process still continues, but my loved ones and I get better at it all the time.

Stacee L. Reicherzer

I was introduced to feminist theory and RCT during my graduate studies at St. Mary's University in San Antonio, Texas. I was interning at the local gay and lesbian community center, which offered no-fee counseling services to lesbian, gay, bisexual, transgender (LGBT), and other persons in need. Many of the people with whom I worked were extremely poor and came from backgrounds of profound marginalization. I saw larger issues at work in their lives that were systemic and themed around power disparities, injustice, trauma, and humiliation, and I struggled to find a theory that really explained how to address a survivor within system-wide oppression.

I had begun working on a textbook with my faculty mentor about RCT's application in work with LGBT communities. In doing so, I started to really connect the dots and directly apply this model of growth-fostering connection, mutual empathy and empowerment, and social justice as a means for change with my clients. I found that RCT, as a specific counseling focus of feminist theory, gave me a means for connecting with my clients in a way that really fostered what they saw as strength-based and wellness-enhancing change. For me, this is at the very core of what it means to be a counselor.

ADDITIONAL RESOURCES

Books

Jordan, J. V. (1997). *Women's growth in diversity: More writings from the Stone Center*. New York: Guilford Press.

Jordan, J. V., Kaplan, A., Miller, J. B., Stiver, I., & Surrey, J. (1991). *Women's growth in connection: Writings from the Stone Center*. New York: Guilford Press.

Jordan, J. V., Walker, M., & Hartling, L. M. (Eds.). (2004). *The complexity of connection: Writings from the Stone Center's Jean Baker Miller Training Institute*. New York: Guilford Press.

Miller, J. B. (1987). *Toward a new psychology of women* (2nd ed.). Boston: Beacon Press.

Miller, J. B., & Stiver, I. P. (1997). *The healing connection: How women form relationships in therapy and in life*. Boston: Beacon Press.

Robb, C. (2007). *This changes everything: The relational revolution in psychology*. New York: Picador.

Walker, M., & Rosen, W. B. (Eds.). (2004). *How connections heal: Stories from relational-cultural therapy*. New York: Guilford Press.

Website

The Jean Baker Miller Training Institute. (2013). Retrieved from http://www.jbmti.org

REFERENCES

American Psychiatric Association. (2013). *Diagnostic and statistical manual of mental disorders* (5th ed.) Washington, DC: Author.

Anzaldúa, G. (2007). *Borderlands/la frontera: The new mestiza* (3rd ed.). San Francisco: Aunt Lute Books.

Bryant-Davis, T., Cooper, K., Marks, A., Smith, K., & Tilman, S. (2011). Sexual assault recovery in the aftermath of the Liberian Civil War: Forging a sister between feminist psychology and feminist theology. *Women and Therapy, 34*(3), 314–330. doi:10.1080/02703149.2011.580689

Budgeon, S. (2011). *Third wave feminism and the politics of gender in late modernity.* New York: Palgrave Macmillan.

Cannon, K. B., Hammer, T. R., Reicherzer, S., & Gilliam, B. J. (2012). Relational-cultural theory: A framework for relational competencies and movement in group work with female adolescents. *Journal of Creativity in Mental Health, 7*(1), 2–16. doi:10.1080/15401383.2012.660118

Collins, P. (2008). *Black feminist thought* (2nd ed., reprint). New York: Routledge.

Comstock, D. L., Hammer, T. R., Strentzsch, J., Cannon, K., Parsons, J., & Salazar, G. (2008). Relational-cultural theory: A framework for bridging relational, multicultural, and social justice competencies. *Journal of Counseling and Development, 86*(3), 279–287. doi:10.1002/j.1556-6678.2008. tb00510.x

Copeland, V. C., & Butler, J. (2007). Reconceptualizing access: A cultural competence approach to improving the lives of African-American women. *Social Work in Public Health, 23*(2–3), 35–58. doi:10.1080/19371910802148263

Davis, A. Y. (1983). *Race, class, and gender.* New York: Vintage Books.

Davis, A. Y. (1999). *Blues legacies and Black feminism: Gertrude "Ma" Rainey, Bessie Smith, and Billie Holiday.* New York: Vintage Books.

Davis-Gage, D., Kettman, J. J., & Moel, J. (2010). Developmental transition of motherhood: Treating postpartum depression using a feminist approach. *Adultspan, 9*(2), 117–126.

Fedele, N. M. (2004). Relationships in groups: Connections, resonance, and paradox. In J. V. Jordan, M. Walker, & L. M. Hartling (Eds.), *The complexity of connection* (pp. 194–219). New York: Guilford Press.

Friedan, B. (1963). *The feminine mystique.* New York: W. W. Norton.

Frieze, I. H. (2008). Social policy, feminism, and research on violence in close relationships. *Journal of Social Issues, 64*(3), 665–684. doi:10.1111/j.1540-4560.2008.00583.x

Gangoli, G. (2007). Immorality, hurt, or choice: How Indian feminists engage with prostitution. *Journal of Politics, 9*(1), 1–19. doi:10.1080/14616740601066184

Garcia Coll, C. (1992). *Cultural diversity: Implications for theory and practice* (Working Paper No. 59). Wellesley, MA: Wellesley Centers for Women.

Garcia Coll, C., Surrey, J. L., & Weingarten, K. (1998). *Mothering against the odds: Diverse voices of contemporary mothers.* New York: Guilford Press.

Gilligan, C. (1982). *In a different voice: Psychological theory and women's development.* Cambridge, MA: Harvard University Press.

Gillis, S., Howie, G., & Munford, R. (2007). *Third wave feminism: A critical interpretation* (2nd ed.). New York: Palgrave MacMillan.

Gilmore, S. (2007). *Feminist coalitions: Historical perspectives on second-wave feminism in the United States.* Chicago: University of Illinois Press.

Goldberg, R. M., Smith-Adcock, S., & Dixon, A. L. (2011). The influence of the mass media on relational aggression among females: A feminist counseling perspective. *Journal of Aggression, Maltreatment, and Trauma, 20*(4), 376–394. doi:10.1080/10926771.2011.568995

Herman, J. L. (1981). *Father-daughter incest.* Cambridge, MA: Harvard University Press.

Heywood, L., & Drake, J. (1997). *Third wave agenda: Being feminist, doing feminism.* Minneapolis: University of Minnesota Press.

hooks, b. (2000). *Feminism is for everybody: Passionate politics.* Cambridge, MA: South End Press.

Horney, K. (1993). *Feminine psychology.* New York: W. W. Norton.

Jordan, J. V. (1991). The meaning of mutuality. In J. V. Jordan, A. G. Kaplan, J. B. Miller, I. P. Stiver, & J. L. Surrey (Eds.), *Women's' growth in connection* (pp. 81–96). New York: Guilford Press.

Jordan, J. V. (Ed.). (1997). *Women's growth in diversity: More writings from the Stone Center*. New York: Guilford Press.

Jordan, J. V. (2002). *Learning at the margin: New models of strength* (Working Paper No. 98). Wellesley, MA: Wellesley Centers for Women.

Jordan, J. V. (2003). *Valuing vulnerability: New definitions of courage* (Working Paper No. 102). Wellesley, MA: Wellesley Centers for Women.

Jordan, J. V. (2004a). Relational resilience. In J. V. Jordan, M. Walker, & L. M. Hartling (Eds.), *The complexity of connection* (pp. 28–46). New York: Guilford Press.

Jordan, J. V. (2004b). Toward competence and connection. In J. Jordan, M. Walker, & L. Hartling (Eds.), *The complexity of connection* (pp. 11–25). New York: Guilford Press.

Jordan, J. V. (2009). *Relational-cultural therapy*. Washington, DC: American Psychological Association.

Jordan, J., Kaplan, A. G., Miller, J. B., Stiver, I., & Surrey, J. L. (1991). *Women's growth in connection: Writings from the Stone Center*. New York: Guilford Press.

Jordan, J., Walker, M., & Hartling, L. (Eds.). (2004). *The complexity of connection: Writings from the Stone Center's Jean Baker Miller Training Institute*. New York: Guilford Press.

Kahn, J. S. (2011). Feminist therapy for men: Challenging assumptions and moving forward. *Women and Therapy, 34*(1–2), 59–76. doi:10.1080/02703149.2011.532458

Liang, B., Tracy, A., Taylor, C. A., Williams, L. M., Jordan, J. V., & Miller, J. B. (2002). The relational health indices: A study of women's relationships. *Psychology of Women Quarterly, 26*, 25–35.

Lorde, A. (2007). *Sister outsider*. Berkeley, CA: Crossing Press.

Matebeni, Z. (2009). Feminizing lesbians, degendering transgender men: A model for building lesbian feminist thinkers and leaders in Africa? *Souls, 11*(3), 347–354. doi:10.1080/10999940903088978

Miller, J. B. (1976). *Toward a new psychology of women*. Boston: Beacon Press.

Miller, J. B. (1986). *What do we mean by relationships?* (Working Paper No. 22). Wellesley, MA: Wellesley Centers for Women.

Miller, J. B. (1988). *Connections, disconnections, and violations* (Working Paper No. 33). Wellesley, MA: Wellesley Centers for Women.

Miller, J. B. (2003). *Telling the truth about power* (Working Paper No. 100). Wellesley, MA: Wellesley Centers for Women.

Miller, J. B., & Stiver, I. P. (1991). *A relational reframing of therapy* (Working Paper No. 52). Wellesley, MA: Wellesley Centers for Women.

Miller, J. B., & Stiver, I. P. (1994). *Movement in therapy: Honoring the "strategies of disconnection"* (Working Paper No. 65). Wellesley, MA: Wellesley Centers for Women.

Miller, J. B., & Stiver, I. P. (1995). *Relational images and their meanings in psychotherapy* (Working Paper No. 74). Wellesley, MA: Wellesley Centers for Women.

Miller, J. B., & Stiver, I. P. (1997). *The healing connection: How women form relationships in therapy and in life*. Boston: Beacon Press.

Moraga, C., & Anzaldúa, G. (1983). *This bridge called my back: Writings by radical women of color*. New York: Kitchen Table Press.

Moschkovich, J. (1983). "But I know you, American woman." In C. Moraga & G. Anzaldúa (Eds.), *This bridge called my back* (pp. 79–84). New York: Kitchen Table/Women of Color Press.

Norsworthy, K. L. (2011). Swimming upstream: Feminist liberatory work within South Thailand communities in conflict. *Women and Therapy, 34*(3), 242–260. doi:10.1080/02703149.2011.580666

O'Mahoney, J. M., & Donnelly, T. T. (2010). A postcolonial feminist perspective inquiry into immigrant women's mental health care experiences. *Issues in Mental Health Nursing, 31*(7), 440–449. doi:10.3109/01612840903521971

Paris, R., & Dubus, N. (2005). Staying connected while nurturing an infant: A challenge of new motherhood. *Family Relations: Interdisciplinary Journal of Applied Family Studies, 54*(1), 73–83. doi:10.1111/j.0197-6664.2005.00007.x

Patton, J., & Reicherzer, S. L. (2010). Inviting "Kate's" authenticity: Relational-cultural theory applied in work with a transsexual sex-worker of color using the ACA Transgender Competencies. *Journal of LGBT Issues in Counseling, 4*(3–4), 214–227. doi:10.1080/15538605.2010.524856

Reicherzer, S. L. (2011). Eye movement desensitization and reprocessing in counseling a male couple. *Journal of EMDR Practice and Research, 5*(3), 111–120. doi:10.1891/1933-3196.5.3.111

Robb, C. (2007). *This changes everything: The relational revolution in psychology*. New York: Picador.

Singh, A. A., & Hays, D. G. (2008). Feminist group counseling with South Asian women who have survived intimate partner violence. *Journal for Specialists in Group Work, 33*(1), 84–102.

Smith, B. (2000). *The truth that never hurts: Writings on race, gender, and freedom*. New York: Routledge.

Spivak, G. (1988). Can the subaltern speak? In C. Nelson & L. Grossberg (Eds.), *Marxism and the interpretation of culture* (pp. 271–316). Urbana: University of Illinois Press.

Tantillo, M. (2006). A relational approach to eating disorders multifamily therapy group: Moving from difference and disconnection to mutual connection. *Families, Systems, and Health, 24*(1), 82–102. doi:10.1037/1091-7527.24.1.82

Tantillo, M., & Sanftner, J. L. (2010). Measuring perceived mutuality in women with eating disorders: The development of the Connection-Disconnection Scale. *Journal of Nursing Measurement, 18*(2), 100–119. doi:10.1891/1061-3749.18.2.100

Trepal, H. C., Boie, I., & Kress, V. E. (2012). A relational cultural approach to working with clients with eating disorders. *Journal of Counseling and Development, 90*(3), 346–356. doi:10.1002/j.1556-6676.2012.00043.x

Trice-Black, S., & Foster, V. A. (2011). Sexuality of women with young children: A feminist model of mental health counseling. *Journal of Mental Health Counseling, 33*(2), 95–111.

Tucker, C., Smith-Adcock, S., & Trepal, H. C. (2011). Relational-cultural theory for middle school counselors. *Professional School Counseling, 14*(5), 310–316. doi:10.5330/PSC.n.2011-14.310

Turner, C. W. (1987). *Clinical application of the Stone Center theoretical approach to minority women* (Working Paper No. 28). Wellesley, MA: Wellesley Centers for Women.

Walker, M. (1999). *Race, self, and society: Relational challenges in a culture of disconnection* (Working Paper No. 85). Wellesley, MA: Wellesley Centers for Women.

Walker, M., & Miller, J. B. (2001). *Racial images and relational possibilities* (Talking Paper No. 2). Wellesley, MA: Wellesley Centers for Women.

Walker, M., & Rosen, W. B. (2004). *How connections heal: Stories from relational-cultural therapy*. New York: Guilford Press.

Family and Couples Therapy

Rebecca M. Goldberg

But, Leona—I don't get it—you are constantly complaining about Tom's lack of attention and the fact that he is disengaged from you—from your life together— and yet . . . you hang in there? If it is that bad and you are not getting anything out of the relationship, isn't it time to pull the plug? Why would you stay in a bad situation?

The suggestion, or at least the question, presented by Leona's friend seems reasonable. If an individual is unhappy in a situation, shouldn't he or she make a decision to effect change in that situation or remove himself or herself from it? While the question and the implied recommendation seem clear and simple, life is neither always clear nor often simple.

When looking at a couple—in this case, Leona and Tom—we certainly want to understand the unique needs and dispositions of the individuals, but we also need to understand the unique entity of "Leona-n-Tom" as a couple and how the rules, goals, and patterns of that entity both serve and thwart the needs of the individuals.

For a theorist approaching counseling from a systems perspective, the focus is on the couple or family coming together and uniting their efforts toward healthy interactions and relationships. An individual cannot be considered without also considering the main entity to which he or she belongs: family.

In this chapter, you will be introduced to the main theorists in family and couples therapy, as well as different modalities thereof. You will learn about trends in family/ couples therapy, including areas being developed further, as well as issues concerning professional identity, family/couples therapists' views on human nature, and basic therapeutic characteristics and assumptions. This chapter will also review research supporting family/couples theory constructs and interventions, application to diverse populations and children, strengths and limitations, and therapeutic process. This chapter includes a case application as well as resources for further information. Specifically, after reading this chapter you will be able to do the following:

1. Identify the elements that make family/couples counseling unique from individual theories

2. Describe application of family/couples therapy as it relates to a variety of potential clients

3. Explain therapeutic process and applications of family/couples therapy, including therapeutic goals, the process of change, interventions, assessment strategies, and focus and intentionality of sessions

INTRODUCTION

Historical Background

While the other theories presented within this text may point to a specific founder or foundress, the development and history of family/couples counseling is quite rich and diverse. That history, and the models to be presented within this chapter, has been tinted by the work of many creative and competent professionals, some of whom are identified in the next section. While this listing does not do justice to each person's contribution or to all those who have added to the literature, it is representative of the type of influence that has given shape to a family/couples approach to counseling.

Profiles of Main Figures

Nathan Ackerman

Nathan Ackerman (1908–1974) wrote *The Psychodynamics of Family Life* (1958). He began promoting the family systems perspective in the 1930s, encouraging psychiatrists to address family dynamics through investigation of family processes. Ackerman encouraged therapists to involve themselves with client families and confront covert problems such that they become open issues.

Alfred Adler

Alfred Adler (1870–1937) founded the school of individual psychology and penned the first major psychology book in the United States, *Understanding Human Nature* (1927/1959). He believed that family of origin plays a central role in terms of impact on an individual's personality. Adler purported that personality must be considered in a unified fashion and that individuals should be viewed wholly from integrated perspectives. All personal dimensions of clients are viewed as indivisible and interrelated. The individual is best understood when viewed within the context of his or her environments, including society, culture, and family.

Gregory Bateson

Gregory Bateson (1904–1980) wrote "The Cybernetics of 'Self'" (1971), investigated dysfunctional patterns of communication, and introduced the concepts of cybernetics and the double bind. Bateson's double bind theory purports that one instance of communication may have two conflicting interpretations that lead to confusion and miscommunication.

Ivan Boszormenyi-Nagy

Ivan Boszormenyi-Nagy (1920–2007) wrote *Foundations of Contextual Therapy* (1987) and founded contextual family therapy, in which problems within interpersonal relationships are addressed with loyalty, commitment, equity, and reciprocity. Boszormenyi-Nagy emphasized the importance of investigating family relational patterns spanning decades.

Murray Bowen

Murray Bowen (1913–1990) wrote *Family Therapy in Clinical Practice* (1978) and created multigenerational family therapy, also known as Bowenian family therapy. Bowen included all family members in the therapeutic process, promoting constructive collaboration for problem resolution. He believed that, for a family to meaningfully change its current problems, interpersonal relationships and transgenerational family patterns must be analyzed and confronted. Bowen recommended that the multigenerational family therapist consider no fewer than three generations of family relationship patterns when attempting to understand and assist client families. Triangulation is a concept most associated with Bowen, who placed emphasis on the multigenerational family therapist as a neutral party in the counseling relationship. Triangulation implies an uneven subsystem within the family system or therapy setting, in which two individuals create a scapegoat of the third person, successfully ganging up on him or her. Triangulation serves to ease anxiety and reduce tension for two members of a triad, while increasing anxiety and tension for the third member.

John Gottman

John Gottman (1942–present) coauthored *The Seven Principles for Making Marriage Work* (Gottman & Silver, 1999) and researched how couples approach conflict within their relationships as it relates to promoting healthy interactions. He found that partners who use a 5:1 ratio of positive interactions to negative interactions have more functional relationships than those individuals who have higher rates of negative interactions. Gottman is also credited with identifying communication styles and coping mechanisms that are destructive and predict relationship failure.

These couple-conflict types are referred to as the Four Horsemen of the Apocalypse: contempt, criticism, defensiveness, and stonewalling. Couples who have higher rates of negative interactions are more likely than those who follow the 5:1 ratio to use these communication styles with each other. When one member of a partnership acts in the *contemptuous* style, he or she communicates disrespectfully through the use of ridicule, sarcasm, and negative nonverbal behaviors (e.g., eye rolling, making unpleasant faces). This can involve showing disregard for one's partner during a stressful event, such as an argument. *Criticism* occurs when an individual confronts and blames his or her partner in a manner that feels like an attack. The criticism involves the partner's personality and character qualities instead of a specific behavior or wrongdoing. Individuals use *defensiveness* when they feel the need to protect themselves from a partner's attacks, which they tend to feel are unwarranted. When one partner acts defensively, it is often the result of feeling accused of something he or she did not do. *Stonewalling* occurs when one partner withdraws from the other, ignoring the relationship and ceasing to engage in relating interpersonally. Conflict is avoided with a sense of condemnation and self-righteousness.

Jay Haley

Jay Haley (1923–2007) cowrote *Techniques of Family Therapy* (Haley & Hoffman, 1968) and is credited with creating strategic family therapy, which focuses on solving problems in the present. Haley promoted the ideas that power must be accumulated during therapy and that clients need direction to encourage movement through the therapeutic process above and beyond insight.

Salvador Minuchin

Salvador Minuchin (1913–1990) wrote *Families and Family Therapy* (1974) and created structural family therapy, the main concern of which is the hierarchical structure within the family. Minuchin believed that every family has a structure composed of rules of engagement for family members. Structure may be well organized, promoting clear communication and patterns of interpersonal relationships among family members, or it can be unorganized, which encourages erratic interactions among individuals within a family.

Virginia Satir

Virginia Satir (1916–1988) wrote *Conjoint Family Therapy* (1964), promoting the idea of a therapist seeing both partners in a relationship at the same time. She created the human validation process model of family systems therapy, also referred to as the communications approach. The goals include promotion of personal growth and self-esteem, and connection with other members of the family system and subsystems through congruent interpersonal relationships and communication. Satir was known for her use of innovative techniques and therapeutic interventions, including family maps, family sculpting, reframing, and metaphor.

She also characterized four communication stances that individuals exhibit when experiencing stress: blaming, irrelevant, placating, and super reasonable. When individuals adopt the *blaming* stance, they tend not to accept personal responsibility or admit accountability for problems, instead accusing others of being culpable for stress-inducing behaviors and situations. When the *irrelevant* stance is utilized, individuals throw focus from the stress to other topics not directly related to it, creating a situation in which the family system becomes distracted from the problem, thus not addressing it. An individual who uses the *irrelevant* stance may act inappropriately or erratically to divert the family's attention away from the stressful situation. When individuals *placate*, they attempt to appease or pacify the problematic situation, often taking the blame for things that go wrong in the family. When placating, the problem can seem less stressful than it really is, such as using a euphemism instead of directly labeling an event (e.g., referring to a rape as "the bad thing that happened" or "that awful occurrence"). This will temporarily lower the family's stress but will limit their ability to cope long-term. When being *super reasonable*, individuals will deny themselves from feeling emotions, instead encouraging themselves to think and act rationally and intelligently. True identity of self is discouraged from emerging so that a person's cognitive presence is greater than that of his or her feelings, stunting full engagement with the family during stressful times.

Carl Whitaker

Carl Whitaker (1912–1995) coauthored *The Family Crucible* (Napier & Whitaker, 1978) and is noted for creating experiential family therapy, an approach that encourages play, spontaneity, and creativity as vital characteristics of the therapeutic process. Whitaker revolutionized traditional therapy by including spouses and children in the therapeutic process. He promoted the idea of making unconscious material conscious for the client family, a classic psychoanalytic method, but also focused on present orientation to therapy.

Areas of Development and Recent Trends

Recently, more collaborative models have been added to family/couples therapy, including feminism, multiculturalism, and postmodernism. Similarities among these new models are the egalitarian nature of the counseling relationship, the assumption that the client is the expert on his or her own life, and a perspective of social action on the therapist's behalf. Therapy is cooperative, with a co-constructive relationship. There is a focus on bringing multiple viewpoints to the therapeutic process so the client has various alternatives by which to make new decisions and implement change in his or her life. Formal assessment is not utilized by the therapist, who also understands the inherent power involved in entering a family system. The feminist, multicultural, and postmodern family/couples therapist does not take center stage in the system, instead adopting a perspective of genuine curiosity and inquisitiveness and taking a not-knowing stance.

Additionally, family/couples therapy will have to progress and change as the makeup of the typical family changes. Family/couples therapists must be prepared to work with what used to be considered nontraditional families and couples but is now becoming more typical of the client family. In the future, family therapists will see more instances of families without children, children being raised by extended family members or guardians, blended families with remarried parents and stepchildren, children being reared by one or more gay parents, families with aging and elderly members, homeless families, multigenerational families, and children from single-parent households. Similarly, couples therapy will include more clients from interfaith marriages, dual-career partnerships, same-sex partnerships and marriages, and interracial and intercultural relationships. Family/couples therapists must be equipped to work with changing dynamics of families as they relate to roles of women, single parents, blended families, and same-sex couples; failure to do so will result in inability to adequately help the increasing range of client families coming to therapy.

Professional Identity

The family/couples therapist must consider crucial family factors, such as physical and mental health histories, transgenerational traditions and patterns, socioeconomic status, and issues surrounding multiculturalism and diversity to best assist the client throughout treatment. The practitioner has to be holistic and place the client family in context to facilitate successful therapeutic engagement and progress. She or he must maintain an optimistic orientation and hope that change can occur. The feeling of hope promotes reassurance for clients that their therapist believes their situation can and will improve, which serves as motivation for clients to continue working through therapy. The therapist reinforces the client family's attempts at change, encouraging them to try new behaviors and different means of interaction and to take calculated risks to promote therapeutic progress. This is an essential role played by the family/couples therapist, who identifies and communicates areas of strength and support within and outside the family system to further engender the client family's understanding of their potential, which leads to hope for personal growth and change. It is important to link family members to appropriate external support systems to enhance positive change. This may include services such as the United Way, Alcoholics Anonymous, or Mothers Against Drunk Driving.

When encountering resistance within an individual client or among the members of the client family, the family/couples therapist must attempt to understand the resistance, rather than fight it, and try to engage the clients so they will not continue to distance themselves from the therapist and process of therapy. Family/couples therapy is often unsuccessful when done passively. The family/couples therapist does not wait for spontaneous change to occur or for insight to bring about change. Therapists must be dynamic and actively involved in the therapeutic process to facilitate effective treatment and model proper engagement. It is important for the family/couples therapist also to model appropriate boundaries for the client family. This is often accomplished in the beginning of therapy by setting ground rules for sessions (e.g., only one person at a time is allowed to talk, no name calling). The therapist continues to model boundaries by maintaining professional distance throughout the therapeutic relationship and upholding those original rules.

The professional family/couples therapist is aware of ethical guidelines and practices accordingly. Two important sources of professional ethical codes for family/couples therapists are the American Association for Marriage and Family Therapy's (AAMFT, 2012) *Code of Ethics* and the International Association for Marriage and Family Counselors' "Ethical Code" (Hendricks, Bradley, Southern, Oliver, & Birdsall, 2011). Principles of professional family/couples therapists must include responsibility to clients, students and supervisees, research participants, and the profession as a whole; confidentiality; professional competence and integrity; and appropriate financial arrangements and advertising of services (AAMFT, 2012). Family/couples therapists avoid exploitative or unprofessional dual relationships, sexual intimacy with current and former clients, bartering with clients for services, and practicing outside of their scopes of competence (AAMFT, 2012). Family/couples therapists maintain nondiscriminative approaches to clients, report unethical conduct of other professionals, protect their records in accordance with the law, engage in pro bono work, and advertise truthful representation of services (AAMFT, 2012).

OVERVIEW OF FAMILY AND COUPLES THERAPY

View of Human Nature

Family/couples therapy focuses on relational interactions and how they affect clients. To work with families/couples, counselors must adopt systems perspectives in which they attempt to understand clients within contexts of their familial relations. Each family member is inexorably intertwined with all other members; individual behaviors, development, and habits are affected by interactions with others. Family structure plays an important role in clients' presenting problems and clinical symptoms, as they are often functions of the family's ineffective coping mechanisms. In addition, the family's inability to cope productively with life problems can produce maladjustment in individual clients, which is often reinforced by unhealthy family patterns.

Basic Characteristics and Assumptions

The family system can impact individual symptoms and should be addressed holistically; counselors view clients from total-person perspectives, considering multiple life domains. Holism promotes the integration of multidimensional aspects of clients' lives, a concept that also forms the basis of family systems. Interactions among family members must be considered and addressed holistically, because every family member affects all other members within the unit; all systemic elements are interconnected.

In addition to family members affecting one another, the family system affects its environment and, reciprocally, environment affects family. It is also important to note that the family system comprises multiple subsystems, in addition to being viewed as one overall unit. Subsystems include individuals, dyads, and small groups within the total family system, including parent–child, siblings, and spouses or partners. Subsystems should be considered separately as affecting (and being affected by) the whole system as well as other subsystems.

Families and subsystems must be considered within the context of their established levels of boundaries. A boundary is the imaginary border between information and knowledge of one family or subsystem and its environment or other subsystems. Boundaries determine what communication is permitted between family or subsystem and their milieus, ranging from open to closed. Open boundaries indicate higher levels of information being transferred; closed boundaries denote information being transmitted neither in nor out of the family. A counselor must be prepared, for example, to work with a family whose boundaries are closer to the closed end of the continuum, as is the case for some clients of diverse backgrounds from collectivistic cultures. This can make the process of rapport building and data gathering more difficult.

Research Supporting Theoretical Constructs and Interventions

For decades, researchers have attempted to investigate the nature of family/couples therapy in relation to effectiveness of theoretical constructs and interventions. In comparison to individual therapy, family therapy has been shown to be more effective in dealing with problems that involve family members (Gurman, 1983). Similarly, conjoint couples therapy is more effective at treating marital issues than is individual therapy (Gurman, 1983). The majority of clients—between 66% and 75%—benefit from participation in family/couples therapy (Carr, 2010). Family therapy has been proven to be cost-effective for treatment of severe mental health disorders (Carr, 2010). Utilizing family therapy for treating schizophrenia, for example, can offset costs associated with inpatient care by providing psychoeducation and training (i.e., communication, coping skills, crisis management, and problem solving) for the family and facilitation of occupational adjustment (Goldstein & Miklowitz, 1995; McFarlane, 2004). In addition, behavioral couple therapy can be used to treat depression, as improvement in marital satisfaction is correlated with improvement in depression symptoms and change in levels of depression (Beach & O'Leary, 1992). Family therapy has also been shown to be effective when applied to treatment of problems related to disruptive behaviors among children and adolescents (Carr, 2010). For adults, family therapy is beneficial for issues surrounding substance abuse, interpersonal relationship distress, and symptoms related to mood and anxiety (Carr, 2010). Family/couples therapy is noted as being among the strongest approaches for adults and adolescents suffering from drug abuse (Rowe, 2012).

Combination of individual and family therapies is beneficial in various circumstances. When a family member is coping with substance use, implementation of family therapy in conjunction with an individual focus is supported by research as an effective means of treatment (Carr, 2010). In addition, family-based interventions coupled with pharmacotherapy lead to better treatment outcomes than using medication alone (Carr, 2010). This has been proven true for children with attention-deficit hyperactivity disorder, as well as adults diagnosed with schizophrenia, bipolar disorder, and alcohol abuse (Carr, 2010).

Use With Diverse Populations and Children

The role of family therapist is that of teacher or consultant to the family (Corey, 2012), which is beneficial with diverse populations and children who might expect more direction and guidance through therapy. In addition, some clients from diverse cultural backgrounds will prefer family therapy over individual counseling because of the collectivistic nature of their upbringings and lifestyles (Corey, 2012). A benefit of family/couples therapy with clients from multicultural backgrounds is that it takes into account how external forces affect individuals (Corey, 2012). Clients are not blamed for the situations in which they find themselves, such as oppression, sexism, and patriarchy. Rather, these are functions of the systems of which clients are members and must be taken into consideration during therapy. The family/couples therapist has the following qualities that make him or her particularly effective when working with clients from diverse backgrounds: sensitivity to similarities and differences between self and client families, life experience working with clients from various cultural populations, genuine acceptance of cultural variabilities, innovation and creativity, specificity with regard to treatment planning and implementation of action plans, and ability to intervene with resistance (Gladding, 2010).

Family counseling can be particularly beneficial for use with children who present a variety of concerns. These might include problems associated with being a member of a single-parent household due to death, divorce, or a parent otherwise being partnerless;

a blended family as a result of remarriage; or cultural diversity that creates distance between children and their communities (Gladding, 2010). Children tend to approach therapy with the understanding that problems exist but need to be changed, which can be done in the context of cooperation in family therapy (Moore & Seu, 2011). The warm, welcoming nature of the family therapist is particularly important when working with children, as they need to feel comforted if they are going to engage in therapy (Moore & Seu, 2011). Children need to feel that their voices and feelings are being heard and respected, and family therapy fulfills this need (Moore & Seu, 2011). In addition, it is more effective to focus on strengths as opposed to weaknesses, a practice inherent to family therapy (Moore & Seu, 2011). Overall, children report family counseling as being helpful with regard to facilitating change within their families, solving preexisting problems, and encouraging their parents to view them differently (Moore & Seu, 2011).

Strengths and Limitations

Strengths of Family and Couples Therapy

Family systems therapy is used extensively in counseling settings because many clients place great value on their families and need to be considered within the context of the family system for optimal treatment to occur. The family systems approach is beneficial in that it does not place blame for existing problems on either the family or individual members (Corey, 2012). It is understood that each family member and subsystem contributes to overall family dynamics, and no single entity is responsible for all dysfunction within the system. When family members are encouraged to be active participants in therapeutic engagement and are included in the processes of hypothesizing, meaning making, and implementing the action plan to facilitate change, they become more invested in therapy as they are empowered to recognize and break unhealthy patterns.

Limitations of Family and Couples Therapy

One potential shortcoming when using a family systems perspective is that the needs of the family can, at times, overshadow the needs of an individual (Corey, 2012). It is important, therefore, that the family therapist remembers to attend to each family member. Also, parents can be noncommittal (i.e., stop attending after a few sessions), which is another major limitation of this approach. An additional limitation occurs when family therapists assume that Western family norms are universal for all client families (Corey, 2012). This does not take into account the broad variations that exist between and among different cultural groups. The notion of individuation or differentiation is supported in family/couples therapy, and that is not always true for clients from diverse cultural backgrounds (Corey, 2012). Promoting individualism, as opposed to collectivism, is taboo for some families and must be considered as a potential deficit in therapy. In addition, clients from diverse cultural backgrounds may have family rules, hierarchies, structures, communication styles, interpersonal relationships, and processes that vary greatly compared with patterns in Western families. The family/couples therapist must be aware of these variations and not impose his or her beliefs, instead treating each client family in context.

THERAPEUTIC PROCESS AND APPLICATIONS

Introduction

As suggested above, there is not a singular proponent of family/couples theory nor is there a singular theory. While there are many common threads to the way those employing a systemic focus conceptualize both case and treatment plans, a vast, rich array of family/couple theories provides unique perspectives and approaches. Those employing a family/couples model share a perspective that the best way to understand an individual is through an assessment of his or her interactions between and among family members. Since there is such a great deal of variation among theories within the systems perspective, review Table 14.1 for processes and applications of the different modalities of family/couples therapy. What follows is a somewhat generic or common focus approach that typifies those theories considered as systems oriented. Family/couples therapy is a collection of works from many contributing theoretical models, as described in this section. Goals for therapy, view of change process, interventions, assessments, and focus all vary according to the specific type of family/couples therapy being practiced. This section will highlight these components of family/couples therapy with a general overview of process and application in relation to the systems perspective.

Table 14.1   Family and Couples Counseling Theory—Not One but Many

Theory	Description	References
Adlerian family therapy	Birth order: • Significantly influences children's development • Accounts for individual likelihood of having certain sets of experiences based on family roles Family constellation: • Used for assessment • Client evaluates his or her prevalent family condition • Includes family atmosphere, relationships, values, and gender roles • Power, boundaries, and rules are especially important Misidentified goals: • Act to motivate individuals within the family system to repeatedly interact negatively	Adler (1931/1958) Adler (1927/1959)

Theory	Description	References
	• Can result in problematic interpersonal relationships • Lead to poor communication Facilitating effective leadership for parents: • Institute and maintain successful leadership styles and skills • Therapist takes on role of coach or model Techniques: • Problem description • Goal identification and disclosure	
Bowenian family therapy (multigenerational family therapy)	Family unit: • A set of associations comprising multiple interpersonal relationships Individuation or differentiation of self: • Process by which clients become aware of self-identity • Members must establish individual identities separate from family unit for healthy functioning • Promotes individual growth and symptom resolution • Aids in reduction of anxiety • Inappropriate differentiation of self or inadequate self-identity results in emotional enmeshment Genograms: • Essential for understanding frameworks of relationships among family members • Maps of individuals and relationships for three or more generations • Historical family-of-origin relational patterns Therapist: • Models objectivity and neutrality • Actively coaches and educates client family	Bowen (1978)

(Continued)

(Continued)

Theory	Description	References
	Techniques: • Definition of family roles • Examination of and connection with family of origin • "I" statements	
Brief family therapy	*Founded at Mental Research Institute.* Family network: • Every family member both influences and is influenced by the entire family system • Interrelated connections formed among individuals who communicate effectively with one another during times of stress to maintain healthy family • Flexible, making necessary changes to functioning as needed Dysfunctional families: • Engage in incongruent communication • Exhibit contradictions between verbal statements and nonverbal behaviors • Stressful situations improperly handled Therapist: • Active therapeutic participant • Organizes and structures treatment • Collects data about family • Assesses hypotheses • Models for family, teaching proper communication skills Techniques: • Effective management styles • Reframing • Homework • Paradoxical injunctions, also called therapeutic double binds	Fall, Holden, and Marquis (2010)

Theory	Description	References
Communications approach (human validation process model)	Family system: • Governed by rules that promote growth and development • Facilitated through proper communication and encouragement of healthy self-esteem Healthy families: • Members attuned to their own emotions • Engage in congruent communication • Individual differences embraced as respectful opportunities for investigation, discovery, and growth rather than threats Dysfunctional families: • Members have not been encouraged to grow and develop • Low self-esteem and poor communication skills • Inferior system functioning • Inappropriate rules and boundaries Therapist: • Authoritative resource • Observer, mentor, facilitator, and active change agent • Promotes the congruence in communication • Warm and empathic • Supports family members but confronts them as needed • Bonds with family through joining • Attacks dysfunction within the system Techniques: • Family mapping • Psychodrama • Reframing • Family sculpting • Family reconstruction	Satir (1964)

(Continued)

(Continued)

Theory	Description	References
Contextual family therapy	Reciprocity: • Each member both contributes to and benefits from the family • Equitable sharing of responsibilities • Balanced relationships • Ecumenical welfare for family system Healthy families: • Equal measures of effort from involved parties • Fair relationships characterized by honesty, commitment, and trust Therapist: • Facilitates psychoeducation • Guides clients through the therapeutic process • Advocates for each client • Uses self-disclosure, directives, and suggestions Therapy: • Ranges from exploratory to confrontational • Family members held accountable for therapeutic involvement and growth	Boszormenyi-Nagy (1987)
Experiential family therapy	Goal: • Motivating client change through enhancement and maintenance of anxiety *There is no specific set of methods recommended for use; rather, the emphasis lies with personal involvement of the therapist, and the relationship is sufficient for change within the family system.* Therapist: • Active participant • Communicates support, empathy, warmth, and hope for change • Creative, engaging, risk taking, and authentic	Napier and Whitaker (1978)

Theory	Description	References
	• Models effective communication skills/strategies Techniques: • Family sculpting • Games • "I" statements	
Imago relationship therapy	Foci: • Affect, behavior, and cognition • Interventions designed to facilitate growth and change Therapist: • Promotes therapeutic engagement by acting as third member of triad • Coaches clients through change process toward understanding and cohesiveness Dysfunctional couples: • Breakdown of connection • Power struggles over competing problems • Dyad members not empathetic with each other and do not see the other's perspective Healthy couples: • Engage in intentional dialogue and communication • Promote clear understanding of each other • Recognize other's worldview as valid	Luquet and Hendrix (2001)
Strategic family therapy	Family rules: • Govern the system • Subsystems comprise power relations among members Dysfunctional families: • Power differentials dictate control over boundaries of relationships	Haley and Hoffman (1968)

(Continued)

(Continued)

Theory	Description	References
	Healthy families: • Cope successfully with struggles of control and stressful situations • Balance between plasticity and immovability in conflict resolution **Treatment:** • Focuses on changing maladaptive behavior patterns that maintain family problems • Therapist guides family during therapeutic engagement **Therapist:** • Uses strategies that are brief, solution-oriented, and focus on process • Authoritative and directive • Addresses issues of power struggles • Assumes the role of temporary family leader facilitating change • Presents focus on problem resolution for current issues **Techniques:** • Reframing • Restructuring • Directives • Paradoxical interventions • Asking clients about solutions to problems they have tried to implement	
Structural family therapy	**Therapy:** • Bringing about change within the family system • Modification of family rules • Development of appropriate boundaries among family members • Creating hierarchy within family structure • Individual problems best considered within context of family patterns	Minuchin (1974) Minuchin and Fishman (1981)

Theory	Description	References
	Healthy families:	
	• Have clear boundaries that delineate rules and acceptable behaviors • Encourage free exchange of information, negotiation and compromise, and bidirectional feedback	
	Boundaries:	
	• Important for family dynamics • Contribute to both separation of individuals and promoting unity thereof	
	Clear boundaries:	
	• Facilitate change while maintaining family stability • Promote individuality and togetherness simultaneously	
	Diffuse boundaries:	
	• Create enmeshment • Improper separation among individuals within family system • Promote dependence	
	Rigid boundaries:	
	• Inflexible • Keep family members isolated from one another • Individuals feel detached from other family members • Do not promote intimacy or healthful interpersonal relationships	
	Techniques:	
	• Setting boundaries • Tracking • Joining with the family	

Therapeutic Goals

The overarching goal for all family/couples therapists is to facilitate change within families such that therapy is no longer necessary, by promoting autonomous, healthfully functioning families that can self-soothe when problems arise. Another goal of family/couples therapy is to include family members in the process of therapeutic engagement and problem resolution, under the assumption that the family affects the individual (and vice versa). These goals are accomplished through different approaches, depending on the specific modality of family/couples therapy being used.

Each model has its own focus of a specific goal for therapeutic engagement, in addition to the general goals of change leading to autonomy and inclusion of family in therapy. In brief family therapy, the main task of the therapist is to encourage change through an active approach that focuses on problem solving. A goal for communications family therapists is restructuring family rules to promote more flexible interactions among members, expanding on ways family members engage in interpersonal relationships. Imago relationship therapists have the goal of aiding clients in establishing and maintaining intentional, committed relationships characterized by intimacy. For structural family therapists, the goal of strengthening the family system through structure is the main concern.

Regardless of the specific type of therapy being practiced, all family/couples therapists also have the following goals for client families: improvement in communication patterns, reduction of conflict and distress among and within family members, growth and development of the family unit as well as individual members, balance of togetherness and separation, and interpersonal relationships characterized by empathy and flexibility.

Change Process

Change tends to be most successful when the whole family receives treatment for a clinical problem, due to the influence of the individual's interpersonal relationships with others in the family unit. Within systems perspective, change within the family necessitates contextual change for successful problem resolution. For problem resolution to occur, acknowledgement and awareness regarding inception and maintenance of existing problems are necessary. For successful change to happen within a family unit, attempted solutions to problems must become the focus of the change process. Two types of change exist: first order and second order.

First-order change happens when adaptations are made to the family system consistent with the system's rules. First-order change comprises solutions to problems that are rational and sensible; we often implement first-order change toward problem resolution by facilitating the opposite of the problem. For example, if a baby is crying, she or he will likely be picked up and soothed so the crying will stop, solving the problem of the crying baby. This is an effective means of problem resolution, but it may be temporary; first-order change will not necessarily cause problems to cease permanently. All change does not need to be exclusively second order to be successful and lasting, but in some instances, second-order change is needed.

Second-order change occurs when rules of the system change, thus changing the system itself. Changing rules creates change in perception, or an individual's view of the problem, which results in opportunity for different behavioral approaches to be applied to the same situations. Consider applying second-order change to the case of the crying baby. In this situation, applying second-order change might result in letting the baby self-soothe instead of immediately picking up the baby when fussy or upset. Allowing the baby to self-soothe creates new behaviors for family members: Parents no longer have to run to the baby every time he or she cries, and the baby increases his or her tolerance for independence and self-reliance. This new contextual experience redefines family rules and creates lasting change to the existing problem.

Interventions

Regardless of the specific types of interventions utilized in family/couples therapy, the family's influence on the individual is likely stronger than that of the therapist. Therefore, the family dynamics should be taken into account so interventions and treatment services are applied accordingly. Without this consideration, the client is not as likely to experience consolidation of learning or successful transfer of information to daily life after therapy is terminated.

Ecomaps

An ecomap is a graphic diagram of family relationships both within the unit and with external support systems. Interpersonal dynamics and psychological, social, and spiritual dimensions are considered when creating this framework. Flow of resources and energy both into and out of the family are identified with respect to how external systems affect the internal family system. Support systems that might be included in an ecomap are extended family, friends, school, work, religious houses of worship (this might mean faith in the religion itself, as well as an individual's religious leader and congregation), medical/health workers (e.g., nurse, physical therapist), and mental health practitioners (e.g., family and couples therapist, social worker). Participation in this intervention permits the client family to become aware of their resources, strengths of their interpersonal and community relationships, and interaction with family members and external systems of which they are also members. Exercise 14.1 invites you to develop your own ecomap.

EXERCISE 14.1

ECOMAPS

- What resources exist in your life? Begin by creating a three-generation genogram of your family of origin.
- Add extended family to the visual map. What do you find helpful about these relationships?
- Do you have neighbors in your community system? How do these relationships benefit you?
- What friends would you add to the list of positive resources?
- Do you belong to a house of worship (i.e., synagogue, temple, church)? How does this connection influence you?
- With whom do you work? Do your coworkers and supervisors support you?
- Do you attend school? How do your classmates and teachers act as resources for you?
- Are you involved in the legal system? Medical system? How do these connections influence your life?
- What other important relationships exist in your life? Do you have a coach who supports you? Perhaps sorority sisters or fraternity brothers with whom you have regular contact? Are you involved in a relationship with a mentor? How do these connections serve as resources for you? In what ways do they differ?

Family Sculpting

Family sculpting is a creation of the client by which he or she reveals a spatial representation of his or her perception of the family. One client is asked to arrange family members in a metaphorical scene by which the client views their relationships at a particular point in time. Family members are placed in a tableau with specific attention paid to how close or far away they are positioned from one another. Case Illustration 14.1 provides one example of this intervention strategy.

CASE ILLUSTRATION 14.1

Family Sculpting

Counselor:	Emily, I notice that, at times, you seem to be left out of the family conversation. Your two older sisters tend to voice their opinions more.
Emily:	No kidding. I can barely get a word in edgewise with these two!
Counselor:	Would you like to participate in an exercise with me?
Emily:	Depends. What is it?
Counselor:	It's called family sculpting, and you'll get to create a life-sized family portrait that addresses your feeling of isolation from the group.
Emily:	How does it work?
Counselor:	I want you to position each one of your family members in relation to one another. You get to place them where you want, how you want them to look—you get to create the whole scene of how you see everyone's relationships and roles in the family.
Emily:	I get to be the boss for once and tell everyone else what to do? I'm totally in!
Counselor:	Start with whomever you want.
Emily:	Mom, I want you to go to the center of the room and try to face everyone at the same time, even if you have to spin around. Look exasperated!
Mom:	(Moves to the center of the room)
Emily:	I like this! Okay, next, Dad, I want you to sit in the far corner and face the wall. Look bored.
Dad:	(Moves to the corner of the room)

Emily:	Okay, Lindsay and May, go to the opposite end of the room. I want you to stand side by side, holding hands. Look happy, smile!
Lindsay:	(Moves to the opposite end of the room)
May:	(Moves to the opposite end of the room)
Counselor:	Now you, Emily—where would you place yourself in this picture?
Emily:	(Stands equidistant from her father and mother) Lindsay and May, I want you to turn your backs to me, but not Mom and Dad. (Her face remains somber.)
Counselor:	Emily, thanks so much for creating this scene for everyone, and thanks to everyone for participating! I would like to process this experience with all of you now, if that's okay. (Family members nod their heads and return to their seats.) What do the different family members' positions mean?
Emily:	Lindsay and May were holding hands because they're best friends. Mom had to spin because she is always juggling a million things at once. Dad was in the corner because he is never home.
Counselor:	Can you talk about the spatial differences between family members with regard to distance?
Emily:	Mom was in the center of the room because she is like the sun—the center of the universe for the family. We are all the planets that orbit her but we all need her to survive. Linds and May were on the opposite side of the room from me because I don't feel close to them, I feel like the outsider of the three sisters.
Counselor:	Please explain the facial expressions as representative of each person at this time.
Emily:	Dad looked bored because that's how he always looks when he's home, like he'd rather be somewhere else. Mom looked exasperated because she is always freaking out about something. Linds and May looked happy because they're together and they like being together.
Counselor:	What about you, Emily?
Emily:	I looked sad because I feel sad when I'm left out.
Counselor:	What would you name this picture?
Emily:	Probably "The Universe as I Know It," or something like that.
Counselor:	What does this scene tell you about your family patterns?
Emily:	That, like the universe, our family did not get this way overnight.
Counselor:	Good point. Let's assess change as it relates to this particular problem.

Genograms

As compared with family sculpting, a genogram is a literal map of the family that illustrates relationships among family members—a type of family tree. Typically, three generations of the family are depicted so the therapist and clients can explore transgenerational patterns that exist within the family. A genogram identifies behaviors such as substance abuse and behavioral addictions, as well as mental health disorders, and levels of boundaries among individuals within an extended family system. The family data in this visual representation can include age, gender, religion, sexual orientation, marital status, education level, career choice, socioeconomic status, and physical health or illness. Lines with various symbols link individuals within the family system, depicting types of relationships, boundaries, and interactional patterns among members, such as enmeshed, loose, or physical abuse. Development of genograms allows clients to tell their stories while providing the family therapist with a visual road map of relationships and patterns that lie within the extended family system. Through this process, the therapist and client family can explore the roots of family problems, which will facilitate present and future changes. Exercise 14.2 invites you to develop your own genogram.

EXERCISE 14.2

GENOGRAMS

- Create a genogram of your family of origin. Include three generations.
- What do you observe about your family structure?
- What relationship patterns stand out to you?
- What significant alliances exist among family members?
- What do you notice about similarities of behaviors exhibited by various family members?
- Do you see any connections between levels of boundaries among family members?
- What do you interpret as major themes existing transgenerationally in your family of origin?

Paradoxical Injunction

This is a type of second-order change by which the context of the problem is redefined, creating a change in the situation and opportunity for alternative methods of approach. This might include symptom prescription, in which the problem is encouraged instead of admonished. Case Illustration 14.2 provides one example of this intervention strategy.

Reframing

Reframing is change in an individual's perception of a particular situation or concern. Reframing removes an old set of rules associated with an issue and replaces them with new contextual guidelines for approach that are reasonable to and achievable by the client

CASE ILLUSTRATION 14.2

Paradoxical Injunction

Session 1: Beginning of Session

Counselor:	(Speaking to mother and son) Can either of you please explain what brings you here?
Grant:	We fight all the time.
Roberta:	It's true. We cannot seem to stop bickering lately over issues both small and large. When we get mad at each other, we both yell at the other one about the issue, and then we do not speak to each other for a while.
Grant:	We have this unspoken agreement that, after our fights, we move on without addressing the problem further. It's better to just get over it.
Counselor:	Will you be willing to try something that I think might help with the arguments? (Mother and son nod their heads) I'd like you to spend 1 hour every afternoon arguing. You are not allowed to fight during any time other than this daily argument appointment. Can you try this? We'll see how the argument appointments are working when we meet again next week. (Mother and son agree.)

Session 2: Beginning of Session

Counselor:	So, how did the prescriptive fighting go this past week?
Grant:	It was weird.
Roberta:	It was strange, indeed, but it went alright. On the first day, we both brought up issues that we had wanted to address earlier, but we saved them for our afternoon argument. The next day, we both started to feel a bit awkward about fighting at a specific time, even if we weren't presently mad at each other.
Grant:	I think the second day's argument was less emotional and intense than the previous day. On the third day, when we met for our argument appointment time, our fight was pretty weak.
Counselor:	What do you mean by "weak"?
Grant:	We were half-heartedly fighting with each other, and after a few minutes, we looked at each other and both began to laugh at the ridiculous nature of the fight.

(Continued)

(Continued)

Roberta:	It's true. Neither of us really felt like we had any reason to argue at that particular point. We couldn't take it seriously.
Grant:	I told her, "I'm not even mad at you right now. How can I yell at you?"
Roberta:	To which I responded, "If we feel silly now for fighting when there is no problem, then we ought to feel really silly for fighting when there is an actual problem and we should be coming together as a family instead of dividing."
Counselor:	Wow, it sounds like the two of you have opened the lines of communication when each has an issue with the other, allowing you both to address the concern instead of yelling about it and then ignoring it.

family. This provides the family with an opportunity to view problems, for instance, from new perspectives, with alternatives they had not previously considered. Case Illustration 14.3 provides one example of this intervention strategy, and Exercise 14.3 gives you a chance to practice this technique.

CASE ILLUSTRATION 14.3

Reframing

Tom:	Leona, you always want to be with me because you don't trust me! You never leave me alone! You don't have to go everywhere I go! Why don't you believe that I'm trustworthy?
Leona:	(Begins to cry) Why don't you want to spend time with me?
Counselor:	Tom, can you tell Leona how you feel now?
Tom:	I feel angry that she doesn't trust me, because I haven't given her any reason to think that I'm cheating on her.
Counselor:	Leona, can you tell Tom how you feel now?
Leona:	I feel rejected. I feel lonely. I'm alone.
Tom:	Always a victim. I know that you have some ulterior motive for all this togetherness.
Leona:	No, that's not true! (Crying harder)

Counselor:	Tom, is it at all possible that Leona wants to be with you frequently because she wants to feel close to you?
Tom:	(Rolls his eyes)
Counselor:	I just want you to consider another possible way of reflecting on this situation. Is it at all possible that Leona just loves being with you?
Tom:	Well, I am pretty fun to be around. . . .
Counselor:	We tend to judge others by their actions, while we judge ourselves by our intentions. Just imagine the possibility that what you perceive is not what the other person intends. I would encourage both of you to attempt to approach a situation like this one differently in the future for more effective communication and interaction with each other.

EXERCISE 14.3

REFRAMING

Come up with alternative ways of thinking about and reflecting on the following scenarios:

1. An older sister accuses her younger sister of stealing her clothes because she wants to deliberately annoy her.

2. A grown man is suspicious of his mother's intentions when she calls his new wife to talk on the phone.

3. A young boy is angry at his father for choosing to spend more time at work than at home with him.

4. A husband and wife think there is something wrong with their marriage because they do not have intercourse as frequently as their friends do.

5. A teenage girl thinks her father does not trust her because he will not allow her to date.

6. A preteen boy feels rejected because his mother and aunt go out to dinner without him.

Focus and Intentionality

Depending on whether family/couples therapy is in the early, middle, or late stages, sessions are focused by different applications of therapeutic processes. Early in therapy, the family/couples therapist is concerned with building rapport and forming bonds with family members, often referred to as joining. The emphasis is on relationships characterized by genuine respect, trust, and empathy in which all parties are actively involved in therapeutic engagement and progress. It is important that, at the beginning of the first session, the family/couples therapist engages the family in informed consent, making clear the limitations of confidentiality, outlining any ground rules for therapy sessions, and demystifying the process for the client family through role induction—explaining how therapy will work and what is expected of participants. The therapist must be willing to address any questions or concerns of the client family to further demystify the process and engage clients in becoming invested in counseling. Clients should be made aware of expectations and included in therapy as active, contributing members. The family/couples therapist needs to be welcoming of each family member, showing desire to join with the family in therapeutic engagement from a perspective of concern and care for overall wellness and healthy functioning. The therapist asks questions that begin with "how" to facilitate understanding of family processes, rather than focusing on content and presenting problems. It is important that, from the very beginning, the family/couples therapist observes the client family to understand established patterns of relational interaction, behavior, cognitions, and affect. Simple counseling skills are utilized to foster engagement and promote an effective working relationship with the client family, skills such as active listening, validation, encouragement, and honest acceptance. Some family/couples therapists use homework assignments to complement the work done during sessions. With managed care limiting the number of times clients can see therapists, homework can be a useful tool to maximize time allowed for therapy.

Once therapeutic joining has been established and the therapist has a greater understanding of the processes of the client family system, he or she will use assessment to gain further comprehension of family data. This is important because it facilitates understanding of which changes need to be made for optimal functioning to exist. This may occur through any number of formal assessment instruments, such as the Parenting Relationship Questionnaire (Kamphaus & Reynolds, 2006), Global Assessment of Relational Functioning (American Psychiatric Association, 2013), Family Environment Scale (Moos & Moos, 1994), and Clinical Rating Scale (Olson, 1993), explained in further detail in the "Assessment Strategies" section of this chapter. Family/couples therapists also use informal means of data gathering, including the circumplex model, family structure typology, genograms, and simple observation and client self-report. Regardless of the type or specific assessment used, the family/couples therapist intends to glean the family's story, facilitating a focus on therapeutic engagement and process. Circular questioning is used, which is relational or interactional in nature, creating meaning for systemic issues presented by the client family.

In the middle stages of family/couples therapy, once rapport has been established and data have been gathered, the therapist engages in the processes of hypothesizing and communicating the meaning he or she understands as a result of encountering systemic issues within the client family. During this time, the focus is still on family process rather than on their problems and concerns. When hypothesizing, the family/couples therapist formulates thoughts about the client family, system, and existing problems or concerns. He or she draws meaning from hypothesis, which is adopted subsequent to family assessment. Some family/couples therapists, particularly from more recent models (i.e., feminism, multiculturalism, and postmodernism), ask the family to collaborate in hypothesizing and meaning making, engaging in bidirectional communication and feedback that fosters client–counselor rapport. To encourage change, the family/couples therapist engages the client family in communication about their understanding of current problems, possible alternative options, benefits and deficits associated with change, and what they will need to do to effect that change. The subjective experiences of all family members are invited to be shared, treated as valid, and included in joint understanding. The family/couples therapist attempts to link all family members to one another so there are no uninvolved peripheral family members.

The late stages of family/couples therapy are when action plans are implemented and change is facilitated. The plan for change might include specific techniques or interventions, including directed homework assignments, paradoxical injunction, and family sculpting. However, importance of techniques weighs more heavily within theories and models that view the therapist as expert, rather than the client. It is more effective to include the client family in the process of agreeing and deciding on which interventions will be most beneficial for their experience. It is important to consider the family's resources when determining the change process, which can be accomplished through using an ecomap, for example. Resources, both within and outside of the family, will contribute to the success of lasting change and need to be identified and utilized to support consolidation of learning for the client family. Change will often occur in small steps, with the client family willing to attempt simpler changes first. Evidence of successful change can often be observed through the family's communication and relational interactions. For example, the client family might begin to engage in healthier communication (listening to one another before responding, not raising their voices when disagreeing) and more positive interpersonal relationships (sharing feelings of love and caring for one another). Once change is effectively taking place and goals are being met, therapy moves toward termination.

The final stage of family/couples therapy, termination, should be something the therapist begins addressing at the beginning of the therapeutic relationship. The therapist is always planning for the time when the weekly counseling sessions will end and the client family will become their own counselors. When the client family conclude their number of sessions permitted by insurance, for example, or when self-pay clients achieve the goals they set for the term of therapy, termination commences. The family/couples therapist reviews the arc of counseling experienced in his or her time with the client family, inviting them to share their perspectives as well. Long-term goals are discussed and established, presuming that the family will continue to work after therapy ends.

Assessment Strategies

Assessment of successful family/couples therapy is measured by progress as defined by the particular model being practiced. Bowenian family therapists consider progress to be concurrent with differentiation of self from other family members, promoting individual, as well as group, functioning. From a brief family therapy perspective, progress occurs when the family can maintain functional unity during stressful times and when individuals communicate with one another clearly and directly. From a communications approach, progress is viewed in terms of honest communication and feelings of self-worth within a family that has set rules but acts flexibly in their application thereof. In contextual family therapy, progress is associated with increased levels of trust and consideration for other family members and shared responsibilities within relationships characterized by flexibility. Experiential therapists view progress within family through stability and balancing autonomy with relational interdependence. Strategic family therapists view parental alliance as crucial to family progress, as well as task accomplishment. The structural family therapy approach views progress as movement toward maintenance of boundaries and hierarchical structure within the family.

In addition to assessing progress differently, various family/couples therapists also use different approaches by which they classify levels of family functioning. One such method is known as the circumplex model. Family functioning is viewed from dimensions of adaptability and cohesion, with expectations of balance for each. Proper family communication facilitates both adaptability and cohesion within healthfully functioning families. Adaptability is assessed by examining family's capability in balancing stability and flexibility. Levels of adaptability include rigid, structured, flexible, and chaotic. Cohesion refers to the family's level of interpersonal interdependence, which ranges from enmeshed to connected to separated to disengaged.

Another method by which family/couples therapists engage in assessment is using typology that denotes family structure as one of three types: closed, open, or random. These subtypes refer to processes by which the family communicates among members and with the outside environment. These are not intended to be value judgments, ascribing superiority to one style over another; rather, these subtypes are designed to help predict certain behaviors or outcomes based on general characteristics associated with each subtype. Closed families promote benefit of the group over any individual. Crucial family elements include clear rules and regulations, internal structure, and power differentials and hierarchy. Behaviors are stable, which creates family patterns; these are maintained through rigid scheduling and communication of expectations. Parents carefully regulate children's contact with their environment, monitoring social media, relationships with friends, and communication with any individual who is not a family member. Children may rebel against parental rules and structure when they are too rigid. Characteristics of the closed family vary greatly compared with the open family, which is democratic both within the family operating style and with regard to its allowance of transmission of information outside of the family. Organization is balanced with flexibility, and family members negotiate with one another to maintain structure. Communication both within and outside of the family is characterized by honesty. Each family member's opinions are respected, and, in return, loyalty to each member and the family as a whole is expected. If the open family becomes too lax in structure, however, they may become a random family, in which family processes are fragmented and individual family members are not necessarily interconnected with one another. The random family does not have enough rules in place to keep it stable and is characterized by unconstant boundaries. Family members' connections with the outside world are not governed or limited, permitting individuals themselves to decide on levels of interaction and depth of interpersonal relationships with one another. The random family becomes problematic when lack of necessary structure leads to chaos.

In addition to the aforementioned evaluation approaches, family/couples therapists can also utilize hard-copy and computerized inventories to assess levels of family functioning and therapeutic success. One example is the Parenting Relationship Questionnaire (Kamphaus & Reynolds, 2006), which is used to examine the parent–child relationship from the parent's perspective and can be utilized with parents of children ages 2 to 18. Another useful assessment is the Family Environment Scale (Moos & Moos, 1994), which measures the socioenvironmental typology of the family, evaluating members as oriented toward personal growth, relationships, or maintenance of family system. The Clinical Rating Scale (Olson, 1993) is intended for use with the circumplex model and measures family cohesion, change, and communication as evidence of growth and therapeutic progress. A widely used measure is called Global Assessment of Relational Functioning and is published in the *Diagnostic and Statistical Manual of Mental Disorders* (American Psychiatric Association, 2013). This scale enables the family/couples therapist to assess the degree to which the family is currently meeting the needs of its members as they relate to problem solving, organization, and emotional climate (American Psychiatric Association, 2013). It is crucial for the family/couples therapist to remember that, when selecting a standardized assessment for use with a client family, he or she must select an instrument designed to measure the area of family functioning he or she is attempting to assess, tests need to have been normed and validated on populations similar to the client family, and instruments should always be used in conjunction with data collected from therapist observation and family report.

Y-CHUN THROUGH THE LENS OF FAMILY/COUPLES COUNSELING

Session 2 (first session after intake)—beginning of session:

Counselor: Thank you so much for coming again this week, Y-Chun.

Y-Chun: I have to admit that I was still nervous coming back.

Counselor: You were nervous, or you are still nervous?

Y-Chun: I was. I mean, I am. Both, I guess.

Counselor: Can you share your feeling of nervousness in the present tense?

Y-Chun: (Takes a deep breath) I am still nervous being back here this week.

Counselor: I appreciate your willingness to try that.

Y-Chun: I have to trust you, I guess.

Counselor: I don't think that you have to trust me. I think that you choose to do so. I give you credit for choosing to trust in me and our relationship. That shows courage and commitment.

Counselor reflection: I choose to replace the word *have* with *choose* because it models accountability for my client.

Y-Chun: (Looks down and smiles softly)

Counselor: Would you like to summarize what we talked about last time?

Y-Chun: Sure. I told you about my weight loss and sleep problems. We talked about my relationships with my family—my parents and my siblings. We talked about my problems in school growing up . . . what else?

Counselor: You also told me about your children, David and Jennifer. You shared with me the story of your cousin raping you and some of the other problems in your life that stemmed from that attack, like the shoplifting and taking money for sex.

Counselor reflection: I choose to recount my client's story to foster rapport by communicating to her that I am listening to her and I remember her unique story.

Y-Chun: I said all that, huh?

Counselor: Yes, and I am still appreciative of your willingness to share this with me. It can't be easy to say these things out loud to someone you just met.

Y-Chun: (Shakes her head)

Counselor: So, do you have an idea of what you would like to accomplish in today's session?

Y-Chun: No, I have never been in counseling before so I don't really know what to expect, or exactly what I am supposed to do . . . I think I need some guidance in that area.

Counselor: Well, I will tell you a little more about my role as a family therapist, and you let me know what questions or concerns come up for you. Does that sound okay?

Counselor reflection: I choose to educate my client about family counseling to facilitate role induction. When my client has information about the therapeutic process, she will be better equipped as an active agent of change.

Y-Chun: Yeah, thanks.

Counselor: Since my focus is family counseling, I tend to think a lot about the relationships in your life, how they affect you and how you affect them, and what patterns have been established through your family.

Y-Chun: What do you mean by "patterns"?

Counselor: Certain behaviors, ways of expressing oneself, interactions among family members, similarities among different people.

Y-Chun: Okay, that makes sense to me. Coming from a background that is half Chinese, we put a lot of emphasis on family and traditions. Usually when I think of traditions, I think of religion and culture, but you're talking about traditions that occur just for my family. I do have one question, though: How can you see only one person—me—and treat me from a family focus?

Counselor:	That's a really good question. Ideally, I would get to see you with your whole family so I can observe these relational interactions for myself. There may be an opportunity at some point for you to bring your family members to session, which we can discuss in further detail later. Regardless of whether I see only you or your entire family, I am still going to be interested in how that whole group has a great deal to do with the person you are today.

Counselor reflection: I hope to impress on my client the importance of focusing on her within the family system so we can attempt to better understand how that has affected who she is today.

Y-Chun:	You really think they affect me that much?
Counselor:	(Nods head) I do. I think that everyone's family affects them greatly, but we're not always aware of how powerful those relationships are.
Y-Chun:	What do you mean by "powerful"?
Counselor:	I'll give you an example. Last week, you told me that you have never really felt a close connection with your children. I also heard you say that you never felt like you had a close relationship with your parents, either. I see a connection between those two sets of relationships.

Counselor reflection: I am attempting to establish patterns between my client and her family members to understand the relationships within the family.

Y-Chun:	I'm screwed up. I know that. My family's screwed up. I know that, too. I guess I just always thought that me being screwed up was my own fault, not that it had anything to do with my family also being screwed up.
Counselor:	That's one way of putting it! (Laughs)
Y-Chun:	(Chuckles) So, we're going to talk a lot about me and my family, huh?
Counselor:	Yes, and also your relationships with people outside of your family. Our upbringings affect those, too.
Y-Chun:	Another area where I'm totally screwed up.
Counselor:	Tell me what you mean by "screwed up."
Y-Chun:	I'm not normal. I don't have close relationships with people, not even my own children! I can't keep a romantic relationship intact because I'm never good enough for any man to want to stay with on a long-term basis. My parents treat me like I'm a loser, which I basically am. (Starts to cry.)
Counselor:	I heard you talk about four important relationships just now: the one with your kids, your parents, a potential partner, and also with yourself. What do you think you would like to change about those relationships?

Counselor reflection: I am using a direct question to establish goals for therapy with my client.

Y-Chun: Everything.

Counselor: (Remains silent, waiting)

Y-Chun: I want to feel closer to my kids and my parents. I'd like to meet a guy that I can be with seriously. I want to feel less angry and upset all the time.

Counselor: Earlier in this session, I asked you what you wanted to accomplish today, and you said you didn't know. It sounds like you just accomplished identifying some goals, which is a really important step in counseling.

Counselor reflection: I want to express to the client that I notice her therapeutic progress, and I want her to be aware of it as well.

Y-Chun: Oh, good! I guess I can do one thing right.

Counselor: I think you can do a lot of things right. It seems like you know how to help yourself better than you realized, or give yourself credit for.

Counselor reflection: I want the client to be aware of her strengths and resources, and to accept responsibility for them.

Y-Chun: So, what's next for goal setting?

Counselor: We start discussing more specifically the objectives of your goals, in which order you think you'd like to address them, how long is reasonable to spend on each part of the goal. The more organized we are, the better we will be able to work through as many components of your goals as possible during the brief time we have together.

Y-Chun: I need as much organization in my life as possible, otherwise nothing gets done.

Counselor: The great thing about organizing goals like this is that we can see achievements when they're happening and also adjust things as needed.

Y-Chun: Basically, we gather a plan of attack.

Counselor: Mm-hmm. We'll start there next week when we meet again. Sound good?

Y-Chun: Sounds good to me.

KEYSTONES

- The nature of family/couples therapy is to view clients as inexorably intertwined with family systems, as well as greater community systems; individuals affect their environments, and environments affect individuals reciprocally.
- The counseling practice is rooted in holism, and the family/couples therapist acts to encourage the family, reinforcing positive attempts at change and therapeutic engagement and progress.

- The client family can both help rectify and exacerbate problems, depending on its focus; established boundaries delineate rules of engagement for family members both inside and outside of the family unit.
- Family/couples therapy has been researched and identified as effective when applied to many presenting concerns and family issues, including interpersonal relationship distress, substance abuse, disruptive behaviors, and mental health diagnoses such as depression, attention-deficit hyperactivity disorder, schizophrenia, and bipolar disorder. Family/couples therapy is also successfully used with diverse cultural populations, as well as children.
- Therapeutic process and application for family/couples therapists varies according to preferred methods of clinical practice. Goals for therapy, view of change process, interventions, assessments, and focus all differ, depending on the style and specific model of the therapist.

We invite you to continue to learn about family/couples therapy by visiting the recommended websites and reading the suggested professional literature (see "Additional Resources" and "References" sections). Consider joining one or more of the listed professional organizations for family/couples therapists. Above all else, continue to educate yourself on the changing nature of families in counseling and how to provide them with optimal services for functional well-being.

REFLECTIONS FROM THE CONTRIBUTOR'S CHAIR

Rebecca M. Goldberg, PhD, is an assistant professor in the Department of Counseling and Educational Psychology at Mississippi State University (MSU). Dr. Goldberg graduated from the University of Florida with a Doctor of Philosophy degree in counselor education in 2009 and her Master of Education and Specialist in Education degrees in mental health counseling and marriage and family therapy in 2006. She received her credential as a licensed professional counselor in the state of Mississippi in 2011. Additionally, Dr. Goldberg has been a certified grief counselor since 2011 and a national certified counselor since 2007. She is the creator and director of the Grief Counseling and Client Support Services Clinic at the MSU College of Veterinary Medicine Animal Health Center, where she counsels individuals, couples, and families on issues surrounding death and dying, grief and loss, and the human–animal bond as it relates to companion animals. Dr. Goldberg also teaches communication strategies, crisis management, and developmental life span issues to advanced veterinary students, and works as a consultant to the MSU Animal Health Center faculty and staff. Additionally, she provides mental health services to veterinary students at MSU. Dr. Goldberg is the chapter faculty advisor for the Mu Sigma Upsilon chapter of Chi Sigma Iota, an international counseling honors organization for graduate counseling students. She is also faculty advisor for the Jewish Life on Campus Hillel student organization at MSU.

ADDITIONAL RESOURCES

Websites

Ackerman Institute for the Family. (n.d.). Retrieved from http://www.ackerman.org/

American Association for Marriage and Family Therapy. (n.d.). Retrieved from http://www.aamft.org/

American Family Therapy Academy. (n.d.). Retrieved from http://www.afta.org/

Bowen Center for the Study of the Family. (n.d.). Retrieved from http://www.thebowencenter.org/

Family Therapy Resources. (2002). Retrieved from http://www.familytherapyresources.net/

Gottman Relationship Institute. (2013). Retrieved from http://www.gottman.com/

International Association of Marriage and Family Counselors. (2013). Retrieved from http://www.iamfconline.com/

International Family Therapy Association. (n.d.). Retrieved from http://www.ifta-familytherapy.org/

Print

Becvar, D. S. (2012). *Handbook of family resilience.* New York: Springer.

Duncan, B. L., Miller, S. D., Wampold, B. E., & Hubble, M. A. (2010). *The heart and soul of change: Delivering what works in therapy.* Washington, DC: American Psychological Association.

Goldenberg, I., & Goldenberg, H. (Eds.). (2012). *Family therapy: An overview* (8th ed.). Pacific Grove, CA: Thomson Brooks/Cole.

Gottman, J. M. (2001). *The relationship cure: A 5 step guide to strengthening your marriage, family, and friendships.* New York: Three Rivers Press.

Hays, D. G., & Erford, B. T. (2012). *Developing multicultural counseling competence: A systems approach* (2nd ed.). San Antonio, TX: Pearson.

McGoldrick, M., Giordano, J., & Garcia-Preto, N. (2005). *Ethnicity and family therapy* (3rd ed.). New York: Guilford Press.

Pipher, M. (2005). *Reviving Ophelia: Saving the selves of adolescent girls.* New York: Berkley.

Satir, V. (1988). *The new peoplemaking.* Palo Alto, CA: Science and Behavior Books.

Satir, V., Banmen, J., Gerber, J., & Gomori, M. (1991). *The Satir model: Family therapy and beyond.* Palo Alto, CA: Science and Behavior Books.

Schnarch, D. (2002). *Resurrecting sex: Solving sexual problems and revolutionizing your relationship.* New York: HarperCollins.

Schnarch, D. (2009). *Passionate marriage: Keeping love and intimacy alive in committed relationships.* New York: W. W. Norton.

Sue, D. W., & Sue, D. (2012). *Counseling the culturally diverse: Theory and practice* (6th ed.). Hoboken, NJ: John Wiley.

Trozzi, M. (1999). *Talking with children about loss: Words, strategies, and wisdom to help children cope with death, divorce, and other difficult times.* New York: Berkley.

Wiseman, R. (2009). *Queen bees and wannabes: Helping your daughter survive cliques, gossip, boyfriends, and the new realities of girl world.* New York: Three Rivers Press.

Wiseman, R., & Rapoport, E. (2007). *Queen bee moms and kingpin dads: Dealing with the difficult parents in your child's life.* New York: Three Rivers Press.

Yalom, I. (2012). *Love's executioner: And other tales of psychotherapy.* New York: Basic Books.

Film

Baumbach, N. (Director). (2005). *The squid and the whale* [Motion picture]. United States: Samuel Goldwyn Films.

Cholodenko, L. (Director). (2010). *The kids are alright* [Motion picture]. United States: Focus Features.

Coppola, S. (Director). (1999). *The virgin suicides* [Motion picture]. United States: American Zoetrope.

Dahan, O. (Director). (1997). *La vie en rose* [Motion picture]. France: Légende Films.

Dayton, J., & Faris, V. (Directors). (2006). *Little Miss Sunshine* [Motion picture]. United States: Fox Searchlight Pictures.

Haggis, P. (Director). (2004). *Crash* [Motion picture]. United States: Lions Gate Films.

Hallström, L. (Director). (1993). *What's eating Gilbert Grape?* [Motion picture]. United States: Paramount Pictures.

Hovde, E., Maysles, A., Maysles, D., & Meyer, M. (Directors). (1975). *Grey gardens* [Motion picture]. United States: Portrait Films.

Howard, R. (Director). (1989). *Parenthood* [Motion picture]. United States: Imagine Entertainment.

Kaye, T. (Director). (1998). *American history X* [Motion picture]. United States: New Line Cinema.

Mandoki, L. (Director). (1994). *When a man loves a woman* [Motion picture]. United States: Touchstone Pictures.

Pakula, A. J. (Director). (1982). *Sophie's choice* [Motion picture]. United Kingdom: Incorporated Television Company.

Perry, F. (Director). (1981). *Mommie dearest* [Motion picture]. United States: Paramount Pictures.

Redford, R. (Director). (1980). *Ordinary people* [Motion picture]. United States: Paramount Pictures.

Waters, M. (Director). (1997). *The house of yes* [Motion picture]. United States: Bandeira Entertainment.

Winkler, I. (Director). (2001). *Life as a house* [Motion picture]. United States: Winkler Films.

Younger, B. (Director). *Prime* [Motion picture]. United States: Prime Film Productions.

REFERENCES

Ackerman, N. (1958). *The psychodynamics of family life.* New York: Basic Books.

Adler, A. (1958). *What life should mean to you.* New York: Capricorn. (Original work published in 1931)

Adler, A. (1959). *Understanding human nature.* New York: Premier Books. (Original work published in 1927)

American Association for Marriage and Family Therapy. (2012). *Code of ethics.* Alexandria, VA: Author.

American Psychiatric Association. (2013). *Diagnostic and statistical manual of mental disorders* (5th ed.). Washington, DC: Author.

Bateson, G. (1971). The cybernetics of 'self': A theory of alcoholism. *Psychiatry: Journal for the Study of Interpersonal Processes, 34*(1), 1–18.

Beach, S. R. H., & O'Leary, K. D. (1992). Treating depression in the context of marital discord: Outcome and predictors of response for marital therapy vs. cognitive therapy. *Behavior Therapy, 23*(4), 507–528.

Boszormenyi-Nagy, I. (1987). *Foundations of contextual therapy: Collected papers of Ivan Boszormenyi-Nagy, MD.* New York: Brunner/Mazel.

Bowen, M. (1978). *Family therapy in clinical practice.* Northvale, NJ: Jason Aronson.

Carr, A. (2010). Ten research questions for family therapy. *Australian and New Zealand Journal of Family Therapy, 31*(2), 119–132.

Corey, G. (2012). *Theory and practice of counseling and psychotherapy* (9th ed.). Belmont, CA: Thomson Brooks/Cole.

Fall, K. A., Holden, J. M., & Marquis, A. (2010). *Theoretical models of counseling and psychotherapy* (2nd ed.). New York: Routledge.

Gladding, S. T. (2010). *Family therapy: History, theory, and practice* (5th ed.). Upper Saddle River, NJ: Merrill Counseling.

Goldstein, M. J., & Miklowitz, D. J. (1995). The effectiveness of psychoeducational family therapy in the treatment of schizophrenic disorders. *Journal of Marital and Family Therapy, 21*(4), 361–376.

Gottman, J. M., & Silver, N. (1999). *The seven principles for making marriage work.* New York: Three Rivers Press.

Gurman, A. S. (1983). Family therapy research and the "new epistemology." *Journal of Marital and Family Therapy, 9*(3), 227–234.

Haley, J., & Hoffman, L. (1968). *Techniques of family therapy.* New York: Basic Books.

Hendricks, B. E., Bradley, L. J., Southern, S., Oliver, M., & Birdsall, B. (2011). Ethical code for the International Association of Marriage and Family Counselors. *Family Journal, 19*(2), 217–224. doi:10.1177/1066480711400814

Kamphaus, R. W., & Reynolds, C. R. (2006). *Parenting relationship questionnaire* [Measurement instrument]. San Antonio, TX: Pearson.

Luquet, W., & Hendrix, H. (2001). Imago relationship therapy. In F. M. Dattilio (Ed.), *Case studies in couple and family therapy* (pp. 401–426). New York: Guilford Press.

McFarlane, W. (2004). *Multifamily groups in the treatment of severe psychiatric disorders.* New York: Guilford Press.

Minuchin, S. (1974). *Families and family therapy.* Boston: Harvard University Press.

Minuchin, S., & Fishman, H. C. (1981). *Family therapy techniques.* Cambridge, MA: Harvard University Press.

Moore, L., & Seu, I. B. (2011). Giving children a voice: Children's positioning in family therapy. *Journal of Family Therapy, 33*(3), 279–301. doi:10.1111/j.1467-6427.2011.00556.x

Moos, R. H., & Moos, B. H. (1994). *Family environment scale manual* [Measurement instrument]. Palo Alto, CA: Consulting Psychologists Press.

Napier, A. Y., & Whitaker, C. (1978). *The family crucible.* New York: Harper & Row.

Olson, D. H. (1993). *Clinical rating scale for the circumplex model of marital and family systems* [Measurement instrument]. St. Paul: University of Minnesota, Department of Family Social Science.

Rowe, C. L. (2012). Family therapy for drug abuse: Review and updates 2003–2010. *Journal of Marital and Family Therapy, 38*(1), 59–81. doi:10.1111/j.1752-0606.2011.00280.x

Satir, V. (1964). *Conjoint family therapy: A guide to theory and technique.* Palo Alto, CA: Science and Behavior Books.

SECTION III

Looking to the Future

CHAPTER 15

Seeking Integration

Adam Zagelbaum, Maureen Buckley,
Shana Friedman, and Kalia Gurnee

*I have a lot on my mind, but I think I am willing to focus on these things for the
first time in a long time, and start doing something about them.*

Though this anonymous client may have always known at some level that issues and problems had gotten in the way of reaching certain goals, being able to recognize the deeper concerns associated with the issues and actionable steps to work through them can be important progress toward reaching these goals. As you will see in the chapter that follows, different therapeutic techniques and approaches can be applied to such a client. Counselors must also recognize where the client is in terms of readiness to use these methods during the course of therapy to facilitate the client's steps toward making and maintaining change.

The current chapter reviews integrative psychotherapy, a framework that proposes the use of multiple models and approaches in the formulation of the counseling process. After reading this chapter, you will be able to do the following:

1. Understand the routes by which counseling professionals integrate theories into the counseling process

2. Describe the stages of change and how they can unfold

3. Identify what types of techniques and methods are deemed most suitable for the stages of change

PROFILE OF MAIN FIGURES

When discussing the issue of integrative theories, one would be hard-pressed to identify a single representative or main figure. In Table 15.1, we have presented a representative sample of those theories and theoreticians who are attempting to achieve effective integration. As evident, the approaches are quite diverse.

Table 15.1 Sampling of Integrative Theories

Theory	Focus	Reference
Multimodal therapy	Technically eclectic model targeting seven modalities (BASIC ID)	Lazarus (2005)
Systematic treatment selection	Integrates the type of therapist, strategy of treatment, and type of psychotherapeutic intervention	Beutler and Harwood (2000)
Cyclical psychodynamics	Integrates psychodynamic, behavioral, and family systems theories	Wachtel (1993)
Cognitive analytic therapy	Integrates object-relations theory and cognitive psychotherapy	Ryle (1990)
Assimilative psychodynamic psychotherapy	Employs cognitive, behavioral, and humanistic techniques within a relationally oriented approach	Stricker and Gold (2006)
Transtheoretical model of change	Draws from a biopsychosocial model that uses various techniques applied at different times during the therapeutic process, depending on the client's stage of change	Prochaska and DiClemente (1984)
Three stage model	Uses techniques from client-centered theory to assist clients with the exploration of their issues, psychodynamic theory to assist clients with developing insight into their issues and strategies to address them, and behavioral theory to assist clients with taking active approaches toward handling said issues	Hill (2004)
Multitheoretical psychotherapy	Uses biopsychosocial, psychodynamic, interpersonal, constructivist, systemic, multicultural, and feminist theoretical principles to develop techniques	Brooks-Harris (2008)
Cognitive-behavioral assimilative integration	Uses cognitive-behavioral theory and related strategies to assist clients with interpersonal awareness, emotional functioning, and deeper levels of insight associated with each of these domains	Castonguay, Newman, Borkovec, Holtforth, and Maramba (2005)

While truly impossible to represent each of these theories adequately, we have attempted to integrate the work of the aforementioned individuals into this chapter and its application to the case of Y-Chun. The authors also wish to note that the work of John Norcross (2005) has been adapted and integrated into this chapter to provide what is believed to be a comprehensive framework by which to best understand theories that seek integration.

INTRODUCTION TO PSYCHOTHERAPY INTEGRATION

Over the course of its history, the field of counseling has seen a steady expansion in the number of theoretical approaches available to practitioners. At present, the count resides somewhere in the neighborhood of 400 different theoretical systems (Nuttall, 2002, p. 251). Yet, as the profession evolved, it became more common, and more acceptable, to openly question whether any one theory holds the key to understanding all of human behavior and, thus, what constitutes efficacious psychological treatment. In essence, a chronicle of psychotherapy integration details a measured progression from a few questioning voices to a full-scale movement, prompted in part by practitioners experiencing the limitations of their respective orientations out in the world of therapeutic practice.

For many, the history of counseling theory begins in the early 20th century, with the emergence of classical Freudian theory. This orientation dominated the stage for decades, despite early disagreements and alterations by a number of Freud's former followers. While the field remained solidly psychoanalytic for decades, it can be argued that, at present, there are four key foundational schools of therapy (psychoanalytic, cognitive-behavioral, humanist-existential, and transpersonal; Nuttall, 2002, p. 251).

As ideas regarding the nature of therapeutic intervention branched from the early psychoanalytic base, there was a steady undercurrent of opinions from many experienced clinicians that, while no single theory held all the answers, features of specific theoretical systems were useful for specific types of clients. As these voices gained strength and influence, aided by opportune contextual conditions, the notion of theoretical rapprochement or integration solidified into a distinct conceptual system currently known as psychotherapy integration. In its broadest sense, psychotherapy integration strives to move beyond the limitations of pristine theoretical models by exploring how the various theories complement one another and where they meet in agreement (Lampropoulos, Spengler, Dixon, & Nicholas, 2002).

A common explanation of psychotherapy integration as a theoretical concept is the use of multiple models and approaches to provide clients with an enhanced, but efficient, form of counseling and psychotherapy (Norcross, 2005). In other words, the form of counseling can be provided with various tools, models, skills, and techniques rooted in various theoretical schools, but the issues explored during the counseling and therapy process are sprouting from the same vine. At first glance, some individuals may view this concept as random or miscellaneous, but by locating the common points that each technique or exercise can bring out of a client, the therapeutic process can become more holistic, diverse, and rich because of the insights and details uncovered along the way.

Historical Background

An oft-cited starting point for the integration movement is a 1932 address by French to the American Psychiatric Association, which was later published in the *American Journal of Psychiatry* (Goldfried & Newman, 1992). French's (1933) case focused on the potential complementarity between psychoanalysis and Pavlovian conditioning. This was the opening salvo that invited theoreticians to begin considering theoretical integration.

As the counseling profession matured, psychotherapy effectiveness became fodder for debate (see, for example, Eysenck, 1952). This debate led many to question whether specific techniques were best suited for specific presenting concerns, thus allowing for consideration of crossing theoretical boundaries in search of technical, if not theoretical, integration, refined to target those approaches that best served a variety of presenting issues.

In the late 1970s, the quest for fundamental efficacious elements emerged as a specific area of attention (Goldfried & Newman, 1986). It became more mainstream for clinicians to express the belief that no one approach perfectly met the needs of all clients and to recognize the key role of outcome research in creating useful treatment plans targeted to a particular client.

The 1980s, in particular, were characterized by the expansion of cross-orientation dialogue in the form of professional conferences, publications, and journal special issues. In fact, this decade is considered the time when psychotherapy integration became a defined movement (Goldfried & Newman, 1992). A notable landmark is the 1983 founding of the Society for the Exploration of Psychotherapy Integration. This international, interdisciplinary organization fosters the development and evaluation of integrative psychotherapy approaches. The organization works to create dialogue among clinicians, researchers, and theorists and provides educational opportunities for such communication through its publication, the *Journal of Psychotherapy Integration,* and its annual conference.

As psychotherapy integration took the form of a recognized movement, "integration by design" replaced "eclecticism by default" (Norcross & Prochaska, 1988, p. 173). Attention was now paid to issues such as training and supervision, as well as outcome research specific to psychotherapy integration (Goldfried & Newman, 1992). With a paradigm of "integration by design" serving to guide reflection, practitioners soon found that they could dip into the realms of other disciplines for meaningful intervention strategies. Fields such as anthropology, sociology, religion/spirituality (Corwin, Wall, & Koopman, 2012), holistic health and medicine, and yoga are just some of the many areas integrative psychotherapists use to assist clients (Barnett & Shale, 2012). One example of such a broad-based approach is complementary and alternative medicine. This approach engages techniques such as dietary supplements, meditation, chiropractic, aromatherapy, massage therapy, yoga, progressive muscle relaxation, spirituality, religion and prayer, movement therapy, acupuncture, Reiki, biofeedback, hypnosis, and music therapy (Barnett & Shale, 2012) to significantly enhance the ways personal issues are being addressed in the therapeutic process. So, just as theoretical shifting has occurred within the psychological sciences to integrate postmodernist and non-Western philosophies (See Chapter 16), psychotherapeutic integrationists are shifting toward other disciplines in ways that purposefully and strategically assist clients in making personal changes.

Psychotherapy integration has a long history, and today the movement is closely aligned with the scientist-practitioner model, emphasizing the role of using outcome research to inform clinical practice (Lampropoulos et al., 2002). It is no surprise, then, that a future direction for the movement is research specifically targeting the efficacy of integrative treatment approaches.

Overview of Psychotherapy Integration

As noted above and depicted in Table 15.1, psychotherapy integration represents a broad and diverse field of study. One approach to organizing the work clusters the theory and research around four areas of emphasis: common factors, technical eclecticism, assimilative integration, and theoretical integration (Lampropoulos et al., 2002; O'Hara & Schofield, 2008).

This section provides a brief overview of each route, along with short descriptions of models that can be used to illustrate comparison and contrast points. Given page constraints, each approach cannot be presented in its fullness; as such, readers are referred to the references and additional resources provided at the end of this chapter to expand their understanding of integrative models.

Common Factors

Common factor advocates investigate the elements shared or "common" to all effective models, including empathy, warmth, and the therapeutic alliance (Lambert & Barley, 2002), as well as rehearsal and adoption of new behavior, catharsis, and positive client expectations (Grencavage & Norcross, 1990). While initially targeting core conditions such as empathy, warmth, and the therapeutic alliance, additional common factors have been added to the mix, such that one empirically derived model identified three clusters of common factors: (1) bond, (2) information, and (3) role (Tracey, Lichtenberg, Goodyear, Claiborn, & Wampold, 2003).

Adherents to the common factors model do not assume these factors are sufficient, in and of themselves, for effective treatment (Imel & Wampold, 2008). What those with a common factors approach hold is that the strategies employed are provided with rationale that makes them credible to the client and helps the client make sense of the presenting problem. The nature of the rationale may vary in accordance with the context in which treatment takes place, including the counselor's theoretical orientation as well as the client's worldview and belief system (Castelnuovo, Faccio, Molinari, Nardone, & Salvini, 2004; Imel & Wampold, 2008). One method that best represents this perspective is Miller, Duncan, and Hubble's (2004) client-directed outcome informed therapy (CDOI).

CDOI emphasizes the value of ongoing client feedback to outcome. Within this approach, the client's perspective serves as the main source of credibility and effectiveness. A counselor using the CDOI approach would use brief assessment instruments such as the Session Rating Scale (SRS) and the Outcome Rating Scale (ORS) to elicit the client's feedback on each session, and would then discuss the results obtained from these measures in the session (Miller et al., 2004). Such feedback allows for adjustments to the relationship or approach to ensure that future sessions are more beneficial to the client (Robinson, 2009).

Assimilative Integration

Those adopting an assimilative integration approach employ a wide variety of techniques that remain consistent with their theoretical orientation. The assimilative integration route requires therapists to anchor their approaches in one main theory so that when different techniques from other theoretical approaches are used, they are incorporated into the therapeutic process in a way that is the most authentic and clear to all parties. As such, a counselor embracing assimilative integration may conceptualize a depressed client from a primarily narrative perspective, while incorporating in his or her counseling sessions an array of treatment techniques ranging from the empty chair of Gestalt theory to the cognitive debating promoted by rational emotive behavior therapy. The key is that the techniques be used in service of the theory anchoring use of the technique. So for the counselor attempting to help a client "re-story" his or her life and current difficulties, as would be central to a narrative theory, the empty-chair strategy or use of cognitive debating would simply be seen as facilitative to that restoring process.

Technical Eclecticism

Like assimilative integration, technical eclecticism involves using an array of techniques borrowed from various theoretical orientations. This model differs from assimilative integration in that it does not depend on a unifying theoretical underpinning, focusing instead on research-driven practice. Arnold Lazarus (2005), a key figure in this approach, suggested that using an approach that is "data-based and open to verification and disproof . . . one may then borrow, purchase, pilfer, and import *methods and techniques* (not theories) from diverse sources so as to harness their specific power" (p. 150). So for the technically eclectic counselor, it would not matter, for example, if a narrative theme connected all the techniques for the client. A technically eclectic therapist would take more of the position that as long as a proper technique, verified through scientific investigation on relevant populations, is being used to assist the client, the process of change can occur.

Theoretical Integration

This route seeks to develop a "meta-theory" that can pull aspects of two or more theories together in a unified approach (Norcross, 2005; O'Hara & Schofield, 2008). One example is Ryle's (2005) cognitive analytic therapy model, which pulls from cognitive psychotherapy and object relations theory. A counselor working from this model would spend time assessing the client's early experiences, focusing on childhood patterns of behavior as they relate to current difficulties. The client would then receive a "reformulation letter" detailing the counselor's understanding of the client's difficulties. The treatment would then move on to detailing the sequences that maintain the client's presenting problem, with the goal of helping the client break free of these patterns. Another model, the transtheoretical model of change, integrates biopsychosocial and sometimes biopsychosocial-spiritual elements in the understanding and directing of purposeful change (Corwin et al., 2012). This model is discussed in more detail later in this chapter.

Multitheoretical Framework

The multitheoretical framework organizes several theories regarding how a client's systems and change processes interact to make progress toward therapeutic goals (Brooks-Harris, 2008; Norcross, 2005). One example of this approach is provided by Brooks-Harris (2008): multitheoretical psychotherapy (MTP).

MTP notes the significant amount of influence biological, interpersonal, cognitive, emotional, cultural, social, and behavioral variables have on clients and, as such, encourages therapists to draw on multiple theories addressing these domains. It is not, however, a random selection of any given variable or theoretical approach at any moment that provides the direction therapy takes. Rather, it is a scientifically based approach that encourages therapists to study particular markers for change that clients can display. In other words, markers for change help therapists devise *strategy-based* and *relationally focused* responses to client needs that help address a variety of presenting problems. As long as therapists are using approaches that come from an informed perspective (intentional); appropriately capture the interaction of thoughts, feelings, behaviors, and contextual systems in which clients exist (multidimensional); and draw from a variety of theoretical positions (multitheoretical), they are considered to be integrationist under the MTP approach (Brooks-Harris, 2008).

Caveat Before Proceeding

It should be clear that many are attempting to find meaningful, valid approaches to integration. It should also be clear that, to date, there is no *one* commonly held method, theory, or orientation to integration. The wide diversity of approaches makes the discussion to follow difficult. As such, and in response to the uniqueness of the common case—the case of Y-Chun, to which an integrated theory will be applied—the authors have chosen to focus the discussion on one integrative approach, that of the transtheoretical model of change. The other routes are no less effective or relevant than the multitheoretical framework when addressing issues of psychotherapeutic integration, but Y-Chun's particular background information and presenting issues appear to fit well with the use of various therapeutic techniques integrated into Prochaska and DiClemente's (2005) transtheoretical approach.

View of Human Nature From a Transtheoretical Frame of Reference

Prochaska and DiClemente (2005) view clients as self-initiated change agents who are also influenced and affected by biopsychosocial factors. Though these factors are meant to be complementary to one another, they are not always in states of equilibrium. The better the balance one can have between internal and external drives, the greater the likelihood one can take appropriate actions to accomplish goals and maintain an action plan that allows for functional existence (Prochaska & Norcross, 2003). These levels of balance progress through five basic stages—precontemplation, contemplation, preparation, action, and maintenance—which ultimately lead to change (Prochaska & DiClemente, 1984). Prior to presenting these basic stages, it may be helpful for you to complete Exercise 15.1.

EXERCISE 15.1

NEW YEAR'S RESOLUTION

Directions: Perhaps you, like so many others, make New Year's resolutions. Perhaps last year, it was a resolve to relax more, lose some weight, exercise more, save money, or pay down debt. Regardless of your resolution, it most likely signaled a desire to change. Often, even the best-intended resolutions go unfulfilled. Select one of your resolutions that you were *not* successful in meeting.

Write down that resolution: _____
_____

Now respond to each of the following, writing your answers down:

1. What was the reason for your selecting that resolution? Was it at the suggestion of another? Was it because of an experience you were having at the time (e.g., bathing suit a little tight), or was there no clear reason? Identify your reason:

   _____

   _____

2. Prior to engaging in the change process, did you identify the costs (physically, psychologically, socially, etc.) as well as benefits? If you did, were there any unexpected costs or benefits?

3. Did you set clear goals, perhaps breaking the overall goal into small steps?

4. Did you develop a plan that was easy for you to implement given all the other demands on your time and energy and the resources you had available?

5. Did others support you in your goal and your action to achieve that goal, or were they stumbling blocks by their words, actions, or lack of support?

As you read on about the various stages of change, return to your answers and identify the stage at which your efforts to change fell apart. Further, identify what you could do to facilitate similar change in the future.

Precontemplation exists when clients are not serious about wanting to change or about seeking proper assistance to do so (Prochaska & DiClemente, 1984, 2005). Perhaps they are psychologically guarding themselves through a sense of denial; perhaps they are not experiencing any physical symptoms of particular concern; perhaps they are socially enabled not to view their behaviors as problematic. This is not to say that other people in the client's world do not see a need for change, but the individual client is not able to take ownership of these problematic concerns (Prochaska & Norcross, 2003). Because the client has not fully accepted that there is a need for change, counselors may often encounter marked resistance from clients in the precontemplation stage.

Consider Chris (Case Illustration 15.1), an 18-year-old college student who has been able to manage the demands of his studies with ease but finds that his social life is lacking the same balance.

CASE ILLUSTRATION 15.1

Chris

Despite his academic achievements, Chris is terribly homesick and is considering moving back home to attend the local community college. He spoke to his academic advisor, citing an inability to fit in with his peers. At his advisor's suggestion, Chris is visiting the university counseling center before making a final decision about his education.

Chris: I just don't fit in here. I can't make any friends.

Counselor: Do you mean in your classes?

Chris: It's not just class. I just can't fit in no matter what I do. No one will talk to me. All I do is go to class and go back to the dorm.

Counselor: What about your roommate? Do you get along with him?

Chris: Yeah, he's cool, but I don't really see him. I have morning classes, and he has afternoon classes. He is busy every evening doing things with his friends or going to club meetings or to watch football games. We don't really see each other.

Counselor: Well, you said that you two get along. Have you ever thought it might be fun to go to a football game or even just to the dining commons with him?

Chris: He asks me if I want to go with him to get dinner, but I don't know anyone. He knows lots of other people here on campus. That just seems weird sitting with him and all his friends when I don't know anyone.

Counselor: Yes, it can be awkward sometimes making conversation with people you don't know very well. Have you ever thought about taking him up on his offer to go eat together at the dining commons?

Chris: Why would I do that?

Counselor: I was just wondering if maybe, since you get along well with your roommate, you might also get along well with some of his friends.

Chris: There's no point. They'll just think I'm lame for tagging along. I've been here almost a month, and I can't make friends. Going to dinner with him isn't going to change things.

As Chris is in the precontemplation stage, the counselor should not be surprised that he is resistant to all suggestions. Even the counselor's observations about Chris's budding friendship with his roommate are ignored. As long as Chris remains in the precontemplation stage, he is unaware that his antisocial behaviors are most likely contributing to his difficulty developing relationships with his peers.

Contemplation exists when clients are becoming more aware of personal consequences related to their actions but are still debating whether or not to head in the direction of long-term change (Prochaska & DiClemente, 1984, 2005). Perhaps the short-term costs are not outweighing the long-term sacrifices and discomforts that are likely to be part of the change process at this point. Further consideration of pros and cons of change becomes essential during this stage (Prochaska & Norcross, 2003).

Preparation exists when clients have determined there is a need for change and start to seek out strategies and resources that can initiate the change process (Prochaska & DiClemente, 1984, 2005). The action stage occurs when clients are not only engaging in the change process but also believe that they are capable of bringing about change (Prochaska & Norcross, 2003). These two stages seem to be based on clients' becoming mentally and physically aware of what is not working for them and their daily routines, coupled with support and encouragement from those around them to make changes. To further illustrate these stages, it may also be helpful to complete Exercise 15.2.

EXERCISE 15.2

ASSIGNMENT PROCRASTINATION

Directions: Throughout your academic career, you have probably experienced numerous deadlines. With competing priorities, it can sometimes be tempting to put projects off until the last minute. Think about the last time you procrastinated on a major assignment, and respond to each of the following questions.

1. What was the reason behind your procrastination? How do you typically approach tasks like this?

2. How did you cope with the pressure of the deadline? Did you take any actions such as withdrawing from the class or asking the professor for more time? How did you motivate yourself to get started?

3. What was your first step to begin this assignment? Did you break up the project into small steps or tackle it all at once?

4. How easy was it to take that first step? What did it mean for you to take action? How did this process impact your future plans about future assignments; would you repeat this process again?

5. How did others, if any, perceive your procrastination? Did peers also struggle with completing the assignment, or were you the only one who put the task off?

As you further consider how the actions of change unfold, refer back to your answers. Think about how you were able to take action to complete an assignment you knew had to be done, and how successfully completing actions can lead to the maintenance stage.

Maintenance exists when clients have reached a "new normal" in their lives and are actively working to avoid situations or triggers that could return them to earlier stages (Prochaska & DiClemente, 1984, 2005). This does not mean that clients have reached a resolution, but they are physically and mentally in a state of being positively different from the ways they felt prior to making long-term changes. It is also important to note that relapse and regression are not indicators of failure but, rather, are normal parts of the process that clients and counselors must be prepared to handle along the road to change (Prochaska & Norcross, 2003). Clients who are able to handle relapse and regression are said to accept these conditions as setbacks but not immovable obstacles. Thus, human nature is viewed as a challenging dynamic by which people are overcoming conditions that create feelings of inadequacy, beliefs of hopelessness and/or helplessness, and social judgment (Prochaska & DiClemente, 1984, 2005). However, individuals can draw from various systems to adjust and deal with these conditions and take personal responsibility for what actions they take to establish longer periods of healthier behaviors and decision making. To further illustrate how the maintenance stage and relapse prevention can be impacted by systems, we suggest completing Exercise 15.3.

EXERCISE 15.3

COMMUNITY GENOGRAM

Directions: If you have ever been successful in making a big change in your life, chances are you relied on the support of others and possibly avoided some triggers or settings that could be obstacles to your maintaining the change(s). For example, if you are trying to lose weight through diet and exercise, you may need to avoid certain places—such as fast-food restaurants—and may surround yourself with certain people to assist with your goals—such as running-club members or community groups that play recreational sports.

A community genogram can serve as a visual representation of the support systems that exist. Think about all the individuals in your life and the places you go when you need support for a change you have made or are attempting to make. Some individuals may include family members, friends, a spouse, or other partner. Coworkers, clergy members, neighbors, teachers, and classmates are also possibilities. Some places may also be included on the genogram, such as school, church, social groups, and clubs. Create a community genogram of the people and places you would turn to if you needed support. You can draw a map of your neighborhood to help with your visual.

(Continued)

(Continued)

Now respond to each of the following, writing your answers down:

1. Who did you select to create your support system? What was the reason for selecting these individuals?

2. What places did you include on your genogram? What was your reason for including these places?

3. If you have not done so already, draw connecting lines to indicate the strongest relationships between you and the resources on your genogram. What similarities exist among these resources? Are there connections between any of the resources?

4. How will your resources help you?

5. How does it feel to know you have this support system?

Consider your support system as you think about the maintenance stage. Consider how knowing you have a robust support system and plentiful resources might be beneficial if you were experiencing relapse or regression.

Basic Characteristics and Assumptions

In the same way biopsychosocial and sometimes spiritual factors are meant to be complementary to one another (Corwin et al., 2012), the transtheoretical approach assumes that different psychotherapeutic systems are complementary as well. Thus, different theories are meant to best serve clients depending on their stage and level of change (Norcross, 2005). At the earlier stages, such as precontemplation and contemplation, clients are best served by using techniques focused on identifying symptoms and situational factors that signify obstacles or blocks to client change (Brooks-Harris, 2008). Many clients at this stage and level of change struggle to engage in therapy because of physical symptoms, perceived situational obstacles, and lack of motivation to take proactive steps toward overcoming perceived and related obstacles (Sue & Sue, 2008). Motivational interviewing is said to accomplish this task because of its ability to frame data into client-centered statements and perspectives that allow for clients to consciously evaluate the pros and cons of behavioral change as well as their need to be active agents in the change process (Dunn, Deroo, & Rivara, 2001; Norcross & Beutler, 2010). Also, because of its intended supportive nature, motivational interviewing can be implemented in the therapy process as early as the intake interview and/or initial session to present clients with a nonjudgmental space to express their ambivalence toward change (Miller & Rollnick, 1991). Although the process of change requires a long-term commitment, clients in the initial stages of change are often focused on short-term steps that allow them to feel comfortable with beginning the process. The following exchange (see Case Illustration 15.2) highlights this point.

CASE ILLUSTRATION 15.2

Small Steps

In the following scenario, Chris has begun to realize that some of his behaviors may be preventing him from developing friendships at college. By asking Chris to consider the risks and rewards of changing his behavior, as well as the obstacles that stand in his way, the counselor is allowing Chris to engage actively in the process of change.

Chris: (Sighs) I want to make friends and feel like I belong. That's just so hard here. I've never had to go out of my way to make friends before.

Counselor: I know it's tough, Chris. It's clear you want to meet people and develop friendships here at school. I wonder, what is standing in your way?

Chris: (Pauses) I dunno. Everyone already has friends here. It's just hard to break into those groups. It's hard to put myself out there.

Counselor: You were telling me about how your roommate has been inviting you to hang out with his friends. Does that make it easier?

Chris: Yeah, I am worried if I do try and meet new people they won't like me.

Counselor: Yes, it is a risk that you may not get along with everyone you meet. It sounds like you're saying that this fear of getting rejected by your roommate's friends is holding you back.

Chris: I guess so. I mean, I live with him. If they don't like me, then what? He's my only friend here. What if I screw that up, too?

Counselor: So you are afraid that his friends may not like you, and he may reject you as well?

Chris: Yeah.

Counselor: Well, you've told me about one of the risks if you try to meet new people. What could be a potential benefit of putting yourself out there?

Chris: Well, I'd have friends.

Counselor: And what do friends bring into your life? What are the rewards of having friends?

Chris: I'd get to go to football games and parties with people. If you have friends, you always have someone to talk to. If I needed help with studying, I might have friends who could help me. I wouldn't be lonely anymore.

Although Chris (in Case Illustration 15.2) is still experiencing anxiety about establishing relationships with his peers, he is beginning to realize that if he does not step outside of the security of his dormitory, he may never achieve the meaningful friendships he desires. In this session, Chris was able to identify his fear of rejection as an obstacle he must move past. Although he did not develop a concrete plan of action, Chris was able to articulate both his hopes and fears—an important step in building motivation to change.

At the preparation, action, and/or maintenance stages, clients who are symptom and/or situation focused are best served through behavioral approaches and exposure therapy (Brooks-Harris, 2008; Norcross, 2005; Prochaska & DiClemente, 1984), because these approaches involve seeing more of a direct relationship between personal action and consequence. Also, because resistance to change is still a part of the process, the notion of taking action and/or physically engaging in steps toward change helps provide clients with signs and signals that their decisions and work are making a difference.

Clients who are experiencing more intrapersonal conflicts, as opposed to reactions at a symptom/situational level, are said to benefit more from psychoanalytic work at the precontemplation and/or contemplation stage(s) (Brooks-Harris, 2008; Norcross & Beutler, 2010). At this point in therapy, the processes of consciousness raising and dramatic relief may help clients address blocks or obstacles preventing them from seeing a need for change (Prochaska & DiClemente, 2005). We will illustrate these processes in a moment, but at this time, readers should mostly be aware that during the initial stages of therapy, unconscious blocks may be getting in the way of viewing change as a possible process, and increasing self-knowledge along with knowledge of the presenting problem appears to be an effective method by which to help clients engage in therapy. Existential therapy is often used for these clients at the contemplation stage (Brooks-Harris, 2008). The need to consider long-term outcomes can require significant examination of one's life and the conflicts associated with making long-term changes. Issues related to personal meaning and existence, which often arise at this point in therapy, are best served through existential exercise. Gestalt therapy is best suited for these clients at the preparation stage (Brooks-Harris, 2008; Norcross & Beutler, 2010). The action-oriented and confrontational nature of this approach is said to best engage clients in a responsibility-driven dialogue that can be used as self-talk and motivation to initiate behavioral and emotional change. As a result, the use of behavioral therapy and exposure therapy can also allow for the action and maintenance stages to come about more effectively (Brooks-Harris, 2008; Norcross & Beutler, 2010).

As previously noted, clients can revisit any of these stages at any point due to relapse or regression, and counselors should be able to assess and reapproach clients in need of the appropriate interventions as a result of the therapeutic relationship. Clients, however, must remain active and engaged in the relationship and the change process to regain their progress and reach desired goals. Even upon termination, counselors should remain available for follow-up and support purposes, with the understanding that clients are capable of keeping the process of change alive even when relapse occurs (Brooks-Harris, 2008; Norcross & Beutler, 2010).

Research Supporting Theoretical Constructs and Interventions

The transtheoretical approach has been applied and studied in various empirically driven ways for a variety of presenting problems. Physical addictions and issues such as obesity (Carels et al., 2007), smoking cessation (DiClemente et al., 1991), and alcoholism (DiClemente,

Bellino, & Neavins, 1999) are among the most prominently researched presenting problems treated with transtheoretical techniques and approaches. However, recent studies have also focused on other issues, such as financial education (Shockey & Seiling, 2004), academic learning strategies (Dembo & Praks Seli, 2004; Pettay & Hughey, 2011), and workplace morale, health, and safety (Barrett, Haslam, Lee, & Ellis, 2004). Numerous studies can be cited in this section, all of which provide significant support for the stages of change model, the transtheoretical approach, and the timing for which certain interventions appear to work best during the therapeutic process. Readers are strongly encouraged to read more seminal works, such as Prochaska, DiClemente, and Norcross's (1992) article, to truly understand the extensive research and theory supporting these constructs.

Use With Diverse Populations and Children

As with many theories, research validating the effectiveness of the transtheoretical approach with diverse populations needs to be expanded. The model has been reported as effective in guiding treatment for Asian children with issues of obesity and smoking cessation (Chen, Horner, & Percy, 2003), as well as with adolescents making decisions regarding sexual behavior (Grimley & Lee, 1997). An extensive review in support of this model's effectiveness with diverse populations can be found in Prochaska and Norcross (2010).

Strengths and Limitations

As is the case with each of the integrative theories, the transtheoretical approach allows for a truly interactionist perspective when conceptualizing a client's issues. The biopsychosocial nature of the theory does not limit the roots of presenting problems to a strictly nature or strictly nurture viewpoint, and it also helps clients understand that the process of change is not a simple one that can be addressed by a purely problem-solving method. It also gives the client a significant amount of responsibility and agency when making determinations to change (Norcross & Beutler, 2010). While we present this as a positive, it is important to note that not all cultures emphasize individualism and personal agency.

It is also important to note that although a wealth of research supports the use of integrationist perspectives such as the transtheoretical model for treating addictions, a lesser amount of research exists regarding nonaddictive behaviors and issues (Corwin et al., 2012). However, the prominence and adaptability of this research has provided enough applicability outlets for this model when it comes to addressing nonaddictive behaviors and issues that many therapists and counselors view eclecticism in a way that benefits a diversity of clients, which not only showcases the strengths of such an approach but also shows how professionals can aspire to the ethics and standards of practice that guide the social and humanistic guidelines of the counseling and psychological field.

THERAPEUTIC PROCESS AND APPLICATION

As part of the change process, the client must first recognize that he or she is experiencing a problem or concern. Once awareness of the problematic behavior is achieved, the individual can begin to implement new cognitive and behavioral strategies to create change. Rather than focusing exclusively on either inner thoughts or behaviors, the client combines awareness with action to produce real change. The therapist assists clients with achieving their goals by determining which stage of change they are currently in and then helping them move through the subsequent stages by achieving set tasks (Prochaska & DiClemente, 2003; Prochaska & Norcross, 2003). These set tasks are a combination of thoughts and behaviors that define each stage; although there is no prescribed amount of time a client must spend at each stage, achieving the specific tasks is necessary for moving through the therapeutic process. Once the therapist has determined the stage the client is in, it is necessary to apply the appropriate processes of change for maximum effectiveness. Processes of change are actions or interventions that influence the thoughts, feelings, and behaviors of individuals (Prochaska, 2000; Prochaska & DiClemente, 2003; Prochaska & Norcross, 2003). As stated previously, different processes of change, which hail from various psychotherapeutic systems, are suited to different stages of change.

Interventions and Change Process

Prochaska, DiClemente, and Norcross (1992) outlined 10 distinct processes of change that individuals use to make adjustments in their lives: consciousness raising, dramatic relief, environmental reevaluation, self-reevaluation, self-liberation, social liberation, counter-conditioning, stimulus control, reinforcement management, and helping relationships. Consciousness raising is the act of making observations and increasing awareness about the self and one's problems. Dramatic relief involves talking about or role-playing an individual's feelings related to his or her concerns (Prochaska, 2000; Prochaska et al., 1992). Both consciousness raising and dramatic relief are appropriate intervention techniques for clients trying to move from the precontemplation to the contemplation stage (Prochaska & DiClemente, 2003; Prochaska & Norcross, 2003). For clients who initially deny that they are experiencing problems or who come to therapy involuntarily, consciousness raising may help them become more aware of their struggles. The counselor can pose questions such as, "What is working in your life? What is not working?" This will begin a conversation and analysis that may lead to insight into the problem areas of the client's life. As insight occurs, the counselor may use bibliotherapy, assigning books, essays, poetry, or passages that may resonate with the client and foster further awareness (Prochaska, 2000; Prochaska & DiClemente, 2003). During this process, the client may become aware of emotional memories, relationships, and situations that should be addressed. Here, the counselor might use dramatic relief. For example, if the client experienced a traumatic event and was unable to process the event at the time, the counselor might ask if the client is comfortable sharing his or her feelings. If the client has a tumultuous relationship with a family member, the counselor could suggest a role play to allow the client an opportunity to practice expressing what he or she would like to say to this person within the safe setting of a counseling session. As dramatic relief is a cathartic process, the client may be better prepared to move into the contemplation stage after participating in this intervention. The process and impact of dramatic relief are presented in Case Illustration 15.3.

CASE ILLUSTRATION 15.3

Dramatic Relief

In the following scenario, Chris starts to process some of the emotions that have become obstacles during his first month at college. The counselor uses dramatic relief, allowing Chris to experience these emotions again and also achieve catharsis from the process.

Chris: (Voice raised) I'm just so angry with myself! Why is it so hard for me to fit in? I've never had a problem with it my whole life!

Counselor: I can hear that you are feeling very upset about how you are fitting in here at college. You mentioned you are angry with yourself. Will you tell me more about that?

Chris: I just don't understand why for the first time in my life I am having such a hard time. Sometimes I just panic when I meet new people. What if they don't like me? What if they think I'm stupid?

Counselor: Panic?

Chris: Not panic, I guess. I'm just, I guess scared. I don't feel confident here. I'm just worried what everyone thinks about me. I've been here a month, and my roommate is the closest thing I have to a friend. People must think I'm pathetic. I think I'm pathetic. (Starts to cry.)

Counselor: Chris, I don't think you are pathetic. I think you moved across the country because you were accepted to a very challenging academic program. This move is a really big change for you.

Chris: I just didn't realize moving here was going to be such a challenge. I was so excited to go to college and then the week before I came out here I started worrying about being so far from home. I was sad that I had to leave my friends. I wanted to tell my parents I changed my mind and didn't want to go.

Counselor: What did you tell your parents?

Chris: I didn't say anything. I pretended I was happy and excited. I didn't want them to be disappointed in me. Every time they call I tell them everything is great.

Counselor: What would you like to tell your parents?

Chris: I dunno. I want to tell them it's tough here. My classes are great, but I'm lonely. I don't want to go home, but I wish I could. I think if I talked to them now, they would just tell me to stick with it.

When Chris was preparing to move away from home, he encountered troubling feelings but ignored them because he was worried about what his parents and friends would think. Now, 1 month later, he is starting to realize the impact of these emotions on his ability to form relationships at school. The process of dramatic relief has allowed Chris the space to express feelings he has ignored: anger, fear, and sadness. The counselor also initiated a brief role play to allow Chris to think about what he might say if he chose to be honest with his parents about his feelings.

Self-reevaluation is the process of analyzing one's self-concept and self-esteem, especially with regard to the current concern, whereas environmental reevaluation is the examination of the effects of one's problems on the external environment (Prochaska et al., 1992). Use of these cognitive interventions is effective during the contemplation stage, as the client attempts to discern which attitude and behavioral alterations are necessary to meet his or her goals. For example, once a problem has been acknowledged, the counselor can help the client explore the consequences of the problem by asking questions such as, "What effects does this problem have on your children/family/relationships/job?" This process is further developed in the following case illustration (Case Illustration 15.4).

CASE ILLUSTRATION 15.4

Self-Reevaluation

Now that Chris is aware that his fears are inhibiting his social life, the process of self-reevaluation can help him see what his life could be like once change occurs.

Chris: Coming to college was worse than I imagined. I'm out of my element. I'm not confident here. I feel so scared and overwhelmed just thinking about trying to meet all these new people, but I can't stay in my dorm room all day.

Counselor: Chris, you've said that these feelings of fear and the worry of being rejected are holding you back and keeping you from making friends. What other effects are these fears having on your life?

Chris: My parents know something is wrong. They keep asking about my friends, and I have nothing to tell them. They know I'm lying, and I feel guilty about lying.

Counselor: So this fear is also affecting your relationship with your parents. What effects does this have on your schoolwork?

Chris: I didn't think there was any effect at first. I was doing really well on all my assignments, but then one of my professors said she was concerned because I do not participate much in class. After she said that, I started wondering if I have what it takes to be here. I'm not confident I can keep my grades up.

Counselor: What happens if you get a bad grade in the class?

Chris:	I could lose my scholarship. I worked so hard to get here. I can't lose that.
Counselor:	You have worked very hard, Chris. I wonder, if you woke up tomorrow feeling confident and not afraid at all, what would be different?
Chris:	(Pauses) Well, I would go have breakfast with my friends before going to class. I would have no problem raising my hand in class. I'd take the lead on group projects. I'd have a 4.0 GPA or better. After class I would hang out around the dorm with my friends. Maybe I'd have a girlfriend.
Counselor:	That seems very different than what your life is like right now. Tell me, how would you feel if that's what your life was like tomorrow?
Chris:	I'd feel great. I wouldn't have this knot in my stomach. I'd walk taller, for sure. I'd be relaxed and not so overwhelmed. I wouldn't just *be* confident. I'd *feel* confident.

Although Chris had initially realized his social life was impeded by fear and lack of confidence, he was also able to see that his relationship with his parents and his schoolwork were being negatively impacted as well. The counselor asked Chris to consider the possibility of a brighter future, focusing not only on external effects Chris could see but also encouraging Chris to think about how these changes would make him feel. By dreaming about a possible future, Chris may become more open to the idea of making a change.

Self-liberation occurs in the preparation stage, as clients believe they have the ability to change and make a commitment to specific changes that can be implemented (Prochaska & Norcross, 2003). In contrast to solely focusing on concerns, social liberation is the awareness and furthering of positive behaviors in the client's life. Here is an opportunity to focus on the client's strengths, passions, and motivations. Social liberation is the act of doing good for society (Prochaska et al., 1992). Explore positive likes, behaviors, and activities with the client. Does the client love animals? Volunteer at a local animal shelter? Participate in religious or spiritual activities? Is the client passionate about social justice? Find a local nonprofit, religious, and/or spiritual group, and learn how to get involved in community activities. Social liberation gives both clients and counselors ways to explore alternatives to problem areas in life by focusing on clients' positive strengths.

As clients move into the action stage, they begin to utilize processes that reinforce their commitment to changing their attitudes and behaviors. Counterconditioning occurs when the individual chooses an alternate activity to replace the problem behavior, and stimulus control is the ability to repress the need to engage in the problem behavior, even when situations arise that would typically trigger the concern. Reinforcement management occurs when the individual is rewarded for remaining committed to changing behaviors. The process of helping relationships refers to sharing the experiences of changing with a trusted individual or group; this is especially valuable during the action and maintenance stages (Prochaska, 2000; Prochaska et al., 1992). As the client progresses and adheres to his or her action plan, the counselor can use praise and encouragement as reinforcement management for the client. Thus, to maximize the effectiveness of the transtheoretical model and assist the client in achieving his or her goals, the therapist matches the client's current stage of change with the appropriate processes of change and corresponding interventions.

Y-CHUN THROUGH A TRANSTHEORETICAL LENS

Now that we have established a basic understanding of the transtheoretical model, including the view of human nature, basic characteristics, therapeutic goals, and interventions, we can take a closer look at the application of such an integrated approach by examining the case of Y-Chun. Y-Chun is a 35-year-old nontraditional college student born to a Polish father and Chinese mother. She has two half-siblings and is mother to a 15-year-old boy and 12-year-old girl. She has come to counseling at the suggestion of her doctor after experiencing a number of physical symptoms: headaches, upset stomach, difficulty sleeping, and short temper. During the intake session, Y-Chun discloses that she feels stressed, overwhelmed, empty, and isolated; she talks of her poor relationships with her parents, half-siblings, children, and intimate partners. She also discloses that her cousin raped her when she was 16 years old, and she has never been able to tell anyone because she was worried she would be blamed or accused of lying. Y-Chun divulges that she has many concerns and would like to "figure this out" but that she doesn't "know where to begin." The initial session ends with the counselor suggesting that perhaps Y-Chun knows more about how to begin than she thinks she does: "I think you have already begun. Coming here—sharing as you have—was courageous." Y-Chun and the counselor plan to meet the following week.

Already, Y-Chun has begun to progress through the stages of change naturally, before ever setting foot in the counselor's office. This is consistent with the basis of the transtheoretical model, as the approach mirrors not only the change that occurs during psychotherapy but also the natural progress among individuals who create change for themselves (Petrocelli, 2002). Y-Chun has demonstrated awareness that there are aspects of her life that require change, and she has taken steps to initiate change by visiting her primary physician, considering her doctor's advice to seek counseling, making the phone call to set up the appointment, keeping the appointment, and being open with the counselor during the initial interview. These may seem like small steps to take, but they demonstrate a self-directed motivation to change, an important factor in the beginning stages of the transtheoretical model.

The counselor encouraged the steps Y-Chun took to seek counseling and create changes in her life by recognizing that she had already begun the process to "figure this out." Throughout the first session, the counselor was able to integrate the transtheoretical approach into the initial intake questioning. The counselor encouraged Y-Chun to begin to explore what problems or concerns she sees in her life. The counselor's questions led to consciousness raising, or awareness of some concerns. As the sessions progress, the counselor can continue to raise Y-Chun's awareness by exploring more triggers and obstacles in Y-Chun's life. For example, they might further explore the triggers in the relationship between Y-Chun and her parents or between Y-Chun and her children. The counselor also encouraged dramatic relief, another intervention applied in the early stages of counseling for clients in the precontemplation and contemplation stages. Y-Chun disclosed that her cousin raped her, and she discussed experiences with racism, sexism, and isolation. The counselor helped Y-Chun begin to express her emotions and feelings about her experiences, which is an important precursor to moving into the contemplation stage (Prochaska & Norcross, 2003). Because Y-Chun has experienced so much hurt in her life, the dramatic relief will play an important role in future sessions as well. Y-Chun's admission of feeling alone and unable to talk with others signals the real need for catharsis and emotional relief from her painful experiences. To encourage Y-Chun to talk about her feelings, the counselor might say, "I hear you saying that you experienced many hurtful things in your life but that you couldn't talk with anyone about how these things affected you or made you feel. I wonder if you would be comfortable sharing with me what you wish you could have said or could say?" The counselor could offer to role-play with Y-Chun so she can express her feelings. Perhaps the counselor could take on the role of one of Y-Chun's parents, as Y-Chun describes the isolation she felt when she experienced racism and was told it was her fault or how she could not talk about being raped for fear of being blamed. By utilizing dramatic relief, the counselor will give Y-Chun a safe place to work through this hurt and a voice she has lacked for so long.

Assessment Strategies

Although the counselor integrated the transtheoretical approach into Y-Chun's initial intake questioning, continued assessment is an important part of the therapeutic relationship. Since relapse and regression are assumed with the transtheoretical approach, the counselor must frequently assess the client to ensure treatment plans are appropriate. Additionally, it is vital to make sure the client continues to be involved and engaged in the process.

One of Y-Chun's main concerns involves her difficulty connecting with her family of origin, children, and romantic partners. As Y-Chun makes changes in her thoughts and behavior to strengthen these relationships, or faces obstacles on the path to change, her perception of her relationships may change. The counselor may find it helpful to use a family genogram (McGoldrick, Gerson, & Petry, 2008) as an assessment tool. Since Y-Chun has identified a certain hierarchal structure in her family, creating a genogram early in the therapeutic process will help the counselor and Y-Chun track the evolution of these relationships. Subsequent genograms may be completed as Y-Chun progresses through the stages of change.

Another benefit of using a family genogram is to help the counselor better understand Y-Chun's bicultural identity. Y-Chun's father is an immigrant from Poland, and Y-Chun's mother is Chinese American. Creating a genogram with Y-Chun may help reveal previously undisclosed feelings about her Polish background. It is unclear how this part of her cultural background, or her father's experiences as an immigrant, may have impacted her childhood. The sacrifices made to immigrate, coupled with difficulties expressing emotion, are sometimes significant matters that contribute to experiences of Polish immigrant clients who seek therapy (Folwarski & Smolinski, Jr., 2005). Some of these matters may reveal themselves as the narrative of the genogram unfolds, or they may not be what Y-Chun identifies as the most central to her self-identity or presenting problems. Allowing for this open discussion of her bicultural identity, however, can form a decent working alliance and help counselor and client understand what therapeutic path(s) to follow (McGoldrick, Giordano, & Garcia-Preto, 2005). So, although we cannot ignore Y-Chun's multicultural identity, for the purposes of this chapter, we are interpreting Y-Chun as primarily identifying with her Asian identity; we also view the fact that Y-Chun was bullied as a child due to her Asian American heritage as reason to explore this piece of her identity further.

When working with individuals from collectivist societies it may be culturally competent to consider factors beyond family of origin. A community genogram (Rigazio-DiGilio, Ivey, Kunkler-Peck, & Grady, 2005) is a holistic approach that allows the counselor to understand how the client is impacted by work, school, friends, religious/spiritual influences, community organizations, societal norms, and cultural influences. For an Asian American client such as Y-Chun, considering the external community of origin is equally as important as considering the family of origin.

Due to the collaborative nature of the transtheoretical approach, it is important for the counselor to assess if Y-Chun feels she is benefiting from the continued therapeutic relationship. Johnson, Miller, and Duncan's (2000) Session Rating Scale (SRS) helps measure the therapeutic alliance based on self-report of the client. Miller and Duncan's (2000) Outcome Rating Scale (ORS), works in tandem with the SRS and allows the client to rate his or her feelings as well as relationships. The ORS is a self-report of the following four areas: overall sense of well-being, personal well-being, family and close relationships, and social interactions outside of the family. This measure can be completed quickly at the start of a therapy session and can provide valuable insight into how the client perceives his or her overall well-being and relationships. This tool may be helpful in working with Y-Chun, as she has presented with myriad physical symptoms and also concerns about connecting with her family and romantic partners.

Beyond the counselor's application of the integrated approach to the initial intake, Y-Chun's background gives more insight into how her case fits within the framework of the transtheoretical model. Because individuals are seen as self-initiated change agents, counseling with the transtheoretical approach gives Y-Chun power to change her own life, something she has lacked in the past. It balances Y-Chun's own internal power with external environmental factors, acknowledging real obstacles and encouraging realistic goals and results (Prochaska et al., 1992).

This integrative approach is also appropriate because it is not a one-size-fits-all therapy. Individuals may be more or less ready for change in different aspects of their lives. The counselor has the ability to match Y-Chun's current stage of change with the appropriate processes of change, or interventions. This allows therapy to be individualized to Y-Chun's needs and supportive of her own drive for change and growth.

The transtheoretical model is also an appropriate multicultural approach (Chen et al., 2003; Prochaska & Norcross, 2003). Consistent with many Asian American individuals who seek counseling, Y-Chun first approached her doctor (and then counselor) with concerns of physical symptoms such as inability to sleep, upset stomach, and headaches (Lee & Mock, 2005; Sue & Sue, 2008). Sue and Sue (2008) explain that many Asian Americans express psychological distress through physical symptoms, believing that the physical symptoms are causing the emotional turmoil. Using the process of consciousness raising, the counselor can help Y-Chun understand the relationship between her physical symptoms and emotional distress. Sue and Sue (2008) suggest asking clients how their physical symptoms are influencing their emotions and daily life. This is a culturally sensitive and appropriate approach, showing respect for the client's physical complaints while also exploring psychological distress. Therapists may use a psychoeducational approach with Y-Chun because education and learning are esteemed by many Asian Americans (Lee & Mock, 2005) and Y-Chun is currently pursuing a college education. The counselor may ask, "What do you notice in your body when you feel angry/sad/stressed?" Then they can discuss how to recognize triggers and how to substitute alternatives when Y-Chun is experiencing a debilitating physical symptom and emotion. For example, with help and information from the counselor, Y-Chun might learn to recognize, "When my body feels tense, it makes me stressed, so I will try the deep breathing exercises or meditation techniques that I just learned to try to decrease my tension and stress." Furthermore, it is also suggested that many Asian American clients expect that counselors are experts in their role who help individuals create concrete solutions for their problems (Lee & Mock, 2005; Sue & Sue, 2008). In the early stages of therapy, the counselor can support Y-Chun in implementing small changes to achieve short-term goals, which is both multiculturally and therapeutically appropriate and effective.

Consciousness raising can be used to discuss the connection between external stressors and intrapersonal conflicts. One of the ways the counselor can work with Y-Chun is by encouraging her to self-monitor her physical symptoms and any emotional antecedents. Tools such as a self-monitoring sheet or journal are helpful in not only understanding the link between seemingly unrelated events but also taking responsibility for behaviors and initiating change (Murphy & Dillon, 2008). For example, a small first step in Y-Chun improving her relationship with her father might be speaking up when she feels as though he is not treating her like an adult. In the following scenario, the counselor shares his or her observations to help raise Y-Chun's awareness of the behaviors that may contribute to her stress.

Counselor: Reviewing your journal, when was the last time you experienced a headache?

Y-Chun: It was last Thursday evening.

Counselor: What happened right before you got the headache?

Y-Chun: (Consulting her journal) I told David he could stay up after he finished his homework and watch TV. My father told him it was bedtime and sent David to bed.

Counselor: What did you do when your father sent David to bed?

Y-Chun: I didn't say anything, but I wanted to scream. My father shouldn't make the rules for my children—I should!

Counselor: It sounds like you were very angry.

Y-Chun: I was, but I didn't let my father know. I just sat there at the table stewing. Then my head started killing me. I wish I could have just said how I felt.

Counselor:	Wow. That sounds like a very intense interaction. From what you have shared with me over the past few weeks, it sounds like you tend to get headaches when you feel as if your father is parenting your children. It also sounds like you feel frustrated that you cannot express your thoughts with your father.

The counselor uses consciousness raising to help Y-Chun become aware that her stressful interactions with her father, and her difficulty communicating her feelings to him, may be contributing to her headaches and other health concerns. The counselor may continue to provide feedback on Y-Chun's monitoring data and also provide education on the connection between mind and body. Through education, feedback, and continuing to track her symptoms, Y-Chun may start to notice the relationship between her physical well-being and situational triggers.

Once the counselor has conceptualized the case, he or she can begin to focus subsequent sessions to help Y-Chun achieve the change she desires. The counselor can help Y-Chun continue to move toward contemplation by increasing her awareness beyond her "lack of relationships" with her parents, half-siblings, children, and men by discussing what she wants and how she can attain what she wants out of her relationships. The counselor can continue to encourage dramatic relief as necessary during this time.

In the case of Y-Chun, there has already been significant dramatic relief—on her anger about being bullied as a child, the disclosure of her rape at age 16, and her tears over feeling alone and disconnected from everyone. Although she has begun to explore these difficult feelings, additional dramatic relief may prove beneficial as she progresses into the contemplation stage. In the following scenario, the counselor initiates a role play with Y-Chun.

Counselor:	Tell me about what your father said to David.
Y-Chun:	My father came into the room and told David, "It's time to go to sleep." David was upset and yelled at my father. He got angry with David for being disrespectful. He said, "My house, my rules."
Counselor:	What did you do while this was happening?
Y-Chun:	I just sat there at the kitchen table finishing my homework.
Counselor:	How were you feeling at that moment?
Y-Chun:	I felt guilty for not standing up for David, since I was the one who said he could stay up later. I was so angry with my father. He acts like he is David's father and completely ignores that I make the rules for David.
Counselor:	You sound very angry that your father overstepped his boundaries. What would you have wanted to say to your father in this situation?
Y-Chun:	I would have told him that I had given David permission to stay up later and that he is my son so I should be the one to make the rules.
Counselor:	That's great, Y-Chun! It sounds like you have already put a lot of thought into your response. Would you be willing to do a role play to practice this? I will pretend to be your father, and you can have an opportunity to practice saying what is on your mind. How does that sound?

It is important to allow Y-Chun the choice to participate in this role play. As with any part of the transtheoretical approach, the client's involvement keeps strategies in line with the client's own abilities (Murphy & Dillon, 2008). By allowing Y-Chun to feel in control, her confidence will build and she will be better prepared to set and achieve goals. During the role play, it is important for the counselor to be warm and encouraging as Y-Chun experiments with new ways of communicating her feelings. Modeling positive feedback will, in turn, help Y-Chun develop positive self-talk.

At the precontemplation stage, the counselor assumes the role of the "nurturing parent" (Prochaska & Norcross, 2003, p. 535). The therapist is an expert in the process of change and encourages the client to become more aware of her concerns (Prochaska & DiClemente, 2003). The role of counselor will evolve as Y-Chun moves through the five stages. In the contemplation stage, the client begins to use self-reevaluation and environmental reevaluation to analyze how she feels about her concerns, what she values, and how she is affecting the people around her. Here, the counselor helps Y-Chun discover her values and desire for change by taking on the role of the "Socratic teacher" (Prochaska & Norcross, 2003, p. 535). Which values are most important to Y-Chun? What new behaviors will she strive toward? What will keep her centered? What habits will she let go of? How will her progress affect her relationships and the people around her? By determining her triggers and obstacles while acknowledging her values and the need for change, Y-Chun is moving toward the preparation stage.

In the middle stages of therapy, Y-Chun moves into the preparation stage of change. It is at this stage where Y-Chun will commit to taking action to make changes in her life. Note that Y-Chun will determine which changes will be made; the therapist is careful not to insert his or her own values on Y-Chun. The individual must be self-driven to set realistic goals and take small, determined steps toward those goals; the therapist acts as an expert in the change process and supports Y-Chun along the way. In the preparation stage, the individual develops an action plan and the counselor supports the plan as an "experienced coach" (Prochaska & Norcross, 2003, p. 535). At this stage, the counselor will use cognitive interventions such as self-liberation, which allows Y-Chun to embrace her own power to change her life. This involves boosting Y-Chun's self-efficacy while also helping her acknowledge real-world obstacles (Prochaska & DiClemente, 2003; Prochaska & Norcross, 2003). By focusing on Y-Chun's strengths, the counselor encourages Y-Chun to believe in her own success. What can you do to be successful? What might get in the way? What will you tell yourself if that happens, and how will you stay on track? Tell me about a time when you were successful. What did you do to make that happen? Using this positive frame of reference allows Y-Chun to be prepared to follow through with her action plan even when external factors appear to block her path. Y-Chun must have the internal drive for change and belief in herself that she can change as she prepares to implement behavioral changes.

Y-Chun is striving to feel less alone and more connected to both her family and the general community. Coming from a collectivistic culture, Y-Chun is deeply aware of her community and also a number of social justice issues that have restricted her in the past. Social liberation is not only a culturally appropriate intervention but may be particularly helpful for Y-Chun, as she will be able to see the tangible impacts of her efforts. Volunteering at a women's day shelter or at her children's schools are a couple of examples of how Y-Chun can progress toward attaining her goals while also addressing social justice issues.

In the following example, Y-Chun and the counselor are discussing her recent volunteer experience at a local women's day shelter.

Counselor:	Tell me about the program where you chose to volunteer.
Y-Chun:	It was a drop-in daytime shelter for homeless women and their children. They serve food, provide clothing and toiletries, and have staff there to help the women find jobs, housing, and health care. One of the rules of the shelter is that if you go there you have to be working toward finding a stable place to live.
Counselor:	That sounds like an amazing program! What did you do there?
Y-Chun:	The first day, I only served food. The next week, the staff was pretty busy, so I helped getting the women settled. I helped them fill out the intake forms. Some of these women are in really bad situations.
Counselor:	That must have been hard to hear about. How was that for you?
Y-Chun:	It was hard, especially when I realized the women were a lot like me. They are single parents, and some of them are going to school full-time! In some ways, the only way I was different was that I have a place to sleep at night.
Counselor:	How did it feel to notice those similarities?
Y-Chun:	I don't know . . . it was really surprising at first. I ended up talking to one mother who also has a daughter with cerebral palsy. I ended up telling her about Jennifer, how much of a struggle it can be for me. She cried. She said she had never spoken to another single mom with a daughter like hers.
Counselor:	Y-Chun, that is such a powerful moment. What was that like for you?
Y-Chun:	I felt like I helped her and . . . maybe she helped me. I'd never spoken to another single mom with a disabled daughter either.

As Y-Chun works to change her life, supporting those also involved in the change process can help build connections and decrease isolation. These small interactions within the community will build Y-Chun's confidence as she works toward creating meaningful interactions within her immediate family. Additionally, as Y-Chun realizes she is positively impacting the lives of others, her belief in her own abilities will be strengthened.

In addition to using cognitive strategies, the counselor can introduce behavioral interventions to support the transition from the preparation to the action stage. Behavioral strategies help Y-Chun stick with her action plan, even as old triggers and external obstacles arise (Prochaska & Norcross, 2003). Stimulus control helps Y-Chun remove or avoid old triggers from her environment, while counterconditioning is electing to choose an alternate behavior over a problem one (Prochaska et al., 1992). If, for example, Y-Chun is focusing on her relationship with her children and part of her action plan is to limit the number of times she yells at her children, she could work with her counselor to develop alternate options to yelling. One option might be to recognize the triggers that precede the yelling, and at that point, to walk out of the room to collect her thoughts. Another option would be to take several deep breaths before responding to her children when she is angry. As Y-Chun practices new strategies, the counselor's responsibility is to help her recognize success as it occurs. For example, after yelling at her children for not completing their homework, Y-Chun might recognize that her anxiety over her own schoolwork is precipitating this reaction. The counselor could then invite Y-Chun to explore these feelings: "How did it feel to recognize that trigger for the first time?" Y-Chun and her counselor should work together to develop realistic alternatives that Y-Chun is committed to implementing.

Another behavioral strategy that is appropriate is reinforcement management. Reinforcement management is a tool that involves being rewarded for implementing the action plan (Prochaska et al., 1992). The behavioral approaches are an integral part of the counseling intervention at the action stage because they give Y-Chun real alternatives to work with in the face of situations that trigger old habits and problems. Because the action plan, alternative behaviors, and goals are Y-Chun's, Prochaska and Norcross (2003) see the counselor's role more as a "consultant" (p. 535) at this stage of therapy. Y-Chun is the one implementing the changes in her life, and the counselor offers encouragement and another perspective if difficulties arise along the way.

An individual is said to be in the action stage once he or she has changed the problem behavior for anywhere from 1 day to 6 months (Prochaska & Norcross, 2003). Thus, as Y-Chun is altering her problematic behaviors and successfully replacing them with new, positive behaviors, she is in the action stage. Once these changes are successful for at least 6 months, Y-Chun will transition to the maintenance stage, in which she attempts to continue her progress and limit relapse. Here, the counselor will help Y-Chun remember all the new strategies and coping mechanisms she has learned and implemented throughout the course of therapy. These new cognitive and behavioral skills, such as self-reevaluation, counterconditioning, and stimulus control, will continue to be the foundation of her maintenance plan. Prochaska and Norcross (2003) suggest that a vital component of successful maintenance is that the client feels a strong reassurance that through the changes made, he or she is developing into the individual he or she aspires to be. During maintenance, it may be helpful to revisit previous assessments completed with Y-Chun. The changes in assessment scores throughout the course of therapy will help Y-Chun understand that she has changed. This concrete data can be an encouraging sign as Y-Chun works toward her final sessions of therapy. Conversely, if the data are not encouraging, this may point toward relapse and regression. The counselor can encourage Y-Chun's internal motivation to maintain her progress by discussing how she identified her values in early sessions, chose to modify her behavior to better attain those values in "middle" sessions, and is now achieving those values through maintenance of her successful cognitive, emotional, and behavioral modifications.

Because relapse and regression are common occurrences in the maintenance stage (Prochaska & Norcross, 2003), it is vital to discuss with Y-Chun what situations may trigger a relapse, how to cope with a relapse, and why a relapse is not a failure but, rather, a surmountable obstacle in the process of change. In Y-Chun's initial sessions, she spoke of the stress and hopelessness she felt due to her poor relationships and her multiple roles and responsibilities. As Y-Chun approaches termination, it is important to discuss how she might cope with stressful situations, especially if she feels more overwhelmed than usual. If Y-Chun does fall back on old habits and problematic behavior, she needs to have the cognitive mind-set that setbacks are normal and she can continue to work toward successful behavior change. Many individuals who relapse feel like failures and are ashamed (Prochaska & Norcross, 2003). The counselor can explain the normal nature of relapses and help Y-Chun reframe a relapse as a setback, not a failure.

In the case of Y-Chun, it is culturally appropriate for the counselor to provide relevant community resources as additional means of support. For a client such as Y-Chun, appropriate referrals could include agencies that provide support for single parents or services to children with disabilities. Y-Chun could also be referred to a center for sexual assault survivors or victims of domestic violence. There are numerous Chinese and Chinese American Community Centers throughout the country, and referral to a local chapter may help facilitate more connections within the community.

Another important tool for Y-Chun is to know that she can return to counseling for periodic booster sessions if she starts to struggle after termination. Along with booster sessions, Y-Chun can also identify other people in her life who act as a support network when she needs encouragement. For Y-Chun, this network will likely grow as she grows, because lack of relationship is a main concern for her over the course of her sessions. As her relationships improve, she will start to build her own support network. Knowing that termination does not mean being cut off from support may be a helpful reminder as she strives to maintain the progress she has made. Reviewing new skills, building up self-esteem and self-efficacy, affirming values, and discussing coping mechanisms for relapse will allow Y-Chun to terminate the counseling relationship armed with the knowledge and strategies she needs to continue her change process and maintain her success.

KEYSTONES

- Integrative psychotherapy strives to form approaches that blend theories, disciplines, and related techniques so clients can be effectively and efficiently guided through the change process.
- Four routes to achieving integration are common factors, technical eclecticism, theoretical synthesis, and assimilative integration.
- Common factor advocates investigate the elements shared or "common" to all effective methods, including empathy, warmth, and the therapeutic alliance.
- Technical eclecticism involves using an array of techniques borrowed from various theoretical orientations, focusing on research-driven practice.
- Theoretical synthesis seeks to develop a "meta-theory" that can pull aspects of two or more theories together in a unified approach.
- The assimilative integration route requires therapists to anchor their approaches in one main theory.

PROFESSIONAL IDENTITY

Psychotherapy integration is more than just trying out various techniques from the grab bag of options. It is a reflection of a coherent professional (Norcross & Prochaska, 1988). Although, as described previously, an integrationist orientation may be actualized in different ways, the approach is distinguished by a commitment to blending theories and techniques to create counseling interventions personalized to the unique needs of the individual client. Techniques are not applied in a vacuum but, rather, utilized with mindfulness regarding their link to theory.

As outlined by Castonguay (2006), the path to an integrationist professional identity may not be smooth and, in fact, may be marked by periods of significant confusion, especially given training "bias" toward major theoretical orientations. Castonguay observed that the major theoretical orientations tend to have affiliated training institutions, along with systematic training methods, and he contended that more work is needed to develop psychotherapy integration training programs.

The question of timing for psychotherapy integration training is important (Castonguay, 2005; Consoli & Jester, 2005). Questions remain as to whether, developmentally, it is best to introduce integration concepts from the start or later in training. While Consoli and Jester (2005) argued for introduction in the second semester of a master's program, Castonguay (2005) advocated training in the integrative model more toward the end of advanced training.

Castonguay (2005, 2006) outlined a model psychotherapy integration training program that encompasses five phases:

1. Preparation

2. Exploration

3. Identification

4. Consolidation

5. Integration

In this model, *preparation* entails instructing new trainees regarding basic therapeutic skills and the general principles of intervention (e.g., relationship factors). The *exploration* stage fosters the study of various theoretical orientations. Students in the *identification* stage work to incorporate a more in-depth understanding of a particular theoretical school. This orientation-specific expertise is sharpened further in the *consolidation* phase. Finally, at the stage of *integration*, typically at the internship level and beyond, students are encouraged to expand on their chosen theoretical model of change by incorporating elements of other orientations. The aim of this expansion is to attend to potential blind spots or limitations in the primary orientation, keeping an open mind to all potential avenues of therapeutic efficacy.

REFLECTIONS FROM THE CONTRIBUTOR'S CHAIR

Our program at Sonoma State University subscribes to tenets of social justice and advocacy for diverse individuals and families, and we felt a particular connection to a theoretical perspective that represents these elements. It also informs some of the research and applications we use in our work. For example, I (Dr. Zagelbaum) have worked with immigrant clients and their families and found integrative theories to be helpful when orienting such clients to the counseling process, especially if the process of counseling is held in a different regard within their country of origin. The integrative approach places more emphasis on the process of change, which allows for clients to experience a parallel process with those of transition within their new country, and helps clients recognize various resources available to them along this journey. Shana has worked with individuals experiencing transitional issues with respect to entering college and, in some cases, being first-generation college students. Kalia, during the course of her training as a preservice school counselor, encountered schoolchildren and family members who were transitioning among grade levels, family situations, and communities. In each case, being able to use different theoretical techniques under the umbrella of an integrationist perspective allows for clients to better embrace change and gain motivation to pursue more changes because of the different ways change can be made possible. Though we mainly focus on transtheoretical approaches, this is primarily because we are significantly involved with school counseling roles and settings where other forms of integration may not be as readily implemented due to various restraints and constraints.

Both Dr. Zagelbaum and Dr. Buckley draw on various aspects of an integrationist orientation. In keeping with the common factors approach, we train students to recognize and foster the core foundational elements believed to be at the heart of all psychotherapies, such as counselor/client relationship and active exploration procedures. We also train our students with the scientist-practitioner perspective and encourage careful consideration of the latest research on counseling efficacy for our student counselors. As our students work to develop their professional identities and theoretical orientations, we encourage them to try on various orientations for size and then work with them as they integrate this learning into a personal theoretical orientation, or personal "meta-theory."

We believe that theoretical techniques and interventions with clients can be as varied as the individuals and systems who seek services, but to best apply these techniques within a counseling relationship, counselors must understand where clients are in terms of readiness for change, familiarity with the counseling process, and the capacity to understand that the process of change is not often a smooth and predictable one. We hope that this chapter provides the insight and clarity we believe integrationist theories give to clients as diverse as Y-Chun.

ADDITIONAL RESOURCES

Beutler, L. E., Consoli, A. J., & Lane, G. (2005). Systematic treatment selection and prescriptive psychotherapy: An integrative eclectic approach. In J. C. Norcross & M. R. Goldfried (Eds.), *Handbook of psychotherapy integration* (2nd ed., pp. 121–143). New York: Oxford University Press.

Castonguay, L. G., Newman, M. G., Borkovec, T. D., Holtforth, M. G., & Maramba, G. G. (2005). Cognitive-behavioral assimilative integration. In J. C. Norcross & M. R. Goldfried (Eds.), *Handbook of psychotherapy integration* (2nd ed., pp. 241–260). New York: Oxford University Press.

Lazarus, A. A. (2005). Multimodal therapy. In J. C. Norcross & M. R. Goldfried (Eds.), *Handbook of psychotherapy integration* (2nd ed., pp. 105–120). New York: Oxford University Press.

Miller, S. D., Duncan, B. L., & Hubble, M. A. (2005). Outcome-informed clinical work. In J. C. Norcross & M. R. Goldfried (Eds.), *Handbook of psychotherapy integration* (2nd ed., pp. 84–102). New York: Oxford University Press.

Norcross, J. C. (2005). A primer on psychotherapy integration. In J. C. Norcross & M. R. Goldfried (Eds.), *Handbook of psychotherapy integration* (2nd ed., pp. 3–23). New York: Oxford University Press.

Stricker, G., & Gold, J. (2005). Assimilative psychodynamic psychotherapy. In J. C. Norcross & M. R. Goldfried (Eds.), *Handbook of psychotherapy integration* (2nd ed., pp. 221–240). New York: Oxford University Press.

REFERENCES

Barnett, J. E., & Shale, A. J. (2012). The integration of complementary and alternative medicine (CAM) into the practice of psychology: A vision for the future. *Professional Psychology: Research and Practice, 43*(6), 576–585.

Barrett, J. H., Haslam, R. A., Lee, K. G., & Ellis, M. J. (2004). Assessing attitudes and beliefs using the stage of change paradigm: Case study of health and safety appraisal within a manufacturing company. *International Journal of Industrial Ergonomics, 35,* 871–887.

Beutler, L., & Harwood, T. M. (2000). *Prescriptive psychotherapy: A practical guide to systematic treatment selection.* London: Oxford University Press.

Brooks-Harris, J. E. (2008). *Integrative multitheoretical psychotherapy.* Boston: Houghton Mifflin.

Carels, R. A., Darby, L., Cacciapaglia, H. M., Konrad, K., Coit, C., Harper, J., et al. (2007). Using motivational interviewing as a supplement to obesity treatment: A stepped-care approach. *Health Psychology, 26,* 369–374.

Castelnuovo, G., Faccio, E., Molinari, E., Nardone, G., & Salvini, A. (2004). A critical review of empirically supported treatments (ESTs) and common factors perspective in psychotherapy. *Brief Strategic and Systemic Therapy European Review, 1,* 208–224.

Castonguay, L. G. (2005). Training issues in psychotherapy integration: A commentary. *Journal of Psychotherapy Integration, 15,* 384–391.

Castonguay, L. G. (2006). Personal pathways in psychotherapy integration. *Journal of Psychotherapy Integration, 16,* 36–58.

Castonguay, L. G., Newman, M. G., Borkovec, T. D., Holtforth, M. G., & Maramba, G. G. (2005). Cognitive-behavioral assimilative integration. In J. C. Norcross & M. R. Goldfried (Eds.), *Handbook of psychotherapy integration* (2nd ed., pp. 241–260). New York: Oxford University Press.

Chen, H., Horner, S., & Percy, M. (2003). Cross-cultural validation of the stages of the tobacco acquisition questionnaire and the decisional balance scale. *Research in Nursing and Health, 26*(3), 233–243.

Consoli, A. J., & Jester, C. M. (2005). A model for teaching psychotherapy theory through an integrative structure. *Journal of Psychotherapy Integration, 15,* 358–373.

Corwin, D., Wall, K., & Koopman, C. (2012). Psycho-spiritual integrative therapy: Psychological intervention for women with breast cancer. *Journal for Specialists in Group Work, 37*(3), 252–273.

Dembo, M., & Praks Seli, H. (2004). Students' resistance to change in learning strategies courses. *Journal of Developmental Education, 27*(3), 2–11.

DiClemente, C., Bellino, L., & Neavins, T. (1999). Motivation for change and alcoholism treatment. *Alcohol Research and Health, 26*(2), 86–92.

DiClemente, C., Prochaska, J., Fairhurst, S., Velicer, W., Velasquez, M., & Rossi, J. (1991). The process of smoking cessation: An analysis of precontemplation, contemplation, and preparation stages of change. *Journal of Consulting and Clinical Psychology, 59*(2), 295–304.

Dunn, C., Deroo, L., & Rivara, F. P. (2001). The use of brief interventions adapted from motivational interviewing across behavioral domains: A systematic review. *Addiction, 96,* 1725–1742.

Eysenck, H. J. (1952). The effects of psychotherapy: An evaluation. *Journal of Consulting Psychology, 16,* 319–324.

Folwarski, J., & Smolinski, J., Jr. (2005). Polish families. In M. McGoldrick, J. Giordano, & N. Garcia-Preto (Eds.), *Ethnicity and family therapy* (pp. 741–755). New York: Guilford.

French, T. M. (1933). Interrelations between psychoanalysis and the experimental work of Pavlov. *American Journal of Psychiatry, 89,* 1165–1203.

Goldfried, M. R., & Newman, C. F. (1986). Psychotherapy integration: An historical perspective. In J. C. Norcross (Ed.), *Handbook of eclectic psychotherapy* (pp. 25–61). New York: Brunner/Mazel.

Goldfried, M. R., & Newman, C. F. (1992). A history of psychotherapy integration. In J. C. Norcross & M. R. Goldfried (Eds.), *Handbook of psychotherapy integration* (pp. 46–93). New York: Basic Books.

Grencavage, L. M., & Norcross, J. C. (1990). Where are the commonalities among the therapeutic common factors? *Professional Psychology: Research and Practice, 21,* 372–378.

Grimley, D. M., & Lee, P. A. (1997). Condom and contraceptive use among a random sample of female adolescents: A snapshot in time. *Adolescence, 32,* 771–779.

Hill, C. (2004). *Helping skills: Facilitating exploration, insight, and action.* Washington, DC: American Psychological Association.

Imel, Z. E., & Wampold, B. E. (2008). The importance of treatment and the science of common factors in psychotherapy. In S. D. Brown & R. W. Lent (Eds.), *Handbook of counseling psychology* (4th ed., pp. 249–266). Hoboken, NJ: John Wiley.

Johnson, L. D., Miller, S. D., & Duncan, B. L. (2000). *The Session Rating Scale 3.0.* Chicago: Authors.

Lambert, M. J., & Barley, D. E. (2002). Research summary on the therapeutic relationship and psychotherapy outcome. In J. C. Norcross (Ed.), *Psychotherapy relationships that work: Therapist contributions and responsiveness to patients* (pp. 17–32). New York: Oxford University Press.

Lampropoulos, G. K, Spengler, P. M, Dixon, D. N., & Nicholas, D. R. (2002). How psychotherapy integration can complement the scientist-practitioner model. *Journal of Clinical Psychology, 58*(10), 1227–1240.

Lazarus, A. A. (2005). Is there still a need for psychotherapy integration? *Current Psychology: Developmental, Learning, Personality, Social, 24*(3), 149–152.

Lee, E., & Mock, M. R. (2005). Asian families: An overview. In M. McGoldrick, J. Giordano, & N. Garcia-Preto (Eds.), *Ethnicity and family therapy* (pp. 269–301). New York: Guilford Press.

McGoldrick, M., Gerson, R., & Petry, S. (2008). *Genograms: Assessment and intervention.* New York: W. W. Norton.

McGoldrick, M., Giordano, J., & Garcia-Preto N. (2005). *Ethnicity and family therapy* (3rd ed.). New York: Guilford Press.

Miller, S. D., & Duncan, B. L. (2000). *The Outcome Rating Scale.* Chicago: Authors.

Miller, S. D., Duncan, B. L., & Hubble, M. A. (2004). Beyond integration: The triumph of outcome over process in clinical practice. *Psychotherapy in Australia, 10*(2), 2–19.

Miller, W. R., & Rollnick, S. (1991). *Motivational interviewing: Preparing people to change* (2nd ed.). New York: Guilford Press.

Murphy, B. C., & Dillon, C. (2008). *Interviewing in action in a multicultural world.* Belmont, CA: Thompson Brooks/Cole.

Norcross, J. C. (2005). A primer on psychotherapy integration. In J. C. Norcross & M. R. Goldfried (Eds.), *Handbook of psychotherapy integration* (2nd ed., pp. 3–23). New York: Oxford University Press.

Norcross, J. C., & Beutler, L. E. (2010). Integrative psychotherapies. In R. J. Corsini & D. Wedding (Eds.), *Current psychotherapies* (9th ed., pp. 502–535). Belmont, CA: Brooks/Cole.

Norcross, J. C., & Prochaska, J. O. (1988). A study of eclectic (and integrative) views revisited. *Professional Psychology: Research and Practice, 19,* 170–174.

Nuttall, J. (2002). Imperatives and perspectives of psychotherapy integration. *International Journal of Psychotherapy, 7,* 249–264.

O'Hara, D., & Schofield, M. J. (2008). Personal approaches to psychotherapy integration. *Counseling and Psychotherapy Research, 8,* 53–62.

Petrocelli, J. V. (2002). Processes and stages of change: Counseling with the transtheoretical model of change. *Journal of Counseling and Development, 80,* 22–30.

Pettay, R. F., & Hughey, J. (2011, October). *A mountain to climb: Strategies for working with probationary students.* Paper presented at the National Academic Advising Association 2011 National Conference, Denver, Colorado.

Prochaska, J. O. (2000). Change at differing stages. In C. R. Snyder & R. E. Ingram (Eds.), *Handbook of psychological change* (pp. 109–127). New York: John Wiley.

Prochaska, J. O., & DiClemente, C. C. (1984). Self change processes, self efficacy and decisional balance across five stages of smoking cessation. In *Advances in cancer control—1983* (pp. 131–140). New York: Alan R. Liss.

Prochaska, J. O., & DiClemente, C. C. (2003). The transtheoretical approach. In J. C. Norcross & M. R. Goldfried (Eds.), *Handbook of psychotherapy integration* (pp. 300–334). New York: Oxford University Press.

Prochaska, J. O., & DiClemente, C. C. (2005). The transtheoretical approach. In J. C. Norcross & M. R. Goldfried (Eds.), *Handbook of psychotherapy integration* (2nd ed., pp. 147–171). New York: Oxford University Press.

Prochaska, J. O., DiClemente, C. C., & Norcross, J. C. (1992). In search of how people change: Applications to addictive behaviors. *American Psychologist, 47*(9), 1102–1114.

Prochaska, J. O., & Norcross, J. C. (2003). *Systems of psychotherapy: A transtheoretical analysis* (5th ed). Pacific Grove, CA: Brooks/Cole.

Prochaska, J. O., & Norcross, J. C. (2010). *Systems of psychotherapy: A transtheoretical analysis* (7th ed.). Belmont, CA: Brooks/Cole (Cengage).

Rigazio-DiGilio, S. A., Ivey, A. E., Kunkler-Peck, K. P., & Grady, L. T. (2005). *Community genograms: Using individual, family and cultural narratives with clients.* New York: Teachers College Press.

Robinson, B. (2009). When therapist variables and the client's theory of change meet. *Psychotherapy in Australia, 15*(4), 60–65.

Ryle, A. (1990). *Cognitive-analytic therapy: Active participation in change: A new integration in brief psychotherapy.* Chichester, UK: John Wiley.

Ryle, A. (2005). Cognitive analytic therapy. In J. C. Norcross & M. R. Goldfried (Eds.), *Handbook of psychotherapy integration* (2nd ed., pp. 196–217). New York: Oxford University Press.

Shockey, S., & Seiling, S. (2004). Moving into action: Application of the transtheoretical model of behavioral change to financial education. *Financial Counseling and Planning, 15*(1), 41–52.

Stricker, G., & Gold, J. (2006). *A casebook of psychotherapy integration.* Washington, DC: American Psychological Association.

Sue, D. W., & Sue, D. (2008). *Counseling the culturally diverse: Theory and practice* (5th ed.). Hoboken, NJ: John Wiley.

Tracey, T. J. G., Lichtenberg, J. W., Goodyear, R. K., Claiborn, C. D., & Wampold, B. E. (2003). Concept mapping of therapeutic common factors. *Psychotherapy Research, 13,* 401–413.

Wachtel, P. L. (1993). *Therapeutic communication: Principles and effective practice.* New York: Guilford Press.

CHAPTER 16

East Meets West

Integration and Complementation

Michael G. Laurent and Shengli Dong

There are many trees that boast of their strength. The strength of the bamboo tree is in its ability to bend. Whereas, there are many different trees in the world, there are many definitions to what strength is.

—Famous Chinese saying

It is possibly best that this saying does not have a direct person/author attached to it. Since much of Eastern psychology has been passed down through oral histories, it is seen more as coming from a collective, rather than something created by an individual. A counseling theory in Asian psychology will not be structured in the same linear fashion as in Western psychology. While much attention has been paid to the differences between Eastern and Western approaches to business practices, political organization, and consumer habits, the same is not true when it comes to the area of psychology and counseling.

Cross-cultural misunderstandings exist whenever "East meets West" in counseling offices. Discussing cross-cultural considerations in counseling is challenging, because on one hand the counselor must be aware of his or her biases and cultural stereotypes and eliminate them in counseling; on the other hand, he or she must explore and discuss the differences between the client's Eastern and Western experiences. This chapter addresses the unique perspective on counseling as emanating from the history, philosophies, and culture serving as foundation for both Western and Eastern psychology. Further, this unique perspective is highlighted by way of application to the case of Y-Chun.

After reading this chapter, the reader will be able to do the following:

1. Describe the differences in goals, interpretations of change, interventions, and evaluations in counseling according to the Western and Eastern perspectives

2. Identify key historical and philosophical movements that have guided Western psychology

3. Explain specific historical, religious, and philosophical influences on Eastern psychology

4. Differentiate the values and philosophies between Western and Eastern culture/history

5. Identify cross-cultural themes/considerations as applied to the case of Y-Chun

OVERVIEW

There are two general perspectives when it comes to the issue of cross-cultural counseling and the research supporting cross-cultural practices: *etic* and *emic*. Adams et al. (2010) explain that an *etic* tradition looks at all cultures in more of a universalistic way, where we as people are more alike than unalike. Here, there is more focus on clients' sharing similar human characteristics—for example, we all cry, we all feel depressed, we all want to belong, and so on. This approach also believes that the person doing the research or working in clinical settings can be "color-blind" and can easily be a member of a group outside of that culture. This can be contrasted with the *emic* tradition, which approaches research and practice from more of a culture-specific perspective, one that sees cultures as uniquely separate and distinctive. From this perspective, one might argue that apples and oranges, while both fruit, cannot be lumped into the same category. In this respect, not all clients are the same, not all women react the same, and not all Asians are alike, for instance. Therefore, the study of these different cultures must be explored individually to understand the true characteristics of each population.

Being aware and respectful of cultural uniqueness is essential for all ethical counselors. Awareness and sensitivity are what find grounding in an understanding of the history and development of both Eastern and Western perspectives.

WESTERN PHILOSOPHY/PSYCHOLOGY

Before there was something known as Western psychology, Western philosophy shaped the minds of the people of Europe and the Mediterranean. Philosophers studied the principles underlying conduct, thought, and the nature of the universe. These philosophical assumptions and principles gave shape to what we now know as Western psychology and, as such, are important to review.

Alchemy and Gnosticism (the Beginnings)

Western philosophy grew out of alchemy (a science predating chemistry) and gnosticism (a theology that maintained that knowledge, not faith, was the way to salvation). As Taylor, Hare, and Barnes (2001) noted, these perspectives took form in the work of Socrates, Plato, and Aristotle, philosophers who have greatly influenced Western thought. Socrates promoted the ideas that truth, justice, and beauty were objective and that men had innate understandings of their existence (Taylor et al., 2001). Socrates employed deductive reasoning and logic to advance his ideas—two elements that continue to be mainstays of our own scientific approach.

Plato was a student of Socrates and, through his writings, continued Socrates's philosophy. He was also influenced by Pythagoras and was chiefly responsible for creating what many believe to be the first organized institution of higher learning in the Western world. Along with his own student, Aristotle, he continued to advance the academy into what closely resembled the Western university system. Aristotle is credited with establishing types of scholarly research that have survived to the present day (Goodrich, 2011).

From Philosophy to Psychology

The foundation of scholarly research, belief in objective reality, and value of employing deductive reasoning to "know" and "understand" that objective reality served as the context from which Western psychology came to life.

The history of Western psychology is filled with "schools of thought." And while many of the psychological theories (i.e., psychoanalysis, humanism, behaviorism, etc.) have their own unique focus and are expressed in other parts of this text, these models also share commonalities in their philosophical origins. A review of the early history of psychology will show how this early philosophical approach to knowing and understanding was given form in the psychological laboratory of Wilhelm Wundt (Wade & Tavris, 2010).

Wundt placed the study of thoughts, feelings, and behaviors in the same arena as the study of natural sciences. Like the early natural scientists, he believed that we can understand our subject—in this case, human nature—by identifying its smallest units, its structures. While promoting this "structuralism" as an early orientation in psychology, others, such as William James, challenged psychology to look at the purpose and function behind the element of thought or unit of behavior (Wade & Tavris, 2010). Thus, in addition to structuralism, the school of functionalism served as the foundation for the emerging field of psychology. While each school was unique, they all shared belief in the use of an emerging "scientific" approach to understanding, an approach founded on the early Western philosophies of Socrates, Plato, and Aristotle.

The theories presented within the text can be identified as illustrations of Western psychology. They have their origins with people who are European, American, and White, and reflect values and worldviews of the highly industrialized cultures. As such, they were influenced by the values permeating those cultures. As McGoldrick and Giordano (2005) noted, these cultures are primarily individualistic and monochronic (meaning they place a heavy emphasis on time, such as with deadlines, due dates, appointments, etc.). Lee (2000) suggested that these principles have been handed down to shape some of the objectives in Western psychology, such as individual responsibility, encouragement to confront others with feelings, concentration on the biological/nuclear family, emphasis on self-fulfillment and self-development, mastery over the environment/nature, and an orientation that pays more attention to the present and the future than to the past. This focus appears to have served acculturated Americans well—for example, in their quests to make their relationships more expressive and democratic. It has also empowered more people to conquer their problems with a "fight-back" attitude and to feel less shame and stigma from the mention of mental illness (Wade & Tavris, 2010). But as we describe later in this chapter, this focus is but one perspective on knowing and understanding the human condition. Exercise 16.1 will help you more fully understand the principles of such a Western orientation.

EXERCISE 16.1

REFLECTING FROM A WESTERN PERSPECTIVE

Directions: Think about a problem you've been having in the past few weeks. Identify the amount of power you believe you have in helping change that problem by rating your ability to change on a scale from 0 to 10—0 meaning no power whatsoever and 10 meaning complete and total control. Now, come up with at least three short goals toward changing this problem, and mention the time frame in which the goals will be completed.

Much of what we take as "truth" and obvious realities—be it the nature and origin of anxiety or depression; the accepted view of human nature; or even buzz words or hot topics such as *best practices*, *empirical evidence*, and *evidence-based interventions*—are rooted in a Western-biased perspective. This perspective emphasizes objectivity over subjectivity, cause and effect over randomness, and treatment (as control) over the natural unfolding of life. The subtle values—biases—imbued within Western psychology are evident in the following example (see Case Illustration 16.1).

CASE ILLUSTRATION 16.1

Susan

Susan is a 22-year-old, single American woman. She is living with her parents, who could be considered upper middle class. Susan is troubled by the fact that she is still living at home with her parents. She has begun working and is paying for her own expenses, but she feels as though her parents still treat her like a child. She's afraid to tell her parents how she feels and would rather avoid conflict.

While the case in the example is neither unique nor overly elaborate, it challenges the reader to begin to conceptualize the issues the client, Susan, is confronting, as well as goals and methods for moving to a more preferred scenario. If Susan is engaged with a "traditionally" Western-oriented counselor, that counselor might be inclined to assist her in seeing the value of being forthright and genuine about her feelings. This counselor might support Susan in developing the skills and attitude necessary for asserting herself with her parents. The counselor may see Susan's concerns about independence as a healthy, normative mind-set and, as such, encourage her to move into her own place. While all this may seem "normal," the challenge is to recognize that all that we deem "normal" is colored by our Western values and may not be universally held as truth.

EASTERN PSYCHOLOGY

In any discussion of Eastern culture, it is essential *not* to approach the explanations of prototypes of Eastern culture as stereotypes or to "lump" the great expanse of people into a monolithic heap. It is all too easy for many Westerners to assume that all Asians are the same or that Eastern philosophy and religion are "cool" or "exotic" or "mysterious." Such a view point is demeaning and reflective of a sense of superiority. Why is it "exotic" or "mysterious," as opposed to an alternative, valid prism of truth-knowledge and the human condition?

An Overview

Jones-Smith (2012) offered a generalization that while Asian culture is usually characterized as introverted, collectivist, and mystical, the West is seen as rational, extroverted, and individualistic. The author noted that Carl Jung described the West as a culture of "doing" and perceived the East as a culture of "passive being." This characteristic of "doing" takes form, in the Western culture, with people tending to solve problems by applying thoughts and actions; in the Eastern culture, people tend to solve problems through engaging in contexts or being in the moment. Wade and Tavris (2010) also noted that Eastern psychology usually refers to Asian countries with more of a focus on collectivism and polychronic customs (less emphasis on time and more on relationships with people and the environment). Lee (2000) contended that, despite the countless differences between Asian groups, a number of cultural similarities are important to consider. In these cultures, an individual, she stated, is a product of all the generations of her or his family, and there are clear roles and positions in that family hierarchy based on age, gender, and social class. While Western civilization has led to an emphasis on autonomy, free will, competition, and materialism, ancient Asian principles can still be seen in values rooted in cooperation, fatalism, and unity (Tweed & Lehman, 2003).

The Role of Eastern Religions and Philosophies

To understand Eastern cultures, or even counseling for that matter, one must understand that religions and philosophies play a huge role in defining Asian cultures. In the East, various philosophies exist. Among them, the most influential are Buddhism, Confucianism, Taoism, and Hinduism. One specific example of where Eastern religion intertwines with Eastern philosophy is Hinduism. Said to be "the oldest living religion," Hinduism does not have a single founder and is actually more of a conglomeration of diverse traditions. It includes a variety of laws and prescriptions of "daily morality" based on karma (the connection between actions and their consequences), dharma (where law, order, and harmony equal reality), samsara (the cycle of birth, life, death, and rebirth), and yogas (pathways or practices) (Brodd, 2003). Vedas, the oldest philosophical writings and first kernels of Hinduism, emphasize that the world of apparent reality is a world of illusion, which is perceived to be the root of problems (*maya*) experienced by human beings (Brodd, 2003). The merge of the finite self with the ultimate reality will yield enlightened consciousness to deal with the problem of *maya*. In contrast to Western approaches, Hinduism looks inward to find a reliable answer.

Buddhism was founded in India but spread to Tibet, China, and most parts of the world. According to Buddhism, suffering is an inherent part of human life, caused by craving for pleasure and aversion to pain from birth to death (Smith & Novak, 2003). Buddha is inside each of us, and emancipation and enlightenment can be achieved through personal effort and intelligence. The "Four Noble Truths" were directly aimed at explaining the causes for human suffering and ways to solve it. The first is the diagnosis of the symptom, the second is the determination of its cause, the third is the cure for the disease when the cause has been removed, and the fourth describes the medicine or treatment that will bring about the cure. Other concepts included in this religion are karma (which reminds us of the causes and eventual effects of our deeds and actions), reincarnation (a process that recycles humans through stages of heavenly beings, humans, ghosts, animals, and hells), nirvana (the destination where suffering is eliminated and complete enlightenment is achieved), and the perpetual attainment of compassion and wisdom (Yeung & Lee, 1997). Compared with the Western linear sense of reality, Buddhism holds that everything is in constant flux; thus, there is no inherent or fixed nature to any object or experience. Freedom from suffering is possible and can be achieved through the Noble Eightfold Path (Brekke, 1999).

Confucian virtue and thinking have been influenced by Buddhist ideas (Confucianism, 2013). Confucianism is considered as being closer to humanism (an attitude concerned with human beings, their achievements, and their interests), rather than a traditional religion or theology. Confucius and his followers taught that man is the center of the universe but cannot live alone. They promoted that the ultimate goal is individual happiness, which can be achieved only through peace with others. In fact, Confucian teaching calls for the abolition of war and the development of world unity. *Ren*, *yi*, and *li* are the most basic Confucian ethics and focus on cultivation and maintenance of virtue (Craig, 1998). *Ren* is translated to mean love, goodness, humanity, and an obligation to altruism and humane treatment of others within a family, community, or organization. It can also be expressed in the Confucian version of the ethic of the Golden Rule: "Do not do unto others what you would not have them do unto you." *Yi* refers to upholding moral disposition and righteousness to do beneficence. *Li* is a system of standards and norms to evaluate how an individual should behave and act appropriately in a community, such as filial piety (Craig, 1998).

Compared with individualism in the West, a person educated under Confucianism is expected to recognize and follow his or her roles in various environments (Confucianism, 2013). Individuals with a collectivist mind-set will sacrifice personal interest for the sake of family and country, and strive for academic and business excellence and success. Confucian virtue and thinking were also heavily influenced by beliefs and traditions from Taoist and Buddhist ideas. The doctrines of Confucianism, Buddhism, and Taoism were often melded together (Confucianism, 2013).

Tao is referred to as meaning "The Way." Major principles from this theology are that life is good and a strong connection exists between the spirit and the body. Taoists believe in establishing harmony with nature through acceptance, simplicity, compassion, reliance on experience, and living in the moment beside others. Chinese alchemy, feng shui, Chinese martial arts, Zen Buddhism, traditional Chinese medicine, and breath training all seem to have been influenced by Taoism.

Taoist ethics emphasizes *wu-wei* (action through nonaction), "naturalness," simplicity, spontaneity, compassion, moderation, and humility (Taoism, 2013). *Wu-wei* is considered the leading ethical concept in Taoism, and it is usually translated as "nonaction" or "action without intent or will" (Van Voorst, 2005). This is quite different from the "doing" upheld in the West.

Comparison in Philosophies Between East and West

An individual's will is not considered the root of the problem unless it is in disaccord with the rhythm of the natural universe (Fasching & deChant, 2001). "By wu-wei, the sage seeks to come into harmony with the great Tao, which itself accomplishes by nonaction" (Van Voorst, 2005, p. 170).

In the West, early philosophies were impacted by the concept of "God as the King of the Universe." This view posits that the natural world obeys laws created by God. Thus, the functions of philosophy and science were to discover the laws that governed the universe (Gordon, 2004).

In Eastern philosophy, the natural world follows nature, which is the natural law. Humans may look for patterns and the flow of the universe. Any "laws" thus detected are the human perception—or a way of organizing our beliefs, which are not the underlying basis of phenomena being observed (Gordon, 2004).

Thus, the approaches to understanding reality differ greatly between the Eastern and Western philosophies. In the West, understanding reality involves application of symbolic thoughts, such as mathematics, formulas, or words. This means that nature of the reality can be discovered through the process of "doing," such as thinking and behaviors. In contrast, the Eastern philosophy believes that "thinking distracts us from understanding reality." The world perceived through our senses is a world of illusion—impermanent, misleading, and unreliable.

The moment we tend to move our attention away from reality (such as nature's rhythms and laws) to the world of symbols (thoughts, formulas, and words), a gap emerges between the symbols and the reality they represent. In the Eastern approaches, the nature of reality is discovered by being in the experience (experiencing it directly), without thoughts. It uses various meditative processes such as meditation, *qigong*, and yoga.

Compared with the popular linear view of the universe and life in the West, the circular view of the universe based on the observation of eternal reoccurrence in life is more valued in the East. Individuals in the East are more inner-world dependent: They tend to believe that events in the universe are interconnected, and they search for truth by examining within themselves and becoming part of the universe through right living and meditation. For example, a college student is experiencing anxiety interacting with her new classmates. She is introverted and not comfortable talking with a counselor about this issue. She recalls combating her anxiety using cognitive-behavioral therapy and other modern counseling approaches, which tend to regard anxiety as a negative symptom that needs to be gotten rid of. The more she focuses on eliminating the anxiety (by doing), the more anxiety she is experiencing. Instead, her counselor suggests that she should apply meditation and tai chi. These approaches help the client be in the moment and aware of the impact of breathing on her body and mind when she is experiencing anxiety. After a few sessions, the student feels relieved and accepts the fact that anxiety is part of a human being's natural feelings. Thus, she can focus on constructive activities while holding and accepting the anxiety's presence.

An individual is an indispensable part of the universe, and each person needs to recognize and follow his or her roles in society and be willing to sacrifice personal interests for the sake of his or her family, community, or country. Collectivism is highly valued over individualism (East Versus West, n.d.). Read the example in Case Illustration 16.2, and see if you can identify the elements of the Eastern school of thought and how that might affect counseling.

CASE ILLUSTRATION 16.2

Jin Jung

Jin Jung is an 18-year-old freshman from China, attending her second year at a major university in America. She's doing well in her general education classes, but she is not sure what major to declare. She was told by the career office that she should take the Strong Interest Inventory and discuss the results with a counselor. What should the counselor consider, outside of the data from the Strong Interest Inventory? What cultural considerations must a counselor be aware of regarding the importance of the family before discussing career choices with Jin Jung? What other ways would counseling Jin Jung be different compared with counseling students born in America who follow more American cultural traditions?

Eastern philosophy has a strong influence in psychological orientations and clinical practices. Various scholars such as Jung and Suzuki have tried to integrate and bridge Buddhism and psychoanalysis (Suzuki, 1991). Albert Ellis (1991) admitted that many of the principles in the theory of rational emotive psychotherapy were originally stated by ancient Taoist and Buddhist thinkers. Mindfulness practices, mindfulness-based stress reduction, yoga, dialectical behavioral therapy, and acceptance and commitment therapy have all been influenced by Eastern philosophies and thought. Many famous psychologists such as Jung and Fritz Perls studied Eastern philosophies such Zen Buddhism and I Ching (Drob, 1999; Wulf, 1996).

Human Nature: Collectivism and Naturalism

In examining human nature from the Eastern philosophical perspective, collectivism and naturalism are two overarching themes. Human beings are considered an indispensable part of the universe, and people are connected (and transpersonal), which is reflected in the thought of collectivism. This collectivism, in combination with respect to authority figures, may be expressed in different forms: locality or filial piety and respect to persons with status in family, tribe, community, or country—such as teachers, counselors, parents, and leaders; sacrifice of personal interest for the sake of family or country; or striving for academic and business excellence and success. Collectivism and community are preferred over individualism. The well-being and welfare of the family and community are valued over individual rights and interests. The harmony within the group is considered most important (Triandis, 1995). Individuals from collective societies regard disclosure of personal problems as bringing guilt and shame on their family members and community (Leong & Lau, 2001). We invite you to complete the following exercise to identify your belief in human nature.

EXERCISE 16.2

BELIEFS ABOUT HUMAN EXPERIENCE

Directions: The following are some statements about human nature. Use the scale from 0 to 3 to measure where you are. Circle only one number for each statement (3 = strong belief, 2 = some belief, 1 = little or no belief, 0 = no answer, meaning it is unknown or impossible for you to determine). There are no right or wrong answers.

1. People are controlled by human nature. 0 1 2 3

2. People can control human nature. 0 1 2 3

3. People control the physical world. 0 1 2 3

4. People are controlled by the physical world. 0 1 2 3

5. One's sense of responsibility rests in the self. 0 1 2 3

6. One's sense of responsibility rests in the group. 0 1 2 3

7. Responsibility for decisions lies with each individual. 0 1 2 3

8. Responsibility for decisions is a function of group or resides in a role the individual fills. 0 1 2 3

9. Mind and body exist separately. 0 1 2 3

10. Mind and body work together. 0 1 2 3

Add Questions 2, 3, 5, 7, and 9, and then Questions 1, 4, 6, 8, and 10. Higher scores in the first group of questions tend to represent the mainstream North American culture, emphasizing individualism, while higher scores in the second group of questions tend to represent Eastern culture, emphasizing collectivism. (Note: Adapted from McGrath & Axelson, 1999.)

Naturalism is defined as the viewpoint that laws of nature operate in the universe and that human behavior should be in accordance with the rhythm of the universe. Naturalism is attuned to Taoism, in which human behaviors and acts are suggested to follow the way of nature. *Wu-wei* epitomizes naturalism with its "action through nonaction." Case Illustration 16.3 highlights this concept of action through nonaction.

CASE ILLUSTRATION 16.3

Confrontation

Yu-Heung is a 21-year-old Chinese employee at a company where he has worked for only 2 months. He hears that someone in the next office does not like him. Stan, one of Yu-Heung's coworkers, tells Yu-Heung that he should immediately confront the other employee to find out specifically what the problem is. Why might confrontation be an important reflection of Stan's culture? If Yu-Heung were to do nothing, how might that be reflective of Chinese culture? Can Yu-Heung's nonaction be seen as a form of action?

View of Mental Health

Philosophical and cultural teachings normally affect an individual's beliefs on the nature and origin of mental health and shape attitudes toward individuals with mental illness (Abdullah & Brown, 2011). Mental health issues, in the traditional (Western) belief system, are considered to be caused by a lack of emotional harmony or conflict with the environment, or by evil spirits. According to Buddhist beliefs, problems in our lives are usually related to transgressions committed in the past, because the previous life and future life are as much a part of the life cycle as the present life is (Kramer, Kwong, Lee, & Chung, 2002). Our suffering, anxiety, and stress are attributed to trying to hold on to things that are constantly changing and shifting and our ignorance and craving for pleasure (Lopez, 2001). In many Asian cultures, mental health issues are often stigmatized and regarded with a sense of guilt and shame because mental illness tends to be explained as a manifestation of spiritual or moral weakness. In Asian cultures, emotional self-control and conformity to norms are highly valued.

Western thinking and philosophy were built on three fundamental foundations: separation of mind and matter (which leads to the separation of mind and body), Greek reductionism, and a deterministic–monotheistic worldview (Kimura et al., 2005). The separation of mind from matter enabled the material sciences to challenge medieval mysticism and undergo vigorous development. However, this Western thinking leads to a "linear" philosophical system, which believes that the future is predictable. Both life and the universe are essentially "nonlinear." Many of the current problems in our lives are attributed to people's attempts to understand the nonlinear, "unpredictable" occurrences of life through a linear, "predictable" lens (Ohnishi & Ohnishi, 2009). See Table 16.1 for a comparison of Eastern and Western philosophical values and beliefs.

Table 16.1   Comparisons of Eastern and Western Values and Philosophies

	Western Values and Philosophies	Eastern Values and Philosophies
Relation orientation	Individualism is stronger (an individual respects independence and is true to self-interests). An individual is deemed an independent part of the universe and society.	Collectivism is stronger (an individual respects interdependence; is loyal to family, community, and organization; and tends to sacrifice personal interests for the sake of the family and community). An individual is deemed an indispensable part of the universe and society.
Causal perception	Takes a linear view of the causal effect, focusing on the role of the individual and discrete events.	Takes a circular view of the causal effect, valuing the interconnectedness of the person and his or her environment and believing in the eternal recurrence of the universe.
Perception of reality	Reality is tangible and predictable and deemed a service to God, fortune and fame, etc.	Eternal reality is intangible and fleeting and deemed beyond the realities that surround us.
Pursuit of reality	Reality is sought through external exploration and self-dedication to *wei* (action), such as cognitions and behaviors (i.e., goal setting for success, fame, vision, achievement, etc.)	Reality is sought through inner exploration and awareness; self-liberation and development can be achieved through eliminating the false self and discovering the true self by becoming an integral part of the universe and society through means of *wu-wei* (nonaction), such as meditation, yoga, and other traditional practices.
Perception of emotions	Positive emotions are pursued vigorously, and negative emotions are targeted for elimination through application of cognition and behaviors.	Emotions (both positive and negative) are deemed integral to human experience. They should not be shunned away; however, they should be kept in balance and harmony through meditation.

THERAPEUTIC PROCESS AND APPLICATION

Goals of Counseling

The goals in counseling as related to Western approaches usually focus on achieving measureable benefits or symptom relief. Traditional therapists from this cultural perspective usually start with a baseline of behavior. Specific goals are then developed with the client, as the counselor asks questions such as, "What would you like to see change in your life?"

"What would you specifically like us to work on?" "Where would you like to see yourself a year from now? Six months from now? By next week?" Many therapists are trained to design detailed treatment plans for each client, and some agencies and insurance companies will punish the therapist if the work with a client is not outlined in specific, technical terms.

Eastern approaches focus on acceptance, going with the flow, and practicing responsible behaviors. The goal of counseling is to help clients give up the idea of controlling the uncontrollable. The more we cling to the illusion of controlling the unpredictable and uncontrollable, the more we turn our attention away from the basic activities that sustain us (self-care, relationships, and responsibilities) to handle our feelings. Soon, the only things getting our attention are our issues and desire to feel better. The harder we try, the more desperate, hopeless, stuck, and frustrated we become ("Japanese Psychology," n.d.).

Thus, the focus is accepting our feelings instead of attempting to change them. Once in tune with our feelings and accepting of them, we find that we can take actions and make plans without first changing our feeling state. Normally, the action naturally leads to changes in feelings.

The Therapeutic Process of Change

Western interpretations of therapeutic change are traditionally measured by examining the results. Whether by using quantitative or qualitative feedback, the focus is on the effect, the consequence, or the conclusion, and less attention is paid to the journey. Therapists use Likert scales ("on a scale from 1 to 10") and an abundance of feedback/evaluation forms to measure change by looking directly at the client's current condition or satisfaction. But many of these tools have difficulties putting "change" in a historical or cultural context. Western practices appreciate setting goals and rewarding achievement. But are there some times when change should be left to evolve? Or maybe the change needs to come in terms of the way the problem is perceived, and not necessarily in the form of a specific reward or punishment. Even medication has been seen as a "quick fix" to achieve change.

Eastern therapeutic practices, including Morita therapy, help individuals accept the internal fluctuations of thoughts and feelings and ground behaviors in reality and the here and now. A cure or solution is not defined by the alleviation of discomfort or the attainment of an ideal feeling state but, rather, by taking constructive actions (such as setting up goals and achieving them) to help an individual live a full and meaningful life and not be over-possessed by one emotional state ("Morita Therapy," n.d.). Morita therapy helps clients accept negative emotions (such as anxiety) as a natural part of emotional experiences while pursuing constructive living, rather than being preoccupied with attempts to eliminate the negative symptoms and emotions. Morita practices include exposure, ritual prevention, goal seeing, and diary keeping.

A 27-year-old man has experienced anxiety for the past 3 years. He trembles and cannot write in front of others, which negatively affects his work. His therapist recommends that he take daily activities under supervision, while experiencing the anxiety. The purpose is to encourage the client to engage in daily constructive activities rather than be preoccupied with attempts to eliminate the anxiety or fear. The client becomes tense and trembles when engaged in group practices. The therapist does not think the trembling and tension are a major issue, encourages the client to engage in constructive activities, and provides the client with positive feedback each time he completes the constructive activities, even though he exhibits certain levels of anxiety. With 2 months of practice, the client engages in more group practices and exposures and becomes less anxious and less preoccupied with the anxiety and tremors. The client loses almost all fear of writing in front of others and communicates much better with his colleagues.

Interventions and Evaluations

From a Western perspective, reinforcement schedules are popular interventions to use with clients. Whether trying to change the conduct or performance of a child or improve the occupational or personal lives of adults, Western psychology might emphasize looking at rewards and punishments. Children get stickers for good behavior. Employees get bonuses for productiveness on the job. In most cases, the pay-off is given to the individual, not the group. Solution-focused therapy has been used by many therapists who wish to help clients with the immediate concerns in their lives. A counselor might be used to help the individual conquer the system but not necessarily to become part of the system. In this culture, self-efficacy usually refers to the pride in one's own personal (individual) accomplishments, and success is determined by individual grades, independent wealth, and self-acquired talents.

Mindfulness practice is one of the effective interventions that originated from Eastern philosophy. Mindfulness includes many practices such as tai chi, *qigong*, sitting and walking meditation, mindfulness-based cognitive therapy (Segal, Williams, & Teasdale, 2002), mindfulness-based stress reduction, dialectical behavior therapy, acceptance and commitment therapy, and yoga. These practices help individuals focus on the present and the purpose, free of judgment. In addition, individuals are invited to accept uncontrollable aspects of their lives and take responsible actions to handle these experiences. Mindfulness practices have been found effective in substantially reducing symptoms of anxiety and comorbid depressive symptoms (Vollestad, Nielsen, & Nielsen, 2012), and in achieving positive treatment effects with posttraumatic stress disorder (Thompson & Waltz, 2010). Mindfulness practices help individuals live in the reality of their experiences rather than being restricted by delusions, anxiety, and fear of those experiences.

In Japan, Shintoism is less of a religion and more of a mixture of history, folklore, and mythology. It flourished throughout Japan even though it did not have a historical founder, date of creation, definite sacred text, or isolated set of beliefs. Yamakage (2006) suggested that it originated back in the 3rd century B.C. with the Yayoi culture in Japan. The primary writings of Shintoism include *Kojiki* (a record of ancient matters that explain Shinto history), *Rikkokushi* (a series of national chronicles of Japan), and *Jinno Shotoki* (an extended study of Shinto policy and the history of Japan). Ancient Chinese writings show the word *Shinto* to mean "Way of the Gods" and the word *Kami* to mean spirits or deities. A key feature of these semireligious spirits is that they can be expressed as human-like, animistic (objects having souls), or part of natural forces in the world (such as mountains, rivers, lightning, wind, waves, trees, etc.). Shinto theology advocates for absolute loyalty to the Sovereign Emperor of Japan (a direct descendent and representative of the highest God), respect for ancestors, and obedience to the State. And while Shintoism has been directly linked to the historical and political advancement of Japan, it has spread to many parts of the world, and its influence can even be seen in such pursuits as flower arrangement, architecture and design, art, and sumo wrestling (Yamakage, 2006).

Identifying examples of Eastern equivalencies to counseling or mental health is more difficult. Welwood (1993) looked at psychotherapy in Japan and said that, while Westerners see this primarily as a "mental" process, Japanese see healing as coming from a more spiritual place. Leong, Lee, and Chang (2008) noticed that while couples counseling is popular in Western cultures, Eastern cultures view the extended family (not just the couple) as more important. They also saw that while Western counseling seeks to make everyone in the family equal, authoritative dynamics in Asian families should be recognized and respected. McGoldrick and Giordano (2005) pointed out that one of the reasons for Asians to seek mental health services is on referral from their medical physicians treating physical complaints. They add that many Asians are not eager to seek out counseling for stress, suffering, and depression, even though stressors such as immigration, acculturation, and loss disrupt their functioning. Hac and Long (2004) found that many of the Asian immigrants to America may be trying to cope with serious psychiatric syndromes such as posttraumatic stress disorder, in addition to the challenges of acculturation. Lee (2000) also pointed out that while many Asian countries are changing and becoming more industrialized and progressive in their own right, many Asian Americans are still shaped by shame and obligation in relation to their families. Cohen, Wolf, Panter, and Insko (2011) cited that Asian women were the most prone to feelings of guilt and shame compared with other subpopulations. But Hsu (1971) stated that such feelings in the Asian culture are still needed to perpetuate an interdependent, peaceful, and harmonious relationship within the family.

Y-CHUN THROUGH A CROSS-CULTURAL LENS

Like most case studies, the value in such research can come from the rich, descriptive examples some of the narrative information provides. While this cannot be generalized to a large group, it does provide interesting insight for cross-cultural psychologists. Dissection of this case can take on many meanings, depending on the place of incision. Cross-cultural psychologists might start with Y-Chun's biracial identity and closely examine the literature that not only shows a small amount of similarity between Western and Asian culture but also points to the conflicts between Chinese and American identities when combined (Ferber, 1995; Houston, 1997; Lou, Lalonde, & Wilson, 2011). According to Takaki (2010), physical characteristics such as eye shape and color can be used to discriminate against and tease children who do not fit the "norm." It is not clear that this was the case for Y-Chun, but the case notes don't seem to reflect a healthy discussion regarding the blending of her two cultures. So a sense of pride growing up is not apparent for Y-Chun. Kim and Park (2008) noted that cultural identity is a crucial force in an Asian or Asian American child's life and that freedom to explore these feelings without shame is the best indicator that the child will grow up feeling more secure. Developmental psychologists such as Feldman (2008) suggest that the most crucial time in the development of cultural identity is around the time of adolescence (or right before). It would be interesting for the therapist to learn some of the client's perceptions of her biracial identity during that time. A hurtful experience for Y-Chun regarding cultural identity can explain low self-esteem and diminished self-efficacy throughout her life. Counselors, especially those with a similar cultural background to Y-Chun's, may help Y-Chun bolster her cultural pride through networking with individuals who have similar experiences and backgrounds, or may refer her to community resources that can assist her in expressing her cultural identity without feeling judged.

When addressing some of the developmental issues in this case, there could be different ways of looking at Y-Chun's moving back into her parents' home. While McGoldrick and Giordano (2005) might find it a sign of collectivism in an extended family, Newman and Newman (2010) might look at Y-Chun's age (38 at the time of the case note) and offer the explanation that "boomerang kids" today, such as Y-Chun, are not bringing their children to live with the grandparents for cultural benefit but, instead, because of a damaged economy leaving no alternatives. Since her siblings appear to be more successful and independent, Y-Chun may feel like a "burden" to her parents. Both Western- and Eastern-trained therapists will be concerned with how Y-Chun feels about this, but the difference is the Western therapist might be more confronting and less patient with the process. A counselor from the Western cultural perspective may need to understand the Y-Chun whose culture is more rooted in the collectivist orientation, in which the multigenerational relationship and roles of individuals in the family system are highly valued. This multicultural awareness and competency are needed to build trust and rapport with the client for goal setting and further interventions.

The transcripts of the intake reveal that Y-Chun may have an eating disorder and issues surrounding body image, despite the lack of literature on this concern as it affects Asian populations. Another difference between the Western and Asian cultures is that body image is even more forbidden as a subject of discussion among Asian women (Haynie, 2007). Counselors may introduce Y-Chun to mindfulness-based cognitive therapy/yoga/tai chi or refer her to professionals in her community who have expertise in these areas. The walking meditation may be particularly useful in dealing with a potential eating disorder that may be attributed to stress and in helping Y-Chun integrate some physical/mental routine into her life to cope with the life stress and challenges.

The topic of Y-Chun's education was also touched on in the interview. Lee (2000) warned that while Asian parents may be supportive (and sometimes overinvolved) in their children's education, many of these parents are disappointed if a child strays away from majors such as math, science, and engineering and into fields such as Y-Chun's chosen focus, liberal arts, where the parents see no guaranteed connection to a successful profession.

Another issue that would be treated differently by the Western versus Eastern cultures involves the lack of a father figure for Y-Chun's children. Western psychology has been looking at single-parent homes and homes without fathers. Women who are single parents in Western cultures are beginning to be viewed in a positive light (Hill, 1998). But most of this research has been focusing on African American mothers, and there has been hardly any mention of this arrangement in the Asian and Asian American populations. Since the shame factor is greater for women from an Eastern culture, it is less likely for an Asian woman, such as Y-Chun, to seek parenting assistance (Armas, 2001). In fact, Kok and Liow (1993) state that many women in Y-Chun's situation would choose suicide rather than live with the shame of coming home to their ancestors with children born out of wedlock. Counseling professionals need to highlight the strengths Y-Chun demonstrated to keep her family intact and to manage her work and school in the face of these adverse situations. Thus, some dialectical behavior approaches such as meditation can assist Y-Chun in recognizing her own untapped strengths and abilities and can bring pride to her achievements. These gains could bolster her cultural identity and self-efficacy.

A counselor or therapist must always consider depression and suicide when working with a client whose life stressors are as extreme as Y-Chun's—from her experimentation with drugs to her running away from home to her shoplifting and being sexually assaulted by a cousin. Given these facts, Y-Chun should be assessed for depression and suicidality. Chen, Chen, and Chung (2002) reported that Asian women have the highest suicide rate compared with other women in the United States and that much of this is related to the cultural bias and stigma that accompanies Asian women's perception that their depression is a personal weakness or moral failing. In an interview on National Public Radio, Duldulao (2009) explained that the reason why suicide is such a common option for Asian women is that they come from an achievement-oriented culture in which failure is not acceptable. She went on to say that mental disorders/mental illnesses are seen as failure and seeking treatment as an admission of failure.

The National Alliance on Mental Illness (2009) recommended Western-oriented therapies such as cognitive-behavioral therapy and interpersonal therapy to change the negative attributional biases of a person with depression. But Sue and Sue (2003) warned that a Western therapist might be affected by her or his own biases if she or he does not incorporate the worldview of the client's culture. So (2005) contended that understanding an Asian client's spiritual place in the world and sometimes considering nontraditional therapies may be necessary to help the client heal. Santee (2007) expanded on this to suggest that the therapist working with Chinese Americans must become familiar with many of the principles of Chinese philosophy. In terms of helping Asian American women, "there are three well-established types of treatment for depression: medications, psychotherapy and electroconvulsive therapy (ECT)" (National Alliance on Mental Illness, 2009, p. 1). But Duldulao (2009) argued that Asian American women will not use these services as long as there continues to be a "lack of culturally competent and culturally sensitive mental health clinicians out there." She went on to note that "there's a very, very small number of Asian-American therapists and counselors, let alone folks who understand the struggles that second-generation Asian-American folks go through." Professionals could integrate Morita therapy in the counseling process—inviting Y-Chun to accept the uncontrollable aspects of her life (what happened in the past) instead of being consumed by her attempts to control them. This may free her from fruitless thoughts and encourage her to invest time in taking more responsible actions and making plans, such as taking care of herself physically and mentally and caring for her children.

Another important piece of information from the interview is that Y-Chun was referred to counseling by a physician. Congruent with the research over the years regarding Asian Americans (Chen et al., 2002; Haynie, 2007; Houston, 1997; Kim, 2005; Kim & Park, 2008; Kok & Liow, 1993; Lee, 2000; Leong et al., 2008; Lou et al., 2011; McGoldrick & Giordano, 2005; Nikolchev, 2010; Paterson, 2006; Santee, 2007; Son, Ellis, & Yoo, 2012; Sue & Sue, 2003; Suinn, 2010),

Y-Chun originally sought help for physical symptom relief. Cross-culturally competent counselors must realize that the resistance that exists for many Asian American women is an important part of the therapy that should be not only acknowledged but respected (Wang & Kim, 2010). Taking into consideration Y-Chun's level of readiness to recognize her mental health issues and the close integration between body and mind, professionals may suggest that the client engage in some culturally appropriate interventions such as *qigong*, tai chi, or meditation, along with counseling. The counselor's stance could help establish his or her credibility through recognizing the client's cultural background and underlying counseling issues.

Issues surrounding gender roles are evident in Y-Chun's family. McGoldrick and Giordano (2005) asserted that Asian families will have a more difficult time accepting female family members who act as or assume the responsibilities of "head of house." A Westernized therapist should be careful not to assume that these inequalities will be easy to resolve. At various times in the interview with Y-Chun (see Chapter 3), it appears as though the therapist is coming mostly from an emotionally focused or solution-focused theoretical orientation. When the counselor asks, "Well, if you are doing these things—and we assume that you are getting something out of it . . . what might that be?" it likely sounds appropriate to a therapy that seeks taking responsibility for one's actions. But cross-cultural therapists, especially those working with Asian Americans, might find this type of question to be too confronting and disrespectful. Kim and Park (2008) might suggest that this question is blaming Y-Chun for what's occurred in her life when she is already coming from a shame-based existence. Sue and Sue (2003) might have found that if the therapist in the interview asked more about Y-Chun's family traditions and customs, he or she might obtain more of an understanding of how Y-Chun sees herself in relation to her family and others. Wang and Kim (2010) noted that many therapists have an overreliance on verbal interview techniques and that culturally competent therapists need to go beyond that. They might recommend nontraditional activities for Y-Chun, such as keeping a journal, bringing in photographs, or talking about artwork, to define her way of being and healing.

McGoldrick and Giordano (2005) believe that when working with Asian clients in a counseling setting (such as with Y-Chun), the first step is for the therapist to engage in consciousness raising about his or her own racial biases and ethnocentrism. They went on to state that the second step is to seek out cultural knowledge, which means that it's never too late to learn about the current research on work with Chinese Americans, Japanese Americans, Filipino Americans, etc. The third step is maintaining professional rapport so the Asian client feels respected, without coming across too casual. Clients are sometimes, consciously and unconsciously, testing the therapist with their statements on identity, acculturation, and bilingualism/biculturalism. If the client, consciously or unconsciously, feels that the therapist does not validate this information, the therapy will likely fail. Wade and Tavris (2010) give an example and note that bilingual/bicultural children who naturally go through "code switching," (the back-and-forth processing between a person's languages or cultures) need teachers and counselors who are accepting and supportive. McGoldrick and Giordano (2005) specifically suggested that while many traditional Western therapeutic approaches are based on individuation, independence, self-disclosure, verbal expression of feeling, and long-term, insight-oriented therapy, Asian American clients (such as Y-Chun) may have values based more on interdependence, self-control, repression of emotions, and short-term, results-oriented solutions.

PROFESSIONAL IDENTITY

Coming From a Western Orientation

Looking back at my interactions with my clinical supervisor, Shiong-Shiong, at the University of Southern California, I realized that my connection with him formed when he allowed me to explain my existence and identity. He was Chinese and born in China. I was African American and born in South Central Los Angeles. The modeling of acceptance he demonstrated helped me see how I needed to be more patient with others. He was the first supervisor I had who took time to study African history, and from there we talked about similarities between Asian and African cultures. Despite the fears I had the first day of intern orientation, I felt that my training had become a tremendous success.

Shiong-Shiong's patience and mindfulness seemed to come from an Eastern mind-set, which was much different from the Western practice I was used to. My frantic pace always included consuming two café mochas a day in the clinic, rushing from department to department on campus, and forcing myself into a jammed schedule of back-to-back appointments. But I will never forget Shiong-Shiong's supervision, which began every morning with a 1-hour meeting, before the clinic opened, to meditate and practice tai-chi exercises. On the first day of tai-chi practice, there I was, this 210-pound African American male and former basketball player with no previous experience in that area, having difficulty even getting my body into the weird physical positions I was asked to hold. Later, I finally learned the value of "chi" (the center of one's being) as a different way to treat the mind and body connection. Shiong-Shiong taught me more than I could ever have imagined, and his effect on me will show in my work for the rest of my life. It's amazing how much we can be affected by another's cultural experience, if we let it happen.

Shiong-Shiong would state that it is important to include an emic perspective in our work with clients, which means that each culture be seen as separate and unique. He illustrated this by telling me that Western psychology reminded him of a big stick that is beaten over the client's head to push or change him or her. He shared with me the quote used at the beginning of this chapter, which refers to bamboo. The bamboo's strength, he repeated, comes from its ability to bend with the wind and current. Other cross-cultural therapists could learn something from this, especially on how to be more flexible when working with clients from different backgrounds.

Coming From an Eastern Orientation

I came to the United States from the other side of the Pacific Ocean (China) in 2004 to pursue a graduate program in counseling. The institution I attended was located in a small town in the Midwest. I took a group counseling course in the first semester and was the only international student in the class. Dr. Scott Wickman (the instructor of the class) used a Bingo activity as a warm-up exercise. I had no idea what Bingo was and just nervously observed what others were doing. Marshaling up all my courage, I asked one of the male students, who was 6 feet tall and very strong, one of the items on the Bingo chart: "Were you a football cheerleader in high school?" He looked at me oddly and said, "No." Later in the class, the students were asked to bring up famous TV shows and their hosts/hostesses in group discussion. My classmates vehemently discussed their favorite U.S. TV shows. I was the only one left out of the conversation. I felt frustrated and started to blame myself for my ignorance on these topics.

Two of my classmates brought up the issue through the online discussion forum and suggested adding diverse topics so I could get involved in the class discussions. I had mixed feelings on this. On one hand, I felt thankful because these two classmates cared for me. On the other hand, I felt upset because my "ignorance" was brought to light. Furthermore, I did not want to be the person to rock the boat; so I made an announcement through the online discussion forum: I am okay and want to learn new stuff to eliminate my "ignorance."

After sending out the e-mail, I started to debate with myself. Should I keep my real thoughts to myself or let the class know my true feelings? I had a lot of concerns, plus my own personal style in handling the issue. It took me a long while to decide my next step, probably the toughest decision to make: telling the class what was going on in my mind. I ended my disclosure with the lyrics to the song "Leaving on a Jet Plane," by American country singer John Denver. The melody in the song actually comes from a Peking opera. It was one of the most memorable class experiences I had.

When reflecting back on this event, I recognize my racial identity development journey and become aware of the importance of multicultural counseling philosophies and approaches, such as tai chi, yoga, meditations, and so on. Being an individual from the East with a lot to learn about modern counseling theories and practices, I also have the responsibility and pleasure to share with my colleagues and counselors-in-training Eastern philosophies and associated counseling practices.

KEYSTONES

This chapter addressed the following topics:

- The early Western philosophical assumptions and principles provided the foundation for psychology today.
- The theories of Western psychology are deeply rooted in the Western cultures and reflect the values and worldviews of the highly industrialized countries.
- Similar to physical sciences Western psychology believes in empirical evidence, best practice, and evidence-based interventions which are culturally oriented and biased.
- The difference between the Eastern culture and the Western culture in terms of problem solving may exist in that the former achieves the goal through engaging in contexts or being in the moment while the later emphasizes "doing".
- Religions and philosophies play a significant role in the Eastern psychology, and Hinduism, Buddhism, Confucianism, and Taoism are some examples of where Eastern religions intertwine with Eastern philosophies.

REFLECTIONS FROM THE CONTRIBUTOR'S CHAIR

Michael G. Laurent

As a scientist and practitioner, I have found the need to continually emphasize the role of culture in a client's experience. I believe that while coursework in counseling programs articulates theory from Freud to Ellis, cross-cultural studies are assumed but not programmed throughout graduate curriculum. I feel that some "traditional" theories may or may not be effective when counseling people from a non-Western culture. But with the growing diversity in our communities and the many mental health issues affecting people from all backgrounds, it is necessary to use some "nontraditional" methods when looking at methods of healing. I have made it my mission to learn as much as possible from "different" cultures and to integrate "different" perspectives into my practice. In particular, I advocate that Eastern perspectives on health and well-being be included in research and clinical practices. I actively help others gain more cross-cultural counseling experiences, and I strongly contend that cross-cultural competence is not just a "good intention" but, instead, must represent an evolving skill.

Shengli Dong

Eastern philosophies and associated counseling practices and Western philosophies and counseling practices are two important and indispensable aspects of counseling knowledge and skills. The relation between them mirrors the relation between Yin and Yang: Each depends on and supplements the other. However, the Eastern counseling practices and philosophies have not gained the recognition they should. As a counselor educator and researcher, integration of Eastern and Western counseling practices has always fascinated and intrigued me.

ADDITIONAL RESOURCES

McAuliffe, G. (2009). *Culturally alert counseling: An introduction*. Thousand Oaks, CA: Sage.
   This multimedia kit includes a six-DVD set on working with African American, Asian, Latino/Latina, conservative religious, and gay/lesbian youth clients.

Pennsylvania State University. (2010). *Multicultural counseling* [DVD]. University Park: Author.
   This DVD includes seven different counseling vignettes reflecting multicultural counseling sessions.

Pope-Davis, D., Prieto, L., Reynolds, A., & Vasquez, L. (Producers). (2000). *Vignettes of culturally different counseling: Working with clients different than you* [DVD]. Framingham, MA: Microtraining.

REFERENCES

Abdullah, T., & Brown, T. L. (2011). Mental illness stigma and ethnocultural beliefs, values, and norms: An integrative review. *Clinical Psychology Review, 31,* 934–948.
Adams, M., Blumenfeld, W., Castaneda, C., Hackman, H., Peters, M., & Zuniga, X. (2010). *Readings for diversity and social justice* (2nd ed.). New York: Routledge.

Armas, G. G. (2001, July 13–19). Census: Asian Americans have fewer single mothers. *AsianWeek*.

Brekke, T. (1999). The religious motivation of the early Buddhists. *Journal of the American Academy of Religion, 67,* 849–866.

Brodd, J. (2003). *World religions.* Winona, MN: Saint Mary's Press.

Chen, J., Chen, H., & Chung, H. (2002). Depressive disorders in Asian American adults: Case-based reviews. *Western Journal of Medicine, 176*(4), 239–244.

Cohen, T. R., Wolf, S. T., Panter, A. T., & Insko, C. A. (2011). Introducing the GASP Scale: New measure of guilt and shame proneness. *Journal of Personality and Social Psychology, 10*(5), 947–966.

Confucianism. (2013, September 19). *Wikipedia.* Retrieved from http://en.wikipedia.org/wiki/Confucianism

Craig, E. (1998). *Routledge encyclopedia of philosophy* (Vol. 7). London: Routledge.

Drob, S. L. (1999). Jung and the Kabbalah. *History of Psychology, 2,* 102–118.

Duldulao, A. (Interviewee). (2009, September 23). Asian-American women more likely to attempt suicide [Radio broadcast]. *NPR.* Retrieved from http://www.npr.org/templates/story/story.php?storyId = 113114107

East Versus West. (n.d.). Census data revisited. Retrieved from http://www.1000ventures.com/business_guide/crosscuttings/cultures_east-west-phylosophy.html

Ellis, A. (1991). *Reason and emotion in psychotherapy.* New York: Carol Publishing Group.

Fasching, D. J., & deChant, D. (2001). *Comparative religious ethics: A narrative approach.* Oxford, UK: Blackwell.

Feldman, R. S. (2008). *Development across the life span* (5th ed.). Upper Saddle River, NJ: Pearson/Prentice Hall.

Ferber, A. L. (1995). Exploring the social construction of race: Sociology and the study of interracial relationships. In A. L. Ferber (Ed.), *American mixed race: The culture of micro-diversity* (pp. 115–167). Lanham, MD: Rowman & Littlefield.

Goodrich, S. (2011). *The great Greek philosophers: Socrates, Plato and Aristotle.* Bayside, NY: A. J. Cornell.

Gordon, O. (2004). Eastern philosophy. In B. Moore & K. Bruder (Eds.), *Philosophy: The power of ideas* (6th ed.). New York: McGraw-Hill.

Hac, P. M., & Long, D. (2004). Psychology in Vietnam. *The Psychologist, 17*(2), 70–71.

Haynie, D. (2007, June 30). Asian American women, stereotypes, and eating disorders. *Audrey Magazine.*

Hill, R. B. (1998). *The strengths of African American families: Twenty-five years later.* Lanham, MD: University Press of America.

Houston, H. R. (1997). Between two cultures: A testimony. *Amerasia Journal, 23*(1), 149–156.

Hsu, F. (1971). *Under the ancestor's shadow: Kinship, personality, and social mobility in China.* Stanford, CA: Stanford University Press.

Japanese psychology. (n.d.). *Morita School of Japanese Psychology.* Retrieved from http://moritaschool.com/content/japanese-psychology

Jones-Smith, E. (2012). *Theories of counseling and psychotherapy: An integrative approach.* Thousand Oaks, CA: Sage.

Kim, B., & Park, Y. S. (2008). East and Southeast Asian Americans. In G. McAuliffe (Ed.), *Culturally alert counseling: A comprehensive introduction* (pp. 189–217). Thousand Oaks, CA: Sage.

Kim, Y. S. E. (2005). Guidelines and strategies for cross-cultural counseling with Korean American clients. *Journal of Multicultural Counseling and Development, 33,* 217–231.

Kimura, H., Nagao, F., Tanaka, Y., Sakai, S., Ohnishi, S. T., & Okumura, K. (2005). Beneficial effects of the Nishino breathing method on the immune activity and stress level. *Journal of Alternative Complementary Medicine, 11,* 285–291.

Kok, A. J., & Liow, S. J. R. (1993). Case studies of help seeking behavior among Asian single parents in Singapore. *Counseling Psychology Quarterly, 6*(4), 303–316.

Kramer, E. J., Kwong, K., Lee, E., & Chung, H. (2002). Cultural factors influencing the mental health of Asian Americans. *Western Journal of Medicine, 176,* 227–231.

Lee, E. (2000). *Working with Asian Americans: A guide for clinicians.* New York: Guilford Press.

Leong, F. T., & Lau, A. S. (2001). Barriers to providing effective mental health services to Asian Americans. *Mental Health Services Research, 3,* 201–214.

Leong, F. T. L., Lee, S., & Chang, D. (2008). Counseling Asian Americans. In P. B. Pedersen (Ed.), *Counseling across cultures* (6th ed.). Thousand Oaks, CA: Sage.

Lopez, D. S. (2001). *The story of Buddhism: A concise guide to its history and teachings.* New York: HarperCollins.

Lou, E., Lalonde, R., & Wilson, C. (2011). Examining a multidimensional framework of racial identity across different racial groups. *Asian Journal of Psychology, 2*(2), 79–90.

McGoldrick, M., & Giordano, J. (2005). *Ethnicity and family therapy.* New York: Guilford Press.

McGrath, P., & Axelson, J. A. (1999). *Accessing awareness and developing knowledge: Foundations for skill in a multicultural society* (3rd ed.). Belmont, CA: Brooks/Cole.

Morita therapy. (n.d.). *Morita School of Japanese Psychology.* Retrieved from http://moritaschool.com/content/morita-therapy

National Alliance on Mental Illness. (2009). *Asian American women and depression: Fact sheet.* Retrieved from http://www.nami.org/Template.cfm?Section = Women_and_Depression&Template = / ContentManagement/ContentDisplay.cfm&ContentID = 88886

Newman, B., & Newman, R. (2010). *Development through life: A psychosocial approach.* Belmont, CA: Wadsworth/Thomson.

Nikolchev, A. (2010, October 12). Among Asian-American women, a little known battle with depression. *Need to Know on PBS.* Retrieved from http://www.pbs.org/wnet/need-to-know/health/among-asian-american-women-a-little-known-battle-with-depression/4200/

Ohnishi, S. T., & Ohnishi, T. (2009). Philosophy, psychology, physics, and practice of ki. *Evidence-Based Complementary Alternative Medicine, 6,* 175–183.

Paterson, J. (2006, June). When East meets West. *Counseling Today.* Washington, DC: American Counseling Association. Retrieved from http://ct.counseling.org/2006/01/ct-online-when-east-meets-west/

Santee, R. G. (2007). *An integrative approach to counseling: Bridging Chinese thought, evolutionary theory, and stress management.* Thousand Oaks, CA: Sage.

Segal, Z. V., Williams, J. M. G., & Teasdale, J. D. (2002). *Mindfulness-based cognitive therapy for depression: A new approach to preventing relapse.* New York: Guilford Press.

Smith, H., & Novak, P. (2003). *Buddhism: A concise introduction.* New York: HarperCollins.

So, J. K. (2005). Traditional and cultural healing among the Chinese. In R. Moodley & W. West (Eds.), *Integrating traditional and healing practices into counseling and psychotherapy* (pp. 100–110). Thousand Oaks, CA: Sage.

Son, E., Ellis, M., & Yoo, S. (2012). Clinical supervision in South Korea and the United States: A comparative descriptive study. *Counseling Psychologist, 20*(10), 1–18.

Sue, D. W., & Sue, D. (2003). *Counseling the culturally diverse.* New York: John Wiley.

Suinn, R. M. (2010). Reviewing acculturation and Asian Americans: How acculturation affects health, adjustment, school achievement, and counseling, *Asian American Journal of Psychology, 1*(1), 5–17.

Suzuki, D. T. (1991). *An introduction to Zen Buddhism.* New York: Grove Press.

Takaki, R. (2010). A different mirror. In W. Adams, W. J. Blumenfeld, C. Castenada, H. Hackman, M. Peters, & X. Zuniga (Eds.), *Readings for diversity and social change* (pp. 67–73). New York: Routledge.

Taoism. (2013, September 23). *Wikipedia.* Retrieved from http://en.wikipedia.org/wiki/Taoism

Taylor, C. C., Hare, R. M., & Barnes, J. (2001). *Greek philosophers*. New York: Oxford University Press.

Thompson, B. L., & Waltz, J. (2010). Mindfulness and experiential avoidance as predictors of posttraumatic stress disorder avoidance symptom severity. *Journal of Anxiety Disorders, 24,* 409–415.

Triandis, H. C. (1995). *Individualism and collectivism.* Boulder, CO: Westview Press.

Tweed, R. G., & Lehman, D. R. (2003). Confucian and Socratic learning. *American Psychologist, 58*(2), 148–149.

Van Voorst, R. E. (2005). *Anthology of world scriptures.* Belmont, CA: Thomson Wadsworth.

Vollestad, J., Nielsen, M. B., & Nielsen, G. H. (2012). Mindfulness- and acceptance-based interventions for anxiety disorders: A systematic review and meta-analysis. *British Journal of Clinical Psychology, 51,* 239–260. doi:10.1111/j.2044-8260.2011.02024.x

Wade, C., & Tavris, C. (2010). *Psychology* (9th ed.). Upper Saddle River, NJ: Pearson.

Wang, S., & Kim, B. S. K. (2010). Therapist multicultural competence, Asian American participants' cultural values, and counseling process. *Journal of Counseling Psychology, 57*(4), 394–401.

Welwood, J. (1993). *Awakening the heart: East/West approaches to psychotherapy and the healing profession.* Boston: Shambhala.

Wulf, R. (1996, November). The historical roots of Gestalt therapy theory. *Gestalt Dialogue: Newsletter of the Integrative Gestalt Centre.* Retrieved from http://www.gestalt.org/wulf.htm

Yamakage, M. (2006). *The essence of Shinto: Japan's spiritual heart* (P. de Leeuw & A. Rankin, Eds.). Tokyo: Kodansha International.

Yeung, W., & Lee, E. (1997). Chinese Buddhism: Its implications for counseling. In E. Lee (Ed.), *Working with Asian Americans: A guide for clinicians* (pp. 452–463). New York: Guilford Press.

Index

SAGE researchmethods

The essential online tool for researchers from the world's leading methods publisher

Find exactly what you are looking for, from basic explanations to advanced discussion

More content and new features added this year!

"I have never really seen anything like this product before, and I think it is really valuable."

John Creswell, University of Nebraska–Lincoln

Discover **Methods Lists**— methods readings suggested by other users

Watch video interviews with leading methodologists

Explore the **Methods Map** to discover links between methods

Search a custom-designed taxonomy with more than 1,400 qualitative, quantitative, and mixed methods terms

Uncover more than 120,000 pages of book, journal, and reference content to support your learning

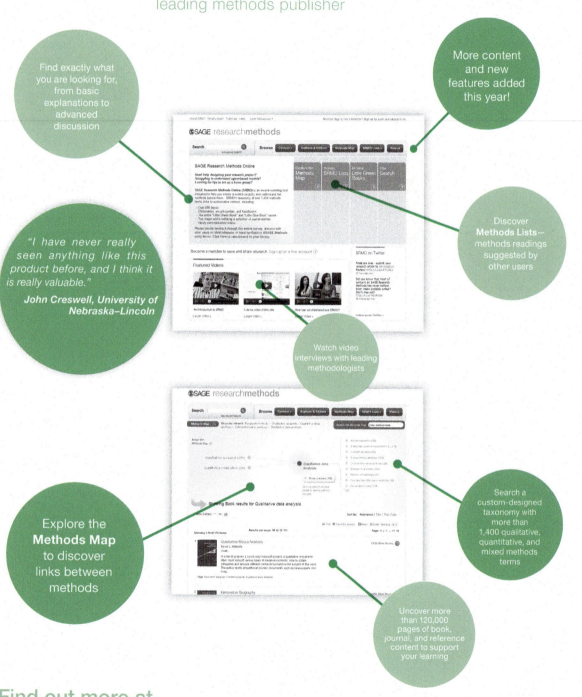

Find out more at
www.sageresearchmethods.com